Happy Holidays to our Clients and Friends:

The Financial Services Office (FSO) continues to grow to meet the needs of the marketplace. Ernst & Young's commitment to the financial services industry can be seen in the significant investment and dedicated resources it has brought together within the FSO. Our professionals have in-depth knowledge of the financial services industry and understand the pressures these companies face in executing their strategies. Our combination of resources and competencies has established us as a market leader in delivering assurance, tax, and advisory services to the asset management, banking, capital markets, and insurance sectors. We welcome the opportunity to assist you in meeting the demands of a challenging business environment.

We present this 2006 Zagat Survey New York City Restaurant Guide as a token of our appreciation for your continued support this past year. Zagat is widely recognized as the authority on consumer-survey based dining content. With valuable and engaging reviews and ratings, Zagat will help you enjoy all the great restaurants that New York has to offer.

All of us in the FSO wish you good health, happiness, and prosperity in the New Year.

Stephen R. Howe, Jr.
Managing Partner
Financial Services Office
Ernst & Young LLP

ZAGATSURVEY®

2006

NEW YORK CITY RESTAURANTS

Editors: Curt Gathje and Carol Diuguid

Coordinator: Larry Cohn

Published and distributed by
ZAGAT SURVEY, LLC
4 Columbus Circle
New York, New York 10019
Tel: 212 977 6000
E-mail: newyork@zagat.com
Web site: www.zagat.com

Acknowledgments

We thank Siobhan Burns, Erica Curtis, Daphne Dennis, Mikola De Roo, Lynn Hazlewood, Charlotte Kaiser, Laura Mitchell, Bernard Onken, Steven Shukow, Miranda Van Gelder and Laura Vogel. We are also grateful to our associate editor, Griff Foxley, and editorial assistant, Jason Briker, as well as the following members of our staff: Betsy Andrews, Caren Weiner Campbell, Reni Chin, Victoria Elmacioglu, Schuyler Frazier, Jeff Freier, Shelley Gallagher, Randi Gollin, Leah Hochbaum, Natalie Lebert, Mike Liao, Dave Makulec, Donna Marino, Emily Parsons, Robert Poole, Josh Rogers, Troy Segal, Robert Seixas, Thomas Sheehan, Joshua Siegel, Daniel Simmons, Carla Spartos, Erinn Stivala and Sharon Yates.

Contents

About This Survey

Here are the results of our *2006 New York City Restaurant Survey,* covering 2,003 restaurants as tested, and tasted, by 30,911 local restaurant-goers. This guide reflects the fact that dining in New York has never been better. When compared to other major cities for which we have guides – e.g. London, Paris, Tokyo – it is fair to say that NYC is now the preeminent restaurant city in the world.

This marks the 27th year that Zagat Survey has reported on the shared experiences of diners like you. What started in 1979 as a hobby involving 200 of our friends rating NYC restaurants purely for fun has come a long way. Today we have over 250,000 active surveyors and now cover entertaining, golf, hotels, resorts, spas, movies, music, nightlife, shopping and tourist attractions. These guides are all based on consumer surveys. They are also available on PDAs, cell phones and by subscription at zagat.com.

By regularly surveying large numbers of avid customers, we hope to have achieved a uniquely current and reliable guide. More than a quarter-century of experience has verified this. In effect, this is the restaurant industry's report card, with each place's ratings and review being a free-market study of its own consumers. Hopefully, restaurateurs will use their ratings and reviews as a way to improve their performance so as to better serve their customers in the future. This year's NYC participants dined out an average of 3.4 times per week, meaning this *Survey* is based on roughly 5.4 million meals. Of these 30,000 plus surveyors, 53% are women, 47% men; the breakdown by age is 17% in their 20s; 28%, 30s; 19%, 40s; 20%, 50s; and 16%, 60s or above. Our editors have done their best to summarize these surveyors' opinions, with their comments shown in quotation marks. We sincerely thank each of these people; this book is really "theirs."

To help you find NYC's best meals and best buys, we have prepared a number of lists. See Most Popular (page 9), Top Ratings (pages 10–19) and Best Buys (pages 20–22). In addition, we have provided 48 handy indexes and have tried to be concise.

Finally, we invite you to participate in our upcoming *Surveys*. Just register at zagat.com. Each participant will receive a free copy of the resulting guide (or a comparable reward) when published. Your comments and even criticisms of this guide are also solicited. There is always room for improvement with your help. Just contact us at newyork@zagat.com.

New York, NY
October 17, 2005

Nina and Tim

Nina and Tim Zagat

What's New

Undressing for Dinner: Ten years ago, one was expected to dress for dinner at better restaurants – jacket and tie were *de rigueur*. Today, they are *de rigor mortis,* with ties required only at the Rainbow Room and 21 Club. Even that symbol of fine dining, the tablecloth, is becoming something of a rarity. The final collapse of all formality could be seen at the Miami imports BED New York and Duvet, two mattress-lined lairs that allow one to *eat in bed in public.*

A Good Year: With 247 noteworthy openings vs. only 83 closings, this was another strong year for the restaurant industry. (In comparison, just three years ago, there were 186 openings and 104 closings.) While this growth has been seen at every level, major players have continued to build their empires, to wit: Jean-Georges Vongerichten (Perry Street), Bobby Flay (Bar Americain), Danny Meyer (The Modern), Nobu Matsuhisa (Nobu 57), Michael Cetrulo (Piano Due), Scott Conant (Alto), Shelly Fireman (Bond 45), Kurt Gutenbrunner (Thor), Drew Nieporent (Centrico), David Pasternack (Bistro du Vent), Laurent Tourondel (BLT Fish, BLT Prime) and Patricia Yeo (Sapa).

No Fluke: This year's strong performance is no fluke. It is part of an ongoing culinary revolution. In fact, 27 of New York City's 50 Top Food rated restaurants opened in the past 10 years, and only three of the top-rated spots, Peter Luger, La Grenouille and the Four Seasons, even existed when we started our surveys back in 1979. Furthermore, this growth has extended to the outer boroughs, where nine of the top 50 are located.

Cream of the Crop: Thomas Keller's phenomenon, per se, took Most Impressive Debut honors, vaulting to the No. 3 Food ranking, as well as No. 1 for Service. Other big winners this year included Le Bernardin (Top Food), Daniel (Top Decor) and Gramercy Tavern (Most Popular).

Costs Steady: The costs of dining out held remarkably steady in the past year, with the average meal clocking in at $37.61, up only 0.4% over last year's $37.45. While NY remains the country's most expensive dining city, it's still a bargain compared to overseas capitals like London ($67.69), Paris ($62.97) and Tokyo ($70.64). The city's 20 most expensive places averaged a whopping $112.49 check, up 23% from last year, mostly due to the mega-pricing of newcomers Masa (average price $356) and per se ($201). Absent these two, the average price would be only $92.49.

Neighborhoods Watch: Times Square got more Vegas-like with three new vast powerhouses, Bolzano's, Bond 45 and the transplanted Hard Rock Cafe. Park Slope's Fifth Avenue heated up with an astonishing eight newcomers, most notably Applewood, Brooklyn Fish Camp and Tempo.

The Bronx Is Up: Bronx borough president Adolfo Carrión Jr. spearheaded a campaign to include more of his constituency's outposts in this guidebook. The good people of that fine borough have spoken, and as a result we've doubled the number of Bronx entries herein. Roberto's was voted No. 1 in the borough, for the sixth year running.

BBQ's Smokin': For years, barbecue fanatics had few serious options beyond Virgil's and Pearson's, but the 2002 arrival of Blue Smoke aroused renewed interest in the genre. This time out, yearling Daisy May's was voted best in town, amid a rash of hot arrivals with 'cue names such as Bone Lick Park, Dinosaur, Rib, RUB and Smoked.

Eastern Aesthetics: Asian restaurants used to be underdecorated. Not any more. Seven out of the Top 20 Decor scorers this year were Asian: Asiate, Kittichai, Matsuri, Megu, Sapa, Spice Market and Tao, not to mention newcomers like Koi, Mainland, Ninja and Nobu 57.

Fortune Cookie: Haute Chinese cooking, in hibernation for some years, seems on the brink of a revival. Harbingers of the future include East Side newcomer Mainland and TriBeCa's 66 as well as two forthcoming, as yet unnamed, restaurants in Ian Schrager's Gramercy Park Hotel and in the Time Cafe space on Lafayette Street.

Final Curtains: Notable closings included America, Chez Es Saada, Gus' Place, Layla, Le Cirque 2000, La Metairie, Le Madri, the Oak Room, the Palm Court, Patria and Union Pacific. The perils of cloning became apparent with the fast closings of twins of Jubilee, Mama's Food Shop, Morrell's, Nebraska Steak, Ony, Ruth's Chris and Westville.

Coming Attractions: 2006 is shaping up to be quite a year: in the Chelsea/Meatpacking District, there will be Buddakan, Stephen Starr's spin-off of his Philly smash; Craftsteak, a sibling cloned from Tom Colicchio's Vegas steakhouse; Del Posto, a mega-Italian from the Batali-Bastianich team; and Morimoto, featuring Iron Chef Masaharu Morimoto. In Midtown, two world-renowned chefs, London's No. 1 rated Gordon Ramsay and Paris' three-star Joël Robuchon, plan first-time NY beachheads. Equally anticipated are Thomas Keller's Bouchon Bakery, and Charlie Trotter's yet-to-be-named seafood house, both in the Time Warner Center; a Blue Ribbon Sushi offshoot near Columbus Circle; a Megu clone in the Trump World Tower; a Rosa Mexicano spin-off near Union Square; and a reborn Le Cirque in the new Bloomberg Tower. That's a lot to chew on!

New York, NY
October 17, 2005

Nina and Tim Zagat

Ratings & Symbols

Name, Address, Phone Number & Web Site

Zagat Ratings

Hours & Credit Cards

F	D	S	C
▽ 23	9	13	$15

Tim & Nina's ◑ 🎟 ⊅

4 Columbus Circle (8th Ave.), 212-977-6000;
www.zagat.com

Open 24/7, this "literal dive" in the Columbus Circle subway station offers one-of-a-kind "Chinese-German dining" where an "hour after you eat you're hungry for more sweet-and-sour schnitzel"; fans ignore its "Bauhaus meets Mao's house" look and the staff's "yin-yang" uniforms (lederhosen for men, cheongsam for women) and say it's "some cheap trip", even if you must "shout to order when the trains come in."

Review, with surveyors' comments in quotes

Top Spots: Places with the highest overall ratings, popularity and importance are listed in BLOCK CAPITAL LETTERS.

Hours: ◑ serves after 11 PM
🎟 closed on Sunday

Credit Cards: ⊅ no credit cards accepted

Ratings are on a scale of **0** to **30**. Cost **(C)** reflects our surveyors' estimate of the price of dinner with one drink and tip.

F	Food	D	Decor	S	Service	C	Cost
23		9		13		$15	

0–9	poor to fair	**20–25** very good to excellent
10–15	fair to good	**26–30** extraordinary to perfection
16–19	good to very good	▽ low response/less reliable

For newcomers or survey write-ins listed without ratings, the price range is indicated as follows:

I	$25 and below	**E**	$41 to $65
M	$26 to $40	**VE**	$66 or more

Most Popular

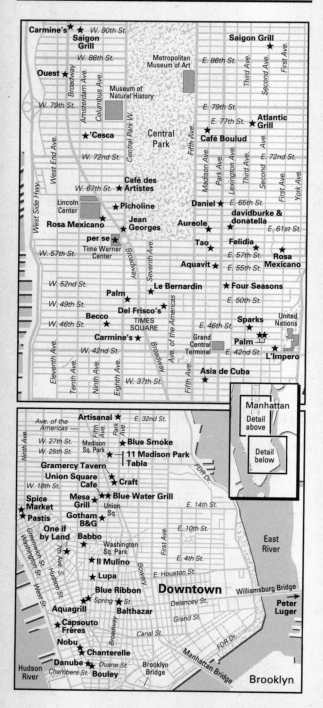

subscribe to zagat.com

Most Popular

Each of our surveyors has been asked to name his or her five favorite restaurants. The following list reflects their choices followed in parentheses by last year's rankings.

1. Gramercy Tavern (1)
2. Union Square Cafe (2)
3. Babbo (7)
4. Daniel (3)
5. Le Bernardin (11)
6. Gotham Bar & Grill (4)
7. Blue Water Grill (5)
8. Bouley (8)
9. Peter Luger (6)
10. Nobu (10)
11. Jean Georges (9)
12. Balthazar (12)
13. per se (–)
14. Eleven Madison Park (13)
15. Four Seasons (17)
16. Spice Market (–)
17. Aureole (14)
18. Tabla (19)
19. Chanterelle (16)
20. Rosa Mexicano (22)
21. Artisanal (20)
22. Aquavit (18)
23. Il Mulino (25)
24. Carmine's (24)
25. Café Boulud (36)
26. Picholine (29)
27. Craft (15)
28. Atlantic Grill (21)
29. Aquagrill (27)
30. Felidia (44)
31. Ouest (23)
32. Pastis (48)
33. One if by Land (40)
34. 'Cesca (33)
35. Tao (42)
36. Blue Smoke (–)
37. L'Impero (35)
38. Asia de Cuba (28)
39. Blue Ribbon* (39)
40. Palm* (32)
41. davidburke & donatella (–)
42. Café des Artistes (30)
43. Lupa* (34)
44. Saigon Grill (45)
45. Del Frisco's (–)
46. Becco (–)
47. Sparks (26)
48. Danube (38)
49. Mesa Grill (31)
50. Capsouto Frères (–)

It's obvious that many of these popular places are also among the city's most expensive, but everyone loves a bargain. Fortunately, New York City has an abundance of wonderful ethnic restaurants and other inexpensive spots that fill the bill. Thus, we have listed 100 Best Buys on page 20 and over 200 Prix Fixe and Pre-Theater Menus on pages 21–22. Also bear in mind that New York's outer borough restaurants often charge less than half what the same meal would cost in Manhattan.

---

* Indicates a tie with restaurant above

Top Ratings

Excludes places with low voting, unless indicated by a ▽.

Top Food

28 Le Bernardin
Daniel
per se
Bouley
Sushi Yasuda
Gramercy Tavern
Nobu
Peter Luger (Bklyn)
27 Jean Georges
Gotham Bar & Grill
Chanterelle
Babbo
Café Boulud
Sushi of Gari
La Grenouille
Masa
Tomoe Sushi
Roberto's (Bronx)
Grocery (Bklyn)
Il Mulino
Aureole
Pearl Oyster Bar
Union Square Cafe
Annisa
Veritas

Sushi Seki
Atelier
Picholine
Danube
Alain Ducasse
Di Fara (Bklyn)
26 Saul (Bklyn)
March
Tasting Room
Poke
Trattoria L'incontro (Queens)
Aquagrill
Il Giglio
L'Impero
Sripraphai (Queens)
Four Seasons
Oceana
Al Di La (Bklyn)
Blue Hill
Milos
Jewel Bako
Craft
Lupa
Grimaldi's (Bklyn)
Honmura An

By Cuisine

American
28 per se
Gramercy Tavern
27 Gotham Bar & Grill
Aureole
Union Square Cafe
Annisa

American (Regional)
27 Pearl Oyster Bar/NE
24 Roy's NY/Hawaii Fusion
Mesa Grill/SW
22 Carl's Steaks/Philly
Michael's/CA
21 Tropica/FL

Barbecue
23 Daisy May's
22 Dinosaur BBQ
21 Blue Smoke
20 Virgil's Real BBQ
16 Brother Jimmy's
Pearson's

Brasseries
25 Café Gray
24 Brasserie LCB
23 Artisanal
Balthazar
22 L'Absinthe
21 Brasserie 8½

Cafes
27 Café Boulud
Union Square Cafe
26 River Café
24 Stone Park Café
Park Avenue Cafe
22 Café des Artistes

Caribbean/West Indies
23 A/*Caribbean*
Café Habana/*Cuban*
22 Maroons/*Carib.*
21 Hispaniola/*Dominican*
Havana Chelsea/*Cuban*
Cuba/*Cuban*

Chinese
24 Mr. K's
Oriental Garden
Shun Lee Palace
Canton
23 Tse Yang
Shun Lee West

Coffeehouses
22 Ferrara
Grey Dog's Coffee
20 Le Pain Quotidien
Once Upon a Tart
Cafe Lalo
19 Edgar's Cafe

Continental
26 Four Seasons
25 Petrossian
22 Café Pierre
21 Chadwick's
Caffé/Green
20 Kings' Carriage Hse.

Delis
24 Barney Greengrass
23 Second Ave Deli
Katz's Deli
22 Mill Basin Kosher
21 Carnegie Deli
20 Stage Deli

Dessert
26 La Bergamote
25 ChikaLicious
24 Sweet Melissa
Payard Bistro
Amy's Bread
23 Veniero's

French
28 Le Bernardin
Daniel
Bouley
27 Jean Georges
Chanterelle
Café Boulud
La Grenouille
Atelier
Alain Ducasse
26 Montrachet
25 Tocqueville
Fleur de Sel
Le Perigord

Greek
26 Milos
25 Periyali
Onera
24 Taverna Kyclades
Avra Estiatorio
23 Thalassa

Hamburgers
24 burger joint/Parker M.
23 Corner Bistro
22 Island Burgers
Shake Shack
21 Rare B&G
20 McHales

Indian
25 Tamarind
dévi
24 Chola
Dawat
23 Banjara
Hampton Chutney

Italian
27 Babbo
Roberto's
Il Mulino
26 Trattoria L'incontro
Il Giglio
L'Impero
Al Di La
Lupa
Scalini Fedeli
25 Piccola Venezia
Felidia
Don Peppe
Pó

Japanese
28 Sushi Yasuda
Nobu
27 Donguri
Sushi of Gari
Masa
Tomoe Sushi
Sugiyama
Sushi Seki
26 Poke
Jewel Bako
Kai
Honmura An
Blue Ribbon Sushi

Korean
25 Hangawi
23 Woo Lae Oak
22 Gahm Mi Oak
21 Won Jo
DoHwa
Dok Suni's

Kosher
23 Second Ave Deli
22 Mill Basin Kosher
Chennai Garden
21 Prime Grill
Pongal
20 Abigael's

Top Food

Mediterranean
27 Picholine
25 Convivium Osteria
Tempo
24 A.O.C. Bedford
Red Cat
Harrison

Mexican
25 Itzocan
24 Mexicana Mama
Pampano
23 Hell's Kitchen
Maya
Mi Cocina

Middle Eastern
23 Zaytoons
Taboon
22 Mamlouk
Moustache
21 Sahara
Persepolis

Noodle Shops
26 Honmura An
23 Soba-ya
22 Big Wong
21 Great NY Noodle
Pho Viet Huong
Pho Bang

Pizza
27 Di Fara
26 Grimaldi's
25 Lombardi's
Denino's
24 Joe's Pizza
23 Pizza 33

Seafood
28 Le Bernardin
27 Pearl Oyster
26 Aquagrill
Oceana
Milos
25 Jack's Luxury Oyster

South American
22 Churrascaria Plataforma
Chimichurri Grill
Caracas Arepa
SushiSamba
Novecento
21 Sipan

Southern/Soul
23 Amy Ruth's
22 Great Jones Cafe
Maroons
21 Ida Mae
Miss Mamie's/Maude's
20 Kitchenette

Spanish
25 Casa Mono
24 Tía Pol
23 Bolo
Sevilla
22 Sala
El Faro

Steakhouses
28 Peter Luger
25 Sparks
Strip House
Wolfgang's Steak
24 BLT Steak
Ruth's Chris
Del Frisco's
Palm
MarkJoseph
Dylan Prime
Uncle Jack's
Post House
Morton's

Thai
26 Sripraphai
24 Wondee Siam
23 Joya
Vong
Holy Basil
Kittichai

Turkish
23 Turkish Kitchen
Ali Baba
21 Pasha
Beyoglu
Uskudar
20 Sip Sak

Vegetarian
25 Hangawi
23 Gobo
Candle 79
22 Vatan
Chennai Garden
21 Pongal

Vietnamese
23 Saigon Grill
Bao 111
Nha Trang
O Mai
22 Nam
Doyers Vietnamese

Wild Cards
27 Danube/*Austrian*
26 Wallsé/*Austrian*
25 Aki/*Japanese-Jamaican*
Aquavit/*Scandinavian*
23 Zum Stammtisch/*German*
Nyonya/*Malaysian*

By Special Feature

Bargain Dinner
28 Sushi Yasuda ($21)
26 Montrachet ($35)
25 Ouest ($29)
23 Chez Michallet ($33)
21 Becco ($22)
    Kitchen 22/82 ($25)

Bargain Lunch ($20–$25)
27 Jean Georges
    Gotham Bar & Grill
26 Eleven Madison
    Tabla
25 Tocqueville
    Fleur de Sel

Breakfast
26 Norma's
24 Payard Bistro
    Barney Greengrass
23 Balthazar
    Fifty Seven 57
21 City Hall

Brunch
26 Aquagrill
    Eleven Madison
    River Café
    Wallsé
25 davidburke & donatella
    JoJo

Buffets
25 Aquavit (Sun.)
24 Chola
23 Turkish Kitchen (Sun.)
22 Chennai Garden
    Shaan
    Diwan

Business Dining
28 Le Bernardin
27 Gotham Bar & Grill
    Union Square Cafe
26 Four Seasons
    Milos
24 Bayard's

Celebrations
28 Bouley
26 Four Seasons (Pool Rm)
    River Café
23 Terrace in the Sky
20 Rainbow Room
15 Tavern on the Green

Child-Friendly
23 Zum Stammtisch
    L & B Spumoni Gardens
20 Virgil's Real BBQ
    London Lennie's
19 Tony's Di Napoli
    Serendipity 3

Hotel Dining
27 Jean Georges/Trump
    Café Boulud/Surrey
    Atelier/Ritz-Carlton CPS
    Alain Ducasse/Essex Hse.
26 Norma's/Parker Meridien
25 Triomphe/Iroquois

Late Dining
26 Blue Ribbon Sushi
25 Blue Ribbon
24 'ino
23 Balthazar
    Raoul's
22 Wollensky's Grill

Meet for a Drink
27 Jean Georges
    Gotham Bar & Grill
26 L'Impero
25 Bond Street
24 Town
23 Bar Masa

Newcomers/Top Rated
25 dévi
    Modern, The
    Onera
    Tempo
    Gari
24 Stone Park Café
23 Applewood
    Ama
    Abboccato
22 Lure Fishbar
    Frankies 457
    BLT Fish
    Dinosaur BBQ

Other Major Arrivals
    Alto
    Bar Americain
    BLT Prime
    Brooklyn Fish Camp
    etcetera etcetera
    Falai
    Koi (Bryant Park)
    Nobu 57
    Perry Street
    Piano Due
    Shaburi
    Spigolo
    Thor

People-Watching
23 Balthazar
    Fresco by Scotto
22 Il Cantinori
    Nam
    Mercer Kitchen
    Da Silvano

Top Food

Power Scenes
28 Nobu
Peter Luger
27 Jean Georges
26 Four Seasons (lunch)
23 Smith & Wollensky
22 Gabriel's

Private Rooms for Parties
28 Le Bernardin
Daniel
per se
27 La Grenouille
Picholine
Alain Ducasse
26 Four Seasons
Blue Hill
25 Café Gray
24 Bayard's
Del Frisco's
23 Il Buco
22 21 Club

Pub Dining
23 Keens
22 Wollensky's Grill
21 Spotted Pig
Bridge Cafe
20 J.G. Melon
Piper's Kilt

Quick Bites
23 Hampton Chutney
22 Shake Shack
City Bakery
21 Westville
Dishes
20 Good Enough to Eat

Quiet Conversation
28 Le Bernardin
per se
27 Chanterelle
Atelier
Picholine
25 Tocqueville

Raw Bars
26 Aquagrill
24 Blue Water Grill
23 Ocean Grill
Shaffer City
Neptune Room
22 Lure Fishbar

Singles Scenes
25 Blue Ribbon
24 Town
Asia de Cuba
23 Balthazar
22 Tao
Spice Market

Sleepers▽
27 Agnanti
Kuruma Zushi
26 Pizza Gruppo
Eliá
25 Sushi Ann
Tanoreen

Sunday's Best
28 Bouley
Gramercy Tavern
27 Gotham Bar & Grill
Café Boulud
26 Blue Hill
Lupa

Tasting Menus
28 Le Bernardin ($135+)
Daniel ($125)
per se ($175)
Bouley ($85)
Gramercy Tavern ($98)
27 Jean Georges ($125)

Trendy
26 L'Impero
25 davidburke & donatella
Casa Mono
Jack's Luxury Oyster Bar
23 Matsuri
22 Lure Fishbar
Shake Shack
Spice Market
21 Spotted Pig
Freemans
Pastis
20 5 Ninth
Ono

24-Hour
22 Gahm Mi Oak
21 Kum Gang San
Wo Hop
20 Gray's Papaya
Bereket
19 Veselka

Winning Wine Lists
28 Daniel
27 Union Sq. Cafe
Veritas
Alain Ducasse
26 Oceana
Eleven Madison
Montrachet
25 Felidia
Sparks
Cru
24 Bayard's
22 21 Club
Tribeca Grill

By Location

Chelsea
24 Da Umberto
    Tía Pol
    Red Cat
    Biltmore Room
23 Gascogne
    Matsuri

Chinatown
24 Oriental Garden
    Canton
23 New Green Bo
    Nha Trang
22 Peking Duck Hse.
    Grand Sichuan

East Village
26 Tasting Room
    Jewel Bako
25 ChikaLicious
    Itzocan
    Prune
    Perbacco

East 40s
28 Sushi Yasuda
26 L'Impero
25 Sparks
24 Nanni
    Hatsuhana
    Pampano

East 50s
27 La Grenouille
26 March
    Four Seasons
    Oceana
25 Felidia
    Aquavit

East 60s
28 Daniel
27 Aureole
    Sushi Seki
26 Kai
25 davidburke & donatella
    JoJo

East 70s
27 Café Boulud
    Sushi of Gari
24 Campagnola
    Lusardi's
    Payard Bistro
23 Sette Mezzo

East 80s
27 Donguri
26 Poke
25 Etats-Unis
    Erminia
    Sistina
24 Sushi Sen-nin

East 90s & 100s
25 Itzocan
23 Nick's
21 Don Pedro's
    Sarabeth's
    Vico
20 Pascalou

Financial District/Seaport
24 Bayard's
    Roy's NY
    MarkJoseph
22 Delmonico's
21 Fino
    Cabana

Flatiron District
28 Gramercy Tavern
27 Veritas
26 Craft
25 Periyali
    Fleur de Sel
    Tamarind

Garment District
24 Uncle Jack's
23 Keens
22 Gahm Mi Oak
21 Frankie & Johnnie
    Won Jo
    Ida Mae

Gramercy/Madison Park
26 Eleven Madison
    Tabla
25 Casa Mono
    Yama
23 I Trulli
    Novitá

Greenwich Village
27 Gotham Bar & Grill
    Babbo
    Tomoe Sushi
    Il Mulino
    Pearl Oyster Bar
    Annisa
26 Blue Hill
    Lupa
    Wallsé
25 Aki
    Cru
    Mas
    Strip House

Harlem
23 Amy Ruth's
22 Dinosaur BBQ
21 Patsy's Pizzeria
    Miss Mamie's/Maude's
    Rao's
18 Bayou

Top Food

Little Italy
23 Il Palazzo
Il Cortile
Nyonya
Pellegrino's
22 Angelo's
Ferrara

Lower East Side
24 71 Clinton Fresh
wd-50
ápizz
23 'inoteca
Katz's Deli
22 Salt

Meatpacking District
23 Old Homestead
22 Spice Market
21 Son Cubano
Pastis
20 Macelleria
5 Ninth

Murray Hill
25 Hangawi
Wolfgang's Steak
24 Asia de Cuba
23 Artisanal
Mishima
Villa Berulia

NoHo
25 Bond Street
23 Il Buco
22 Sala
Great Jones Cafe
Five Points
21 Quartino

NoLita
25 Lombardi's
23 Café Habana
22 Peasant
21 Public
Cafe Gitane
Rice

SoHo
26 Aquagrill
Honmura An
Blue Ribbon Sushi
25 Blue Ribbon
24 L'Ecole
Fiamma Osteria

TriBeCa
28 Bouley
Nobu
27 Chanterelle
Danube
26 Il Giglio
Scalini Fedeli

Union Square
27 Union Sq. Cafe
25 Tocqueville
24 Blue Water
22 Olives
20 Spice
Whole Food Café

West 40s
25 Triomphe
db Bistro Moderne
24 Sushi Zen
Del Frisco's
Sushiden
Sea Grill

West 50s
28 Le Bernardin
27 Sugiyama
Atelier
Alain Ducasse
26 Milos
Norma's

West 60s
28 per se
27 Jean Georges
Masa
Picholine
25 Café Gray
23 Shun Lee West

West 70s
25 Onera
Gari
24 'Cesca
23 Ocean Grill
21 Scaletta
Pomodoro Rosso

West 80s
25 Ouest
24 Celeste
Barney Greengrass
23 Neptune Room
Aix
Nëo Sushi

West 90s & Up
24 Gennaro
Pisticci
Max
23 A
Saigon Grill
Terrace in the Sky

Outer Boroughs

Bronx
27 Roberto's
24 Pasquale's Rigoletto
23 Dominick's
22 Riverdale Garden
   F & J Pine
21 Madison's

Brooklyn: Bay Ridge
24 Areo
23 Pearl Room
   Tuscany Grill
22 Chianti
   Embers
21 Chadwick's

Brooklyn: Heights/Dumbo
26 Grimaldi's
   Henry's End
   River Café
25 Noodle Pudding
23 Queen
21 Five Front

**Brooklyn: Carroll Gardens/
Boerum Hill/Cobble Hill**
27 Grocery
26 Saul
24 Osaka
   Sweet Melissa
23 Joya
   Quercy

Brooklyn: Park Slope
26 Al Di La
   Blue Ribbon Sushi
25 Convivium Osteria
   Rose Water
   Blue Ribbon
   Tempo

Brooklyn: Williamsburg
28 Peter Luger
23 DuMont
   Diner
22 Bamonte's
   SEA
21 Relish

Brooklyn: Other
28 Garden Cafe
27 Di Fara
23 Franny's
   Nyonya
   L & B Spumoni Gardens
   Zaytoons

Queens: Astoria
26 Trattoria L'incontro
25 Piccola Venezia
24 Taverna Kyclades
23 Telly's Taverna
   718
22 Christos

Queens: Other
26 Sripraphai
25 Don Peppe
   Park Side
24 Tournesol
   Uncle Jack's
23 Manducatis

Staten Island
25 Denino's
   Trattoria Romana
23 Angelina's
19 American Grill
   Lento's
   Marina Cafe

Top Decor

28 Daniel
Rainbow Room
Danube
Four Seasons
27 per se
River Café
Asiate
La Grenouille
Megu
Kittichai
Tao
Alain Ducasse
Le Bernardin
Spice Market
Chanterelle
Matsuri
26 One if by Land
Suba
Sapa
Bouley
Aureole
Café des Artistes
FireBird
Hangawi
Eleven Madison

Modern, The
Jean Georges
Gramercy Tavern
Kings' Carriage Hse.
Café Botanica
Fifty Seven 57
25 Town
Boat House
Atelier
Water's Edge
Thalassa
Gotham Bar & Grill
March
Tavern on Green
Tabla
Asia de Cuba
View, The
Bayard's
Biltmore Room
EN Japanese
Terrace in the Sky
Lure Fishbar
Scalini Fedeli
24 Aquavit
Ono

Gardens

A.O.C.
Barbetta
Barolo
Battery Gardens
Bottino
Bryant Park Grill
Cávo
Convivium Osteria
Da Nico
Five Front
Gascogne
Gnoccho Cafe
Grocery

I Coppi
I Trulli
Le Jardin Bistro
Miracle Grill (E. Village)
Paradou
Park, The
Patois
Pure Food and Wine
Surya
Tavern on the Green
VaTutto
ViceVersa
Vittorio Cucina

Great Rooms

Alain Ducasse
Asiate
Atelier
Bayard's
Biltmore Room
Capital Grille
Craft
Daniel
Danube
FireBird
Four Seasons
Gramercy Tavern
La Grenouille
March

Matsuri
Megu
Milos
Modern, The
Mr. K's
Nobu 57
per se
Sapa
Scalini Fedeli
66
Spice Market
Suba
Tao
Town

Romance

Aix
Alain Ducasse
Aureole
Café Pierre
Chanterelle
Chez Josephine
Chez Michallet
Convivium Osteria
Danube
davidburke & donatella
Erminia
Il Buco
JoJo
La Grenouille
Le Gigot
Le Refuge
L'Impero
March
Mark's
One if by Land
Periyali
Petrossian
Piano Due
Piccola Venezia
Place, The
Primavera
Rainbow Room
River Café
Scalini Fedeli
Suba
Terrace in the Sky
Water's Edge

Views

Asiate
Battery Gardens
BED New York
Boat House
Café Gray
Foley's Fish House
Gigino at Wagner Park
per se
Pete's Downtown
Rainbow Room
River Café
Sea Grill
Terrace in the Sky
View, The
Water Club
Water's Edge

Top Service

28 per se
Le Bernardin
Daniel
27 Gramercy Tavern
La Grenouille
Chanterelle
Four Seasons
Atelier
Alain Ducasse
Bouley
Jean Georges
26 Aureole
Danube
Union Square Cafe
Café Boulud
Gotham Bar & Grill
Veritas
March
Annisa
25 Picholine
River Café
Tasting Room
Oceana
Masa
Eleven Madison

Scalini Fedeli
Le Perigord
Babbo
Mr. K's
Grocery
24 Hangawi
Aquavit
Mas
Blue Hill
Nobu
One if by Land
Tabla
Mark's
Piccola Venezia
Erminia
Bayard's
L'Impero
Montrachet
Saul
Il Giglio
Acappella
Tocqueville
Craft
Jewel Bako
Henry's End

Best Buys

Full-Menu Restaurants

Alice's Tea Cup/*Eclectic*
Bereket/*Turkish*
Big Wong/*Chinese*
Brennan & Carr/*American*
Chennai Garden/*Indian*
Cubana Café/*Cuban*
Daisy May's/*bbq*
Doyers/*Vietnamese*
El Malecon/*Dominican*
Excellent Dumpling/*Chinese*
Fresco on the Go/*Italian*
Friendhouse/*Asian*
Gahm Mi Oak/*Korean*
Goodies/*Chinese*
Great NY Noodle/*Chinese*
Joya/*Thai*
Kitchenette/*Southern*
L & B Spumoni/*Italian*
La Taza de Oro/*Puerto Rican*
Mama's Food/*American*
Mee Noodle/*Chinese*
Mill/*Korean*
Mill Basin/*Kosher*
Momofuku/*noodles*
New Green Bo/*Chinese*
Nha Trang/*Vietnamese*
Nyonya/*Malaysian*
Old Devil Moon/*Southern*
Olive Vine/*Middle Eastern*
Penelope/*American*
Pepe... To Go/*Italian*
Pho Bang/*Vietnamese*
Pho Viet Huong/*Vietnamese*
Planet Thailand/*Thai*
Pump/*Health Food*
Republic/*Asian*
Rice/*Eclectic*
Saigon Grill/*Vietnamese*
SEA/*Thai*
Sripraphai/*Thai*
Sweet-n-Tart/*Chinese*
Tierras/*Colombian*
Tuk Tuk/*Thai*
Veselka/*Ukrainian*
Whole Foods/*Eclectic*
Wondee Siam/*Thai*
X.O./*Chinese*
Zabar's Cafe/*Eclectic*
Zaytoons/*Middle Eastern*
Zeytuna/*Eclectic*

Specialty Shops

Amy's Bread/*baked goods*
A Salt & Battery/*fish 'n' chips*
Au Bon Pain/*baked goods*
BB Sandwich/*sandwiches*
Better Burger/*burgers*
Blue 9 Burger/*burgers*
burger joint-PM/*burgers*
Burritoville/*Mexican*
Cafe Lalo/*desserts*
Caracas/*arepas*
Carl's/*cheese steaks*
ChikaLicious/*desserts*
Chipotle/*Mexican*
Chop't Creative/*salads*
Corner Bistro/*burgers*
Cosí/*sandwiches*
Cosmic Cantina/*burritos*
Cozy Soup/*burgers*
Denino's/*pizza*
Di Fara/*pizza*
Dishes/*sandwiches*
Dumpling Man/*dumplings*
Emack & Bolio's/*ice cream*
Ess-a-Bagel/*deli*
F & B/*European hot dogs*
Ferrara/*Italian pastry*
Gray's Papaya/*hot dogs*
Grey Dog's/*coffeehse*
Grilled Cheese/*sandwiches*
Grimaldi's/*pizza*
Hale & Hearty/*soup*
Hampton Chutney/*Indian*
Island Burgers/*burgers*
Joe's Pizza/*pizza*
La Bergamote/*bakery*
Little Italy Pizza/*pizza*
Once Upon a Tart/*sandwiches*
Papaya King/*hot dogs*
Peanut Butter/*sandwiches*
Pizza 33/*pizza*
Press 195/*sandwiches*
Rickshaw/*dumplings*
Roll-n-Roaster/*sandwiches*
71 Irving Place/*coffeehse*
Shake Shack/*burgers*
Sweet Melissa/*pastry*
teany/*sandwiches*
Two Boots/*pizza*
Veniero's/*Italian pastry*
'wichcraft/*sandwiches*

Bargain Prix Fixe Menus
Lunch

Abboccato	$29	Le Colonial	35
Artisanal	25	Lenox Room	20
Asiate	35	Le Perigord	32
Atlantic Grill	20	L'Impero	34
Aureole	35	Levana	30
Avra Estiatorio	26	Luxia	15
Baldoria	27	Madison Bistro	22
Basta Pasta	15	Manhattan Grille	13
Bay Leaf	14	Mercer Kitchen	20
Beacon	28	Michael Jordan's	23
Becco	17	Milos	35
Bistro du Nord	15	Molyvos	24
Bombay Palace	14	Montparnasse	20
Bouley	35	Montrachet (Fri.)	20
Brasserie LCB	26	Mr. K's	25
Café Botanica	26	Nick & Stef's	35
Café des Artistes	25	Novitá	20
Cafe Luxembourg	26	Ocean Grill	20
Café Pierre	36	Odeon	24
Capsouto Frères	20	Orsay	29
Cascina	17	Park Bistro	25
Chiam	21	Patsy's	32
Chin Chin	20	Petrossian	24
Chola	14	Pó	30
Chur. Plataforma	31	Queen	24
Cibo	27	René Pujol	24
Cinque Terre	26	Riingo	20
Cipriani Downtown	35	Salaam Bombay	14
Darbar	11	San Domenico	30
davidburke/donatella	20	Sapphire Indian	13
Dawat	14	Sardi's	30
Delegates' Dining	25	Seppi's	24
Diwan	14	Shaan	15
Duane Park Cafe	22	Shun Lee Palace	20
Eleven Madison Park	25	Silverleaf Tavern	18
Felidia	30	66	20
FireBird	29	Sushi Yasuda	21
Fleur de Sel	25	Tabla	25
Frère Jacques	22	Tamarind	20
fresh	20	Tartine	13
Gallagher's Steak	20	Tavern on the Green	34
Gascogne	20	Terrace in the Sky	25
Gigino	23	Thalia	17
Giovanni	30	Tocqueville	20
Giorgio's/Gramercy	15	Town	28
Gotham Bar & Grill	25	Trata Estiatorio	18
Hangawi	33	Tse Yang	26
Honmura An	18	Turkish Kitchen	14
Il Menestrello	33	21 Club	33
Jean Georges	24	Ulrika's	22
Jewel of India	16	Utsav	15
JoJo	20	Vong	20
Kings' Carriage Hse.	19	V Steakhouse	20
La Mangeoire	23	Water Club	21
La Mediterranée	22	Water's Edge	29
La Petite Auberge	17	Yuka	18
L'Ecole	20	Zoë	20

Bargain Prix Fixe Menus
Dinner

PT = pre-theater only; where two prices are listed, the first is for pre-theater and the second is for normal dinner hours.

Abboccato/PT	$35	La Mangeoire	26/29
Akdeniz	18	La Mediterranée	27/30
Aki/PT	26	La Petite Auberge	25
Alouette/PT	22	Lavagna/PT	25
Amuse	35	Le Boeuf à la Mode	38
A.O.C. Bedford/PT	29	L'Ecole	32
Artisanal	35	Le Madeleine/PT	30
Atlantic Grill/PT	26	Lenox Room/PT	35
Au Coin de Feu	27	Le Singe Vert/PT	24
Avra/PT	35	Le Tableau/PT	26
Baldoria	35	Levana	30
Bay Leaf/PT	21	Luxia/PT	29
Becco	22	Madison Bistro	29
Bistro du Nord/PT	19	Mamlouk	35
Bombay Palace	30	Manhattan Grille/PT	27
Brasserie 8½	35	Métisse/PT	25
Brasserie Julien/PT	25	Michael Jordan's/PT	23
Brasserie LCB/PT	39	Molyvos/PT	35
Bryant Park Grill/PT	30	Montparnasse/PT	20
Café Botanica/PT	38	Montrachet	35
Candela/PT	20	Ocean Grill/PT	25
Capsouto Frères	35	Odeon/PT	28
Cascina/PT	25	O Mai	35
Cebu/PT	19	Ouest	29
Chelsea Bistro/PT	30	Park Bistro/PT	25
Chez Michallet	23/33	Pascalou/PT	19
Chez Napoléon	25	Payard Bistro/PT (Sat.)	34
Chin Chin	35	Petrossian/PT	31
Cibo	30	Queen/PT	24
Del Frisco's/PT	31	Russian Samovar/PT	28
Eastern King	20	San Domenico/PT	33
English is Italian	39	Saul	30
etcetera etcetera	30	Seppi's/PT	32
Frère Jacques/PT	25	Shaan/PT	22
Garden Cafe	30	Sharz Cafe/PT	19
Gascogne/PT	27	Sumile/PT	35
Gavroche/PT	19	Sushi Yasuda	21
Gigino	28	Table d'Hôte/PT	23
Giorgio's/Gramercy/PT	25	Tavern on the Green/PT	38
Giovanni	30	Thalia/PT	35
Hangawi	38	Tocqueville/PT	38
Henry's End/PT	22	Trata Estiatorio/PT	20
Il Menestrello	40	21 Club/PT	38
Indochine/PT	25	Ulrika's	22
Jacques Brasserie/PT	22	Utsav/PT	23
Jarnac	34	Vatan	23
Jewel of India/PT	22	ViceVersa/PT	35
Jules/PT	20	Village	25
Kitchen 22/82	25	Vivolo/PT	24
La Baraka	24/33	Vong/PT	38
La Belle Vie/PT	22	Water Club/PT	39
La Boîte en Bois/PT	32	Yuka	18

Restaurant Directory

A ⊠⊅ | 23 | 12 | 19 | $24 |

947 Columbus Ave. (bet. 106th & 107th Sts.), 212-531-1643
"Quirky" Morningside Heights BYO where the "inventive", all-organic French-Caribbean eats proffered in "thimble"-size environs are deemed "worth the smush"; seriously "cheap" tabs for "tasty" treats mean the "wait can be forever", but there's a "good bar next door" to help time pass.

A&B Lobster King House ◑ | ▽ 19 | 11 | 15 | $26 |

1 Mott St. (Bowery), 212-566-0930
If you "thought there were only three ways to cook" crustaceans, you don't know this Chinatown seafooder serving the "best lobster" every way imaginable; though carpers crab about "debatable feng shui" and "long weekend waits", all applaud the rock-bottom prices.

Abboccato | 23 | 21 | 22 | $60 |

Blakely Hotel, 136 W. 55th St. (bet. 6th & 7th Aves.), 212-265-4000; www.abboccato.com
"Well-crafted" Italian dishes to "wake the taste buds", including some "new twists on the old favorites", distinguish this "terrific newcomer" from the Livanos family (Molyvos, Oceana); factor in "attentive" service and a "date-worthy" space "convenient to City Center" and most agree it's "just what Midtown needed."

Abigael's | 20 | 14 | 17 | $48 |

1407 Broadway (bet. 38th & 39th Sts.), 212-575-1407; www.abigaels.com
This "tasteful" Garment District "standby" is touted for "varied" kosher New American fare at "not-too-exorbitant" prices; kvetchers who find the menu and main dining room "missing zip" suggest "stick to the upstairs" Pan-Asian–accented annex.

Above | 19 | 20 | 19 | $50 |

Hilton Times Sq., 234 W. 42nd St., 21st fl. (bet. 7th & 8th Aves.), 212-642-2626
Theatergoers applaud the "dependable" New American fare and "smooth" service offered at this "quiet" retreat perched 21 stories above the "Times Square madness"; opinions differ on the view ("beautiful" vs. "so-so") and the hotel setting ("elegant" vs. "strange"), but there's no dispute about the "expensive" tabs.

Acappella ⊠ | 24 | 21 | 24 | $65 |

1 Hudson St. (Chambers St.), 212-240-0163; www.acappella-restaurant.com
"Absolutely fabulous food" and "Oscar-worthy performances" from an "extremely attentive" staff light up this "dark" yet "elegant" TriBeCa Italian; yes, it can "make an expense account blush", but at least the signature "wicked" postprandial grappa's free.

Acqua Pazza ⊠ | 21 | 20 | 21 | $52 |

36 W. 52nd St. (bet. 5th & 6th Aves.), 212-582-6900; www.acquapazzanyc.com
"Fine food" and "elegant service" draw Midtowners seeking a "great business lunch" to this "stylish" Italian, but its "calming atmosphere" also lures locals in search of a "delicious" (albeit "high-priced") dinner in a room "quiet enough for conversation."

Adä | ▽ 24 | 23 | 22 | $49 |

208 E. 58th St. (bet. 2nd & 3rd Aves.), 212-371-6060; www.adanyc.com
Thanks to "refined" nouvelle "tweaks", this East Midtown "maharajah's hideaway" towers "above NYC's usual Indian" fare; the "muted" room and "warm" service are ideal for "quiet conversation", but that may be because its "pricey" tabs keep it "less crowded."

Aesop's Tables

▽ 22 | 18 | 19 | $41

1233 Bay St. (Maryland Ave.), Staten Island, 718-720-2005;
www.aesopstables.net
For "quirky" "Village" vibes on Staten Island, this petite "mom's kitchen" is a "pleasant surprise" with a "creative" Med–New American menu and "delightful" garden; it's "holding its own" as an area "winner", though a few say "underwhelming food" is the moral here.

Afghan Kebab House

18 | 10 | 16 | $22

764 Ninth Ave. (bet. 51st & 52nd Sts.), 212-307-1612
1345 Second Ave. (bet. 70th & 71st Sts.), 212-517-2776
74-16 37th Ave. (bet. 74th & 75th Sts.), Queens, 718-565-0471
"Cost-conscious" turbanites tout this "consistent" Afghan threesome's "filling", "nicely spiced" grilled meats and "budget" BYOB option; sticklers say the "humble surroundings" tend to "fall flat", but the "authenticity" and "value" "do the job if you want a kebab."

Agave

20 | 19 | 18 | $37

140 Seventh Ave. S. (bet. Charles & W. 10th Sts.), 212-989-2100;
www.agaveny.com
Something of a "New Age" cantina done up in "adobe" "neutrals", this West Villager ropes in "young, smiling faces" with "nontraditional" Southwestern fare that's "well executed" if "not overly exciting"; despite occasional "inattentive service", "potent" margaritas from the "great tequila list" keep things "cheery."

Agnanti

▽ 27 | 15 | 20 | $31

19-06 Ditmars Blvd. (19th St.), Queens, 718-545-4554;
www.agnantimeze.com
A "hike" to Astoria it may be, but this "real taverna's" "eclectic menu" of "fresh" Greek "home cooking" rewards travelers with "the stuff of dreams" at "reasonable prices"; the setup's as "simple" as "a bit of the Plaka", but "caring" hospitality keeps it "packed" and "gregarious."

Agozar!

▽ 18 | 17 | 17 | $31

324 Bowery (Bleecker St.), 212-677-6773; www.agozarnyc.com
This "casual" "li'l" Cuban is where NoHo's "cool folks" "explore" the possibilities of "down-home" Latin eats and "killer mojitos"; despite the "lively salsa" spirit, however, contras contend its "not distinguished" foodwise and "too small" for comfort.

Aix

23 | 22 | 21 | $61

2398 Broadway (88th St.), 212-874-7400; www.aixnyc.com
"Aix-cellent" is the word for this "first-class" French Upper Westsider, where Didier Virot's "rich", "accomplished" food is "paired expertly with wines" and "unobtrusive service"; some who "aix-pect a lot" for the "platinum" prices deem it "uneven", but for the *majorité* it's "worth every franc", er euro.

Aja ◓

21 | 23 | 19 | $43

1068 First Ave. (58th St.), 212-888-8008
"Nice feng shui" marks this Asian "hideaway" by the Queensboro Bridge, serving appealing Eastern eats ("solid sushi" included) in "artful" environs featuring a sub-floor goldfish pond and "beatific" "Buddha statue"; likened to a "mini-Tao", it's an "ambitious" upstart in a usually "sleepy" neighborhood.

Akdeniz ⊠

▽ 22 | 14 | 21 | $26

19 W. 46th St. (bet. 5th & 6th Aves.), 212-575-2307;
www.akdenizturkishusa.com
No one deniz that this "friendly" Midtowner's $17.95 prix fixe dinner is a "steal" for "well-prepared" Turkish fare; given its popularity as one

"of the better" "simple" meze joints, even loyalists fez up that the "narrow space" really "should expand."

Aki
| 25 | 13 | 22 | $40 |

181 W. Fourth St. (bet. Barrow & Jones Sts.), 212-989-5440
"Go figure", but this Village sushi specialist's unprecedented Japanese-Jamaican "blend" yields "consistently" "incredible" "treats" that "definitely convince" the "adventurous"; the "attention to detail" includes "charming service", though "very cozy" quarters offer barely enough seating to "fight over."

Aki Sushi
| 19 | 12 | 18 | $30 |

121 E. 27th St. (bet. Lexington Ave. & Park Ave. S.), 212-213-9888
366 W. 52nd St. (bet. 8th & 9th Aves.), 212-262-2888
1425 York Ave. (bet. 75th & 76th Sts.), 212-628-8885
"Quick" picks for "satisfactory" Japanese, these "itty bitty" "local sushi" stops serve "reliable" rolls at "reasonable prices"; there are "no lines", meaning walk-ins "can get a seat", but the "ambiance isn't much" so some suggest "stick to takeout" or "fast delivery."

ALAIN DUCASSE ⊠
| 27 | 27 | 27 | $179 |

Essex House, 155 W. 58th St. (bet. 6th & 7th Aves.), 212-265-7300;
www.alain-ducasse.com
"One of the best in NYC", Alain Ducasse's "fantastical" Central Park South "Shangri-la" "elates" diners who "feel like overindulging" with "hours" of culinary "wizardry" (courtesy of new exec chef Tony Esnault) and "unparalleled" service in the "most glamorous" of surroundings; "positively stunning" might equally describe the overall experience and the bill, but "win the Lotto" and "go for it" – "this isn't just food, it's theater."

Al Bustan
| 20 | 15 | 18 | $40 |

827 Third Ave. (bet. 50th & 51st Sts.), 212-759-5933; www.albustanny.com
The "genuine" goods for "meze in Midtown", this "traditional" Lebanese "lives up to" its reputation as a rare breed with "quality" "grazing" in "generous portions"; allies attest "they treat you well", though it's a pita about the "bland decor."

Alcala
| ▽ 22 | 17 | 21 | $50 |

342 E. 46th St. (bet. 1st & 2nd Aves.), 212-370-1866; www.alcalarestaurant.com
Renamed but "much the same" as ever, this "intimate" East Midtown "Spanish alcove" achieves acclaim for its "authentic" Basque-based dishes washed down with "full-bodied" "Iberian wines"; fans of the "quiet" "charm" declare "it's all good", if "pricey", for "neighborhood-type" dining.

AL DI LA
| 26 | 19 | 21 | $41 |

248 Fifth Ave. (Carroll St.), Brooklyn, 718-783-4565;
www.aldilatrattoria.com
A "perennial favorite" with a "cultish" Park Slope following, this "bustling" "taste of Venice" plies "superlative", "gently priced" cuisine in a "cramped" but "convivial" room; with "no reservations" and a "full house" al di time, the "round-the-corner wine bar" is "a lifesaver" during those inevitable "mind-boggling waits."

Aleo
| 22 | 20 | 22 | $42 |

7 W. 20th St. (5th Ave.), 212-691-8136; www.aleorestaurant.com
Perhaps it's the "unlikely" side-street location that keeps it "less well-known", but cognoscenti call this Flatiron Med-Italian a "find" for "flavorful", "fairly fared" food served by "eager-to-please" sorts; what's more, the "comfortable" scene comes complete with a "pretty", "date haven" "back garden."

Alexandra ◐
▽ | 20 | 16 | 15 | $38

455 Hudson St. (bet. Barrow & Morton Sts.), 212-255-3838
"Locals" "welcome" this "warm" West Village newcomer for its "good"
American bistro menu and "unpretentious" airs; when busy the "cozy"
"storefront" space "can be cramped" and service "hurried", but few
find fault after factoring "what they're charging."

Alfama
| 23 | 21 | 23 | $45

551 Hudson St. (Perry St.), 212-645-2500; www.alfamarestaurant.com
This "top-notch" West Village Portuguese is a "professional" yet
"relaxed" "charmer" with a menu of "well-executed" "regional"
highlights and "seamless" expat service; add a "massive" port list
and a "Wednesday night fado" crooner and it's as "authentic" as a
"trip to Lisbon" yet cheaper than the cab ride to JFK.

Al Forno Pizzeria
| 20 | 12 | 16 | $21

1484 Second Ave. (bet. 77th & 78th Sts.), 212-249-5103
Fulfill that "urge for a thin crust" at this Upper East Side pizzeria,
a "consistent", "kid-friendly" "staple" providing "fresh" brick-oven
pies that "never break the bank"; the faithful find it fine enough "to
rival Patsy's" – "without the wait."

Alfredo of Rome
| 19 | 18 | 19 | $46

4 W. 49th St. (bet. 5th & 6th Aves.), 212-397-0100; www.alfredos.com
The "signature fettuccini" that feeds its "popularity" may be traditional,
but this midpriced Rock Center Southern Italian looks "contemporary"
down to caricaturist Al "Hirschfeld's murals"; given that it's popular
with the "tourists", some locals seek "better options."

Algonquin Hotel Round Table
| 16 | 22 | 20 | $51

*Algonquin Hotel, 59 W. 44th St. (bet. 5th & 6th Aves.), 212-840-6800;
www.algonquinhotel.com*
For a "fond look back" at Dorothy Parker, Robert Benchley and the
"gang", many surveyors treasure this "fabled" Theater District hotel
as a "nostalgia" trip; however, the "heavy-handed" American food is
"not up to the price", so others opt for the Oak Room's "wonderful
cabaret" or drinking in the "beautiful", wood-paneled lobby.

Alias
| 21 | 16 | 20 | $41

76 Clinton St. (Rivington St.), 212-505-5011
Behind its "cool bodega" exterior, this "tiny" Lower Eastsider produces
"quality" "variations" on "comforting" American fare at an "entirely
reasonable" cost; despite sharing "tight quarters" with "chatty"
crowds, most diners don't disguise their liking for its "winning ways."

Ali Baba
| 23 | 14 | 17 | $25

*212 E. 34th St. (2nd & 3rd Aves.), 212-683-9206;
www.alibabaturkishcuisine.com*
"Tell your stomach to open sesame" at this Murray Hill Turk, a "hectic"
"neighborhood favorite" (now in "bigger new" digs) that's decreed
"the real thing" for "mouthwatering" "delights" like kebabs and
"Turkish pizza"; seekers of "value" vow "come hungry, leave happy."

Alice's Tea Cup
| 19 | 20 | 16 | $23

*102 W. 73rd St. (bet. Amsterdam & Columbus Aves.), 212-799-3006;
www.alicesteacup.com*
296 City Island Ave. (Hawkins St.), Bronx, 718-885-0808
Site of "girlie gatherings" for "ages 8–80", this West Side tearoom (with
a City Island "sipster" sister) offers an "entertaining" "Wonderland
theme", an "array" of brews and "scrumptious" nibbles; though the
staff's "reliable as the Cheshire Cat" and the milieu may be a tad
"precious", most customers are suited to a tea.

Aliseo Osteria del Borgo ⊅   ▽ 23 | 21 | 22 | $37

665 Vanderbilt Ave. (bet. Park & Prospect Pls.), Brooklyn, 718-783-3400
"A real gem" in Prospect Heights, this "warm" restaurant/enoteca looks to Central Italy's Marche region for its "amazing" "country fare" and "well-selected" wines; the "whimsical owner" "makes you feel at home" in a "studio apartment"–size space where regulars report enjoying "good times."

Alma   22 | 21 | 19 | $33

187 Columbia St., 2nd fl. (Degraw St.), Brooklyn, 718-643-5400;
www.almarestaurant.com
"Not your typical Mexican", this "find" "brings *vida* to Carroll Gardens" with its "imaginative" "high-end" food and "yowza" margaritas; "special" mention goes to the "roof deck", which is "the place to be" for "dazzling" "shipyard" and Lower Manhattan "skyline" views.

Alouette ●   20 | 17 | 19 | $42

2588 Broadway (bet. 97th & 98th Sts.), 212-222-6808
Flocks of Upper West Side Francophiles find "unexpected" "refuge" at this "simple" bistro where "fine" "classics" are "cheerfully served" in "unhurried" style; it's an "asset" at a "reasonable price", though "*coude à coude*" seating may be too "intimate" at times.

Alta   22 | 21 | 17 | $42

64 W. 10th St. (bet. 5th & 6th Aves.), 212-505-7777; www.altarestaurant.com
Highly regarded for "inventiveness", this Village Mediterranean's "impressive range" of tapas and "quirky wine list" are "delectable" even if tabs for those "tiny" plates "can be alta too"; with the "romantic" back room's balcony and "roaring fire" to distract from "sometimes lagging" service, contented customers call it "a keeper."

Alto ⊠   ▽ 24 | 23 | 23 | $92

520 Madison Ave. (enter on 53rd St., bet. Fifth & Madison Aves.),
212-308-1099; www.altorestaurant.com
Scott Conant's "fabulous" "fresh take on Italian" showcases "surprising flavors" from the Alto Adige region and an "enviable" wine cellar suggested by a wall of bottles; an ambiance of "beautiful" "formality" complements this "unusual" – and unusually "expensive" – new high "concept" Midtown outing.

Ama   23 | 20 | 20 | $48

48 MacDougal St. (bet. King & Prince Sts.), 212-358-1707; www.amanyc.com
Dining *donna* "Donatella Arpaia does it again" with "lots of love" at her "sleek", "chic" new Italian, a "stylish" amalgam of SoHo "hip" and "superb" "homemade tastes" from the Puglia region; its "trendy" but "serene" "white decor" may seem "minimal", but it's already attracting maximal "attention."

Amarone ●   19 | 14 | 19 | $38

686 Ninth Ave. (bet. 47th & 48th Sts.), 212-245-6060
An "affordable" "pre-theater standby" "just where it's needed", this "down-to-earth" Hell's Kitchen Italian supplies "decent red-sauce" pastas and "fast service" to ensure you "make the curtain"; it's liable to be "noisy and rushed" since the "straightforward" act plays to a "packed" house.

American Grill   19 | 17 | 21 | $42

420 Forest Ave. (bet. Bard Ave. & Hart Blvd.), Staten Island, 718-442-4742;
www.americangrill.org
Staten Islanders hit the "big city without the boat ride" at this "lively" local "favorite", where the "predictable" American menu's show of "patriotism" is "popular" with all parties; tabs may run "high", but

the "cheery" vibe and "consistent" "quality" are "much needed" in the area.

Amici Amore I

▽ 21 18 20 $38

29-35 Newtown Ave. (30th St.), Queens, 718-267-2771;
www.amiciamore1.com
You'll feel "like one of the family" at this Astoria "neighborhood" Italian, a go-to for affordable, "large, tasty portions" of "solid" "standards"; *amici* attest you "gotta love" the "hospitality" even if it's a little less "homey" since they attached the "steakhouse next door."

Amma

23 17 21 $40

246 E. 51st St. (bet. 2nd & 3rd Aves.), 212-644-8330; www.ammanyc.com
Reaching "the highest caste in Indian food", this "welcoming" East Midtown "hideaway" caters to "sophisticated tastes" with a "broad range" of "delicious" choices that "tells you you're not on Sixth Street"; it's "not the cheapest", but fans declare "Amma believer!"

Ammos ●

– – – M

20-30 Steinway St. (bet. 20th Ave. & 20th Rd.), Queens, 718-726-7900;
www.ammosnewyork.com
This new Astoria Greek is making a flap with "the freshest seafood on land", served by "attentive" staffers in a rustically "upscale" room with wood beams and candlelight; despite a "middle-of-nowhere" locale, it packs the alimentary ammo to "quickly become" a "heavyweight in its class."

Amuse

– – – E

108 W. 18th St. (bet. 6th & 7th Aves.), 212-929-9755; www.amusenyc.com
With the departure of chef-owner Gerry Hayden, the menu of this Chelsea New American has become more conventional and no longer follows its former mix-and-match, Craft-like approach; still, its sleek, modern setting and circa-1889 bar remain intact.

Amy Ruth's

23 12 17 $23

113 W. 116th St. (bet. Lenox & 7th Aves.), 212-280-8779;
www.amyruthsrestaurant.com
Wear "an adjustable belt" to Carl Redding's "hopping" Harlem Southerner, where the "sinful" likes of chicken 'n' waffles and ribs 'n' layer cake are smack "on the money"; the "cafeterialike decor" and "slow" (but "sweet") service "in no way suggest the quality", but the "line outside" does.

Amy's Bread

24 12 17 $12

250 Bleecker St. (bet. Carmine & Leroy Sts.), 212-675-7802
Chelsea Mkt., 75 Ninth Ave. (bet. 15th & 16th Sts.), 212-462-4338
672 Ninth Ave. (bet. 46th & 47th Sts.), 212-977-2670
www.amysbread.com
"One *can* live by bread alone" at this "tempting" trio, whose "superior" "array" of "artisanal loaves" and calorific "baked goodies" are all a "carb addict" kneads; even with "compact" quarters and "moody" service, they're almost "too popular", and a Village "hearth" now offsets the loss of the Upper East Side outlet.

Angelica Kitchen ∅

20 14 17 $23

300 E. 12th St. (bet. 1st & 2nd Aves.), 212-228-2909;
www.angelicakitchen.com
To go through vegan "detox" try this East Village "old-timer", serving "macrobiotic" "at its tastiest" and most "uncompromising" in a "hippie" "haven" worthy of "Berkeley"; though it "satisfies" the "virtuous", skeptics say "spacey" staffers and "bland" eats can be less than angelic.

Angelina's
23 | 19 | 22 | $53

26 Jefferson Blvd. (Annadale Rd.), Staten Island, 718-227-7100;
www.angelinasristorante.com

"Ultimate hostess" Angelina Malerba brings "a little Manhattan" to
Staten Island at this "classy" Italian, where the "fabulous" food and
"warm" ambiance belie the "strip-mall" exterior; then again, the cost
is "a bit over the top" for the underwhelming location.

Angelo & Maxie's ●
21 | 19 | 19 | $51

233 Park Ave. S. (19th St.), 212-220-9200; www.angelo-maxies.com

You can "feel the testosterone" at this Flatiron "beeffest", where
"boisterous" "boiler room boys" "with Blackberries" convene for
"massive hunks of meat", "man-size drinks" and "deafening" banter;
"solid if unexceptional", it's "entertaining" for a "big party" "without
the crazy prices" of its competitors.

Angelo's of Mulberry Street ●
22 | 16 | 19 | $41

146 Mulberry St. (bet. Grand & Hester Sts.), 212-966-1277;
www.angelomulberry.com

"There's a reason" this Little Italy landmark has "been around
forever": "garlicky" "old-style Southern Italian" that's "done right"
and served by "traditional" types who "truly know the drill"; loyalists
who "savor every bite" shrug off the plain room and "touristy" "droves"
as "to be expected."

Angelo's Pizzeria
21 | 13 | 15 | $22

1697 Broadway (bet. 53rd & 54th Sts.), 212-245-8811
1043 Second Ave. (55th St.), 212-521-3600
117 W. 57th St. (bet. 6th & 7th Aves.), 212-333-4333

A "nice change from greasy slices", this pizza trio's "ultrathin" "coal-
fired" pies are "right up there" for "well-topped" "crispiness"; though
the "hapless staff" and "basic" decor detract, these "budget" places
"fill an important niche" in high-rent Midtown.

Angon on the Sixth
▽ 23 | 14 | 17 | $28

320 E. Sixth St. (bet. 1st & 2nd Aves.), 212-260-8229; www.angon.biz

It's "seventh heaven" on Sixth Street thanks to this "real-deal" East
Village Indian, where a "cult following" extols the "high-level"
"homestyle" cooking as a "rare treat" at "reasonable prices"; some
cite "uneven" service, but it's a clear "standout" on the block.

Angus McIndoe ●
17 | 16 | 20 | $39

258 W. 44th St. (bet. B'way & 8th Ave.), 212-221-9222;
www.angusmcindoe.com

The "Broadway buzz" will "make your head turn" at this "tri-level"
Theater District American, a "busy" "star-stalking" "joint" where the
thespian "'in' crowd" "meets, greets and eats" in "loud", "convivial"
style; it offers "respectable" if "basic" chow, but "you don't come
here for the food."

Anh
20 | 15 | 17 | $26

363 Third Ave. (bet. 26th & 27th Sts.), 212-532-2858;
www.anhrestaurant.com

As an anh-est "neighborhood" eatery, this Gramercy Vietnamese
offers tasty "takes on the old standbys" and "alert service" in "small",
"quiet" surroundings; those in-the-know call it a "favorite" for
"reliable" dining "on the cheap", so "why don't more people know?"

Annie's
17 | 15 | 16 | $27

1381 Third Ave. (bet. 78th & 79th Sts.), 212-327-4853

Join the weekend brunch line "the night before" or face "brutal"
waits at this Upper East Side American, home to "hearty" "comfort

food" in "upgraded diner" digs; it's a "family" favorite, though the "no-stroller policy" riles a few "Burberry-clad moms."

ANNISA
27 | 23 | 26 | $65

13 Barrow St. (bet. 7th Ave. S. & W. 4th St.), 212-741-6699;
www.annisarestaurant.com
"Stealth superstar" Anita Lo "works her magic" at this "civilized" Villager, which "enchants the senses" with "smart" New American "artistry", "gracious service" and "spare, elegant" decor; a "wowed" crowd urges "raise your credit card limit" – it's "worth the splurge."

A.o.C. ◑
18 | 17 | 17 | $36

314 Bleecker St. (Grove St.), 212-675-9463; www.aocnyc.com
Villagers favor this "pleasant" French for its "modestly" priced bistro "basics" and "splendid" year-round garden perfect for weekend brunch; if the staffers can be a tad "neglectful", supporters just give it the Gallic shrug – hey, at least they're "friendly."

A.O.C. Bedford
24 | 21 | 22 | $51

14 Bedford St. (bet. Downing & Houston Sts.), 212-414-4764;
www.aocbedford.com
This "special little place" in the Village is "worth seeking out" for its "thoughtful menu" of "excellent" Southern European dishes, "wonderful wine" list and "attentive" staff; as for the space, one diner's "tight" is another's "cozy"; N.B. it's BYO on Sundays and Mondays.

ápizz ☒
24 | 21 | 22 | $41

217 Eldridge St. (bet. Rivington & Stanton Sts.), 212-253-9199;
www.apizz.com
"Oft overlooked" but "worth" scouting out, this "offbeat" Lower East Side "grotto" focuses on "distinctive" Italian dishes ("pizza is a must") "masterfully cooked" in a "wood-burning oven"; the "friendly service" and "reasonable" tabs also "please" those "in on the secret."

Applewood
23 | 19 | 21 | $44

501 11th St. (bet. 7th & 8th Aves.), Brooklyn, 718-768-2044;
www.applewoodny.com
Boasting an "on-target" New American menu, this new Park Sloper makes "ambitious" use of "seasonal, organic ingredients" that complement its "farmhouse interior" and "warm" service; critics cite "modest" portions and "Manhattan prices", but it's "already a neighborhood favorite."

AQ Cafe ☒
▽ 21 | 15 | 13 | $19

Scandinavia House, 58 Park Ave. (bet. 37th & 38th Sts.), 212-847-9745;
www.aquavit.org
It's "Aquavit on a budget" at Marcus Samuelsson's cafeteria-style Murray Hill "lunch spot", a "generous" "Scandinavian taste treat" if you don't mind "Nordic-spartan decor" and toting "your own tray"; for a "Swedish meatball fix" or a cheap "change of pace", it "can't be beat."

AQUAGRILL
26 | 19 | 22 | $54

210 Spring St. (6th Ave.), 212-274-0505
"If you like fish", it's "piscatorial heaven" at this "tried-and-true" SoHo "crowd-pleaser", known for a "top-shelf" raw bar and other "right-off-the-boat" seafood served by a "smart" staff; though "not cheap", it's "always packed" with a pleasing crowd.

AQUAVIT
25 | 24 | 24 | $68

65 E. 55th St. (bet. Madison & Park Aves.), 212-307-7311; www.aquavit.org
Only "the waterfall is missed" in the "elegantly" "streamlined" new East Side setting of Marcus Samuelsson's transplanted "Nordic

nirvana", which "continues to shine" with "innovative", "beautifully crafted" Scandinavian fare; service from real "pros" and "housemade aquavits" round out this "culinary wonder", "if you can affjord it."

Arabelle
▽ | 25 | 26 | 27 | $71

Plaza Athénée Hotel, 37 E. 64th St. (Madison Ave.), 212-606-4647; www.arabellerestaurant.com
A "quiet haven" "at the high end", the Plaza Athénée's French-American "secret" is a "soothing" synthesis of "fine" food, "formal" chandeliered surroundings and "classic" "fawning" service; the "old-world" style suits "older" fans who say it "deserves more recognition."

Areo ●
24 | 19 | 19 | $47

8424 Third Ave. (bet. 84th & 85th Sts.), Brooklyn, 718-238-0079
"One of Bay Ridge's hottest spots", this "real Italian" is famed for its "terrific food" and "high decibel levels"; while you "wait forever to be seated", the "overdressed locals" with "slicked-back 'do's" and "big hair" will keep you "entertained."

Arezzo ☒
22 | 17 | 20 | $48

46 W. 22nd St. (bet. 5th & 6th Aves.), 212-206-0555; www.arezzony.com
It's hard to understand why this Flatiron Tuscan remains "undiscovered" given its "delightful" food, "enthusiastic service" and "spare but attractive" space; while well-wishers hail it as a "neighborhood find", others answer the "prices outstrip the surroundings."

Arqua
23 | 20 | 21 | $50

281 Church St. (White St.), 212-334-1888
To "escape TriBeCa attitude" try this "family-run" Northern Italian, a deservedly longtime "standby" serving "deliciously" "nuanced" food in an "airy", rusticated room where it's "easy to talk"; "solicitous" staffers who "know their job" ensure it "delivers" ("very well").

Arté
17 | 17 | 18 | $41

21 E. Ninth St. (bet. 5th Ave. & University Pl.), 212-473-0077
"Neighborhood" regulars rely on this "quaint", "convenient" Villager for "typical Italian" eats "awash in sauce" and served with "old-school" civility; though "nothing special", it's a "warm setting" "summer or winter" thanks to the fireplace and "garden out back."

Arté Café
18 | 18 | 17 | $32

106 W. 73rd St. (bet. Amsterdam & Columbus Aves.), 212-501-7014; www.artecafenyc.com
"The secret's out" on this "sturdy", "economical" Italian, where "decent" pasta and "amazing" prix fixe deals promise "casual" "carb-loading" close to Lincoln Center; snobs sniff at "standard" fare and service, but "with these prices, how can you complain?"

Artie's Deli
18 | 11 | 15 | $21

2290 Broadway (bet. 82nd & 83rd Sts.), 212-579-5959; www.arties.com
Modeled after an "old-style deli", this Upper Westsider boasts "noisy" crowds, "harried service" and "heart-stopping" noshes like the "signature pastrami"; it's not only as "bright" and "kid-friendly" as "Epcot", but hungry locals also report it "hits the spot" at a "decent price."

ARTISANAL
23 | 20 | 20 | $50

2 Park Ave. (enter on 32nd St., bet. Madison & Park Aves.), 212-725-8585
"Holy cheese!", Terrance Brennan's "cavernous" Murray Hill brasserie focuses on "celestial" fromage, with "beaucoup options" from "all over the world" paired with 160 "fab wines by the glass"; the French milieu,

"cacophony" and "cheese whiz" service are a "heady" experience, and there's even a "retail counter" for goods to go.

Arturo's Pizzeria ◗

22 | 12 | 15 | $22

106 W. Houston St. (Thompson St.), 212-677-3820
If "coal-fired pizza" is "the real thing", this "old-time" Village Italian is "right on the mark", plying "awesome" pies amid wall-to-wall "kitsch" with "live jazz accompaniment"; "nostalgic" types tout the "wonderfully dumpy" digs, but warn that it may be "cramped" at times.

A Salt & Battery

18 | 9 | 15 | $15

112 Greenwich Ave. (bet. 12th & 13th Sts.), 212-691-2713
80 Second Ave. (bet. 4th & 5th Sts.), 212-254-6610
www.asaltandbattery.com
"Would-be Brits and lonesome Limeys" satisfy their "cravings" for fish 'n' chips at these low-budget twins where "everything's deep-fried", even Mars Bars; the East Side outlet offers seating, while the West Village "hole-in-the-wall" screams "takeout."

ASIA DE CUBA

24 | 25 | 20 | $56

Morgans Hotel, 237 Madison Ave. (bet. 37th & 38th Sts.), 212-726-7755;
www.chinagrillmanagement.com
You'd better "wear all black" and cop an "attitude" at this "action"-packed Murray Hill Asian-Cuban, an "über-sleek" "Philippe Starck–designed beauty" matching "exciting" food with "attentive" (if "haughty") service; it's "hard to beat for heat" even with "tourists and wannabes" thinning the "Euro-model"/"power broker" crowd, but "save up" because "feeling special" "will cost you."

ASIATE

23 | 27 | 23 | $82

Mandarin Oriental Hotel, 80 Columbus Circle, 35th fl. (60th St.),
212-805-8881; www.mandarinoriental.com/newyork/
Reaching "dazzling heights", the Mandarin Oriental Hotel's "luxe" Japanese-French "perch" with "million-dollar views" of Central Park showcases chef Nori Sugie's "inspired", "exotic" "artistry" in an "ethereal" window-lined space; service disputes aside ("superb" vs. "uneven"), it's "worth every dime" of the "trust-fund" tabs.

Assaggio

19 | 17 | 19 | $36

473 Columbus Ave. (bet. 82nd & 83rd Sts.), 212-877-0170
When "you're in the neighborhood", this Upper West Side Italian is a "cheerful", "consistent" spot for "homemade pasta" at a "fair price"; it's a "relaxing" "hangout" with "pleasant" "outside seating" to assuage critics of the "limited" offerings.

ATELIER

27 | 25 | 27 | $95

Ritz-Carlton Central Park, 50 Central Park S. (6th Ave.), 212-521-6125;
www.ritzcarlton.com
"Dignified" dining "for adults" is the métier at the Ritz-Carlton Central Park's "plush" New French, where chef Alain Allegretti's "seamless" takeover is evident in the "stellar" food ("changed my life"); offering a "stately environment" where the "charming" servers "have ESP", it caters to a necessarily well-heeled clientele.

ATLANTIC GRILL ◗

22 | 19 | 20 | $47

1341 Third Ave. (bet. 76th & 77th Sts.), 212-988-9200;
www.brguestrestaurants.com
"Always hopping" with a "sea" of stylish neighbors, Steve Hanson's "standout" Upper Eastsider is a "staple" for "first-rate fish" served by a "cordial", "competent" crew "at decent prices"; it "delivers" "satisfaction" with "no surprises", but there's often "quite a wait" at the bar.

Au Bon Pain ⊅

14 | 8 | 11 | $11

684 Broadway (W. 3rd St.), 212-420-1694
58 E. Eighth St. (Mercer St.), 212-475-8546
122 E. 42nd St. (bet. Lexington & Park Aves.), 212-599-8643
Macy's Department Store, 151 W. 34th St. (7th Ave.), 212-494-1091
Manhattan Tower, 600 Lexington Ave. (bet. 52nd & 53rd Sts.), 212-223-8679
Port Authority, 625 Eighth Ave. (bet. 40th & 41st Sts.), 212-502-4823 ◑
1 State St. Plaza (Water St.), 212-952-9098
6 Union Sq. E. (14th St.), 212-475-0453
125 W. 55th St. (bet. 6th & 7th Aves.), 212-246-6518
World Financial Ctr., 200 Liberty St. (West St.), 212-962-9421
www.aubonpain.com

"Help yourself" to "soup and sandwiches on the fly" at these "hectic" "no-brainers", where the mundane "munchies" are "handy in a pinch" and "trendier than Dunkin' Donuts"; but expect "utilitarian" setups with service so "surly" it's "almost French."

Au Coin du Feu

– | – | – | M

222 Lafayette St. (Spring St.), 212-226-7676

It's "easy to walk past" this new NoLita "French joint" given its narrow candlelit space, but it's hard to pass up a "surprisingly great meal" at such a "reasonable price"; the cordial expat staff would be equally at home at the Riviera original.

August ◑

23 | 21 | 20 | $43

359 Bleecker St. (bet. Charles & W. 10th Sts.), 212-929-4774;
www.augustny.com

Known for "hearty" "seasonal" specialties straight from the wood oven, this Village regional European "gem" would be a "winner" "for any month"; it's a "loudish" "shoebox" with "close tables", but its "picture-perfect" rusticity ("courtyard" included) is "inviting" all year.

Au Mandarin

19 | 14 | 18 | $30

World Financial Ctr., 200-250 Vesey St. (West St.), 212-385-0313;
www.worldfinancialcenter.com/dining/

In a "white-linen" setting, this WFC Chinese "fixture" suits "all the suits" who keep it "bustling" for "business lunch"; it may be a tad "overpriced", but it's "quick on the go."

AUREOLE ☒

27 | 26 | 26 | $81

34 E. 61st St. (bet. Madison & Park Aves.), 212-319-1660;
www.charliepalmer.com

Charlie Palmer and chef Dante Boccuzzi remain "at the top of their game" at this "unforgettable" East Side townhouse duplex, where the "lovingly prepared" New American fare sets the "gold standard" down to the "masterpiece" desserts; "highbrow" surroundings and "classy service" bolster its "mythical status", so go for a "splurge" or aim for "value" via the $35 lunch prix fixe.

Austin's Steakhouse ☒

▽ 21 | 19 | 21 | $54

8915 Fifth Ave. (90th St.), Brooklyn, 718-439-5000;
www.austinssteakhouseny.com

Casual carnivores "trek" to this "low-key" Bay Ridge steakhouse to put away "prime steak" in simple digs noteworthy mostly for their "really good vibe"; meanwhile antis protest "Manhattan prices" for a cowdown that's not up to the top rank.

Avra Estiatorio ◑

24 | 21 | 21 | $52

141 E. 48th St. (bet. Lexington & 3rd Aves.), 212-759-8550; www.avrany.com

Channeling "the Aegean right in to Midtown", this Greek seafooder offers "classic" preparations of "incredibly fresh" fish; "you feel right at home" amid the "friendly" "din" of the indoor/outdoor space, but "be careful" of "pricing by the pound."

Azafran ●
21	19	20	$43

77 Warren St. (bet. Greenwich St. & W. B'way), 212-284-0578; www.azafrannyc.com

"You can't top the tapas" at this "smooth" TriBeCa Spaniard "hot spot" presenting such an "outstanding" variety it's "hard to pick a favorite"; it's commended for "intriguing" eating, but watch out for "tight" seating and tabs that "sure add up" fast.

Azucar ●
–	–	–	M

939 Eighth Ave. (56th St.), 212-262-5354; www.azucarnyc.com

A little Havana heat spices up the area just south of Columbus Circle courtesy of this new midpriced Cuban; in addition to the island-esque setting and occasional live music, dinner comes with a bonus: a gratis, hand-rolled cigar made on premises.

Azul Bistro ●
▽ 23	19	19	$37

152 Stanton St. (Suffolk St.), 646-602-2004

It's easy to "love being a carnivore" at this "affordable" Lower East Side Argentinean, where the "first-rate" steaks and "interesting wines" are so "genuine" it's like being "back in B. A."; though "remote", it's a "relaxed" alternative for blue-chip beef.

Azuri Cafe ⊅
▽ 23	3	8	$12

465 W. 51st St. (bet. 9th & 10th Aves.), 212-262-2920

Those who "overlook" "service without a smile" from the "meshuga" owner esteem this "tiny" Westsider for its "remarkable", inexpensive Israeli fare; the "attitude" and "sardine can" setup suggest "takeout."

BABBO ●
27	24	25	$70

110 Waverly Pl. (bet. MacDougal St. & 6th Ave.), 212-777-0303; www.babbonyc.com

"There is no hype" at Mario Batali and Joe Bastianich's Villager voted the *Survey*'s No. 1 Italian, just "unbeatable" "originality" in the "intense flavors" that amount to "pure bliss" for "capacity" crowds; "exemplary" service, "impressive wines" and the "rollicking" "vibrance" of the carriage house surroundings help make it "the place to be", so keep "redialing" because getting reservations here is "a blood sport."

Babu ●
▽ 23	21	22	$62

99 MacDougal St., downstairs (bet. Bleecker & W. 3rd Sts.), 212-979-2228

For a "traditional" taste of Calcutta, this Village Indian upstart "artfully" concocts "excellent" Bengali cuisine in a simple but "sexy" subterranean space; newfound followers claim it's a "pleasant change" from what's found elsewhere.

Bacchus ●
▽ 20	15	19	$33

409 Atlantic Ave. (Bond St.), Brooklyn, 718-852-1572

At this "little" Boerum Hill bistro, you'll find "sturdy French" cooking and "sweet service" à la the "Left Bank"; it "gets pretty packed" (especially for Wednesday's "two-for-one" entree special), with crowds overflowing into the "lovely" bacch garden.

Baldoria
21	17	20	$54

249 W. 49th St. (bet. B'way & 8th Ave.), 212-582-0460; www.baldoriamo.com

"Regular people" who "can't get in to Rao's" find "the next best thing" at Frank Pellegrino Jr.'s Theater District Italian, a "commendable" source of "damn good" "old-school" dishes and "cheerful service"; fans assemble "en masse" in the "big and noisy" duplex space to take in the "easygoing" "*Sopranos*/Sinatra vibe."

BALTHAZAR ◗
23 | 23 | 20 | $51

80 Spring St. (bet. B'way & Crosby St.), 212-965-1414; www.balthazarny.com
Still "the quickest way to Paris", Keith McNally's "insanely popular" SoHo brasserie "never loses its edge", doing a "phenomenal job" from the "prototypical" decor to the "pitch-perfect" French fare and "energetic" staff; offering "megawatts of electricity", it draws everyone from a "gossipy" "who's who" to "fanny-packed tourists", so prepare for a "claustrophobic" "hubbub" and "expect to wait unless you're Madonna."

Baluchi's
18 | 14 | 16 | $25

283 Columbus Ave. (bet. 73rd & 74th Sts.), 212-579-3900 ◗
224 E. 53rd St. (bet. 2nd & 3rd Aves.), 212-750-5515
111 E. 29th St. (bet. Lexington Ave. & Park Ave. S.), 212-481-3861
1149 First Ave. (63rd St.), 212-371-3535
104 Second Ave. (6th St.), 212-780-6000
1565 Second Ave. (bet. 81st & 82nd Sts.), 212-288-4810
1724 Second Ave. (bet. 89th & 90th Sts.), 212-996-2600
193 Spring St. (bet. Sullivan & Thompson Sts.), 212-226-2828
240 W. 56th St. (bet. B'way & 8th Ave.), 212-397-0707
263 Smith St. (Degraw St.), Brooklyn, 718-797-0707
www.baluchis.com
"Sure it's a chain", but these "fail-safe" havens for "Indian in a pinch" are "naan too bad" for a "competent" "fix" of "the basics" at "modest prices" (viz. the "wallet-friendly" half-off "lunch deal"); though "predictable", the "trusty" formula "holds its own."

Bamonte's
22 | 16 | 21 | $37

32 Withers St. (bet. Lorimer St. & Union Ave.), Brooklyn, 718-384-8831
After 100 years, this Williamsburg "throwback" is still "keeping it real" with "no-nonsense" "red-sauce Italian" and "local color" "so classic it's nearly a cliché"; "gruff" waiters boost the "old-time" feel, and if it "isn't too inventive", "without a doubt" it remains "something special."

Banania Cafe ⊘
21 | 18 | 18 | $29

241 Smith St. (Douglass St.), Brooklyn, 718-237-9100
As an "anchor of Smith Street", this "sweet little" Cobble Hill French bistro is a local go-to for "creative" bites that are "tough to beat" "for the money"; the "relaxed" ambiance turns "terminally crowded" come weekend brunch, but it's still "worth the wait."

Banjara ◗
23 | 15 | 18 | $30

97 First Ave. (6th St.), 212-477-5956; www.banjaranyc.com
"Don't even turn onto Sixth Street" advise allies of this "impressive" East Village Indian, where the "vividly spiced" food and "attentive" service easily outpace the competition's; even the "decor's fancier" than the norm, so though tabs run "slightly more", "this one's a keeper."

Bann
– | – | – | E

350 W. 50th St. (bet. 8th & 9th Aves.), 212-582-4446
A Zen-like walkway takes diners from a trendy front lounge to a dining temple made ethereal by gossamer screens and bamboo at this theatrical Midtown West Korean inside Worldwide Plaza; the open kitchen specializes in upscale BBQ and other options good for sharing.

Bann Thai
20 | 18 | 20 | $27

69-12 Austin St. (Yellowstone Blvd.), Queens, 718-544-9999; www.bannthairestaurant.com
Fanns go "out of the way" to this "inviting" Forest Hills Thai for "super" food spiced "the way it should be" and served with "a smile"; if skeptics scoff "overpriced", "you'd pay double" for the "quality" in Manhattan.

Bao Noodles ⊄
20 15 16 $26

391 Second Ave. (bet. 22nd & 23rd Sts.), 212-725-6182
Bringing Bao 111's "subtlety" to Gramercy, this "casual" Vietnamese draws devotees with "Hue delicious" "classics" at "moderate" tabs; the seating's so "close" you'll "lock chopsticks with your neighbors", but it's a "treat" given the "sparse selection" hereabouts.

Bao 111 ◐
23 19 17 $39

111 Ave. C (bet. 7th & 8th Sts.), 212-254-7773; www.bao111.com
A "shining star" among "high-end Vietnamese", this East Villager attracts a "hipper-than-thou crowd" for "ultratasty" food and sakes; despite the "squished space" and "portions befitting models", most agree it's "hard not to love" this "original."

Bar Americain ◐
▽ 24 25 23 $61

152 W. 52nd St. (bet. 6th & 7th Aves.), 212-265-9700; www.baramericain.com
Star chef Bobby Flay "works his magic" with an "upscale take" on "classic" regional American at this Midtown newcomer, fielding a "fresh", "imaginative menu" in a brasserie setting (the former JUdson Grill space, made over by David Rockwell); add a staff of "professionals", and early handicappers predict "another winner."

Baraonda ◐
18 17 16 $45

1439 Second Ave. (75th St.), 212-288-8555; www.baraondany.com
See the East Side's "wilder side" at this "high-energy" Italian, a "major meet market" where "good-looking" Euros share their "joie de vivre"; the menu of "staples" is "better than you'd expect", but it's the "hopping scene" that "stands out."

Barbès ◐
22 19 22 $40

21 E. 36th St. (bet. 5th & Madison Aves.), 212-684-0215
An "unexpected" Murray Hill "oasis", this "inviting" French-Moroccan does "delightful" specialties in a "warm, low-lit" Casbah-like room; the "sweet staff" "treats you royally", though cries of "please lose a table" are in vain.

Barbetta ◐
20 23 20 $57

321 W. 46th St. (bet. 8th & 9th Aves.), 212-246-9171; www.barbettarestaurant.com
"Like stepping back in time", this "rococo" Restaurant Row centenarian offers outstanding, "traditional" Northern Italian plus "polished" service in "ornate" townhouse digs; though "slightly faded", it "still charms", and romeos regard the "enchanting garden" as a surefire "closer."

BarBossa ◐⊄
– – – M

232 Elizabeth St. (bet. Houston & Prince Sts.), 212-625-2340
There's no space to samba, but this pint-size NoLita cantina is a picture-perfect patch of Brazil, serving a short menu of Italian-accented Carioca cuisine; with white tile walls and doors that open to the street, you can almost feel the Copacabana breeze.

Barbuto
19 16 15 $46

775 Washington St. (bet. Jane & W. 12th Sts.), 212-924-9700; www.barbutonyc.com
Follow "the 'in' crowd" to Jonathan Waxman's "relaxed" West Village Italian, where the "well-executed" "Greenmarket" menu is "not the typical boring pasta" and the "cool industrial" space offers "lively" "people-perusing"; "spotty service" aside, it's a "keeper."

Barking Dog
16 14 15 $22

150 E. 34th St. (bet. Lexington & 3rd Aves.), 212-871-3900

(continued)

(continued)

Barking Dog

1678 Third Ave. (94th St.), 212-831-1800 ⊅
1453 York Ave. (77th St.), 212-861-3600 ⊅

To "kibble" "with your pooch" check out these "kid- and dog-friendly" East Side "stepped-up diners", serving "all-American food" that's "not arf bad"; some mutter about "no frills" and "plenty of noise", but they're "cheap and easy" and "you won't leave hungry."

barmarché ●

| ▽ | 18 | 18 | 16 | $36 |

14 Spring St. (Elizabeth St.), 212-219-2399

"Pretty people" are pretty keen on this "saucy new" NoLita bistro, where "buttercream walls" and "ambient lighting" lend a "Euro vibe" to the "tasty" New American fare; but for the "aloof" staffers "flirting with each other", it's a "cozy" refuge for the "styled" set.

Bar Masa ●🅕

| 23 | 20 | 20 | $76 |

Time Warner Ctr., 10 Columbus Circle, 4th fl. (60th St. at B'way), 212-823-9800; www.masanyc.com

For a "mini-Masa experience" there's this annex offering the "inspired" sushi at "survivable prices"; though the "unimpressed" stress the "tiny portions" and still sizable bill, there's one obvious attraction: "you can get in."

Barna

| – | – | – | M |

Hotel Giraffe, 365 Park Ave. S. (26th St.), 212-532-8300; www.barnarestaurant.com

Say *hola* to "unusual Spanish specialties" at this Gramercy newcomer, where the eats are enhanced by "interesting" wines, "knowledgeable" service and weekend flamenco; patrons can head "below the street" to the dark, "attractive" main room or up to the roof deck.

Barney Greengrass ⊅

| 24 | 6 | 14 | $25 |

541 Amsterdam Ave. (bet. 86th & 87th Sts.), 212-724-4707; www.barneygreengrass.com

"The authenticity is second to none" at this "vintage" Upper Westsider, a "treasure" trove of "world-class" "deli-cacies", e.g. "sublime" Nova, bagels and bialys; the "wall-to-wall" weekend "masses" admit it's "run-down", "brusque" and possibly "overpriced", but given "such deli-ciousness", plus the possibility of "takeout", "who cares?"

Barolo ●

| 18 | 21 | 18 | $51 |

398 W. Broadway (bet. Broome & Spring Sts.), 212-226-1102; www.nybarolo.com

It's easy to catch "spring fever" in the "spacious garden" at this sprawling SoHo Italian; critics call it "pricey" for "ordinary food" and "inattentive" service, but naturalists insist the outdoor "scene" "sets it apart" if you want to "eat, drink and be merry."

Bar Pitti ●⊅

| 22 | 14 | 17 | $36 |

268 Sixth Ave. (bet. Bleecker & Houston Sts.), 212-982-3300

"Don't forget your oversized sunglasses" at this "bustling" Village sidewalk Italian, where the "always hip" "scene is as enjoyable" as the "great chow"; it's an "easygoing" place to "dine alfresco", "spot celebs" and "not blow the budget" ("pitti it's not bigger").

BarTabac ●

| 18 | 19 | 16 | $28 |

128 Smith St. (Dean St.), Brooklyn, 718-923-0918

"Every neighborhood should have" a "hangout" like this "communal" Boerum Hill French bistro, a "staple on Smith Street" for "simple" bites at "moderate prices"; cynics cite "borderline" eats and "fickle" service, but most simply say "*je l'adore.*"

Basso Est ●
21 14 21 $35

198 Orchard St. (Stanton St.), 212-358-9469; www.bassoest.com
Esteemed as "a real find", this "quaint" "little" Lower East Side
"sleeper" wins applause for its "superb" "fresh" Italian fare, delivered
by a "downright affectionate staff" at "basso prices"; though not much
to look at, it has plenty of well-wishers out for an "intimate" bite.

Basta Pasta
21 17 20 $37

37 W. 17th St. (bet. 5th & 6th Aves.), 212-366-0888
"Italian with a Japanese accent" ("who knew?") proves to be a
"harmonious" "concept" at this "quirky" Flatiron entry, which adds
Eastern accents to "mouthwatering pasta" "favorites"; toss in the
"ultrafriendly" Japanese staffers and prepare for a "treat."

Battery Gardens
19 22 18 $49

SW corner of Battery Park (State St.), 212-809-5508;
www.batterygardens.com
"Ah, the view" sigh "even the most jaded" at this duplex Battery Park
venue "overlooking Lady Liberty" and the harbor; though the Asian-
inflected New American menu is quite good, it's the panorama that
will most "impress."

Bayard's ⊠
24 25 24 $64

1 Hanover Sq. (bet. Pearl & Stone Sts.), 212-514-9454; www.bayards.com
"Romance in the Financial District" is not an oxymoron thanks to this
French-American "surprise" housed in the "transporting" circa-1851
India House; wonder chef Eberhard Müller (ex Le Bernardin and
Lutèce) brilliantly employs produce "from his own North Fork farm" and
owner Harry Poulakakos' "famed cellar" adds "outstanding" wines
all served via a "pro" staff; "it doesn't get much better than this";
N.B. a private club at lunchtime, it also boasts "elegant" party rooms.

Bay Leaf
20 18 18 $35

49 W. 56th St. (bet. 5th & 6th Aves.), 212-957-1818;
www.bayleafny.com
A "solid" Midtown "standby" offering "better-than-average" Indian
fare, "efficient service" and "comfortable" quarters; if the regular
menu's "a bit pricier" than the competition, the "outstanding" $13.95
lunch buffet remains a "best buy."

Bayou
18 16 17 $34

308 Lenox Ave. (bet. 125th & 126th Sts.), 212-426-3800;
www.bayouinharlem.com
For "a change of pace", soul-food seekers head up the stairs to this
"hidden" Harlem "gem" for its "tasty", modestly priced Cajun-Creole
eats and "easy vibes"; critics say it's "nothing exceptional" and needs
to "try harder."

BB Sandwich Bar
19 3 11 $7

120 W. Third St. (bet. MacDougal St. & 6th Ave.), 212-473-7500
The "best $4 you'll ever spend" gets you a "juicy, saucy", "addictive"
Philly cheese steak at this one-item Villager ("just say how many you
want"); the downsides are the lack of "real decor or service."

Beacon
22 22 21 $56

25 W. 56th St. (bet. 5th & 6th Aves.), 212-332-0500;
www.beaconnyc.com
Waldy Malouf has a "winning formula" in this "stylish-without-
being-faddy" multilevel Midtown New American, where the
"wood-fired grill" coaxes "wonderful flavor from fish and fowl alike";
prices can be "steep", but the prix fixe menus, including lunch,
are "excellent values."

Beast ▽ 18 | 18 | 19 | $31

638 Bergen St. (Vanderbilt Ave.), Brooklyn, 718-399-6855
"There's nothing beastly" about this affordable Prospect Heights
newcomer housed in a long-abandoned tavern; a "friendly" staff and
"flavorful" Med-inspired tapas give it the "potential" to become
a local staple.

BECCO ◐ 21 | 17 | 20 | $42

355 W. 46th St. (bet. 8th & 9th Aves.), 212-397-7597; www.becconyc.com
"Eat till you bust" is the mantra at Joe Bastianich's Restaurant Row
Italian beloved for its all-you-can-eat pasta "extravaganza" and
"amazing" $20-and-under wine list; despite a recent expansion, it's
still a "madhouse" before showtime as one of "NYC's best values."

BED New York ◐ ▽ 17 | 24 | 17 | $52

530 W. 27th St., 6th fl. (bet. 10th & 11th Aves.), 212-594-4109; www.bedny.com
Maybe there's "a reason mom and dad never let you eat in bed",
but that hasn't slowed the "boisterous" rooftop "scene" at this
West Chelsea newcomer where often intertwined diners recline on
mattresses and nibble "pricey" Franco–New American bites.

Bella Blu 19 | 17 | 17 | $46

967 Lexington Ave. (bet. 70th & 71st Sts.), 212-988-4624
"Bustling" "any day of the week", this East Side Northern Italian lures
its stylish local crowd with "food that never disappoints" (including
"wonderful brick-oven pizzas") and an "upbeat" ambiance; just
"remember to ask the price of the specials."

Bella Via ▽ 20 | 18 | 20 | $34

47-46 Vernon Blvd. (48th Ave.), Queens, 718-361-7510;
www.bellaviarestaurant.com
In an area "sorely lacking in choices", this Long Island City Italian is
a "welcome" source for "real-deal" housemade pastas and brick-
oven pizzas; "reasonably spaced tables" facilitate conversation, and
nearby piers offer *bella* Manhattan "skyline views."

Bellavitae ◐ ▽ 24 | 20 | 23 | $47

21 Minetta Ln. (bet. MacDougal St. & 6th Ave.), 212-473-5121;
www.bellavitae.com
"Simple, punchy flavors" and "welcoming" staffers have helped to
make this new Village Florentine wine bar a "winner"; its "passionate"
young owners even import "the salad greens from Italy."

Belleville 20 | 21 | 16 | $35

350 Fifth Ave. (5th St.), Brooklyn, 718-832-9777
"*La belle France*" meets Park Slope at this "lively" "favorite" that fits the
"1930s Parisian bistro" model to a T, with a "beautiful tiled floor", zinc
bar and "solid", "gently priced" menu; even though the staff doesn't
always "have its act together", it's a nifty "neighborhood asset."

Bellini ⊠ 22 | 20 | 22 | $54

208 E. 52nd St. (bet. 2nd & 3rd Aves.), 212-308-0830
A "sure bet" in East Midtown, this "sophisticated" Italian appeals to
the "expense-account set" with its "well-prepared" Neapolitan fare
and "conversation-friendly" atmosphere; even if owner Donatella
Arpaia now has new ventures that divide her time, the "pro" staff
"still brings it home."

Bello ⊠ 20 | 16 | 19 | $44

863 Ninth Ave. (56th St.), 212-246-6773; www.bellorestaurant.com
A "rose in a thorny neighborhood", this Hell's Kitchen "standby"
dispenses "classic" "stick-to-your-ribs" Italian at prices that "won't

break the bank"; factor in free parking and a $32.95 pre-theater menu and it's no wonder it's usually "busy."

Bello Sguardo

21	18	20	$37

410 Amsterdam Ave. (bet. 79th & 80th Sts.), 212-873-6252

Making "delicious" ports of call around the Mediterranean, this Upper Westsider proffers a "wonderful selection" of small plates in "cozy" quarters; if it's "hard to choose" among the many options, "reasonable prices" mean you can "go with a group and order them all."

Belluno

∇ 21	18	22	$43

340 Lexington Ave. (bet. 39th & 40th Sts.), 212-953-3282

The "Grand Central crowd" touts this midpriced Murray Hill Northern Italian duplex as a "steady performer for both lunch and dinner"; points also go to the "doting" staff and owner who extend "warm welcomes" to all.

Ben & Jack's Steakhouse ⊠

–	–	–	VE

219 E. 44th St. (bet. 2nd & 3rd Aves.), 212-682-5678;
www.benandjackssteakhouse.com

Hoping to match the success of their former employer, a pack of Peter Luger alums has opened this new Grand Central–area chop shop offering choice cuts served by a staff out of central casting; pricing is ambitious, the decor is not.

Ben Benson's

22	17	21	$61

123 W. 52nd St. (bet. 6th & 7th Aves.), 212-581-8888

"Nirvana for carnivores", this manly Midtown moohouse moves many a "mighty good cow" in "noisy" quarters staffed by "pushy" but "knowledgeable" waiters; in other words, it's perfect for a "boys' night out", especially if someone else is paying.

Ben's Kosher Deli

18	11	14	$21

209 W. 38th St. (bet. 7th & 8th Aves.), 212-398-2367
Bay Terrace, 211-37 26th Ave. (211th St.), Queens, 718-229-2367
www.bensdeli.net

"Come hungry and leave stuffed" with "doggy bag" in tow at this kosher deli duo in the Garment District and Bayside; though "bubbe may not be impressed" by the "diner-style" decor, "rushed" service and "homogenized" fare, the majority roars "pass the pastrami!"

Beppe ⊠

23	20	21	$52

45 E. 22nd St. (bet. B'way & Park Ave. S.), 212-982-8422; www.beppenyc.com

"Tuscan farmhouse" warmth, Cesare Casella's "wood-oven" fare and "well-selected" vinos add up to "pricey" but "wonderful experiences" at this usually "packed" and "noisy" Flatiron Northern Italian; most agree the service is "terrific", except during the busiest hours.

Bereket ●⊘

20	5	13	$11

187 E. Houston St. (Orchard St.), 212-475-7700

To cap a night of "hard clubbing" stop in at this Lower East Side "self-service" Turk, where "unbeatably priced" kebabs and other "Istanbul street" favorites "heal the drunken soul" and fuel "taxi drivers" 24/7; though the decor's nothing to "get high on", "lines wrap the block at 2 AM."

Beso

20	14	17	$25

210 Fifth Ave. (Union St.), Brooklyn, 718-783-4902

Perennially "packed" with "young" Park Slopers at "fabulous brunch", this "vibrant" Nuevo Latino's secret is "palate-pleasing" fare and "perfect" fruit drinks; sure, they could "improve the decor and service", but still it's a puzzle why business is "weak at dinner."

Bette
461 W. 23rd St. (bet. 9th & 10th Aves.), 212-366-0404

| − | − | − | E |

From nightlife queen Amy Sacco (Bungalow 8) comes this chic new boîte in Chelsea's London Terrace featuring a self-described 'European grill' menu served amid salute-to-the-'70s decor; be prepared for a beautiful crowd of varying degrees of celebrity.

Better Burger

| 15 | 11 | 14 | $13 |

178 Eighth Ave. (19th St.), 212-989-6688 ●
587 Ninth Ave. (bet. 42nd & 43rd Sts.), 212-629-6622
1614 Second Ave. (84th St.), 212-734-6644 ●
561 Third Ave. (37th St.), 212-949-7528
www.betterburgernyc.com

"Quick, convenient" and comparatively "healthy", these "slick" fast-fooders please "diet-conscious peeps" with "guilt-free" organic burgers ("both carnie and veggie") and "condiments galore"; traditionalists "let down" by the "hype" ask "better than what?"

Bettola ●

| ▽ 21 | 16 | 19 | $34 |

412 Amsterdam Ave. (bet. 79th & 80th Sts.), 212-787-1660

The Upper West Side "needs more like" this "friendly" "place to sit and relax" according to locals "addicted" to its "tasty" thin-crust pizzas and other midpriced Italian standbys; if inside is a little "close", the tables on Amsterdam offer ample elbow room.

Beyoglu ●

| 21 | 17 | 18 | $33 |

1431 Third Ave. (81st St.), 212-650-0850

"For a change from pasta peddlers and noodle houses", Upper Eastsiders turn to this "delightful" Turk to "feast" on "cheap", "satisfying" meze; service can be "slow", but no one minds waiting when the "weather's nice and they set up seating outside."

Bianca ⊄

| ▽ 23 | 18 | 20 | $36 |

5 Bleecker St. (bet. Bowery & Elizabeth St.), 212-260-4666

This "quaint" NoHo "gem" "stands out in the land of 1,000 Italians" thanks to its "delightful" "authentic" Emilia-Romagnan specialties, "moderate" prices and "warm" service; it's "highly recommended for a date", but it takes no reservations so "get there early" to avoid the "crowds."

Bice ●

| 20 | 19 | 19 | $55 |

7 E. 54th St. (bet. 5th & Madison Aves.), 212-688-1999;
www.bicenewyork.com

"Go to see, be seen" and sample "upscale" Northern Italian fare at this "high-energy Euro" lair in Midtown; if service can be "snobby" and tabs "expensive", it's always "enjoyable" to "sit outside and have a drink", so don "your best suit, buy a Rolex off the street and join the scene."

Big Nick's Burger Joint ●

| 17 | 5 | 13 | $15 |

2175 Broadway (77th St.), 212-362-9238

The menu of "cheap" diner eats is "Old Testament"–size at this "dingy little" 24/7 "institution", but it's the "big", "burgertastic" patties that win Upper Westsiders' hearts; if the space and staff aren't universally appreciated, there's always takeout.

Big Wong ⊄

| 22 | 4 | 11 | $12 |

67 Mott St. (bet. Bayard & Canal Sts.), 212-964-0540

"Jury duty" turns into good verdicts when lunch breaks at this "authentic" C-town BBQ and congee specialist allow diners to "eat for less than the cost of a Starbucks latte"; those "depressed" by the "cafeteria"-like setup just "head straight to the take-out counter."

Bill Hong's

| 23 | 13 | 19 | $45 |

227 E. 56th St. (bet. 2nd & 3rd Aves.), 212-751-4048;
www.billhongs.com
At this "wonderful taste of the past" in East Midtown, the decor's "decidedly tired" but the "old-fashioned" Cantonese dishes are "ever fresh"; tabs are "pricey" compared to Chinatown, but then "you don't last this long" (51 years) "without delivering the goods."

Biltmore Room

| 24 | 25 | 20 | $66 |

290 Eighth Ave. (bet. 24th & 25th Sts.), 212-807-0111;
www.thebiltmoreroom.com
Chef Gary Robins "wows" jaded palates with his "exciting" creations at this forever-booked, high-priced Chelsea Eclectic–New American, whose "exquisite" setting "glitters" with trappings from the old Biltmore Hotel; for those who say the "awkward" dining room seating "could be more comfy", there's always the "winning" front bar and its "noisy" "young scene."

Biricchino ⊠

| 20 | 12 | 17 | $38 |

260 W. 29th St. (8th Ave.), 212-695-6690
Madison Square Garden–goers count this Northern Italian eatery–cum–"housemade sausage" specialist as a "rare find" in an area with "slim pickings"; never mind the "lousy" decor and "brisk" service, just focus on the "well-prepared" and "reasonably priced" eats.

Bistro Cassis

| 21 | 18 | 20 | $39 |

243 W. 14th St. (bet. 7th & 8th Aves.), 212-871-6020;
www.bistrocassisnyc.com
A "solid bet", this "Left Bank"–esque Chelsea French bistro turns out "reliable" classics ferried by a "charming" (if "overworked") staff; factor in "hard-to-beat" prices and it's no wonder it "becomes a scene on weekends."

Bistro du Nord

| 19 | 16 | 17 | $42 |

1312 Madison Ave. (93rd St.), 212-289-0997
"Slim Upper Eastsiders" say it's "worth squeezing into" this "snug" Carnegie Hill "boîte" for "fine French bistro" food; though service wavers between "efficient" and "indifferent", the prix fixe menus consistently offer "excellent value."

Bistro du Vent ●

| 21 | 17 | 19 | $50 |

411 W. 42nd St. (bet. 9th & 10th Aves.), 212-239-3060
"Ooh-la-la" – the team behind Esca (Pasternack-Batali-Bastianich) has jumped from Italy to France with this Theater District newcomer that's been "packed" from day one with show-goers and others enjoying bistro favorites "done right"; as for the "slice-of-Paris" decor, it's "authentic" right down to the "deafening" acoustics.

Bistro Les Amis ●

| 20 | 17 | 19 | $39 |

180 Spring St. (Thompson St.), 212-226-8645;
www.bistrolesamis.com
"Undiscovered" by the SoHo masses, this "cozy" French standby's "tiny tables" are just the place to "unwind" over "reasonably priced" "down-home bistro fare" served by a "refreshingly unpretentious" staff; regulars say "sit outside on a warm day and people-watch."

Bistro Le Steak ●

| 17 | 14 | 17 | $41 |

1309 Third Ave. (75th St.), 212-517-3800; www.bistrolesteak.com
Vive Le Steak enthuse "low-budget romantics" who satisfy beefy cravings at this East Side bistro that perhaps is "not of top steakhouse caliber", but then "neither are its prices"; given the "crowded" main room, diners in-the-know ask for the "less-noisy" glassed-in terrace.

Bistro 61 ◗
▽ 20 16 21 $38

1113 First Ave. (61st St.), 212-223-6220
At this "tiny, comfy" East Side newcomer with a "Parisian feel", the "clever old-record-album menus" may be "unwieldy", but the "fairly priced" French bistro classics listed within them are "appealing"; locals are already calling it a "needed" and "welcome" addition to the area.

Bistro St. Mark's
21 19 16 $39

76 St. Marks Ave. (bet. Flatbush & 6th Aves.), Brooklyn, 718-857-8600
A Park Slope "favorite", this "down-to-earth" bistro is beloved for its "high-quality" fare and "reasonable prices" (especially the "bargain" $25 prix fixe on Monday nights); service that can "take forever" rankles less when out on the "lovely" patio.

Bistro Ten 18
19 18 18 $34

1018 Amsterdam Ave. (110th St.), 212-662-7600; www.bistroten18.com
With a "view of St. John the Divine and a fireplace", this moderately priced American bistro "can't go wrong" in the culinary "wilds" of Morningside Heights; most give it "high fives", citing "quality" cuisine, "attentive" service and an "easy" vibe, but a few find it "unpredictable."

Bivio
18 17 15 $44

637 Hudson St. (Horatio St.), 212-206-0601; www.bivionyc.com
Despite the high "trendiness" quotient, fans insist the "focus is on the food, not just the scene" at this "fun" Village Italian manned by a sometimes "slow" staff; if "tight seating" means "you feel like you're in your neighbor's lap", that's not necessarily a detraction given the "cool" clientele.

Black Betty ◗
▽ 19 12 17 $22

366 Metropolitan Ave. (Havemeyer St.), Brooklyn, 718-599-0243; www.blackbetty.net
It's mostly "about the vibe" at this "hip" Williamsburg "hole-in-the-wall", but revelers who "overlook" its "cozy" dining room are "missing out" on "tasty" Med–Middle Eastern eats at "great prices"; what's more, there's pleasant patio seating in warm weather.

Black Duck
▽ 19 17 19 $45

Park South Hotel, 122 E. 28th St. (bet. Lexington Ave. & Park Ave. S.), 212-448-0888; www.parksouthhotel.com
"Hidden" in a Gramercy hotel is this "decidedly laid-back" seafooder with a "quiet" atmosphere that allows diners to "carry on a conversation" and even kindle "romance" over quite good New American cuisine; live jazz on weekends further enhances the mood.

Black Pearl ⌨
– – – M

14 Ave. A (bet. Houston & 2nd Sts.), 212-358-7583; www.blackpearlnewyork.com
There's a new lobster roll in town via this New England–style East Village seafooder that offers traditional shack fare for reasonable tabs, served in a spacious, no-frills interior or in the backyard.

Bliss
▽ 22 17 15 $35

45-20 Skillman Ave. (46th St.), Queens, 718-729-0778; www.blissgardens.com
A "much-needed upscale addition" to Sunnyside, this "cozy", well-priced American has blissful early visitors reporting that the chef can "flat out cook"; hopefully the "inattentive" service is simply part of this promising newcomer's "growing pains."

Blockhead's Burritos
18 11 16 $17

954 Second Ave. (bet. 50th & 51st Sts.), 212-750-2020

(continued)

Blockhead's Burritos

1563 Second Ave. (bet. 81st & 82nd Sts.), 212-879-1999
499 Third Ave. (bet. 33rd & 34th Sts.), 212-213-3332
Worldwide Plaza, 322 W. 50th St. (bet. 8th & 9th Aves.), 212-307-7029
www.blockheads.com

"Burritos as big as your head" are the specialty of this Mexican mini-chain whose "reliably" "tasty" eats "can't be beat" given the "south-of-the border prices"; after a "fantastic margarita" or two, the "spotty service" and dull decor are easy to overlook.

BLT Fish

22 | 20 | 20 | $54

21 W. 17th St. (bet. 5th & 6th Aves.), 212-691-8888; www.bltfish.com

Part of Laurent Tourondel's expanding BLT school, this new Flatironer's "incredible" seafood brings back "summers on Cape Cod"; really two eateries in one, it includes a glorified "clam shack" on the first floor for lobster rolls and the like, while the "formal", *très* cool" upstairs offers "pricier", more "elegant" fare.

BLT Prime

▽ 27 | 23 | 23 | $72

111 E. 22nd St. (bet. Lexington Ave. & Park Ave. S.), 212-995-8500;
www.bltprime.com

The latest in chef Laurent Tourondel's "BLT empire", this "delightful" new Gramercy chophouse follows "pretty much the same formula" as its siblings, with an "expensive", "Craft-like" menu divided into mains, sides and sauces; early visitors are giving it high ratings, though a few cite "loud" acoustics and service lapses as "wrinkles" to be ironed out.

BLT Steak ⊠

24 | 21 | 22 | $69

106 E. 57th St. (bet. Lexington & Park Aves.), 212-752-7470; www.bltsteak.com

Giving a "twist to the steakhouse" template ("no sawdust and geriatric waiters" here), chef Laurent Tourondel's "classy" Midtown eatery attracts a "sleek moneyed crowd" for "melt-in-your-mouth" meat and "excellent sides" offered strictly à la carte; prime "people-watching" helps distract from constant crowds, "ear-splitting" noise levels and "steep" prices.

bluechili ◐

20 | 19 | 17 | $39

251 W. 51st St. (bet. B'way & 8th Ave.), 212-246-3330; www.bluechilinyc.com

Straddling the restaurant-lounge divide, this Theater District "find" offers "creative" Pan-Asian cooking plus "playful" drinks; the "mod yet comfortable" space pleases its "funky" clientele, but "throbbing music" and "lighting that changes color" can give you the blues.

Blue Fin ◐

22 | 23 | 19 | $52

W Times Square Hotel, 1567 Broadway (47th St.), 212-918-1400;
www.brguestrestaurants.com

"Seafood lovers" thank Steve Hanson for this "sleek", "cavernous" "godsend in Times Square" because once "past the pretty people at the bar" they encounter "terrific" fin fare and sushi; the only drawbacks are "well-meaning but uneven" service and "megaphone"-worthy noise levels.

BLUE HILL

26 | 22 | 24 | $65

75 Washington Pl. (bet. 6th Ave. & Washington Sq. W.), 212-539-1776;
www.bluehillnyc.com

"Integrity is key" at this Village New American where the chefs "follow ingredients from farm to plate", seducing a necessarily well-heeled "mature crowd" with "simple but sublime" preparations; most are also "charmed" by the "modern townhouse setting" and service "so good you won't mind" the "pricey tab."

Blue 9 Burger ◐⇱
92 Third Ave. (bet. 12th & 13th Sts.), 212-979-0053;
www.blue9burger.com

| | 19 | 6 | 11 | $9 |

This East Villager does a "decent job of pulling off" an "adaptation" of California's In-N-Out Burger, purveying never-frozen "yummy, messy and cheap" patties plus "crispy fries" with "magical" "dipping sauces"; the "no-nonsense" setting argues for "takeout."

BLUE RIBBON ◐
97 Sullivan St. (bet. Prince & Spring Sts.), 212-274-0404
280 Fifth Ave. (bet. 1st St. & Garfield Pl.), Brooklyn, 718-840-0404
www.blueribbonrestaurants.com

| | 25 | 19 | 22 | $48 |

"God save the Brombergs" cry the legions who dine till "after midnight" on "top-notch" New American "comfort" fare and "outstanding" raw bar choices at this no-reservations Village "original" and its Brooklyn offshoot; the staff "makes newcomers feel like regulars and regulars like royalty", so don't let the "big tariffs" and "crazy waits" deter.

Blue Ribbon Bakery
33 Downing St. (Bedford St.), 212-337-0404; www.blueribbonrestaurants.com

| | 24 | 19 | 20 | $39 |

"A true winner", this "funky" Village New American's "irreproachable" "artisinal" loaves arrive "straight from the basement oven" to accompany delightful dishes ordered from a "broad" menu; brunch is a "favorite" weekend event, but "bring a book" to while away the "long wait."

Blue Ribbon Sushi ◐
119 Sullivan St. (bet. Prince & Spring Sts.), 212-343-0404
278 Fifth Ave. (bet. 1st St. & Garfield Pl.), Brooklyn, 718-840-0408
www.blueribbonrestaurants.com

| | 26 | 19 | 21 | $50 |

A "perennial" sushi-lovers' "heaven", this decade-old SoHo Japanese (with a Brooklyn satellite) focuses on "glisteningly" "fresh" fish; it's best enjoyed when someone else pays, and the wait for a seat can be a "sting", but if you "go during off hours, you'll be delighted."

BLUE SMOKE
116 E. 27th St. (bet. Lexington Ave. & Park Ave. S.), 212-447-7733;
www.bluesmoke.com

| | 21 | 17 | 19 | $39 |

You can find "fantastic" BBQ, "gracious service" and live jazz "without having to travel to a Red State" at Danny Meyer's Gramercy "smokehouse"; though some Southerners scoff "only Yanks pay this much for ribs", the "long waits" for a table speak for themselves.

Blue Star Oyster Bar
254 Court St. (bet. Degraw & Kane Sts.), Brooklyn, 718-858-5806

| | 20 | 15 | 17 | $30 |

One of the "cooler options" in Cobble Hill, this "unpretentious", "cute dinerlike" seafooder serves "very fresh fish" and a "great" weekend brunch; service is "variable", but never mind because the vibe and prices are right.

BLUE WATER GRILL ◐
31 Union Sq. W. (16th St.), 212-675-9500; www.brguestrestaurants.com

| | 24 | 22 | 21 | $50 |

"Never disappoints" declare devotees of Steve Hanson's Union Square anchor where "consistently" "top-shelf" seafood, a "dramatic", "airy" former bank setting, "prompt" service and live jazz downstairs combine to "winning effect"; despite "waits even with reservations" and serious "noise levels", it's still "perfect for dates" and "alfresco" brunches.

Boat Basin Cafe ◐
W. 79th St. (Hudson River), 212-496-5542; www.boatbasincafe.com

| | 12 | 20 | 12 | $24 |

To "escape the city" without leaving the West Side visit this Hudson River–side cafe where "simple" American grill food is enhanced by "peerless" sunset views; just "don't be in a rush", especially during "meet-market happy hour"; N.B. May–October only.

Boat House   17 | 25 | 17 | $48

Central Park, enter on E. 72nd St. (Central Park Dr. N.), 212-517-2233; www.thecentralparkboathouse.com
NYers "get romantic just thinking about" this New American beside the Central Park boat pond that's "ideal" on "a beautiful spring or fall day"; though the food's only "acceptable" and service "indifferent", most agree it's "worth a visit" if only for "cocktails by the dock."

Bobby Van's Steakhouse   23 | 18 | 21 | $62

131 E. 54th St. (bet. Lexington & Park Aves.), 212-207-8050
230 Park Ave. (46th St.), 212-867-5490 ☒
www.bobbyvans.com
At these East Side chop shops a "mix of commuters and suits on expense accounts" devour "top-grade" "steers" in "cacophonous" digs; if a few have beefs with "brusque" service and "silly prices", others shrug "not top-tier but not bad either."

Boca Chica   20 | 15 | 16 | $27

13 First Ave. (1st St.), 212-473-0108
"Raucous" "early 20s" types downing "killer" tropical cocktails keep this East Village South American "packed most nights"; its "tasty" fare may be something of an "afterthought" and the "din" deafening, but to most it's "worth the wait and the squish."

Bogota Latin Bistro   – | – | – | M

141 Fifth Ave. (bet. Lincoln & St. John's Pls.), Brooklyn, 718-230-3805; www.bogotabistro.com
Midpriced dishes from Colombia and Costa Rica are on the roster of this new Park Slope Pan-Latin whose colorful digs sport whirling fans and tropical plants; the back deck is a great place to get lost with a pitcher of coconut mojitos.

Boi ☒   21 | 18 | 20 | $39

246 E. 44th St. (bet. 2nd & 3rd Aves.), 212-681-6541; www.boi-restaurant.com
"Slightly upscale" in price and demeanor, this "friendly" Vietnamese is a welcome pocket of "calm" near "frenetic" Grand Central; it serves "modern" "riffs on classic" dishes plus "inventive desserts", drawing a "nice mix" of "business diners" and "UN" sorts as customers.

Bolo   23 | 20 | 21 | $53

23 E. 22nd St. (bet. B'way & Park Ave. S.), 212-228-2200; www.bolorestaurant.com
Spanish wine and tapas aficionados relive their "*ensalada* days" at Bobby Flay's "exquisitely different" Flatiron Iberian that, despite the chef's "celebrity" status, is still somewhat "unsung"; the "up there" prices can be avoided via the bargain prix fixe lunch.

Bolzano's ◗   – | – | – | E

1515 Broadway (45th St.), 212-302-2250; www.bolzanosrestaurant.com
Times Square's latest is this pricey new Italian brasserie that's already famed for its signature spaghetti-in-a-meatball dish; the large, vaguely retro-looking space is both tourist- and theatergoer-friendly, with bonus alfresco Shubert Alley seating.

Bombay Palace   19 | 19 | 19 | $35

30 W. 52nd St. (bet. 5th & 6th Aves.), 212-541-7777
A "good bet" after visiting MoMA, this spacious Midtown Indian tops buffet-surfers' lists since the "tasty" lunch spread is a "fantastic bargain", service "friendly" and tables "amply spaced"; the separately

owned, Kama Sutra–themed K Lounge upstairs is "a good place for a drink."

Bombay Talkie
20 | 20 | 17 | $35

189 Ninth Ave. (bet. 21st & 22nd Sts.), 212-242-1900
"Setting the scene for a great night", this Chelsea newcomer draws local "hipsters" for "delectable Indian street eats" and "divine" cocktails in a "Bollywood-glam" setting; despite "ditzy" service, "high prices" and "small portions", it's "fun overall."

Bond 45
19 | 20 | 18 | $50

154 W. 45th St. (bet. 6th & 7th Aves.), 212-869-4545;
www.bond45.com
Housed in the former Bond's clothing store, this "wacky, touristy" new Theater District Italian from Shelly Fireman proffers "generous portions" of "above-average" classics to match its "huge" dimensions; still, "so-so service" and "echoing noise" make some feel the prices are out of scale.

Bond Street ●
25 | 22 | 19 | $60

6 Bond St. (bet. B'way & Lafayette St.), 212-777-2500
To "bond" with a "young, good-looking crowd" over "outstanding sushi", check out this "super-trendy" bi-level NoHo Japanese; "haughty" service and "astronomical prices" temper enthusiasm, but "canoodling" with a "date" in the "sceney" downstairs lounge helps warm the blood.

Bone Lick Park Bar-B-Que ●
∇ 14 | 14 | 15 | $26

75 Greenwich Ave. (bet. Bank St. & 7th Ave. S.), 212-647-9600
Something is a "first for the area", this "retro-cute" newcomer set in a West Village storefront slings "cheap" BBQ with a slew of Southern sides; while some say it's "surprisingly good", to others it's a "work in progress" with meats that "need more smoke and fire."

Bonita ●
∇ 22 | 18 | 19 | $20

338 Bedford Ave. (bet. S. 2nd & 3rd Sts.), Brooklyn, 718-384-9500
When hankering for "perfect tacos" and other "satisfying" south-of-the-border fare, "hipsters" head for this "fun", "warm"-hearted Williamsburg Mexican; however, high quality for low tabs can produce "long waits."

Boom ●
∇ 19 | 18 | 18 | $36

152 Spring St. (bet. W. B'way & Wooster St.), 212-431-3663
Offering "good basic Italian", this pleasingly "dark" SoHo bistro is also "great for a quiet drink" in the early evening; however, "late-night" a "young" crowd collects for live and DJ-driven music producing a "lively" scene that "can get crazy on weekends."

Borgo Antico ●
19 | 17 | 20 | $40

22 E. 13th St. (bet. 5th Ave. & University Pl.), 212-807-1313;
www.borgoanticonyc.com
There's "nothing flamboyant" about this Village Italian, but the locals say the food's "well prepared" and "reasonably" priced; its townhouse setting's "relaxing", especially since "nobody rushes you."

Bottega del Vino
∇ 21 | 21 | 21 | $59

7 E. 59th St. (bet. 5th & Madison Aves.), 212-223-3028;
www.bottegadelvinonyc.com
A replica of the famed "Verona original", this upscale Midtown wine bar's "authentic" food is backed by an "endless list" of choice vintages; those looking to keep their tabs under control opt for the casual front area's "superb" panini, pastries and espresso.

Bottino
19 | 18 | 18 | $41

246 10th Ave. (bet. 24th & 25th Sts.), 212-206-6766;
www.bottinonyc.com
"Far afield on 10th Avenue", this "stylish" Chelsea Italian "caters to local gallery-arty-chic" types who tout the "excellent martinis" and "consistently good" food; casanovas suggest the "romantic garden" makes "any blind date more appealing."

Bouillabaisse 126
∇ 23 | 16 | 19 | $34

126 Union St. (bet. Columbia & Hicks Sts.), Brooklyn, 718-855-4405;
www.bouillabaisse126.com
It's "back and better than ever" declare devotees of this Carroll Gardens revival of Neil Ganic's erstwhile eatery known for its "wonderful", moderately priced seafood-centric French menu; most "welcome" its return even if there's room for improvement in the "sardine"-size setup.

BOULEY ●
28 | 26 | 27 | $87

120 W. Broadway (Duane St.), 212-964-2525;
www.bouleyrestaurants.com
Star chef David Bouley is back at the top of his game at this "triumphant" TriBeCan serving "spectacular" New French cuisine in a lovely "vaulted" space via a "stealthily attentive" "pro" staff; connoisseurs "clear their credit cards" for this "mind-blowing" but "expensive" experience, or capitalize on the "extraordinary prix fixe lunch" deal.

Bouterin
20 | 22 | 21 | $59

420 E. 59th St. (bet. 1st Ave. & Sutton Pl.), 212-758-0323
For a "touch of Provence", Sutton Place denizens look to this "secret", predictably "pricey" "enclave"; its "tchotchke-filled" space with "gorgeous flowers" everywhere strikes some as impossibly "quaint" while others find it suited for a "bridal or baby shower."

Brasserie ●
20 | 22 | 19 | $48

100 E. 53rd St. (bet. Lexington & Park Aves.), 212-751-4840;
www.restaurantassociates.com
To "impress out-of-town guests" or "a date" with your appreciation for modern "design" take them to this deservedly "popular" Midtown French brasserie; just about everyone likes the "sleek", *Jetsons*-esque space, but a few fault the prices and "indifferent" service.

Brasserie 8½
21 | 23 | 21 | $53

9 W. 57th St. (bet. 5th & 6th Aves.), 212-829-0812;
www.restaurantassociates.com
"Bankers" and "Carnegie Hall" ticket-holders praise this "glamorous" "subterranean" Midtown brasserie for its "enjoyable" eats, comfy booths and "thrilling" cocktails; only prices give pause.

Brasserie Julien ●
17 | 19 | 17 | $41

1422 Third Ave. (bet. 80th & 81st Sts.), 212-744-6327;
www.brasseriejulien.com
A blend of "solid" French brasserie fare, art deco–inspired decor and live jazz on weekends makes this Upper Eastsider a local "favorite"; still, as ratings show, both food and service could use some work.

Brasserie LCB
24 | 22 | 24 | $66

60 W. 55th St. (bet. 5th & 6th Aves.), 212-688-6525
"Somewhere between a brasserie and a formal French" restaurant, chef Jean-Jacques Rachou's more "casual" yet still "pricey" revamp of La Côte Basque still turns out "quintessential quenelles" and other "perfect classics" ferried by "pro" waiters; however, the graying clientele is torn as to whether this redo is "better, brighter and more fun" than before, or merely "missing the old elegance."

Bravo Gianni ●
23 | 14 | 21 | $61

230 E. 63rd St. (bet. 2nd & 3rd Aves.), 212-752-7272
"*Bravissimo,* Gianni" applaud "well-heeled" patrons "charmed" by their host's "tableside manner" at this East Side "blast from the past" serving top of the line "old-school" Italian; some find it a bit "frayed" and expensive, but most appreciate its "Rat Pack"–era style.

Brawta Caribbean Café
∇ 20 | 13 | 14 | $22

347 Atlantic Ave. (Hoyt St.), Brooklyn, 718-855-5515
"Fresh", "vibrant" and "inexpensive", this Boerum Hill Caribbean dispenses "flavorful", "hearty" eats; laid-back (translate: slow) service and unimpressive decor are the only drawbacks.

Bread
18 | 17 | 15 | $33

20 Spring St. (bet. Elizabeth & Mott Sts.), 212-334-1015
Bread Tribeca
301 Church St. (Walker St.), 212-334-8282; www.breadtribeca.com
"Trendy but solid" Ligurian food is the deal at this "well-priced" TriBeCa Italian whose "slick setting" features big "floor-to-ceiling" windows; "loud" "weekend mobs" and "flaky" service lead locals to tout "takeout"; P.S. the bite-size NoLita original specializes in panini.

Breeze
– | – | M

661 Ninth Ave. (bet. 45th & 46th Sts.), 212-262-7777; www.breezenyc.com
Hip new Hell's Kitchen arrival with a musical motif, from the turntable-topped stainless-steel bar to the CD-case menus; the kitchen spins out well-priced Thai grub with some Gallic grace notes.

Brennan & Carr ● ⇄
19 | 7 | 13 | $15

3432 Nostrand Ave. (Ave. U), Brooklyn, 718-646-9559
"Beating the chains" since 1938, this Sheepshead Bay "fixture" traffics in "juice-drenched" roast beef sandwiches that require "extra napkins" plus "a good book" to read "while on line"; given the "divey" digs, it's no wonder many say "it tastes best eaten in one's car."

Bricco
19 | 17 | 19 | $40

304 W. 56th St. (bet. 8th & 9th Aves.), 212-245-7160; www.bricconyc.com
"Great for a date" or a "pre-theater" meal, this "unpretentious" Westsider features a roster of "tempting" Italian options, including "marvelous brick-oven pizzas"; with "cozy" digs and "moderate" prices, it deserves to be more than a "locals' secret."

Brick Cafe
20 | 21 | 19 | $29

30-95 33rd St. (31st Ave.), Queens, 718-267-2735; www.brickcafe.com
Grateful Astoria denizens favor this "rustic-feeling" Franco-Italian bistro for a "relatively upscale" yet "reasonably priced" meal; outdoor seating in warmer months "makes this place all the better."

Brick Lane Curry House
21 | 15 | 15 | $29

306-308 E. Sixth St. (2nd Ave.), 212-979-2900; www.bricklanecurryhouse.com
A "home away from home for Brit curry-lovers", this East Village Indian "isn't kidding when it talks about its hottest dish" – "you get a free beer if you can finish it"; if slightly "higher priced" than others on the block, its food quality justifies the extra few bucks.

Bridge Cafe
21 | 17 | 19 | $42

279 Water St. (Dover St.), 212-227-3344
For a "relaxing escape" without leaving the Financial District, try this "delightful" New American in one of the "oldest taverns in the city" (circa 1794) tucked "under the Brooklyn Bridge"; happily the food's as "up-to-date" as the mood is "antiquated."

Bright Food Shop

20 | 10 | 16 | $25

216-218 Eighth Ave. (21st St.), 212-243-4433

A "diner with a kick", this "one-of-a-kind" Chelsea "treasure" tenders a "tasty" "true fusion" of "Mexican, Asian and who knows what" in "basic" quarters; locals appreciate it as a rare source for "good", "cheap" eats in an "ever-changing neighborhood."

Brio

18 | 13 | 16 | $38

786 Lexington Ave. (61st St.), 212-980-2300; www.brionyc.com

Handy to Bloomingdale's, this "sleeper-keeper" Italian is "ideal for a shopper's lunch" of "fresh", "great-value" pastas or pizzas from its round-the-corner annex, Brio Forno; however, the less-enthused fault "uneven" food and service "slow as a Sicilian afternoon."

Brooklyn Diner USA ●

16 | 14 | 15 | $29

212 W. 57th St. (bet. B'way & 7th Ave.), 212-977-2280; www.brooklyndiner.com

"Quantity is king but there's quality too" at Shelly Fireman's "nouveau diner" that is more true to its Midtown locale than its moniker; despite "inattentive" service and a "touristy" profile, it's "always packed" with "NYers" who recognize a good deal.

Brooklyn Fish Camp ⊠

– | – | – | M

162 Fifth Ave. (Degraw St.), Brooklyn, 718-783-3264; www.brooklynfishcamp.com

The same luscious lobster rolls and other fairly priced New England shore classics that made Mary's Fish Camp a Manhattan hit turn up at its new Park Slope satellite; outgrowing its guppy-size sire, it boasts a long dining room and spacious back patio.

Brother Jimmy's BBQ

16 | 11 | 14 | $23

428 Amsterdam Ave. (bet. 80th & 81st Sts.), 212-501-7515 ●
Grand Central, lower level (42nd St. & Vanderbilt Ave.), 212-661-4022
1485 Second Ave. (bet. 77th & 78th Sts.), 212-288-0999 ●
1644 Third Ave. (93rd St.), 212-426-2020 ●
www.brotherjimmys.com

Don your "dirtiest jeans" and "Southern-U" sweatshirt before "diving into" the ribs and fixin's at this "rowdy" BBQ chain; the setup's vintage "frat basement" and the staff's most noted for "tight pants", but fans insist that you get lots of bang for your bucks.

Bruckner Bar & Grill ●

– | – | – | M

1 Bruckner Blvd. (3rd Ave.), Bronx, 718-665-2001

Set in a former industrial building in Mott Haven, this "diamond in the rough" has a "regular" "semi-hipster" crowd of "artist" types who come to eat "decent", affordable "Americana" and then "work it off at the billiard table."

Bruculino ●

18 | 15 | 19 | $35

225 Columbus Ave. (70th St.), 212-579-3966

This Upper West Side "standby" works "after a movie" or for weekend brunch and in summer offers outdoor tables for "watching passersby"; some say "you can do better" at its sibling, Pomodoro Rosso, but "when the wait's too long" it's a "quick, comfortable" alternative.

Bruno ⊠

23 | 19 | 24 | $57

240 E. 58th St. (bet. 2nd & 3rd Aves.), 212-688-4190; www.brunosnyc.com

It's "always a pleasure to dine" at this "steady", "clubby", "costly" Midtown Southern Italian where the classic fare's "top-notch" and owner Bruno and his crew know how to "take care of their customers"; a few allege it's getting "tired", but most agree it "still charms year after year."

Bryant Park Grill/Cafe
| 17 | 22 | 17 | $43 |

*behind NY Public Library, 25 W. 40th St. (bet. 5th & 6th Aves.),
212-840-6500; www.arkrestaurants.com*

For "happy hour at sunset" with prime "pickup" potential, "you can't
beat" the Cafe at this "urban oasis" with alfresco tables in Bryant
Park; the Grill's American food is "second" to the backdrop, though,
and "noise", "high prices" and "spotty" service can rankle.

B. Smith's Restaurant Row
| 18 | 19 | 19 | $45 |

320 W. 46th St. (bet. 8th & 9th Aves.), 212-315-1100; www.bsmith.com

"Gracious" Barbara Smith's Restaurant Row Eclectic is an "upbeat"
"staple" with a "Southern slant" that puts "yummy" "twists" on familiar
"favorites"; it remains a "solid pre-theater" pick, though some say it's
a tad "old hat" and could use "more zing."

Bubba Gump Shrimp Co. ●
| 14 | 16 | 17 | $29 |

1501 Broadway (bet. 43rd & 44th Sts.), 212-391-7100; www.bubbagump.com

"Based on the movie *Forrest Gump*", this low-priced Times Square
American has no shortage of "big shrimp"–loving fans; if the food
quality "falls below sea level" and the "corn-fed" staff can grate, at
least the "trivia quizzes" make the "kids giggle and the tourists smile."

Bubby's
| 18 | 14 | 15 | $27 |

120 Hudson St. (N. Moore St.), 212-219-0666
1 Main St. (bet. Plymouth & Water Sts.), Brooklyn, 718-222-0666
www.bubbys.com

For the "home cooking" that people "born after 1970 dreamed about
but never got", this "family-oriented" TriBeCa American (with a Dumbo
offshoot) is a "forever favorite"; it's most "popular" for weekend
brunch, though "long waits", "screaming kids" and "slow" service
are part of the deal.

Bukhara Grill
| 21 | 17 | 19 | $35 |

217 E. 49th St. (bet. 2nd & 3rd Aves.), 212-888-2839

Offering a "broad swath of dishes beyond the typical", this "cavernous"
Indian overseen by a "watchful but unobtrusive" staff attracts Midtown
lunchers with its "plentiful", "affordable" buffet; devotees add it's
also "a pleasure to have dinner" here.

Bull & Bear ●
| 20 | 20 | 20 | $55 |

*Waldorf-Astoria, 570 Lexington Ave. (49th St.), 212-872-4900;
www.waldorfastoria.com*

A "classic of its type", this Midtown steakhouse draws "suspender"-
wearing carnivores for "reliable" slabs and drinks from an "old-school"
barkeep who "doesn't believe in watering 'em down"; N.B. it has just
reopened after extensive (post-*Survey*) renovations.

Bull Run
| 19 | 17 | 18 | $42 |

*Club Quarters Hotel, 52 William St. (Pine St.), 212-859-2200;
www.bullrunwallstreet.com*

Thirsty Wall Streeters pack this "aptly named" New American "after the
market closes", and it also works for "power lunches"; however, even
admirers allow that its "expensive" eats, while "fine for the Financial
District", might not "make the cut elsewhere."

Burger Heaven
| 16 | 9 | 14 | $16 |

9 E. 53rd St. (bet. 5th & Madison Aves.), 212-752-0340
20 E. 49th St. (bet. 5th & Madison Aves.), 212-755-2166
804 Lexington Ave. (62nd St.), 212-838-3580
291 Madison Ave. (bet. 40th & 41st Sts.), 212-685-6250
536 Madison Ave. (bet. 54th & 55th Sts.), 212-753-4214

(continued)

Burger Heaven
1534 Third Ave. (bet. 86th & 87th Sts.), 212-722-8292
www.burgerheaven.com

Perhaps not quite heaven, this longtime "local" chain remains a "family"-friendly "favorite" for its "sinfully good" burgers plus "great milkshakes"; despite the "no-frills" settings, "lunchtime hassle" and "rushed" service, it runs circles around most of the fast-fooders.

Burger Joint ●∅

∇ 21 | 9 | 14 | $13

241 Third Ave. (bet. 19th & 20th Sts.), 212-228-1219

For a "quick fix", hit this new Gramercy patty purveyor (no relation to its Parker Meridien namesake), where the "teeny-tiny" burgers are "a good deal"; both decor and menu are "minimal", but the service is "fast and friendly", and those "bite-size" sliders are "pretty damn tasty."

burger joint at Le Parker Meridien ●∅

24 | 10 | 13 | $13

Le Parker Meridien, 119 W. 56th St. (bet. 6th & 7th Aves.), 212-708-7414;
www.newyork.lemeridien.com

"The secret's out" about this "quirky", "low-atmosphere" source for "first-class" patties that's "tucked" behind "thick curtains" in the lobby of an otherwise posh Midtown hotel; insiders "go at off times" to avoid "long lines" and "tight" seating.

Burritoville

17 | 7 | 13 | $12

298 Bleecker St. (7th Ave. S.), 212-633-9249
144 Chambers St. (bet. Greenwich St. & W. B'way), 212-571-1144
625 Ninth Ave. (44th St.), 212-333-5352 ●
141 Second Ave. (bet. 8th & 9th Sts.), 212-260-3300 ●
1487 Second Ave. (bet. 77th & 78th Sts.), 212-472-8800 ●
866 Third Ave. (52nd St.), 212-980-4111
36 Water St. (Broad St.), 212-747-1100
166 W. 72nd St. (bet. Amsterdam & Columbus Aves.), 212-580-7700 ●
352 W. 39th St. (9th Ave.), 212-563-9088
264 W. 23rd St. (bet. 7th & 8th Aves.), 212-367-9844 ●
www.burritoville.com

The key words are "fast, cheap and good" at this Tex-Mex chain specializing in "mammoth", "gut-busting" San Francisco–style burritos; those turned off by "zero atmosphere" and "spotty service" opt for "speedy, reliable delivery."

Butai

– | – | – | M

115 E. 18th St. (bet. Irving Pl. & Park Ave. S.), 212-387-8885

Gramercy gets another Japanese eatery in this newcomer that specializes in izakaya, or "tapas-style" small plates, backed by a broad sake selection; its bi-level setting includes a candlelit upstairs dining room and a sleek first-floor lounge.

Butter ●▨

18 | 24 | 18 | $53

415 Lafayette St. (bet. Astor Pl. & 4th St.), 212-253-2828;
www.butterrestaurant.com

Though the New American food's deemed "decent", "it's all about the atmosphere" at this ever-"trendy" Village "pretty-people" magnet; more "subdued" than the "crowded" "scene" in the lounge is the "beautifully designed" wood-paneled upstairs dining room.

Cabana ●

21 | 18 | 18 | $34

South Street Seaport, 89 South St., Pier 17, 3rd fl. (bet. Fulton & John Sts.),
212-406-1155

(continued)

(continued)

Cabana
1022 Third Ave. (bet. 60th & 61st Sts.), 212-980-5678
107-10 70th Rd. (bet. Austin St. & Queens Blvd.), Queens, 718-263-3600
"It's a fiesta every day" at these "hot, hot, hot" Cubans, where a "loud, happy" crowd downs "addictive" mojitos and "spicy" Nuevo Latino eats; there's "always a line" on weekends, but at least at the Seaport location there's a "wonderful pier view" to take in as you wait.

Cacio e Pepe
22 | 17 | 20 | $35
182 Second Ave. (bet. 11th & 12th Sts.), 212-505-5931
"Cute and intimate", this "friendly" Roman trattoria "stands apart" from the other East Village Italians thanks to its "delicious", "surprisingly authentic" dishes and "excellent-value" prices; P.S. there's a "gorgeous garden out back."

Cafe Asean ⊽
22 | 15 | 19 | $26
117 W. 10th St. (bet. Greenwich & 6th Aves.), 212-633-0348
"Vibrant", "exotically spiced" dishes "from all over Southeast Asia" are served by "sweethearts" at this "affordable" Village "gem"; the decor's "unassuming" and space "cramped", making the "adorable" back garden "a big draw."

Café Botanica
20 | 26 | 22 | $57
Essex House, 160 Central Park S. (bet. 6th & 7th Aves.), 212-484-5120
The "outstanding view" is the thing at this "airy" Med–New American overlooking Central Park, but the "delicious food" and "gracious" service also please many; yes, it's "a splurge", but the $38 prix fixe is "an excellent deal", and the "wonderful" weekend brunch is "a must."

CAFÉ BOULUD
27 | 23 | 26 | $75
Surrey Hotel, 20 E. 76th St. (bet. 5th & Madison Aves.), 212-772-2600;
www.danielnyc.com
"Aren't we lucky" sigh sated surveyors at Daniel's "more relaxed, more modern" but still "luxurious" East Side sister after experiencing the "exquisite", "imaginative" French cuisine, served against an "elegantly understated" backdrop by an "unobtrusive, courteous" staff; it all adds up to "a class act" that's "among NYC's most celebrated" – and that describes the clientele too.

Cafe Centro ☒
19 | 17 | 18 | $43
MetLife Bldg., 200 Park Ave. (45th St. & Vanderbilt Ave.), 212-818-1222;
www.restaurantassociates.com
"Popularity" and "convenience" ensure that this Grand Central–area cafe's a "noisy" "zoo at lunchtime", but things become more "quiet and refined" at dinner; "quality" midpriced Mediterranean cuisine and "warm" service make it a "welcome oasis" in a busy zip code.

Cafe Con Leche
17 | 12 | 15 | $22
424 Amsterdam Ave. (bet. 80th & 81st Sts.), 212-595-7000
726 Amsterdam Ave. (bet. 95th & 96th Sts.), 212-678-7000
The "cheap", "tasty", "stick-to-your-ribs" Cuban-Dominican fare at this Upper West Side duo "hits the spot" and may be "one of the city's best bargains"; those who object to the simple "seedy" setup note there's "really fast delivery" and "takeout too."

Café de Bruxelles ◑
20 | 16 | 18 | $39
118 Greenwich Ave. (13th St.), 212-206-1830
After 20-plus years, this "old West Village fave" still satisfies with its "seriously delicious" Belgian classics (notably the moules frites) washed down with "super" "trappist brews"; the room's a bit "threadbare", but its "charm remains intact."

CAFÉ DES ARTISTES ◐
22 | 26 | 23 | $66

1 W. 67th St. (bet. Columbus Ave. & CPW), 212-877-3500;
www.cafenyc.com

"One of the city's treasures", George and Jenifer Lang's venerable "institution" near Lincoln Center exudes "old-world elegance and class" thanks to its "ornate" belle epoque interior resplendent with Howard Chandler Christy's "intoxicating" "frolicking nymph" murals; factor in "excellent" French food and "caring" service, and it's "the ultimate in romantic dining" – pass the ring, please.

Café du Soleil ◐
∇ 23 | 23 | 17 | $44

2723 Broadway (104th St.), 212-316-5000

Upper Westsiders who've discovered this "wonderful" Provençal newcomer call it a "ray of sunshine" in an "up-and-coming" area; its airy, high-ceilinged space also appeals, but some say service still suffers from a kink or two.

Cafe Español ◐
19 | 15 | 17 | $31

172 Bleecker St. (bet. MacDougal & Sullivan Sts.), 212-505-0657
78 Carmine St. (bet. Bedford St. & 7th Ave. S.), 212-675-3312
www.cafeespanol.com

Sangria slurpers "say *si*" to these separately owned Village Spaniards, where "modest" settings don't detract from the "humongous portions" of Iberian "homestyle cooking"; a "super-nice staff" and "reasonable prices" (especially the "lobster deal") complete the picture.

Café Evergreen
20 | 12 | 17 | $29

1288 First Ave. (bet. 69th & 70th Sts.), 212-744-3266

"Why schlep to Chinatown" when you can get such "top-shelf" dim sum and other Chinese specialties at this "spacious, comfortable" Upper Eastsider boasting a surprisingly "amazing" wine list; still, nitpickers note the decor could use a little "freshening up."

Café Fiorello ◐
20 | 16 | 18 | $46

1900 Broadway (bet. 63rd & 64th Sts.), 212-595-5330;
www.cafefiorello.com

Fans fete this "festive" Lincoln Center–facing "favorite" for "hearty Italian" including an "unsurpassed antipasto" bar and "outstanding" super-thin pizzas; sure, it's a bit "expensive" and a "madhouse before curtain time", but when you add in the sidewalk seating, the bottom line is "bravo!"

Café Frida
20 | 17 | 16 | $35

368 Columbus Ave. (bet. 77th & 78th Sts.), 212-712-2929

"Worth a trip for the guacamole alone", this "wonderful" Upper West Side Mexican wins favor with "potent margaritas" and "fresh", "surprisingly good" fare; "upbeat" atmosphere aside, casanovas say its "dark", "rustic" interior makes it a "seductive" date place.

Cafe Gitane ◐⇆
21 | 16 | 15 | $24

242 Mott St. (Prince St.), 212-334-9552

Morocco via Paris, this "cramped", "cheap" NoLita "charmer" may be "Eurotrash central", but "in a great way"; its "model"/"über-hipster" habitués hasten to hit the walk-up window for "the best espresso" when it's too "packed" to snag a table.

CAFÉ GRAY ☒
25 | 22 | 23 | $78

Time Warner Ctr., 10 Columbus Circle, 3rd fl. (60th St. at B'way),
212-823-6338; www.cafegray.com

"Thank goodness" "he's back" cry fans of chef Gray Kunz, whose Asian-accented French brasserie in the Time Warner Center is declared a "winner" thanks to its "brilliant" cuisine featuring "powerful flavor combinations" backed by "unusual wines" and "exceptional" service; however, when it comes to the "stunning" David Rockwell–designed space overlooking Central Park, some surveyors can't help but ask "why did they put the kitchen in front of the view?"

Café Habana ⏺
23 | 12 | 14 | $23

17 Prince St. (Elizabeth St.), 212-625-2001
"Always crowded, and for good reason", this "happening" NoLita Cuban-Mexican lures "cool" types with its "cheap", "divine" eats dispensed by a "supermodel-in-training" staff; those who can't abide the "dreadful waits" hit the "easy" take-out annex "around the corner."

Cafe Joul
18 | 12 | 18 | $39

1070 First Ave. (bet. 58th & 59th Sts.), 212-759-3131
For "simple, fresh" renditions of French bistro classics, Sutton Place locals turn to this "welcoming" "neighborhood" place; however, grumbles about "high prices" for "just-ok" eats and "no decor" may explain its "sleeper" status.

Cafe Lalo ⏺≠
20 | 19 | 12 | $19

201 W. 83rd St. (bet. Amsterdam Ave. & B'way), 212-496-6031
"Tremendously crowded" and "touristy" since *You've Got Mail* made it famous", this West Side cafe serves a sybarite-satisfying selection of "succulent sweets"; sadly, "sloow" service stirs sour sentiments.

Cafe Loup ⏺
18 | 17 | 19 | $40

105 W. 13th St. (bet. 6th & 7th Aves.), 212-255-4746
The "friendly buzz" at this Village vet is due to a loyal "local crowd" that returns regularly for "hearty bistro fare" and "warm service"; the room may be "slightly stodgy", but it's as "comfortable" as "your favorite broken-in jeans."

Cafe Luluc ⏺≠
19 | 16 | 17 | $26

214 Smith St. (Baltic St.), Brooklyn, 718-625-3815
"Paris-quality food for Brooklyn prices" sums up this "unpretentious" Cobble Hill French bistro that produces "great brunches, late-night snacks" and everything in between; insiders say "the back garden is the way to go."

Cafe Luxembourg ⏺
21 | 18 | 19 | $48

200 W. 70th St. (bet. Amsterdam & West End Aves.), 212-873-7411
"It just gets better with age" attest the legion fans of this "classiest dame" near Lincoln Center, where "excellent bistro" classics and a "lively", "comfortable" ambiance draw a "sophisticated" crowd; "noisy" conditions and "occasional celeb" sightings are part of the "bustling" appeal.

Cafe Mogador ⏺
22 | 17 | 16 | $23

101 St. Marks Pl. (bet. Ave. A & 1st Ave.), 212-677-2226
"Vibrant and friendly", this East Village Moroccan is a "neighborhood mainstay" thanks to its "fantastic", "budget"-priced tagines and such; it's "always hopelessly crowded" with "young, hip" types who don't seem to mind that the service is "sometimes harried."

Café Pierre
22 | 25 | 23 | $71

Pierre Hotel, 2 E. 61st St. (5th Ave.), 212-940-8195
With its "elegant", gray satin setup, smooth "formal service" and first-rate classic cuisine, this East Side French-Continental makes a "quietly sophisticated" retreat for breakfast, lunch or dinner, high tea or cocktails; it's "expensive", but to most such "top-notch experiences" are "splurge"-worthy, especially after 8 PM when the "phenomenal" Kathleen Landis is on piano.

Cafe Ronda

| 19 | 15 | 17 | $30 |

249-251 Columbus Ave. (bet. 71st & 72nd Sts.), 212-579-9929; www.caferonda.com

At this "friendly" West Side Med–South American, the Uptown-priced, hearty food and "Downtown vibe" attract an "eclectic mix" of folks; especially "fun for brunch", it please locals who attest its "small" space is "always busy for a reason."

Café Sabarsky

| 22 | 24 | 19 | $38 |

Neue Galerie, 1048 Fifth Ave. (86th St.), 212-288-0665; www.wallserestaurant.com

Kurt Gutenbrunner's "perfect period piece" of pre-war Vienna in the Neue Galerie showcases "*wünderbar* desserts" and other outstanding Austrian bites; the "impeccable" interior is enhanced by "glamorous park views", which make the "interminable waits" easier to endure.

Cafe S.F.A.

| 18 | 17 | 16 | $30 |

Saks Fifth Ave., 611 Fifth Ave., 8th fl. (bet. 49th & 50th Sts.), 212-940-4080

To "rest your feet" while shopping at Saks, head for this "convenient, relaxing" cafe, where the light American fare's "surprisingly good" and not too pricey; hold out for "a seat by the window" to best enjoy the view of "Rockefeller Center and St. Pat's."

Cafe Spice

| 18 | 14 | 15 | $26 |

Grand Central, lower level (42nd St. & Vanderbilt Ave.), 646-227-1300
72 University Pl. (bet. 10th & 11th Sts.), 212-253-6999
54 W. 55th St. (bet. 5th & 6th Aves.), 212-489-7444
www.cafespice.com

Fans flock to this "terrific" Indian trio for "modern, fresh" food "packed with bold taste"; "hip, trendy" interiors add appeal, especially for the "NYU students" at the Village branch, while the takeout-only outpost in Grand Central is a commuter's boon.

Café St. Bart's

| 15 | 21 | 16 | $34 |

109 E. 50th St. (Park Ave.), 212-888-2664; www.cafestbarts.com

The "divine" alfresco setting on the steps of St. Bartholomew's Church comes as a "blessed surprise" at this Park Avenue American; even those who find the staff "indifferent" and the "country club"–esque fare "just ok" enjoy the chance to sit outside and watch the suits parade by.

Cafeteria ●

| 18 | 17 | 14 | $28 |

119 Seventh Ave. (17th St.), 212-414-1717

"LA comes to Chelsea" via this "hip" "modern greasy spoon" where the "upscale comfort food" is on 24 hours a day; some say it's "all scene and no substance", citing "snobby" service and "mediocre" eats, but the fact that it's "always busy" speaks for itself.

Cafe Trevi ●

| ▽ 18 | 15 | 19 | $45 |

1570 First Ave. (bet. 81st & 82nd Sts.), 212-249-0040; www.cafetrevi.com

A "neighborhood" "favorite" on the Upper East Side, this comfortable "old-school Italian" offers "well-prepared" specialties "graciously served"; however, while some say the "new owners have done a fabulous job", its ratings suggest otherwise.

Cafe Un Deux Trois ●

| 16 | 15 | 16 | $40 |

123 W. 44th St. (bet. B'way & 6th Ave.), 212-354-4148; www.cafeundeuxtrois.biz

"Solid bistro fare" and a spirit of fun have made this Times Square French "a pre- or post-theater standby" for more than 25 years; it's "starting to look a little tattered", but the "inexpensive" tabs and "quick" service help keep it "lively" – and "loud."

Caffe Bondi
∇ | 22 | 19 | 20 | $37

1816 Hylan Blvd. (Dongan Hills Ave.), Staten Island, 718-668-0100;
www.bondiny.com

Declared "a delightful surprise" for "authentic Sicilian" at "value"
prices, this new Staten Island Italian also boasts a "lovely" dining room
and "courteous" service; no wonder early visitors are welcoming it
to the neighborhood.

Caffe Buon Gusto
18 | 14 | 17 | $29

236 E. 77th St. (bet. 2nd & 3rd Aves.), 212-535-6884
1009 Second Ave. (bet. 53rd & 54th Sts.), 212-755-1476
151 Montague St. (bet. Clinton & Henry Sts.), Brooklyn, 718-624-3838
www.caffebuongustoonline.com

Locals turn to this "relaxed, leisurely" Italian trio for "decent",
"reasonably priced" meals in "friendly, down-to-earth" environs;
perhaps the experience is "sort of generic", but most people appreciate
it as a "simple but reliable" standby.

Caffe Cielo ●
20 | 17 | 20 | $41

881 Eighth Ave. (bet. 52nd & 53rd Sts.), 212-246-9555

"The food's always on the money" at this "enjoyable" "Theater
District stalwart" where the classic Italian dishes are backed up by a
"welcoming", "warm and efficient" staff; if a few shrug "nothing
special", they are easily outvoted.

Caffe Grazie
18 | 16 | 18 | $44

26 E. 84th St. (bet. 5th & Madison Aves.), 212-717-4407; www.caffegrazie.com

"A short walk from the Met", this "spiffy little" Italian cafe offers
"dependable" fare that's "attentively served" but perhaps "a little
expensive"; still, both locals and tired tourists treat this "townhouse"
"treasure" as a "home away from home."

Caffe Linda ⊠
19 | 13 | 18 | $32

145 E. 49th St. (bet. Lexington & 3rd Aves.), 646-497-1818

A "find" in bustling Midtown, this "intimate", understated Italian
serves "surprisingly good" pastas and such at "reasonable prices";
often "crowded and noisy" at lunchtime, it's more relaxed at dinner,
and at any meal the "accommodating" staff "makes you feel at home."

Caffé on the Green
21 | 22 | 20 | $48

201-10 Cross Island Pkwy. (bet. Clearview Expwy. & Utopia Pkwy.),
Queens, 718-423-7272; www.caffeonthegreen.com

Bayside's "delightful" "local classic" overlooking the Throgs Neck
Bridge has what it takes: a "beautiful" setting ("Rudolph Valentino's
former summer home"), "quality" Italian-Continental cuisine and
"courteous" service; all agree it's "perfect for parties" and "weddings",
assuming "you have the bucks."

Caffe Rafaella ●
18 | 18 | 13 | $22

134 Seventh Ave. S. (bet. Charles & W. 10th Sts.), 212-929-7247

Rafaella on 9th ●

178 Ninth Ave. (21st St.), 212-741-3230

"Delectable desserts" are the way to go at this Italian "stalwart" that's
a "cozy" perch for Village "people-watching" or "conversations over
coffee"; never mind if the savory fare's just "serviceable" and the
"aloof" service isn't even that; N.B. there's a smaller offshoot in Chelsea.

California Pizza Kitchen
16 | 12 | 15 | $22

201 E. 60th St. (bet. 2nd & 3rd Aves.), 212-755-7773; www.cpk.com

Ok, it's a chain, but "for a no-fuss, basic meal", even die-hard NYers
admit they "love" the "designer pizza" and "awesome salads" at this

Left Coast import near Bloomie's; just be warned that it's a magnet for "screaming kids", and oh that decor – "so '80s!"

Calle Ocho
21 | 23 | 19 | $45

446 Columbus Ave. (bet. 81st & 82nd Sts.), 212-873-5025;
www.calleochonyc.com
"When you can't get to Miami", stop by this West Side Nuevo Latino where "pretty people" nibble "awesome", slightly "pricey" eats in "sexy", "cavernous" digs; "exotic" drinks and "terrific music" fuel the "high-energy" scene, which can get pretty "raucous" on weekends.

CamaJe ●
▽ 22 | 17 | 18 | $33

85 MacDougal St. (bet. Bleecker & Houston Sts.), 212-673-8184;
www.camaje.com
"Wonderful French-American bistro fare comes in "cozy" quarters at this "laid-back" Village "refuge"; factor in "reasonable prices" and "terrific cooking classes and wine tastings", and it's a puzzle why it remains largely "undiscovered."

Cambalache
– | – | – | M

406 E. 64th St. (bet. 1st & York Aves.), 212-223-2229
From the owner of the Upper West Side's Pampa comes this cross-town Argentine, whose colorful lounge, subdued peach-toned dining room and spacious back garden exude a graceful Latin air; the menu's predictably meat-focused, with a selection of traditional tapas to round things out.

Campagnola ●
24 | 19 | 22 | $59

1382 First Ave. (bet. 73rd & 74th Sts.), 212-861-1102
"They take care of their customers" with "highest-quality" "old-school Italian" fare and "primo" wines at this dark, classy East Side "scene"; still, some show signs of serious "sticker shock", which may be especially painful if it's true that "only regulars are treated well" here.

Canaletto
21 | 17 | 21 | $50

208 E. 60th St. (bet. 2nd & 3rd Aves.), 212-317-9192
"Fresh and plentiful" Italian classics dispensed by an "excellent" staff are the reasons to go to this "pleasant", "upscale" East Side Italian; it's declared a neighborhood standby, even if a few dismiss the experience as "somewhat generic" and on the expensive side.

Candela
18 | 22 | 18 | $39

116 E. 16th St. (bet. Irving Pl. & Park Ave. S.), 212-254-1600
"A zillion shimmering candles" light this "cavernous", "Gothic" Union Square East New American that's "very romantic, or very dark, depending on your mood"; the "tasty" fare's "almost an afterthought", but who cares if "you can't see it" – just "bring a date", "snag a booth" and "cuddle."

Candle 79
23 | 21 | 22 | $39

154 E. 79th St. (bet. Lexington & 3rd Aves.), 212-537-7179;
www.candlecafe.com
"Veggie goes upscale" at this Upper East Side "organic haven" offering "creative" dishes so "delectable" they could "convert carnivores into vegolas"; the "attentive staff" and "chic", "luxurious atmosphere" light up those "looking for a fine-dining" experience.

Candle Cafe
21 | 13 | 19 | $28

1307 Third Ave. (bet. 74th & 75th Sts.), 212-472-0970; www.candlecafe.com
"Heaven" for "health nuts", and a good bet "if you need to detox", this little East Side cousin of Candle 79 serves "hearty" vegan dishes full of "fresh, bright flavors" plus desserts defining "rich decadence";

despite no-frills quarters, fair prices for quality food and service keep the place crowded.

Canton ⊄

24	13	21	$42

45 Division St. (bet. Bowery & Market St.), 212-226-4441

You can "eat yourself into nirvana" at this Chinatown Cantonese class act if you just "sit back" and tell hostess Eileen Leong "to surprise you"; the food is "always top-form", so even though it's a tad "pricey" and the decor could use "jazzing up", "you're in for a treat."

Canyon Road

20	17	17	$33

1470 First Ave. (bet. 76th & 77th Sts.), 212-734-1600; www.arkrestaurants.com

"Energetic" "thirtysomethings" "dressed to a T" head for this East Side Southwestern cantina to down "tasty" eats and get "cross-eyed" on margaritas "served in a glass your fish could live in"; though often "crowded", the "mood lighting" and "relaxed" vibe make it a "perfect date place."

Capital Grille

23	23	23	$59

Chrysler Ctr., 155 E. 42nd St. (bet. Lexington & 3rd Aves.), 212-953-2000; www.thecapitalgrille.com

"Amazing" steaks so "tender" you "don't need teeth" are the hallmark of this Midtown outpost of an Atlanta chain, where "chipper" staffers serve a "power" clientele in "striking" quarters within the "Philip Johnson–designed" Trylon Towers; its "clubby" feel extends to "costly" prices, so it's best to go when "the boss is paying."

CAPSOUTO FRÈRES

24	23	23	$52

451 Washington St. (Watts St.), 212-966-4900; www.capsoutofreres.com

Located "halfway to Joisey" in "the middle of nowhere" (aka west TriBeCa), this "glorious oasis of civility" has delivered "delicious" French bistro fare for decades; its "pretty", red brick–walled "high-ceilinged room" provides all the "creature comforts", with "unpretentious" yet "delightful" service "icing the cake."

Caracas Arepa Bar

22	12	18	$14

91 E. Seventh St. (1st Ave.), 212-228-5062; www.caracasarepabar.com

If "on a quest" for "cheap", "quality" "munchies", try this "teeny" East Village Venezuelan's "addictive" arepas (stuffed corn-flour cakes); so what if it feels a bit like "dining in a confessional" – it's a "winner."

Cara Mia

20	15	18	$33

654 Ninth Ave. (bet. 45th & 46th Sts.), 212-262-6767; www.nycrg.com

A Hell's Kitchen "favorite", this "charming" Italian offers "well-made" pastas and other classics in "quaint" quarters; even though "sardines may have more room" than the diners here, "quality" and "decent" prices keep both locals and theatergoers coming back.

Carino

21	14	22	$31

1710 Second Ave. (bet. 88th & 89th Sts.), 212-860-0566

The "lovingly prepared" "old-school" Southern Italian served at this Upper Eastsider will leave you "with a smile", especially when Mama Carino is there to take "good care of you"; it's "not fancy", but anyone craving that "homey", "grandma's-kitchen" feel will be in "heaven."

Carl's Steaks

22	6	14	$11

79 Chambers St. (bet. B'way & Church St.), 212-566-2828
507 Third Ave. (34th St.), 212-696-5336 ●⊄
www.carlssteaks.com

The "mouthwatering cheese steaks" at this Murray Hill purveyor of "greasy goodness" are "as close to Philly as you can get" "without taking the Jersey Turnpike"; given the "unpretentious" space with few seats, another plus is that its "addictive" sandwiches "survive delivery": N.B. a TriBeCa branch opened recently.

CARMINE'S
20 | 15 | 17 | $36

2450 Broadway (bet. 90th & 91st Sts.), 212-362-2200
200 W. 44th St. (bet. B'way & 8th Ave.), 212-221-3800 ●
www.carminesnyc.com

"King garlic" reigns at this "legendary" Southern Italian duo where the red-gravy fare is served "family-style" in "bust-your-gut" portions; for full enjoyment, "go with a group" and "team taste", but plan on "long lines" because these "raucous parties" are "perpetually packed."

Carne
19 | 17 | 16 | $35

2737 Broadway (105th St.), 212-663-7010; www.carnenyc.com
A "hot spot" for the Upper West Side, this modestly priced steakhouse delivers "tried-and-true" dishes plus a "cool" "Downtown vibe"; surveyors appreciate that a new chef has taken the menu "a step up", but the staff is still often "nowhere to be found."

Carnegie Deli ●≠
21 | 9 | 13 | $25

854 Seventh Ave. (55th St.), 212-757-2245; www.carnegiedeli.com
"Killer" "overstuffed" sandwiches "only a python could get its jaws around" lure NYers and "tourists" alike to this "hectic" Midtown "deli heaven"; noshers crammed "elbow-to-elbow" should expect "fast, efficient and rude" service that's as "classic" as the "can't-beat-it" cheesecake at this quintessential NYC "landmark."

Carol's Cafe ⊠
▽ 25 | 17 | 20 | $51

1571 Richmond Rd. (bet. Four Corners Rd. & Seaview Ave.), Staten Island, 718-979-5600; www.carolscafe.com
"Charming" chef Carol Frazzetta is constantly conjuring "delicious", "creative" dishes at her Staten Island Eclectic, meaning that "every visit is a new experience"; just know this tasteful "touch of Manhattan in a sleepy suburb" comes with accordingly "expensive" tabs.

Casa ●⊠
▽ 23 | 17 | 19 | $38

72 Bedford St. (Commerce St.), 212-366-9410
"Warm and hip" is a hard combo to pull off, but this "intimate" Village Brazilian manages it with a stylishly "simple" setting and "friendly" staff offering "on-the-mark" advice; still, it's the "delicious", "authentic" cuisine, "terrific" caipirinhas and modest prices that fill this casa.

Casa La Femme North ●
▽ 20 | 22 | 17 | $50

1076 First Ave. (bet. 58th & 59th Sts.), 212-223-2322
Still going strong as a "sultry date spot", this Egyptian near the Queensboro Bridge offers "surprisingly good" edibles nearly on par with the "imaginative decor" featuring "tented tables" and "rose petals on the floor"; belly dancing completes the "exotic", if "expensive", picture.

Casa Mia
20 | 17 | 20 | $34

225 E. 24th St. (bet. 2nd & 3rd Aves.), 212-679-5606
This "friendly" Gramercy Italian delivers "like grandma's" repasts with "hearty" "classic" fare and "homey" digs; given the "caring" service and "affordable" tabs, it's no wonder it's a local "favorite."

Casa Mono ●
25 | 18 | 20 | $46

52 Irving Pl. (17th St.), 212-253-2773
"Is there anything Mario Batali can't do?" marvel those "dazzled" by this Gramercy Spaniard specializing in "wonderfully inventive" small plates ("don't call them tapas"); such "spectacular" nibbles are "worth every cent and bumped elbow" in its "dollhouse" of a dining room; N.B. there's a wine bar/waiting room, Bar Jamón, around the corner.

Casbah Rouge ⦿

_– – – M_

2841 Broadway (bet. 110th & 111th Sts.), 212-932-2222;
www.casbah-rouge.com

Adding some verve to colorless Morningside Heights, this exotic new Moroccan from the Le Souk folks purveys midpriced exotica in a multichambered crimson setting; after-dinner hookahs and belly dancers lend nightlife appeal.

Cascina ⦿

_18 17 18 $38_

647 Ninth Ave. (bet. 45th & 46th Sts.), 212-245-4422;
www.cascina.com

"Service is quick and friendly" at this "rock-solid", "homey" Hell's Kitchen Italian providing "pleasant", "unpretentious", affordable pre-theater meals; the "rustic" quarters are warmed by a "wood-burning oven", not to mention "good wines" from the restaurant's own label.

Caserta Vecchia

_▽ 21 15 20 $27_

221 Smith St. (bet. Baltic & Butler Sts.), Brooklyn, 718-624-7549;
www.casertavecchiarestaurant.com

Though sometimes "overlooked", perhaps because of its "unassuming exterior", this "friendly" Carroll Gardens Italian is locally noted for its "thin-crust, fresh-ingredient" "brick-oven" pizzas; the "lovely garden out back" is yet another endearment.

Casimir ⦿

_20 20 16 $34_

103-105 Ave. B (bet. 6th & 7th Sts.), 212-358-9683

"Left Bank and Alphabet City sensibilities" meld in this "dark, romantic" French bistro to create a "cool, young", "hip" vibe; the "savory" fare is an "excellent value", and if you "bring your attitude shield" you might even enjoy the "cute" staff.

Caviar & Banana

_18 19 18 $50_

12 E. 22nd St. (bet. B'way & Park Ave. S.), 212-353-0500;
www.chinagrillmgt.com

The site of the Jeffrey Chodorow/Rocco DiSpirito reality TV show, _The Restaurant,_ has been reborn as this "very Brazilian" Flatiron venture from Chodorow and Claude Troisgros; though early visitors report some "rough edges", between the "lively decor" and menu of "tasty", "shareable" dishes, at least "you won't be bored."

Caviar Russe

_▽ 25 24 25 $91_

538 Madison Ave., 2nd fl. (bet. 54th & 55th Sts.), 212-980-5908;
www.caviarrusse.com

"Ladies who lunch very, very well" climb to "the height of luxury" at this Midtown New American "caviar speakeasy"; the "decadent" eggs and seafood platters are priced like the "works of art" they are, but no one minds given the "exquisite" setting and "impeccable" service.

Cávo ⦿

_19 25 18 $38_

42-18 31st Ave. (bet. 42nd & 43rd Sts.), Queens, 718-721-1001;
www.cavocafelounge.com

Groupies gush over the three-story waterfall and "gorgeous" garden at this "bustling", "upbeat" (read: "noisy") Astoria Greek; the "modern", midpriced cuisine is deemed "delish", but go "early" because in the "late-night" hours the crowd is mostly there "to dance and drink."

Cebu ⦿

_▽ 22 21 20 $33_

8801 Third Ave. (88th St.), Brooklyn, 718-492-5095

Bay Ridge night-owls say "you can't beat" this "quaint", cost-conscious Continental that's "great for a late meal" as the kitchen's "open till 3 AM"; the setup includes a "bustling bar area" and a "quiet", "romantic back room" where a fireplace warms winter nights.

Celeste ⌀
24 | 12 | 17 | $33

502 Amsterdam Ave. (bet. 84th & 85th Sts.), 212-874-4559

"Amazing quality" and "low prices" add up to a fanatic following for this Upper West Side Neapolitan; yes, it's "crowded and noisy", the "cash-only" policy "can be a hassle" and no reservations "often means a wait", but its fans could care less.

Cellini ⌧
22 | 18 | 22 | $49

65 E. 54th St. (bet. Madison & Park Aves.), 212-751-1555; www.cellinirestaurant.com

"They really take care of you" at this "gracious" Midtown Northern Italian that "can be counted on" for "good", "old-fashioned" pasta and veal dishes with a bit of "flair"; "hopping" business lunches here cede to more "romantic" repasts in the dinner hours.

Cendrillon
20 | 17 | 20 | $37

45 Mercer St. (bet. Broome & Grand Sts.), 212-343-9012; www.cendrillon.com

"Jaded Manhattanites" and other "adventure"-seekers track down "truly unique fare" at this "peaceful" SoHo Filipino-Asian; surveyors report that the "fascinating assortment" of "flavorful", "imaginative dishes" is always "served with care" – and at agreeable prices.

Centolire
20 | 21 | 19 | $57

1167 Madison Ave. (bet. 85th & 86th Sts.), 212-734-7711

Elegant Eastsiders enthuse over the "sophisticated" experience at Pino Luongo's "posh" East Side Italian "duplex"; his "high-level" Tuscan cooking and a trip in the glass elevator to the "handsome" upstairs dining room can be costly, but the $24.50 prix fixe lunch is "a great deal", and just seeing your fellow diners is worth the price of admission.

Centrico
– | – | – | M

211 W. Broadway (Franklin St.), 212-431-0700; www.myriadrestaurantgroup.com

Drew Nieporent's latest, this TriBeCa Mexican might feel a bit austere with its high ceilings and big windows but it's usually too crowded to notice; the food's creative (credit chef Aarón Sanchez), the mood's festive (thanks to the frozen margarita machine) and the price is right.

'CESCA
24 | 22 | 21 | $56

164 W. 75th St. (Amsterdam Ave.), 212-787-6300; www.cescanyc.com

Chef Tom Valenti of Ouest fame has gone "beyond wow" at this "smart"-looking Southern Italian, where the "hearty, rustic" dishes come with "bold and complex flavors" via a "fantastic" crew; the bourgeoise scene may be overly "vibrant" at times and tabs are high, but the main problem is "getting a reservation."

Chadwick's
21 | 18 | 21 | $40

8822 Third Ave. (89th St.), Brooklyn, 718-833-9855

"Wonderfully old-school", this Bay Ridge American serves "good" steaks and seafood in a "publike" setting; the "gracious" staff and "welcoming atmosphere" make this a "great local haunt" for "the young at heart."

Chance
▽ 21 | 19 | 19 | $36

223 Smith St. (Butler St.), Brooklyn, 718-242-1515; www.chancecuisine.com

A post-*Survey* chef and menu change put the Food rating in question for this "interesting" Asian fusion yearling in Boerum Hill, but the "modern decor" with "rolling waterfall" and "Hong Kong–nightclub" vibe remain; in warmer months check out the "small patio in back."

Chanpen Thai ▽ 19 | 13 | 19 | $23
761 Ninth Ave. (51st St.), 212-586-6808; www.chanpenthai.com
"Flavorful" food and "sweet service" make this Hell's Kitchen Thai a good bet "for quick bites or large meals", and "for very little money" too; "fresh flowers" aside, some find the atmosphere "a bit drab."

CHANTERELLE ⌧ 27 | 27 | 27 | $91
2 Harrison St. (Hudson St.), 212-966-6960; www.chanterellenyc.com
"The height of understated luxe", David and Karen Waltuck's TriBeCa French standby combines "flawless" cuisine, a "serene", "airy" dining room dressed with "breathtaking floral displays" and "faultless" "choreographed" service; fans call it a "first-class trip" to "heaven-on-earth", but suggest "saving up" in advance or checking out the "pure perfection" $43 prix fixe lunch.

Charles' Southern-Style Kitchen ▽ 24 | 5 | 15 | $16
2839 Eighth Ave. (151st St.), 212-926-4313
For "amazingly tasty" fried chicken and other "down-home" favorites, check out this Harlem soul fooder; although "nothing to look at", it's a big "bargain", besides, who "eats food like this anywhere fancy"?

Chat 'n Chew ◑ 17 | 14 | 15 | $22
10 E. 16th St. (bet. 5th Ave. & Union Sq. W.), 212-243-1616
When an "urge for old-time" "comfort food" strikes, this Union Square cafe's "cheap" "grub" "hits the spot"; admittedly the "homespun decor" is "tacky" and service "sketchy", but that "crazy-good mac 'n' cheese" "keeps everyone coming back", especially the kids.

Chef Ho's Peking Duck Grill 22 | 15 | 19 | $27
1720 Second Ave. (bet. 89th & 90th Sts.), 212-348-9444
"Wonderful Peking duck" stars on the menu at this "superior" Upper East Side Chinese; the "touches of class" here includes "prompt, polite service", for prices only a "smidge higher" than Chinatown.

Chelsea Bistro 21 | 19 | 20 | $45
358 W. 23rd St. (bet. 8th & 9th Aves.), 212-727-2026; www.chelseabistro.com
This "adorable" Chelsea "stalwart" "pleases" with "tasty" bistro standards served by a "welcoming staff"; the "Gallic atmosphere" is "relaxed, quiet" and "romantic", whether in the "cozy" main room or the greenhouse room in back.

Chelsea Grill 19 | 14 | 17 | $25
135 Eighth Ave. (bet. 16th & 17th Sts.), 212-242-5336
675 Ninth Ave. (bet. 46th & 47th Sts.), 212-974-9002 ◑
"One of the last old NY pubs" in the area, this "no-nonsense" Chelsea stalwart serves the likes of "famously good" "hefty burgers" and "super waffle fries"; the scene's "just rowdy enough to be fun", and if that doesn't suit, the "cool enclosed garden" may; N.B. there's a new branch in the Theater District.

Chelsea Ristorante 20 | 17 | 20 | $34
108 Eighth Ave. (bet. 15th & 16th Sts.), 212-924-7786; www.chelsear.com
"Pleasant" waiters at this "casual", "reliable" Chelsea Italian dispense "surprisingly good" food, much of it from a wood-burning oven, including pizzas that are a "real treat"; it gets an "A for effort", and "very affordable" prices score high marks too.

Chemist Club Grill ◑ – | – | – | E
Dylan Hotel, 52 E. 41st St. (bet. Madison & Park Aves.), 212-297-9177; www.dylanhotel.com
The Grand Central area gets another steakhouse via this Dylan Hotel newcomer set in a former science hall and retaining much of its period

detail; the all-day menu features Americana for breakfast and lunch, and pricey dinnertime surf 'n' turf.

Chennai Garden

| 22 | 12 | 17 | $20 |

129 E. 27th St. (bet. Lexington Ave. & Park Ave. S.), 212-689-1999; www.chennaigarden.com

"Vegans", the observant and other "enlightened" types tout this Gramercy Indian for "interesting vegetarian" and kosher options, including "captivating curries"; the decor's "a little dingy", but the menu's a "fantastic value" topped by the $5.95 prix fixe take-out lunch.

Chestnut

| 21 | 18 | 20 | $38 |

271 Smith St. (bet. Degraw & Sackett Sts.), Brooklyn, 718-243-0049; www.chestnutonsmith.com

"Simple" seasonal cuisine "with a modern edge" is fittingly served in "modest yet cool" digs at this "charming" Carroll Gardens New American; its "fine service", "reasonable" prices and "lovely garden" all cause fans to wonder why it "doesn't get more credit."

Chez Jacqueline

| 20 | 17 | 19 | $45 |

72 MacDougal St. (bet. Bleecker & Houston Sts.), 212-505-0727

"A typical neighborhood place – if you live in Nice", this "casual" Village French bistro offers "solid fare" for "grown-ups" served by an "attentive" staff; though its "small" quarters "get crowded quickly", there's "charming outdoor seating."

Chez Josephine ●

| 21 | 21 | 21 | $49 |

414 W. 42nd St. (bet. 9th & 10th Aves.), 212-594-1925; www.chezjosephine.com

"Legendarily charming host" Jean-Claude Baker's "joie de vivre sets the tone" at this Theater District French bistro–cum–"homage to Josephine Baker", his adoptive mother; besides the pricey tabs, "out-of-the-ordinary" repasts here include "delicious" (if "unadventurous") rations, "lavish" "bordello" decor and a "terrific piano player."

Chez Michallet

| 23 | 19 | 22 | $51 |

90 Bedford St. (Grove St.), 212-242-8309

"Big-time pleasure" comes in a "tiny" package at this "upscale" French bistro "on a quaint Village corner"; its "delightful", classic dishes, "courteous" service and "charming" setting add up to "super-romantic" repasts.

Chez Napoléon ☒

| 20 | 13 | 21 | $41 |

365 W. 50th St. (bet. 8th & 9th Aves.), 212-265-6980; www.cheznapoleon.com

The "worn charm" of this Theater District "throwback" suits longtimers who "love" its "solid", "old-school" French bistro fare and "authentic" "Left Bank" feel; equally endearing is the "pleasant" staff that ensures "you'll make your curtain" with both time and money to spare.

Chiam Chinese Cuisine

| 21 | 18 | 20 | $43 |

160 E. 48th St. (bet. Lexington & 3rd Aves.), 212-371-2323

"East meets West" at this "upmarket" Midtown Chinese where an "outstanding" wine list encourages pairings with the "imaginative", "well-presented dishes"; its "calm", "lovely" room is conducive to "business conversation", which is fortunate since an "expense account" comes in handy when the bill arrives.

Chianti

| 22 | 17 | 20 | $37 |

8530 Third Ave. (86th St.), Brooklyn, 718-921-6300

Take your pick of "tasty" dishes served "family-style" or in "individual portions" at this "solid" Bay Ridge Italian where you're treated like you're "part of the family"; such "friendly service" makes requesting "off-the-menu" items seem like "no problem."

ChikaLicious ●
25 | 19 | 23 | $21

203 E. 10th St. (bet. 1st & 2nd Aves.), 212-995-9511; www.chikalicious.com
"Subtle little mouthfuls of delight" are the forte of this "tiny" East Village dessert "theater" where the "brilliant concept" is a three-course, prix fixe–only menu of "sublime" sweets plus "perfect wine pairings"; there's often "a long wait", but addicts advise "it's worth it."

Chimichurri Grill ●
22 | 15 | 20 | $44

606 Ninth Ave. (bet. 43rd & 44th Sts.), 212-586-8655;
www.chimichurrigrill.com
"Steak is what it's about", so "get ready to be wowed" by "marvelous meats" bathed in the namesake sauce at this Argentinean in Hell's Kitchen; factor in "polite" service and "reasonable" prices, and the only rub is the "shoebox"-size space.

China Grill
23 | 21 | 19 | $52

CBS Bldg., 60 W. 53rd St. (bet. 5th & 6th Aves.), 212-333-7788;
www.chinagrillmgt.com
"Theatergoers, bankers and tourists" mingle at this "still-trendy" Midtown Asian purveying pricey fusion fare "at its best"; the handsome, "cavernous" space fuels the "party" mood, so while you may need "cast-iron eardrums" to deal with the "din", it's all very "entertaining."

China 1 ●≠
17 | 19 | 14 | $29

50 Ave. B (4th St.), 212-375-0665; www.china1nyc.com
The "crowd is hot and the drinks strong" at this "retro Chinese" East Villager; though the cooking gets mixed notices, fans say the "seductive" setting and downstairs "party" lounge are real bonuses.

Chin Chin ●
23 | 18 | 21 | $47

216 E. 49th St. (bet. 2nd & 3rd Aves.), 212-888-4555; www.chinchinny.com
"The crowd always looks happy" at this longtime "gourmet" Midtown Chinese where "familiar" dishes manage to seem "fresh and different" thanks to their "beautiful preparation"; "superior" service further justifies the "high-end" price tag.

Chino's ≠
▽ 20 | 18 | 19 | $26

173 Third Ave. (bet. 16th & 17th Sts.), 212-598-1200; www.chinosnyc.com
An "awesome addition" to Gramercy, this stylish newcomer's inexpensive small-plate menu offers a "delicious" "twist on traditional Asian fare"; though the sleek interior is "smaller than some NYC studio apartments", there's still room for a "hopping bar scene."

Chipotle
19 | 11 | 15 | $11

2 Broadway (Whitehall St.), 212-344-0941
55 E. Eighth St. (bet. B'way & University Pl.), 212-982-3081
150 E. 52nd St. (bet. Lexington & 3rd Aves.), 212-755-9754
150 E. 44th St. (bet. Lexington & 3rd Aves.), 212-682-9860
680 Sixth Ave. (bet. 21st & 22nd Sts.), 212-206-3781
19 St. Marks Pl. (bet. 2nd & 3rd Aves.), 212-529-4502
200 Varick St. (bet. Houston & King Sts.), 646-336-6264
9 W. 42nd St. (bet. 5th & 6th Aves.), 212-354-6760
304 W. 34th St. (8th Ave.), 212-268-4197
185 Montague St. (Court St.), Brooklyn, 718-243-9109
www.chipotle.com
"McDonald's did it right" with these fast-food Mexicans that offer "belt-busting" burritos "you create yourself" from "quality" ingredients; they have "hungry hordes" at lunchtime, but luckily service is "*rápido.*"

ChipShop ●
19 | 14 | 17 | $19

129 Atlantic Ave. (bet. Clinton & Henry Sts.), Brooklyn, 718-855-7775

(continued)

ChipShop/CurryShop ≠

381-383 Fifth Ave. (bet. 6th & 7th Sts.), Brooklyn, 718-832-7701
www.chipshopnyc.com

"Bloody brilliant!" cry "expats and Anglophiles" wowed by this new
"true Brit" pub in Brooklyn Heights and its Park Slope progenitor
(where curries are still served); at both, a "cheerful staff" dispenses
"authentic" fish 'n' chips and other English "throwbacks" washed
down with imported suds.

Cho Dang Gol
▽ 23 | 15 | 18 | $27

55 W. 35th St. (bet. 5th & 6th Aves.), 212-695-8222

"Wonderful" tofu "made fresh" stars in many of the "spicy, tasty"
dishes at this Garment District Korean, where a "helpful staff" guides
"the uninitiated"; though the "faux-tropical" decor strikes some as
"dreary", most surveyors say the modest prices and "peaceful"
ambiance make up for it.

Chola
24 | 15 | 20 | $36

232 E. 58th St. (bet. 2nd & 3rd Aves.), 212-688-4619; www.pappadums.com

"First-timers and foodies alike" are bound to enjoy the "outstanding"
regional dishes on this East Side Indian's "huge" menu; still, it's the
"amazing" $13.95 lunch buffet that garners the most acclaim.

Chop't Creative Salad
21 | 10 | 14 | $12

60 E. 56th St. (bet. Madison & Park Aves.), 212-750-2467 ☒
24 E. 17th St. (bet. B'way & 5th Ave.), 646-336-5523
www.choptsalad.com

With a "mind-boggling" array of "ingredients and dressings" tossed
and chopped to order, these "hot spots" are "standouts in a sea of
salad bars"; it's "easy to get carried away with the toppings" and
blow your lunch budget, but you'll "enjoy every bite of it."

Chow Bar
20 | 18 | 18 | $39

230 W. Fourth St. (W. 10th St.), 212-633-2212

"Fearsome" "ginger martinis" pave the way for "tasty Asian fusion"
chow at this "hopping" West Villager; sure, the "party atmosphere"
may overshadow the edibles, but it's "ideal for meeting up with friends."

Christos
22 | 17 | 20 | $43

41-08 23rd Ave. (41st St.), Queens, 718-777-8400

"Greek butcher shop" by day, "comfortable" steakhouse by night,
this "Astoria treasure" was renovated post-*Survey* and has a new
seafood emphasis, but it still offers the same "slabs of happiness"
and "wonderful sides" that are its signature; "very efficient" service
and an "excellent wine list" round out the experience.

Chubo
▽ 22 | 15 | 18 | $44

6 Clinton St. (bet. Houston & Stanton Sts.), 212-674-6300; www.chubo.com

"A real chef" "artfully" crafts "superb" Eclectic fare at this "tiny"
Lower East Side $34 prix fixe place, which is "sceney" but "without
pretense"; though the decor could be better, most surveyors can't
seem to get enough of it.

Churrascaria Plataforma ●
22 | 19 | 21 | $54

221 W. Broadway (bet. Franklin & White Sts.), 212-925-6969
316 W. 49th St. (bet. 8th & 9th Aves.), 212-245-0505
www.churrascariaplataforma.com

You may "feel a little barbaric" after enacting the "glutton's dream" at
these "festive" Brazilian "meat smorgasbords", where "affable",
"sword"-happy waiters slice "endless" "hot-off-the-grill" hunks at
tableside; just remember, you "have to know when to call it quits."

Cibo

| 20 | 20 | 21 | $43 |

767 Second Ave. (bet. 41st & 42nd Sts.), 212-681-1616

"Cordial" service in an "attractive", "large and airy" space near Tudor City contributes to the "quietly peaceful" air of this "solid" Tuscan–New American; it's particularly popular because you can "actually hear the person sitting across from you."

Cilantro ●

| 17 | 15 | 16 | $28 |

1321 First Ave. (71st St.), 212-537-4040
1712 Second Ave. (bet. 88th & 89th Sts.), 212-722-4242
www.cilantronyc.com

"The chips are worth the trip" say fans of these Upper East Side Southwesterners, who wash them down with "delectably strong", "generous margaritas"; no wonder it's "easygoing" all-around at this provider of "affordably priced" "decent" grub.

Cinque Terre

| ▽ 19 | 18 | 19 | $50 |

Jolly Madison Towers, 22 E. 38th St. (bet. Madison & Park Aves.), 212-867-2260; www.jollymadison.com

"Interesting" Italian "regional" cuisine is "well represented" at this "lovely little" Ligurian "tucked away" in a Murray Hill hotel lobby; if it seems "underpatronized", "pricey" tabs may be the reason, but the bonus is there's almost "always a table."

Cipriani Dolci ●

| 18 | 19 | 16 | $43 |

Grand Central, West Balcony (42nd St. & Vanderbilt Ave.), 212-973-0999; www.cipriani.com

"Perched above" "the comings and goings" of the Grand Central Concourse, this Italian offers "classic" dishes plus the "simple pleasure" of people-watching; even if the prices are high, to most it's "worth it" because the "scenery below always fascinates."

Cipriani Downtown ●

| 21 | 19 | 19 | $59 |

376 W. Broadway (bet. Broome & Spring Sts.), 212-343-0999; www.cipriani.com

It's "all about the scene" at this SoHo Cipriani outpost, where a "stunning crowd" of "Euros", "local imposters" and "models pretending to eat" gathers to be "fabulous" while sipping "divine Bellinis" and grazing on "good" Italian food "elbow-to-elbow"; it's "costly", but even after several years it's "still white-hot."

Circus

| ▽ 20 | 19 | 19 | $46 |

132 E. 61st St. (bet. Lexington & Park Aves.), 212-223-2965; www.circusrestaurante.com

Ensconced in "new digs", this Midtown Brazilian still offers "hearty" fare and potent caipirinhas that leave indulgers with "trouble focusing"; the "congenial" vibe's enlivened by a "whimsical" "circus motif", making for a "pleasant diversion" after a Bloomie's spree.

Cité ●

| 22 | 20 | 21 | $58 |

120 W. 51st St. (bet. 6th & 7th Aves.), 212-956-7100; www.citerestaurant.com

The "famous" "all-you-can-drink" wine dinners are a "fantastic bargain" at this "perfect Midtown steakhouse" where an "unfailingly patient" staff serves "a big business crowd" in "attractive, non-clubby" quarters; if you like cow with your wine, this is the right cité.

Cité Grill ●▨

| 20 | 19 | 20 | $49 |

120 W. 51st St. (bet. 6th & 7th Aves.), 212-956-7262; www.citerestaurant.com

It's "easy in, easy out" at this Midtown grill that's more "relaxed" than its next-door sibling, serving near "Cité-caliber" fare perfect for "a bite after work" or "pre-theater"; "liberal drinks" fuel a "busy scene" at the bar.

Citrus Bar & Grill
20 | 19 | 18 | $37

320 Amsterdam Ave. (75th St.), 212-595-0500; www.citrusnyc.com
It "helps to be under 30" at this West Side Latin-Asian "hot spot" where the kitchen produces an "exciting blend of flavors", but most "go for the scene", "swanky cocktails" and "nice outdoor seating."

City Bakery
22 | 13 | 14 | $18

3 W. 18th St. (bet. 5th & 6th Aves.), 212-366-1414
Beware the buffet and salad bar at Maury Rubin's Flatiron bakery lest you "ruin your appetite" for the "heavenly" pastries; it would all be "utter bliss" but for the "glorified cafeteria" setting and service.

City Crab & Seafood Co.
17 | 14 | 16 | $41

235 Park Ave. S. (19th St.), 212-529-3800
"If it swims", you can find it at this fairly priced Flatiron fish bar where "boisterous" patrons "whack away at crabs with mallets"; the "ersatz seashore decor" could use some "sprucing" and service can be "crabby", but overall it's "satiating."

City Hall ⌧
21 | 21 | 21 | $53

131 Duane St. (bet. Church St. & W. B'way), 212-227-7777
"Masters of the universe" "rub elbows" with "top city brass" at Henry Meer's "posh" TriBeCa surf 'n' turf "classic" serving "consistently" "well-done" fare; though not cheap, quality is written all over this place, starting with the first-rate food and including the "loftlike space" that "exudes old NY."

City Lobster & Crab Co.
18 | 16 | 17 | $47

121 W. 49th St. (bet. 6th & 7th Aves.), 212-354-1717; www.citylobster.com
A "good standby for business lunches", this formulaic Radio City–area seafooder dispenses "ample amounts" of "fresh" fin fare "with minimal fuss"; though critics call it "rather humdrum", it's nice to have around.

coast ⌧
▽ 20 | 15 | 17 | $38

110 Liberty St. (Church St.), 212-962-0136;
www.freshshorecoast.com
"Desperate Wall Streeters" in search of "a good option" find this new "cousin to Fresh and Shore" a "godsend", offering "wonderful" seafood at "affordable" rates; in front is "a marvelous" "fish market to boot", so it's only the "industrial" decor that gets mixed notices.

Coco Pazzo
23 | 21 | 21 | $64

23 E. 74th St. (bet. 5th & Madison Aves.), 212-794-0205
"All's right with the world" now that chef "Mark Strausman's back" at this handsome, comfortable East Side Northern Italian; every night you can find a "glittering", celeb-centric crowd "dressing up" to graze on "well-prepared classics"; it may be "pricey", but it's very popular and thus always "busy."

Coco Roco
20 | 14 | 15 | $26

392 Fifth Ave. (bet. 6th & 7th Sts.), Brooklyn, 718-965-3376
"Hands-down the best" dish on this Park Slope Peruvian's menu is the "mouthwatering" rotisserie chicken, but everything is "good, plentiful and cheap"; yes, the decor "leaves something to be desired", ditto the "poor service", but then there's always "delivery."

Cocotte
22 | 18 | 19 | $37

337 Fifth Ave. (4th St.), Brooklyn, 718-832-6848
Park Slopers tout this French–New American for its "homey" vibe, "flavorful" fare and particularly "lovely brunch"; service can be "slow", but at least "you won't feel rushed"; P.S. the "cozy" back wine bar is a "destination in itself."

Coffee Shop ◐

16 | 14 | 12 | $27

29 Union Sq. W. (16th St.), 212-243-7969

The "fabulosity" factor's high at this "mobbed" Union Square Brazilian-American, where "pretty good" fare is delivered by "bored" "model wannabes"; the "decor could use a little TLC" too, but nobody notices much given the plentiful "eye candy."

Col Legno ◐

▽ 19 | 13 | 18 | $36

231 E. Ninth St. (bet. 2nd & 3rd Aves.), 212-777-4650

"A regular haunt" for East Villagers seeking a little "Tuscan cool", this "unsung" standby offers "tasty" eats including "brick-oven specialties" ("exemplary pizza", anyone?) at "fair prices"; the "oddly configured room" is definitely "not flashy", but "who cares?"

Columbus Bakery

19 | 13 | 11 | $16

474 Columbus Ave. (bet. 82nd & 83rd Sts.), 212-724-6880
957 First Ave. (bet. 52nd & 53rd Sts.), 212-421-0334
www.arkrestaurants.com

"Awesome" baked goods and "superior" light fare "packs 'em in" to these crosstown bakery/cafes; even those put off by "the stroller brigade", "chaotic" lines and "cranky staff" admit it's "good for a nosh."

Comfort Diner

16 | 12 | 15 | $21

214 E. 45th St. (bet. 2nd & 3rd Aves.), 212-867-4555
25 W. 23rd St. (bet. 5th & 6th Aves.), 212-741-1010

"The name says it all" at these diners dispensing "nostalgia" in the form of "'50s" "home-cooking" classics that are just the thing "if you're having a rough day"; ergo, you're likely to "leave with a smile."

Compass

21 | 22 | 20 | $56

208 W. 70th St. (bet. Amsterdam & West End Aves.), 212-875-8600;
www.compassrestaurant.com

Perhaps "the chefs keep changing" at this West Side New American, but the food's "consistently wonderful" according to advocates of its "creative" dishes served in "sleek, sexy" environs by an "attentive" staff; the less-impressed indicate it's "still finding its way."

Convivium Osteria

25 | 24 | 21 | $43

68 Fifth Ave. (bet. Bergen St. & St. Marks Ave.), Brooklyn, 718-857-1833

"Very convivial" indeed, this "little wonder" in Park Slope "continues to astound" with its "excellent" "offbeat" Portuguese, Italian and Spanish dishes and its winning wines; darkly "atmospheric" and "romantic", it's a "great place to linger" and, in warm weather, the garden is "delightful."

Copper Chimney

– | – | – | M

126 E. 28th St. (bet. Lexington Ave. & Park Ave. S.), 212-213-5742;
www.copperchimney.com

Melding traditional Indian tastes with modern looks, this bi-level Gramercy newcomer features a dimly lit, banquette-equipped first floor topped by a cocktail lounge and private dining room; its $11, three-course lunch special is an easy way to get to know it.

Coppola's ◐

19 | 16 | 17 | $34

378 Third Ave. (bet. 27th & 28th Sts.), 212-679-0070
206 W. 79th St. (bet. Amsterdam Ave. & B'way), 212-877-3840
www.coppolas-nyc.com

These "no-guesswork" "neighborhood Italian joints" provide "good, reliable eats" of the "bountiful", "affordable" variety; fans find them "cozy", but there are those who think they're "better for delivery" given their so-so decor and service.

Cornelia Street Cafe ◐   19 | 15 | 18 | $33
29 Cornelia St. (bet. Bleecker & W. 4th Sts.), 212-989-9319;
www.corneliastreetcafe.com
A "cozy bohemian vibe" permeates this modestly priced Village
French-American that "keeps it real" while serving "reliably good
cafe" classics, hosting "jazz and poetry" performances in the
basement and offering "delightful" sidewalk seating; in sum, "the
parts add up to a great time" here.

Corner Bistro ◐≠   23 | 9 | 12 | $15
331 W. Fourth St. (Jane St.), 212-242-9502
It's "crowded and loud", but the myriad fans of the "mouthwatering"
bargain burgers at this "classic Village dive" "wouldn't change a
thing"; just "have a beer while you wait" for that "juicy", "grilled-
to-perfection" patty.

Cortina   ▽ 19 | 14 | 20 | $35
1448 Second Ave. (bet. 75th & 76th Sts.), 212-517-2066;
www.ristorantecortina.com
The "attentive" chef-owner creates a "warm", "inviting" feeling at this
"small" Upper East Side neighborhood place serving "fresh", "solid"
Northern Italian fare followed by formidable desserts.

Cosette   20 | 14 | 21 | $36
163 E. 33rd St. (bet. Lexington & 3rd Aves.), 212-889-5489
"Enthusiastic", "quick" service "makes up for" "dowdy" decor at
this Murray Hill French "sleeper" whose "butter-laden" "*ancienne*
cuisine" completes the "pleasant experience"; better still, you leave
"well satisfied" but "without taking a financial hit."

Cosí   17 | 11 | 12 | $13
841 Broadway (13th St.), 212-614-8544 ◐
2160 Broadway (76th St.), 212-595-5616
60 E. 56th St. (bet. Madison & Park Aves.), 212-588-1225
Paramount Plaza, 1633 Broadway (51st St.), 212-397-9838
257 Park Ave. S. (21st St.), 212-598-4070
498 Seventh Ave. (bet. 36th & 37th Sts.), 212-947-1005
504 Sixth Ave. (13th St.), 212-462-4188 ◐
700 Sixth Ave. (bet. 22nd & 23rd Sts.), 212-645-0223
11 W. 42nd St. (bet. 5th & 6th Aves.), 212-398-6662
World Financial Ctr., 200 Vesey St. (West Side Hwy.), 212-571-2001
www.getcosi.com
Additional locations throughout the NY area
"It's all about the flatbread" at these "ubiquitous" "grab-and-go"
eateries where the "chewy", "addictive" stuff is "so good it elevates"
the "interesting fillings" inside; too bad seats can be "hard to come
by" and the "apathetic service" comes "without a smile."

Cosmic Cantina ◐≠   19 | 9 | 14 | $12
101 Third Ave. (bet. 12th & 13th Sts.), 212-420-0975
"Big, rockin' burritos" made with "healthful", organic ingredients
head the list of "late-night munchies" at this East Village Mexican;
"packed with college kids", the "casual" setup's "nothing to look at",
but it's "cheap" and "fun to sit outside with a pitcher of beer."

Counter ◐   21 | 20 | 19 | $32
105 First Ave. (bet. 6th & 7th Sts.), 212-982-5870
Inside the "pearly gates" of this "classy" East Village vegetarian there's
"terrific" fare "flavorful" enough "for any meat eater" plus "organic
wines"; given the "hip, pretty setting", "patient, friendly staff" and
modest prices, it's not surprising that the vibe here is "mellow."

Country Café

∇ 20 | 16 | 21 | $36

69 Thompson St. (bet. Broome & Spring Sts.), 212-966-5417;
www.countrycafesoho.com
Something of a "neighborhood secret", this "charming" French–North
African "off-the-beaten-SoHo" path serves "enjoyable" food for
"decent prices"; though it "doesn't offer much" in the way of decor,
the ambiance is "cozy" and "quiet" enough for romantics.

Cowgirl

16 | 18 | 16 | $26

519 Hudson St. (10th St.), 212-633-1133; www.cowgirlnyc.com
For "a rootin'-tootin' good time", West Villagers head to this "hokey",
low-budget Southwestern and devour "down-home" eats "served up
big, Texas-style"; by day it's "loaded with kids", but come nighttime it
hosts a "deafening bar scene."

Cozy Soup & Burger ●

18 | 8 | 16 | $15

739 Broadway (Astor Pl.), 212-477-5566
Hungry "insomniacs" and "late-night revelers" tout this round-the-
clock "quintessential" Village diner for its "amazing" "burgers that
need two hands" and "out-of-this-world split-pea soup"; as for its
"unadorned" digs and "gruff" service, you get what you pay for.

CRAFT

26 | 24 | 24 | $69

43 E. 19th St. (bet. B'way & Park Ave. S.), 212-780-0880
Acolytes attest that "Tom Colicchio is a god" and his Flatiron eatery a
"foodie's heaven", where patrons "mix and match" from among
"simple" yet "sublime" New American dishes; the room's "serene", and
an "exemplary staff" helps solve its "riddle" of a menu, so though the tab
can be "staggering", it's "worth it" when "every meal's memorable."

Craftbar

23 | 19 | 20 | $47

900 Broadway (bet. 19th & 20th Sts.), 212-461-4300
Craft's "casual" sibling, this Flatiron New American offers "a lighter",
less-pricey menu; still, the "market-fresh ingredients" "shine through"
in "delicious" dishes, and if the "new digs" are "less intimate", at
least you can still "walk in on impulse."

Creole

∇ 20 | 17 | 20 | $39

2167 Third Ave. (118th St.), 212-876-8838; www.creolenyc.com
Already "popular", this "friendly" newcomer to East Harlem has hit on
the "perfect combination" of "marvelous" spicy Creole specialties and
nightly jazz; early patrons, wowed by the "ambiance and concept",
only wish "they had a bigger menu."

Crispo ●

23 | 19 | 19 | $42

240 W. 14th St. (bet. 7th & 8th Aves.), 212-229-1818
Full of "robust flavors", the Northern Italian food at this "hopping"
Villager is served in "warm, romantic" quarters that light up an
otherwise "drab" block; add "affordable" wines and a "transporting"
"outdoor garden" and you've got a clear winner.

Croton Reservoir Tavern ⊠

∇ 19 | 16 | 19 | $36

108 W. 40th St. (bet. B'way & 6th Ave.), 212-997-6835;
www.crotonreservoirtavern.com
"Not your standard pub grub" say patrons who've found this "surprise
treat", "solid value" Times Square New American; the classic tavern
setting makes a perfect "little hideaway" for "quick business meals."

Cru ⊠

25 | 22 | 24 | $82

24 Fifth Ave. (9th St.), 212-529-1700; www.cru-nyc.com
The "extraordinary", "telephone book–size" wine list tops it all at this
Village Med, but chef Shea Gallante's "shockingly delicious" cuisine

"isn't far behind"; factor in "cosmopolitan-chic" decor and excellent service, and it's no surprise it's "*très cher*", yet deemed "worth it" by most; P.S. try out the small plates that are served in the "lively", "more casual", walk-in front room.

Cuba ◐
21 | 20 | 18 | $32

222 Thompson St. (bet. Bleecker & W. 3rd Sts.), 212-420-7878; www.cubanyc.com
"Simple but delicious" Cuban fare, "mojitos by the pitcher" and "Latin rhythms belting" make this little Villager a "lively" scene; still, service can be "sketchy", especially on "live music" nights.

Cuba Cafe
19 | 17 | 18 | $31

200 Eighth Ave. (bet. 20th & 21st Sts.), 212-633-1570; www.chelseadining.com
"Right on" mojitos rule at this "funky", "festive" Chelsea Cuban; the combo of "better-than-expected" "traditional" dishes and "great prices" has made it "a local hangout"; P.S. check out the "excellent sandwiches" at lunchtime.

Cubana Café ♥
20 | 16 | 18 | $23

110 Thompson St. (Prince St.), 212-966-5366 ◐
272 Smith St. (Degraw St.), Brooklyn, 718-858-3980
"Down, dirty and delicious", these "unpretentious" Village–Cobble Hill cafes are "a screaming value", serving up "home cooking à la Cuba" plus "delicious fruity cocktails"; however, demanding diners declare "they've got to find more space."

Cube 63 ◐
▽ 25 | 17 | 22 | $34

63 Clinton St. (bet. Rivington & Stanton Sts.), 212-228-6751; www.cube63.com
"Such a find" yet "so easy to miss", this "funky" BYO Lower East Side Japanese lures "young" sushi-lovers with "fresh", "delicious rolls" complemented by a "concerted effort to please"; given these attributes, it's no surprise that it's often crowded.

Cub Room
17 | 18 | 16 | $45

131 Sullivan St. (Prince St.), 212-677-4100; www.cubroom.com
An ever-"trendy" "SoHo hang" that's "reliable" for New American "comfort food"; the "fun bar" draws kudos from all, but those put off by its "pricey" bites wonder whether it's running "on cruise control."

Cucina di Pesce ◐
18 | 14 | 17 | $26

87 E. Fourth St. (bet. Bowery & 2nd Ave.), 212-260-6800; www.cucinadipesce.com
"Large portions and small checks" (especially the "incredible" $10.95 early-bird) are the appeal at this "good" ol' East Village Italian standby whose "crowded" digs scream "shabby-chic"; those unimpressed with the kitchen's handiwork shrug "you get what you pay for."

Cupping Room Café ◐
17 | 15 | 16 | $28

359 W. Broadway (bet. Broome & Grand Sts.), 212-925-2898; www.cuppingroomcafe.com
"Cozy, comfortable and convenient", this "welcome SoHo respite" is an "authentic NY eatery" with "no disappointments or surprises"; "reasonably priced", "enjoyable" American comfort fare, especially the "worth-the-wait" weekend brunches, is the secret to its longevity.

Curry Leaf
21 | 12 | 17 | $24

99 Lexington Ave. (27th St.), 212-725-5558
151 Remsen St. (bet. Clinton & Court Sts.), Brooklyn, 718-222-3900
www.curryleafnyc.com
The "Kalustyan's pedigree shows" at this "cut-above" Indian duo, where "classic", "well-spiced" dishes come in "portions that are just

right", with prices to match; the decor may be strictly "no-frills", but "relaxed", "pleasant" service curries further favor.

Cyclo
| 18 | 15 | 17 | $31 |

203 First Ave. (bet. 12th & 13th Sts.), 212-673-3957
"Delicate" yet "down-to-earth" Vietnamese-Thai food more than "compensates for the tight squeeze" at this East Village standby, while lighting that's a bit more "dim" than romantic, "spotty service" and "modest portions" are overlooked given the "equally modest prices."

Da Andrea
| 24 | 17 | 22 | $34 |

557 Hudson St. (bet. Perry & W. 11th Sts.), 212-367-1979;
www.biassanot.com
The "space is small, but the appeal is huge" at this "rustic" West Village Northern Italian thanks to its "delicious" "homestyle" fare, "welcoming" staff and "comfortable"atmosphere; factor in "beyond-affordable prices", and it's no wonder that "lines form out the door" nightly.

Da Antonio ☒
| ▽ 22 | 19 | 23 | $56 |

157 E. 55th St. (bet. Lexington & 3rd Aves.), 212-588-1545
"Caring" "veteran waiters" recite the "staggering specials list" at this multilevel "*autentico*" East Midtown Italian; live piano music adds to the "old-time" feel, so the only problem is you may "leave with a thin wallet."

Da Ciro
| 21 | 16 | 19 | $38 |

229 Lexington Ave. (bet. 33rd & 34th Sts.), 212-532-1636;
www.dacironyc.com
Maybe Murray Hill's "best-kept secret", this "comfortable", "old-school" Italian offers "earthy", "tasty" classics as well as "fantastic" "gourmet pizza" from its brick oven; it may be "overpriced" and "noisy", but it pleases "those who are tired of me-too" fare.

Da Filippo
| 21 | 17 | 21 | $50 |

1315 Second Ave. (bet. 69th & 70th Sts.), 212-472-6688;
www.dafilipporestaurant.com
"Super-charming" owner Carlo Meconi and his crew "take great care of everyone" at this "low-key", "comfortable" East Side Northern Italian; the "bountiful menu" is most "satisfying", so no one minds if it's a bit "pricey."

da Giacomo
| ▽ 23 | 21 | 21 | $59 |

156 E. 64th St. (Lexington Ave.), 212-308-1300
An offshoot of its longstanding Milan namesake, this East Side townhouse Italian with several "relaxing" dining rooms is deemed a "great addition" to the area; early visitors cite "excellent" fare (including seafood dishes that "sparkle") as well as expensive tabs.

Daisy May's BBQ USA ☒
| 23 | 5 | 13 | $17 |

623 11th Ave. (46th St.), 212-977-1500; www.daisymaysbbq.com
"Heaven's in Hell's Kitchen" at this "amazing" "BBQ jernt" serving "mind-boggling" ribs, pulled pork and such (voted NYC's best) at "bargain" prices; it's counter service–only, but at least it has outdoor tables, "good delivery" and a flotilla of lunch carts.

Dakshin Indian Bistro
| ▽ 21 | 11 | 19 | $24 |

1713 First Ave. (bet. 88th & 89th Sts.), 212-987-9839
"Delicious", suitably spiced Indian eats and an "outstanding $6.95 lunch buffet" attract Upper Eastsiders to this "tiny hole-in-the-wall"; what's more, the staff "aims to please", and a recent redo should quell complaints of "so-so" decor.

Dallas BBQ ◗ | 15 | 8 | 13 | $19 |

3956 Broadway (166th St.), 212-568-3700
261 Eighth Ave. (23rd St.), 212-462-0001
132 Second Ave. (St. Marks Pl.), 212-777-5574
1265 Third Ave. (bet. 72nd & 73rd Sts.), 212-772-9393
27 W. 72nd St. (bet. Columbus Ave. & CPW), 212-873-2004
180 Livingston St. (bet. Hoyt & Smith Sts.), Brooklyn, 718-643-5700
www.dallasbbq.com

"Bring a large appetite" and a powerful thirst to this BBQ chain, 'cuz the "giant portions" of chicken and ribs are matched by the "massive" drinks; sure, it's "boisterous" and "jammed", but "quick" service and "insanely low prices" make it a "staple."

Danal | 21 | 21 | 17 | $34 |

90 E. 10th St. (bet. 3rd & 4th Aves.), 212-982-6930

"Quirky bohemian decor" complete with a "quaint" garden makes this "charming" East Village "refuge" a "great date place"; "delicious", "reasonably priced" French-Med fare (including an "appealing" brunch") rounds out the "pleasant experience."

Da Nico | 20 | 17 | 19 | $33 |

164 Mulberry St. (bet. Broome & Grand Sts.), 212-343-1212

"Luscious" "old-world Italian" and "tons" of it is the hallmark of this Little Italy "classic"; all agree that the "fabulous", "fairy-lit" "courtyard" garden is "a summer treat" worthy of the "long waits."

DANIEL ☒ | 28 | 28 | 28 | $108 |

60 E. 65th St. (bet. Madison & Park Aves.), 212-288-0033; www.danielnyc.com

"If only life were as perfect as dinner" at "artiste" Daniel Boulud's East Side "luxurious temple" of "fine dining", where the "flawless" New French fare is "enthralling", the wines "wonderful", service "seamless" and the "exquisite" room (voted No. 1 for Decor in this *Survey*) "adorned with gorgeous flowers"; *bien sûr,* the cost is on par with "Ivy League tuition", but gourmets recommend that you "throw caution to the winds and order the tasting menu."

DANUBE ◗☒ | 27 | 28 | 26 | $82 |

30 Hudson St. (bet. Duane & Reade Sts.), 212-791-3771;
www.bouleyrestaurants.com

Chef David Bouley's "magical Klimt dreamland" in TriBeCa offers "transporting experiences" in a "soigné" setting that befits the "sublime" French-accented Viennese fare and "fantastic wines"; with "outstanding" service completing an "enchanting evening" here, it comes as no surprise that tabs are "expensive"; P.S. be sure to make time for a pre-dinner cocktail in the "elegant lounge" and keep in mind the downstairs party space for your next fete.

Darbar | ▽ 21 | 18 | 19 | $35 |

152 E. 46th St. (bet. Lexington & 3rd Aves.), 212-681-4500;
www.darbarny.com

You'd better "skip breakfast" to take full advantage of the "sensational" $9.95 lunch buffet at this "gracious" East Midtown Indian; the food is "flavorful" and "authentic", service "attentive" and the bi-level setting supplies "great atmosphere."

Darna | ▽ 20 | 20 | 17 | $37 |

600 Columbus Ave. (89th St.), 212-721-9123

"Kosher can mean 'delicious'" declare "happy" fans of the "fabulous" midpriced French-Moroccan cuisine on offer at this "exotic" Upper Westsider; there are grumbles about "inconsistent service", but for most that doesn't dampen the "pleasant" experience.

Da Silvano ◗

22 | 17 | 18 | $57

260 Sixth Ave. (bet. Bleecker & Houston Sts.), 212-982-2343;
www.dasilvano.com
"Swarming with celebrities", Silvano Marchetto's Village "scenester"
serves "top-notch Tuscan" to "common folk as well", but getting a
"charming sidewalk" table may mean "promising your first-born";
"gawking" rights can "max out your card" too, so the budget-minded
move next door to the "better-priced" annex.

Da Tommaso ◗

21 | 13 | 19 | $41

903 Eighth Ave. (bet. 53rd & 54th Sts.), 212-265-1890; www.datommaso.com
For a "relaxed" meal near the Theater District, this Northern Italian
fills the bill with "hearty", "old-world" dishes; the "pleasant owner"
makes sure "everything goes well", and though it's not "glitzy", the
"right" prices keep it a "favorite."

Da Umberto ⊠

24 | 18 | 22 | $55

107 W. 17th St. (bet. 6th & 7th Aves.), 212-989-0303
"A respite from the ills of the world", this "elegant" Chelsea "classic"
offers "superlative" Tuscan cooking dispensed by a "solicitous" staff;
a few feel it's "slightly pricey" and perhaps "past its prime", but most
maintain it's "one of the best Italians in the city."

DAVIDBURKE & DONATELLA

25 | 23 | 23 | $74

133 E. 61st St. (bet. Lexington & Park Aves.), 212-813-2121;
www.dbrestaurant.com
Chef-cum-"magician" David Burke "earns the buzz" about his
East Side New American, a "grand culinary experience" featuring
"marvelous" entrees followed by "whimsical" desserts; the "chic"
multilevel space is a fitting foil for its stylish clientele, the service
overseen by Donatella Arpaia is "excellent", and even if the prices
lean toward the "ridiculous", the prix fixe lunch is a "terrific value."

Dawat

24 | 18 | 21 | $45

210 E. 58th St. (bet. 2nd & 3rd Aves.), 212-355-7555
For "high-end Indian fare", this East Midtowner is "still a favorite"
thanks to Madhur Jaffrey's "delicious" dishes delivered by a "caring"
staff; surveyors split over the decor ("lovely" vs. "needs freshening"),
but agree the prices, though "not Sixth Street", are "worth the splurge."

Dazies

▽ 21 | 18 | 19 | $44

39-41 Queens Blvd. (40th St.), Queens, 718-786-7013;
www.daziesrestaurant.com
"Queens power-lunchers" gravitate to this Italian standby both for its
"excellent" classic dishes and "*molto* friendly" staff; detractors decry
the "dated decor" and "Manhattan prices", but even they admit the
"piano player is pleasing."

db Bistro Moderne

25 | 22 | 23 | $60

City Club Hotel, 55 W. 44th St. (bet. 5th & 6th Aves.), 212-391-2400;
www.danielnyc.com
For a "regal meal" before a show, don't miss Daniel Boulud's "French
bistro deluxe" in the Theater District; besides "superb" food (including
that "famous" $29 burger) there's a "wonderful" staff that "treats
even tourists with finesse"; though still "steep", prices are lower than
at Boulud's other venues, and the $42 prix fixe is a "great value."

Deborah

21 | 15 | 20 | $36

43 Carmine St. (bet. Bedford & Bleecker Sts.), 212-242-2606;
www.deborahlifelovefood.com
Deborah Stanton's West Village "hideaway" has "earned a cult
following" for its "creative", "budget-friendly" New American edibles;

the "tiny" quarters can be "cramped" and "hectic", but the "great garden" and "welcoming" staff compensate.

Dee's Brick Oven Pizza   23 | 17 | 19 | $24
107-23 Metropolitan Ave. (74th Ave.), Queens, 718-793-7553
"Everyone in Forest Hills is happy" that the "El Dorado" of brick-oven pizzerias and Mediterranean pastas has moved to this "new, larger location" without any menu missteps; "friendly" service and "fair prices" are further dee-lights.

DeGrezia 🖾   23 | 22 | 23 | $59
231 E. 50th St. (bet. 2nd & 3rd Aves.), 212-750-5353
Though "often overlooked", this "charming" East 50s basement-level "haunt" continues to offer "excellent" Italian fare and an "exceptional wine list"; it's a bit "expensive" and the menu's "not adventurous", but business diners laud its "unbeatable" service and "quiet" ambiance.

Delegates' Dining Room 🖾   ▽ 18 | 21 | 17 | $38
United Nations, 4th fl. (1st Ave. & 45th St.), 212-963-7626
"Magnificent East River views" and the chance to "hobnob" with "UN officials" are the draw at this East 40s Eclectic; while the $25 weekday-only lunch buffet can be a "treat" or merely "blah", diplomatic sorts say "you must do it at least once"; P.S. "bring your photo I.D. to get through security."

DEL FRISCO'S ◐   24 | 23 | 22 | $64
1221 Sixth Ave. (49th St.), 212-575-5129; www.delfriscos.com
"You can't go wrong" at this Midtown "steakhouse to end all steakhouses" purveying "premium" beef, "phenomenal" wines and desserts to make you "hug the chef"; a "knockout" setting and "attentive" staff further help justify "king"-size tabs, though budget-watchers ballyhoo the $34.95 pre-theater deal.

Delhi Palace   ▽ 24 | 12 | 16 | $22
37-33 74th St. (bet. Roosevelt & 37th Aves.), Queens, 718-507-0666
"Bombay dreams" come true at this Jackson Heights Indian "secret" where the "super-cheap" food is arguably "better" than "more heralded" spots nearby; "fancy" it's not, but the "great $8.95 buffet" lunch and "fast" service make it a local "favorite."

Della Rovere 🖾   ▽ 21 | 19 | 19 | $56
250 W. Broadway (Beach St.), 212-334-3470
Faced with tough local competition, this "spacious" new TriBeCa Italian specializes in Venetian-style tapas, "standout pastas" and offers 100 wines by the glass; "warm Tuscan" decor and "enthusiastic" service win praise, but some say it's "still working out the kinks."

Delmonico's 🖾   22 | 22 | 21 | $57
56 Beaver St. (bet. Broad & Williams Sts.), 212-509-1144;
www.delmonicosny.com
"Pinstriped" types craving a "taste of old NY" fancy this "historic" Financial District chop shop where "flavorful" steaks are served by a "sterling" staff as in the days of Diamond Jim Brady; if a few parvenus protest it's "stuffy" and "overpriced", more consider it a "legend."

Delta Grill ◐   19 | 15 | 17 | $30
700 Ninth Ave. (48th St.), 212-956-0934
For "tasty", "spicy" Cajun-Creole "comfort food" at "affordable" prices, po' boys and girls head to this Hell's Kitchen "surprise"; loyalists laud the "laid-back" vibe and "fab" roadhouse decor, but the "cramped" quarters and "patchy" service have some singing the blues.

De Marco's
▽ 18 10 13 $18

146 W. Houston St. (MacDougal St.), 212-253-2290
Proponents proclaim this Village newcomer to be progressing to the "pizza pantheon"; even those critics "let down" by "spotty quality" can't resist the slices available from the "express" counter around the corner.

Demetris Seafood ●
▽ 23 15 20 $30

32-11 Broadway (bet. 32nd & 33rd Sts.), Queens, 718-278-1877
"Excellent", "exceptionally fresh" grilled seafood and other "memorable" Greek specialties at "bargain prices" make this "undiscovered gem" "worth the trip" to Astoria; the staff's "willing to please" and there's "wonderful" live music Thursday–Saturday.

Denino's Pizzeria ⊄
25 10 18 $17

524 Port Richmond Ave. (bet. Hooker Pl. & Walker St.), Staten Island, 718-442-9401
"Nobody does pizza better" than this "family-friendly" "Staten Island icon", which produces "incredible" thin-crust pies; after eating, hunker down with a "cheap beer" in the "time-warp" bar or "walk across the street to Ralph's Ices" ("a must").

Dervish Turkish ●
19 16 19 $33

146 W. 47th St. (bet. 6th & 7th Aves.), 212-997-0070; www.dervishrestaurant.com
The prix fixe menus "can't be beat" at this Theater District "authentic", "clean-your-plate-good" Turk; though it gets "hectic" pre-curtain, the "helpful" staff maintains a "pleasant" vibe that also makes it "worth a whirl."

Deux Amis
20 16 20 $43

356 E. 51st St. (bet. 1st & 2nd Aves.), 212-230-1117
"You're never a stranger" at this Midtown East French bistro since the "congenial host" "makes everyone feel special"; what's more, the food's "delightful" and there's a "lively bar scene" "early and late."

DÉVI
25 23 22 $55

8 E. 18th St. (bet. B'way & 5th Ave.), 212-691-1300; www.devinyc.com
"Even the okra dazzles" at this Flatiron "haute Indian", where chefs Suvir Saran and Hemant Mathur create "extraordinary" cuisine; it may be "expensive", but no one minds much given the "gorgeous" bi-level space and "gracious" service; P.S. insiders say the "tasting menu's the way to go."

Diablo Royale ●
– – – M

189 W. 10th St. (bet. Bleecker & W. 4th Sts.), 212-620-0223; www.diabloroyale.com
Vending made-to-order Mexicana, this red-hot Village taqueria fuels its nightly fiesta with frozen margaritas and communal seating; despite the authentic eats, don't expect cantina pricing – salsa and jalapeños are à la carte here.

Diamond on Eighth
▽ 23 13 15 $24

6022 Eighth Ave. (60th St.), Brooklyn, 718-492-6888
Fka Jade Plaza, this "aircraft hangar"–size Sunset Park Cantonese is still the "quintessential dim sum" place, serving "terrific" "cart-pushed" tidbits to weekend "mobs"; "waiting for a table" can feel like "a subway car at rush hour", but seriously low tabs compensate.

DI FARA ⊄
27 4 10 $12

1424 Ave. J (15th St.), Brooklyn, 718-258-1367
"It's worth a trip from anywhere" to sample "master craftsman" Dominic De Marco's "world-class" pizzas (voted No. 1 in this *Survey*) at this

circa-1963 Midwood parlor; though the waits are "interminable", they are fully justified.

Dim Sum Go Go

21 | 13 | 15 | $21

5 E. Broadway (Chatham Sq.), 212-732-0797
"Go go a little off Chinatown's beaten path" and be "rewarded" with "fresh" dim sum at this "dumpling lovers' delight"; some lament the "lack of carts" and detect a "Westernized" bent, but all appreciate the "easy-on-the-pocket" tabs.

Diner ◐

23 | 18 | 18 | $28

85 Broadway (Berry St.), Brooklyn, 718-486-3077
"Hipsters" and "yuppies" alike choo-choose this New American in a former Pullman car in Williamsburg for its "amazing burgers", "well-priced" specials and "impressive" wines; service can be "friendly" or "arch" and the digs "cramped", but trainspotters tout it as "one of Brooklyn's best."

Diner 24 ◐

17 | 17 | 15 | $27

102 Eighth Ave. (15th St.), 212-242-7773; www.diner24.com
"Decent" "designer diner eats" draw Chelsea brunchers and late-night "clubbers" to this "moderately priced" 24/7 American yearling; the "cool", "airy" space pleases "preening" locals, but though the staffers are "cute", they can also be "snooty."

Dinosaur Bar-B-Que

22 | 18 | 19 | $26

646 W. 131st St. (12th Ave.), 212-694-1777; www.dinosaurbarbque.com
"Your diet is so over" at this "upstate import" where the "bodacious" BBQ favorites at "bargain prices" are an "awesome addition to the West Harlem scene"; "over-the-top" "biker-shtick" decor, a "super" staff and "great beers on tap" help fuel the "festive" vibe.

Dishes

21 | 12 | 13 | $16

6 E. 45th St. (bet. 5th & Madison Aves.), 212-687-5511 ☒
Grand Central, lower level (42nd St. & Vanderbilt Ave.), 212-808-5511 🖨
"Divine" soups, "superb sandwiches" and "upscale" salad bars "set the standard" at this Midtown "lunch temple" duo; despite "endless lines" and "cramped" seating, they're a "lifesaver" for local workers; N.B. Grand Central is open on weekends.

District

20 | 19 | 20 | $55

Muse Hotel, 130 W. 46th St. (bet. 6th & 7th Aves.), 212-485-2999; www.themusehotel.com
An "oasis" amid the "hubbub of Times Square", this "find" offers first-rate New American fare in a "stylish" David Rockwell–designed setting; critics knock the pre-theater prix fixe as "limited" and "expensive", but not the "wonderful" service.

Divino ◐

19 | 15 | 20 | $38

1556 Second Ave. (bet. 80th & 81st Sts.), 212-861-1096; www.divinoristorante.net
"Copious portions" of "well-executed" Italian fare have gained a "loyal following" for this East Side "stalwart"; perhaps the "room could use a face-lift", but the "gracious" staff and "romantic piano music" consistently produce "pleasant experiences."

Diwan

22 | 18 | 19 | $35

Helmsley Middletowne, 148 E. 48th St. (bet. Lexington & 3rd Aves.), 212-593-5425; www.diwanrestaurant.com
"Not your typical curry house", this East Midtown Indian offers "rich", "flavorful" dishes including a fab lunch buffet for only $13.95; service

is "accommodating" and the clientele, heavy on suits, seems to like the "upscale" digs for their "corporate" feel.

Django ⊠

| 20 | 23 | 20 | $51 |

480 Lexington Ave. (46th St.), 212-871-6600

Though "perfect for a business lunch", this "unsung" Midtowner really "comes alive at night" when the Moroccan-inspired bi-level space serves as a "flirty" backdrop for first-class French-Med fare ferried by a sterling staff; still, some seem shell-shocked about the prices.

Docks Oyster Bar

| 19 | 16 | 17 | $45 |

2427 Broadway (bet. 89th & 90th Sts.), 212-724-5588
633 Third Ave. (40th St.), 212-986-8080
www.docksoysterbar.com

These "affordable" Midtown–Upper West Side "fixtures" "deliver" with "savory", "straightforward" seafood and "terrific" raw-bar fare washed down by "superb" martinis; despite sometimes-"harried" service and a "high noise-to-pleasure ratio", to most they're a "shore thing."

DoHwa

| 21 | 18 | 18 | $39 |

55 Carmine St. (bet. Bedford St. & 7th Ave. S.), 212-414-1224;
www.dohwanyc.com

Whether you "grill your own" BBQ or order a "delicious" prepared dish, "you can't go wrong" at this "upscale" Korean catering to Village "hipsters" with its "sleek" setting and "attentive" service; it may be "pricier" than its K-town ilk, but "you get what you pay for."

Dok Suni's ◐⇥

| 21 | 15 | 17 | $30 |

119 First Ave. (bet. 7th St. & St. Marks Pl.), 212-477-9506

Still kickin' "after all these years", this East Village "standby" slings "fantastic" Korean dishes in "cozy", "dimly lit" quarters; "reasonable" tabs help explain why "low-key" "locals" are willing to brave the "long waits" for a table.

dominic ⊠

| ▽ 19 | 19 | 20 | $45 |

349 Greenwich St. (bet. Harrison & Jay Sts.), 212-343-0700;
www.dominicnyc.com

Aka John Villa's dominic, this "relaxed" TriBeCa Italian–New American splits surveyors: admirers insist it "should be busier", but antis allege it's "uneven" and "overpriced"; all can agree the roast suckling pig, a holdover from its old Portuguese incarnation, is "a must."

Dominick's ⇥

| 23 | 9 | 17 | $34 |

2335 Arthur Ave. (bet. Crescent Ave. & E. 187th St.), Bronx, 718-733-2807

You "sit at communal tables", "let the waiter tell you what you eat" and "pig out" on "heavenly" "red-sauce" Southern Italian at this Bronx "landmark"; just "be prepared to wait", rub elbows with the world and "bring cash" – it's all part of the "legendary experience."

Don Giovanni ◐

| 18 | 12 | 15 | $24 |

214 10th Ave. (bet. 22nd & 23rd Sts.), 212-242-9054
358 W. 44th St. (bet. 8th & 9th Aves.), 212-581-4939
www.dongiovanni-ny.com

"Great pizzas and pastas" "unpretentiously" presented are the mainstay of these "casual" West Side Italians; nobody's singing arias over the "flaky service" or dreary decor, but for an "affordable" "quick bite" in "friendly" environs, they "can't be beat."

Donguri

| 27 | 17 | 26 | $55 |

309 E. 83rd St. (bet. 1st & 2nd Aves.), 212-737-5656

Here's hoping a recent change in ownership won't alter this "tiny jewel on the Upper East Side", where the "transcendent" Japanese cuisine (sans sushi) is served with a "loving touch"; portions are "Lilliputian" and the "check hurts", but most say the "quality's unmatched."

Don Pedro's
21 | 18 | 19 | $35

1865 Second Ave. (96th St.), 212-996-3274; www.donpedros.net
The Latin-Caribbean fare and "outstanding cocktails" at this Yorkville "favorite" serve as an "antidote" to the area's same old, same old; all appreciate its "friendly" service, "lively" ambiance and "good" prices.

Don Peppe ⇨
25 | 10 | 18 | $40

135-58 Lefferts Blvd. (149th Ave.), Queens, 718-845-7587
It's "worth the schlep" to Ozone Park for the "superlative" Italian classics "served family-style" at this "crowded", cash-only "garlic *paradiso*"; there's "no decor to speak of", but diehards declare the "lack of atmosphere *is* atmosphere", and besides, it's a "true bargain."

Dos Caminos
21 | 21 | 18 | $42

373 Park Ave. S. (bet. 26th & 27th Sts.), 212-294-1000
475 W. Broadway (Houston St.), 212-277-4300
www.brguestrestaurants.com
"*Dos* thumbs up" for Steve Hanson's *muy* "popular" Mexicans known for their "irresistible" guacamole and "fantastic" margaritas; the "upscale", "sultry" settings suit "scenesters" who in turn contribute to the "great people-watching."

Downtown Atlantic
▽ 20 | 17 | 19 | $31

364 Atlantic Ave. (bet. Bond & Hoyt Sts.), Brooklyn, 718-852-9945
"You can count on" this "comfortable" Boerum Hill New American for well-prepared "mainstays" as well as "fantastic" baked goods made on the premises; "moderate prices", "welcoming" service and an "awesome" brunch are other reasons "locals love it."

Doyers Vietnamese
22 | 7 | 16 | $17

11-13 Doyers St. (Chatham Sq.), 212-513-1521
"A veritable feast" of "delicious" Vietnamese victuals awaits those who track down this "hidden gem" on an "out-of-the-way" Chinatown block; a "dollar stretches very far here", so never mind the "dive" decor.

Duane Park Cafe
22 | 18 | 22 | $49

157 Duane St. (bet. Hudson St. & W. B'way), 212-732-5555
"What a sweet place" declare TriBeCa denizens of this "standby" for "stellar" New American fare and "gracious" service in "calm", "flower-filled" environs; it may look a bit "tired", but it deserves more attention.

Due ◐⇨
21 | 16 | 20 | $41

1396 Third Ave. (bet. 79th & 80th Sts.), 212-772-3331
Being greeted "like family" pleases patrons of this "unpretentious" Upper East Side Northern Italian, where the "irresistible" dishes come at "fair prices"; just remember they take "no plastic."

Duke's
16 | 13 | 15 | $24

99 E. 19th St. (Park Ave. S.), 212-260-2922
Southern bar food competes for attention with "cheap" suds, "TVs at every turn" and "underdressed waitresses" at this "down-and-dirty" Gramercy "faux" "roadhouse"; in short, if you're a "twentysomething" "frat boy", "this is the place to be."

DuMont
23 | 18 | 19 | $29

432 Union Ave. (bet. Devoe St. & Metropolitan Ave.), Brooklyn, 718-486-7717;
www.dumontrestaurant.com
"Teeming with hipsters", this "laid-back" Williamsburg New American with "an emphasis on comfort food" has become a local "staple"; those

who gripe about "overcrowding" should seek out the "lovely back garden", though even it gets "tight" during "popular weekend brunch."

Dumpling Man ◑   19 | 10 | 14 | $11

100 St. Marks Pl. (bet. Ave. A & 1st Ave.), 212-505-2121; www.dumplingman.com
Get "dumplings on demand" at this "eat-and-run" shop where the "tasty snacks" are prepared right "in front of your eyes" and serve as "low-budget" meals for many a "value"-oriented East Villager; however, the "bare-bones setting" means many "order it to go."

Duvet ◑⬤☒   ▽ 17 | 23 | 16 | $51

45 W. 21st St. (bet. 5th & 6th Aves.), 212-989-2121; www.duvetny.com
You can "eat at conventional tables", but at this new Flatironer the "decadent" "gimmick" is "dining in bed" "South Beach"–style; the scene's as "sexy" as the "solid" New American bites are "pricey", though cynics yawn it's "nothing to get all wrapped up in."

Dylan Prime   24 | 23 | 22 | $58

62 Laight St. (Greenwich St.), 212-334-4783; www.dylanprime.com
"Seductive" "anti-steakhouse" decor sets this "date-friendly" TriBeCa "carnivorium" apart from the competition; better still, the food is also superb and there's an "ultracool bar" that supplies "amazing" cocktails to its attractive, "young" crowd; N.B. a nearby sibling, Devan, is scheduled to open shortly.

Earl's   15 | 15 | 14 | $24

560 Third Ave. (37th St.), 212-949-5400
"Big screens" meet "big food" at this low-budget Murray Hill Southern newcomer slinging "truly casual meals" of BBQ and other "down-home essentials" that "go well with beer"; it's just the place to "catch a game" and soak up some "festive", "noisy, rocking" atmosphere.

East Buffet ◑   19 | 15 | 12 | $27

42-07 Main St. (Maple Ave.), Queens, 718-353-6333; www.eastusa.com
It's "hard to resist gorging" on the "wonderful array" of "Eclectic-Asian" dishes (more than 200) at this Flushing buffet where "every minute you spent on the No. 7 train is rewarded 1,000 times over"; it can get "wild on Saturday nights", so the $10.99 lunch may be the way to go.

Eastern King   – | – | – | I

1395 Second Ave. (bet. 72nd & 73rd Sts.), 212-628-8652
A simple stone fountain marks the entrance of this stark, spacious Upper East Side Chinese-Japanese newcomer; in addition to a lengthy menu of Szechuan dishes, it offers a hard-to-beat $19.99 all-you-can-eat sushi deal every night of the week.

East Lake ◑   21 | 12 | 14 | $25

42-33 Main St. (Franklin Ave.), Queens, 718-539-8532
"Excellent dim sum" and Cantonese "seafood at its best" highlight the "good-value" menu at this "crowded" Flushing vet where service is "speedy" if sometimes "unfriendly"; it's "the more the merrier" here – "bring more people" and "you get to order more dishes."

East Manor   ▽ 20 | 16 | 14 | $25

46-45 Kissena Blvd. (Laburnum Ave.), Queens, 718-888-8998; www.eastusa.com
A popular Flushing "wedding palace", this cavernous Chinese serves "wonderful dim sum" and "banquet-style" dishes; maybe the "chandelier"-laden setup's a tad "gaudy" and service "could use improvement", but the fact that it's "always crowded" speaks for itself.

East of Eighth ◗
17 | 16 | 18 | $29

254 W. 23rd St. (bet. 7th & 8th Aves.), 212-352-0075; www.eastofeighth23.com
"Hang with the boys" at this Chelsea Eclectic where the "decent", "well-priced" comfort food tastes even better in the "gorgeous garden"; entertainment comes via drag artiste Hedda Lettuce (twice weekly), not to mention the "colorful crowd" at the bar.

E.A.T.
19 | 10 | 13 | $37

1064 Madison Ave. (bet. 80th & 81st Sts.), 212-772-0022; www.elizabar.com
"Ladies who lunch" meet "well-heeled" "museumgoers" at Eli Zabar's popular East Side "coffee shop" to nibble "high-quality" light fare and baked goods; even fans sometimes wonder if it's worth the "chaotic service", "crazy-tight seating" and "trademark" high prices.

Eatery ◗
19 | 17 | 17 | $29

798 Ninth Ave. (53rd St.), 212-765-7080; www.eaterynyc.com
A Hell's Kitchen "favorite", especially at "popular brunch", this "sleek", "stark", "noisy-as-heck" New American produces "affordable" "gourmet comfort food" served by "hip" staffers; to avoid "long waits" and "tight" "real estate", consider "lightning-fast delivery."

Ecco ⊠
22 | 19 | 21 | $52

124 Chambers St. (bet. Church St. & W. B'way), 212-227-7074
"It's all about the old school" at this TriBeCa Italian where "well-prepared", "unfussy" classics come via a "hospitable" staff; its "dark, woody" interior lined in "comfy booths" is enhanced by an "excellent Sinatra wannabe" at the piano on weekends.

Edgar's Cafe ◗⊟
19 | 18 | 15 | $19

255 W. 84th St. (bet. B'way & West End Ave.), 212-496-6126
The "delectable desserts" are "dangerous" at this Edgar Allan Poe–themed Upper West Side cafe where "a first date could lead to marriage"; though the sandwiches and other savories may be less risky, they come at a "languid pace."

Edison Cafe ⊟
15 | 9 | 13 | $19

Edison Hotel, 228 W. 47th St. (bet. B'way & 8th Ave.), 212-840-5000
"Fancy it's not", but this "run-down" Theater District "icon", aka the Polish Tea Room, dispenses "tasty" "Jewish soul food" for "cheap"; "rushed, distracted, irritable servers" don't deter "actors, directors and writers" from making it a beloved B'way "hangout."

Eemo ◗
– | – | – | I

107 First Ave. (bet. 6th & 7th Sts.), 212-505-7974
Sushi shares center stage with the bibimbop at this new Korean whose large-for-the-East-Village space is appointed with dark-wood booths; look for unusual roll combinations like crab, walnut and avocado.

Eight Mile Creek ◗
▽ 19 | 15 | 18 | $37

240 Mulberry St. (bet. Prince & Spring Sts.), 212-431-4635; www.eightmilecreek.com
"Who knew kangaroo could taste so good?" marvel "daring" diners savoring "a taste of Australia" at this Little Italy "Ozzie" outpost; more casual eats (burgers and such) are offered in the "relaxed" "downstairs pub" and "romantic" garden.

EJ's Luncheonette
16 | 11 | 14 | $21

447 Amsterdam Ave. (bet. 81st & 82nd Sts.), 212-873-3444 ⊟
432 Sixth Ave. (bet. 9th & 10th Sts.), 212-473-5555
1271 Third Ave. (73rd St.), 212-472-0600 ⊟
These "faux-'50s" diners deal in "breakfast the way it should be", "terrific soda fountain" treats and other "tasty" "staples"; despite the

"screaming kid" factor, there's always a wait for "popular" brunch, a fact that "baffles" the "nothing-to-get-excited-about" clique.

Elaine's ●

| 12 | 13 | 13 | $48 |

1703 Second Ave. (bet. 88th & 89th Sts.), 212-534-8103

The renowned Elaine Kaufman presides nightly over this Upper East Side Italian-American "institution", where "potential star sightings" and the chance to appear on Page Six the next day help make up for "poor" service and "forgettable" food; "love it or hate it", all agree "it's a scene."

El Charro Español

| ▽ 23 | 14 | 22 | $40 |

4 Charles St. (bet. Greenwich Ave. & 7th Ave. S.), 212-242-9547

"Absolutely reliable" after 80 years in its "cozy subterranean" West Village lair, this "old-fashioned" Spaniard continues to serve "hearty portions" of "straightforward" "standards" and draw praise for the paella Valenciana, which, unlike the decor, needs no "sprucing up."

El Cid

| 22 | 12 | 18 | $35 |

322 W. 15th St. (bet. 8th & 9th Aves.), 212-929-9332

"Get there early" because this "tiny" Chelsea Spaniard "fills up fast"; between the "knockout sangria" and "terrific tapas", "everyone has a good time", happily overlooking "cramped seating" and "dive" decor that's just "grungy enough to keep out the right people."

Elephant, The ●

| 21 | 18 | 15 | $34 |

58 E. First St. (bet. 1st & 2nd Aves.), 212-505-7739; www.elephantrestaurant.com

"If you can squeeze in" to this "pocket-size" East Village Thai-French, you'll discover "Euros" downing "hipster drinks" and "scrumptious", fairly fared food; it's "way too loud" and some say the staff's "stuck-up", but never mind because it's "still happening and chic."

Elephant & Castle ●

| 18 | 14 | 17 | $25 |

68 Greenwich Ave. (bet. 6th & 7th Aves.), 212-243-1400; www.elephantandcastle.com

"A hangout since forever", this "tiny", "friendly" Village American is just the thing "when you want 'simple'"; especially apt for "brunch-lovers" and those looking to "linger" over a "cup of joe and a paper", it leaves nearly everyone "full and happy."

ELEVEN MADISON PARK

| 26 | 26 | 25 | $63 |

11 Madison Ave. (24th St.), 212-889-0905; www.elevenmadisonpark.com

A "shining star" in the city's "culinary galaxy", Danny Meyer's "fine-tuned" New American on Madison Square Park continues to produce "exquisite" cuisine backed by a "fabulous wine list" and a "smashing" art deco interior featuring "breathtaking vaulted ceilings"; add in "unobtrusive", "mind-reading" service and it's clear why this is a "favorite place to splurge"; N.B. founding chef Kerry Heffernan is leaving to take over Meyer's new catering operation.

El Faro ●

| 22 | 11 | 18 | $35 |

823 Greenwich St. (Horatio St.), 212-929-8210

"Elegant in a dilapidated way", this Village "classic" "hasn't changed in decades", which suits fans of its "authentic" retro-style Spanish fare and "ancient", "dimly lit" quarters; "old-timers" appreciate that it shows "no hint" of ceding to "nearby Meatpacking" trendiness.

Eliá

| ▽ 26 | 19 | 22 | $46 |

8611 Third Ave. (bet. 86th & 87th Sts.), Brooklyn, 718-748-9891

Bay Ridgers craving a "taste of the Mediterranean" head for this "courteous" Greek taverna whose "unassuming" setup belies its "fantastic seafood" and other "extremely well-done" traditional dishes; although "pricey", "it's worth every penny."

Elias Corner ●⚭⌗   22 | 9 | 14 | $34
24-02 31st St. (24th Ave.), Queens, 718-932-1510
"Simplicity is the key" at this Astoria Greek, where the "ambrosial fish" is so fresh you'd swear it was "caught while you ate your appetizer"; sure, aesthetics are "lacking", as are menus, credit cards and "manners", but all's forgiven given "prices you can't beat."

Elio's ●   22 | 17 | 19 | $55
1621 Second Ave. (bet. 84th & 85th Sts.), 212-772-2242
It's "great to be an insider" at this "clubby" Upper East Side Italian "jammed" with "celebs and CEOs" "chatting" over "terrific" eats; few dispute that the space is "tight" and prices "maddening", but as for the service, it's either "snobby" or "attentive" depending on who you are.

El Malecon   21 | 7 | 15 | $16
764 Amsterdam Ave. (bet. 97th & 98th Sts.), 212-864-5648
4141 Broadway (175th St.), 212-927-3812 ●
5592 Broadway (231st St.), Bronx, 718-432-5155 ●
The "wonderful aroma" of "moist and juicy" rotisserie chicken lures "eager crowds" to these "vibrant" Uptown Dominicans where hearty, rustic repasts come at "phenomenal" prices; still, the "basic" digs cause many to go the "delivery" route.

elmo   15 | 19 | 15 | $31
156 Seventh Ave. (bet. 19th & 20th Sts.), 212-337-8000
"Chic boys" convene at this "ultramodern" Chelsea New American where the "reliable comfort food" is "ok", but the "flirtatious" "scene" and "faboo martini lounge" downstairs are really the point; just "bring a megaphone if you want to talk."

El Parador Cafe ⌕   21 | 16 | 20 | $39
325 E. 34th St. (bet. 1st & 2nd Aves.), 212-679-6812;
www.elparadorcafe.com
"Everyone's treated like a regular" at this "traditional" Murray Hill Mexican with a "friendly", "old-fashioned air" that makes for "very relaxing" dining; perhaps the "trapped-in-the-'50s" decor is a bit "tired", but "superior" cuisine and "classy" service make that easy to overlook.

El Paso Taqueria   ▽ 21 | 10 | 17 | $19
64 E. 97th St. (Park Ave.), 212-996-1739
1642 Lexington Ave. (104th St.), 212-831-9831 ●
There are "no frills" and none needed for fans of the "*muy delicioso*" "homestyle" Mexican at this "*autentico*" Upper East Side twosome where the "fresh" goods are a "great value"; aesthetes suggest doing takeout or delivery as "an even better experience."

El Pote ⌕   21 | 12 | 20 | $36
718 Second Ave. (bet. 38th & 39th Sts.), 212-889-6680
"Above-average paella" and other hearty, "flavorful Spanish" classics served by an "old pro" staff are what keep this "little" Murray Hill "hideaway" going; yes, it's a "crowded", "ancient-looking place", but diehards insist it fits like any old-shoe "favorite."

El Quijote ●   19 | 14 | 17 | $38
226 W. 23rd St. (bet. 7th & 8th Aves.), 212-929-1855
"Split a vat of paella" or order the "superb" lobster "bargain" – they're "not stingy on the servings" at this "been-around-forever" Chelsea Spaniard; it's a "NYC institution" that's "tacky in the best way", even if it's also a bit of "a madhouse."

El Rancho ●∅

429 E. Tremont Ave. (Park Ave.), Bronx, 718-294-4380

A "new kid in town", this "friendly" Italian in the "huge", "lovely" old Bronx Savings Bank building has yet to be discovered; however, its pleasing menu, which is heavy on surf 'n' turf options and Mexican-accented dishes, won't break the bank.

El Rey del Marisco ●

1779 Webster Ave. (175th St.), Bronx, 718-299-7707

– – – M

Although it's frequently crowded, our surveyors are not yet familiar with this Bronx Continental specializing in, as the name suggests, seafood; the maritime focus is also reflected in its decor, which is done up in blues with ocean scenes.

Emack & Bolio's ∅

25 9 16 $7

389 Amsterdam Ave. (bet. 78th & 79th Sts.), 212-362-2747 ●
52 Cooper Sq. (bet. 6th & 7th Sts.), 212-253-0539
1564A First Ave. (bet. 81st & 82nd Sts.), 212-734-0105
56 Seventh Ave. (bet. 13th & 14th Sts.), 212-727-1198 ●
73 W. Houston St. (W. B'way), 212-533-5610 ●
21-50 31st St. (bet. Ditmars Blvd. & 21st Ave.), Queens, 718-278-5380
www.emackandbolios.com

"On a hot day – or any day" – these "Beantown"-based ice cream parlors are beloved for their "awesome", "inventive" flavors; even though you may "need an installment plan to pay for a cone", "indulge" and "your mouth will thank you."

Embers

22 14 18 $41

9519 Third Ave. (bet. 95th & 96th Sts.), Brooklyn, 718-745-3700

Bay Ridge residents tout this "tiny", "casual" steakhouse vet for its "great-deal" "thick, juicy" beef and ribs; the decor's "lacking" and thanks to the no-rez policy "be prepared to wait" to "squeeze in", but "efficient" service keeps things moving.

Empire Diner ●

15 15 13 $23

210 10th Ave. (22nd St.), 212-243-2736

At this "retro" "Chelsea landmark" they dish up "classic diner" "grub" and rich desserts 24/7; drop in while "gallery hopping", for a "late-night nosh after hitting the clubs" or join the "patrons with pooches" for brunch at the "seasonal" sidewalk tables.

Empire Szechuan

15 8 14 $21

2574 Broadway (97th St.), 212-663-6004 ●
2642 Broadway (100th St.), 212-662-9404 ●
4041 Broadway (bet. 170th & 171st Sts.), 212-568-1600 ●
193 Columbus Ave. (bet. 68th & 69th Sts.), 212-496-8778 ●
15 Greenwich Ave. (bet. Christopher & W. 10th Sts.),
212-691-1535 ●
173 Seventh Ave. S. (bet. Perry & W. 11th Sts.), 212-243-6046 ●
381 Third Ave. (bet. 27th & 28th Sts.), 212-685-6215
251 W. 72nd St. (bet. B'way & West End Ave.), 212-873-2151 ●

"Still pluggin' along", this Chinese chain continues to offer "reliable, if ordinary", eats at "pretty-cheap" prices, and some branches have added sushi to the "phone book"–size menu; however, "zero" ambiance and "lackluster service" argue for delivery.

Employees Only ●

∇ 18 20 18 $40

510 Hudson St. (bet. Christopher & W. 10th Sts.), 212-242-3021;
www.employeesonlynyc.com

Already "ridiculously popular", this "sophisticated" European West Village newcomer with a "speakeasy" feel is "decked out" in "atmospheric" "deco decor" that's only enhanced by its "cool crowd"; the food is "surprisingly good", but most say the "amazing" "mixology" takes center stage.

English is Italian
20 | 22 | 20 | $54

622 Third Ave. (40th St.), 212-404-1700; www.chinagrillmgt.com
"Go with a group" to Todd English's cavernous new "family-style" Midtown Italian to best enjoy the "all-you-can-eat" prix fixe format that amounts to "an embarrassment of culinary riches"; think "Carmine's on steroids", and you'll get an idea of what this is like.

EN Japanese Brasserie ●⊠
22 | 25 | 19 | $51

435 Hudson St. (Leroy St.), 212-647-9196; www.enjb.com
"Vastness and simplicity" mark the "beautiful" setting of this "stylish" West Village newcomer where sushi "isn't the main attraction" – rather it's the "real-deal" izakaya cuisine (think "Japanese-style tapas"), including "luscious" "housemade tofu"; meals here are a "wonderfully different" experience, albeit one that comes at "Tokyo prices."

Ennio & Michael
▽ 22 | 16 | 22 | $43

539 La Guardia Pl. (bet. Bleecker & W. 3rd Sts.), 212-677-8577
"An uncomplicated menu" of "classic" Italian dishes "cooked to perfection" is proffered by "the perfect hosts" of this "quiet" NoHo "neighborhood standby"; a "courteous" staff and "comfortable" setting mean you're sure to feel "at home."

En Plo
▽ 22 | 15 | 18 | $41

103 W. 77th St. (Columbus Ave.), 212-579-7777;
www.enplonyc.com
"Fresh grilled fish", "pure and simple" is the deal at this West Side Greek seafooder; thrill-seekers might "wish the decor was more stimulating", but most just appeciate the "quiet", neighborly vibe.

Enzo's
▽ 23 | 14 | 20 | $34

1998 Williamsbridge Rd. (Neill Ave.), Bronx, 718-409-3828
"Follow the line" for "good-as-it-gets" "red-sauce" repasts at this Bronx Italian that's "a step ahead" of the typical "old-fashioned" neighborhood joints; sure, it "could use more mood", but who cares when the crew is so "friendly."

Epicerie ●
▽ 20 | 19 | 16 | $32

170 Orchard St. (bet. Rivington & Stanton Sts.), 212-420-7520
"Chic but not trendy", this "casual" Lower East Side French bistro serves up *cuisine typique* with "minimal hoopla"; "Euro house music" keeps things "on the noisy side" and getting served "can take an eon", but all's forgiven when the "very reasonable" tab arrives.

Epices du Traiteur
20 | 16 | 19 | $38

103 W. 70th St. (Columbus Ave.), 212-579-5904
The "subtle" Tunisian-Med cuisine is "just exotic enough" at this "palatably priced" "congenial" "oasis" near Lincoln Center; while it can get "cramped", in summer there's always the "peaceful back patio."

Erawan
23 | 19 | 17 | $33

42-31 Bell Blvd. (bet. 43rd Ave. & Northern Blvd.), Queens, 718-428-2112;
www.erawanthai.com
213-41 39th Ave. (Bell Blvd.), Queens, 718-229-1620;
www.erawan-seafoodandsteak.com
"A cut above the usual Thai", this Baysider gets high marks for "fresh", "beautifully prepared" dishes at "reasonable" prices; complaints that its "popularity" and "tight" quarters add up to long "waits" may be answered by the arrival of a sibling on 39th Avenue.

Erminia ⊠
25 | 24 | 24 | $59

250 E. 83rd St. (bet. 2nd & 3rd Aves.), 212-879-4284
"Love is in the air" at this Upper East Side Italian where "fantastic" Roman dishes, "intimate", "candlelit" digs and "impeccable" pro service add up to "the most romantic" dining around – "you only need to remember the ring" and your credit rating.

Esca ●
24 | 19 | 21 | $62

402 W. 43rd St. (9th Ave.), 212-564-7272; www.esca-nyc.com
There's nowhere like this "chic" Theater District Italian where "fresh-off-the-boat" catch and pastas are "perfectly prepared" by chef David Pasternack; as with others in the Batali-Bastianich empire, it can be "harder to get into than Fort Knox", but despite "hefty pricing" and "tepid service", its "distinctive preparations" are worth the effort.

Esperanto ●
21 | 18 | 18 | $30

145 Ave. C (9th St.), 212-505-6559
"Lively, crowded and loud", this East Village Nuevo Latino swarms with "young" locals savoring its "killer mojitos" and "tasty" eats at "Lower East Side prices" (including an "amazing" $10 brunch deal); other draws are live Brazilian music and "great outdoor seating."

ESPN Zone
12 | 19 | 13 | $28

1472 Broadway (42nd St.), 212-921-3776; www.espnzone.com
"The game is always on" at this three-story sports bar–cum–"tourist mecca" in Times Square, where the "basic" American grub is secondary to the "trillion big-screen TVs"; sure, it's "gimmicky", but to "kids and fanatics" it's "the ultimate" – "all sports all the time."

Ess-a-Bagel
24 | 6 | 14 | $9

359 First Ave. (21st St.), 212-260-2252
831 Third Ave. (bet. 50th & 51st Sts.), 212-980-1010
www.ess-a-bagel.com
"Humongous", "toothsome" bagels and "top-notch schmears" have made this East Side deli duo a "NYC legend"; "depressing" decor, "ornery" service and a "highly caloric" product do nothing to deter devotees who gladly endure "daunting" "weekend waits."

Essex ●
18 | 19 | 16 | $28

120 Essex St. (Rivington St.), 212-533-9616; www.essexnyc.com
Something of a "zoo" during its "unbeatable" "three-drink" Sunday brunch, this Lower East Side New American regularly hosts a "hip, young scene", particularly at the bar; "frazzled" service is easy to take given its "cheap", "surprisingly good" "Jewish/Latin"-accented eats.

Etats-Unis
25 | 17 | 22 | $54

242 E. 81st St. (bet. 2nd & 3rd Aves.), 212-517-8826
"A rarity on the Upper East Side", this "special" New American produces "truly sophisticated" (if "pricey") fare delivered by an "exceptional" staff; those less enamored of its "tight quarters" opt for the roomier, "more casual" wine bar across the street.

etcetera etcetera ●
▽ 22 | 19 | 22 | $48

352 W. 44th St. (bet. 8th & 9th Aves.), 212-399-4141; www.etcrestaurant.com
Recently opened as a second act from the "ViceVersa folks", this dramatic Theater Districter presents its "fresh, creative" Italian fare against a "sleek, modern" stage set staffed by a "charming" crew.

Ethiopian Restaurant
20 | 13 | 21 | $25

1582 York Ave. (bet. 83rd & 84th Sts.), 212-717-7311
At this Upper East Side Ethiopian the "tasty", "cheap" fare is served in "authentic" fashion ("no cutlery, that is"); while the "homey" digs

are basic, there's outdoor seating in summer and a "personable staff" to keep things "enjoyable."

Ethos ◑
21 | 17 | 18 | $36

495 Third Ave. (bet. 33rd & 34th Sts.), 212-252-1972
Poseidon would be proud of the "pristine whole fish" served fresh off the grill at this Murray Hill Hellenic; perhaps the "cozy" room's "not big on decor", but it's manned by a staff that "wants to please you."

Euzkadi
▽ 20 | 18 | 17 | $34

108 E. Fourth St. (bet. 1st & 2nd Aves.), 212-982-9788;
www.euzkadirestaurant.com
"You almost forget you're in NYC" upon entering this "small" East Village "find" for "fragrant" Basque food at "easy-on-the-wallet" prices; "everyone-looks-sexy lighting" enhances the "lively" mood, as does the "friendly" service and "live flamenco music" on Monday nights.

Evergreen Shanghai
18 | 11 | 15 | $23

10 E. 38th St. (bet. 5th & Madison Aves.), 212-448-1199
63 Mott St. (bet. Bayard & Canal Sts.), 212-571-3339 ⊟
Some of "the best juicy buns" going can be found at these "quality dim sum" specialists, which also offer above-average Shanghai-style dishes; "the value's hard to beat", so never mind the "harried" service and "bus station"–worthy decor.

Excellent Dumpling House ⊟
19 | 6 | 13 | $15

111 Lafayette St. (bet. Canal & Walker Sts.), 212-219-0212
A "one-trick pony" it may be, but it's a good trick at this Chinatown "hole-in-the-wall" beloved for its "fabulous" soup dumplings; "rock-bottom prices" and super-"quick" service make it a perennial "jury duty" pick, decor be damned.

Extra Virgin
23 | 18 | 19 | $39

259 W. Fourth St. (bet. Charles & Perry Sts.), 212-691-9359
This Village Med yearling has quickly become a local "favorite" thanks to its "simple, tasty" fare at "affordable" prices; a "lively crowd" packing into "teensy" digs makes for "tight, noisy" conditions, but the "wonderful" weekend brunch is a bit more sane.

Fairway Cafe
20 | 8 | 12 | $33

Fairway, 2127 Broadway, 2nd fl. (74th St.), 212-595-1888
"The convenience of eating and shopping can't be beat" at this "casual" cafe above the famed Upper West Side grocer, where "delicious" breakfasts and lunches cede to "excellent" "bare-bones" steakhouse" dinners; however, a few who "miss Mitchel London" insist it "used to be better."

Falai
▽ 24 | 21 | 19 | $45

68 Clinton St. (bet. Rivington & Stanton Sts.), 212-253-1960
This new Lower East Side Italian is already garnering high praise for its "creative", "sure-handed" cuisine and "modern" "white-on-white" decor; relatively "reasonable prices" allow followers to forget it's "the size of a sardine can."

F & B
19 | 12 | 15 | $11

150 E. 52nd St. (bet. Lexington & 3rd Aves.), 212-421-8600
269 W. 23rd St. (bet. 7th & 8th Aves.), 646-486-4441
www.gudtfood.com
"Euro street food" is the concept at these "hip" counter-service dispensers of "designer hot dogs", "fantastic frites" and other "upscale" bites; maybe they're a bit costly for the genre, but "how many other fast-food joints serve" champagne splits and Belgian beer?

F & J Pine Restaurant ● ⊘ ⇗

22 | 18 | 19 | $32

1913 Bronxdale Ave. (bet. Morris Park Ave. & White Plains Rd.), Bronx, 718-792-5956

"Enormous portions" of "Italian home cooking" and frequent "Yankee" sightings are the appeal at this circa-1970 "Bronx landmark"; an expansion hasn't quelled the "interminable waits" on weekends, when fans line up for "family-style" "feasts."

FELIDIA

25 | 22 | 23 | $67

243 E. 58th St. (bet. 2nd & 3rd Aves.), 212-758-1479; www.lidiasitaly.com

"Creativity abounds" at chef Lidia Bastianich's "beautiful" East Side townhouse, where "wonderful pastas" and other "authentic" Italian dishes are matched by a "fantastic wine list"; the prices can be "intimidating", but its "inviting" decor and "top-notch" service have customers cheering "brava Lidia!"

Félix ●

18 | 17 | 15 | $37

340 W. Broadway (Grand St.), 212-431-0021; www.felixnyc.com

Perennially a Euro "scene", this SoHo bistro is also known for its "killer" Sunday brunch; in summer "large windows" that open to the street keep things "airy" and allow for "great people-watching", and oh, yes, "the food's ok too."

Ferdinando's Focacceria ☒ ⊘ ⇗

▽ 22 | 12 | 17 | $23

151 Union St. (bet. Columbia & Hicks Sts.), Brooklyn, 718-855-1545

"May it last another 100 years" cheer Carroll Gardeners enamored of this circa-1904 "staple" for "authentic Sicilian dishes" as "tasty" as they are "reasonable"; the "no-frills service and ambiance" don't keep regulars or newcomers from "feeling at home."

Ferrara ●

22 | 16 | 15 | $18

195 Grand St. (bet. Mott & Mulberry Sts.), 212-226-6150; www.ferraracafe.com

"Holy cannoli!" – the "Italian pastries are endless" at this circa-1892 Little Italy "landmark" for "after-dinner" coffee and treats; its slightly "flashy" interior teems with "tourist"-studded "crowds" and it's not cheap, but it's a much beloved "NY tradition" all the same.

FIAMMA OSTERIA

24 | 24 | 23 | $62

206 Spring St. (bet. 6th Ave. & Sullivan St.), 212-653-0100; www.brguestrestaurants.com

At Steve Hanson's "multilevel" SoHo "stunner", the "posh" interior is a fitting foil for "fiamm-azing" pastas and other "hard-to-beat" Italian dishes; yes, the "prices are out of sight", but "stellar service" helps seal the "truly memorable" experiences, which are "worth the splurge."

50 Carmine

22 | 16 | 19 | $45

50 Carmine St. (bet. Bedford & Bleecker Sts.), 212-206-9134

"Renowned" chef Sara Jenkins has left, but this Village Northern Italian remains a "neighborhood favorite" thanks to its "delicious housemade pastas" and other "fresh" fare; the staff's "assiduously polite" while working the "pretty room", which is "cozy" to some, "tight" to others.

Fifty Seven Fifty Seven

23 | 26 | 23 | $67

Four Seasons Hotel, 57 E. 57th St. (bet. Madison & Park Aves.), 212-758-5757; www.fourseasons.com

A "cathedral-like" I.M. Pei–designed space "attracts a galaxy of glitterati" to this New American in Midtown's Four Seasons Hotel; host to high-wattage "business" breakfasts and lunches plus "an active bar at cocktail time", it "remains one of the city's great power scenes" – albeit "for those with deep pockets."

Fig & Olive Kitchen ●   – – – M
808 Lexington Ave. (62nd St.), 212-207-4555; www.fig-and-olive.com
A "promising new" Upper Eastsider, this "sleek" Med's devotion to
olive oil is evident in its extra virgin–doused dishes as well as the
selection of bottles offered for sale; early visitors say its "delightful
atmosphere" is as inviting for "drinks and a snack" as for a full meal.

F.illi Ponte ☒   20 19 20 $56
39 Desbrosses St. (West Side Hwy.), 212-226-4621; www.filliponte.com
"Out of the way" in West TriBeCa, this veteran Italian affords
"spectacular views" of the Hudson at sunset, not to mention the "NY
Trapeze School" at lunchtime; true, it's "not inexpensive", but the
"old-school" fare "meets expectations", as do the "pro waiters."

Finestra   ▽ 19 16 22 $37
1370 York Ave. (73rd St.), 212-717-8594
The kind of "welcoming" "local place" every neighborhood should
have, this "small" Yorkville Italian serves as a "quiet" standby for
"well-priced" trattoria standards served by a "super" staff; live guitar
music adds to the "pleasant" ambiance on weekends.

Fino ☒   21 16 20 $44
4 E. 36th St. (bet. 5th & Madison Aves.), 212-689-8040; www.finon36.com
1 Wall Street Ct. (Pearl St.), 212-825-1924; www.finowallstreet.com
Both the Murray Hill and roomier Wall Street locations of this "gracious,
old-world Italian" keep 'em "coming back" with "enjoyable" classic
fare and "take-good-care-of-you" service; now if only they'd "lighten
up the atmosphere."

Fiorentino's   20 13 18 $31
311 Ave. U (bet. McDonald Ave. & West St.), Brooklyn, 718-372-1445
Hungry Gravesenders get lots of "good basic food for a great price" at
this "old-time Italian"; there's usually a "wait" and it gets "crowded",
"loud and raucous" during prime times, but that doesn't stop the
faithful from "coming back again and again."

FireBird   21 26 21 $58
365 W. 46th St. (bet. 8th & 9th Aves.), 212-586-0244;
www.firebirdrestaurant.com
"What's Russian for heaven?" muse "pampered" patrons of this
Restaurant Row duplex where cuisine "fit for a czar" comes via a
"pro staff" as smooth as the "amazing" honey-infused vodka; if the
tab leaves you "feeling like a serf", just remember the $40 prix fixe.

Firenze ●   19 17 20 $43
1594 Second Ave. (bet. 82nd & 83rd Sts.), 212-861-9368; www.firenzenyc.com
"A cut above your usual neighborhood Italian", this "welcoming"
Upper East Side Tuscan's "tasty" fare is dispensed by a "wonderfully
friendly" staff; the quarters have a "cozy" feel, but locals hope it remains
a bit of a "secret" because of its "too-small" dimensions.

Fish ●   21 14 18 $37
280 Bleecker St. (Jones St.), 212-727-2879
"It's a treat to drop anchor" at this Village "quasi–New England fish
house" where the "well-prepared, no-frills" seafood tastes "straight
from the briny"; it may be "lacking decor", but the prices are modest.

Five Front   21 19 20 $35
5 Front St. (Old Fulton St.), Brooklyn, 718-625-5559;
www.fivefrontrestaurant.com
"Amazingly sited" under the Brooklyn Bridge in a "quaint" 1835 building
with "fab outdoor seating", this Dumbo New American offers "quality",

"well-priced" fare ferried by a "lovely" staff; N.B. a $22 prix fixe is served on Monday, Wednesday and Thursday evenings.

5 Ninth ●

| 20 | 22 | 17 | $57 |

5 Ninth Ave. (bet. Gansevoort & Little W. 12th Sts.), 212-929-9460; www.5ninth.com

Chef Zak Pelaccio creates "culinary adventures" amid "Meatpacking District flash" at this "rustic" "little townhouse" Eclectic, where "spotty" service doesn't keep the "crowds" from cramming into the "cool" but "cramped" digs; even those who find it "too much of a scene" can't resist its "sweet garden"; P.S. "bring your black Amex."

Five Points ●

| 22 | 21 | 20 | $45 |

31 Great Jones St. (bet. Bowery & Lafayette St.), 212-253-5700; www.fivepointsrestaurant.com

This "NoHo hipster hangout" is firmly established thanks to its affordable "well-crafted" Med–New American cuisine and "warm" service; the "serene" atmosphere is also appreciated, though at the "terrific" Sunday brunch, it can get "noisy."

Fives

| ▽ | 21 | 23 | 22 | $66 |

Peninsula Hotel, 700 Fifth Ave. (55th St.), 212-903-3918; www.peninsula.com

"Tranquility" awaits at this "well-kept secret" in Midtown's Peninsula Hotel, a "lovely" choice for a "business meeting" or "ladies' lunch" featuring "better-than-good" French–New American fare; there's a "big price tag" attached, but the wine bar offers lighter, less-costly fare.

Flea Market Cafe ●

| 20 | 19 | 15 | $28 |

131 Ave. A (bet. 9th St. & St. Marks Pl.), 212-358-9282

Aside from the "views of Tompkins Square Park", this "bustling" Alphabet City "favorite" feels "straight from Paris' Latin Quarter", offering "well-executed" bistro classics consumed amid "cool flea-market trinkets"; "reasonable" prices make up for "mediocre" service.

Fleur de Sel

| 25 | 20 | 23 | $65 |

5 E. 20th St. (bet. B'way & 5th Ave.), 212-460-9100; www.fleurdeselnyc.com

Cyril Renaud creates "wonderful Brittany" cuisine at his Flatiron District French where the "excellent" dishes and "superb" wines come in "elegant", "romantic", "recently updated" quarters manned by a "caring" staff; all in all it's "perfect" for a "dinner splurge", though those in-the-know especially tout the $25 prix fixe lunch.

Flor de Mayo ●

| 20 | 9 | 16 | $20 |

484 Amsterdam Ave. (bet. 83rd & 84th Sts.), 212-787-3388
2651 Broadway (101st St.), 212-663-5520

"Amazing roasted chicken" in "huge", "cheap" portions has made this Upper West Side Peruvian-Chinese duo a local "favorite" despite decidedly "no-nonsense" digs; "lightning-fast service" carries through to "speedy" delivery, so no wonder it's a "staple for ordering in."

Flor de Sol ●✉

| 20 | 21 | 18 | $40 |

361 Greenwich St. (bet. Franklin & Harrison Sts.), 212-366-1640

"Dark", "candlelit" quarters create a "sexy", "romantic" mood at this TriBeCa Spaniard, and "great live music" and "fantastic" sangria add to the "swoon" factor; "crowded" conditions might be a downer, but oh, what a "good-looking" crowd.

Florent ●⊄

| 19 | 13 | 16 | $29 |

69 Gansevoort St. (bet. Greenwich & Washington Sts.), 212-989-5779; www.restaurantflorent.com

The "original Meatpacking District eatery", this 20-plus-year-old bus station–style French bistro is "still crazy popular after all these years";

"tasty", inexpensive fare served 24/7 draws a "fierce and fabulous" crowd that happily overlooks "close quarters" and "spotty" service.

Flor's Kitchen
19 | 12 | 16 | $22

149 First Ave. (bet. 9th & 10th Sts.), 212-387-8949
170 Waverly Pl. (bet. 6th & 7th Aves.), 212-229-9926
"Delicious" arepas and seviche are among the "tasty" Venezuelan "comfort" offerings at these "simply" appointed "favorites"; "reasonable prices" take the sting out of "unavoidable waits" to get in and "slow" service from the otherwise "accommodating" staff.

Foley's Fish House
20 | 23 | 21 | $55

Renaissance NY Hotel, 714 Seventh Ave., 2nd fl. (bet. 47th & 48th Sts.), 212-261-5200; www.foleysfishhouse.com
For a "surreal out-of-body, into-billboard experience", try this "pricey" Times Square seafooder where "dimly lit" digs allow diners to feel one with "the lights and colors" outside; the food and service are "very good", but "you're paying for the view" here, so "enjoy it."

Fontana di Trevi ⊠
20 | 17 | 20 | $41

151 W. 57th St. (bet. 6th & 7th Aves.), 212-247-5683; www.fontanaditrevi.com
Good (if "routine") Northern Italian fare ensures that this "unassuming" "old standby" across from Carnegie Hall maintains a loyal following; if some find its decor a bit "tired", none complain about its "value."

Fornino
▽ 21 | 14 | 18 | $21

187 Bedford Ave. (N. 7th St.), Brooklyn, 718-384-6004
Chef Michael Ayoub (ex Cucina) is winning Williamsburg hearts with "fantastic" wood-fired pizzas at this "casual" new low-budget Neapolitan; its "arty" space showcasing the chef's own blown-glass pieces plus a climate-controlled garden make it a good fit for the area.

44
19 | 23 | 16 | $52

Royalton Hotel, 44 W. 44th St. (bet. 5th & 6th Aves.), 212-944-8844; www.royaltonhotel.com
It's "not as trendy as it used to be", but this "cool" "Starck"-designed French–New American in Midtown's Royalton Hotel makes a smart "pre-theater" choice; ignore the waiters' "attitude" and check out those famously "wondrous bathrooms", or just bask in the now-"quiet" atmosphere.

44 & X Hell's Kitchen ◗
21 | 18 | 19 | $42

622 10th Ave. (44th St.), 212-977-1170; www.44andX.com
A "bright spot" in a culinarily challenged area, this Hell's Kitchen New American slings "comfort food with a twist" in "modern", "simple" digs; it's "jammed" with locals and "pre-theater" diners who like the "friendly" "boy-toy" waiters nearly as much as the "delicious" eats.

FOUR SEASONS ⊠
26 | 28 | 27 | $82

99 E. 52nd St. (bet. Lexington & Park Aves.), 212-754-9494; www.fourseasonsrestaurant.com
"You pay for perfection" at this Midtown Continental where the clientele "exudes class and power" and the Philip Johnson–designed interior remains "the height of sleek sophistication" "after over 40 years"; whether you make the "lunch scene" in the Grill Room or go for an "elegant special-occasion dinner" in the Pool Room, the "superb" cuisine and "exquisite" service ensure "you know you've made it."

14 Wall Street ⊠
19 | 20 | 19 | $50

14 Wall St., 31st fl. (bet. Broad St. & B'way), 212-233-2780
Situated in "J.P. Morgan's former penthouse", this Financial District French "in the sky" draws "suits" who savor its "very good" food,

"efficient" service and "astounding views" (with matching "way up there" prices); here "bullish" lunches give way to "quiet" evenings and the occasional "wedding reception."

Fragole

▽ 22 | 18 | 21 | $27

394 Court St. (bet. Carroll St. & 1st Pl.), Brooklyn, 718-522-7133; www.fragoleny.com
This "friendly" Carroll Gardens "nook" satisfies locals "again and again" with "unbeatable housemade pastas" and other "flavorful" Italian fare at "price-is-right" rates; "interesting" specials, "half-price wine" nights and a "perfect back garden" add up to "happy eating."

Franchia

▽ 23 | 22 | 21 | $32

12 Park Ave. (bet. 34th & 35th Sts.), 212-213-1001; www.franchia.com
"Peaceful vibes" reign at this "welcoming" Murray Hill "temple of Zen calm" that's both a teahouse and a vegetarian Korean eatery; it offers "tasty" fare as well as a "lovely introduction to the ceremony of tea", so while some say it's "a little pricey" for the genre, to most it's "a great find."

Francisco's Centro Vasco ●

20 | 12 | 17 | $40

159 W. 23rd St. (bet. 6th & 7th Aves.), 212-645-6224
Bring "earplugs and a megaphone" to this "old-school" Chelsea Spaniard whose "no-frills" interior hosts "one big" sangria-fueled "party"; "lobster-lovers" form "lines out the door" for its "huge" crustaceans at "great prices", so be prepared to "claw your way" in.

Frank ●⊅

23 | 14 | 15 | $29

88 Second Ave. (bet. 5th & 6th Sts.), 212-420-0202; www.frankrestaurant.com
"Go early or late" if you want to nab a table at this "tiny", "overcrowded" "bargain" East Village Italian that's like "Sunday dinner" "at your uncle's", complete with "delish" "homestyle" Italian food; "spotty" service and "dive" decor complete the family-dinner milieu.

Frankie & Johnnie's Steakhouse ⊠

21 | 14 | 20 | $53

269 W. 45th St. (bet. B'way & 8th Ave.), 212-997-9494 ●
32 W. 37th St. (bet. 5th & 6th Aves.), 212-947-8940
www.frankieandjohnnies.com
Both the original 1920s "upstairs speakeasy" in "Theaterland" and its newer, more spacious Garment District spin-off specialize in surefire-"satisfying" steaks supported by the standard sides; "stoic" waiters who "know what they're doing" add to the "old-NY" feel.

Frankies 457 Court Street Spuntino

22 | 20 | 19 | $28

457 Court St. (bet. 4th Pl. & Luquer St.), Brooklyn, 718-403-0033; www.frankies457.com
This "hip", "relaxed" Carroll Gardens Italian newcomer is winning friends fast with "fresh" fare and "lots" of vinos "by the glass"; a "great brunch" and garden seating are more reasons locals latch onto it.

Frank's

21 | 17 | 21 | $54

410 W. 16th St. (bet. 9th & 10th Aves.), 212-243-1349; www.franksnyc.com
It's "testosterone city" at this "old-time" Italian-style chophouse, which just moved a couple of blocks from the Meatpacking District into West Chelsea but remains the same "steak heaven"; staffed by a "witty" crew, it's a "terrific" "ol' boys' type of place" with lots of loyal regulars.

Franny's

23 | 16 | 19 | $31

295 Flatbush Ave. (bet. Prospect Pl. & St. Marks Ave.), Brooklyn, 718-230-0221; www.frannysbrooklyn.com
"Artisanal pizzas" are the province of this outstanding Prospect Heights "brick-oven" pie place, where "gossamer-thin" crusts are

topped with "fresh, high-quality" ingredients (e.g. house-cured meats); the only rub: its "simple, modern" space can get "crowded and noisy."

Frederick's Madison

| | | | E |

768 Madison Ave. (bet. 65th & 66th Sts.), 212-737-7300;
www.fredericksnyc.com

From nightlife kingpin Frederick Lesort (the Lemon, Opia) comes this new Madison Avenue Mediterranean set in the former Cafe Nosidam space; look for an inventive, expensive menu, amiably snappy service and a heavy-duty, air-kissing Euro following.

Fred's at Barneys NY

| 20 | 18 | 16 | $43 |

Barneys NY, 660 Madison Ave., 9th fl. (60th St.), 212-833-2200

For a "high-class shopping break", walk "your Manolos" to this Tuscan–New American inside Barneys that supplies the "Botox" set with "solid" nibbles; "unless the whole room knows your name", you'd "better make a lunch reservation" – and expect "indifferent" service.

Freemans ◗

| 21 | 22 | 17 | $38 |

Freeman Alley (off Rivington St., bet. Bowery & Chrystie St.), 212-420-0012;
www.freemansrestaurant.com

Hidden "at the end of an alley", this Lower East Side New American is "cool" and "old-world" simultaneously, with a "hunting lodge"–like (as in "taxidermy") setup and "creative" yet "down-to-earth" food; the "packed" "rich-and-single" "scene" has in-the-know types "nostalgic" for the days when it "was still a secret."

French Quarter ⌧

| | | | M |

102 E. 25th St. (bet. Lexington Ave. & Park Ave. S.), 212-598-4555;
www.frenchquarterny.com

Chef Luis Cardenas, formerly of Whitestone's Cooking with Jazz, has brought his Cajun-Creole cuisine to this publike Gramercy Park newcomer; the place promises plenty of Mardi Gras–inspired revelry abetted by specialty cocktails and beers of Big Easy origin.

French Roast ◗

| 15 | 14 | 12 | $25 |

2340 Broadway (85th St.), 212-799-1533
458 Sixth Ave. (11th St.), 212-533-2233
www.tourdefrancenyc.com

"Always packed", this 24/7 French bistro duo is "everybody's local" hangout for "decent" Parisian classics at "value" prices; consider the "loud, cramped" quarters and "aloof" service marks of "authenticity."

Frère Jacques

▽ | 19 | 16 | 20 | $42 |

13 E. 37th St. (bet. 5th & Madison Aves.), 212-679-9355

Francophiles have a soft spot for this "little charmer" in Murray Hill that turns out "above-average" Gallic bistro dishes; "friendly" service and "reasonable" tabs round out the "pleasant" experience.

Fresco by Scotto ⌧

| 23 | 19 | 21 | $55 |

34 E. 52nd St. (bet. Madison & Park Aves.), 212-935-3434;
www.frescobyscotto.com

The Scotto clan continues to make patrons feel like "part of the family" at this "noisy, energetic" Northern Italian Midtown "power" spot that's popular with "NBC staffers"; "huge portions" and "friendly" service almost "make you forget what you're spending."

Fresco on the Go ⌧

| 20 | 11 | 13 | $16 |

40 E. 52nd St. (bet. Madison & Park Aves.), 212-754-2700;
www.frescobyscotto.com

"Almost as good as the real Fresco", this Midtown carry-out/"quick-bite" Italian sibling is certainly "cheaper" and possibly more "frenzied";

if you're dropping in for a "fast lunch", "go before or after the noon crush" or you may have to "stare down your boss for his table."

fresh ☒
24 | 21 | 22 | $54

105 Reade St. (bet. Church St. & W. B'way), 212-406-1900;
www.freshshorecoast.com

Its name "couldn't be more apt" gush groupies of TriBeCa's "baby Bernardin", which specializes in "exquisite" yet "no-pretense" seafood that "tastes like you've just caught it"; "friendly, informed service" and a "sparkling" aquariumlike setting soothes the "sole", making this "one great catch" that's worth the arm and a fin.

Friendhouse ◗
19 | 15 | 19 | $22

99 Third Ave. (bet. 12th & 13th Sts.), 212-388-1838

"Wonderfully eclectic", "cheap" eats have gained a local following for this East Village Pan-Asian, whose sushi rolls almost "too big" to eat garner particular praise; diners can opt for the "sleek" dining room, "waterfall"-edged garden or good old "quick delivery."

Friend of a Farmer
17 | 18 | 16 | $27

77 Irving Pl. (bet. 18th & 19th Sts.), 212-477-2188

"Even city people" occasionally need the "little-piece-of-Vermont" experience this "quaint" Gramercy "farmhouse" American delivers; it's a "brunch favorite" featuring "hearty" "home cooking", but foes fault "long lines", "scarce servers" and "too-cute" "country kitsch" decor.

Fuleen Seafood ◗
▽ 24 | 10 | 15 | $25

11 Division St. (bet. Bowery & E. B'way), 212-941-6888

This C-town seafooder overcomes its "loud", "seedy" setup with "melt-in-your-mouth" shore fare prepared Hong Kong–style and served until the wee hours; going with someone who "speaks Cantonese" helps.

Fushimi
▽ 24 | 23 | 21 | $42

2110 Richmond Rd. (Lincoln Ave.), Staten Island, 718-980-5300

"Finally", a "standout" sushi specialist on Staten Island – locals laud this "trendy" Japanese for its "top-notch" fare, "stimulating" decor and "gracious" service; you'd almost swear you were "in the city" – especially when the check arrives.

Gabriel's ☒
22 | 18 | 22 | $55

11 W. 60th St. (bet. B'way & Columbus Ave.), 212-956-4600;
www.gabrielsbarandrest.com

"If you want to avoid" Time Warner Center "glitz" and "tourists", this terrific Tuscan "mainstay" is a "solid choice" that's also "convenient to Lincoln Center"; bravos go to the "routinely" "tasty" cuisine and "warm" service overseen by "hands-on" owner Gabriel Aiello; busy at night, it's more relaxed and less expensive at lunch.

Gahm Mi Oak ◗
22 | 14 | 17 | $22

43 W. 32nd St. (bet. B'way & 5th Ave.), 212-695-4113

"Hit-the-spot" Korean "comfort food", including "amazingly" restorative *sollongtang* (beef, rice and noodle soup), makes this Garment Districter the "place to nurse a cold or a hangover"; low prices and 24/7 hours "bring people back again and again."

Gallagher's Steak House ◗
21 | 17 | 18 | $56

228 W. 52nd St. (bet. B'way & 8th Ave.), 212-245-5336;
www.gallaghersnysteakhouse.com

The "hanging slabs on show" up front "foreshadow" the "hefty portions" (and prices) at this Theater District steakhouse that's been offering "excellent" beef since 1927; if the decor and staff seem not to have changed "since WWII", that's part of the "nostalgic" charm.

Garden Cafe ⌂
28 21 26 $47

620 Vanderbilt Ave. (Prospect Pl.), Brooklyn, 718-857-8863
"The reason to come to Prospect Heights for over 20 years", this New American "jewel box" continues to "charm" with "superb" cuisine full of "unexpected" combinations; in the "caring" hands of husband-and-wife team John and Camille Policastro and their staff, patrons have the "delightful" feeling of dining "at a good friend's home" – albeit one who's a "top-notch" chef.

Gargiulo's
22 19 20 $43

2911 W. 15th St. (bet. Mermaid & Surf Aves.), Brooklyn, 718-266-4891; www.gargiulos.com
In "the heart of Coney Island" this "old-Brooklyn" Italian has been serving "classic" fare that would make "mama proud" for almost a century; the "rococo" space feels like a "wedding hall", complete with "attentive" waiters, and "you can still roll the dice" for a shot at "a free meal."

Gari
25 19 19 $65

370 Columbus Ave. (bet. 77th & 78th Sts.), 212-362-4816
Upper Westsiders "welcome" this sister to Sushi of Gari that has "raised the neighborhood's level of sushi" with "magic-in-your-mouth" fish flown in from Japan; the "polished" digs also meet with approval, but there are grumbles that those "superb" morsels are raising local "credit-card balances."

Gascogne
23 21 21 $47

158 Eighth Ave. (bet. 17th & 18th Sts.), 212-675-6564; www.gascognenyc.com
Fans give a European-style "kiss, kiss" to this "romantic" French "hideaway" in Chelsea with a "lovely garden in back"; "wonderful" bistro fare and "delightful" service "transport" diners who wish to "relive" their "last Gallic jaunt" for just a few hours.

Gavroche
19 15 17 $42

212 W. 14th St. (bet. 7th & 8th Aves.), 212-647-8553; www.gavroche-ny.com
This "cozy" Greenwich Village "newcomer" "charms" locals with its "solid" country French lineup "that hits all the standards", "friendly" service and wallet-friendly "early-bird special"; however, it's the "terrific" "garden in the back" that's the "real find."

Geisha ●⌂
23 22 19 $59

33 E. 61st St. (bet. Madison & Park Aves.), 212-813-1113; www.geisharestaurant.com
Once you get past the "so-Euro-it-hurts" types in the "happening" downstairs bar, there's fine food to be had in the "civilized" dining room of this East Side French-accented Japanese; service may be "a bit spacey", but the "intricate" Asian decor designed by David Rockwell is widely admired.

Gennaro ⇰
24 14 16 $36

665 Amsterdam Ave. (bet. 92nd & 93rd Sts.), 212-665-5348
"Comfort food at comfort prices" is the calling card of this ever-"popular" West Side "neighborhood Italian" whose kitchen "continues to shine" and "occasionally dazzles"; "no reservations" means "come early" or "prepare to wait" – and know that "spotty service" and minimal decor are part of the deal.

Ghenet
▽ 21 14 15 $29

284 Mulberry St. (bet. Houston & Prince Sts.), 212-343-1888; www.ghenet.com
"Huge" platters of well-priced, "terrifically spiced" fare make it "worth getting your hands messy" at this "fun" NoLita Ethiopian where you

"eat with your fingers"; "go with friends" and share, but don't be surprised by the no-frills decor and "slow service."

Giambelli ❶   21 | 18 | 22 | $55

46 E. 50th St. (bet. Madison & Park Aves.), 212-688-2760; www.giambelli50th.com

To "step back in time" try this "upscale" but "aging" Midtown Northern Italian where the "traditional" dishes come via a "professional" formal staff; the "old-fashioned" surroundings "sooth and charm" loyalists, but younger diners say it's time for "a face-lift."

Gigino at Wagner Park   19 | 22 | 16 | $40

20 Battery Pl. (West St.), 212-528-2228; www.gigino-wagnerpark.com

You "can't beat" the "spectacular views" of the "NY Harbor and Statue of Liberty" at this Battery Park Italian, so never mind if the standard offerings are just "good"; go on a "lazy" day when you have time to "watch the ferries" and won't notice the "slow" service.

Gigino Trattoria   21 | 19 | 19 | $42

323 Greenwich St. (bet. Duane & Reade Sts.), 212-431-1112; www.gigino-trattoria.com

This TriBeCa Italian "institution in-the-making" is "popular with locals" as a "welcoming" "refuge" suffused with the "intoxicating aroma" of "scrumptious" pizzas, pastas and the like; an "energetic" vibe and "reasonable prices" are other secrets to its success.

Gino ⊯   19 | 14 | 19 | $44

780 Lexington Ave. (bet. 60th & 61st Sts.), 212-758-4466

"Bring cash" and "have a blast" at this East Side "old-world" Italian where the "garlic-and-red-sauce" fare and "worn" "zebra wallpaper" seem not to have changed "since 1945"; regulars who come every week say the "clubby feeling is great" – "if you're a member", that is.

Giorgione   21 | 19 | 18 | $51

307 Spring St. (bet. Greenwich & Hudson Sts.), 212-352-2269

It may be in the "middle of nowhere", but this "bustling", "stylish" West SoHo Italian co-owned by Giorgio DeLuca (of gourmet store renown) is deemed "worth the trip"; the "fantastic" food makes up for loud "acoustics" and "distracted" service.

Giorgio's of Gramercy   23 | 19 | 21 | $44

27 E. 21st St. (bet. B'way & Park Ave. S.), 212-477-0007; www.giorgiosofgramercy.com

"Tucked away" on a Flatiron "side street", this New American is a local "standby" for "delicious" food at "agreeable prices", and its "romantic" vibe makes it a prime "date" venue too; devotees wonder why it's still somewhat "undiscovered."

Giovanni   ▽ 21 | 18 | 22 | $49

47 W. 55th St. (bet. 5th & 6th Aves.), 212-262-2828; www.giovanni-ristorante.com

Those who like their Northern Italian in "quiet" environs turn to this "subdued" Midtowner where the dishes are "consistently" "on the mark" and the service is "polite"; a few nitpickers say the overall experience lacks "zip", but they are easily outvoted.

Giovanni Venticinque   ▽ 22 | 18 | 23 | $59

25 E. 83rd St. (bet. 5th & Madison Aves.), 212-988-7300

Just "steps away from the Met", this "attractive" trattoria enchants museumgoers and locals alike with "delicious" Northern Italian dishes, "attentive" service and a "warm, homey" atmosphere; true, it's "expensive", but in return you're "treated like gold."

Girasole ●
22 | 18 | 20 | $54

151 E. 82nd St. (bet. Lexington & 3rd Aves.), 212-772-6690
"Popular with the Met staff" and Upper Eastsiders "who can afford" the tabs, this "small, refined" Italian functions almost like "a neighborhood club"; the "better-than-average" (if "unremarkable") fare and "consistently good" service please its "generally older" crowd.

Gnocco Caffe ⇚
23 | 19 | 19 | $33

337 E. 10th St. (bet. Aves. A & B), 212-677-1913; www.gnocco.com
It's "named for the lighter-than-air" fried dough appetizer, so it's no surprise that this "warm" East Village Italian produces a "heavenly" version, as well as other "fresh", "authentic" Emilian specialties at "value" prices; insiders note the "garden in back" "is the place to sit" and philosophize about the meaning of gnoccos in life.

Gobo
23 | 19 | 19 | $30

401 Sixth Ave. (bet. Waverly Pl. & W. 8th St.), 212-255-3242 ●
1426 Third Ave. (81st St.), 212-288-5099
www.goborestaurant.com
"Ethical eaters" and carnivores alike are "wowed" by this "upscale" vegan twosome, insisting "you don't miss the meat" when you're dining on such "delicious" Asian-influenced specialties; the "stylish" interior is manned by an always-"pleasant" staff, and better still, prices are "affordable."

Golden Unicorn
20 | 11 | 13 | $22

18 E. Broadway, 2nd fl. (Catherine St.), 212-941-0911
A little like "eating in Grand Central", this "giant", "bustling" Chinatown "banquet hall" satiates "crowds" with a seemingly endless "parade" of "authentic" dim sum; "reasonable prices" mean for most it's "worth the wait" for a table, but expect "no smiles" from the "cart-pushing" staff.

Gonzo
21 | 17 | 18 | $41

140 W. 13th St. (bet. 6th & 7th Aves.), 212-645-4606
It's all about chef Vincent Scotto's "wonderful", "crackling-thin-crusted" grilled pizzas at this "super-packed" Village Italian whose "spacious, festive" digs include a "nice front bar"; the "noise level" can be high and service "spotty", but for most it's still a "true treat."

good
21 | 15 | 18 | $33

89 Greenwich Ave. (bet. Bank & W. 12th Sts.), 212-691-8080;
www.goodrestaurantnyc.com
"The name says it all" at this West Village New American whose affordable "Southern-influenced" comfort fare, enjoyed in "simple" but "cheery" digs, makes it a local "favorite", especially for "amazing brunch"; "fun drinks" ease the occasional "long waits."

Good Enough to Eat
20 | 16 | 17 | $24

483 Amsterdam Ave. (bet. 83rd & 84th Sts.), 212-496-0163;
www.goodenoughtoeat.com
Brunch lines "halfway down the block" bespeak the "homey" American fare on offer at this "cute" "Vermont-ish" Upper Westsider; impatient sorts go for dinner or during weekday breakfast when "you don't have to wait" and it's "much less hectic."

Goodies
20 | 8 | 15 | $17

1 E. Broadway (bet. Catherine & Oliver Sts.), 212-577-2922
"Fresh, flavorful, fantastic soup buns" are the specialty of this cheaper, "much-less-crowded" Chinatown spin-off of Joe's Shanghai; to enjoy all the goodies you must ignore that it's a "divey" "hole-in-the-wall" with service that's "nothing to brag about."

Googie's ●
14 | 10 | 13 | $21

1491 Second Ave. (78th St.), 212-717-1122
You get "plenty of food for the money" at this "child-crazy", er, "family-friendly" East Side Italian diner that's the site of "enormous lines" at weekend brunch; all hail its "famous shoestring fries" but snipe at "sluggish" service and kinda "shabby" digs.

GOTHAM BAR & GRILL
27 | 25 | 26 | $68

12 E. 12th St. (bet. 5th Ave. & University Pl.), 212-620-4020;
www.gothambarandgrill.com
"Year after year" this Village star "continues to shine brightly" thanks to chef Alfred Portale's "terrific", "towering" New American cuisine, served by a "top-notch" staff in "simple but elegant" surroundings; in short, "everything is grand – including the check", although the $25 lunch prix fixe is "a wonderful thing."

Grace ●
▽ 20 | 19 | 17 | $31

114 Franklin St. (bet. Church St. & W. B'way), 212-343-4200;
www.gracebarandrestaurant.com
"Wall Street" types who frequent this "likable" TriBeCa New American come for the "killer" drinks served at the "beautiful" front bar, but stay for the "tasty, trendy" "appetizer"-size dishes "that go well with a martini."

Grace's Trattoria
19 | 17 | 17 | $40

201 E. 71st St. (bet. 2nd & 3rd Aves.), 212-452-2323
"Fresh is the key word" at this East Side "neighborhood" trattoria where the "delicious" Italian dishes are made from ingredients sourced at "next-door" Grace's Marketplace; however, there are a few grumbles that this "brick-walled" standby is "a little cramped" and "pricey."

Gramercy 24
▽ 21 | 21 | 18 | $48

Marcel Hotel, 323 Third Ave. (24th St.), 212-532-1766; www.gramercy24.com
"Newly opened" in the boutique Marcel Hotel, this earth-toned Gramercy Park seafooder serves sophisticated takes on seafood classics via chef Jeffrey Wilson, formerly of the 21 Club.

GRAMERCY TAVERN
28 | 26 | 27 | $73

42 E. 20th St. (bet. B'way & Park Ave. S.), 212-477-0777;
www.gramercytavern.com
Still "magical" and still the *Survey*'s No. 1 for Popularity, this "flagship of Danny Meyer's fleet" is the "utmost" in "sophisticated dining", from Tom Colicchio's "dazzling", "innovative" American cuisine to the "refined" yet "rustic" stetting to the "flawless", hospitable service; in sum, it's well "worth every penny" ("and it will take a ton of them") as well as the trouble of "getting a reservation" – though if you can't book a "month in advance", the more "affordable", yet equally "charming", "front tavern" takes walk-ins.

Grand Sichuan
22 | 9 | 13 | $22

125 Canal St. (Bowery), 212-625-9212 ⇄
227 Lexington Ave. (bet. 33rd & 34th Sts.), 212-679-9770
229 Ninth Ave. (24th St.), 212-620-5200 ●
745 Ninth Ave. (bet. 50th & 51st Sts.), 212-582-2288
19-23 St. Marks Pl. (bet. 2nd & 3rd Aves.), 212-529-4800
1049 Second Ave. (bet. 55th & 56th Sts.), 212-355-5855
www.thegrandsichuan.com
Fired-up fans say "if you can take the heat" head to this Szechuan "chainlet" specializing in "terrific" "pepper-laden" Chinese dishes; don't expect the "warmth" to extend to the "taciturn" waiters, however, and as for decor – "what decor?"

Gravy ●⌀

− | − | − | I

100-102 Smith St. (bet. Atlantic & Pacific Sts.), Brooklyn, 718-935-1294
Serving low-cost Americana till 2 AM in ultrarelaxed, dinerlike digs, this all-day Boerum Hill spot has become a hipster magnet; though there's also a kids' menu available for junior cool cats, the back garden with its own bar is designed for adults.

Gray's Papaya ●⌀

20 | 4 | 14 | $5

2090 Broadway (72nd St.), 212-799-0243
539 Eighth Ave. (37th St.), 212-904-1588
402 Sixth Ave. (8th St.), 212-260-3532
Eating at these "landmark" "bare-bones hot dog joints" is an essential "part of" living in NYC; "juicy" franks with "snap and sizzle" paired with a "succulent" tropical drink add up to "a full stomach" for "a pittance" – so who needs a seat?

Great Jones Cafe ●

22 | 13 | 16 | $24

54 Great Jones St. (bet. Bowery & Lafayette St.), 212-674-9304;
www.greatjones.com
"Tiny" and "dumpy" it may be, but this NoHo "juke joint" dishes out "terrific" Cajun classics in "down-to-earth" environs that "make you feel welcome"; it's a particular "favorite" for "amazing brunches" awash in "killer Bloody Marys" and surrounded by "local hipsters."

Great NY Noodle Town ●●⌀

21 | 5 | 11 | $15

28½ Bowery (Bayard St.), 212-349-0923
"Steam-fogged windows" hint at the "unsurpassed noodle soups" at this "packed" C-town "favorite" where you slurp "with strangers" at "communal tables"; given the "rock-bottom" prices and late hours, it's easy to forgive the "no-decor" digs and "chaotic" service.

Greek Kitchen

18 | 12 | 15 | $27

889 10th Ave. (58th St.), 212-581-4300
"When you don't want to venture to Astoria", this Hell's Kitchen Greek fills the bill with its "simple", "solid" "homestyle" dishes served in "abundant" portions; however, the "no-frills" setting and sometimes "slow" service make many thankful for the "delivery" option.

Green Field Churrascaria

19 | 16 | 19 | $34

108-01 Northern Blvd. (108th St.), Queens, 718-672-5202;
www.greenfieldchurrascaria.com
"Be ready to eat, and eat" at this soccer field–size Brazilian carnivore's "delight" in Corona, where you "pay one price" and "assorted" "slabs of meat" "keep coming" "until you cry uncle"; there's also a "massive salad bar and hot-dish buffet" for those who can see beyond the bovine bonanza.

Grey Dog's Coffee ●

22 | 17 | 17 | $14

33 Carmine St. (bet. Bedford & Bleecker Sts.), 212-462-0041;
www.thegreydog.com
"Young" Village "hipsters" "looking to mingle" and "nosh" come to this "cute" "San Fran–style" cafe where "compelling people-watching" comes free with the "tasty" coffee, baked goods and light fare; it's a "zoo on weekends", but "snagging a table isn't as tough as it looks."

Grifone ☒

23 | 17 | 23 | $57

244 E. 46th St. (bet. 2nd & 3rd Aves.), 212-490-7275;
www.grifonenyc.com
This "hushed", "upscale" UN-area Northern Italian always "seems to be filled with regulars" drawn by the "excellent" "traditional" dishes, "elegant" ambiance and "first-class" service; up-to-the-minute types yawn it's all a bit too "stuffy" and "sleepy", not to mention "expensive."

Grilled Cheese NYC ●⊘
20 | 11 | 15 | $12

168 Ludlow St. (bet. Houston & Stanton Sts.), 212-982-6600;
www.grilledcheesenyc.com
Sure, "you can make your own at home", but the "fresh, interesting",
"super-cheap" grilled cheese dishes at this "relaxed" Lower East
Side "joint" are "oozing with taste" ("no Kraft Singles here") and
served up with "killer fries"; still, cynics say it's strictly "for slackers."

Grill Room ☒
▽ 20 | 22 | 19 | $50

World Financial Ctr., 225 Liberty St. (West Side Hwy.), 212-945-9400;
www.arkrestaurants.com
"Unbeatable" "Hudson views" draw "corporate types" to this World
Financial Center surf 'n' turfer whose "quiet" atmosphere is "perfect"
for "business entertaining"; tabs "can get pricey" so be sure to "charge
it to the firm"; "too bad it's not open on weekends!"

GRIMALDI'S ⊘
26 | 11 | 15 | $19

19 Old Fulton St. (bet. Front & Water Sts.), Brooklyn, 718-858-4300;
www.grimaldis.com
If there were "a pizza hall of fame", this "modest" Brooklyn "institution"
would be inducted for its "crusty, chewy, covered-in-coal" pies that
reach near-"perfection"; "long" lines are part of the deal, so "bring
an iPod" to while away the wait.

GROCERY, THE ☒
27 | 17 | 25 | $56

288 Smith St. (bet. Sackett & Union Sts.), Brooklyn, 718-596-3335
Now that "the secret's out", you'll need to "book weeks in advance" for
a table at this "very special" Carroll Gardens spot, whose "superb"
"seasonal" New American cuisine crafted and presented by "gracious"
owners Charles Kiely and Sharon Pachter "continues to dazzle";
"caring" service, a "small", "homey" dining room and a "dream-
come-true" back garden all make the experience worth waiting for.

Grotta Azzurra ●
▽ 17 | 15 | 17 | $43

387 Broome St. (Mulberry St.), 212-925-8775;
www.grottaazzurrany.com
Founded in 1908 but revamped recently, this "new old restaurant" in
Little Italy earns mixed reviews for its contemporary takes on Southern
Italian cuisine: "sentimental" types say "*grazie*" for pleasures "past
and present", but critics lament "it's not what it once was."

Gusto
– | – | – | M

60 Greenwich Ave. (Perry St.), 212-924-8000
Midpriced, multiregional Italian fare graces the menu of this attractive
new Village neighborhood place, a bright, black-and-white bistro
that's already bustling; a subterranean wine cellar for more intimate
dining is reportedly in the works.

Gyu-Kaku ●
– | – | – | M

34 Cooper Sq. (bet. Astor Pl. & E. 4th St.), 212-475-2989;
www.gyu-kaku.com
This big, "busy" new East Village link of a Japan-based "grill-it-yourself"
Korean barbecue chain gives patrons the chance to cook everything
from Kobe beef to veggies over a tableside charcoal fire; it's all "lots
of fun" so long as you don't "burn" dinner to "a crisp."

Hacienda de Argentina ●
20 | 21 | 19 | $51

339 E. 75th St. (bet. 1st & 2nd Aves.), 212-472-5300
"It really feels like a hacienda" at this East Side Argentine steakhouse,
where diners savor "mouthwatering" "grass-fed" beef "by candelabra
light"; while "cheaper than flying to Buenos Aires", some say it's "still
a bit pricey."

Haikara Grill

▽ 21 | 16 | 18 | $47

206 E. 63rd St. (bet. 2nd & 3rd Aves.), 212-355-7000
"Not your grandmother's kosher", this East Side haunt for the observant slices and rolls "fresh", "creative" sushi and offers "decent" (albeit pricey) Pan-Asian cooked dishes; a post-*Survey* move to new, roomier digs outdates the above Decor score.

Hakata Grill

20 | 15 | 18 | $32

230 W. 48th St. (bet. B'way & 8th Ave.), 212-245-1020;
www.hakatagrill.com
"When you're strapped for time" "before a play" and "don't want to pay" big bucks, this "bustling" Theater District Japanese is a "good quick place" to grab some "decent" sushi; "efficient service" "ensures" you'll get to your show on time.

Hale & Hearty Soups ⇗

19 | 8 | 13 | $10

55 Broad St. (Beaver St.), 212-509-4100 🌣
Chelsea Mkt., 75 Ninth Ave. (bet. 15th & 16th Sts.), 212-255-2400
Grand Central, lower level (42nd St. & Vanderbilt Ave.), 212-983-2845
849 Lexington Ave. (bet. 64th & 65th Sts.), 212-517-7600
Rockefeller Plaza, 30 Rockefeller Plaza (49th St.), 212-265-2117 🌣
462 Seventh Ave. (35th St.), 212-971-0605 🌣
685 Third Ave. (43rd St.), 212-681-6460 🌣
55 W. 56th St. (bet. 5th & 6th Aves.), 212-245-9200 🌣
49 W. 42nd St. (bet. 5th & 6th Aves.), 212-575-9090 🌣
32 Court St. (Remsen St.), Brooklyn, 718-596-5600 🌣
On its way to becoming the "Starbucks" of lunchtime fare, this "popular" "cafeteria-style" chain offers "creative, tasty", "truly hearty" soups, plus "decent" salads and sandwiches, to "busy" office-workers around town.

Hallo Berlin

19 | 8 | 13 | $21

626 10th Ave. (bet. 44th & 45th Sts.), 212-977-1944
"Grab an indoor picnic table" at this Hell's Kitchen German wurst house and, "if your arteries can handle it", "stuff yourself silly" on "sausages galore", loads of "kraut and onions" and suds to "wash it down"; "budget" prices translate to "no attempt at decor or service."

Hampton Chutney Co.

23 | 10 | 17 | $14

68 Prince St. (bet. Crosby & Lafayette Sts.), 212-226-9996;
www.hamptonchutney.com
The "post-yoga-class" SoHo crowd collects for "cheap-but-delicious" "Indian fusion" dosa wraps, "lightly spiced with curry and a smile", at this tiny storefront; the "only issue" is the "limited seating."

Hangawi

25 | 26 | 24 | $45

12 E. 32nd St. (bet. 5th & Madison Aves.), 212-213-0077;
www.hangawirestaurant.com
Plan to "dine blissfully" at this Murray Hill Korean that takes vegetarian cuisine to "superb" heights and will soothe even "carnivore friends" with its "serene" surroundings and "gentle service"; "you take off your shoes and relax" here, so just "remember to wear clean socks."

Happy Buddha

– | – | – | M

135-37 37th Ave. (bet. Main & Prince Sts.), Queens, 718-358-0079;
www.happybuddha.com
At this Flushing vegetarian Chinese, an upscale reincarnation of the owners' previous same-name eatery, a trio of chefs creates the ambitious fare (including some organic offerings); its sleek, Zen-calm setting, staffed by solicitous servers, features a curving juice bar and 25-ft. waterfall.

Hard Rock Cafe ●
11 | 20 | 13 | $28

1501 Broadway (43rd St.), 212-343-3355; www.hardrock.com
Elvis has left the 57th Street building and moved to Times Square, an apt address for this music-themed tourist magnet; though the "rock memorabilia" is better than the barely "decent" Americana, it's "perfect for kids – you can't hear them and they can't hear you."

Harlem Grill ●●⊠
– | – | – | M

2247 Adam Clayton Powell Jr. Blvd. (bet. 132nd & 133rd Sts.), 212-491-0493
A "terrific addition" to Harlem, replacing the famed jazz club/eatery Well's, this "classy" destination serves a seafood-heavy slate of Southern–New American fare, and early visitors are saying "it's all good"; N.B. a gospel brunch is in the works.

Harrison, The
24 | 21 | 23 | $55

355 Greenwich St. (Harrison St.), 212-274-9310; www.theharrison.com
At once "impressively cool" and "comfortable", this popular TriBeCa Med-American has all the earmarks of a Jimmy Bradley/Danny Abrams creation, from the "soaring" cuisine to the "know-their-stuff" staff to the "smart" space and "stylish" crowd; in sum, it's a "sophisticated" choice that inspires many "repeat" visits.

Haru
21 | 17 | 17 | $37

433 Amsterdam Ave. (bet. 80th & 81st Sts.), 212-579-5655 ●
220 Park Ave. S. (18th St.), 646-428-0989 ●
280 Park Ave. (48th St.), 212-490-9680
1327 Third Ave. (76th St.), 212-452-1028 ●
1329 Third Ave. (76th St.), 212-452-2230 ●
205 W. 43rd St. (bet. B'way & 8th Ave.), 212-398-9810 ●
www.harusushi.com
"Whale-size" sushi is the hallmark of this "too-popular", "loud" Japanese chain, where the staff delivers "fresh, reliable", slightly "pricey" fare at "high speed"; just "hold onto your plate" or you'll be "in and out" before you know it.

Hasaki ●
24 | 15 | 18 | $37

210 E. Ninth St. (bet. 2nd & 3rd Aves.), 212-473-3327; www.hasakinyc.com
"Super-fresh" and "beautifully presented" is how the rolls stack up at this "small" East Village Japanese that sushiphiles swear is the "real thing" and has "the lines to prove it"; number-crunchers note the early evening "twilight special" "can't be beat."

Hatsuhana ⊠
24 | 17 | 21 | $51

17 E. 48th St. (bet. 5th & Madison Aves.), 212-355-3345
237 Park Ave. (46th St.), 212-661-3400
www.hatsuhana.com
This "traditional" Midtown sushi duo has been "going for two decades" on the power of its "wonderful" "classic" offerings and "lovely" service; it's long been a "favorite" of "businesspeople" and others who don't mind the "expensive" price tag or the "never-changing" decor.

Havana Alma de Cuba
∇ 22 | 17 | 20 | $27

94 Christopher St. (bet. Bedford & Bleecker Sts.), 212-242-3800;
www.havanavillagenyc.com
It's easy to "get hooked" on this Village Cuban's formula of "*muy delicioso*" fare, "amazing sangria", "friendly" service and "sexy guitar music"; in summer its "very small" space is augmented with "a big patio out back."

Havana Central
17 | 13 | 15 | $24

151 W. 46th St. (bet. 6th & 7th Aves.), 212-398-7440 ●

(continued)

Havana Central

22 E. 17th St. (bet. B'way & 5th Ave.), 212-414-2298
www.havanacentral.com

It's "Havana" by way of Union Square and Restaurant Row at these "casual", "lively" Cubans that offer a "cafeteria"-style buffet by day but become full-service at dinner; their "authentic" "classics" come for only a "few bucks", which helps to make up for iffy decor and service.

Havana Chelsea ⊄

| 21 | 8 | 14 | $20 |

190 Eighth Ave. (bet. 19th & 20th Sts.), 212-243-9421

"A lot cheaper than going to Miami", a trip to this Chelsea "greasy spoon" yields "mounds and mounds" of "delicious" Cuban "comfort food" at "reasonable prices"; "bring your Lipitor" and "come to eat", "not to admire the scenery or be pampered."

Haveli ◑

| 21 | 17 | 19 | $31 |

100 Second Ave. (bet. 5th & 6th Sts.), 212-982-0533

"Around the corner" from Curry Row, this "comfortable", comparatively "fancy" East Village Indian stands out as a "cut above"; admirers say it must be "blessed" with good "karma."

Hearth

| 24 | 20 | 23 | $57 |

403 E. 12th St. (1st Ave.), 646-602-1300; www.restauranthearth.com

Fans of this East Village Tuscan-American report that "chef-to-watch" Marco Canora (ex Craft) dishes out "innovative" cuisine "bursting with flavor and freshness"; a setting as "cozy as the name implies" and "warm" service offset "small portions" and "pricey" tabs.

Heartland Brewery

| 14 | 13 | 14 | $26 |

Empire State Bldg., 350 Fifth Ave. (34th St.), 212-563-3433
1285 Sixth Ave. (51st St.), 212-582-8244
South Street Seaport, 93 South St. (Fulton St.), 646-572-2337
35 Union Sq. W. (bet. 16th & 17th Sts.), 212-645-3400
127 W. 43rd St. (bet. B'way & 6th Ave.), 646-366-0235 ◑
www.heartlandbrewery.com

This microbrewery chain offers a "fine selection of suds" and "passable" "pub" basics in "crowded", "raucous" spaces that'll have you "remembering your college days"; critics foam c'mon, "it's NYC" – you can "do better than this."

Hedeh ◑▣

| ▽ | 24 | 19 | 20 | $51 |

57 Great Jones St. (bet. Bowery & Lafayette St.), 212-473-8458

The counter chefs greet patrons "with a roaring welcome" at this new NoHo Japanese, and it's a "culinary treat from there on in" say early samplers; with "fresh", "delectable" sushi served in "fun, modern" digs, it's unlikely to fly "under most people's radar" for long.

Heidelberg

| 18 | 16 | 17 | $33 |

1648 Second Ave. (bet. 85th & 86th Sts.), 212-628-2332;
www.heidelbergrestaurant.com

The "last of the old-line Germans in Yorkville" lures schnitzel-hounds and others who crave "hearty staples" dispensed by staffers in "lederhosen" and "dirndls"; its "festive vibe" fueled by "live music" makes the "dowdy" digs feel downright *gemütlich*.

Heights Cafe ◑

| 17 | 16 | 16 | $28 |

84 Montague St. (Hicks St.), Brooklyn, 718-625-5555; www.heightscafeny.com

A "casual" Brooklyn Heights "neighborhood favorite" "near the Promenade", this New American cafe supplies "solid" basics (i.e. "delicious burgers") along with the possibility of outdoor dining; just "don't expect" meals "in a hurry" or the decor to rise above "bland."

Hell's Kitchen
23 | 16 | 18 | $40

679 Ninth Ave. (bet. 46th & 47th Sts.), 212-977-1588;
www.hellskitchen-nyc.com
As "small as a Hell's Kitchen studio", this "upscale Mexican" has
patrons clamoring to "move in" thanks to its "spicy" cuisine with
"nuevo" touches; to alleviate the "heinous waits" and "daunting" din,
a move to larger, down-the-street digs is planned.

Hemsin
▽ 22 | 11 | 18 | $24

39-17 Queens Blvd. (39th Pl.), Queens, 718-482-7998
"Succulent kebabs" and other "flavorful" Turkish-style grilled meats
are reason enough to "hop on the 7 train" and head for this Sunnyside
"joint"; the decor may be "modest", but the tabs are too.

Henry's End
26 | 15 | 24 | $42

44 Henry St. (Cranberry St.), Brooklyn, 718-834-1776; www.henrysend.com
Somewhere between "gourmet cuisine" and "down-home cooking"
lies this veteran Brooklyn Heights New American known for its
"outstanding" menu focused on "all things game"; "cramped"
environs are eased by "friendly" service.

Highline ●
20 | 22 | 17 | $34

835 Washington St. (Little W. 12th St.), 212-243-3339; www.nychighline.com
"Watch the fashion show go by" at this "trendy Thai" on the fringes
of the Meatpacking District, where the crowd's "scantily clad" and the
decor's "futuristic" ("you'll be looking for the orgasmatron"); no one's
there for the food, but it's "surprisingly good" and "totally affordable."

Hip Hop Chow
– | – | – | M

129 Second Ave. (bet. 7th St. & St. Marks Pl.), 212-674-2459;
www.hiphopchow.com
A self-proclaimed embodiment of the East Village's cultural diversity,
this altar to kung fu, hip-hop and graffiti art (check out the cut-glass
light boxes on the wall) dishes out Chinese-accented soul food, a
culinary twist on an oldie intended to get all to holla.

Hispaniola ●
21 | 20 | 18 | $38

839 W. 181st St. (Cabrini Blvd.), 212-740-5222; www.hispaniolarestaurant.com
"Take the A train to 181st Street" to sample this "charming" Washington
Heights Nuevo Latino–Asian that boasts a "Downtown" look and an
"impressive view of the GW Bridge"; the cuisine's "toe-tingling" and
the service "caring", but some say it's "pricey for the neighborhood."

Hк ●
▽ 19 | 20 | 18 | $31

523 Ninth Ave. (39th St.), 212-947-4208
Its "bright, open space fills a void" say admirers of this Hell's Kitchen
New American that dwells "in the dark shadow of Port Authority"; its
"cheap" bistro menu is "spot-on" (especially the "excellent brunch"),
but the service, though via a "cute" staff, is "hit-or-miss."

Holy Basil ●
23 | 19 | 19 | $29

149 Second Ave., 2nd fl. (bet. 9th & 10th Sts.), 212-460-5557
"Slightly fancier than the average Thai", this "dark, sexy" (think
"candles and mirrors") East Villager proffers "delicious" dishes "with
a contemporary twist" dispensed by a "friendly" crew; if servings are
"small", so are the prices.

Home
20 | 17 | 19 | $37

20 Cornelia St. (bet. Bleecker & W. 4th Sts.), 212-243-9579;
www.recipesfromhome.com
"Fresh and organic" American "comfort" cuisine is what comes
out of the kitchen at this "cozy and quirky" Villager overseen by an

"attentive" staff; those who find the "narrow" space "cramped" appreciate its "delightful garden."

HONMURA AN

| 26 | 23 | 24 | $49 |

170 Mercer St., 2nd fl. (bet. Houston & Prince Sts.), 212-334-5253
This "Elysian Fields of noodles and tempura" will make you think you're "in Tokyo rather than SoHo" thanks to its "state-of-the-art soba" "presented like artwork"; given the "beautiful" setup and "wonderful" service, it's no surprise you have to "drop some serious coin."

Hope & Anchor ●

| ▽ 19 | 16 | 18 | $19 |

347 Van Brunt St. (Wolcott St.), Brooklyn, 718-237-0276;
www.hopeandanchordiner.com
"Diner food with an edge" is dispensed by this "cheap", "funky" New American favored by "cool" "Red Hook locals"; popular for "amazing brunch", it "rocks" on weekends when the "drag-queen karaoke" keeps the "good times" rolling.

Houston's

| 20 | 18 | 19 | $34 |

Citigroup Ctr., 153 E. 53rd St. (enter at 54th St. & 3rd Ave.), 212-888-3828
NY Life Bldg., 378 Park Ave. S. (27th St.), 212-689-1090
www.houstons.com
Yes, this "cozy" "upscale" duo's "part of a (gasp!) chain", but devotees say it's "perfect" "for what it's aiming at": "consistently satisfying", modestly priced American fare, served by a "fast", "friendly" staff; no wonder people "line" up to eat here.

HSF

| 19 | 10 | 12 | $23 |

46 Bowery (bet. Bayard & Canal Sts.), 212-374-1319
A dim-sum standby deemed "worth the trip to Chinatown", this "cheap" Cantonese "dumpling heaven" is noted for its "large variety" of "trundling cart"–borne tidbits; just know that the "tremendous space" becomes a "crowded, noisy" "zoo on weekends."

Hudson Cafeteria

| 18 | 22 | 17 | $45 |

Hudson Hotel, 356 W. 58th St. (bet. 8th & 9th Aves.), 212-554-6000;
www.chinagrillmgt.com
Quality "comfort food" is the deal at this "chic" American-Eclectic housed in the Hudson Hotel, where diners sit at "communal tables" in a "dramatic", "high-ceilinged" space, or in the spacious "outdoor garden"; it's "not as hot as it used to be", but no one's broken the news to the "intimidating" staff.

Hue ●▣

| 18 | 21 | 14 | $48 |

91 Charles St. (Bleecker St.), 212-691-4575; www.huenyc.com
"Solely for fabulistas", this West Village Vietnamese's "tasty, fancy" fare is overshadowed by its "beautiful" bi-level space and "eye-candy" crowd; "how-dare-they" prices and "poor" service from a "primping" staff have mere mortals vowing "no Hue."

Hunan Park ●

| 20 | 11 | 17 | $22 |

235 Columbus Ave. (bet. 70th & 71st Sts.), 212-724-4411
Upper Westsiders rely on this "family Chinese" for "surprisingly good" standards offered "cheap"; those turned off by its "tiny", "crowded" digs opt for the "faster-than-a-speeding-bullet" delivery.

Ian

| 23 | 19 | 19 | $54 |

322 E. 86th St. (bet. 1st & 2nd Aves.), 212-861-1993; www.ianrestaurant.com
"A real star" on a culinarily challenged stretch of 86th Street, this Upper East Side New American offers "addictive", "out-of-the-ordinary flavor combos" in a "pleasant" "Downtown"-ish space; the only "kinks" are sometimes-"slow" service and "sky-high" prices "for the area."

Ichiro ◕
▽ | 22 | 16 | 20 | $29

1694 Second Ave. (bet. 87th & 88th Sts.), 212-369-6300; www.ichi-ro.com
"Fantastic", "fresh" sushi in iterations both "traditional and inventive" is the draw at this Upper East Side newcomer that also offers "a wide variety of sake"; "wonderful service" and a "calming" atmosphere make it worth tabs "a tad pricier" than the local competition.

Ici
21 | 20 | 19 | $37

246 DeKalb Ave. (bet. Clermont & Vanderbilt Aves.), Brooklyn, 718-789-2778; www.icirestaurant.com
This "light", "simple yet elegant" modern French bistro in Fort Greene boasts "fresh, amazing" seasonal fare that tastes even better in the "absolutely gorgeous" garden; if service can be "less than organized", the staff's "cheerfully welcoming" attitude makes up for any miscues.

I Coppi
22 | 21 | 20 | $44

432 E. Ninth St. (bet. Ave. A & 1st Ave.), 212-254-2263; www.icoppinyc.com
This "friendly family Tuscan" and its "delight" of an "all-season garden room" are "a nice break from typical cramped East Village Italians"; "delicious", "well-prepared" classics and a staff with "lots of heart" justify the "high" tabs (though the "excellent" prix fixe brunch is "a deal").

Ida Mae ☒
21 | 19 | 17 | $49

111 W. 38th St. (bet. B'way & 6th Ave.), 212-704-0038; www.idamae.com
A "burst of energy" in the Garment District culinary "wasteland", this provider of "delicious" "upscale down-South" fare boasts a "lively" vibe enhanced by a "great jazz band" some nights; if the space is a "little cramped" and service can be "slow", it's still "one of your best bets" in the area.

Ideya
21 | 17 | 18 | $33

349 W. Broadway (bet. Broome & Grand Sts.), 212-625-1441; www.ideya.net
"Reliable" Caribbean bites are washed down with "perfect mojitos" at this "affordable", "feisty" (read: "loud") SoHo scene; the "lounge"-like "step-out-onto-the-beach" decor furthers the "fun" vibe, as do the "cute", "pencil-thin" staffers, even though service can be iffy.

Il Bagatto ◕
24 | 18 | 16 | $34

192 E. Second St. (bet. Aves. A & B), 212-228-0977
"Top-notch" Italian "almost as good as grandma's" is "made with love and attitude" at this "affordable" East Villager; "cramped" quarters, "long waits" and "weird rules" are cons, but, ultimately, the "amazing" eats keep 'em coming back.

Il Bastardo
– | – | – | M

191 Seventh Ave. (bet. 21st & 22nd Sts.), 212-675-5980
From the folks behind Chelsea's Sette comes this new next-door Tuscan eatery/wine bar that specializes in midpriced steak and seafood; the meandering, three-part setup includes a main dining room, cozier rear lounge and a back area for private parties.

Il Buco ◕
23 | 24 | 20 | $53

47 Bond St. (bet. Bowery & Lafayette St.), 212-533-1932; www.ilbuco.com
"Escape NY" upon entering this "Umbrian farmhouse"–like NoHo Med whose "inspired" cuisine and "romantic", "antiques"-filled digs make it "a place to fall and stay in love"; its "educated staff" is one more reason it's "worth" the effort of "getting a table" as well as the "expense" when the check comes.

Il Cantinori ◑

22 21 21 $57

32 E. 10th St. (bet. B'way & University Pl.), 212-673-6044; www.il-cantinori.com
"Romantic lighting", loads of "fresh flowers" and the odd "celeb sighting" fuel the "special-occasion" feel at this "lively" Northern Italian on a "Village side street"; "simply prepared" but "fabulous" fare and "attentive" pro service complete the "luxurious" experience, and justify the "big price tag."

Il Corallo Trattoria ◑

23 13 19 $25

176 Prince St. (bet. Sullivan & Thompson Sts.), 212-941-7119
"Not at all pretentious", this "friendly", "cheap-for-SoHo" Italian specializes in "wholesome, tasty" dishes, including "about a million pastas"; "nothing-fancy" quarters and "a lack of elbow room" are par for the course.

Il Cortile ◑

23 20 20 $48

125 Mulberry St. (bet. Canal & Hester Sts.), 212-226-6060
"Innovative" Italian ("not the same old lasagna and meatballs") comes out of the kitchen at this "very Tony Soprano"–feeling "safe bet" on Mulberry Street; "choose the garden room", take in stride the "uneven" service and know you'll have to "pay to play", and "you'll feel like you're in Italy."

Il Fornaio

21 13 18 $31

132A Mulberry St. (bet. Grand & Hester Sts.), 212-226-8306
"Stick to the basics and you'll be happy" at this "Little Italy joint" where "good old-fashioned red-sauce" Italian is the name of the game; the at-times-"inconsistent" service and "cramped" environment do not detract from the "like-mama's" feeling.

Il Gattopardo

▽ 24 18 23 $59

33 W. 54th St. (bet. 5th & 6th Aves.), 212-246-0412; www.ilgattopardonyc.com
"MoMA next door may have inspired the minimalist decor" of this "undiscovered" "jewel box" where the "heavenly" Neapolitan cuisine, "excellent Italian wine list" and "warm, helpful service" help to allay the inevitable sticker shock.

IL GIGLIO ☒

26 19 24 $67

81 Warren St. (bet. Greenwich St. & W. B'way), 212-571-5555; www.ilgiglionyc.com
It's "always a fabulous meal" at this TriBeCa Italian where the scene's "crowded and boisterous" and the servings of "superior" food "are epic" (it doesn't stop from the "free antipasto while you look at the menu" to the "final complimentary grappa"); legendarily "gracious" and "attentive" service makes up for pricing that may necessitate "a Brinks truck" when it's time to settle the check.

Il Menestrello ☒

22 18 23 $58

14 E. 52nd St. (bet. 5th & Madison Aves.), 212-421-7588
"You know what you're going to get" at this longtime Midtown Italian: "excellent" "traditional" fare served in "sophisticated" style; deemed a "peaceful retreat" despite decor that's "a little tired", it boasts "warm, accommodating" service "so fine-tuned" it's almost invisible.

Il Monello

23 18 22 $55

1460 Second Ave. (bet. 76th & 77th Sts.), 212-535-9310; www.ilmonellonyc.com
Be "transported to another era" at this "formal, serene" "Italian classic" catering to a "well-heeled" East Side clientele with "high-class" (and high-priced) food and service; it's still "excellent" "after all these years", even if a "disappointed" few claim it's "lost its edge."

IL MULINO ⌧
27 | 18 | 24 | $79

86 W. Third St. (bet. Sullivan & Thompson Sts.), 212-673-3783;
www.ilmulinonewyork.com
Visits to this Italian Village "classic" are "a culinary event" featuring "king-size" portions of "heavy, old-fashioned", "sublime" fare served by waiters who are "the epitome of professional"; after landing a "difficult-", if not "impossible-to-get" reservation, hit this "dimly lit" "shoebox" with "plenty of cash", time and appetite, because meals here last "longer than a flight to Italy and cost about the same."

Il Nido ⌧
23 | 18 | 22 | $63

251 E. 53rd St. (bet. 2nd & 3rd Aves.), 212-753-8450
"Old-school" Northern Italian with "a flourish" is the deal at this East Midtown classic where "tableside preparation" is just one of the ways the "pro" waiters "take care of you"; despite digs that are "getting dated", to most it's "worth every dollar" — and that's saying a lot.

Il Palazzo
23 | 18 | 21 | $40

151 Mulberry St. (bet. Grand & Hester Sts.), 212-343-7000
Considered "a cut above the others on Mulberry Street", this "sweet, romantic" Italian is known for its seafood that's "complex and full of flavor"; though it doesn't live up to its name, it does have a "charming" glassed-in garden.

Il Postino ●
22 | 19 | 20 | $60

337 E. 49th St. (bet. 1st & 2nd Aves.), 212-688-0033
"One of Midtown's hidden treasures", this white-tablecloth Italian caters to a smart, necessarily well-heeled crowd with its first-class food and "attentive, old-world" service; everything's ordered from a "verbal" menu longer than Hamlet's soliloquy.

Il Riccio ●
▽ 22 | 14 | 20 | $49

152 E. 79th St. (bet. Lexington & 3rd Aves.), 212-639-9111
Although "it's a squeeze", this "snug little" Upper East Side Italian is "very big in quality and flavor"; its "varied clientele" includes the likes of "Mayor Bloomberg", who you just might find in the "cozy back room."

Il Tinello ⌧
23 | 20 | 23 | $59

16 W. 56th St. (bet. 5th & 6th Aves.), 212-245-4388
A "civilized" "throwback" to a "'60s kind of" Northern Italian, this "gracious" Eastsider has a wealth of devotees who declare its "reliable" cuisine "a blessing for the palate"; it's not universal though, as a few caution that its aura is a bit "dated."

Il Vagabondo ●
18 | 14 | 17 | $38

351 E. 62nd St. (bet. 1st & 2nd Aves.), 212-832-9221; www.ilvagabondo.com
Ok, maybe it's a little "past-a its prime", but this "old-world Italian" on the East Side still has lots to recommend it: "solid" "red-sauce" favorites, "martinis done right" and even a "must-see" "indoor bocce court" that always impresses the youth brigade.

Il Valentino
▽ 18 | 18 | 19 | $55

330 E. 56th St. (bet. 1st & 2nd Aves.), 212-355-0001; www.thesutton.com
"Tucked away on a quiet street", this "old-fashioned" Italian caters to "retired VIPs and their wives" as well as its other Sutton Place neighbors; "enjoyable" live "jazz and swing" is another plus.

Inagiku
23 | 21 | 22 | $58

Waldorf-Astoria, 111 E. 49th St. (bet. Lexington & Park Aves.),
212-355-0440; www.inagiku.com
"If you can't afford dinner" at this "high-class" Japanese in the Waldorf, go for the "reasonable" "lunch-box special" advise admirers of its

"fresh, high-quality" sushi and other delights; "friendly" service and "elegant" (if "none-too-original") decor justify the "pricey" tabs.

Indochine ● | 21 | 20 | 17 | $48 |
430 Lafayette St. (bet. Astor Pl. & E. 4th St.), 212-505-5111
"Still steamin'" after 20-plus years, this French-Vietnamese opposite the Public Theater remains a "lively scene" with "savory" cuisine and "sexy" clientele; "stingy" portions and "intermittent" service aside, it has attained the status of Downtown dining "institution."

Indus Valley | 23 | 16 | 19 | $30 |
2636 Broadway (100th St.), 212-222-9222
Upper Westsiders "rejoice" in the "impeccably authentic", "refined" Indian cuisine at this "neighborhood godsend"; if the "sweet" staff "tries a little too hard to sell the specials", they can be forgiven because "it's all delicious" and inexpensive.

'ino ● | 24 | 15 | 18 | $23 |
21 Bedford St. (bet. Downing St. & 6th Ave.), 212-989-5769;
www.cafeino.com
"Little bites of heaven" abound at this low-budget Village "panini paradise" whose "indulgent rustic sandwiches" go down *delizioso* with "affordable, tasty wines"; unfortunately, this "Mini-Me of restaurants" is often "jam-packed", but few complain because everything tastes so "ridiculously good."

'inoteca ● | 23 | 18 | 20 | $34 |
98 Rivington St. (Ludlow St.), 212-614-0473; www.inotecanyc.com
This "'ino spin-off" with a "Lower East Side sensibility" serves "reasonable" "echt-Italian snacks" and "fantastic" vinos in "roomier" (but still "overcrowded") digs; the "hard-to-read *Italiano* menu" is navigable thanks to a "helpful" staff, and while there's "always a wait" to get in, surveyors say "it's totally worth it."

Inside | ▽ 24 | 19 | 21 | $41 |
9 Jones St. (bet. Bleecker & W. 4th Sts.), 212-229-9999;
www.insideonjones.com
Still "a local secret" despite its "excellent" "contemporary comfort food", this "civilized" Village New American features "incredibly accommodating" service and a "laid-back" vibe that make everyone feel like "an insider."

Intermezzo | 19 | 17 | 19 | $29 |
202 Eighth Ave. (bet. 20th & 21st Sts.), 212-929-3433; www.intermezzony.com
An "affordable", "better-than-average" "neighborhood Italian" that's "a dance away from the Joyce", this Chelsea standby was "recently remodeled" in "high-tech" style; everyone appreciates the "attentive waiters", assuming you can hear them over the "techno-trendy", "noisy" output of the in-house DJ.

Iron Sushi | 20 | 12 | 18 | $28 |
355 E. 78th St. (bet. 1st & 2nd Aves.), 212-772-7680
440 Third Ave. (bet. 30th & 31st Sts.), 212-447-5822
A "large variety of" "genius combo" rolls is the draw at this East Side "neighborhood sushi" twosome; "fair prices", "fresh fish" and a "friendly staff" make "not-so-great decor" easy to overlook, especially since there's "reliable delivery."

Isabella's ● | 20 | 20 | 18 | $39 |
359 Columbus Ave. (77th St.), 212-724-2100; www.brguestrestaurants.com
"To see and be seen on the West Side", head for this Med–New American "fixture" for good food delivered by a "welcoming" staff;

the "awesome brunch" is best enjoyed from the "lovely outside tables" in summer, but enough people know it to produce weekend waits.

Island Burgers & Shakes ⊅
22 | 9 | 14 | $14

766 Ninth Ave. (bet. 51st & 52nd Sts.), 212-307-7934
"Huge", "juicy" burgers and "delicious" chicken churrascos plus "awesome, thick shakes" cost next to nothing at this "surfer"-themed Hell's Kitchen storefront; "crowded" digs and so-so service are the downsides of "popularity" here.

Ithaka
21 | 17 | 19 | $43

308 E. 86th St. (bet. 1st & 2nd Aves.), 212-628-9100; www.ithakarestaurant.com
"Can't-be-beat" grilled fish and other Greek specialties are highlights at this Upper Eastsider supported by a "warm, welcoming host"; regulars note "things taste even better" when the guitar player is performing (Wednesday–Saturday).

I Tre Merli ●
18 | 18 | 17 | $40

463 W. Broadway (bet. Houston & Prince Sts.), 212-254-8699
I Tre Merli Bistro ●
183 W. 10th St. (W. 4th St.), 212-929-2221
www.itremerli.com
With locations "in the heart of SoHo" and on a "cozy" Village corner, this "laid-back" Northern Italian "draws in neighbors" for "simple panini, pastas" and the like backed up by a wine list that "rocks"; it's ideal for "hanging with the pretty people."

I Trulli
23 | 21 | 21 | $53

122 E. 27th St. (bet. Lexington Ave. & Park Ave. S.), 212-481-7372;
www.itrulli.com
A "cozy" "fireplace in winter" and "beautiful garden" in summer make this Gramercy "hideaway" a year-round "romantic" destination; Southern Italian food "at its finest" and "spectacular wines" served by a "warm" staff justify its expense, but budget-watchers can always take advantage of the more affordable "next-door enoteca."

It's a Dominican Thing
▽ 19 | 18 | 19 | $25

144 W. 19th St. (bet. 6th & 7th Aves.), 212-924-3344
Try this "small", "charming" Chelsea newcomer if you want to sample "authentic" Dominican fare in "cute" quarters; given the "anxious-to-please" staff and "not-expensive" tabs, it's no surprise there are already "long waits" at prime times.

Itzocan
25 | 12 | 19 | $28

438 E. Ninth St. (bet. Ave. A & 1st Ave.), 212-677-5856
1575 Lexington Ave. (101st St.), 212-423-0255
"Hip crowds of all ages" favor this East Village Mexican and its Upper East Side offshoot, where the *muy* "authentic" cuisine is "a joy for the taste buds" – and the wallet, given the "reasonable" prices; "tiny" digs make it feel "like eating in a shoebox", but "kind" service compensates.

Ivo & Lulu ⊠⊅
▽ 24 | 13 | 22 | $25

558 Broome St. (bet. 6th Ave. & Varick St.), 212-226-4399
"A hidden treasure near the Holland Tunnel", this "friendly", "spicy" SoHo French-Caribbean delivers "excellent, organic" dishes posted daily on a "limited chalkboard menu"; the "postage stamp"–size digs are basic and "cramped", but it's "amazingly cheap" and "BYO to boot."

Ivy's Cafe ●
20 | 9 | 19 | $26

154 W. 72nd St. (bet. B'way & Columbus Ave.), 212-787-3333
In an "easy-to-miss" "diner"-ish "storefront" dwells this Westsider that caters to "those who can't decide which Asian food they prefer",

Chinese or Japanese; most agree the food is "delicious", but the "gloomy" decor has some saying it's "better for delivery."

Ixta ●
19 | 19 | 15 | $39

48 E. 29th St. (bet. Madison Ave. & Park Ave. S.), 212-683-4833; www.ixtarestaurant.com
"Nuevo spins on old favorites" and "sleek", "Miami"-style decor have locals lining up for this Gramercy Park Mexican; food "vibrant with flavors" and an "exhaustive tequila selection" make the noise, crowds and "pushy service" easy to forgive.

Jack's Luxury Oyster Bar ⊠
25 | 21 | 23 | $72

246 E. Fifth St. (bet. 2nd & 3rd Aves.), 212-673-0338
"Luxury is an understatement" at this "special" East Village French-Continental by way of "New Orleans", given its "magnificent", "meticulous" seafood-oriented cuisine; from the Jewel Bako team, it provides predictably "impeccable" service, and while its "minuscule" bi-level space is "incredibly romantic", some wonder why they didn't provide more legroom "at these prices."

Jackson Diner ⊭
22 | 11 | 15 | $22

37-47 74th St. (bet. Roosevelt Ave. & 37th Rd.), Queens, 718-672-1232
The "lavish" $8.95 buffet brunch is "nirvana" at this Jackson Heights Indian that "lives up to the hype" even if its dining room "looks like a cafeteria" and service is "workmanlike" at best; just "prepare to eat a lot" and "be careful when you ask for extra spice."

Jackson Hole
17 | 10 | 14 | $19

517 Columbus Ave. (85th St.), 212-362-5177 ●
232 E. 64th St. (bet. 2nd & 3rd Aves.), 212-371-7187 ●
1270 Madison Ave. (91st St.), 212-427-2820
1611 Second Ave. (bet. 83rd & 84th Sts.), 212-737-8788 ●
521 Third Ave. (35th St.), 212-679-3264 ●
69-35 Astoria Blvd. (70th St.), Queens, 718-204-7070 ●
35-01 Bell Blvd. (35th Ave.), Queens, 718-281-0330 ●
www.jacksonholeburgers.com
"Gigantic, delicious burgers" mean "you can't go wrong" at this multiboro "greasy spoon" chain that's "a must with children"; low prices compensate for decor and service that "leave much to be desired."

Jacques Brasserie
18 | 17 | 18 | $40

204-206 E. 85th St. (bet. 2nd & 3rd Aves.), 212-327-2272; www.jacquesnyc.com
"Consistent bistro fixes" in a "backstreets-of-Paris" milieu make this "very French" Upper Eastsider a "neighborhood favorite"; it's particularly popular on Mondays when it rolls out the "amazing bargain" of "moules frites and a beer" for $14.95.

Jacques-Imo's NYC
18 | 15 | 17 | $35

366 Columbus Ave. (77th St.), 212-799-0150
Grand Central, lower level (42nd St. & Vanderbilt Ave.), 212-661-4022
"Not the real deal, but close" is the consensus on this New Orleans transplant on the Upper West Side, where "killer" Cajun-Creole cooking (including "heavenly fried chicken") comes in "jammed", "kitschy" quarters with a "party" feel; N.B. there's also a take-out counter in Grand Central.

Jaiya Thai ●
21 | 10 | 14 | $27

396 Third Ave. (28th St.), 212-889-1330; www.jaiya.com
"Wonderful Thai flavors" are the forte of this "cheap" Gramercy "gem" where the uninitiated shouldn't "order more than medium-spicy" lest they "require Tums"; seating's "tight", decor's "minimal" and service is "mediocre", so takeout and delivery are "good options."

Jake's Steakhouse
▽ 24 | 18 | 20 | $45

6031 Broadway (242nd St.), Bronx, 718-581-0182; www.jakessteakhouse.com
"Sterling beef", aged in the owners' own facility, is "juicy and cooked right" at this comfortable, midpriced Bronx steakhouse staffed by an "attentive, friendly" crew; locals consider it a "special-occasion" destination and advise "ask for a table by the window" "overlooking Van Cortlandt Park."

Jane ⬤
22 | 18 | 20 | $37

100 W. Houston St. (bet. La Guardia Pl. & Thompson St.), 212-254-7000; www.janerestaurant.com
There's "nothing plain" about this "delightful" New American on the Village-SoHo border, nor about the "fresh, intriguing" food that suits "all pocketbooks"; despite its "sleek" setup, it has a "neighborhood feel" enhanced by "caring" service.

Japonica
22 | 13 | 19 | $41

100 University Pl. (12th St.), 212-243-7752
It's the "pristinely fresh sushi" and "sweet" servers, not the "nothing-special" ambiance, that keep the "insane crowds" coming to this "longtime" Village Japanese "favorite"; "huge" rolls and equivalent tabs inspire fantasies of "half the size at half the price", but you can't argue with success.

Jarnac
22 | 20 | 23 | $50

328 W. 12th St. (Greenwich St.), 212-924-3413; www.jarnacny.com
"Innovative takes on French standards" served in a "romantic" room endear this "lovely" West Village bistro to locals, who happily "avoid the Meatpacking District hype" nearby; it's "expensive", but a "brilliant host" and "personable chef" ensure that it merits "every penny."

Jasmine
20 | 15 | 17 | $26

1619 Second Ave. (84th St.), 212-517-8854
"Cut-above" Thai dishes in "bountiful portions" have made this "casual" Upper Eastsider a "neighborhood staple"; the staff's "friendly as can be", but "can be slow" and acoustics may be "loud", but those "pretty darn reasonable" checks make up for a lot.

Jean Claude ⊅
23 | 15 | 20 | $41

137 Sullivan St. (bet. Houston & Prince Sts.), 212-475-9232
"Feels like the real deal" but "without the smoke" is the take on this "wonderful", "laid-back" "Left Bank"–style SoHo French bistro; admittedly, it's "small", "dimly lit" and "crowded", but the latter attribute is due to the fact that NYers know a good deal when they eat one.

JEAN GEORGES ⊠
27 | 26 | 27 | $95

Trump Int'l Hotel, 1 Central Park W. (bet. 60th & 61st Sts.), 212-299-3900; www.jean-georges.com
Jean-Georges Vongerichten's "prowess is entirely seductive" at his "opulent" New French flagship on Columbus Circle, where "highly personal cooking from a modern master" is "impeccably presented" to "spectacular" effect; factor in "flawless" service and Adam Tihany's "subtle" "contemporary" design, and the high tabs are fully understandable; if price is a concern, the $20 prix fixe lunch offered in the "less formal Nougatine Room" and on the terrace is probably "the best bargain in town."

Jean-Luc
20 | 20 | 18 | $51

507 Columbus Ave. (bet. 84th & 85th Sts.), 212-712-1700; www.jeanlucrestaurant.com
The "Upper West Side meets TriBeCa" at this "friendly" French bistro boasting a "mellow" Downtown vibe and some seriously

114

good food; a "recent redecoration" has "brightened" things up a bit, while some new, lower-priced dishes may address concerns about overly "pricey" tabs.

Jekyll & Hyde Club
| 10 | 22 | 14 | $31 |

1409 Sixth Ave. (bet. 57th & 58th Sts.), 212-541-9517;
www.jekyllandhydeclub.com
"It's a blast for the kids", what with the "spooky" fun-house setting including a "cast of strange people and machines"; however, grown-ups "beware": this Midtown "haunted house–themed" American is also home to "subpar food", "surly, careless service" and enough tourists to bring out the Hyde in any NYer.

Jerry's
| 19 | 15 | 16 | $31 |

101 Prince St. (bet. Greene & Mercer Sts.), 212-966-9464;
www.jerrysnyc.com
"Still fun", still "casually cool", this veteran SoHo "upscale diner" continues to pull in the "crowds" with its "reliable", "justly priced" New American food and "arty" vibe; though it's fine "for any meal", mavens maintain "brunch is the winner here."

JEWEL BAKO ⊠
| 26 | 22 | 24 | $72 |

239 E. Fifth St. (bet. 2nd & 3rd Aves.), 212-979-1012
JEWEL BAKO MAKIMONO ◐⊠
101 Second Ave. (bet. 5th & 6th Sts.), 212-253-7848
Among "Downtown's crown jewels of sushi", this East Village Japanese slices and rolls "exquisite", "rarefied" fish "as fresh as it comes" in a "tranquil, minimalist" bamboo-lined space; "cool" owners Jack and Grace Lamb ("the kind of hosts you thought disappeared in the '40s") oversee the near-"flawless" service, so the only bone is the "wallet-melting" tab – though there's a more-affordable satellite, Jewel Bako Makimono, around the corner on Second Avenue.

Jewel of India
| 21 | 19 | 21 | $36 |

15 W. 44th St. (bet. 5th & 6th Aves.), 212-869-5544
This "comfortable", "dependable" Midtown Indian's a "favorite" of area office types thanks to its first-rate "traditional" dishes "sizzling with spice" and "bargain" lunch buffet; lots of "smiles" from the "charming" staff offset the fact that that elegant interior is beginning to look like it might need "a face-lift."

Jezebel ⊠
| 19 | 24 | 19 | $47 |

630 Ninth Ave. (45th St.), 212-582-1045; www.jezebelny.com
It's the "Old South" (right down to the "porch swing") at this "romantic" Theater District "belle" where the palatable, "down-home" Southern cooking is "far surpassed" by the "Louisiana" "bordello-chic" decor; "friendly", languid service is part of the show.

J.G. Melon ◐⋑
| 20 | 12 | 16 | $23 |

1291 Third Ave. (74th St.), 212-744-0585
An Upper East Side "icon" of "old-school casual dining", this longtime pub is famed for some of the "best burgers and cottage fries" in town; it's "dingy" and "the staff can be surly", but that doesn't deter "prep-school" types from "lining up" for those "juicy, tasty" patties and a brew.

Jing Fong
| 18 | 13 | 11 | $20 |

20 Elizabeth St. (bet. Bayard & Canal Sts.), 212-964-5256
The "rock-steady dim sum" at this popular Chinatown vet is so "cheap", you may not even mind the service from "Indy 500"–worthy "cart-pushers"; though its "grand ballroom–size" space had a "recent face-lift", faultfinders feel "it still looks the same."

Joe Allen ◗

326 W. 46th St. (bet. 8th & 9th Aves.), 212-581-6464;
www.joeallenrestaurant.com

This "archetypal" Theater District "pre- or post"-play "mainstay" is "wonderful" for dining on simple, straightforward "pub-type" fare while "looking out for Broadway stars" at the next table; "fast-paced" service and a famous collection of "flop" show posters complete the scene; N.B. a new upstairs bar offers sandwiches and other light bites.

Joe's Ginger ⊟

113 Mott St. (bet. Canal & Hester Sts.), 212-966-6613
25 Pell St. (Doyers St.), 212-285-0333

Joe's Shanghai

9 Pell St. (bet. Bowery & Mott St.), 212-233-8888 ◗ ⊟
24 W. 56th St. (bet. 5th & 6th Aves.), 212-333-3868
136-21 37th Ave. (bet. Main & Union Sts.), Queens, 718-539-3838 ⊟

"Bring on the soup dumplings" cheer the legion fans of this "authentic, excellent Shanghai" chain and its signature soup-filled buns; service can be "grumpy" and the digs "dumpy", but just close your eyes and savor "lots of food for little money."

Joe's Pizza

7 Carmine St. (bet. Bleecker St. & 6th Ave.), 212-255-3946;
www.famousjoespizza.com ◗
137 Seventh Ave. (bet. Carroll St. & Garfield Pl.), Brooklyn, 718-398-9198

"True NY pizza" is the deal at these super-"cheap" "joints" slicing "thin, crispy-crust" pies with the "perfect ratio of sauce and cheese"; "what-decor?" interiors and "busy, limited" service are a small price to pay for "sublime slices" that are a "late-night-out must."

Joe's Place ◗

1841 Westchester Ave. (Thieriot Ave.), Bronx, 718-918-2947

The "Regency of the Bronx", this spacious, white-tablecloth Spaniard caters to the borough's "power brokers" with Latin-inflected surf 'n' turf dishes; pluses are frequent live music in the lounge, modest prices and hosts "who make you feel like you're dining in their home."

John's of 12th Street ⊟

302 E. 12th St. (2nd Ave.), 212-475-9531

Bathed in "old-school charm" and "red sauce", this East Village Italian "straight out of an old movie" set "still holds up" for "basic" edibles and service; sure, it's "cramped and dingy" by day, but at night its "candles and cozy corners" appeal to "romance"-minded types.

John's Pizzeria ◗

278 Bleecker St. (bet. 6th & 7th Aves.), 212-243-1680 ⊟
408 E. 64th St. (bet. 1st & York Aves.), 212-935-2895
260 W. 44th St. (bet. B'way & 8th Ave.), 212-391-7560

"Pizza the way God intended" comes out of the "huge brick oven" at this "tried-and-true" Village pie parlor and its offshoots; sure, "lines can be long", and "competitors" arguably offer "better service", but to the "crispy-crust" faithful it's "the best, bar none"; P.S. "no slices!"

JoJo

160 E. 64th St. (bet. Lexington & 3rd Aves.), 212-223-5656;
www.jean-georges.com

"Go, go" urge acolytes of Jean-Georges Vongerichten's "culinary wizardry" at this East Side modern French bistro providing "sumptuous" meals on two floors of a "gorgeously appointed townhouse" with servers who "really know their stuff"; yes, it's "expensive", but the $20 prix fixe lunch is a "bargain."

Jolie
▽ 21 | 20 | 21 | $38

320 Atlantic Ave. (bet. Hoyt & Smith Sts.), Brooklyn, 718-488-0777;
www.jolierestaurant.com
"*C'est très jolie*" is the word on this Boerum Hill newcomer specializing
in "lovingly prepared" "hearty" French fare; service is "efficient and
friendly" and the garden's a "gem", so never mind the few who yawn
it's "not very original."

Josephina ◗
19 | 16 | 18 | $43

1900 Broadway (bet. 63rd & 64th Sts.), 212-799-1000;
www.josephinanyc.com
"On target for pre-opera" dining, this American-Eclectic "across from
Lincoln Center" delivers "bright, fresh" eats at "affordable prices";
perhaps it won't "knock your socks off", but the decor is "pleasant"
and staffers "handle the theater crowd like pros."

Josephs Citarella ☒
23 | 22 | 20 | $62

1240 Sixth Ave. (49th St.), 212-332-1515; www.josephscitarella.com
"Exceedingly fresh, delicious fish" "imaginatively" prepared lures
seafood-lovers to this bi-level "white-tablecloth" outpost of the
"landmark" grocer, which provides an island of "calm amid the
chaos of Rock Center"; "caring" service helps take the bite out
of "expensive" tabs.

Joseph's Restaurant ☒
▽ 21 | 13 | 20 | $46

3 Hanover Sq. (Pearl St.), 212-747-1300; www.josephsdowntown.com
"Expense-account" types favor this Hanover Square "old-school
Italian" that's "easy to miss" but "worth seeking out" for "delicious"
standards; the formal service is "consistently good", even if the
"basement location" is "in need of a makeover."

Josie's
20 | 16 | 17 | $30

300 Amsterdam Ave. (74th St.), 212-769-1212 ◗
565 Third Ave. (37th St.), 212-490-1558
www.josiesnyc.com
These "yuppie-meets-hippie" Eclectics lend a "little California chic"
to the city's health food scene; "excellent prices", especially for the
"quality and portions", help make up for the "loud", "packed" settings
and service that can get "overwhelmed" at times.

Joya ⇗
23 | 19 | 19 | $21

215 Court St. (Warren St.), Brooklyn, 718-222-3484
The "delicious, inventive Thai" fare at this "crazy-popular" "scene"
livens up "an otherwise sedate part of Cobble Hill"; the "hip, young
environment", "wonderful back garden" and "amazing bang for the
buck" mean it's often "noisy" with "long waits" that are "no Joya."

Jubilee
21 | 15 | 19 | $45

347 E. 54th St. (bet. 1st & 2nd Aves.), 212-888-3569;
www.jubileeny.com
Though you "always have to mussel your way in" to this "cramped"
Sutton Place French bistro, the signature "wonderful" moules frites
reward the effort; add a "friendly", neighborly ambiance and "fair
prices" (for the locale), and you've got a party every night.

Jules ◗
20 | 20 | 17 | $35

65 St. Marks Pl. (bet. 1st & 2nd Aves.), 212-477-5560
"Live jazz is the kicker" at this East Village French "institution" that's
"still going strong" as a "lively" source for "tasty", "reasonably
priced" bistro classics, especially the "fab brunch"; habitués say
the "real"-deal Gallic setup feels "like being in France", right down to
the "surly service."

Julian's

| 18 | 17 | 17 | $35 |

802 Ninth Ave. (bet. 53rd & 54th Sts.), 212-262-4800

This "likable" Italian is a "Hell's Kitchen neighborhood fixture" that also makes a "cozy find" for Broadway theatergoers; perhaps it's "nothing special", but the food's "well prepared" and in warm weather it's "nice to sit outside and watch the people" along Ninth Avenue.

Junior's

| 17 | 9 | 14 | $21 |

Grand Central, lower level (42nd St. & Vanderbilt Ave.), 212-983-5257
386 Flatbush Ave. (DeKalb Ave.), Brooklyn, 718-852-5257 ◗
www.juniorscheesecake.com

"It's all about the cheesecake" at this recently renovated (but still old-school) Downtown Brooklyn "institution", though it also serves "classic greasy diner fare"; just keep in mind that the "lines are anything but junior"; N.B. there's a satellite location in Grand Central.

Kai

| 26 | 24 | 25 | $73 |

Ito En, 822 Madison Ave., 2nd fl. (bet. 68th & 69th Sts.), 212-988-7277; www.itoen.com

"The epitome of Zen", this expensive East Side "boutique Japanese" specializes in "authentic", "beautifully presented" kaiseki cuisine; the staff "treats you like an honored guest", which is another reason to "take someone you want to impress."

Kam Chueh ◗

| ▽ 25 | 10 | 18 | $26 |

40 Bowery (bet. Bayard & Canal Sts.), 212-791-6868

"Don't bother with the menu" – just "ask for the fresh-from-the-tank" fish at this "excellent Chinatown standby" staffed by a "helpful" crew; there's "no decor" to speak of and tight seating means you'll "get cozy" with your neighbor, but you can't do better for less.

Kang Suh ◗

| ▽ 20 | 12 | 16 | $32 |

1250 Broadway (32nd St.), 212-564-6845

"Above-average Korean BBQ" is "loads of fun" at this 24-hour Garment District eatery that is long on ingredients, but short on decor and service; traditionalists bemoan the fact that "the charcoal grills have been replaced by gas."

Kapadokya

| ▽ 20 | 16 | 17 | $26 |

142 Montague St., 2nd fl. (bet. Clinton & Henry Sts.), Brooklyn, 718-875-2211

"Reasonably priced Turkish" delights (especially "fresh kebabs") are the draw at this "upstairs" Brooklyn Heights "change of pace" that "overlooks bustling Montague Street"; some say the weekend belly dancers are "good, clean fun", but to others they're just "annoying."

Katsu-Hama

| 22 | 11 | 15 | $25 |

11 E. 47th St. (bet. 5th & Madison Aves.), 212-758-5909; www.katsuhama.com

Fans of the "juicy, tender" cutlets fried at this Midtowner know "there's more to Japanese cuisine than sushi"; true, the "decor isn't the greatest", but most don't mind because it feels "like stepping into Tokyo" for a "simple" "bargain" meal.

Katz's Delicatessen

| 23 | 9 | 12 | $20 |

205 E. Houston St. (Ludlow St.), 212-254-2246; www.katzdeli.com

A Lower East Side "icon" and a "NY must", this "quintessential deli"–cum–"Lipitor heaven" has been dispensing "unparalleled" corned beef and pastrami since 1888; "ragged" decor, "brusque" service, "tourist-trap" tendencies and "Hollywood prices" be damned – one bite of a signature "mile-high sandwich" and "you'll know how Sally felt."

Keens Steakhouse

| 23 | 22 | 21 | $58 |

72 W. 36th St. (bet. 5th & 6th Aves.), 212-947-3636; www.keenssteakhouse.com

"A true guy's place", this "classic steakhouse" near Madison Square Garden is known for its "impeccable" meat (including the "must-have" mutton chop), 200-plus "single-malt collection" and "old-world charm" abetted by a zillion antique "clay pipes hanging from the ceiling"; "class-act" service helps justify the tabs, while the memorabilia-filled rooms upstairs are perfect for private parties.

Kelley & Ping

| 17 | 15 | 15 | $25 |

127 Greene St. (Prince St.), 212-228-1212
340 Third Ave. (25th St.), 212-871-7000
www.kelleyandping.com

To "fuel your SoHo shopping expedition", stop by this Pan-Asian noodle shop that serves its "cheap", "quick", "flavorful" fare "cafeteria-style" at lunch and full-service at dinner; the recently opened Gramercy branch is deemed "a great addition" to the area.

Khyber Grill

| ∇ 21 | 18 | 21 | $34 |

230 E. 58th St. (bet. 2nd & 3rd Aves.), 212-339-0050; www.khybergrill.com

Formerly a Bukhara Grill outpost, this "chic" Midtown Indian has a new menu and wine list, but it continues to offer "fresh", "well-seasoned" fare and "crisp" service; those who gripe that it's "pricey" for the genre should try the $13.95 lunch buffet.

Killmeyer's Old Bavaria Inn

| ∇ 18 | 18 | 17 | $27 |

4254 Arthur Kill Rd. (Sharrotts Rd.), Staten Island, 718-984-1202;
www.killmeyers.com

The "beer flows like water and the bratwursts are huge" at this "pub"-like Staten Islander that's a little "like a German Epcot", right down to the "costumes" and live "oompah" music in summer; regulars say it's best "when the biergarten is open."

Kings' Carriage House

| 20 | 26 | 22 | $54 |

251 E. 82nd St. (bet. 2nd & 3rd Aves.), 212-734-5490;
www.kingscarriagehouse.com

Set in an "enchanting little carriage house", this Upper East Side Continental makes the "perfect hideaway" for "ladies who lunch" (by day) and those "in love" (by "candlelit" evening); "impeccable" service completes the "special-treat" experience, and though you pay for it, "bargain"-seekers tout the $18.95 prix fixe lunch.

Kin Khao

| 21 | 18 | 18 | $35 |

171 Spring St. (bet. Thompson St. & W. B'way), 212-966-3939;
www.kinkhao.com

SoHo shoppers and "pretty people" mix at this "down-to-earth" Thai where the "flavorful" dishes are surprisingly well priced; as for the "packed" setting, it strikes some as "romantic" but others say it's "too dark to see."

Kitchen & Cocktails ◐

| – | – | – | M |

199 Orchard St. (bet. Houston & Stanton Sts.), 212-420-1112;
www.kitchenandcocktailsny.com

One part kitchen, two parts cocktails, this Orchard Street newcomer proffers creative drinks and gussied-up pub grub at moderate tabs; during warmer months, French doors open to the street adding to its welcoming feel, while a downstairs adjunct offers more private dining.

Kitchen 22 ⊠

| 21 | 18 | 19 | $36 |

36 E. 22nd St. (bet. B'way & Park Ave. S.), 212-228-4399

(continued)

(continued)

Kitchen 82

461 Columbus Ave. (82nd St.), 212-875-1619
www.charliepalmer.com

"Charlie Palmer's best" for the "budget" set is available at this dinner-only New American duo where you get "three fabulous courses" for "only $25" (and it now offers à la carte dishes too); its "utilitarian" but "hip" space can get "jam-packed", so "come early."

Kitchen Club   ▽ 23 | 19 | 23 | $46

30 Prince St. (Mott St.), 212-274-0025; www.thekitchenclub.com

A "haven in a tumultuous city", this NoLita French-Japanese enjoys a "very loyal" following for its "delightful" "eclectic" fare "served by people who care" in "warm" quarters; "everyone's greeted by" the "unique" owner's dog, Chibi, for whom the "great little" adjacent sake bar is named.

Kitchenette   20 | 14 | 16 | $21

1272 Amsterdam Ave. (bet. 122nd & 123rd Sts.), 212-531-7600
80 W. Broadway (Warren St.), 212-267-6740

"Dee-lish" "down-home cookin'" comes in "gingham"-"kitsch" quarters at this popular Uptown-Downtown Southern duo; "waits can be long" for its specialty "artery-clogging country brunch", but once inside service is "friendly and fast" and tabs "cheap."

KITTICHAI   23 | 27 | 20 | $57

60 Thompson Hotel, 60 Thompson St. (bet. Broome & Spring Sts.),
212-219-2000; www.kittichairestaurant.com

"Eye candy" abounds ("patrons, staff, decor") at this "sexy" Rockwell-designed Thai in SoHo's "swanky" 60 Thompson Hotel; fortunately the "feast for the senses" extends to the "exquisite" "modern" cuisine and "incredible cocktails", though given all the "distractions" it's no wonder service can be "absentminded."

Klong ●   ▽ 21 | 21 | 19 | $22

7 St. Marks Pl. (bet. 2nd & 3rd Aves.), 212-505-9955; www.klongnyc.com

Its name means 'canal' in Thai, hence the "water theme" of this new "industrial-chic" Siamese "in the midst of the St. Marks" madness; "savory" eats served by a "pleasant" staff include both traditional and Westernized dishes, all at enticingly "cheap" prices.

Knickerbocker Bar & Grill ●   20 | 17 | 20 | $44

33 University Pl. (bet. 8th & 9th Sts.), 212-228-8490;
www.knickerbockerbarandgrill.com

"Old-school is still cool" at this "reliable Villager" where "tasty steaks" and other hearty New American dishes come with a side of "great live jazz" on weekends; "friendly" service adds to the "homey" (if slightly "shopworn") ambiance, though too bad it's so "crowded and noisy."

Kodama ●   18 | 10 | 18 | $29

301 W. 45th St. (bet. 8th & 9th Aves.), 212-582-8065

Maybe it's "not a destination", but this "reliable" Hell's Kitchen Japanese is just right for a "quick dinner before the theater" thanks to its "decent" sushi and noodle dishes served at a "fast and furious" pace; the "factorylike" decor is par for the course.

Koi   ▽ 25 | 17 | 21 | $37

175 Second Ave. (11th St.), 212-777-5266; www.koisushinyc.com

"Sushi-lovers rejoice" – chefs from the late, lamented Iso are slicing and rolling at this East Village successor, where diners "don't need a loan" to enjoy "wonderful fresh fish"; the "owners greet you like old friends", bringing warmth to the "crowded", "too-brightly-lit" room.

Koi
▽ 24 23 18 $61

Bryant Park Hotel, 40 W. 40th St. (bet. 5th & 6th Aves.), 212-921-3330; www.koirestaurant.com

A spin-off of the LA original, this pricey Asian fusion newcomer in the Bryant Park Hotel is "very sexy" – both the eye-poppingly "trendy" decor and the "hot" "young" crowd – and early visitors say its "innovative" food lives up to the "scene"; "kinks" still to be worked out include "shaky" service.

Komegashi
▽ 21 22 18 $50

928 Broadway (bet. 21st & 22nd Sts.), 212-475-3000; www.komegashi.com

"Japanese ingredients prepared in a French manner" is the concept at this "truly innovative" Flatiron newcomer whose "too-cool" space includes cushy booths and high ceilings; "not-inexpensive" prices are justified by "friendly pro" service, if not by the "tiny portions."

Korea Palace ⊠
18 13 17 $33

127 E. 54th St. (bet. Lexington & Park Aves.), 212-832-2350; www.koreapalace.com

"Reliably good Korean" cuisine (plus some "Japanese options") is the output of this "solid", moderately priced Midtown BBQ specialist; it boasts a "professional, English-speaking staff" – though it always "helps to speak Korean" – so never mind if the decor's less than royal.

Kori ⊠
▽ 21 18 21 $31

253 Church St. (bet. Franklin & Leonard Sts.), 212-334-4598

For "high-end Korean" in "low-key" environs, TriBeCa locals tout this "neighborhood favorite"; the "vibrant" cuisine and "creative cocktails" have a fitting backdrop in the modern, "well-decorated" space, and "excellent-value" prices round out the endorsement.

Ko Sushi
19 14 18 $29

1329 Second Ave. (70th St.), 212-439-1678
1619 York Ave. (85th St.), 212-772-8838
www.newkosushi.com

"Quality sushi" that "won't break the bank" brings Upper Eastsiders back to this "dependable" Japanese duo; considered "a step above the ordinary" joints, it boasts "pleasant feng shui" and "friendly" service, but it's probably not worth "going out of your way."

Kuma Inn ●◐⊄
▽ 21 13 19 $36

113 Ludlow St., 2nd fl. (bet. Delancey & Rivington Sts.), 212-353-8866; www.kumainn.com

"Thaipino? Filithai?" ask diners unsure of how to peg this "romantic" Lower East Side Thai-Filipino "hidden" in a "tiny, dark", "second-floor" space; "mouthwatering" tapas at "light prices", "great sakes" and "friendly, efficient" service mean "you can't go wrong" here.

Kum Gang San ●
21 16 17 $30

49 W. 32nd St. (bet. B'way & 5th Ave.), 212-967-0909
138-28 Northern Blvd. (bet. Bowne & Union Sts.), Queens, 718-461-0909

"For a little bit of Seoul", check out these 24/7 Koreans where the "memorable" BBQ and other "spicy, flavorful" dishes are delivered by a "harried yet efficient" gang; it's "great" "fun for groups" and 3 AM hunger attacks.

Kuruma Zushi ⊠
▽ 27 16 23 $111

7 E. 47th St., 2nd fl. (bet. 5th & Madison Aves.), 212-317-2802

"If you can find it" (without a sign around) "there's no fresher" fish than at this Midtown mezzanine Japanese with "H&R Block"–style decor but "incredible" fare that's "no neophyte's sushi"; sure, it's "super-expensive", but just remember, it's "a bargain compared to Masa."

Kyma ◑
18 | 15 | 17 | $40

300 W. 46th St. (8th Ave.), 212-957-8830

"Solid Greek fare" (including good grilled fish) and convenience for "pre-theater dining" earns this "peaceful" Midtown Hellenic a faithful following; "quick", curtain time–sensitive service means the "nothing-to-write-home-about" decor is beside the point.

La Baraka
21 | 17 | 23 | $40

255-09 Northern Blvd. (Little Neck Pkwy.), Queens, 718-428-1461; www.labarakarest.com

"Enjoy a kiss-kiss from owner Lucette" at this "charming" Little Neck French where the "old-fashioned, hearty" classics are matched with "welcoming, attentive" service; most appreciate the "warm" atmosphere, even if the decor might use some "redoing."

La Belle Vie ◑
17 | 17 | 17 | $34

184 Eighth Ave. (bet. 19th & 20th Sts.), 212-929-4320; www.chelseadining.com

A far cry from its "sceney" Chelsea neighbors, this "unassuming" French bistro suits "locals" who favor its "modest" "comfort" classics and "enjoyable outdoor seating"; "pleasant" and affordable as it is, many say ultimately "it's nothing to write home about."

La Bergamote ⇗
26 | 13 | 14 | $13

169 Ninth Ave. (20th St.), 212-627-9010

"Excepting the City of Lights", "some of the best pastries anywhere" come from this "authentic" French bakery/cafe in Chelsea where "rich", "pure ingredients" result in "heavenly" offerings; so-so service strikes the only sour note.

La Boîte en Bois
20 | 16 | 20 | $48

75 W. 68th St. (bet. Columbus Ave. & CPW), 212-874-2705

An "efficient pre-theater machine" near Lincoln Center, this tiny "rustic" French standby has long been putting out "well-prepared" classics that, if you go for the $32 prix fixe, are also a "bargain"; as to the space, however, one diner's "intimate" and "cozy" is another's "crowded" and "claustrophobic."

La Bonne Soupe ◑
18 | 14 | 16 | $28

48 W. 55th St. (bet. 5th & 6th Aves.), 212-586-7650; www.labonnesoupe.com

As the name would suggest, "incredible soups" headline the menu of "reliable" French bistro standards at this Midtown "chestnut"; "excellent prices", a "low-key" vibe and "friendly" service mean its "somewhat cramped" quarters are easily overlooked.

La Bottega ◑
18 | 20 | 13 | $38

Maritime Hotel, 88 Ninth Ave. (17th St.), 212-243-8400; www.themaritimehotel.com

"It's all about the scene" at this "trendy" Italian in Chelsea's Maritime Hotel, where the pizzas are a "sure bet" but hard to notice given the "distractingly hot" crowd; though the "model" servers look good in the "faux-trattoria" interior or on the "unbeatable" outdoor patio, they leave a lot to be desired when you're hungry.

L'Absinthe
22 | 23 | 20 | $60

227 E. 67th St. (bet. 2nd & 3rd Aves.), 212-794-4950

"One almost expects Toulouse-Lautrec" to walk through the door at this "French-as-they-come" East Side brasserie with "savory" cooking, a "pro" staff and "lovely" "belle epoque" trappings; just "wear your Chanel to fit in" and be ready for "*l'attitude*", le "noise" and "*très cher*" tabs.

La Cantina

▽ 22 | 15 | 20 | $41

38 Eighth Ave. (Jane St.), 212-727-8787

You "order from the blackboard" at this West Village Italian where the "delicious" fare comes in "tiny" digs that "mercifully" remain "relatively undiscovered" (though there are "waits on weekends"); most find the "hands-on" chef-owner-host "charming", if "a little overzealous."

La Cantina Toscana

▽ 23 | 13 | 21 | $46

1109 First Ave. (bet. 60th & 61st Sts.), 212-754-5454

Say "taxi, take me to Firenze" and you may end up at this East Side "rare outpost of actual Tuscan" fare specializing in "impeccably prepared", "hard-to-find game" dishes and "impressive wines"; a "homey" feel and "sweet" service round out the "surprisingly wonderful" experience.

Lady Mendl's

▽ 21 | 27 | 24 | $40

Inn at Irving Pl., 56 Irving Pl. (bet. 17th & 18th Sts.), 212-533-4466; www.innatirving.com

Bring your "best manners" to this "ladylike" "white-glove" Gramercy tearoom, a "quiet haven" where "Martha" look-alikes indulge in a "mélange" of brews and "elegant" bites in a "period" setting; but take a "rich aunt" to pick up the bill.

La Esquina ●

– | – | – | M

106 Kenmare St. (Lafayette St.), 646-613-7100

Aiming to be all things to all comers, this midpriced NoLita Mexican packs three separate venues into one *pequeño* corner: on street level sits a brightly lit taco stand and an adjacent cozy cantina, but the place to be is the grottolike, hipster-heavy downstairs restaurant/lounge.

La Flor Bakery & Cafe ∄

▽ 24 | 16 | 17 | $25

53-02 Roosevelt Ave. (53rd St.), Queens, 718-426-8023

Serving "bargain" Mexican-Eclectic fare, this "vibrant neighborhood place" is deemed "worth the ride on the 7 train" for its "decadent desserts" alone; yes, it's "tiny, tiny, tiny", and seems "consistently understaffed", but satisfied surveyors say it's simpatico.

La Focaccia

22 | 19 | 19 | $35

51 Bank St. (W. 4th St.), 212-675-3754

Known for its "addictive" "namesake bread" from the "wood-burning oven", this "pretty" West Village Italian also boasts "pleasant" service and "great values"; no wonder Match.com types call it "a perfect first-date spot."

La Giara

20 | 15 | 18 | $35

501 Third Ave. (bet. 33rd & 34th Sts.), 212-726-9855; www.lagiara.com

A "capable Italian" "tucked amid the joints" of Murray Hill, this "neighborhood place" offers a few "twists on the classics", "great service" and an alluring $19.95 prix fixe dinner "that includes wine"; it can get "a bit loud", but in "good weather" there's "outdoor seating."

La Gioconda

22 | 15 | 19 | $39

226 E. 53rd St. (bet. 2nd & 3rd Aves.), 212-371-3536; www.lagiocondany.com

"High-quality", "homestyle" Italian is the draw at this "cozy, quiet" Midtowner "tucked away" in an "unassuming brownstone" space so "tiny", there "isn't enough room to change your mind"; still, "delightful service" ensures that repasts here feel "like a long, warm embrace."

La Goulue ●

20 | 20 | 18 | $57

746 Madison Ave. (bet. 64th & 65th Sts.), 212-988-8169

For years now "*le tout* Mad Ave" (i.e. "the air-kiss crowd") have flocked to this "pricey" East Side French bistro to nab outside tables and "watch NYC stride past"; however, you don't get to be an "institution" like this without "decent" food and "fantastic, authentic" decor.

LA GRENOUILLE ⊠

27 | 27 | 27 | $88

3 E. 52nd St. (bet. 5th & Madison Aves.), 212-752-1495; www.la-grenouille.com

"Regal, elegant and timeless", this East Side French classic is one of the city's "last grande dames", supplying "superb" cuisine in "beautiful" quarters with "sublime fresh flower displays"; "memorable wines", "gracious" black-tie service and the chance to experience "a treasured remnant of old NY" conspire to make the $87 prix fixe dinner feel like a bargain; N.B. there's an upstairs private party space.

La Grolla

21 | 14 | 19 | $41

413 Amsterdam Ave. (bet. 79th & 80th Sts.), 212-496-0890

Specializing in cooking from Val d'Aosta ("the very northern section of Italy"), this "Upper West Side hideaway" offers "delicious", slightly "different" dishes in "grown-up, quiet" (if "cramped") environs; better still, "a nicer staff can't be found" and the prices are "reasonable for what you get."

Lake Club

▽ 16 | 23 | 18 | $44

1150 Clove Rd. (Victory Blvd.), Staten Island, 718-442-3600; www.lake-club.com

It's under new ownership, but "location, location, location" remains the draw at this Staten Island Italian seafooder, whose "picturesque" lakeside views "make everything taste better"; despite "so-so" dining for "prices this high", the "pretty" site is "popular with parties."

La Lanterna di Vittorio ●

▽ 21 | 22 | 20 | $24

129 MacDougal St. (bet. W. 3rd & W. 4th Sts.), 212-529-5945

This "charming refuge from the rush of modern life" near Washington Square has endured for nearly 30 years on the power of its "classic" "homey Italian desserts and great coffee"; "a little romantic, a little beatnik", it's ideal for "NYers (or tourists) in love."

L'Allegria ●

18 | 14 | 18 | $34

623 Ninth Ave. (44th St.), 212-265-6777; www.lallegriarestaurant.com

As a Theater District "fallback" that's "close to the shows", this "casual" Italian supplies "acceptable staples" and a "friendly" vibe; though the "tight", "slapdash interior" is a drawback, at least it "won't blow your budget."

La Locanda dei Vini

22 | 15 | 21 | $43

737 Ninth Ave. (bet. 49th & 50th Sts.), 212-258-2900

Still something of an "undiscovered treasure", this Hell's Kitchen Italian "looks like a dive", but those in-the-know call it a "dependable" standby for "quality" "real-deal" food and "friendly" service; best of all, it's a "convenient" "pre-theater" choice.

La Lunchonette

22 | 15 | 19 | $39

130 10th Ave. (18th St.), 212-675-0342

Perfect post–"gallery-hopping", this veteran Chelsea French bistro turns out "honest" fare (including possibly the "best cassoulet in town") served by a staff bent on "making you happy"; given its "unexpectedly good" repasts, who cares if the decor's a bit "strange"?

La Mangeoire

19 | 19 | 20 | $47

1008 Second Ave. (bet. 53rd & 54th Sts.), 212-759-7086

Like a walk in the "French countryside", this East Side bistro has been doling out "solid fare" and "friendly" service for 30 years; factor in "excellent brunches" and "value" pricing and it's "easy to see why" it stays a "favorite."

Lamarca ⌧
▽ | 20 | 9 | 16 | $19

161 E. 22nd St. (3rd Ave.), 212-674-6363
"Hearty, homemade pastas" priced for "value" hit the marca at this "small", "no-nonsense" Gramercy Italian with an "easy" take-out area; it's "reliable" enough to excuse the "bland decor", though many find it odd that "they take weekends off."

La Masseria ●
▽ | 22 | 21 | 21 | $49

235 W. 48th St. (bet. B'way & 8th Ave.), 212-582-2111
In an area rife with ristorantes, this "rustic" yearling stands out due to "better-than-average" Southern Italian fare, e.g. "delicious pasta" and "wonderful tiramisu"; the "helpful" service seals its rep as a "great addition to the Theater District" even if it is on the pricey side.

La Mediterranée
18 | 14 | 18 | $45

947 Second Ave. (bet. 50th & 51st Sts.), 212-755-4155;
www.lamediterraneeny.com
"Comfortable as a French chapeau", this East Midtown bistro is a fit with fans thanks to "consistent" fare served "without ostentation"; some say it's "past its prime", but its "mature" followers are content that "nothing's changed" here.

La Mela ●
19 | 10 | 17 | $34

167 Mulberry St. (bet. Broome & Grand Sts.), 212-431-9493;
www.lamelarestaurant.com
"Bring your appetite" and a "group" to this "rip-roaring" Little Italy "party" that's renowned for its $32 "no-menu" prix fixe offering family-style Italiana served "at a dizzying pace"; sure, it's "touristy", but it's "always entertaining."

La Mirabelle
21 | 17 | 22 | $45

102 W. 86th St. (bet. Amsterdam & Columbus Aves.), 212-496-0458
Your "maiden aunt" will find "no surprises" at this "classic" French Westsider, just a "quiet" repast of "old-fashioned" "melt-in-your-mouth food"; though the crowd and decor may be *un peu* "mature", it's "homey" enough to remain a "perennial."

Lan ●
▽ | 23 | 17 | 19 | $38

56 Third Ave. (bet. 10th & 11th Sts.), 212-254-1959; www.lan-nyc.com
Sushiphiles savor the "awesome" fish, but this East Village Japanese also satisfies those with a yen for "delicious" sukiyaki or shabu-shabu; no matter what your taste, the "no-attitude" service and "affordable" cost make it a "real find."

Land
22 | 17 | 18 | $26

450 Amsterdam Ave. (bet. 81st & 82nd Sts.), 212-501-8121;
www.landthaikitchen.com
"Authentic" Thai lands on the Upper West Side at this "ambitious" newcomer where the "food's amazing and so's the price" – even if the space approximates a "walk-in closet"; P.S. "if you can't get a seat, take it home."

L & B Spumoni Gardens
23 | 10 | 16 | $17

2725 86th St. (bet. 10th & 11th Sts.), Brooklyn, 718-449-6921;
www.spumonigardens.com
"Go for the squares" at this "legendary", "totally retro" Bensonhurst pizzeria/ice cream parlor that's famed for "fabulous" Sicilian slices and "can't-pass-up" spumoni; it's "cheap" and thus "always mobbed", with a bonus "summer staple" patio.

Landmarc ◐

23 | 21 | 23 | $47

179 W. Broadway (bet. Leonard & Worth Sts.), 212-343-3883;
www.landmarc-restaurant.com

A "hot ticket in TriBeCa", this "inviting" bi-level bistro features "splendid, nonfussy" French fare with "Italian flair" from chef-owner Marc Murphy; plan to "arrive early" since "they don't take reservations" and the "minimal" wine markups encourage lingering.

Landmark Tavern

– | – | – | I

626 11th Ave. (46th St.), 212-247-2562

Back after a hiatus, this circa-1868 pub in Way West Hell's Kitchen serves the likes of scotch eggs and soda bread on its inexpensive Irish-American menu; happily, its seen-it-all 19th-century decor remains intact, most notably its marvelous mahogany bar.

L'Annam ◐

18 | 12 | 16 | $21

393 Third Ave. (28th St.), 212-686-5168
121 University Pl. (13th St.), 212-420-1414

"Simplicity" sums up these "brusque" but "efficient" Vietnamese that churn out "generous" helpings of "tasty standards" at price tags tailored to "student budgets"; the "minimal" decor is "no thrill", but they'll deliver "by the time you put the phone down."

La Paella

20 | 18 | 16 | $33

214 E. Ninth St. (bet. 2nd & 3rd Aves.), 212-598-4321

Couples get "romantic" over "perfect" paella and "fuzzy" from "fantastic" sangria at this midpriced, "Gothically Spanish" East Villager; despite "slow" service and "dark", "tight" digs, the tapas are "tasty."

La Palapa ◐

20 | 17 | 18 | $33

359 Sixth Ave. (bet. Washington Pl. & W. 4th St.), 212-243-6870
77 St. Marks Pl. (bet. 1st & 2nd Aves.), 212-777-2537
www.lapalapa.com

You'll "never want to leave" these Nuevo Mexicanos that "surprise" with "flavorful" food and "snappy" margaritas (except perhaps to get away from the "ear-splitting" din); while "sizable portions" satisfy, some still wonder "should chorizo cost that much?"

La Petite Auberge

20 | 15 | 21 | $43

116 Lexington Ave. (bet. 27th & 28th Sts.), 212-689-5003

This longtime Gramercy bistro offers "well-done" "old-school" French fare and "*comme il faut*" service; the "tiny", "dated" room may be a "throwback to yesteryear", but stalwarts "hope it stays like that forever" – including the moderate prices.

La Pizza Fresca Ristorante

23 | 16 | 17 | $35

31 E. 20th St. (bet. B'way & Park Ave. S.), 212-598-0141;
www.lapizzafrescaristorante.com

"Authentic Neapolitan pizza" is the signature of this "upscale" Flatiron Italian, augmented by "delicious pasta"; servicewise, "you'd get it quicker if you hopped a plane", and pricewise, it's "not inexpensive."

La Ripaille ◐

▽ 19 | 17 | 20 | $45

605 Hudson St. (bet. Bethune & W. 12th Sts.), 212-255-4406

There are plenty of reasons why this Village bistro "survivor" has "been around forever": besides its "charming owner", there's the affordable, "on-target" cooking, "no-rush atmosphere" and country French setting.

La Rivista ◐⊠

19 | 16 | 19 | $42

313 W. 46th St. (bet. 8th & 9th Aves.), 212-245-1707; www.larivistanyc.com

Remarkably "laid-back" for the Theater District, this durable Italian still "gets you out" by showtime sated with "ample portions" of "hearty" eats; add "discount parking" and a "piano player after eight" and it's "not bad" at all.

La Taza de Oro ⊠≢
18 | 5 | 15 | $14

96 Eighth Ave. (bet. 14th & 15th Sts.), 212-243-9946
The "real deal" for "workingman's" grub, this Chelsea "hole-in-the-wall" holdout plies "gigantic", "bargain" helpings of "flavorful" Puerto Rican "soul food" and "great cafe con leche"; for a "no-nonsense", "no-frills" lunch counter, it's really impressive.

Lattanzi ●⊠
22 | 19 | 21 | $51

361 W. 46th St. (bet. 8th & 9th Aves.), 212-315-0980; www.lattanzinyc.com
"Not your usual red-sauce joint", this Restaurant Row Italian serves "surprisingly solid" fare, including "not-to-be-missed" Roman Jewish items like fried artichokes; more "low-key" after the "rush to make the curtain", it's a "repeater" even if it's a tad tabby.

Lavagna
24 | 18 | 21 | $39

545 E. Fifth St. (bet. Aves. A & B), 212-979-1005; www.lavagnanyc.com
This "intimate" East Villager proffers a "superb" Italian menu and a wine list "studded with hidden gems"; the "addicting" eats and "value" could be a "life-changing find" – except everybody's "already found it."

La Vela
18 | 15 | 18 | $34

373 Amsterdam Ave. (bet. 77th & 78th Sts.), 212-877-7818
Maybe it's "unrecognized" by non-locals, but Westsiders tout this "low-key" trattoria for *"molto bene"* Tuscan cooking that "won't break the bank"; sure, the genre is "predictable", but that's why it's a "safe bet."

La Villa Pizzeria
22 | 15 | 18 | $24

261 Fifth Ave. (bet. 1st St. & Garfield Pl.), Brooklyn, 718-499-9888
Key Food Shopping Ctr., 6610 Ave. U (bet. 66th & 67th Sts.), Brooklyn, 718-251-8030
Lindenwood Shopping Ctr., 82-07 153rd Ave. (bet. 82nd & 83rd Sts.), Queens, 718-641-8259
"Informal" types hype this "family-oriented" trio for their "outstanding" wood-oven pizza and other inexpensive Italian "staples" served in "generous" portions; the "generic mall" decor is no thrilla, but they're "always busy" nonetheless.

La Vineria
∇ 21 | 15 | 20 | $41

19 W. 55th St. (bet. 5th & 6th Aves.), 212-247-3400;
www.lavineriarestaurant.com
"In a sea of fancy-schmancy" joints, this "rough-hewn" Midtown cucina's "mouthwatering" Italian fare and "charming" service are a welcome change of pace; the "extensive wine" selection is a bonus.

LE BERNARDIN ⊠
28 | 27 | 28 | $100

155 W. 51st St. (bet. 6th & 7th Aves.), 212-554-1515; www.le-bernardin.com
"Still nonpareil", Maguy LeCoze's "world-class" Midtown French is "hallowed" ground for "sophisticated" dining and an "unequaled" practitioner of the "high art of seafood subtlety"; chef Eric Ripert's "exquisite" fare (rated No. 1 in this *Survey*) arrives in "spacious", "understated" environs where the "classical" service is as "flawless" as "clockwork"; granted, prices may be steep, but it's worth a "home equity loan" for a "profound event" that "lingers in the memory", and the $49 lunch conveys the same experience for far less.

Le Bilboquet
20 | 15 | 15 | $50

25 E. 63rd St. (bet. Madison & Park Aves.), 212-751-3036
"French accents" come in handy at this air-kissing East Side bistro, a *"très petit"* "piece of Paris" serving "underrated" food that overcomes

the "indifferent service" and "tight" seating; it's a Euro "hot spot" where the "expat élan" is always *amusant*.

Le Boeuf à la Mode
20 19 21 $51

539 E. 81st St. (bet. East End & York Aves.), 212-249-1473
"Nouvelle is an unknown word" at this Yorkville "fixture", an "old-style" French bistro where "grown-ups" relax over "rock-solid" dishes and "genteel service"; though hardly à la mode, its "sedate" ways have stood the "test of time."

Le Charlot ●
▽ 19 15 15 $50

19 E. 69th St. (bet. Madison & Park Aves.), 212-794-1628
Known as a "hideaway" for "chic" East Side Euros, this "pocket-size" French bistro furnishes "passable food", "buzzy" atmospherics and a new sidewalk cafe; but "they cater to regulars", so "major attitude" is part of the package.

L'Ecole ☒
24 20 23 $43

French Culinary Institute, 462 Broadway (Grand St.), 212-219-3300; www.frenchculinary.com
They've "done their homework" at the French Culinary Institute's SoHo showcase for "burgeoning chefs", where the prix fixes are "unbeatable" given the "top-notch" cooking; "eager-to-please" service makes it a "best bet" to stay at the "head of the class."

Le Colonial
21 23 19 $50

149 E. 57th St. (bet. Lexington & 3rd Aves.), 212-752-0808
Like a trip to "old Saigon", this East Side Franco-Vietnamese purveys "terrific" food matched with "exotic elegance" out of a "Graham Greene novel"; for a few the "romance" is "a little tired", but insiders report that the "Indochina feel" is "better" in the upstairs lounge.

Le Gamin
20 17 14 $22

536 E. Fifth St. (bet. Aves. A & B), 212-254-8409 ●
258 W. 15th St. (bet. 7th & 8th Aves.), 212-929-3270 ●
556 Vanderbilt Ave. (Dean St.), Brooklyn, 718-789-5171
www.legamin.com
These "saucy little Frenchies" are an "asset" for "light bistro staples" and café au lait served in "hubcap"-size cups; they're "comfortable" for a "time out", but plan on a long one given the "frazzled" service.

Le Gigot
25 19 23 $50

18 Cornelia St. (bet. Bleecker & W. 4th Sts.), 212-627-3737
"Oh-so-French", this "delicious" Village bistro radiates "charm plus" as it works "culinary magic"; it's an "inviting rendezvous" that's likely to "melt your date", though some complain their style is "cramped" by the *petite* quarters.

Le Jardin Bistro
21 18 19 $40

25 Cleveland Pl. (bet. Kenmare & Spring Sts.), 212-343-9599; www.lejardinbistro.com
The "gorgeous" garden with "trellises of real grapes" at this "well-priced" NoLita French bistro is a great rendezvous for a "summer romance"; given the "authentic" food and "unpretentious" style, it's an "easy" option for any season.

Le Madeleine
20 19 19 $44

403 W. 43rd St. (bet. 9th & 10th Aves.), 212-246-2993; www.lemadeleine.com
This "long-running" Hell's Kitchen French bistro draws theatergoers hungry for "well-prepared country classics"; despite a "hectic", "sardine"-like setup, moderate prices and "competent" staffers "get you to the show on time" still solvent.

Le Marais

20 | 14 | 16 | $50

150 W. 46th St. (bet. 6th & 7th Aves.), 212-869-0900
"Useful" before a show, this kosher French steakhouse is a Theater District "standby" for "darn good" meats and frites; critics kvetch about the "charmless" service and "crowded" room, but it's a great opportunity to "observe and splurge at the same time."

Le Monde ●

17 | 18 | 14 | $30

2885 Broadway (bet. 112th & 113th Sts.), 212-531-3939; www.lemondenyc.com
Packed with "college" types scarfing "respectable" French food, this Morningside Heights brasserie not only offers "roomy" digs but "outside tables" as well; the service may be "flaky" and some find it "uninspired", but in a dining "wasteland", it "does the job."

Lemongrass Grill

17 | 13 | 16 | $21

37 Barrow St. (7th Ave. S.), 212-242-0606
2534 Broadway (bet. 94th & 95th Sts.), 212-666-0888
9 E. 13th St. (bet. 5th Ave. & University Pl.), 646-486-7313 ●
138 E. 34th St. (bet. Lexington & 3rd Aves.), 212-213-3317
84 William St. (Maiden Ln.), 212-809-8038
156 Court St. (bet. Dean & Pacific Sts.), Brooklyn, 718-522-9728
61A Seventh Ave. (bet. Berkeley & Lincoln Pls.), Brooklyn, 718-399-7100
www.lemongrassgrill.com
"If you're not fussy", this "workhorse" chain churns out "middle-of-the-road" Thai at "fair prices" with "fast-food" efficiency; still, many forsake the "spartan" setups for "super-speedy" delivery.

Lenox Room

19 | 21 | 20 | $50

1278 Third Ave. (bet. 73rd & 74th Sts.), 212-772-0404; www.lenoxroom.com
"Dapper" host Tony Fortuna "makes the rounds" at this East Side New American, a "clubby" enclave where well-heeled locals settle in for "fine food" and "conversation" in "conservative" digs; it also has an "active" side when "Biff and Buffy do martinis" in the "upscale bar."

Lentini ●

▽ 20 | 16 | 20 | $56

1562 Second Ave. (81st St.), 212-628-3131; www.lentinirestaurant.com
"Not your typical pasta mill", this Upper Eastsider is a "find" for "well-prepared Italian" dishes purveyed in "quiet" environs with "plenty of elbow room"; to admirers it's a "mystery" why it's so "little known", though "high" prices may be a clue.

Lento's

19 | 10 | 16 | $24

7003 Third Ave. (Ovington Ave.), Brooklyn, 718-745-9197 ⊟
289-291 New Dorp Ln. (Richmond Rd.), Staten Island, 718-980-7709;
www.lentossi.com
31 Victory Blvd. (Bay St.), Staten Island, 718-447-2744 ⊟
Maybe it's just an "unrenovated tavern", but this "age-old" Bay Ridge Italian is renowned for "ultrathin", "oh-so-crispy" pizza; Staten Island now has twin spin-offs, but the original is the "better choice" – so long as you "don't look around" too much.

L'Entrecote ⊠

20 | 15 | 23 | $45

1057 First Ave. (bet. 57th & 58th Sts.), 212-755-0080
"If you can't go to Paris", this "pocket-size" Sutton Place bistro provides "agreeable" traditional Gallic steaks and the "warmest welcome this side of the Seine"; "old-school" down to its *plus que* "close" quarters, it "never changes – but who cares?"

Le Pain Quotidien

20 | 16 | 14 | $20

ABC Carpet & Home, 38 E. 19th St. (bet. B'way & Park Ave. S.), 212-673-7900
(continued)

(continued)

Le Pain Quotidien

252 E. 77th St. (bet. 2nd & 3rd Aves.), 212-249-8600
10 Fifth Ave. (8th St.), 212-253-2324
1336 First Ave. (bet. 71st & 72nd Sts.), 212-717-4800
100 Grand St. (bet. Greene & Mercer Sts.), 212-625-9009
833 Lexington Ave. (bet. 63rd & 64th Sts.), 212-755-5810
1131 Madison Ave. (bet. 84th & 85th Sts.), 212-327-4900
922 Seventh Ave. (58th St.), 212-757-0775
50 W. 72nd St. (bet. Columbus Ave. & CPW), 212-712-9700
www.painquotidien.com

"Tip-top organic goodies" "hit the spot" at these Belgian bakery/cafes, a "Euro-ish farmhouse" franchise sporting "signature communal tables"; "slapdash service" can be a pain, but they're a "pleasant change" from the usual ("Starbucks who?").

Le Perigord

25 | 21 | 25 | $72

405 E. 52nd St. (bet. FDR Dr. & 1st Ave.), 212-755-6244; www.leperigord.com

One of the last French "bastions of refinement", this Sutton Place "grande dame" provides "excellent" cuisine and a "courtly staff" led by owner Georges Briguet; surveyors report that the comfortable, baroque setting exudes a combination of "warmth" and "old money" not easily found nowadays.

Le Pescadou ◗

▽ 18 | 15 | 19 | $46

18 King St. (6th Ave.), 212-924-3434

To "shut out the city", visit this SoHo French seafooder that's a "mainstay" for its "worthy" bouillabaisse alone; the "outgoing" owner makes it a "club for locals", so even if some say the food's "nothing special", it's "charming" all the same.

Le Refuge

21 | 20 | 21 | $53

166 E. 82nd St. (bet. Lexington & 3rd Aves.), 212-861-4505;
www.lerefugeinn.com

"Aptly named", this "quiet" bistro nestled in an East Side townhouse offers "just the right dose of class" with its "rustic antique" decor, "sophisticated" French fare and "polished service"; for most, it's a "best-known secret" where "reliable" quality comes at serious tabs.

Le Refuge Inn ⇔

▽ 25 | 22 | 23 | $50

Le Refuge Inn, 586 City Island Ave. (bet. Beach & Cross Sts.), Bronx, 718-885-2478; www.lerefugeinn.com

Urban refugees can't resist this "romantic" "getaway" on "scenic City Island" that recently relocated to a "renovated Victorian house"; in addition to "true French" cuisine plus "expert" service, there are also "country inn" guestrooms upstairs for those who "want to linger."

Le Rivage

20 | 16 | 20 | $41

340 W. 46th St. (bet. 8th & 9th Aves.), 212-765-7374;
www.lerivagenyc.com

"Tried and true" for "solid" grub and "unstuffy service", this French vet also offers a dinner prix fixe "bargain" that's "better than most on Restaurant Row"; despite shrugs about the "ordinary" style, it's a "predictable" performer that's geared to curtain time.

Le Sans Souci

▽ 21 | 21 | 18 | $36

44-09 Broadway (bet. 44th & 45th Sts.), Queens, 718-728-2733;
www.lesanssouci.net

Les locals laud this "excellent change of pace for Astoria", an "authentic", "cozy" French bistro featuring "delicious" cooking via Brittany and "right-on hospitality"; the farmhouse setup with "stone walls and an open kitchen" helps justify "the trek."

Les Enfants Terribles ◐   ▽ 21 | 20 | 18 | $37

37 Canal St. (Ludlow St.), 212-777-7518; www.lesenfantsterriblesnyc.com
For "something a little different" on the Lower East Side, check out this "hopping" French-African joint where the "creative" vittles, "tasty" potables and overall "sex appeal" are certified "the coolest"; indeed, "les hipsters" keep the "limited" square footage "packed."

Les Halles ◐   21 | 17 | 16 | $42

15 John St. (bet. B'way & Nassau St.), 212-285-8585
411 Park Ave. S. (bet. 28th & 29th Sts.), 212-679-4111
www.leshalles.net
"*Vive le boeuf*" should be the motto of these "jumping" French bistros that are the "fiefdoms" of "media star" Anthony Bourdain – and the "real deal" for "killer" steaks and "fabulous" frites; even if the "harried" service is "too Parisian" and the acoustics too "noisy", "dollar for dollar" you "can't go wrong" here.

Le Singe Vert ◐   19 | 17 | 16 | $36

160 Seventh Ave. (bet. 19th & 20th Sts.), 212-366-4100
Just say *oui* to a modestly priced "taste of Paree" at this *très français* Chelsea bistro that's "dependable" for "decent" dining amid "jovial" company; it's Gallic right down to the "snooty service", and so "noisy" that you should "bring a date who reads lips."

Les Moules   – | – | – | M

35-02 Ditmars Blvd. (35th St.), Queens, 718-204-6186;
www.lesmoulesny.com
As the name suggests, mussels take center stage – they appear in at least 20 dishes – at this simply designed Astoria Med that offers up complimentary pita and tapas before the meal; there's also a long wooden bar where you can sample a wide selection of imported beers.

Le Souk ◐   17 | 22 | 13 | $37

47 Ave. B (bet. 3rd & 4th Sts.), 212-777-5454; www.lesoukny.com
"Not a place for deep discussions", this "loud" East Village Moroccan is a "young" folks magnet, where the "scene" and the "belly dancers" overwhelm the "decent" grub and "inadequate service"; in short, expect "more spectacle than sustenance" here.

Le Tableau   23 | 15 | 21 | $40

511 E. Fifth St. (bet. Aves. A & B), 212-260-1333; www.letableaunyc.com
East Villagers call this "endearing" French bistro their "local favorite" for "exceptional food" and "gracious" service at "refreshing prices"; just "try not to eavesdrop" in the petite, "convivial" room, now all the more "cramped" since it's been "discovered."

Levana   ▽ 18 | 15 | 16 | $55

141 W. 69th St. (bet. B'way & Columbus Ave.), 212-877-8457;
www.levana.com
If you're going glatt kosher and "don't want deli", try this Lincoln Center–area New American where "unusual" dishes like venison and bison come in "plentiful" portions; still, despite the "innovative" ideas, doubters deem it "pricey" and "underwhelming."

Lever House   23 | 24 | 22 | $72

390 Park Ave. (enter on 53rd St., bet. Madison & Park Aves.), 212-888-2700;
www.leverhouse.com
Leveraging its "hype" as one of the "power joints of the moment", this "buzzing", "ultramodern" Midtowner flaunts a "futuristic" design that works well with chef Dan Silverman's New American menu; it's emerging as a "challenger to the Four Seasons", with "deafening" acoustics and "deep-pocket prices" to be expected.

L'Express ◐

| 17 | 15 | 13 | $28 |

249 Park Ave. S. (20th St.), 212-254-5858; www.lexpressnyc.com
"Lively young night-owls" make this 24/7 Flatiron bistro a "hub" for
"post–bar hopping quickies", keeping it "packed at random hours";
though it's basically a "dressed-up diner" with "plausible" French eats
and "ditzy" service, most surveyors express fondness for the "scene."

Le Zie 2000 ◐

| 22 | 15 | 19 | $36 |

172 Seventh Ave. (bet. 20th & 21st Sts.), 212-206-8686; www.lezie.com
"Mama never made it as good" as this Chelsea Italian, dubbed the
"real thing" for "honest" Venetian-inspired basics at "gentle" prices;
the "capable" execution "sure packs them in", even if the room
"needs a decorator."

Le Zinc ◐

| 19 | 17 | 17 | $41 |

139 Duane St. (bet. Church St. & W. B'way), 212-513-0001; www.lezincnyc.com
A "neighborhood" hangout with TriBeCa "edge", this "funky", "well-
priced" French bistro sired by Chanterelle boasts "hearty" food and
"arty" decor defined by "vintage posters"; it "hits the spot" when you
"want something easy" and zinc nothing of "service snafus."

Lil' Frankie's Pizza ◐⇄

| 23 | 16 | 16 | $24 |

19-21 First Ave. (bet. 1st & 2nd Sts.), 212-420-4900
The "super pizza" attains "thin-crust perfection" at this "affordable"
East Village scion of Frank's, and followers are "happily surprised" by
the "home-cooked" Italian offerings too; a "laid-back" "local
favorite", it's now expanded into a "more comfortable" space.

Lili's Noodle Shop & Grill

| 17 | 14 | 15 | $22 |

Embassy Suites, 102 North End Ave. (Vesey St.), 212-786-1300
1500 Third Ave. (bet. 84th & 85th Sts.), 212-639-1313
200 W. 57th St. (enter on 7th Ave., bet. 56th & 57th Sts.), 212-586-5333
This "efficient", as in affordable, Chinese mini-chain "hits the spot"
with "monstrous bowls" of the "noodles you crave" plus a number of
"appetizing staples"; to skirt the "curt" service and inauspicious decor,
consider delivery – the "fastest in the Occident."

Lima's Taste

| ▽ 21 | 11 | 14 | $29 |

122 Christopher St. (Bedford St.), 212-242-0010 ◐
432 E. 13th St. (bet. Ave. A & 1st Ave.), 212-228-7900
www.limastaste.com
"Surprise" your taste buds with a "foray into authentic Peruvian fare"
at this "small, dark" East Villager where the food's easily affordable,
"wholesome" and "filling"; "very drinkable sangria" offsets the
"unremarkable" decor and "amateur" service; N.B. the West Village
location is new and unrated.

Lime Leaf

| 18 | 14 | 17 | $25 |

2799 Broadway (108th St.), 212-864-5000; www.limeleaf-nyc.com
"Sorely needed" for a "solid Thai" fix, this way Upper Westsider
caters to "Columbia professors" and other "neighborhood" types
with its "well-executed" food and "calming atmosphere"; with few
rivals for the limelight, the "intimate" digs are "usually pretty full."

L'IMPERO ⊠

| 26 | 24 | 24 | $68 |

45 Tudor City Pl. (bet. 42nd & 43rd Sts.), 212-599-5045; www.limpero.com
"Artful" chef Scott Conant's "glorious riffs" on Italian fare are the
"stuff of dreams" at this "elegant" Tudor City outpost, a "high-end",
"grown-up" respite where the "sleek", "modern" setting is matched
by "polished", "simpatico" service; it's imperially "expensive", but
the $58 prix fixe is such an "incredible deal" that most "can't wait
to go back."

Lisca ∅
▽ 20 | 16 | 20 | $40

660 Amsterdam Ave. (bet. 92nd & 93rd Sts.), 212-799-3987
An "exciting newcomer", this Upper West Side Tuscan "shines" with "delightful" traditional cooking (including "lots of fresh seafood") and "personal service" in "bright" digs; though "not cheap", at least it's a chance to "skip the lines across the street at Gennaro."

Little Giant
▽ 26 | 21 | 22 | $40

85 Orchard St. (Broome St.), 212-226-5047; www.littlegiantnyc.com
"Great things come in small packages" at this "inspired" Lower Eastsider with a New American menu featuring "occasionally daring" dishes; it's a "haven" for "happening" types, with "groovy" looks and an "enthusiastic staff" that together should help it make the big time.

Little Italy Pizza ☒
22 | 8 | 14 | $10

1 E. 43rd St. (bet. 5th & Madison Aves.), 212-687-3660
11 Park Pl. (bet. B'way & Church St.), 212-227-7077
180 Varick St. (bet. Charlton & King Sts.), 212-366-5566
55 W. 45th St. (bet. 5th & 6th Aves.), 212-730-7575
To enjoy a "slice of life", try these "pizza-on-the-run" fixtures where connoisseurs commend the "classic" thin-crust version with "hard-to-top" toppings; "long lunch lines" make the "cramped" quarters "a little crazy", but at least the mobs "move quickly" and the price is right.

Lobster Box
19 | 16 | 18 | $40

34 City Island Ave. (Belden St.), Bronx, 718-885-1952; www.lobsterbox.com
Finatics consider this "picturesque", "high-volume" City Island "mainstay" overlooking the Sound a "summer must" for feasting on the "usual" seafood hits; critics call the formula "trite and true" and feel the place is "living on past glory."

Locanda Vini & Olii
▽ 22 | 25 | 22 | $42

129 Gates Ave. (Cambridge Pl.), Brooklyn, 718-622-9202;
www.locandany.com
Cognoscenti go "out of the way" for the "home-cooked" Tuscan food at this "unexpected" Clinton Hill "gem" that matches "excellent" eating with "intriguing" wines and "devoted" service; the "former pharmacy" space has lots of "retro" allure, even if the "doses are small" here.

Lodge ●
− | − | ± | M

318 Grand St. (Havemeyer St.), Brooklyn, 718-486-9400;
www.lodgenyc.com
Shabby-chic Williamsburg and rustic Adirondack lodge collide at this American set on a prime Grand Street corner; look for modern twists on classic standards, moderate pricing and a setting heavy on the wood paneling and antler chandeliers.

Lombardi's ∅
25 | 12 | 15 | $21

32 Spring St. (bet. Mott & Mulberry Sts.), 212-941-7994
Diehards happily make the "pilgrimage" to this "nostalgic" NoLita entry in the "pizza pantheon", where the "delicate" "crisp-crust" pies easily "live up to their rep"; there's "breathing room" in the "spartan" setting, but given such "sublime" eating, "who needs decor?"

Londel's Supper Club
▽ 19 | 17 | 18 | $32

2620 Frederick Douglass Blvd. (bet. 139th & 140th Sts.), 212-234-6114;
www.londelsrestaurant.com
Owner Londel Davis keeps everyone "feeling right at home" at this Harlem Southern "staple", safeguarding the "fine art of soul food" with "always good" renditions of the classics; supporters say the "lively atmosphere", "personable" staff and "jazz nights" keep "bringing you back."

London Lennie's
20 | 16 | 17 | $39

63-88 Woodhaven Blvd. (bet. Fleet Ct. & Penelope Ave.), Queens, 718-894-8084; www.londonlennies.com

It's "the real thing" declare the "old-timers" at this "boisterous" family fish house, a Rego Park "throwback" that consistently nets the "freshest" seafood around at moderate prices; in addition to the "huge", "noisy" setup, expect "crowds" (and a "wait") on weekends.

Long Tan ●
19 | 19 | 18 | $27

196 Fifth Ave. (bet. Berkeley Pl. & Union St.), Brooklyn, 718-622-8444; www.long-tan.com

"Cooler than your average Thai", this Park Sloper features an "innovative menu" offering some "unusual" options at "fair prices"; its "young hipster" following fawns over the "mod", "minimalist" design and "perfect drinks."

Lorenzo's
▽ 22 | 21 | 21 | $47

Hilton Garden Inn, 1100 South Ave. (off Staten Island Expwy.), Staten Island, 718-477-2400

Something of a "surprise" awaits at this "ambitious" American in Staten Island's Hilton Garden Inn, where a "charming" team serves up Italian-accented standards; with live entertainment in the works, it's like a trip to "Manhattan without all the hassle", but with nearly the same tabs.

Lo Scalco ●▯▧
▽ 26 | 25 | 24 | $65

313 Church St. (bet. Lispenard & Walker Sts.), 212-343-2900

A "touch of class" in TriBeCa, this "lovely new" Italian "surprises at every turn" by putting "heart and soul" into its "inventive" cooking and "sweet", "discreet" service; the "austere" setting is uncrowded (perhaps because of its rather steep pricing), but it won't be "undiscovered" for long.

Los Dos Molinos ▧
18 | 16 | 15 | $32

119 E. 18th St. (bet. Irving Pl. & Park Ave. S.), 212-505-1574

"Margaritas big enough to swim in" soothe the "burn" of the "seriously spicy" grub at this Gramercy Southwestern, a "vibrant" fiesta favored by "under-30" types; its "gimmicky" style and "cheesy Arizona decor" hardly dampen the high-energy goings-on; N.B. don't miss the custom-made guacamole.

LoSide ●
– | – | – | I

157 E. Houston St. (bet. Allen & Eldridge Sts.), 212-254-2080; www.losidediner.com

A lime-green-and-white neon sign looming above Houston Street beckons passersby into this tongue-in-cheek tribute to the diner; a hipster-friendly slice of old-fashioned Americana, it's a place for retro-politans to savor greasy-spoon staples priced on the lo side.

Lotus ▧
17 | 23 | 14 | $54

409 W. 14th St. (bet. 9th Ave. & Washington St.), 212-243-4420; www.lotusnewyork.com

Diners may wind up "chowing down to the beat" at this Meatpacking District nightclub where "sceney" sorts unwind in "dark", "sexy" environs; though a bit "expensive", the Pan-Asian menu is "better than you'd expect" – but "who goes there for the food" anyway?

Loulou
▽ 24 | 20 | 21 | $33

222 DeKalb Ave. (bet. Adelphi St. & Clermont Ave.), Brooklyn, 718-246-0633

You can count on this "relaxed" Fort Greene Gaul to garner "ooh-la-la's" for providing a "delightful" taste of Brittany "right in the neighborhood"; since the "intimate" digs can get "very crowded", the "charming garden" may be the "best way" to go.

Luca   20 | 16 | 20 | $38

1712 First Ave. (bet. 88th & 89th Sts.), 212-987-9260; www.lucatogo.com
Yorkville locals find it "hard to resist" chef Luca Marcato's "addictive" cooking at this "casual", midpriced Northern Italian where the "rustic" fare comes with "flair" but the "storefront" decor "could definitely improve"; N.B. they've just opened Cavatappo, a new wine bar nearby.

Lucien ●   22 | 17 | 18 | $39

14 First Ave. (1st St.), 212-260-6481
It doesn't get much "more Parisian" than this "nifty little" East Village bistro, the "genuine article" for "flavorful" (if "not novel") French dishes in "informal" digs buffeted by "constant hustle"; "affordable" prices atone for the "so tight" seating.

Lucy's Latin Kitchen   18 | 20 | 16 | $42

ABC Carpet & Home, 35 E. 18th St. (bet. B'way & Park Ave. S.), 212-475-5829
"Latin lovers" get cozy at this "fancy" Flatiron Mexican BBQ joint, an "innovative" purveyor of "A-ok" cuisine and "terrific" cocktails against an "attractive" backdrop of "primary colors"; proponents pardon "slow" service and praise its "potential", while contras consider it "expensive for what it is."

Ludo ●   – | – | – | E

42 E. First St. (bet. 1st & 2nd Aves.), 212-777-5617; www.ludonyc.com
Formerly Chez Es Saada, this reinvented East Villager serves an expensive Eclectic menu sprinkled with Med-Eclectic dishes; the plain-Jane upstairs bar barely hints at the atmospheric, grottolike dining rooms below, complete with canoodle-worthy nooks.

Luke's Bar & Grill ●⊄   17 | 13 | 17 | $25

1394 Third Ave. (bet. 79th & 80th Sts.), 212-249-7070
"Solid" as a rock, this "friendly" Eastsider is a "fixture" for American pub grub, especially if you're "into burgers"; with a "cool staff" and "lively" regulars, it's a "typical" neighborhood hangout for brews and simple food for young and old alike.

Luna Piena   18 | 17 | 18 | $38

243 E. 53rd St. (bet. 2nd & 3rd Aves.), 212-308-8882; www.lunapienanyc.com
Admirers are "luna struck" by the "hospitality" at this "down-to-earth" Midtown Italian, serving "affordable" "homemade" pastas in a "simple" setting sans "crazy crowds"; even if the eating's "not spectacular", the "pretty" outdoor terrace is a "big draw."

LUPA ●   26 | 18 | 22 | $48

170 Thompson St. (bet. Bleecker & W. Houston Sts.), 212-982-5089; www.luparestaurant.com
Aka the "baby Babbo", this *molto* popular" Villager from the Batali-Bastianich-Denton team is a "bohemian" Roman trattoria where "lusty, soul-warming" "peasant food" at "midrange" cost is served by a "super-smart staff"; it "hits on all cylinders", but the "hectic crush", "cacophony" and "long waits" may knock you for a lupa.

Lupe's East L.A. Kitchen ⊄   – | – | – | I

110 Sixth Ave. (Watts St.), 212-966-1326
Casual TriBeCa cantina serving Californian-style Mexican fare in a diner-esque, linoleum-and-Formica setting; service may be on the relaxed side, but then again so are the prices.

Lure Fishbar   22 | 25 | 20 | $57

142 Mercer St., downstairs (Prince St.), 212-431-7676; www.lurefishbar.com
"Ahoy!", this "shipshape" SoHo seafooder has an "eye for detail" that extends to both the "succulent" fin fare and "handsome" "luxury-

yacht" decor; with a "lively" crew on board, it's "engaging" enough to lure "well-dressed" folk – even if prices go slightly "overboard."

Lusardi's ◑ | 24 | 19 | 22 | $55

1494 Second Ave. (bet. 77th & 78th Sts.), 212-249-2020; www.lusardis.com
"Old-fashioned" sorts keep this "classy" East Side Northern Italian "always full", since it's a "mainstay" for "consistent", "high-quality" food and "top-notch" service; "decades"-long devotees concede both the "close" seating and the fact that it "pays to be a regular" here.

Luxia ◑ | 19 | 16 | 18 | $42

315 W. 48th St. (bet. 8th & 9th Aves.), 212-957-0800; www.luxianyc.com
A "lesser-known" Theater District pick, this "small hideaway" offers "decent" Italian chow with a "healthy bent" via "organic, free-range" ingredients, not to mention a back garden "oasis" and "huge fruit martinis"; overall, it's an "unpretentious find" on "touristy" turf.

Luz | – | – | – | M

177 Vanderbilt Ave. (bet. Myrtle Ave. & Willoughby St.), Brooklyn, 718-246-4000; www.luzrestaurant.com
Fort Greene turns out for upscale but easy *comidas* and well-crafted cocktails at this Nuevo Latino with recessed lighting, orange accents and sidewalk seating; take in the Brooklyn-style blend of liveliness and relaxation, sip a frothy pisco sour and see *la luz.*

Luzia's | 17 | 14 | 17 | $33

429 Amsterdam Ave. (bet. 80th & 81st Sts.), 212-595-2000
It's "change-of-pace" time on the Upper West Side at this "authentically Portuguese" niche serving "generous" portions of "interesting" specialties in plain-Jane digs; the "friendly" staff "tries hard" and costs are modest, yet skeptics say "nothing special" is going on.

Macelleria ◑ | 20 | 18 | 18 | $49

48 Gansevoort St. (bet. Greenwich & Washington Sts.), 212-741-2555
Lodged in a "converted Meatpacking District warehouse", this "solid" Italian chop shop "keeps it real" with "awesome" steak/pasta combos and a "rustic feel" abetted by a "charming wine cellar"; it's "easier to get into than most" nearby, but beefs include "noise", "brusque" service and pricey tabs.

Madiba | ▽ 18 | 20 | 19 | $33

195 DeKalb Ave. (Carlton Ave.), Brooklyn, 718-855-9190; www.i-shebeen.com
Adventurers are drawn to this "exotic yet approachable" Fort Greene original purveying the "unusual tastes" of "down-home" South Africana; the "bush outpost" look sets the "very chill" tone, and sporadic jams from "local bands" enhance the "funky flavor."

Madison Bistro | 19 | 16 | 18 | $43

238 Madison Ave. (bet. 37th & 38th Sts.), 212-447-1919; www.madisonbistro.com
Both locals and "lucky travelers" find "Paris personified" at this "subdued" Murray Hill bistro, a "civilized haven" for "enjoyable" French fare and "welcoming" service, but "no theatrics"; "pocket-friendly" prix fixes curb the otherwise "pricey" tabs.

Madison's | 21 | 18 | 20 | $36

5686 Riverdale Ave. (259th St.), Bronx, 718-543-3850
For "reliable" Italian cooking, this is Riverdale's "hands-down winner" thanks to a "sophisticated" menu that "surprises" many, matched by a "friendly staff" and "classy, comfortable" accommodations; even better, it's quite affordable.

Maggie Brown ≠

21 22 18 $24

455 Myrtle Ave. (bet. Washington & Waverly Aves.), Brooklyn, 718-643-7001
Clinton Hillers welcome this "funky" new arrival where "super"
Eclectic–New American comfort food with a "twist" arrives in a space
featuring the "thrown-together" feel of "grandma's living room"; most
agree it's "much needed" for the "reasonable prices" alone.

Magnifico ⊠

20 14 19 $45

200 Ninth Ave. (22nd St.), 212-633-8033
From the "cordial greeting" to the "robust" food, they "aim to please" at
this ambitiously named Chelsea Northern Italian, an "underappreciated
surprise" set in "inconspicuous" digs; partisans applaud the "down-
to-earth" style, though a few find the "standard" fare a bit "insignifico."

Magnolia

20 17 17 $27

486 Sixth Ave. (12th St.), Brooklyn, 718-369-4814; www.magnoliabrooklyn.com
Though sometimes "overlooked", this "mellow", pleasingly priced Park
Slope "neighborly" nook provides "quality" New Americana from a
"patron-oriented" staff; it's "homey without much flourish", but the
Friday jazz and "great brunch" deal make it "more than acceptable."

Mainland

– – – E

1081 Third Ave. (64th St.), 212-888-6333; www.mainlandnyc.com
Peking duck from a wood-burning oven is the star at this showy (and
pricey) new East Side Chinese; given the modern menu, voluptuous
setting and silky service, some see it as a harbinger of the return of
upscale Chinese food to NYC.

Malagueta

▽ 26 15 21 $26

25-35 36th Ave. (28th St.), Queens, 718-937-4821; www.malagueta.com
The "creative" kitchen gives "native Brazilian" dishes a "sophisticated
twist" at this Astoria location; for a modest "local" overseen by
"accommodating" expats, it's a "real treat" – as is the "value."

Malatesta Trattoria ●≠

▽ 21 17 19 $30

649 Washington St. (Christopher St.), 212-741-1207
"Hidden away" in the far West Village, this "vibrant" trattoria is a
"staple" where "hot waiters" serve "hearty" Italian fare in "casual"
quarters with a "breezy", "open-air" feel; aficionados attest it's "worth
the walk" for a *buono* meal at an "amazing price."

Maloney & Porcelli ●

23 19 21 $60

*37 E. 50th St. (bet. Madison & Park Aves.), 212-750-2233;
www.maloneyandporcelli.com*
"Paul Bunyan"–size portions mark this "premium-priced" Midtown
steakhouse "old boys' club" that's also known for its "unbelievable
crackling pork shank" served by a "brisk" staff; surveyors say it "rivals
the best", and there's a great private party space to boot.

Mamá Mexico ●

20 17 18 $33

2672 Broadway (bet. 101st & 102nd Sts.), 212-864-2323
214 E. 49th St. (bet. 2nd & 3rd Aves.), 212-935-1316
www.mamamexico.com
"Great guacamole!", this "over-the-top" pair are "nacho ordinary
Mexicans" given the "perpetual party" vibe complete with "roving
mariachi bands" and "free-flowing tequila"; the "fantastic" food is
nearly overlooked amid the "absurdly loud" conditions.

Mama's Food Shop ⊠≠

21 10 13 $14

200 E. Third St. (bet. Aves. A & B), 212-777-4425; www.mamasfoodshop.com
"Mama expects a big appetite" at this "down-home" East Village
American known for its mac 'n' cheese served in helpings that could

"feed a small nation"; the "best-buy" prices are a "dream", but "no-frills" digs and service make it a "delivery staple."

Mamlouk ● | 22 | 19 | 19 | $40 |

211 E. Fourth St. (bet. Aves. A & B), 212-529-3477
Practical patrons plan to pace themselves at this "little" East Villager that provides a "barrage" of "delicious" Middle Eastern "treats" via a six-course, $35 "blowout"; "sexy" lighting sustains the Moroccan mood, even though they "did away with the hookah."

Mancora ● | ▽ 19 | 14 | 19 | $26 |

99 First Ave. (6th St.), 212-253-1011
176 Smith St. (bet. Warren & Wyckoff Sts.), Brooklyn, 718-643-2629
For a "flavorful change of pace", these price-conscious, cross-borough Peruvians purvey plentiful portions of "authentic" specialties (including a notable rotisserie chicken); "smiling" service ups the appeal, but expect a "very basic" backdrop.

Mandarin Court | 20 | 8 | 14 | $19 |

61 Mott St. (bet. Bayard & Canal Sts.), 212-608-3838
Admirers go for the "excellent" dim sum at this "cheap" Chinatown stalwart, despite the "run-down" interior and "hit-or-miss" service; its "solid" food and low tabs draw droves who "come early" on weekends.

Mandoo Bar | 19 | 14 | 17 | $22 |

71 University Pl. (bet. 10th & 11th Sts.), 212-358-0400
2 W. 32nd St. (bet. B'way & 5th Ave.), 212-279-3075
www.mandoobar.com
"Can-do" depots for "genuine but accessible" Korean "staples", these low-budget, strictly "informal" sources of "luscious" "dumplings galore" get their customers "in and out satisfied"; regulars report that it's hard to get more for less.

Manducatis | 23 | 13 | 20 | $42 |

13-27 Jackson Ave. (47th Ave.), Queens, 718-729-4602
A "hidden treasure" from the "old school", this "family-owned" Long Island City vet vends "top-notch", "red-sauce" Italiana via a "sincere" staff that's "happy to have you"; if the decor "needs a complete overhaul", the "hearty" eating and warm greeting ensure it "endures."

Manetta's ☒ | ▽ 23 | 16 | 19 | $32 |

10-76 Jackson Ave. (49th Ave.), Queens, 718-786-6171
The "crispy" wood-fired pizza and "homemade pastas" tempt fans to this "friendly" Long Island City Italian slinging "simple fare" for "reasonable" dough; it's "not fancy", but it's one "neighborhood favorite" that's "worth a trip."

Mangia ☒ | 20 | 13 | 13 | $20 |

16 E. 48th St. (bet. 5th & Madison Aves.), 212-754-0637
Trump Bldg., 40 Wall St. (bet. Nassau & William Sts.), 212-425-4040
50 W. 57th St. (bet. 5th & 6th Aves.), 212-582-5554
22 W. 23rd St. (bet. 5th & 6th Aves.), 212-647-0200
www.mangiatogo.com
"Fancy-schmancy" pit stops for the "office set", this "cafeteria-style" Med foursome features a "mind-blowing variety" of "haute" chow; the "quality" and "convenience" are a "godsend", but "cheap it ain't" and "mobbed" it is.

Mangiarini | 19 | 13 | 17 | $33 |

1593 Second Ave. (bet. 82nd & 83rd Sts.), 212-734-5500; www.mangiarini.com
There's a "tiny bit of Italy" at this space-challenged Eastsider known for its "impressive" blend of "traditional yet creative" cooking; the

"stark", "thigh-to-thigh" space "leaves much to be desired", but "affordability" and taste are the payoffs.

Manhattan Grille
20 | 18 | 19 | $56

1161 First Ave. (bet. 63rd & 64th Sts.), 212-888-6556; www.themanhattangrille.com

Long an "accommodating respite", this "steady" East Side steakhouse matches "large portions" of "basic" beef with a comfortable, "old-fashioned" "country club atmosphere"; sure, "it'll cost you", but the "no-fuss" approach suits our surveyors "just fine."

Manhattan Ocean Club
24 | 21 | 22 | $65

57 W. 58th St. (bet. 5th & 6th Aves.), 212-371-7777; www.manhattanoceanclub.com

Awash in "posh", this "unsinkable" Midtowner stays "on the mark" with "premier seafood" and "impeccable" service; a "tasteful" space festooned with "Picasso plate" displays, it may "require a second mortgage" but what else would you expect for "the best"?

Mara's Homemade
18 | 9 | 18 | $31

342 E. Sixth St. (bet. 1st & 2nd Aves.), 212-598-1110; www.marashomemade.com

Crawfish in season are "flown in fresh" and "done up tasty" at this Curry Row Cajun-Creole "surprise", a "low-key" "little mom-and-pop shop" specializing in "traditional N'Awlins" cookin'; some surveyors shrug "unimpressive", but the "down-home" eating is "legit."

MARCH
26 | 25 | 26 | $90

405 E. 58th St. (bet. 1st Ave. & Sutton Pl.), 212-754-6272; www.marchrestaurant.com

The "ultimate in class", this "stylishly seductive" East Side New American allows you to "customize" from "showstopping" chef Wayne Nish's "brilliant" tasting menu while the "gracious" staff "spoils you"; given the fact that this "lovely townhouse" is the "perfect place to propose", few mind "going for broke" here.

Marco Polo Ristorante
20 | 18 | 20 | $39

345 Court St. (Union St.), Brooklyn, 718-852-5015; www.marcopoloristorante.com

You'd better slip on a "pinky ring" to fit in at this Carroll Gardens Italian stalwart, a "standout" for "traditional" cuisine and "Brooklyn flavor"; still, what's "old-world charm" to some is "pretentious" to others.

Maremma ●🅢
– | – | – | M

228 W. 10th St. (bet. Bleecker & Hudson Sts.), 212-645-0200; www.maremmanyc.com

Tuscany goes Texan with dishes like the 'Sloppy Giuseppe' at this new Villager that's corralling crowds of clued-in cowpokes with Cesare Casella's 'spaghetti western' cooking; moderate tabs and a friendly vibe make folks feel at home in this range.

Maria Pia
20 | 16 | 18 | $36

319 W. 51st St. (bet. 8th & 9th Aves.), 212-765-6463; www.mariapianyc.com

Ticket-holders applaud the "sweet" staff for its "timely" handling of "pre-show hordes" at this Theater District vendor of "authentic" Italian grub; though "not unique", at least it's "economical."

Marina Cafe
19 | 21 | 18 | $40

154 Mansion Ave. (Hillside Terr.), Staten Island, 718-967-3077; www.marinacafegrand.com

A "sprawling view" of Great Kills Harbor is "definitely the draw" at this Staten Island fixture for "classic" "fresh seafood"; some snub the "hit-or-miss" food, but the "attractive nautical decor" and "waterfront" deck "make everything taste better."

Marinella
▽ 23 | 16 | 22 | $40

49 Carmine St. (Bedford St.), 212-807-7472
"Old-fashioned in the best sense", this "hidden" West Villager is a longtime local locus for "consistently wonderful" Italian cooking abetted by blackboard specials and "personalized service"; regulars report that "everyone's treated like family" here.

Marion's Continental ●
▽ 17 | 19 | 19 | $32

354 Bowery (bet. 4th & Great Jones Sts.), 212-475-7621
This "campy" Bowery bistro–cum–"retro lounge" now sports a more "modern look", but it's still a "wacky" joint where the "X-rated cocktail menu" – if not the "fair" American fare – wins "raves"; as an "amusing sideshow", it can be a "fabulous" scene with lots of "noisy" goings-on.

Mario's
21 | 14 | 19 | $39

2342 Arthur Ave. (bet. 184th & 186th Sts.), Bronx, 718-584-1188
An "endearing" veteran, this circa-1919 Bronx "icon" still supplies "real Southern Italian" cooking "served with charm"; maybe the "retro" decor "doesn't work anymore", but let's face it, it's always "wonderful to be on Arthur Avenue."

MarkJoseph Steakhouse ⌧
24 | 17 | 22 | $62

261 Water St. (off Peck Slip), 212-277-0020; www.markjosephsteakhouse.com
Whether a "carnivore's paradise" or a "cardiologist's nightmare", this Financial District chop shop delivers "perfectly prepared" steaks and sides; "understated decor", "knowledgeable" service and "bull-market prices" complete the picture.

Mark's
23 | 24 | 24 | $66

Mark Hotel, 25 E. 77th St. (Madison Ave.), 212-879-1864;
www.mandarinoriental.com
"Civilized" lunches and "splendid" afternoon teas are a given at this Edwardian-style French-American dining room in the "highbrow" Mark Hotel; while the "theatrical" service makes many feel like a "king", it's best enjoyed if you "don't look at the prices."

Markt ●
19 | 18 | 17 | $41

401 W. 14th St. (9th Ave.), 212-727-3314; www.marktrestaurant.com
"Mussels and Belgian beer" make for "happiness" at this "big", "buzzing" brasserie known for its "long drinking bar" and "subpar service"; scenesters say "you can't get a better view" of "the Meatpacking District show" than from its "perfect sidewalk seats."

Maroons
22 | 16 | 19 | $34

244 W. 16th St. (bet. 7th & 8th Aves.), 212-206-8640
"Spice and tradition" meet cute at this "cheap and cheerful" Chelsea Southern-Caribbean hybrid where the "flavorful home cooking" and "funky" setup add a "dash of color to the neighborhood."

Marseille ●
20 | 19 | 19 | $48

630 Ninth Ave. (44th St.), 212-333-3410; www.marseillenyc.com
"Well-prepared twists on standard brasserie fare" fill out the menu of this "upscale" Hell's Kitchen French-Med set in a "stylish", window-wrapped room; despite the "noise", most leave "pleasantly surprised."

Mars 2112
9 | 20 | 13 | $30

1633 Broadway (51st St.), 212-582-2112; www.mars2112.com
Best for "10-year-old boys" or "people from Orlando who want a taste of home", this Martian-themed Theater District "amusement park"

vends "forgettable" Americana in "hokey" digs; a "space simulator" ride and camera-ready aliens provide the atmosphere.

Maruzzella ◐
21 | 15 | 21 | $36

1483 First Ave. (bet. 77th & 78th Sts.), 212-988-8877
Despite the "small" setting, this "cozy" Eastsider attracts an ardent following with "tasty" Italian food at "can't-be-topped" prices; while the staff is "friendly" but "unobtrusive", service definitely picks up "if you speak Italian."

Mary Ann's
15 | 12 | 14 | $24

2452 Broadway (bet. 90th & 91st Sts.), 212-877-0132
116 Eighth Ave. (16th St.), 212-633-0877 🖙
80 Second Ave. (5th St.), 212-475-5939 🖙
1503 Second Ave. (bet. 78th & 79th Sts.), 212-249-6165 ◐
1803 Second Ave. (93rd St.), 212-426-8350
107 W. Broadway (bet. Chambers & Reade Sts.), 212-766-0911 ◐
For "sloppy, cheesy" Tex-Mex grub on the "cheap", these "lively" outposts "hit the spot"; sure, service is "perfunctory" and a "hosing down" wouldn't hurt, but no one cares after a "wicked" margarita.

Mary's Fish Camp 🖾
24 | 12 | 17 | $39

64 Charles St. (W. 4th St.), 646-486-2185; www.marysfishcamp.com
Experience a "group hug" at this way popular West Village seafooder where the fish is "so fresh it might bite", ditto the staff; "luscious lobster rolls" and other deceptively "simple" offerings explain the "killer lines"; N.B. a sibling, Brooklyn Fish Camp, has just opened in Park Slope.

Mas ◐🖾
25 | 24 | 24 | $74

39 Downing St. (bet. Bedford & Varick Sts.), 212-255-1790
A "true find", chef/owner Galen Zamarra's "romantic" New American Villager lures a "sexy adult" clientele with an "intricate" seasonal menu while a "deft" staff works the "postmodern farmhouse"–style room; it's already a "favorite for celebrations", especially if "someone else is paying."

MASA 🖾
27 | 23 | 25 | $356

Time Warner Ctr., 10 Columbus Circle, 4th fl. (60th St. at B'way), 212-823-9800;
www.masanyc.com
Like a "trip to the moon" for "sushi worshipers", this Time Warner Center Japanese (renowned as "NY's most expensive restaurant") is overseen by star chef Masayoshi Takayama who offers exquisite, "Tokyo"-worthy, kaiseki-style dinners, best taken at the counter "to get the full show"; some find the mas-ive prices hard to swallow (it's a $350 prix fixe before drink, tax and tip), but most feel it's more than "worth every Benjamin."

MATSURI ◐
23 | 27 | 20 | $56

Maritime Hotel, 369 W. 16th St. (9th Ave.), 212-243-6400;
www.themaritimehotel.com
Set in an "ultraluxurious" "aircraft hangar"–esque space, this "stunning" Japanese beneath Chelsea's Maritime Hotel lives up to its looks with chef Tadashi Ono's "always good and sometimes magical" offerings; sure, the "price tags are a little steep" but the "sexy people running around" don't seem concerned.

Maurizio Trattoria
▽ 22 | 16 | 21 | $43

35 W. 13th St. (bet. 5th & 6th Aves.), 212-206-6474
"Less is more" at this "charming" Village Northern Italian yearling where the "simplicity" of its "hearty" dishes is matched with wines from a "short but good list"; it's especially convenient for "New School staffers" and "Quad Cinema"–goers.

Max ◑⊭
24 | 16 | 16 | $26

1274 Amsterdam Ave. (123rd St.), 212-531-2221
51 Ave. B (bet. 3rd & 4th Sts.), 212-539-0111
www.max-ny.com
"Amazing pastas" at "amazing prices" account for the popularity of these separately owned Uptown/Downtown Italians; the "cash-only", "packed-in-like-sardines" scene and "spotty service" don't seem to trouble its "hungry student" following.

Maxie
▽ 23 | 21 | 24 | $35

516A Third Ave. (bet. 34th & 35th Sts.), 212-685-3663
A "wonderful new addition" to Murray Hill, this "elegant" French-influenced Japanese features "high-quality sushi" and "skilled chefs", abetted by "professional service" and moderate prices; add in an "upscale" design, and it's easy to see why its prognosis is so favorable.

Maya
23 | 20 | 20 | $48

1191 First Ave. (bet. 64th & 65th Sts.), 212-585-1818; www.modernmexican.com
Those whose "Mexican cravings go beyond salsa and chips" tout this "fancy" Eastsider for "beautifully presented" "gourmet" fare good enough to "impress someone from San Antonio"; though the price point and "noise level" detract, the hostesses are "nice to look at."

Mayrose
15 | 10 | 13 | $22

920 Broadway (21st St.), 212-533-3663; www.mayrose-nyc.com
A Flatiron "alternative to trendy, pricey places", this "glorified diner" has "something for everyone" on its expansive American menu; a recent "face-lift has improved" its looks, but you'll still need to "battle the crowds for weekend brunch."

Maz Mezcal
21 | 17 | 18 | $35

316 E. 86th St. (bet. 1st & 2nd Aves.), 212-472-1599; www.mazmezcal.com
Yorkville gets a "real Mexican" jolt via this "cheery", "bustling" cantina featuring "better-than-usual" chow paired with "even more amazing margaritas"; "affordable" tabs make it very "family friendly", though "weekend mobs" may cause "auditory overload."

McCormick & Schmick's
19 | 18 | 19 | $48

1285 Sixth Ave. (enter on 52nd St., bet. 6th & 7th Aves.), 212-459-1222; www.mccormickandschmicks.com
This local outpost of the "high-end seafood chain" has quickly become a "good Midtown backup" thanks to its "well-prepared" fish and "perky" service; but foes fret over the franchise feel, saying it "could just as easily be in Kansas City or Spokane."

McHales ◑⊭
20 | 9 | 16 | $20

750 Eighth Ave. (46th St.), 212-997-8885
"Tasty", "frisbee-size" burgers are the name of the game at this "real deal" Theater District spot, a stagehands' "hangout bar" that's "refreshingly un-chichi"; "manageable" prices make up for the "mediocre" service and "dark", "seedy" setting.

Mediterraneo ◑
18 | 15 | 15 | $36

1260 Second Ave. (66th St.), 212-734-7407; www.mediterraneonyc.com
"Some of the best sidewalk dining on the East Side" can be had at this "sceney" Italian where the "serviceable" grub and "flirty" staff take a backseat to mighty stellar "people-watching"; still, what's "hip and lively" for some is "noisy and crowded" to others.

Mee Noodle Shop
17 | 5 | 13 | $14

219 First Ave. (13th St.), 212-995-0333
795 Ninth Ave. (53rd St.), 212-765-2929

(continued)

Mee Noodle Shop

547 Second Ave. (bet. 30th & 31st Sts.), 212-779-1596
922 Second Ave. (49th St.), 212-888-0027

These "fast and furious" Chinese joints offer an "infinite" variety of "cheap", "aromatic" noodle dishes that will "warm you up"; still, many "stick with takeout" to bypass the "abrupt" service and "overlit" decor.

Meet

| 17 | 18 | 15 | $45 |

71-73 Gansevoort St. (Washington St.), 212-242-0990;
www.the-meet.com

"Take a date" to this semi-"swanky" Meatpacking District Med that's the kind of place where the crowd's young and the "food's fine but the party's better"; "expensive drinks" blot out the "spaced-out service."

MEGU ◑

| 24 | 27 | 22 | $102 |

62 Thomas St. (bet. Church St. & W. B'way), 212-964-7777;
www.megunyc.com

"Everything's over the top" at this "much-hyped" TriBeCa Japanese, from the "unbelievable" theatrical setting arranged around a dramatic "ice Buddha sculpture" to the "menu as long as a book"; while the food's "fantastic" and the service seamless, regulars advise you "eat slowly to savor the flavors" – and to blunt the shock of those "ouch"-inducing mega-prices.

MeKong

| 18 | 15 | 15 | $27 |

44 Prince St. (bet. Mott & Mulberry Sts.), 212-343-8169
259 Fifth Ave. (Garfield Pl.), Brooklyn, 718-788-1210 ◑

These "versatile" pho factories in NoLita and Park Slope dish out "light, refreshing" Vietnamese fare at "can't-be-beat" prices; though the "quality varies" and service is "disorganized", the "laid-back" vibe works for both "dates and larger parties."

Melba's

| – | – | – | I |

300 W. 114th St. (8th Ave.), 212-864-7777

Serving up American comfort food with soul, this roomy Harlem eatery is outfitted with antique chandeliers, church pew–like benches and long tables, and boasts a tile-bedecked bar; here local cheap-eats seekers are joined by Columbia students willing to make the trek across Morningside Park.

Melt ◑

| – | – | – | M |

440 Bergen St. (bet. 5th St. & Flatbush Ave.), Brooklyn, 718-230-5925

A sleek New American addition to Park Slope's budding culinary scene that may make you melt with its attractive minimalist decor, creative eats and reasonable prices – especially on Tuesdays, when 20 bucks buys you a five-course tasting menu,

Meltemi

| 18 | 14 | 19 | $45 |

905 First Ave. (51st St.), 212-355-4040

Like a "short trip to the Greek Islands", this "low-key" Sutton Place Hellenic offers a "simple", seafood-centric menu along with the possibility of some "UN celeb"–spotting; "hefty" tabs and the "need for more ambiance" are downsides.

Menchanko-tei ◑

| 19 | 10 | 16 | $21 |

131 E. 45th St. (bet. Lexington & 3rd Aves.), 212-986-6805
43-45 W. 55th St. (bet. 5th & 6th Aves.), 212-247-1585

They "use their noodle" to good effect at these crosstown dispensers of "filling, tasty" ramen dishes that draw a crowd heavy with "Japanese salarymen"; despite "indifferent service" and "so-so" decor, they're tough to top when you want it "cheap, quick" and filling.

Mercadito
▽ | 24 | 19 | 19 | $35

179 Ave. B (bet. 11th & 12th Sts.), 212-529-6490
100 Seventh Ave. S. (Grove St.), 212-647-0410 ◗
Really "tasty" tapas-style items are purveyed at these "refreshingly different" Mexicans where "cucumber margaritas and designer tacos" make fans feel "frisky"; sure, the price of the "small plates can add up", but most customers consider the quality-cost quotient to be high.

Mercer Kitchen ◗
22 | 22 | 19 | $53

Mercer Hotel, 99 Prince St. (Mercer St.), 212-966-5454;
www.jean-georges.com
Jean-Georges Vongerichten's signature double bill of "beautiful food and beautiful people" works well at this "subterranean" SoHo French–New American; if "touch-and-go" service and "expensive" tabs are off-putting, remember that "seeing and being seen has its price."

Mermaid Inn
22 | 18 | 20 | $41

96 Second Ave. (bet. 5th & 6th Sts.), 212-674-5870;
www.beanstalkrestaurants.com
Suckers for seafood "throw down their anchors and come to rest" at this "casual" East Villager from the Red Cat/Harrison team, where the bait includes "heavenly" lobster rolls, an "economical" wine list and a "bonus garden"; N.B. thankfully, they now take reservations.

MESA GRILL
24 | 20 | 20 | $52

102 Fifth Ave. (bet. 15th & 16th Sts.), 212-807-7400; www.mesagrill.com
"Still sailing along with sass and flash", Iron Chef Bobby Flay's "original" Flatiron Southwestern whips up "full-of-surprises" dishes washed down with "killer margaritas"; maybe it's "time for a face-lift", but the "expansive" layout and "high ceilings" help with the "noise problem."

Meskerem
20 | 9 | 16 | $23

164 Amsterdam Ave. (67th St.), 212-799-2501 ◗
124 MacDougal St. (bet. Bleecker & W. 3rd Sts.), 212-777-8111
468 W. 47th St. (bet. 9th & 10th Aves.), 212-664-0520 ◗
Bring "an appetite and clean hands" to these utensil-free Ethiopians where the "delicious" stews are "scooped up" on flatbread; good "bang for the buck" makes up for "sorry decor" and "brusque service."

Métisse
20 | 17 | 20 | $41

239 W. 105th St. (bet. Amsterdam Ave. & B'way), 212-666-8825
Something of a "sleeper", this midpriced Upper West Side French "hideaway" boasts a "devoted" Columbia-faculty following, with "reliably good" food and an "excellent" early-bird deal; service is so "professional" that the staff is usually "better dressed than the guests."

Metrazur ⊠
20 | 22 | 18 | $48

Grand Central, East Balcony (42nd St. & Park Ave.), 212-687-4600;
www.charliepalmer.com
"Above the crowd but near the train", Charlie Palmer's newly renovated, "open-air" New American is perched on a mezzanine with a "dazzling" view of Grand Central Concourse's "hustle and bustle"; while the food's reliably good, service is "slow" and an "expense account is a plus."

MetroCafe & Wine Bar
18 | 15 | 17 | $34

32 E. 21st St. (bet. B'way & Park Ave. S.), 212-353-0800;
www.metrocafenyc.com
A "wide menu" and an even "wider wine list" are the draws at this "unpretentious", "under-the-radar" Flatiron American serving an "odd mix" of "diner-style" items (plus dim sum at the bar); while decor and service could use some help, no one's complaining at these prices.

Metropol ◐
∇ | 18 | 18 | 17 | $41

234 W. Fourth St. (10th St.), 212-206-8393; www.metropolnewyork.com
In the old La Metairie digs comes this new Village French bistro that earns mixed notices: fans say it's already a "local favorite" (especially "late-night") and tout the "great renovations", but foes yawn "ho-hum", citing a "limited menu" and, as of yet, "amateurish" service.

Metsovo ◐
17 | 18 | 17 | $39

65 W. 70th St. (bet. Columbus Ave. & CPW), 212-873-2300
"Romance"-minded types request a "fireside table" at this Lincoln Center–area Greek, a neighborhood "sleeper" where you can "always get a table"; the food may be "uneven", but after dinner insiders descend to Shalel, the "seductive lounge downstairs."

Mexicana Mama ⊁
24 | 11 | 17 | $31

525 Hudson St. (bet. Charles & W. 10th Sts.), 212-924-4119
"Mind-blowingly creative", this "adventurous" Village Nuevo Mexican prepares "*fantastico*", "affordable" chow in a space recalling a "studio apartment"; natch, it's "cramped and hectic", but at least the "intense margaritas will make you forget how long you waited to get in."

Mexican Radio ◐
20 | 15 | 17 | $30

19 Cleveland Pl. (bet. Kenmare & Spring Sts.), 212-343-0140; www.mexrad.com
This "hopping" NoLita Mexican cantina draws "trendy" types with "cheap 'n' tasty" food and "knock-your-socks-off" margaritas; despite "decor as cheesy as the nachos", it's a swell "place for a party."

Mezzaluna ◐
20 | 14 | 17 | $40

1295 Third Ave. (bet. 74th & 75th Sts.), 212-535-9600; www.mezzalunany.com
"Great for when you don't want to cook" (though "not for a special occasion"), this East Side Italian features "tasty" pizzas and pastas in "cramped", "noisy" digs; "service is hardly attentive despite the close quarters", but at least the "clientele is well dressed."

Mezzogiorno ◐
20 | 17 | 18 | $40

195 Spring St. (Sullivan St.), 212-334-2112; www.mezzogiorno.com
At its "best when the windows are open", this "pleasant" SoHo Italian seems better known for "people-watching" than for its "consistently good" pastas and pizzas; "unhurried" service adds to the leisurely air.

Michael Jordan's
The Steak House NYC
21 | 21 | 19 | $60

Grand Central, West Balcony (42nd St. & Vanderbilt Ave.), 212-655-2300; www.theglaziergroup.com
The "huge" steaks at this "brand-name" chop shop may do a "full-court press on your arteries", but ultimately it's the "primo locale" – a mezzanine overlooking Grand Central Concourse – that "steals the show"; as for pricing, it helps to have just "hit Lotto."

Michael's
22 | 21 | 22 | $60

24 W. 55th St. (bet. 5th & 6th Aves.), 212-767-0555; www.michaelsnewyork.com
Be prepared for a "traffic jam" of "media mavens" at this Midtown Californian that's a bona fide "power scene" at breakfast and lunch; dinner's a more "quietly elegant" affair, though "just being there" makes nobodies feel like "big shots."

Mi Cocina
23 | 18 | 19 | $43

57 Jane St. (Hudson St.), 212-627-8273
There's "nothing rice-and-beans" about this "serious", "always crowded" Village Mexicano where amigos "happily eat their way up

and down the menu"; sure, it can cost "*mucho dinero*", but you'll be so well fed you may "need help getting out of your chair."

Mill Basin Kosher Deli
22 | 16 | 16 | $21

5823 Ave. T (59th St.), Brooklyn, 718-241-4910; www.millbasindeli.com
"Erté fans" and kosher-keepers collide at this Mill Basin Jewish deli offering "generous portions" of "top-grade" meats accompanied by framed "lithographs and other artwork" that's also for sale; it's so "original" that Dalí himself couldn't have done better.

Mill Korean
20 | 14 | 17 | $19

2895 Broadway (bet. 112th & 113th Sts.), 212-666-7653
"Perfect for a bibimbop fix", this "cramped" but "pleasant" Morningside Heights Korean offers "dependable" fare priced for a "student budget"; an "indispensable part of the Columbia scene" for 20 years, it has kept many fed after the university dining halls closed.

MILOS, ESTIATORIO ◕
26 | 23 | 22 | $70

125 W. 55th St. (bet. 6th & 7th Aves.), 212-245-7400; www.milos.ca
"If you can't get to Mount Olympus", this "spectacular" Midtown Greek seafooder is the next best peak with "incredibly fresh fish" "simply prepared" and presented in a "stylish", high-ceilinged space by a "top-notch" staff; to avoid the "hard-to-swallow", by-the-pound prices, some suggest staying with the sensational first courses.

Minado
19 | 14 | 16 | $29

6 E. 32nd St. (bet. 5th & Madison Aves.), 212-725-1333; www.minado.com
"Heaven for gluttons", this modestly priced Murray Hill Japanese "bonanza" features a "mile-long" all-you-can-eat "smorgasbord" of both raw and cooked items; while the "variety never fails to wow first-timers", picky eaters say the "hot stuff is better than the sushi."

Minetta Tavern ◕
19 | 18 | 20 | $41

113 MacDougal St. (bet. Bleecker & W. 3rd Sts.), 212-475-3850
To "escape to gentler times", try this circa-1937 Village Italian "steeped in history", where the food's as "old-school" as the "neighborhoody, warm" vibe; though trendoids yawn "tired", traditionalists say it's "aging gracefully" and "wish the walls could talk."

Mingala Burmese
20 | 10 | 17 | $24

1393-B Second Ave. (bet. 72nd & 73rd Sts.), 212-744-8008
21-23 E. Seventh St. (bet. 2nd & 3rd Aves.), 212-529-3656
For a "change of pace", these East Side/East Village "secrets" serve "top-notch" Burmese fare spiked with plenty of "SE Asian firepower"; few mind the "pizza parlor"–grade decor what with the "Kmart" prices.

Minnow
22 | 16 | 20 | $38

442 Ninth St. (bet. 6th & 7th Aves.), Brooklyn, 718-832-5500;
www.theminnowrestaurant.com
A "jewel among rhinestones", this "consistently inventive" Park Slope seafooder purveys "fish so fresh you'd swear the ocean was in the backyard"; due to its "continuing popularity", they've opened Bar Minnow next door, serving cocktails and "clam shack"–style grub.

Miracle Grill
19 | 17 | 18 | $33

415 Bleecker St. (bet. Bank & W. 11th Sts.), 212-924-1900
112 First Ave. (bet. 6th & 7th Sts.), 212-254-2353 ◕
222 Seventh Ave. (4th St.), Brooklyn, 718-369-4541
"Easy to enjoy", these Southwestern "standbys" offer "tasty" chow and exude "great energy", but "the miracle is being able to walk after the margaritas"; the East Village branch is "all about the garden", while the Park Slope spin-off is too new to rate.

Miriam

| | | | M |

79 Fifth Ave. (Prospect Pl.), Brooklyn, 718-622-2250

Park Slope's Fifth Avenue scene stays simmering with the arrival of this airy, midpriced Middle Eastern; the tables are so small they guarantee an intimate meal, and weekend belly dancing shakes things up.

Mishima

| 23 | 15 | 20 | $32 |

164 Lexington Ave. (bet. 30th & 31st Sts.), 212-532-9596; www.mishimany.com

There's "real", as in really good, sushi to be had at this "hassle"-free Murray Hill Japanese duplex that also vends "equally good" simply cooked items; maybe the decor's "nonexistent", but the mood's "peaceful" and pricing is "reasonable."

Miss Mamie's

| 21 | 11 | 16 | $24 |

366 W. 110th St. (bet. Columbus & Manhattan Aves.), 212-865-6744

Miss Maude's

547 Lenox Ave. (bet. 137th & 138th Sts.), 212-690-3100
www.spoonbreadinc.com

These Harlem exercises in "caloric abandon" lay out "delicious" soul food that "fills your belly" for cheap; if the decor seems "minimal", it's designed to attract "homesick Southerners" who show up regularly and suggest "saving room for dessert."

Miss Saigon

| 18 | 10 | 15 | $24 |

1425 Third Ave. (bet. 80th & 81st Sts.), 212-988-8828

A "great place for an introduction" to all things Vietnamese, this Upper Eastsider provides "delectable", "affordable" fare that's always "reliable"; but given the "lacking decor" and "service without a smile", bear in mind that "they deliver fast."

Miss Williamsburg ⊄

| 20 | 16 | 17 | $31 |

228 E. 10th St. (bet. 1st & 2nd Aves.), 212-228-5355
206 Kent Ave. (bet. Metropolitan Ave. & N. 3rd St.), Brooklyn, 718-963-0802
www.miss-williamsburg.com

The "lasagna alone merits a visit" to this "remote" Williamsburg Italian whose "diner-car" shell belies the "unique" Italian cooking inside and "jewel" of a garden beyond; N.B. its stovetop-less East Village sibling serves a limited menu of oven-baked and cold items.

Mizu Sushi ⌧

| 23 | 16 | 20 | $33 |

29 E. 20th St. (bet. B'way & Park Ave. S.), 212-505-6688

Hailed for its "luscious sushi", this "upbeat" Flatiron Japanese caters to "young, hip" folk with a menu that's "more designer than traditional" (but still "reasonably priced"); the only problem is that "waits are getting longer" since "people are finding out about it."

MJ Grill ⌧

| 18 | 15 | 17 | $41 |

110 John St. (bet. Cliff & Pearl Sts.), 212-346-9848; www.mjgrill.com

"Less formal" and "less expensive" than its sibling, MarkJoseph, this midpriced Financial District American is home to a "noisy lunch crowd" as well as an "after-work bar scene"; just "don't expect to be wowed", and remember it's closed on weekends.

Mo-Bay

| ▽ 20 | 17 | 14 | $26 |

17 W. 125th St. (bet. 5th & Lenox Aves.), 212-876-9300
112 DeKalb Ave. (bet. Ashland Pl. & St. Felix St.), Brooklyn, 718-246-2800
www.mobayrestaurant.com

"Southern cooking meets the islands" at these far-flung Jamaican soul fooders in Harlem and Fort Greene that dish out "huge portions" of "fabulous jerk chicken" on the cheap; "no-frills" scenes and "slow-bay" service keep the take-out business brisk.

Moda

▽ | 19 | 20 | 17 | $46

Flatotel, 135 W. 52nd St. (bet. 6th & 7th Aves.), 212-887-9880;
www.flatotel.com

"Hidden" in a West Midtown hotel, this Med-Italian is a handy option for "business" lunches or after-work drinks at its "cool" outdoor bar; "ultramodern" furnishings help distract from the "inconsistent" cooking and "pleasantly amateurish" service.

MODERN, THE ●

25 | 26 | 22 | $70

Museum of Modern Art, 9 W. 53rd St. (bet. 5th & 6th Aves.), 212-333-1220;
www.themodernnyc.com

"A work of art within a work of art", Danny Meyer's latest "masterpiece" is set in the reopened MoMA, where "everything has style", from chef Gabriel Kreuther's "memorable" French-American food to the "chic", spare setting; the more formal main dining room features a $78, prix fixe–only menu eased by "killer views" of the museum's "serene sculpture garden", but it's easier to score a seat in the still "sexy" (but cheaper) bar area where the eating's à la carte.

Molyvos ●

23 | 20 | 20 | $51

871 Seventh Ave. (bet. 55th & 56th Sts.), 212-582-7500; www.molyvos.com

"Zeus smiles down" on this "surprisingly fine" Midtown taverna, a "different sort of place" with "stylish", "not-your-typical-nautical" decor and "expertly prepared" Greek dishes; it's among the "best pre–Carnegie Hall", and appropriately "pricey."

Momofuku Noodle Bar

20 | 13 | 17 | $20

163 First Ave. (bet. 10th & 11th Sts.), 212-475-7899;
www.eatmomofuku.com

"Counter culture doesn't get much better" than at this East Village noodle nook where fans dig into bowls of "avant-garde ramen" (as well as other Japanese, Korean and Chinese dishes); the "narrow" space may fail the feng shui test, but with tabs this "cheap", no one notices.

Momoya ●

– | – | – | M

185 Seventh Ave. (21st St.), 212-989-4466

This new Chelsea Japanese offers traditional, reasonably priced dishes with the odd unexpected ingredient like jalapeños or hearts of palm; in warm weather its cool, minimalist space opens onto the street for an alfresco feel.

Monkey Bar ☒

18 | 21 | 19 | $52

Elysée Hotel, 60 E. 54th St. (bet. Madison & Park Aves.), 212-838-2600;
www.theglaziergroup.com

"Stylish" types agree this Midtown steakhouse is "fun for a lark", citing "good" grazing in a "retro cool" room recalling an "art deco jungle"; others say the monkeying around is "better at the bar", especially if you're in the market for a "trophy wife."

Mon Petit Cafe

19 | 14 | 17 | $34

801 Lexington Ave. (62nd St.), 212-355-2233; www.monpetitcafe.com

"Popular with the ladies who shop and lunch", this "modest French cafe" is just the ticket "après Bloomingdale's" for "affordable", "classic" Gallic fare; "nonchalant" (maybe even "snippy") service is its downside.

Monsoon ●

19 | 14 | 16 | $27

435 Amsterdam Ave. (81st St.), 212-580-8686

"Highly recommended" Upper Westsider where folks blow in for "consistent, aromatic" Vietnamese vittles with an "Americanized" "low-spice content"; the decor may be cheesy and service "brusque", but prices are "bargain" level and "takeout is as good as eating in."

Monster Sushi
19 | 11 | 16 | $28

535 Hudson St. (Charles St.), 646-336-1833
22 W. 46th St. (bet. 5th & 6th Aves.), 212-398-7707 ⊠
158 W. 23rd St. (bet. 6th & 7th Aves.), 212-620-9131
www.monstersushi.com

You "get a lot of sushi for not too many clams" at these "mid-tier" Japanese triplets known for their "big fat" portions served "without bells and whistles" (like decor and service); ok, "Nobu it isn't", but "at least you can get a table."

Montparnasse ●
20 | 19 | 18 | $43

Pickwick Arms, 230 E. 51st St. (bet. 2nd & 3rd Aves.), 212-758-6633; www.montparnasseny.com

"Pleasant" if "underknown", this East Midtowner provides "classic" bistro items in "faux French" digs; fans feel it "should be more popular", citing "friendly" service and "great-deal" pre-theater prix fixes.

MONTRACHET ⊠
26 | 20 | 24 | $68

239 W. Broadway (bet. Walker & White Sts.), 212-219-2777; www.myriadrestaurantgroup.com

Managing to stay at the "cutting edge" of the TriBeCa restaurant scene, Drew Nieporent's 20-year-old French "delight" shows "real staying power" with its "always consistent" food and service, even if the room is a bit "lacking in style"; "no-corkage-fee Mondays draw an interesting clientele", while Friday's $20 prix fixe lunch is "not to be missed."

Mo Pitkin's ●
– | – | – | M

34 Ave. A (bet. 2nd & 3rd Sts.), 212-777-5660; www.mopitkins.com

Squeezing a lot into its double-decker digs, this new East Villager serves salute-to-the-neighborhood Judeo-Latino dishes in an ironic, '50s-style setting that includes wall caricatures of Downtown celebs; the second-floor performance space is its primary draw, however.

Moran's Chelsea
19 | 20 | 21 | $43

146 10th Ave. (19th St.), 212-627-3030; www.moranschelsea.com

Especially "beautiful during winter with the fireplaces burning", this longtime West Chelsea surf 'n' turf "comfort zone" offers a "steady" surf 'n' turf menu, but it's the "old-world" "mahogany atmosphere" that makes it special; "reasonable prices" lure loyal locals.

Morrell Wine Bar & Cafe
20 | 18 | 19 | $47

1 Rockefeller Plaza (on 49th St., bet. 5th & 6th Aves.), 212-262-7700; www.morrellwinebar.com

The "light" New American menu at this Rock Center cafe pales in comparison to its "extraordinary" wine-by-the-glass list, "lovely" outdoor patio seating and "stiff prices"; having been in the business for decades, no one knows his vintages better than Pete Morrell.

Morton's, The Steakhouse ●
24 | 19 | 22 | $65

551 Fifth Ave. (45th St.), 212-972-3315; www.mortons.com

Maybe "not as dramatic" as some steakhouses, this "clubby", dark wood–paneled Midtown cow palace is still "dependable" for a "beef orgy" at "expense-account" prices; but the pre-meal "show-and-tell" menu presentation is "getting old" – most "already know what a porterhouse is", even if it's wrapped in cellophane.

Moustache ●⊉
22 | 11 | 15 | $22

90 Bedford St. (bet. Barrow & Grove Sts.), 212-229-2220
265 E. 10th St. (bet. Ave. A & 1st Ave.), 212-228-2022

"Trademark" pita-bread 'pizzas' lend an "exotic" touch to these crosstown Village Middle Easterners that are always "densely packed" due to "cheap" pricing for very good food – not the "hole-in-the-wall" looks or "slow" service.

Moutarde ◐

| 18 | 20 | 16 | $36 |

239 Fifth Ave. (Carroll St.), Brooklyn, 718-623-3600

"Tasty if typical" French fare fills out the midpriced menu of this Park Slope "bistro by the book" where the decor lies somewhere between "perfection" and "Epcot Center"; service may be "more Brooklyn than Latin Quarter", but that doesn't stop it from re-creating the "bustle of Paris."

Mr. Chow ◐

| 23 | 21 | 19 | $68 |

324 E. 57th St. (bet. 1st & 2nd Aves.), 212-751-9030;
www.mrchow.com

Sure, this venerable but still "happening" Midtown Chinese offers "fine cuisine" and stark modern decor, but the "real pull" is its "glittery" crowd, a mix of "flashy-trashy" rappers and "Wall Street execs"; regulars "let the waiter do the ordering", which is a bit like investing in a highly leveraged hedge fund.

Mr. K's

| 24 | 23 | 25 | $52 |

570 Lexington Ave. (51st St.), 212-583-1668; www.mrks.com

Devotees feel "like a royal emperor" at this "upscale" Midtown Chinese serving "high-society cuisine at its finest" in a "coolly opulent", "plush pink" setting; "doting service" comes with the territory, along with a "fortune cookie that reads 'big bill.'"

Mughlai ◐

| 19 | 13 | 17 | $32 |

320 Columbus Ave. (75th St.), 212-724-6363

This "down-to-earth" West Side Indian "mainstay" has "been around a long time" thanks to "good, basic" cooking and "fair-deal" prices; even its "nothing-special" decor can't dampen the overall "pleasant" mood.

Mundo ◐∅

| – | – | – | I |

31-18E Broadway (enter on 32nd St.), Queens, 718-777-2829;
www.mundoastoria.com

At this new Astoria eatery, co-owners Guillermo from Argentina and Canalp from Turkey share the best of both worlds in their lovingly crafted menu and space, which feels one part trendy SoHo cafe, one part comfy dinner party; best of all, it's chic but not mondo expensive.

My Most Favorite Dessert Co.

| 18 | 14 | 17 | $34 |

120 W. 45th St. (bet. B'way & 6th Ave.), 212-997-5130;
www.mymostfavorite.com

"Indulge your sweet tooth" at this "always packed" Theater District kosher option that serves "real food too", though the sugary stuff remains the "best part" (and is "worth the extra time at the gym"); "subpar" service and dubious decor are its least favorite features.

Ñ ◐∅

| ▽ 21 | 21 | 19 | $28 |

33 Crosby St. (bet. Broome & Grand Sts.), 212-219-8856

Almost "as small as its name", this "romantic" tapas bar is a "dark, sexy" den offering "hearty" Spanish small plates along with "great sangria"; despite its "secret getaway" status, it's often "hard to find a seat", since SoHo sybarites smell a steal.

Naima ◐

| – | – | – | M |

513 W. 27th St. (bet. 10th & 11th Aves.), 212-967-4392

A new eatery on a hot nightlife street, this West Chelsea Southern Italian offers hearty, midpriced fare matched with regional wines; expect plenty of late-night action (it's open till 2 AM on weekends) and some celeb sightings, given its next-door-to-Bungalow-8 setting.

Nam
| 22 | 20 | 19 | $37 |

110 Reade St. (W. B'way), 212-267-1777
For a "unique take on Vietnamese", fans suggest this TriBeCa "local favorite" that sure "tastes like Saigon"; ok, prices may be a tad "higher than in Chinatown", but the setting's much more "hip", ditto the crowd.

Nana ⊅
| 21 | 19 | 19 | $28 |

155 Fifth Ave. (bet. Lincoln & St. John's Pls.), Brooklyn, 718-230-3749
There's "something for everyone" in the "vast" roster of "delicious" Pan-Asian dishes at this "wallet-friendly" (but "cash-only") Park Sloper; the back garden both "lifts the spirits" and provides an escape from the "loud music" inside.

Nanni ⊠
| 24 | 14 | 24 | $53 |

146 E. 46th St. (bet. Lexington & 3rd Aves.), 212-697-4161
"As traditional as can be", this "charming" Northern Italian near Grand Central has a "throwback style that works", from its "excellent" kitchen to the "feel-like-family" service; the main downside is "not-so-pleasing" pricing.

Napa & Sonoma Steak House
▽ | 21 | 17 | 19 | $50 |

15-01 149th St. (15th Ave.), Queens, 718-746-3446
"Pleasant and friendly", this Whitestone chop shop serves "good" beef enhanced by an "excellent wine list" that does justice to its name; still, some shrug it's a "wannabe big-city steakhouse" that's rather "costly" for the neighborhood.

Naples 45 ⊠
| 17 | 15 | 15 | $32 |

MetLife Bldg., 200 Park Ave. (45th St.), 212-972-7001; www.naples45.com
"Eat and beat it" is the word at this "huge", relatively inexpensive Grand Central Italian that enjoys a "high-turnover" lunch trade thanks to one of the "most authentic Neapolitan pizzas" around (not the "bland" digs and "poor acoustics"); N.B. closed weekends.

Native
▽ | 19 | 18 | 18 | $31 |

101 W. 118th St. (Lenox Ave.), 212-665-2525; www.harlemnative.com
A "great alternative" to Harlem's usual soul food parade, this "adventurous" Eclectic features a globe-trotting menu emphasizing Moroccan and Caribbean items; outdoor seats (a "rarity in this neighborhood") make up for what some see as "spacey" service.

Neary's ◗
| 16 | 12 | 20 | $41 |

358 E. 57th St. (1st Ave.), 212-751-1434
"Quintessential host" Jimmy Neary "embodies Irish hospitality" at this Sutton Place pub that lures "loyal", "mature" types; the "wholesome" American menu is "pretty good", but it's "mostly a bar" where the "atmosphere's the thing" and the customers enjoy seeing each other night after night.

Nebraska Steak House ⊠
▽ | 21 | 13 | 19 | $47 |

15 Stone St. (bet. Broad St. & B'way), 212-952-0620
"Neighborly" yet "relatively unknown", this Financial District chop shop offers "pretty darn good" chops in a "dark, speakeasy"-esque setting; since everything's "à la carte", you may want to go when the Dow is having a good day.

Negril
| 20 | 16 | 15 | $31 |

70 W. Third St. (bet. La Guardia Pl. & Thompson St.), 212-228-9440
362 W. 23rd St. (bet. 8th & 9th Aves.), 212-807-6411 ◗
www.negrilvillage.com
"Authentic" enough to draw a "large Caribbean clientele", this affordable Jamaican pair serves "solid" island food and drink to the

tune of a "reggae" beat; though the Village branch is bigger and more upscale, "slooow service" plagues both.

Nello ◑ | 20 | 18 | 18 | $70

696 Madison Ave. (bet. 62nd & 63rd Sts.), 212-980-9099
Its "Eurotrash" following "thinks they're on the Riviera" at this "popular" Madison Avenue Northern Italian where the "good food" is runner-up to the "too-beautiful-for-mere-mortals" scene; "insane" pricing and "snooty" service diminish the "glamour."

Nëo Sushi ◑ | 23 | 18 | 19 | $57

2298 Broadway (83rd St.), 212-769-1003; www.neosushi.com
"In the same vein as Nobu", this "sophisticated" West Side Japanese is known for "exquisite" sushi plus some "unconventional" but "flavorful" dishes served in modishly "sterile" digs; ok, prices are steep given the "model-size" portions, but at least you "save the hike Downtown."

Neptune Room | 23 | 20 | 20 | $48

511 Amsterdam Ave. (bet. 84th & 85th Sts.), 212-496-4100;
www.theneptuneroom.com
"When you can't make it to the beach", there's always this "welcoming" Upper West Side yearling that supplies "adventurous" seafood and a "terrific raw bar"; "pricey" it may be, but the mood's as "cool and fresh" as the fish.

Nero ◑ | ▽ 17 | 17 | 16 | $39

46 Gansevoort St. (Greenwich St.), 212-675-5224
A "serendipitous" find in the seething Meatpacking District, this new Italian supplies a "small, on-the-money menu" served in "rustic", "earth-toned" digs; early word is it "doesn't have its act together yet", though it's sure "convenient" for nightcrawlers.

New Bo-Ky ⇌ | ▽ 22 | 6 | 12 | $11

80 Bayard St. (bet. Mott & Mulberry Sts.), 212-406-2292
This cheap Chinatown noodle shop may be "nothing to look at" but delivers one helluva "bang for a quick buck" via its "hearty" soups; it's a natural for jury duty, but "bring a pointer – the waiters don't speak much English."

New Green Bo ◑ ⇌ | 23 | 5 | 12 | $16

66 Bayard St. (bet. Elizabeth & Mott Sts.), 212-625-2359
Expect "long lines" for the "luscious" goods at this "absurdly busy" C-town bun-and-soup-dumpling "heaven"; while there's "absolutely no decor" (and not much more service), the price is a downright "steal."

New Leaf Cafe | 22 | 24 | 19 | $38

Fort Tryon Park, 1 Margaret Corbin Dr. (190th St.), 212-568-5323;
www.nyrp.org/newleaf
"Splendid" Fort Tryon Park is the setting for this "picturesque" New American where the food is suitably "tasty and beautifully presented" in a "château"-like room; even better, profits go to a "good cause" – Bette Midler's NY Restoration Project.

New Pasteur ⇌ | ▽ 21 | 6 | 15 | $16

85 Baxter St. (bet. Bayard & Canal Sts.), 212-608-3656
"Jury duty's a pleasure" after lunching at this Chinatown Vietnamese where the "prices are from the 1960s" but the "delicious" fare works for "any decade"; though "hardly the best looking" spot, it's "crowded all the time" for good reason.

Nha Trang | 23 | 7 | 15 | $17

87 Baxter St. (bet. Bayard & Canal Sts.), 212-233-5948

(continued)

Nha Trang

148 Centre St. (bet. Walker & White Sts.), 212-941-9292
"Mountains" of "delicious" Vietnamese fare keep fans flocking to this "crowded" Chinatown duo where the "graceless service" is offset by "awesome" pricing; maybe the "moon has more atmosphere", but the "hectic" pace allows you to happily "eat and run."

Nice

21 | 11 | 17 | $23

35 E. Broadway (bet. Catherine & Market Sts.), 212-406-9510
"Piping hot" Chinese food comes via "steaming carts" at this "busy" C-town Cantonese dim sum palace that's usually "filled with locals"; "fluorescent light and a fish tank" pass for decor, but service is "polite" and prices so low it's, well, "nice."

Nice Matin ●

20 | 19 | 18 | $45

201 W. 79th St. (Amsterdam Ave.), 212-873-6423; www.nicematinnyc.com
With its "cosmopolitan" air and "snazzy" menu, this popular West Side French-Med brasserie is "deservedly difficult to get into"; "unbearable noise" and "full-of-themselves" service come with the territory, but at least the "tight tables make eavesdropping easy."

Nick & Stef's Steakhouse ⊠

20 | 18 | 20 | $55

9 Penn Plaza (on 33rd St., bet. 7th & 8th Aves.), 212-563-4444; www.restaurantassociates.com
A "good bet" for sports fans or "business lunchers", this "solid, no-frills" steakhouse on the north side of Madison Square Garden serves "succulent" chops priced to reflect its "convenient" address; usually "quiet and mellow", it can get "packed pre-game."

Nick and Toni's Cafe

18 | 15 | 16 | $46

100 W. 67th St. (bet. B'way & Columbus Ave.), 212-496-4000
Wood-fired-oven aficionados declare the "dependable" Med fare at this "quiet", "cozy" West Side "standby" is good enough "for a quickie before or after Lincoln Center"; others, citing "dull" looks and "indifferent service", feel it's "too expensive."

Nick's

23 | 13 | 17 | $22

1814 Second Ave. (94th St.), 212-987-5700 ●
108-26 Ascan Ave. (bet. Austin & Burns Sts.), Queens, 718-263-1126 ⊟
"Holy cannoli": this inexpensive Italian duo produces "pizza like it oughta be", with a "thin crust", "fresh toppings", some "brick-oven blackening" and a "light touch with sauce"; they're "very kid-friendly", but "moody service" and "dodgy decor" are downsides.

Nicky's Vietnamese Sandwiches ⊟

▽ 22 | 6 | 15 | $8

150 E. Second St. (Ave. A), 212-388-1088
"Perfection on a roll" is the thing at this "dirt-cheap" East Village Vietnamese where "fresh" (if "strange") ingredients "blend together deliciously"; it seats just six, so most "take their sandwiches and run."

Nicola's ●

22 | 16 | 21 | $53

146 E. 84th St. (Lexington Ave.), 212-249-9850
"Connections count" at this very "social" East Side Italian oozing "old-world charm"; it's "always good for a superb dinner", "especially if they know you", but outsiders sometimes feel like nonmembers.

Night and Day

– | – | – | M

230 Fifth Ave. (President St.), Brooklyn, 718-399-2161
Aiming for the same sophistication that its Cole Porter–inspired name suggests, this Park Slope newcomer serves moderately priced

American fare in a cozy interior or on a sun-drenched deck; a room for live jazz is in the works.

Ninja

— — — VE

25 Hudson St. (bet. Duane & Reade Sts.), 212-274-8500
Something different for TriBeCa, this new subterranean Japanese fusion specialist is done up like a faux feudal mountain village, a mazelike affair with intimate chambers where diners are served by waiters in full Ninja drag; the ambitious, albeit pricey offerings (tasting menus start at $80) overcome the theme park–esque mood.

Niko's Mediterranean Grill ●

19 10 16 $29

2161 Broadway (76th St.), 212-873-7000
The "menu's the size of a coffee table book" at this West Side Greek-Med whose "campy", "dinerlike" digs disguise what is in fact a "hospitable taverna": "huge portions" at "fair prices" make it "one of the best values in the neighborhood."

Nino's ●

23 19 23 $54

1354 First Ave. (bet. 72nd & 73rd Sts.), 212-988-0002
Nino's Tuscany
117 W. 58th St. (bet. 6th & 7th Aves.), 212-757-8630;
www.ninostuscany.com
Featuring "top-of-the-line" Tuscan fare and "entertaining piano players", this "classy" Northern Italian duo exhibits "meticulous" attention to detail; given its prices, it should come as no surprise that it draws a "prosperous" clientele.

Nino's Positano

21 18 22 $48

890 Second Ave. (bet. 47th & 48th Sts.), 212-355-5540
It's "not flashy", but this "old-school" East Midtown Italian serves a "solid", "uncomplicated" menu of "flavorful fare" in "classic", somewhat "stolid", digs; it's a "business lunch" favorite since you can actually "hear your dining partner."

Nippon ▨

▽ 22 15 18 $47

155 E. 52nd St. (bet. Lexington & 3rd Aves.), 212-758-0226;
www.restaurantnippon.com
"Old-fashioned, yes", some critics even say "weary", but this Midtown Japanese has been dispensing "terrific" traditional dishes and some of the "freshest sushi" around since 1963; those were the days when most NYers thought eating raw fish was a fraternity prank.

Nisos ●

18 15 17 $37

176 Eighth Ave. (19th St.), 646-336-8121; www.nisos-ny.com
Count on "good honest" grub from the Mediterranean menu and "fabulous boys everywhere" at this "not fancy" (but not expensive) place in the heart of the "Chelsea strip"; sidewalk seating and indoor "mood lighting" contribute to the happening "bar scene."

NOBU

28 23 24 $78

105 Hudson St. (Franklin St.), 212-219-0500
NOBU, NEXT DOOR ●
105 Hudson St. (bet. Franklin & N. Moore Sts.), 212-334-4445
www.myriadrestaurantgroup.com
Still "off the charts", this TriBeCa "destination" serves "sublime" Japanese-Peruvian fusion fare in "gorgeous" digs liberally garnished with celebs; no surprise, getting a reservation is an "ordeal", but beyond that, the "expert staff" and "astronomical" prices make for an "out of this world" experience; P.S. the next-door adjunct offers the "same level" of dining but is "a tad less expensive" and easier to get into since it only takes walk-ins.

NOBU 57 ●🚫

– | – | – | VE

40 W. 57th St. (bet. 5th & 6th Aves.), 212-757-3000; www.noburestaurants.com
Nobu Matsuhisa's spin-off of his Downtown powerhouse, this must-see-to-believe David Rockwell–designed Midtown duplex is a triumph of theatrical feng shui with a downstairs bar/lounge topped by a spacious, second-floor dining room; look for the same pricey Japanese-Peruvian fusion fare that built the brand, and as for the scene, it's a safe bet to become people-watching central.

Nocello

21 | 17 | 21 | $45

257 W. 55th St. (bet. B'way & 8th Ave.), 212-713-0224
A "winner of the pre-theater derby", this Carnegie Hall–area Italian dispenses a wide range of "old-world" Tuscan "delights" in a "cozy candlelit" space; after the show-goers depart, it's a "wonderful place to linger" when romance is in the air.

NoHo Star ●

18 | 14 | 15 | $30

330 Lafayette St. (Bleecker St.), 212-925-0070; www.nohostar.com
Serving "solid", easily affordable American grub with a "smattering" of Asian dishes at dinnertime, this NoHo "old faithful" is always "dependable"; despite "just-going-through-the-motions" service and digs that show "years of wear and tear", locals are "glad it's still here."

Nonna

20 | 16 | 17 | $34

520 Columbus Ave. (85th St.), 212-579-3194; www.nonnarestaurant.com
Already "popular for good reason", this Italian newcomer offers "down-to-earth" yet "inventive" comfort food; while the "sardine setting" garners mixed reviews, the $19, six-course "Sunday night feast" is a steal.

Nooch

15 | 20 | 14 | $22

143 Eighth Ave. (17th St.), 212-691-8600
So far, this Chelsea newcomer's "knockout", "Hello Kitty"–style design outshines its Pan-Asian menu, with the exception of the "fine noodles"; this first U.S. beachhead of the Singapore chain also boasts "surprisingly cheap" tabs, but "don't expect stellar service."

Noodle Pudding ⊘

25 | 18 | 22 | $33

38 Henry St. (bet. Cranberry & Middagh Sts.), Brooklyn, 718-625-3737
Ok, the "name's a head-scratcher", but the "stupendous" cooking makes this Italian one of the "best in Brooklyn Heights"; although an "accommodating staff" and low prices compensate for the cash-only, no-reservations rules, "good luck finding it": there's "no sign" outside.

Nook ●◗⊘

∇ 24 | 14 | 18 | $28

746 Ninth Ave. (50th St.), 212-247-5500; www.nynook.com
"Good things come in small packages" at this "*really* tiny" Hell's Kitchen Eclectic where the "outstanding" food is served in digs that "live up to its name"; bargain-hunters say its "BYO factor" makes the already "astonishing" prices an even better deal.

Norma's

26 | 19 | 20 | $35

Le Parker Meridien, 118 W. 57th St. (bet. 6th & 7th Aves.), 212-708-7460; www.parkermeridien.com
It's "worth getting up early" to savor the "scrumptious" breakfasts at this Midtown American that's full of "glamorous" folk bent on a "calorie splurge"; just be prepared for long waits and eye-opening tabs.

North Square

23 | 19 | 21 | $43

Washington Sq. Hotel, 103 Waverly Pl. (MacDougal St.), 212-254-1200; www.northsquareny.com
A "civilized atmosphere" prevails at this New American "sleeper" off Washington Square, where "wonderful" food is served in a "cozy"

subterranean dining room; the "affordable" pricing is echoed by its $15 prix fixe jazz brunch.

Notaro

▽ 20 | 15 | 20 | $32

635 Second Ave. (bet. 34th & 35th Sts.), 212-686-3400
From the "always good" Northern Italian food and "unhurried" service to the "bargain-hunter's dream" prix fixes, this Murray Hill "secret" is a "perfect neighborhood" place – even if it could use a "bit of a polish."

Novecento ◐

22 | 18 | 17 | $43

343 W. Broadway (bet. Broome & Grand Sts.), 212-925-4706; www.novecentogroup.com
"Delicious" steaks jazz up the menu at this "unpretentious", almost "bargain" Argentine that's improbably situated "on the trendiest stretch of SoHo"; the ambiance can vary between "barroom" and "Miles Davis chill", but the sound level is almost uniformly "noisy."

Novitá

23 | 18 | 22 | $49

102 E. 22nd St. (bet. Lexington Ave. & Park Ave. S.), 212-677-2222; www.novitanyc.com
"Hidden in plain sight" in Gramercy is this "classy" Northern Italian set in a "pleasant" basement space, though the "lovingly prepared" food is "penthouse" all the way; a "courteous" staff takes the edge off of the "expensive" tabs.

Nyonya ◐⊅

23 | 12 | 14 | $20

194 Grand St. (bet. Mott & Mulberry Sts.), 212-334-3669
5323 Eighth Ave. (54th St.), Brooklyn, 718-633-0808
"Crowds keep coming" to this "boisterous" Little Italy/Sunset Park duo to nosh on "real-deal" Malaysian chow for "cheap"; true, they're "not much" on looks and service can get "snappy", but "where else can you dine on stingray?"

OCEANA ▣

26 | 24 | 25 | $75

55 E. 54th St. (bet. Madison & Park Aves.), 212-759-5941; www.oceanarestaurant.com
Come aboard for "serious dining" at this Midtown seafooder that's "exquisite" from chef Cornelius Gallagher's "delectable" fish to its "serene", "cruise ship"–like feel and "understated yet attentive" staff; N.B. prix fixe–only, except at the bar where à la carte is available.

Ocean Grill ◐

23 | 20 | 20 | $48

384 Columbus Ave. (bet. 78th & 79th Sts.), 212-579-2300; www.brguestrestaurants.com
"Cast your net no further" than this winsome West Side poisson palace where the seafood "couldn't be fresher" and there's a "plentiful raw bar" too; though the brunch is "very popular", whether it's "too noisy" or just a "good buzz" is up to you.

Océo

▽ 18 | 18 | 17 | $57

Time Hotel, 224 W. 49th St. (bet. B'way & 8th Ave.), 212-262-6236; www.oceo.com
A "très chic space" and "unique" Eclectic–New American specialties make this Theater District hotel room a good place to "impress clients" or simply enjoy "conversation" in a "calming atmosphere"; still, "expensive" tabs and "pretentious" airs detract.

Odeon ◐

18 | 17 | 17 | $42

145 W. Broadway (bet. Duane & Thomas Sts.), 212-233-0507; www.theodeonrestaurant.com
"Young, old, singles, families" – "everyone" comes to this "bustling", affordable French-American "workhorse", a circa-1980 TriBeCa scene

that "still rocks" ("go figure"); night-owls credit the "over-40 lighting" and comfortable "deco-ish feel" for its "wee-hours" popularity.

O.G. ◐   ∇ 24 | 17 | 24 | $32

507 E. Sixth St. (bet. Aves. A & B), 212-477-4649; www.ogrestaurant.com
Admirers "can't say enough" about the "sensational" Asian fusion flavors served at this "little" East Village "secret"; even better, the mood's "mellow", the staff "charming" and the price tags extremely "reasonable" given the quality offerings.

Old Devil Moon   19 | 16 | 17 | $21

511 E. 12th St. (bet. Aves. A & B), 212-475-4357; www.olddevilmoon.com
"Sturdy appetites and skimpy wallets" are well served by this "loopy" East Village Southerner where you can "eat down-home without going home"; "white-trash" decor and a "tough" "tattooed" staff add to the "honky-tonk" roadhouse mood.

Old Homestead   23 | 16 | 20 | $62

56 Ninth Ave. (bet. 14th & 15th Sts.), 212-242-9040;
www.theoldhomesteadsteakhouse.com
"NY's oldest steakhouse" (circa 1868) is appropriately set in the Meatpacking District and features "high-quality" beef served in a "testosterone"- and "sawdust"-strewn space by "intimidating" waiters; "lofty price tags" notwithstanding, traditionalists feel it's making a "comeback."

Olives   22 | 22 | 21 | $53

W Union Sq., 201 Park Ave. S. (E. 17th St.), 212-353-8345;
www.toddenglish.com
Expect an "all-around fine-dine" at this "classy", "flavor-filled" Todd English Mediterranean off Union Square where you can watch your meal being prepared in the "interesting open kitchen"; since it's also a "beautiful-people magnet", brace yourself for a "dynamite" bar scene.

Olive Vine Cafe ⇪   18 | 10 | 17 | $16

362 15th St. (7th Ave.), Brooklyn, 718-499-0555
54 Seventh Ave. (bet. Lincoln & St. Johns Pls.), Brooklyn, 718-622-2626
"Pizzas made from fresh-baked pita" are the raisons d'être of these "uncomplicated" Park Slope Mideastern BYOs where the "basic" looks are trumped by dirt-"cheap" prices; happily, the branch closed by fire is back in a new Seventh Avenue location.

Ollie's ◐   16 | 9 | 13 | $21

1991 Broadway (bet. 67th & 68th Sts.), 212-595-8181
2315 Broadway (84th St.), 212-362-3111
2957 Broadway (116th St.), 212-932-3300
200B W. 44th St. (bet. B'way & 8th Ave.), 212-921-5988
For "filling", affordable Chinese or a "tasty noodle fix" at "lightning"-fast speed, this "crazy busy" West Side chain comes in "mighty handy"; trade-offs include "mess-hall" looks and an "expressionless" staff.

O Mai   23 | 18 | 18 | $35

158 Ninth Ave. (bet. 19th & 20th Sts.), 212-633-0550; www.omainyc.com
"Inventive", "upscale Vietnamese" food is served "minimalist style" at this "signless" Chelsea storefront where the "soft lighting" disguises a "tightly packed" scene; given the "polite" service and "reasonable" cost, it's considered a "neighborhood keeper."

Omen ◐   24 | 18 | 22 | $53

113 Thompson St. (bet. Prince & Spring Sts.), 212-925-8923
"Superb" Kyoto-style cuisine is presented at this "original", sushi-free SoHo Japanese where a "cool" crowd relaxes in a "sparse" but

"calming" setting; to avoid "paying royally" for à la carte, stick with the "great-value set menus."

Omonia Cafe ●   18 | 13 | 13 | $17

7612-14 Third Ave. (bet. 76th & 77th Sts.), Brooklyn, 718-491-1435
32-20 Broadway (33rd St.), Queens, 718-274-6650
Offering a taste of "Greek cafe culture", this coffeehouse duo churns out "delectable" desserts and "Euro-style" java; maybe the rest of the Hellenic menu is just "ok", but they're open almost 'round-the-clock for those in need of a "late-night sugar fix."

Once Upon a Tart . . .   20 | 11 | 13 | $14

135 Sullivan St. (bet. Houston & Prince Sts.), 212-387-8869;
www.onceuponatart.com
A "stone's throw from SoHo's crazy melee" lies this cheap, "nostalgia-making" counter-service cafe vending "tasty" pastries and sandwiches in an "impossibly small" space; "sourpuss" service makes many wish they'd "lose the bad karma at the cash register."

One ●   18 | 22 | 15 | $48

1 Little W. 12th St. (9th Ave.), 212-255-9717; www.one1w12.com
The "sexy", "velvet-rope" vibe at this Meatpacking District lounge/ eatery heats up late-night when "scenesters" are drawn in by its "strong" potions and "pounding club music"; while the New American small-plate menu is "surprisingly good", the "party does it one better."

O'Neals' ●   17 | 17 | 18 | $43

49 W. 64th St. (bet. B'way & CPW), 212-787-4663; www.oneals.us
Culture vultures seeking "pre- or post–Lincoln Center" refreshment are glad for the return and "renovation" of this "fancified version of an Irish pub"; "sure 'n' steady" American grub for "moderate" sums and "hard-working" service keep it ever popular.

One 83   ▽ 20 | 19 | 20 | $46

1608 First Ave. (bet. 83rd & 84th Sts.), 212-327-4700;
www.one83restaurant.com
Eastsiders seeking "grown-up" encounters in a "quiet", "relaxing" ambiance favor this "pleasant" Northern Italian where the food's "terrific" and the "covered garden" just plain "magical"; only its prices are cause to pause.

ONE IF BY LAND, TWO IF BY SEA   23 | 26 | 24 | $71

17 Barrow St. (bet. 7th Ave. S. & W. 4th St.), 212-228-0822;
www.oneifbyland.com
What with the "roses, candlelight" and "heavenly piano music", it simply "drips romance" at this "special-occasion" Village New American, once Aaron Burr's carriage house and now "marriage-proposal" central; "sumptuous" prix fixe–only menus and "white-glove service" complete the "magical" experience, though given the serious tabs, would-be grooms should "buy the ring first."

101   19 | 17 | 19 | $37

10018 Fourth Ave. (bet. 100th & 101st Sts.), Brooklyn,
718-833-1313 ●
3900 Richmond Ave. (Amboy Rd.), Staten Island, 718-227-3286
The "bar scene is worth the price of admission" at this Bay Ridge Italian–New American where the scent of "Drakkar Noir" in the air blends well with the "reliably good" food and "gentle prices"; N.B. the Staten Island offshoot is new and still unrated.

107 West   17 | 14 | 17 | $26

2787 Broadway (bet. 107th & 108th Sts.), 212-864-1555

(continued)
107 West
811 W. 187th St. (bet. Ft. Washington & Pinehurst Aves.), 212-923-3311
www.107west.com
In the "sketchy culinary landscape" between the Upper West Side and Washington Heights comes these Cajun Tex-Mexicans purveying "simple" fare for "reasonable" dough in plain-Juanita settings; to circumvent the "sweet but amateur" service, many do takeout.

Onera
| 25 | 21 | 22 | $55 |
222 W. 79th St. (bet. Amsterdam Ave. & B'way), 212-873-0200
Decidedly "not your typical taverna" nor cheap, this "knockout" new Westsider features a "chef who really cares" creating "inspired takes" on Greek classics complemented by a "fascinating" wine list; "artful decor" and "helpful" service make up for the "tight" fit.

Onju
| ▽ 20 | 18 | 22 | $41 |
108 E. Fourth St. (bet. 1st & 2nd Aves.), 212-228-3880; www.onjurestaurant.com
Early visitors to this East Village newcomer declare it's "truly a standout", given its unusual "all-organic" Italian menu and slick but "cozy" setting; still, bean counters claim it's a little "overpriced" given the "minuscule" size of the portions.

Ono
| 20 | 24 | 18 | $60 |
Gansevoort Hotel, 18 Ninth Ave. (enter on 13th St.), 212-660-6766;
www.chinagrillmgt.com
"Leggy girls and the bankers who love them" hook up at Jeffrey Chodorow's "trendy" new Meatpacking District Japanese where the "innovative menu" features both sushi and robata-grilled items; despite "expensive" tabs and "snooty" service, the early word is "oh yes."

Ony ●
| 18 | 16 | 16 | $25 |
357 Sixth Ave. (bet. Washington Pl. & W. 4th St.), 212-414-9885
With the closing of the West Side branch, there's only the Village original remaining of this "satisfying" Japanese noodle nook known for its "piping hot", "create-your-own" menchanko soup; the sushi seems an afterthought, ditto the "frazzled" service.

Orbit East Harlem ●
| ▽ 20 | 13 | 18 | $34 |
2257 First Ave. (116th St.), 212-348-7818; www.orbiteastharlem.com
"Essentially a bar" jazzed up with some "tasty" Eclectic offerings, this "cool" East Harlem "hangout" is best known for its "rollicking" nightly live entertainment; still, some say it's "overpriced for the neighborhood."

Oriental Garden ●
| 24 | 12 | 16 | $29 |
14 Elizabeth St. (bet. Bayard & Canal Sts.), 212-619-0085
"Pick your supper from the tank" ("it swims till it's cooked") at this Chinatown Cantonese seafooder that's "head and shoulders above the rest"; when they roll out the "wonderful dim sum", the "bright lights" and "indifferent" service don't seem so glaring.

Orsay ●
| 18 | 21 | 17 | $53 |
1057 Lexington Ave. (75th St.), 212-517-6400; www.orsayrestaurant.com
"Chichi" types, "old-school Eastsiders" and a few "div-orsays" populate this "classy classic" brasserie oozing "authentic French flair" (right down to the "attitude"); the "interesting menu" offers "solid" selections but somehow the "bill's always higher than you expect."

Orso ●
| 22 | 18 | 20 | $52 |
322 W. 46th St. (bet. 8th & 9th Aves.), 212-489-7212; www.orsorestaurant.com
"People-watching galore" (and some random "celeb sightings") provide the frisson at this "fancy" Theater District Northern Italian

offering "exceptional" fare in "civilized" environs; to break the "tough reservation" barrier, "try it for lunch", when it's "easier on the pocketbook" too.

Osaka

24 | 17 | 20 | $30

272 Court St. (bet. Degraw & Kane Sts.), Brooklyn, 718-643-0044
"Big rolls" and "succulent sushi" are well represented at this "cute" Cobble Hill Japanese complete with a "beautiful garden" for alfresco dining; given the "friendly chefs" and "personable" staff, fans award it the ultimate accolade: "worthy of being in Manhattan."

Osso Buco

16 | 14 | 17 | $33

1662 Third Ave. (93rd St.), 212-426-5422
88 University Pl. (bet. 11th & 12th Sts.), 212-645-4525
"Don't expect designer pasta" at these "family-style" Italians that do offer the opportunity to "overeat" with "plentiful red-sauce" dishes at "reasonable prices"; maybe they're "not the most inventive" thing around, but they work well "when you owe your friends a dinner."

Osteria al Doge ◗

21 | 17 | 19 | $44

142 W. 44th St. (bet. B'way & 6th Ave.), 212-944-3643; www.osteria-doge.com
"You never feel rushed" at this "rustic" Times Square Italian that earns "standing ovations" for its pre-theater performance with "dependable" meals and "on-time" service; applause is muted for the "loud crowds", so insiders opt for the "quieter" balcony seating.

Osteria del Circo ◗

22 | 23 | 21 | $58

120 W. 55th St. (bet. 6th & 7th Aves.), 212-265-3636; www.osteriadelcirco.com
"Getting more attention now that Le Cirque is closed", this similarly "circus-themed" Midtown spin-off run by the Maccioni clan offers "high-flying" dining on "well-edited" Northern Italiana; throw in "formal" yet "friendly" service, and many call it a "celebration of life."

Osteria del Sole ◗

22 | 17 | 20 | $43

267 W. Fourth St. (Perry St.), 212-620-6840
"Gracious owners" preside over this "much loved" Village Italian where Sardinian delicacies with "bright flavors" are served with "sass and style" by a "sunny" staff; foodwise, most agree it's a "good value", but the "Medici"-style wine "markups" are another story.

Osteria Gelsi

▽ 23 | 19 | 20 | $38

507 Ninth Ave. (38th St.), 212-244-0088
Enlivening a "bland" stretch of the Garment District behind Port Authority, this "great newcomer" serves "inventive", "flavorful" Italian dishes from the Puglia region; early reports find it "stylish, comfortable" and a "good value" to boot.

Osteria Laguna ◗

20 | 19 | 19 | $40

209 E. 42nd St. (bet. 2nd & 3rd Aves.), 212-557-0001; www.osteria-laguna.com
"Midtown expensers" and "corporate types" turn up at this "tasty" Italian near the UN for its "enjoyable" specialties and "pleasant" ambiance; sometimes "loud at lunch", it's more "romantic" for dinner, with French doors that open to the street.

Osteria Stella

21 | 21 | 20 | $42

135 W. 50th St. (bet. 6th & 7th Aves.), 212-957-5050; www.osteria-stella.com
Bringing a "touch of class" to Midtown, this "spacious" Northern Italian offers "hearty, traditional" fare along with a "fun-to-watch bar scene"; it's "not too expensive" for the area, though some bemoan the "out-of-control" acoustics.

Ota-Ya
23 | 18 | 20 | $33

1572 Second Ave. (bet. 81st & 82nd Sts.), 212-988-1188;
www.ota-ya.com
Folks tired of being "crammed" in enjoy the "pleasant", "peaceful"
atmosphere at this East Side Japanese where the sushi is "real
quality", the prices "reasonable" and the staff "personable" – "there's
never a wait", either.

Otto ●
22 | 19 | 20 | $36

1 Fifth Ave. (enter on 8th St.), 212-995-9559; www.ottopizzeria.com
Attain "pizza nirvana" at this Batali-Bastianich Village enoteca/pizzeria
where the "upper-class pies" feature "fascinating, fearless" toppings
paired with an "abundant" selection of Italian wines; "loud crowds",
"train terminal" decor and modest tabs complete the pleasing picture.

OUEST
25 | 22 | 23 | $59

2315 Broadway (bet. 83rd & 84th Sts.), 212-580-8700; www.ouestny.com
Still "leading the Upper West Side fine-dining renaissance", chef Tom
Valenti has "mastered the art of upscale comfort food" here with
"wickedly wonderful", "just original enough" New Americana; the
food's "superlatively served" in "sophisticated", "grown-up" digs
dotted with "sexy red leather booths" filled with a fair share of celebs –
so "good luck getting a table."

Our Place
21 | 15 | 20 | $32

141 E. 55th St. (bet. Lexington & 3rd Aves.), 212-753-3900;
www.ourplace-teagarden.com
1444 Third Ave. (82nd St.), 212-288-4888
"First-rate Shanghai" specialties meet "above-average" NY Chinese
"classics" at this "high-end" East Side duo where the service is
"genteel" and the "white-tablecloth" settings "semi-elegant"; "low"
tabs add to their allure.

Outback Steakhouse
15 | 13 | 16 | $31

919 Third Ave. (enter on 56th St., bet. 2nd & 3rd Aves.), 212-935-6400
60 W. 23rd St. (bet. 5th & 6th Aves.), 212-989-3122
1475 86th St. (15th Ave.), Brooklyn, 718-837-7200
Bay Terrace, 23-48 Bell Blvd. (26th Ave.), Queens, 718-819-0908
Queens Pl., 88-01 Queens Blvd. (56th Ave.), Queens, 718-760-7200
www.outback.com
"The Palm it ain't", but if you like it "big and fried", you'll probably like
this "suburban-style", Aussie-themed chophouse chain known for
"cheery" service and "hokey" decor; many say "leave it to the tourists",
but "bloomin' onion" fans want to keep it for themselves.

OYSTER BAR ☒
21 | 17 | 16 | $44

Grand Central, lower level, (42nd St. & Vanderbilt Ave.), 212-490-6650;
www.oysterbarny.com
"History's in the air" at this sprawling, circa-1913 "mollusk-lover's must"
parked "in the bowels of Grand Central" where the "freshest fish",
"terrific pan roasts" and "well-chosen wines" are delivered by a "no-
nonsense" crew; though it can be "noisy" due to the "vaulted tile
ceilings", a meal here is "about as NY as it gets."

Pace
21 | 21 | 19 | $54

121 Hudson St. (N. Moore St.), 212-965-9500;
www.beanstalkrestaurants.com
"More than just another cool scene", this TriBeCa Italian yearling
serves "inventive" fare in a "big open space" as well as at streetside
tables; there are "still a few kinks" and it can definitely "dent the wallet",
but overall, ratings show they're well paced.

Paladar ●

| 18 | 15 | 17 | $32 |

161 Ludlow St. (bet. Houston & Stanton Sts.), 212-473-3535; www.paladar.ws
Lower Eastsiders "on a budget" hit Aarón Sanchez's "jumping" Nuevo Latino for "spicy hot" fare or join the "throngs at the bar" for the "fabulous", cooling mojitos; fans are pleased that it now accepts plastic.

PALM

| 24 | 16 | 21 | $62 |

837 Second Ave. (bet. 44th & 45th Sts.), 212-687-2953 ⊠
840 Second Ave. (bet. 44th & 45th Sts.), 212-697-5198
250 W. 50th St. (bet. B'way & 8th Ave.), 212-333-7256 ●
www.thepalm.com
Fab, "no-nonsense" feasting on "brontosaurus"-size steaks and lobsters is yours at this "well-oiled" trio that epitomizes "NY through and through"; despite "saloon-type" decor and "ornery waiters", they're "excellent for business", particularly on the "company card"; N.B. the original West-side-of-Second-Avenue location is preferred.

Paloma ●

| – | – | – | M |

60 Greenpoint Ave. (bet. Franklin & West Sts.), Brooklyn, 718-349-2400; www.palomanyc.com
Nestled on a quiet Greenpoint street, this new American satisfies those hankering for home cooking with seasonal dishes from an in-kitchen grill pit; the front bar opens to a dining area in back that doubles as a showcase for local artists and filmmakers.

Pampa ●⇗

| 21 | 17 | 17 | $36 |

768 Amsterdam Ave. (bet. 97th & 98th Sts.), 212-865-2929; www.pamparestaurant.com
"Mouthwatering chimichurri" is the topping of choice at this "funky" West Side Argentinean steak place where the "mammoth portions" are a "real deal"; the warm-weather patio is "magical", unlike the no-plastic policy and sometime service.

Pampano

| 24 | 23 | 22 | $53 |

209 E. 49th St. (bet. 2nd & 3rd Aves.), 212-751-4545; www.modernmexican.com
Chef Richard Sandoval and co-owner Placido Domingo have "redefined what Mexican cuisine can be" at this "elegant" Midtowner specializing in "scrumptious" seafood served by a "gracious staff" in "light-filled" environs; add "interesting imbibables" and you get an experience "so good you'll want to sing."

Pam Real Thai Food ⇗

| 23 | 8 | 15 | $20 |

404 W. 49th St. (bet. 9th & 10th Aves.), 212-333-7500; www.pamrealthai.com
"Flurries of garlic" suffuse the "genuine" Thai offerings at this Hell's Kitchen spot whose patrons are "prepared to wait" (no reservations) and who "smile when the bill arrives" ("dirt cheap", but cash only).

Panino'teca 275 ●

| ▽ 24 | 18 | 21 | $21 |

275 Smith St. (bet. Degraw & Sackett Sts.), Brooklyn, 718-237-2728; www.paninoteca275.com
The "coolest sandwich shop" around, this Carroll Gardens place offers "fabulous" main courses as well as "authentic Italian snacks" and "mean cocktails" in "hip" digs; the "huge" back garden is a summer treat, but they're "friendly" and "sweet to children" year-round.

Paola's

| 22 | 17 | 20 | $48 |

245 E. 84th St. (bet. 2nd & 3rd Aves.), 212-794-1890; www.paolasrestaurant.com
"Paola's presence is everywhere" at this East Side Italian standby where an abundance of flowers and "carefully conceived" food is to be

"treasured"; both "romantic" and "comfortable", this "neighborhood gem" continues to be "worth a detour" after 24 years in business.

Papaya King ⊅ | 20 | 4 | 11 | $7
179 E. 86th St. (3rd Ave.), 212-369-0648 ◐
200 W. 14th St. (7th Ave.), 212-367-8090 ◐
121 W. 125th St. (bet. Lenox & 7th Aves.), 212-665-5732
www.papayaking.com
"Crunchy franks with snap" and "fruit drinks you almost chew" make these "landmark" stand-up wiener wonderlands the "king of cheap eats"; fans can't decide what's more interesting, the "inspirational graffiti" on the walls or the characters on line with you.

Paper Moon Milano | 18 | 17 | 19 | $47
39 E. 58th St. (bet. Madison & Park Aves.), 212-758-8600;
www.papermoonrestaurant.com
"Perfect after shopping" or "after work", this "dependable" Midtown Northern Italian from Milan provides "fresh, well-prepared" dishes from a "standard trattoria" menu in quarters that are "more comfortable than chic"; the only downside is the pricing.

Paradou ◐ | 19 | 17 | 18 | $38
8 Little W. 12th St. (bet. Greenwich & Washington Sts.), 212-463-8345;
www.paradounyc.com
"Less hectic" than its Meatpacking District neighbors, this petite French bistro "charmer" with a Provençal patina provides "elegant sandwiches and interesting entrees" paired with an "impressive wine list"; bonus points go to its "enchanting" "year-round" garden.

Paris Commune | 18 | 18 | 16 | $39
99 Bank St. (Greenwich St.), 212-929-0509; www.pariscommune.net
This Village bistro's move from "humble quarters" to a "roomier", "glossy new home" nearby earns mixed notices, as do its "inexpensive French eats": some say "delicious", others "so-so"; despite "service glitches", all agree the brunch is "worth the long lines."

Parish & Co. ◐ | ▽ 21 | 18 | 19 | $41
202 Ninth Ave. (bet. 22nd & 23rd Sts.), 212-414-4988; www.parishandco.com
"Mixing portion sizes" allows for great grazing at this "imaginative", "out-of-the-mainstream" Chelsea New American; the "warm, inviting" ambiance "feels like Cheers with class", right down to occasionally Woody-style "clueless" service.

Paris Match ◐ | – | – | – | M
29 E. 65th St. (bet. Madison & Park Aves.), 212-737-4400
New East Side bistro that does the old-world Paris thing with Bordeaux-hued banquettes, a zinc bar, large mirrors and low lights; conversely, its modern, moderately priced French menu (which includes sushi and sake) is strictly of the moment.

Park, The ◐ | 16 | 24 | 15 | $42
118 10th Ave. (bet. 17th & 18th Sts.), 212-352-3313; www.theparknyc.com
Decor is "first and foremost" (followed by the free-flowing drinks) at this "gorgeous" West Chelsea Med "swankateria" that's equipped with hot tubs, a "glorious garden" and a "tented rooftop deck"; its young fans report moderate tabs, only "passable" fare and "ditzy service."

Park Avalon ◐ | 20 | 21 | 19 | $43
225 Park Ave. S. (bet. 18th & 19th Sts.), 212-533-2500;
www.brguestrestaurants.com
"Snazzy", "city-chic" surroundings laden with "candles and mirrors" serve as a "romantic" backdrop for "mingling singles" at this big

Flatiron New American; the midpriced, "well-flavored" fare "hits the spot", ditto the "truly enjoyable" (albeit "noisy") jazz brunch.

Park Avenue Cafe
24 | 22 | 23 | $64

100 E. 63rd St. (bet. Lexington & Park Aves.), 212-644-1900; www.parkavenuecafe.com
"Chef Neil Murphy's creativity dazzles" diners at this stylish East Side "favorite" where the "ingenious" cuisine and "folksy decor" is an ode to American food; its "money crowd" says the "top-notch" service alone is worth the "high prices" and reports that "the kitchen's chef's table is an experience."

Park Bistro
21 | 18 | 20 | $48

414 Park Ave. S. (bet. 28th & 29th Sts.), 212-689-1360
Everything's "so French" at this "charming", "old-time" Gramercy bistro offering "expertly prepared" food delivered by a "pleasant, capable" staff; the "comfortable", recently "spiffed-up" setting exudes a "lovely vibe", the "crowds" to the contrary.

Park East Grill
∇ 23 | 19 | 19 | $52

1564 Second Ave. (bet. 81st & 82nd Sts.), 212-717-8400; www.parkeastgrill.com
For "wonderful" meats and "super kosher" cooking "to plotz for", Eastsiders head to this steakhouse offshoot of the neighboring butcher shop; "prompt service" is a bonus, but "claustrophobic" wallet-pinchers deride the long, narrow space and prime prices.

Park Place
∇ 20 | 16 | 18 | $34

5816 Mosholu Ave. (B'way), Bronx, 718-548-0977
"Good places are scarce" in Riverdale, so it's "hard to get into" this "well-done" Continental offering "large portions" of "homestyle" food; a "patchwork of rooms" lends some "quirky charm", while other draws include "friendly" service and an "affable" bar scene.

Park Side ●
25 | 19 | 23 | $42

107-01 Corona Ave. (51st Ave.), Queens, 718-271-9321; www.parksiderestaurant.com
Only the "extra lucky" snag weekend tables at this "authentic" Corona Italian where the "savory delights" and "special service" feel like "Manhattan" but come at "Queens prices"; its *Sopranos* extras crowd recommends you catch a "bocce game across the street."

Park Terrace Bistro
∇ 21 | 20 | 20 | $33

4959 Broadway (bet. Isham & 207th Sts.), 212-567-2828; www.parkterracebistro.com
Residents "starved for dining diversity" in the "burgeoning" Washington Heights–Inwood area welcome this newcomer offering a "wonderful" French-Moroccan blend at "inexpensive" tabs; "somewhat kitschy decor" sets the appropriate mood for occasional belly dancing.

Parma ●
22 | 14 | 21 | $52

1404 Third Ave. (bet. 79th & 80th Sts.), 212-535-3520
Eastsiders "swear by" this "unpretentious" Northern Italian "mainstay" where the "classic" menu is "delicious" and the serious tabs softened by "incredible hospitality" (particularly "if they know you"); decor in need of "a little pick-me-up" just got a paint job.

Parsonage
∇ 21 | 22 | 18 | $42

74 Arthur Kill Rd. (Clarke Ave.), Staten Island, 718-351-7879
"Old-world charm" meets "contemporary" American-Continental cooking at this "landmark" Victorian home in "Historic Richmond Town"; despite a staff that "needs training" and that Staten Island address, devotees say "make a day of it" – it's "worth the voyage."

Pascalou
20 | 13 | 17 | $39

1308 Madison Ave. (bet. 92nd & 93rd Sts.), 212-534-7522
"Consistently good" French bistro food keeps them cramming into this "much-loved" Carnegie Hill "miniature" bistro where the "vast menu" is almost "bigger than the seating space"; the volume's "loud", the service "cheery" and the prices a "bargain."

Pasha
21 | 19 | 19 | $38

70 W. 71st St. (bet. Columbus Ave. & CPW), 212-579-8751;
www.pashanewyork.com
An "exotic" air and the "aroma of expertly spiced" dishes "transport you to Istanbul" at this midpriced West Side Turk that "buzzes like a bazaar"; "fast" service makes it "ideal" pre–Lincoln Center.

Pasquale's Rigoletto
24 | 18 | 22 | $38

2311 Arthur Ave. (Crescent Ave.), Bronx, 718-365-6644
"You have to be good to compete" in the "Bronx's Little Italy", and this "friendly" Italian "is up to the challenge", dishing out "excellent, down-home cooking"; the "loud, large" digs bedecked with "murals" and "mirrors" are like a GPS indicating this is Arthur Avenue.

Pasticcio
▽ 20 | 18 | 20 | $35

447 Third Ave. (bet. 30th & 31st Sts.), 212-679-2551; www.pasticcionyc.com
"Good for business meals", "family gatherings" or "romantic dinners", this "intimate" Murray Hill Italian vet has it all covered, with "honest, well-prepared" grub delivered "promptly"; Proseccheria, its eight-seat wine bar specializing in sparkling vinos, is another "plus."

PASTIS ●
21 | 21 | 17 | $43

9 Ninth Ave. (Little W. 12th St.), 212-929-4844; www.pastisny.com
"Celebrities", "socialites", "Eurotrash" and the merely "fabulous" cram into this ever "sizzling" Meatpacking District hub to graze on "flavorful French food" in a "trompe l'oeil version of a Paris bistro"; maybe it's a "lesser Balthazar" with "torturous" waits and "iffy service", but it's still "bliss" to be "in the thick of things" without overspending.

Patois
20 | 18 | 18 | $37

255 Smith St. (bet. Degraw & Douglass Sts.), Brooklyn, 718-855-1535;
www.patoisrestaurant.com
The "grandparent" of the Smith Street scene, this "easygoing", easy-on-the-wallet French bistro is a locus for "wonderful basics"; a fireplace and "pleasant garden" supply the "charm", while the pace can be either "leisurely" or "listless", depending on your mood.

Patroon ⊠
20 | 18 | 20 | $62

160 E. 46th St. (bet. Lexington & 3rd Aves.), 212-883-7373;
www.patroonrestaurant.com
"Good of its genre", Ken Aretsky's New American "power-broker refuge" provides "solid" steakhouse fare and "pro service" in a "refined" if "fraying" Midtown duplex; "cigar lovers" are hip to the "amazing" rooftop, even though it's "strictly expense-account territory."

Patsy's
21 | 16 | 20 | $44

236 W. 56th St. (bet. B'way & 8th Ave.), 212-247-3491; www.patsys.com
"One of Sinatra's old haunts", this simple Southern Italian near Carnegie Hall has been "chugging along" since 1944 with "old-style servers" serving "first-rate", "old-school" eats; some say it's "coasting", but "if it was good enough for Ol' Blue Eyes..."

Patsy's Pizzeria
21 | 12 | 15 | $22

206 E. 60th St. (bet. 2nd & 3rd Aves.), 212-688-9707

(continued)

(continued)

Patsy's Pizzeria

2287-91 First Ave. (bet. 117th & 118th Sts.), 212-534-9783
1312 Second Ave. (69th St.), 212-639-1000
509 Third Ave. (bet. 34th & 35th Sts.), 212-689-7500
67 University Pl. (bet. 10th & 11th Sts.), 212-533-3500
61 W. 74th St. (bet. Columbus Ave. & CPW), 212-579-3000
318 W. 23rd St. (bet. 8th & 9th Aves.), 646-486-7400

For "pizza with pizzazz", this chainlet is a prime player, even if connoisseurs say the separately owned East Harlem original with its coal-fired oven is "the best"; pitfalls include "indifferent service", "no delivery" and "cash only" at most locations.

Paul & Jimmy's

19 16 20 $42

123 E. 18th St. (bet. Irving Pl. & Park Ave. S.), 212-475-9540;
www.paulandjimmys.com

This "old-time" Gramercy "favorite" Italian, family-operated for more than half a century, "hasn't changed in years"; it's a "casual hideaway" where "traditional fare" and "cordial service" make you "feel at home."

Payard Bistro ⊠

24 21 19 $51

1032 Lexington Ave. (bet. 73rd & 74th Sts.), 212-717-5252; www.payard.com

"Set aside some treadmill time" and dig in at François Payard's East Side patisserie/bistro where "desserts are off the charts" and chef Philippe Bertineau's menu is a "showstopper"; it's not cheap and service may be a bit "stiff", but its many assets draw a full house.

Peanut Butter & Co.

20 13 15 $12

240 Sullivan St. (bet. Bleecker & W. 3rd Sts.), 212-677-3995;
www.ilovepeanutbutter.com

"Sweet, gooey childhood memories" are revisited at this Village sandwich shop, a "stick-to-the-roof-of-your-mouth haven" for "PB&J in every way conceivable"; "kids love it" though grinches grumble it's "overpriced for lunch-box fare."

PEARL OYSTER BAR ⊠

27 15 20 $40

18 Cornelia St. (bet. Bleecker & W. 4th Sts.), 212-691-8211;
www.pearloysterbar.com

Habitués of this Village "fantasy of a Maine clam shack" can't say enough about chef Rebecca Charles' "deservedly legendary" lobster roll or her "flawless" preparation of "whatever the fish of the day is"; service is "friendly" and "efficient" but waits can be "horrendous" given the "sardine" space.

Pearl Room

23 21 21 $45

8201 Third Ave. (82nd St.), Brooklyn, 718-833-6666

"No need to venture over the bridge" say Bay Ridge boosters of this "upscale" seafooder offering "standout" cuisine, an "elegant" setting and an "accommodating" staff sans "Manhattan pretension"; "all ages" show up, but it's those "young" things who keep it "noisy."

Pearson's Texas BBQ

16 10 14 $27

170 E. 81st St. (bet. Lexington & 3rd Aves.), 212-288-2700

"On a good day", the "smoky" fare is "delicious" at this low-budget Eastsider where fans are rooting for the new chef to make the BBQ less "hit-or-miss"; on not-good days, it's fine enough "to take the kids."

Peasant

22 21 19 $51

194 Elizabeth St. (bet. Prince & Spring Sts.), 212-965-9511;
www.peasantnyc.com

"Bring your flashlight and a date" to this "dark", "romantic" NoLita Italian purveying pricey, "adventurous" fare; the "wood-oven aroma" and "warm", "sexy" vibe effectively temper the "somewhat silly" menu-in-Italian shtick and occasional "snotty" server.

Peep ⏺

21 | 22 | 18 | $30

177 Prince St. (bet. Sullivan & Thompson Sts.), 212-254-7337;
www.peepsoho.net

The "pink neon" casts a "flattering light" at this "ultramodern" SoHo Thai "hipster joint" that offers "delicious dishes" and "trendy tropical cocktails" for "cheap"; it's also famed for "risqué" bathrooms that allow "people-watching" through a "one-way mirror."

Peking Duck House

22 | 15 | 17 | $33

236 E. 53rd St. (bet. 2nd & 3rd Aves.), 212-759-8260
28 Mott St. (bet. Chatham Sq. & Pell St.), 212-227-1810
www.pekingduckhousenyc.com

"Crispy", "succulent" Peking duck "carved tableside" is the standout dish among otherwise "average" eats at these modestly priced Chinese twins; just "don't expect to be pampered" in either the "upscale"-for-Chinatown digs or the more "spare" East Side outpost.

Pellegrino's ⏺

23 | 17 | 22 | $40

138 Mulberry St. (bet. Grand & Hester Sts.), 212-226-3177

Sure, it's another Little Italy "tourist" destination, but "satisfied patrons" award this moderately tabbed Mulberry Street Italian "top marks" for its *delicioso* fare, "gracious waiters" and "jovial atmosphere"; if you can "grab a table on the street", you can watch a great "sideshow."

Penang

19 | 18 | 16 | $30

240 Columbus Ave. (71st St.), 212-769-3988
1596 Second Ave. (83rd St.), 212-585-3838 ⏺
109 Spring St. (bet. Greene & Mercer Sts.), 212-274-8883
www.penangusa.com

"*Fantasy Island*"–style "bamboo kitsch" sets the mood for good Malaysian fusion with "complex sauces" at this "congested" but "reliable" mini-chain; its "twentysomething crowd" willingly overlooks the "scatterbrained service" in return for "affordable" tabs.

Penelope ⊅

22 | 20 | 20 | $20

159 Lexington Ave. (30th St.), 212-481-3800;
www.penelopenyc.com

A "little country restaurant" tucked into Murray Hill, this "sweet" American has "comfort food nailed down", with "old favorites" served in a "soothing pastel" room by a "friendly" staff; the "brunch lines" can be a "bother", but are eased by "free coffee while you wait."

Pepe Giallo To Go

21 | 10 | 15 | $19

253 10th Ave. (bet. 24th & 25th Sts.), 212-242-6055

Pepe Rosso Caffe

Grand Central, lower level (42nd St. & Vanderbilt Ave.), 212-867-6054

Pepe Rosso To Go

149 Sullivan St. (bet. Houston & Prince Sts.), 212-677-4555

Pepe Verde To Go ⊅

559 Hudson St. (bet. Perry & W. 11th Sts.), 212-255-2221

"*Molto bene*" chow that's about "as cheap as you can get" draws "throngs" to this Italian chainlet; they're "not much on space or looks", and if you can't deal with "annoyed servers", it's "best for takeout."

Peperoncino

▽ 19 | 17 | 18 | $31

72 Fifth Ave. (St. Marks Ave.), Brooklyn, 718-638-4760

"Busy as soon as it opened", this Park Slope newcomer serves such "terrific" Neapolitan brick-oven pies that it has become "another candidate for best pizza in Brooklyn"; expect a setting that's part "rustic countryside", part "urban funk" and always "frenetic."

Pepolino
25 | 17 | 22 | $47

281 W. Broadway (bet. Canal & Lispenard Sts.), 212-966-9983;
www.pepolino.com

"Lip-smacking", "authentic" Northern Italiana served by equally authentic "sexy waiters" have TriBeCans dubbing this "out-of-the-way" eatery "superlative"; despite "deafening" decibels, the "comfort" level has increased since the upstairs was expanded.

Perbacco ◐≠
25 | 18 | 20 | $35

234 E. Fourth St. (bet. Aves. A & B), 212-253-2038

"Mouthwatering" Italian-style tapas enhanced by a "delightful" wine list head the "fine" menu at this "cute" East Village small-plate specialist; it's a "best value", too, but the "secret's out", so expect "terrible lines" at prime times and tight seating once inside.

Periyali ⊠
25 | 21 | 23 | $53

35 W. 20th St. (bet. 5th & 6th Aves.), 212-463-7890;
www.periyali.com

It may have been "outglitzed" by newcomers, but this Flatiron Greek "doyen" still shines with its trademark "fabulous fresh fish"; other "Athenian delights" include a "lovely staff" and a "gorgeous" yet "understated" setting that please its "mature clientele" and justify the rather "pricey" tabs.

Perry Street ◐
– | – | – | E

176 Perry St. (West St.), 212-352-1900; www.jean-georges.com

Jean-Georges Vongerichten's latest offering occupies a coolly elegant, Calvin Klein–style space set in the base of a Richard Meier West Village tower; the petite dining room is mirrored by a succinct New French menu, featuring pared-down versions of dishes from the chef's eponymous flagship.

PER SE
28 | 27 | 28 | $201

Time Warner Ctr., 10 Columbus Circle, 4th fl. (60th St. at B'way),
212-823-9335; www.perseny.com

Thomas Keller's year-old "shrine to food" has acolytes "swooning" over his French–New American tasting menus, a "parade of culinary wizardry" providing "hours of bliss"; kudos also go to the "seamless", "choreographed" service (No. 1 in this *Survey*) and Adam Tihany's design that's "elegance stripped to its essentials", capped by "stunning" Central Park and Columbus Circle views; sure, the price is a "shocker", but "worth every C-note" for a "temporary pass to heaven"; appropriately, getting a reservation takes "divine intervention."

Persepolis
21 | 14 | 18 | $33

1423 Second Ave. (bet. 74th & 75th Sts.), 212-535-1100;
www.persepolisnyc.com

"They can kebab anything" at this "unusual" East Side Persian, though the "subdued flavors" shine brightest in its "aromatic rice dishes" (especially the "must-try" sour-cherry variety); happily, the "drab interior" is balanced by an "obliging owner" and "moderate prices."

Pershing Square
15 | 16 | 15 | $38

90 E. 42nd St. (Park Ave.), 212-286-9600

Conveniently parked opposite Grand Central Station, this "good-looking" American brasserie is a breakfast-and-lunch "business meeting" magnet; despite its "ordinary" pub grub and "poor service", come evening, things pick up when desk jockeys wind down with "after-work cocktails."

Pescatore ●

19 | 16 | 18 | $38

955 Second Ave. (bet. 50th & 51st Sts.), 212-752-7151;
www.pescatorerestaurant.com
"You get your money's worth" at this "reliable" Italian seafooder boasting "pretty darn good" fin fare and "no waiting"; the upstairs balcony seats offer prime East Midtown "people-watching."

Petaluma

18 | 16 | 18 | $42

1356 First Ave. (73rd St.), 212-772-8800; www.petalumanyc.com
Now in its 20th year, this Yorkville Italian "standby" provides consistently good cooking in an "easygoing neighborhood" environment; its "kid-friendly" reputation makes for one "terrific family place" that also "hums whenever Sotheby's has an auction."

PETER LUGER STEAK HOUSE ⌀

28 | 14 | 19 | $66

178 Broadway (Driggs Ave.), Brooklyn, 718-387-7400;
www.peterluger.com
Williamsburg's "utopia of steakdom" is again voted the No. 1 chophouse in this *Survey* – for the 22nd consecutive year – thanks to "buttery soft" meats and "killer sides" served in a faux (verging on funky) "German biergarten" setting; since they "don't take plastic", "bring cash, and plenty of it", and if the "gruff" waiters "mock you for asking for a menu", just "order what everyone else is having" – the "ultimate porterhouse."

Pete's Downtown

▽ 19 | 16 | 19 | $36

2 Water St. (Old Fulton St.), Brooklyn, 718-858-3510
"Great Manhattan skyline views" are "*the* reason to go" to this "pleasant" Dumbo Italian near the Brooklyn Bridge; while it's "not quite the River Cafe" (just across the street), the "good traditional" grub is much more "reasonably priced."

Pete's Tavern ●

13 | 15 | 15 | $28

129 E. 18th St. (Irving Pl.), 212-473-7676; www.petestavern.com
Gramercy's circa-1864 "landmark" tavern dispenses "great NYC flavor" and "decent" pub grub when you want to "keep it simple"; most show up to "soak up the atmosphere" that O. Henry once savored, even if it's gotten a little "dog-eared" since then.

Petite Abeille

19 | 14 | 16 | $25

401 E. 20th St. (1st Ave.), 212-727-1505
466 Hudson St. (Barrow St.), 212-741-6479
134 W. Broadway (Duane St.), 212-791-1360
107 W. 18th St. (bet. 6th & 7th Aves.), 212-604-9350
www.petiteabeille.com
"Convenient", "cozy" and a bit "cramped", this Belgian quartet bats out *magnifique* moules and frites washed down with "specialty brews" for a "good price"; Tintin-themed decor distracts from the "inconsistent" service.

Petrosino ●

▽ 20 | 18 | 17 | $43

190 Norfolk St. (Houston St.), 212-673-3773
"Chic simplicity" marks this Lower East Side Southern Italian offering "tasty", midpriced dishes matched with a "unique" selection of regional wines (a next-door annex, Canapa, serves lighter fare); "lackadaisical service" and "prime-time noise" are the downsides.

Petrossian ●

25 | 24 | 24 | $72

182 W. 58th St. (7th Ave.), 212-245-2214; www.petrossian.com
"Dandy deco" decor sets the "appropriate mood" for the "fabulous" repasts at this French-Continental "temple of class" near Carnegie Hall; renowned as a caviar-and-champagne "mecca", no surprise, it's "expensive", but there is a $24 lunch and $31 dinner prix fixe available.

Philip Marie ◑

21 | 17 | 20 | $41

569 Hudson St. (W. 11th St.), 212-242-6200

Both "affordable" and "delicious", this Village New American is a "solid choice" run by a "wonderful" husband-and-wife team; romantics in the mood for a "phenomenal evening" reserve the "hidden" table for two in the wine cellar.

Philly Slim's Cheesesteaks

▽ 22 | 8 | 15 | $11

789 Ninth Ave. (bet. 52nd & 53rd Sts.), 212-333-3042

"Big, juicy and messy" are the meals at this little Hell's Kitchen newcomer to the "eat-and-run" cheese steak competition; fans feel this joint is "as authentic as you'll get north of Philly", even if the staff needs to take "Customer Service 101."

Pho Bang ⊅

21 | 6 | 13 | $14

6 Chatham Sq. (Mott St.), 212-587-0870
157 Mott St. (bet. Broome & Grand Sts.), 212-966-3797
3 Pike St. (bet. Division St. & E. B'way), 212-233-3947
82-90 Broadway (Elmhurst Ave.), Queens, 718-205-1500
41-07 Kissena Blvd. (Main St.), Queens, 718-939-5520

There's "nothing faux" about these real-deal Vietnamese noodle shops doling out "banging pho" and other "delectable" items at "mind-blowingly cheap" tabs; "dingy" digs and "you-eat-you-leave" service come with the territory.

Phoenix Garden ⊅

22 | 8 | 11 | $26

242 E. 40th St. (bet. 2nd & 3rd Aves.), 212-983-6666

A "little bit of Chinatown" in Murray Hill, this "hidden" Cantonese may "taste like Hong Kong" but looks kind of "shabby"; "cheap" tabs and a BYO policy make up for the "cash-only" rule and "grumpy service."

Pho Viet Huong

21 | 11 | 14 | $17

73 Mulberry St. (bet. Bayard & Canal Sts.), 212-233-8988

Seekers of a "Vietnamese fix on the cheap" hone in on this "authentic" Chinatown spot and its "delicious", "exotic" dishes; it's a natural when on jury duty, but "don't expect decor" or a warm welcome from the sometimes "surly" staff.

Piadina ◑⊅

▽ 20 | 18 | 18 | $31

57 W. 10th St. (bet. 5th & 6th Aves.), 212-460-8017

Whether for a "first date" or "casual dinner", this "candlelit", "cash-only" Village Italian "passes the test", providing "simple, tasty" fare at "reasonable" prices; not quite being able to "see your food" is the only "slight inconvenience."

Piano Due ⊠

– | – | – | E

Equitable Ctr. Arcade, 151 W. 51st St., 2nd fl. (bet. 6th & 7th Aves.), 212-399-9400

From Scalini Fedeli's Michael Cetrulo comes this new, top-drawer Italian hidden on the *piano due* (translation: second floor) of a Midtown breezeway; the lush, vaulted-ceilinged space features all the classics served by a pro staff, while downstairs, Palio Bar and its famed Sandro Chia murals set the mood with heady specialty cocktails.

Piccola Venezia

25 | 17 | 24 | $53

42-01 28th Ave. (42nd St.), Queens, 718-721-8470;
www.piccola-venezia.com

You'll be "fed like there's no tomorrow" at this Astoria Italian where "absolutely delicious" red-sauce specialties "prepared with heart" are delivered by "old-world" waiters; sure, it's "expensive for Queens" and the "decor could use an update", but overall it's still "firing on all 12 cylinders."

Piccolo Angolo

25 | 13 | 22 | $36

621 Hudson St. (Jane St.), 212-229-9177
There's "no pretense, just good food" at this "tiny", ever popular West Village Italian known for its "enthusiastic" staff, led by "omnipresent" owner Renato Migliorini; the frequent "waits" are offset by the "low tabs" and high quality.

PICHOLINE

27 | 24 | 25 | $79

35 W. 64th St. (bet. B'way & CPW), 212-724-8585
"Soigné in every way", Terry Brennan's Lincoln Center French-Med is a "West Side star" with "heavenly food", "gracious hospitality" and a "beautiful" setting, capped by a "not-to-be-missed cheese cart"; although it costs a "pretty penny", Saturday's $28 prix fixe lunch is a "steal", and no matter what the cost, a meal in the private rooms is sure to be happily remembered.

Picket Fence

▽ 20 | 15 | 19 | $26

1310 Cortelyou Rd. (bet. Argyle & Rugby Rds.), Brooklyn, 718-282-6661; www.picketfencebrooklyn.com
An "ambitious" New American offering "excellent" comfort food in a "sorely lacking" Ditmas Park neighborhood; in fair weather, the "charming backyard" helps alleviate the crush in the "matchbox-small", "kid-friendly" digs.

Picnic Market & Café

▽ 23 | 13 | 17 | $27

2665 Broadway (101st St.), 212-222-8222
A spin-off of the Silver Moon Bakery, this new Upper West Side deli/cafe dispenses French fare that's both "imaginative" and "flavorful", and not too expensive; given the limited seating and decor, some say "takeout is your best bet."

Pietrasanta

19 | 13 | 18 | $33

683 Ninth Ave. (47th St.), 212-265-9471; www.pietrasantanyc.com
A longtime "sentimental favorite", this Hell's Kitchen Italian provides "reliable" food in a "tight", "knee-to-knee" setting; if the "homespun" digs are getting a bit "threadbare", tabs remain a "bargain", especially the $10 prix fixe weekend brunch.

Pietro's ⊠

23 | 13 | 22 | $57

232 E. 43rd St. (bet. 2nd & 3rd Aves.), 212-682-9760; www.pietros.com
Perhaps it's "old-fashioned", but this "clubby" Grand Central–area Italian steakhouse suits its "older" following with "big" helpings of "high-quality" fare served by a very "courteous" crew; "up-there" prices and a "tired-looking space" are its only turnoffs.

Pigalle ◗

17 | 17 | 16 | $34

Days Hotel, 790 Eighth Ave. (48th St.), 212-489-2233; www.pigallenyc.com
Night-owls are "bummed" that this "ersatz Parisian" brasserie in the Theater District is no longer open round the clock, but it's still "dependable" for "basic" French chow at "moderate" rates; the staff, however, "needs to attend charm school."

Pig Heaven ◗

19 | 14 | 18 | $32

1540 Second Ave. (bet. 80th & 81st Sts.), 212-744-4333; www.pigheaven.biz
Though the menu's "very porky" at this "above-average" East Side Chinese, there are equally "tasty non-pig items" available too; "swift" service and a "charming" owner compensate for "standard" looks.

Pinch, Pizza by the Inch

19 | 10 | 18 | $18

416 Park Ave. S. (bet. 28th & 29th Sts.), 212-686-5222; www.pizzabytheinch.com
"Customizable pizza" sold by the inch is the "shtick" at this "aim-to-please" Gramercy spot specializing in "crispy square pies" with

"creative" toppings (and other "well-prepared" eats too); critics complain that the tabs "pinch your wallet."

Ping's Seafood ⏺

21 | 12 | 14 | $26

22 Mott St. (bet. Bayard & Pell Sts.), 212-602-9988
83-02 Queens Blvd. (Goldsmith St.), Queens, 718-396-1238

"High-end" Hong Kong–style seafood and "delectable dim sum" draw droves to this "cheap" Chinatown-Elmhurst duo; "nothing special" describes the decor and the "language-barrier" service.

Pink Tea Cup ⏺⬱

20 | 11 | 15 | $21

42 Grove St. (bet. Bedford & Bleecker Sts.), 212-807-6755;
www.thepinkteacup.com

"Stick-to-your-ribs" Southern soul food in all its "fried goodness" is yours at this tiny Village vet providing "excellent calorie-per-dollar value"; as for the staff "attitude", insiders say just "shut up and eat."

Pinocchio

▽ 23 | 14 | 23 | $42

1748 First Ave. (bet. 90th & 91st Sts.), 212-828-5810

With its "hearty", midpriced cooking and "warm service", this "off-the-beaten-track" Yorkville Italian has fans hoping "word doesn't get out" – the "very small" space is already "cramped" enough.

Pintaile's Pizza

19 | 5 | 13 | $15

26 E. 91st St. (bet. 5th & Madison Aves.), 212-722-1967
1443 York Ave. (bet. 76th & 77th Sts.), 212-717-4990
1577 York Ave. (bet. 83rd & 84th Sts.), 212-396-3479

"Ultrathin" whole-wheat crusts and "clever", "California"-esque toppings distinguish the "designer pizzas" dispensed at these Eastsiders; "abrupt service" and "no decor" argue for delivery.

Pipa

21 | 23 | 17 | $40

ABC Carpet & Home, 38 E. 19th St. (bet. B'way & Park Ave. S.), 212-677-2233;
www.abchome.com

Favored by a "young crowd", this "festive" Flatiron Spaniard vends "super sangria" and "tasty" tapas in "sexy", "shabby-chic" digs; "pricey" tabs and "aloof" service are frequently part of the package.

Piper's Kilt ⏺

20 | 12 | 18 | $19

4946 Broadway (207th St.), 212-569-7071
170 W. 231st St. (Albany Crescent), Bronx, 718-548-9539

"When you hanker for a burger" or some "hangover relief", these "funky" Bronx/Inwood joints fill the bill with "better-than-average" pub grub; the "classic Irish bar" decor may verge on "dingy", but at least "all the sports channels are on."

Pisticci

24 | 19 | 20 | $29

125 La Salle St. (B'way), 212-932-3500

"Everybody's a regular" (or made to feel like one) at this cost-conscious Columbia-area Italian offering "big-flavored" dishes in a recently expanded, "home-away-from-home" setting; it's considered a "precious asset" despite the "middle-of-nowhere block."

Pizza Gruppo

▽ 26 | 12 | 18 | $18

186 Ave. B (bet. 11th & 12th Sts.), 212-995-2100

"Olsen twin–thin" crusts and "delish" toppings make this East Village brick-oven pizzeria a "standout"; despite little decor, some say the pies don't travel well and are thus best enjoyed "in house."

Pizza 33 ⏺

23 | 8 | 14 | $11

489 Third Ave. (33rd St.), 212-545-9191
171 W. 23rd St. (bet. 6th & 7th Aves.), 212-337-3661

(continued)

Pizza 33

268 W. 23rd St. (8th Ave.), 212-206-0999

Best known for their "late weekend hours", this pizzeria trio caters to nightcrawlers with a variety of "crunchy" "munchies"; connoisseurs who say the slices are a "bit overpriced" haven't lived in NYC long.

P.J. Clarke's ●

| 18 | 16 | 17 | $32 |

915 Third Ave. (55th St.), 212-317-1616; www.pjclarkes.com

The "epitome of classic NY alehouses", this "creaky" Midtown saloon around since 1884 has a "helluva burger" leading its "pub-grub" parade; while its upstairs adjunct, the Sidecar, is available for "classier" dining, either room is a "triumph for nostalgia."

Place, The

| 22 | 23 | 22 | $45 |

310 W. Fourth St. (bet. Bank & W. 12th Sts.), 212-924-2711; www.theplaceny.com

"Romance is in the air" at this "candlelit", "fireplace-equipped" West Village "trysting place"; fans say the "surprisingly good" Med–New American menu and "soft-spoken" staff will make you "fall in love with whomever you're with – so be careful who you bring."

Planet Thailand ●▱

| 21 | 20 | 16 | $22 |

133 N. Seventh St. (bet. Bedford Ave. & Berry St.), Brooklyn, 718-599-5758

This "hip", "well-priced" Williamsburg "food factory" serves "tasty" Thai-Japanese items from a menu that's as "extensive" as the "sleek room" is "vast"; in contrast to the "energetic" vibe, the staff displays "Buddha-like indifference."

Plate NYC ●

| ▽ 19 | 21 | 19 | $43 |

264 Elizabeth St. (bet. Houston & Prince Sts.), 212-219-9212; www.platenyc.com

A boutique by day, this NoLita newcomer morphs into an "adventurous" purveyor of Latin-Asian small plates at night; despite an "opened-last-week" feel, fans are "transported" by its canopied, year-round garden.

Ploes ●

| ▽ 23 | 21 | 21 | $35 |

33-04 Broadway (33rd St.), Queens, 718-278-1001

This "cheerful", well-served Astoria Greek offers a "vast", "good-value" menu that hits the usual Hellenic bases but adds a large choice of meze; with its arched brick ceiling and terra-cotta-toned walls, the room's "prettier than most."

Pó

| 25 | 16 | 21 | $48 |

31 Cornelia St. (bet. Bleecker & W. 4th Sts.), 212-645-2189; www.porestaurant.com

"Blissfully good" cooking that's "within striking distance of perfect" makes this "slim" Village Italian "tough to get into" (though "smooth service" "keeps the tables turning"); despite "cheek-by-jowl" seating, that $45, six-course tasting menu is a "steal."

Poetessa

| ▽ 21 | 16 | 17 | $37 |

92 Second Ave. (bet. 5th & 6th Sts.), 212-387-0065

Domestic ingredients are the basis of the simple, "imaginatively presented" menu at this new East Villager where the American-influenced Italian fare "won't strain the budget"; the cozy main dining room, outfitted European cafe–style, is enhanced by solid service.

POKE ⊠▱

| 26 | 4 | 17 | $32 |

305 E. 85th St. (bet. 1st & 2nd Aves.), 212-249-0569

"Exceptional sushi" sliced by a "friendly chef" at "bargain" rates is slightly muted by the "grim", "cramped" setup at this East Side

Japanese BYO – but regulars say "if you drink enough sake, you'll think it's Nobu."

Pomodoro Rosso
21 | 15 | 20 | $38

229 Columbus Ave. (bet. 70th & 71st Sts.), 212-721-3009
"More creative" than the typical "red-sauce haunt", this "earthy" Italian near Lincoln Center is "very popular" with waits "almost a guarantee" since they "don't take reservations"; but once you're in, service is "quick" and prices "affordable."

Pongal
21 | 12 | 13 | $24

1154 First Ave. (bet. 63rd & 64th Sts.), 212-355-4600
110 Lexington Ave. (bet. 27th & 28th Sts.), 212-696-9458;
www.pongal.org
"Dosas bursting with flavor" are the calling cards of these "small" South Indians offering "bountiful", "bargain"-priced kosher vegetarian fare; downsides include "early closings" and "rude" service.

Pongsri Thai
20 | 11 | 17 | $23

106 Bayard St. (Baxter St.), 212-349-3132
311 Second Ave. (18th St.), 212-477-2727
244 W. 48th St. (bet. B'way & 8th Ave.), 212-582-3392 ◗
165 W. 23rd St. (bet. 6th & 7th Aves.), 212-645-8808
www.pongsrionline.com
This "easygoing" Thai mini-chain "has the formula right", offering "flavorful" fare for "fabulously cheap" tabs, even if the decor is "low-budget" and service "efficient but not always gracious."

Ponticello
▽ 23 | 19 | 22 | $47

46-11 Broadway (bet. 46th & 47th Sts.), Queens, 718-278-4514;
www.ponticelloristorante.com
For "delicious" Italian cooking, Astorians head to this "old-school winner" where "pro waiters" keep things "seamless" in the recently "perked-up" dining room; while the price tags may be "high for Queens", it's worth a trip for the "daily specials" alone.

Pop Burger ◗
19 | 16 | 14 | $19

58-60 Ninth Ave. (bet. 14th & 15th Sts.), 212-414-8686
The mini-burgers strike some as "couture White Castle" at this Meatpacking District New American featuring a modish, fast-food counter in front and a "groovy", late-night lounge in back; "loud" acoustics and "ditzy" servers are part of the scene.

Popover Cafe
18 | 14 | 16 | $24

551 Amsterdam Ave. (bet. 86th & 87th Sts.), 212-595-8555;
www.popovercafe.com
"Perfect popovers" make for "crazy lines" at this "sweet" West Side brunch magnet; while service can be "lazy" and the rest of the American menu "average", the "unabashedly cute", "teddy bear–laden" digs appeal to sentimentalists.

Portofino Grille
20 | 22 | 21 | $41

1162 First Ave. (bet. 63rd & 64th Sts.), 212-832-4141; www.portofinogrille.com
What's "corny" to some is "romantic" to others at this East Side Italian best known for its "courtyard garden" decor and "twinkling stars in the ceiling"; the "hearty" fare is served by an "anxious-to-please" staff.

Portofino's ◗
▽ 20 | 19 | 19 | $43

555 City Island Ave. (Cross St.), Bronx, 718-885-1220;
www.portofinocityisland.com
Locals like the "whole package" at this "upscale" City Island Italian seafooder, from the "good food" and "reasonable prices" to the

"beautiful" water views; in winter, a "table near the fireplace" is just the ticket.

Positano ⏺
20 | 15 | 19 | $35

122 Mulberry St. (bet. Canal & Hester Sts.), 212-334-9808; www.positanolittleitaly.com

A "step above" the Little Italy tourist joints, this "old-school" Southern Italian offers "better-than-average" cooking, an "accommodating" staff and "reasonable" prices; boosters bypass the "ordinary interior" by dining alfresco on Mulberry Street.

Post House
24 | 19 | 22 | $67

Lowell Hotel, 28 E. 63rd St. (bet. Madison & Park Aves.), 212-935-2888; www.theposthouse.com

A magnet for "movers and shakers" of both sexes, this East Side "beef eater's must" offers "succulent steaks", "wonderful sides" and "stellar wines" in a handsome setting; service is "respectful", and even though you'll pay "top prices", most consider it a privilege to do so.

Posto
▽ 23 | 15 | 18 | $19

310 Second Ave. (18th St.), 212-716-1200

"Fantastic" "paper-thin" pizzas using the "finest ingredients" make this Gramercy greenhorn a "boon to the neighborhood"; the "friendly" service, "cozy", "tavern"-esque quarters and "inexpensive" tabs explain why the main problem is "getting in."

Prem-on Thai ⏺
▽ 22 | 22 | 19 | $35

138 W. Houston St. (bet. MacDougal & Sullivan Sts.), 212-353-2338

The few who have discovered this new Village Thai applaud its "delicious", "elegantly prepared" Siamese fare; "striking" digs and a "friendly" staff justify tariffs that are a little high for Thai.

Press 195 ⊭
20 | 12 | 16 | $17

195 Fifth Ave. (bet. Sackett & Union Sts.), Brooklyn, 718-857-1950; www.press195.com

Panini with "pizzazz" im-presses fans at this "casual" Park Slope cafe, despite the "indifferent" service and "uninspiring" digs; still, the garden's "great for a dawdle" and the sandwiches "good enough to outlast the fad."

Primavera ⏺
24 | 21 | 24 | $66

1578 First Ave. (82nd St.), 212-861-8608; www.primaveranyc.com

"Don't wait for a special occasion" to visit Nicola Civetta's "top-of-the-line" Italian, an East Side standby for "excellent" food, "superb" service and good old "romance"; the ambiance may be a bit formal (jackets suggested) and it's admittedly "pricey", but its "upper-crust" crowd reports being in "heaven" after the first bite.

Prime Grill
21 | 19 | 17 | $61

60 E. 49th St. (bet. Madison & Park Aves.), 212-692-9292; www.theprimegrill.com

"Kosher hipsters" are glatt to eat the "quality chops" and "decent" sushi offered at this "stylish" Midtown steakhouse; though a few oy-sayers find prices "outrageous" and service a "sore point", most report an "all-around satisfying" experience.

Primola
23 | 17 | 21 | $55

1226 Second Ave. (bet. 64th & 65th Sts.), 212-758-1775

This "pretty" East Side Italian supplies "consistently good" fare to "crowds of regulars" who are "treated like kings" (though it helps to be a "captain of industry" or at least dressed like one); in sum, it's a "great neighborhood resource – if you've got the resources."

Provence ◗

| | | | 21 | 21 | 20 | $52 |

38 MacDougal St. (Prince St.), 212-475-7500; www.provence-soho.com
"Authentic" Provençal cooking "at its best" – along with a "romantic" interior, "lovely" all-weather patio and "welcoming" staff – is yours at this longtime SoHo "charmer"; it's "perfect" for a "quiet dinner", even if a few feel it could "use freshening up."

Prune

| | | | 25 | 16 | 21 | $46 |

54 E. First St. (bet. 1st & 2nd Aves.), 212-677-6221
"Even the most jaded palate will be revived" by chef Gabrielle Hamilton's "touch-of-genius" New American menu at this "too tiny" East Villager; "caring" service and a "life-changing" brunch make up for the "cramped" conditions and "long waits" to get in.

Public ◗

| | | | 21 | 24 | 18 | $49 |

210 Elizabeth St. (bet. Prince & Spring Sts.), 212-343-7011;
www.public-nyc.com
In addition to a "super-hip", "library"-like interior and "exotic" International fare (including some "fantastic" Antipodean dishes), this NoLita "surprise" also hosts a "swinging" bar scene; service lapses and premium prices notwithstanding, it's "great for dates and groups."

Pukk

| | | ∇ | 22 | 21 | 22 | $23 |

71 First Ave. (bet. 4th & 5th Sts.), 212-253-2741
"Inventive", "affordable" dishes fill out the all-vegetarian menu of this "fresh" new East Village Thai where "fast" service and a "stylish", "space-age" setting (including the "coolest bathroom") elevate it to "destination" status.

Pump Energy Food

| | | | 19 | 5 | 14 | $13 |

Crystal Pavilion, 805 Third Ave., lower level food court (50th St.),
212-421-3055 🅱
113 E. 31st St. (bet. Lexington Ave. & Park Ave. S.), 212-213-5733
31 E. 21st St. (bet. B'way & Park Ave.), 212-253-7676
40 W. 55th St. (bet. 5th & 6th Aves.), 212-246-6844
112 W. 38th St. (bet. B'way & 6th Ave.), 212-764-2100
www.thepumpenergyfood.com
"Gym bunnies" and "health-food junkies" alike "start their motors" at this "busy" quintet offering "tasty" high-protein, low-fat eats good for both "the body and the wallet"; "coupons for freebies" and "speedy" delivery make up for the no-decor decor.

Punch

| | | | 19 | 18 | 17 | $36 |

913 Broadway (bet. 20th & 21st Sts.), 212-673-6333;
www.punchrestaurant.com
There's "something for everyone" on the "imaginative" menu at this "hidden" Flatiron Eclectic; it may be "no longer trendy", but with "tasty food", "reasonable prices" and "caring service", it's lauded by locals as an "all-around great neighborhood" spot.

Pure Food and Wine

| | | | 20 | 22 | 20 | $46 |

54 Irving Pl. (bet. 17th & 18th Sts.), 212-477-1010; www.purefoodandwine.com
Chef Matthew Kenney coaxes "fantastic" flavors from raw ingredients at this Gramercy vegan "phenomenon" where a "magical" garden and "knowledgeable" service also get raves; still, a few find it a bit expensive "for a restaurant without an electric bill."

Puttanesca

| | | | 18 | 15 | 17 | $35 |

859 Ninth Ave. (56th St.), 212-581-4177; www.puttanesca.com
Those hooked on this "Hell's Kitchen haunt" hail its "hearty", "no-frills" Italian fare, "served with a smile" at "competitive" prices;

though critics call the cooking "uninspired" and the digs "noisy", they admit it's "good for a quickie" pre-theater.

Pylos ◑
23 | 22 | 20 | $39

128 E. Seventh St. (bet. Ave. A & 1st Ave.), 212-473-0220; www.pylosrestaurant.com

"Refined" Hellenic fare is paired with an "excellent all-Greek wine list" at this "upscale" taverna set on a "downscale Alphabet City block"; service is "friendly", prices "reasonable" and the "clay pot–adorned ceiling" makes many "glad they're not in San Francisco."

Q, a Thai Bistro
21 | 19 | 19 | $34

108-25 Ascan Ave. (bet. Austin & Burns Sts.), Queens, 718-261-6599

The "imaginative" "haute Thai" cooking is worth queuing up for at this "tiny", easily affordable Forest Hills "favorite"; a "sweet" setting and "welcoming service" are extra benefits.

Quartino
21 | 19 | 19 | $31

11 Bleecker St. (Elizabeth St.), 212-529-5133 ⊟
21-23 Peck Slip (Water St.), 212-349-4433

"Surprisingly light" Ligurian fare is the calling card of this South Street Seaport "hideaway" and its newer NoHo sibling (which stresses fish and vegetarian dishes); "limited menus" and "laid-back" service are trumped by the "affordable" tabs.

Quatorze Bis
21 | 19 | 19 | $52

323 E. 79th St. (bet. 1st & 2nd Aves.), 212-535-1414

The "Rive Gauche" comes to the East Side via this longtime French "treasure" that's "reliable" for "simple, unpretentious" bistro fare; the attractive, "informal" room and "pleasant" service are also "comforting" — ergo the often "jam-packed" conditions.

Quattro Gatti
19 | 17 | 19 | $41

205 E. 81st St. (bet. 2nd & 3rd Aves.), 212-570-1073

"Still good after all these years", this "relaxed" East Side Italian "deservedly draws crowds" with "reliable cooking", "warm service" and "cozy" quarters (including a "great outdoor space"); some say the cuisine "needs updating", but most defend its "dependability."

Queen
23 | 12 | 20 | $38

84 Court St. (bet. Livingston & Schermerhorn Sts.), Brooklyn, 718-596-5955; www.queenrestaurant.com

"Worth a trip over the bridge", this circa-1958 Brooklyn Heights "favorite of judges and lawyers" offers "voluptuous" Italian fare including "incredible pastas" and the "best" homemade mozzarella; despite "no-frills" digs, it's an "oasis" on commercial Court Street.

Quercy
23 | 18 | 20 | $36

242 Court St. (Baltic St.), Brooklyn, 718-243-2151

"Cobble Hill is blessed" with this "charming" French bistro where the "homey" fare is "fantastic", the staff "couldn't be friendlier" and the "warm" space is "conducive to lingering"; in short, it "deserves to be recognized."

Quintessence
∇ 20 | 15 | 19 | $25

566 Amsterdam Ave. (bet. 87th & 88th Sts.), 212-501-9700
263 E. 10th St. (bet. Ave. A & 1st Ave.), 646-654-1823
www.raw-q.com

"Discerning vegans" and kosher keepers "don't miss the heat" at this raw food double act where the cuisine is "creative" and really "delicious"; doubters deem it "costly for vegetables" and lament the dubious decor.

Rachel's American Bistro ◑
18 | 14 | 18 | $35

608 Ninth Ave. (bet. 43rd & 44th Sts.), 212-957-9050; www.rachelsnyc.com
For "solid" New American fare "with flair" at "bargain" prices, this "Theater District find" comes "highly recommended"; true, it's a bit of a "squeeze", but the vibe is "cozy", service "pleasant" and brunch can be "wonderful."

Radha
– | – | – | I

173 Ludlow St. (bet. Houston & Stanton Sts.), 212-473-3374; www.radharestaurant.com
Cozy booths set the inviting tone at this new Eclectic vegetarian nestled in a narrow Lower East Side storefront; its name honors the Indian goddess of love while its inexpensive menu supplements subcontinental standards with pasta and stir-fries.

Raga
▽ 22 | 18 | 21 | $38

433 E. Sixth St. (bet. Ave. A & 1st Ave.), 212-388-0957; www.raganyc.com
"Gastro-nirvana" comes to the East Village via this Indian "diamond in the rough" where the cooking adds a "splash of French" flavors; "delightful service", "small" but "comfortable" digs and "reasonable" prices round out this standout experience.

Raices
– | – | – | M

25-39 Steinway St. (bet. 25th & 28th Aves.), Queens, 718-204-7711
Amid a dozen kebab joints in Astoria's Little Cairo, this new Nuevo Latino tastefully reminds that lamb isn't the only protein that can be turned on a spit; roasted chicken with Peruvian spices are as vibrant as the tangerine-and-blood-orange interior.

Rain
21 | 21 | 19 | $38

100 W. 82nd St. (bet. Amsterdam & Columbus Aves.), 212-501-0776; www.rainrestaurant.com
From the "savory" Pan-Asian eats to the "sexy", "*Casablanca*"-style tropical decor, this West Side "champ" provides a "true escape"; "moderate" tabs and "prompt" service make devotees all the more "devastated" over the recent closing of its crosstown sibling.

RAINBOW ROOM
20 | 28 | 22 | VE

GE Bldg., 30 Rockefeller Plaza, 65th fl. (enter on 49th St., bet. 5th & 6th Aves.), 212-632-5100; www.rainbowroom.com
This "one-and-only" "celebration" destination perched 65 stories above Rock Center parlays "sensational views", "gorgeous" deco digs, "fine" service and "impressive" Venetian cuisine via the Cipriani dynasty; expect a "dress-up crowd" with deep pockets who can handle the $200 prix fixe dinner (select Fridays and Saturdays) and the $80 brunch buffet (every Sunday).

Rao's ⌦⊘
21 | 16 | 20 | $64

455 E. 114th St. (Pleasant Ave.), 212-722-6709; www.raos.com
"Unless you're connected" to the Governor or the Godfather, "fuhgeddabout" getting into this "outstanding" East Harlem Southern Italian overseen by "charming" owner Frank Pellegrino and patronized by "movie stars" and "central casting" types; but since it's "essentially a private club", most just "buy the sauce" and "pretend."

Raoul's ◑
23 | 19 | 20 | $53

180 Prince St. (bet. Sullivan & Thompson Sts.), 212-966-3518; www.raouls.com
Even "before SoHo was cool", this "magical" French bistro was serving "fabulous" fare in "dark", "romantic" digs (including a garden room designed for "dalliances"); although the space is "tight" and the tabs "expensive", service is "warm" and the "food's worth it."

Rare Bar & Grill ◐
21 | 15 | 16 | $28

Shelburne Murray Hill Hotel, 303 Lexington Ave. (37th St.), 212-481-1999;
www.rarebarandgrill.com
This Murray Hill patty purveyor offers "terrific" "gourmet" burgers (from
foie gras to bison) with "esoteric toppings" in a "buzzing" setting;
though some snipe at service with "attitude", all agree that the rooftop
bar is "*the* place to be" come summertime.

Raymond's Cafe
▽ 19 | 17 | 21 | $34

88 Seventh Ave. (bet. 15th & 16th Sts.), 212-929-1778
"Dependable" American fare at modest prices plus "solicitous" service
make this longtime "Chelsea secret" a place "worth rediscovering"; ok,
the setting "could use some help", but at least it's "comfy" and "calm."

Rectangles ◐
– | – | – | M

1431 First Ave. (bet. 74th & 75th Sts.), 212-744-7470;
www.rectanglesrestaurant.com
This longtime East Villager has relocated to Yorkville, where it offers
the same unusual Yemenite Israeli kosher items (and fair prices) that
made it a Downtown staple; the vaguely medieval setting features
stone walls and antique mirrors.

Red Café
▽ 21 | 17 | 20 | $33

78 Fifth Ave. (bet. Prospect & St. Mark's Pls.), Brooklyn, 718-789-1100
"Good things come in small packages" at this "tiny" Park Slope bistro
offering first-class New American food served by a "gracious" staff;
add "pleasant" ambiance and "good value" and you've got a "keeper."

Red Cat
24 | 20 | 22 | $49

227 10th Ave. (bet. 23rd & 24th Sts.), 212-242-1122; www.theredcat.com
This Way West Chelsea "charmer" that begat a "mini-empire" (the
Harrison, Mermaid Inn) is "still a standout" thanks to its "phenomenal"
New American–Med cuisine at "rational prices" served in "stylish"
but "homey" digs; "high noise levels" aside, it's close to "purr-fect."

Redeye Grill ◐
21 | 19 | 19 | $51

890 Seventh Ave. (56th St.), 212-541-9000; www.redeyegrill.com
"Loud and brassy", Shelly Fireman's "massive" Midtown New American
supplies "pristine" seafood from a "huge menu" in "snazzy" digs; ok,
"it ain't cheap" and it may be a tad "touristy", but "fast", "cheerful"
service makes it busy at all hours.

Red Garlic ◐
20 | 14 | 17 | $28

916 Eighth Ave. (bet. 54th & 55th Sts.), 212-489-5237;
www.redgarlicrestaurant.com
It may not be "much to look at", but this "excellent little storefront"
brings some "hot stuff" to Hell's Kitchen with "consistently delicious"
Thai seafood at "decent prices"; "cramped quarters" notwithstanding,
it remains a "handy" pre-theater pick.

Regency
▽ 19 | 22 | 20 | $64

Regency Hotel, 540 Park Ave. (61st St.), 212-339-4050; www.loewshotels.com
A veritable "who's who" of "CEOs, politicos and celebs" colonizes the
Regency Hotel's dining room for its famed "über power breakfasts";
the New American fare at other meals is "good" (if "overpriced"),
service "fast and efficient" and after dark the space moonlights as
cabaret club Feinstein's.

Regional ◐
– | – | – | I

2607 Broadway (bet. 98th & 99th Sts.), 212-666-1915
At this Upper West Side regional Italian, dishes from around The Boot
come out of a kitchen barely concealed behind frosted glass; aside

from its dark-wood tables and comfy cushioned chairs, orange-and-white lampshades add a splash of color to the well-stocked bar.

Regional Thai
18 | 14 | 16 | $27

1479 First Ave. (77th St.), 212-744-6374
208 Seventh Ave. (22nd St.), 212-807-9872 ◗
"Neighborhood favorites" for "satisfying", "zingy" Thai chow including "creative specials", these vets also offer "kitschy" but "comfy" digs and "courteous" service; naysayers yawn "nothing groundbreaking", but the "bargain prices" still lure locals.

Relish ◗
21 | 20 | 17 | $26

225 Wythe Ave. (bet. Metropolitan Ave. & N. 3rd St.), Brooklyn, 718-963-4546;
www.relish.com
Whether you eat in the "funky", "mint-condition dining car" or "great garden", this Williamsburg "hipster" magnet impresses with "tasty" New American comfort food "on the cheap"; though service can be "slow", the brunch is "awesome" if "you don't mind a wait."

Remi
22 | 22 | 21 | $55

145 W. 53rd St. (bet. 6th & 7th Aves.), 212-581-4242
Set in a "soothing" Adam Tihany–designed space with a huge mural of Venice, this Midtowner maintains its "verve" with "first-rate", Venetian-accented Italian fare for tabs that are fairly "reasonable" given the "pricey neighborhood"; P.S. fans hope the "new owners will keep up" the high standards.

René Pujol
22 | 19 | 21 | $55

321 W. 51st St. (bet. 8th & 9th Aves.), 212-246-3023; www.renepujol.com
For more than 35 years, this French "warhorse" has been an "ideal" Theater District choice for "excellent" cooking and "smooth", "professional" service in "civilized" environs; *c'est vrai*, it's "not cheap", but regulars recommend the "terrific" $44 prix fixe dinner.

Republic
18 | 15 | 15 | $20

37 Union Sq. W. (bet. 16th & 17th Sts.), 212-627-7172;
www.thinknoodles.com
"Noodle lovers unite" at this spacious Union Square stalwart for "delicious" Pan-Asian dishes at "student-friendly" prices; the "communal picnic table seating" and "killer" noise levels are "turn offs", but "lightning-fast" service and "potent" cocktails compensate.

Re Sette
21 | 19 | 18 | $51

7 W. 45th St. (bet. 5th & 6th Aves.), 212-221-7530; www.resette.com
Loyal subjects report that this Midtown Italian turns out "delicious" (albeit "pricey") dishes from the Barese region in a "lovely" Gothic setting; though service can be "inattentive", the King's Table upstairs "can't be beat" for private parties.

Rib
– | – | – | M

357 West St. (bet. Clarkson & Leroy Sts.), 212-336-9330
Parked in a restored West Side Highway diner, this latest entry in the city's BBQ derby boasts affordable South Carolina–style offerings stressing, what else, ribs; the nostalgic setting includes a pleasant back garden for alfresco gnawing.

Ribot
– | – | – | E

780 Third Ave. (48th St.), 212-355-3700
Named after an Italian racehorse, this new Midtowner is quick out of the gate with authentic Mediterranean fare served either in a soaring bi-level space or roomy patio; an upscale, expense-account crowd on weekdays yields to more casual types on weekends.

Rice ⊄

21 17 16 $19

115 Lexington Ave. (28th St.), 212-686-5400 ◗
227 Mott St. (bet. Prince & Spring Sts.), 212-226-5775 ◗
81 Washington St. (bet. Front & York Sts.), Brooklyn, 718-222-9880
www.riceny.com

"There's something for everyone" on the "flavorful" menu of "round-the-world" eats at this "popular" Eclectic trio where "cramped" quarters are overlooked in favor of "bargain" prices; N.B. a Fort Greene outpost in the works.

Rice 'n' Beans

∇ 20 7 17 $22

744 Ninth Ave. (bet. 50th & 51st Sts.), 212-265-4444;
www.ricenbeansrestaurant.com

"Seriously good" Brazilian "comfort food" at "unbeatable prices" transforms this "no-frills", "shoebox-size" Hell's Kitchen space into a "great destination"; "quick service" makes it ideal for pre-theater too.

Rickshaw Dumpling Bar

17 10 14 $13

61 W. 23rd St. (bet. 5th & 6th Aves.), 212-924-9220;
www.rickshawdumplings.com

Those pulling for this "novel" new Flatiron Chinese praise its "singular food focus", the "tasty" traditional dumplings concocted by consulting chef Anita Lo (Annisa); doubters deem the offerings "inconsistent" and the decor minimal, but admit the tabs are "cheap."

Riingo

19 20 18 $56

Alex Hotel, 205 E. 45th St. (bet. 2nd & 3rd Aves.), 212-867-4200; www.riingo.com

Mavens maintain Marcus Samuelsson's East Midtowner supplies "unique" New American–Japanese fare (and "outstanding" sushi), "attentive" service and a "tranquil" hotel setting; but critics complain about "hit-or-miss" dishes at "ridiculous" prices and wonder "what's the fuss about?"

Risotteria

21 11 17 $22

270 Bleecker St. (Morton St.), 212-924-6664; www.risotteria.com

"Every risotto under the sun" (plus "gluten-free baked goods and veggie options") is supplied by this easily affordable Village Italian that thankfully "does all the stirring"; since the place is "tiny" and the "decor's a joke", it may be "better for takeout."

River

18 15 16 $28

345 Amsterdam Ave. (bet. 76th & 77th Sts.), 212-579-1888

"Solid if unspectacular" Thai-Vietnamese items "satisfy cravings in a pinch" at this Westsider; a "faux tropical" setting, "accommodating" service and "decent" pricing keep things flowing nicely.

RIVER CAFÉ

26 27 25 VE

1 Water St. (bet. Furman & Old Fulton Sts.), Brooklyn, 718-522-5200;
www.rivercafe.com

"Dress-up destination" dining doesn't get much better than at Buzzy O'Keeffe's Brooklyn waterfront "jewel" where the New American menu is "heavenly" and the "breathtaking" views of Lower Manhattan plus spectacular flowers and piano music provoke "at least one marriage proposal per night"; though a meal here can be pricey, it's "well worth any expense", especially if you snag a coveted window table.

Riverdale Garden

22 19 18 $42

4576 Manhattan College Pkwy. (242nd St.), Bronx, 718-884-5232;
www.riverdalegarden.com

"Eden" comes to Riverdale at this "ambitious" New American boasting an "innovative", "ever-changing" menu and a "romantic" mien complete with a "beautiful garden"; "spotty service" and "Manhattan prices" get "Bronx cheers", but overall they're doing well.

Riverview
▽ 20 24 20 $50

2-01 50th Ave. (49th Ave.), Queens, 718-392-5000; www.riverviewny.com
A "spectacular view of Manhattan" is the raison d'être of this Long Island City New American that's got "special occasion" written all over it; while a bit "overpriced for the neighborhood", the payoffs include "high standards in food and decor" not found elsewhere in the area.

Roberto Passon ●
▽ 23 15 16 $35

741 Ninth Ave. (50th St.), 212-582-5599
Thanks to "outstanding pastas", "attentive" service and an "arty" mood, this new Italian trattoria is a "welcome addition" to the burgeoning Hell's Kitchen dining scene; when ordered by the glass, the "excellent wines" arrive the Batali way – in quartino carafes.

ROBERTO'S
27 18 22 $45

603 Crescent Ave. (Hughes Ave.), Bronx, 718-733-9503
The "new surroundings" are "marginally better" but the food remains as "stellar" as ever at Roberto Paciullo's relocated "piece of heaven in the Bronx" that's rated the No. 2 Italian in this *Survey*; regulars "time their visit carefully" ("no reservations" taken) and "don't even think of looking at a menu", preferring to let the chef (a "real character") choose for them.

Roc ●
22 21 22 $47

190-A Duane St. (Greenwich St.), 212-625-3333; www.rocrestaurant.com
Everything's "solid as a roc" at this "unassuming" TriBeCa Italian, a "standby" for "well-prepared" meals and "cordial service"; ok, it can be a bit "demanding on the wallet", but then again it's "wonderful on the taste buds."

Rocco
▽ 20 14 19 $38

181 Thompson St. (bet. Bleecker & Houston Sts.), 212-677-0590; www.roccorestaurant.com
Since 1922, this "classic" Village "neighborhood joint" has been dishing out "unpretentious", "old-fashioned" Southern Italiana in "cozy" confines; a "spirited" staff and "value" pricing help explain its longevity.

Rock Center Cafe
19 21 19 $42

Rockefeller Ctr., 20 W. 50th St. (bet. 5th & 6th Aves.), 212-332-7620; www.restaurantassociates.com
Have "lunch with Prometheus" at this Rock Center American located somewhere between "expense-account territory" and the "tourist crossroads" of the world; views of "frolicking ice skaters" make the "reliable" food taste even better, and it now serves breakfast too.

Rocking Horse
21 17 17 $34

182 Eighth Ave. (bet. 19th & 20th Sts.), 212-463-9511
"Above and beyond regular burritos and tacos", this "creative" Mexican serves "sophisticated" stuff in a "fiesta" atmosphere on the rocking Chelsea strip; trouble is, the "chaotic" "party vibe" threatens to unhorse the grub.

Rolf's
17 22 17 $36

281 Third Ave. (22nd St.), 212-477-4750
"Kitsch" connoisseurs commend this Gramercy Park German's "over-the-top" holiday decor as "endearing" (though "wacky" and "tacky" also come to mind); as for the "hearty", moderately priced food, it may be "too heavy for lunch" – especially "if you want to stay awake."

Roll-n-Roaster ◑

| 19 | 7 | 12 | $12 |

64 Third Ave. (11th St.), 212-614-2333
2901 Emmons Ave. (bet. E. 29th St. & Nostrand Ave.), Brooklyn,
718-769-5831 ⌷
www.rollnroaster.com

A "Sheepshead Bay landmark" lands in the East Village via this low-budget, "fast-food" American that "does one thing pretty well": "awesome roast beef sandwiches"; though some shrug "wannabe", at least "you can get cheez on anything you pleez."

Roppongi

| 21 | 15 | 18 | $33 |

434 Amsterdam Ave. (81st St.), 212-362-8182

"Oft overlooked" in favor of its across-the-street competitor, Haru, this "bare-bones" West Side Japanese still slices some surprising sushi for smaller sums than its rival; its other selling point is more basic: you can "usually get a table" here pronto.

ROSA MEXICANO ◑

| 23 | 21 | 20 | $47 |

61 Columbus Ave. (62nd St.), 212-977-7700
1063 First Ave. (58th St.), 212-753-7407
www.rosamexicano.com

"Cut-above" crosstown Mexicans best known for their "signature guacamole" mashed tableside and washed down with "original" pomegranate margaritas that will leave you – and your wallet – "breathless"; a vast new Flatiron branch (in the former America space) is in the works.

Rose Water

| 25 | 19 | 22 | $39 |

787 Union St. (6th Ave.), Brooklyn, 718-783-3800

"Inventive, market-based dishes" are "expertly prepared and served" at this "memorable" Park Slope New American that also decants a "well-thought-out wine list"; although the "minuscule", "B&B"-like space "gets loud fast", this "tiny place has a big heart."

Rossini's ◑

| 22 | 17 | 23 | $52 |

108 E. 38th St. (bet. Lexington & Park Aves.), 212-683-0135;
www.rossinisrestaurant.com

"Out of the past" comes this Murray Hill Northern Italian "throwback" offering a good albeit "pricey" menu and "treat-you-like-a-king" service; "live opera" on Saturdays outperforms the rather "worn" decor.

Rothmann's

| 21 | 19 | 22 | $62 |

3 E. 54th St. (bet. 5th & Madison Aves.), 212-319-5500;
www.rothmannssteakhouse.com

Joining the "crowded steak market", this "macho" Midtown chop shop "imported from the 'burbs" is one that "nobody talks about" much despite its "satisfying" eats and "excellent" service; "no real style" might have something to do with it, or possibly the bull-market pricing.

Roth's Westside Steakhouse

| 19 | 16 | 18 | $48 |

680 Columbus Ave. (93rd St.), 212-280-4103;
www.rothswestsidesteakhouse.com

A "handy location" and lack of local competition draw Westsiders to this "eager-to-please" steakhouse where the meats are "solid" and the staff "friendly"; though critics find things "predictable" and the tabs "out of line for the neighborhood", nightly live music "makes it special."

Rouge

∇ | 20 | 19 | 19 | $38 |

107-02 70th Rd. (Austin St.), Queens, 718-793-5514

"*Très bonne*" is the word on this "traditional" French bistro that's as "authentic" as it gets in Forest Hills while still exuding a "Manhattan quality"; "friendly but not overbearing" service and moderate checks trump the "cramped" digs.

Royal Siam

18 | 11 | 17 | $25

240 Eighth Ave. (bet. 22nd & 23rd Sts.), 212-741-1732
The "spices are right" at this "affordable", "above-average" Chelsea Thai where the "heat can be tailored to your taste" and the decor needs more than tailoring; a few find it a "bit cramped", but then again "many couples like that."

Roy's New York

24 | 20 | 22 | $50

Marriott Financial Ctr., 130 Washington St. (bet. Albany & Carlisle Sts.), 212-266-6262; www.roysrestaurant.com
There's "a refreshing bit of the aloha spirit" (the "waiters smile") at Roy Yamaguchi's Financial District outpost where the "creative" Hawaiian fusion fare features "vibrant flavors"; though "not cheap" and in a "not-happening" locale, it's still "heaven for seafood fans."

RUB BBQ

▽ 19 | 8 | 15 | $27

208 W. 23rd St. (bet. 7th & 8th Aves.), 212-524-4300; www.rubbbq.net
A Kansas City pit master leaps into the red-hot NY BBQ fray with this Chelsea newcomer that just "could be a contender"; they're "still working out the kinks" – i.e. "running out" of menu items early in the evening, which "rubs many the wrong way."

Ruby Foo's ●

19 | 21 | 17 | $41

1626 Broadway (49th St.), 212-489-5600
2182 Broadway (77th St.), 212-724-6700
www.brguestrestaurants.com
Like "dining in a movie set", these "glitzy" West Side Pan-Asian purveyors are decorated in "campy" Shanghai style and are "always crowded and noisy"; while the "surprisingly good" food is better than the "rushed" service, the overall sensation is "amusement park ride."

Rue 57 ●

19 | 19 | 17 | $45

60 W. 57th St. (6th Ave.), 212-307-5656; www.rue57.com
A French brasserie that "unaccountably serves sushi", this more than "serviceable" Midtowner is also known for its "ideal" location near Carnegie Hall and lunches so "crazy busy" that "you can't hear yourself talk"; by the way, it's "now open for breakfast."

Rughetta ☒

23 | 16 | 21 | $39

347 E. 85th St. (bet. 1st & 2nd Aves.), 212-517-3118
"Civilized dining" comes to Yorkville via this "simple" little Southern Italian that's a "step above" the competition; "romantic quarters" and "affordable" pricing make the first-rate, "classic" preparations all the tastier.

Russian Samovar ●

19 | 16 | 17 | $46

256 W. 52nd St. (bet. B'way & 8th Ave.), 212-757-0168;
www.russiansamovar.com
This "decadent" Theater District Russian "cultural experience" may serve a "classic" Continental menu, but the "extensive vodka list" and live music may be the real "stars" of the show; "sit next to Baryshnikov" (a co-owner) and it's even more "intoxicating."

Ruth's Chris Steak House

24 | 20 | 22 | $60

148 W. 51st St. (bet. 6th & 7th Aves.), 212-245-9600; www.ruthschris.com
"Cholesterol be damned" could be the motto of this handsome Theater District link of the New Orleans–bred chain chop shop, known for "tender, juicy" steaks served "sizzling in butter"; it's as "overpriced" as any in the genre, though many admit to still being full "two meals later."

Sabor ◐
18 17 16 $35
1725 Second Ave. (89th St.), 212-828-0003
Though the West Side original is no more, this affordable Yorkville
Nuevo Latino carries on with an "interesting tapas" menu washed down
with "excellent sangria"; but dissenters disparage the "munchkin-
size" portions that can "add up" to real money.

Sachiko's on Clinton ◐
▽ 23 21 20 $50
25 Clinton St. (bet. Houston & Stanton Sts.), 212-253-2900;
www.sachikosonclinton.com
"Ambitious" new Lower East Side Japanese taking "basic ingredients
to a new level", starting with its "house special *kushiage*" (fried-and-
skewered meat and vegetables); adding to its allure is that "hushed,
Zen" setting, which seems less Zen when the bill arrives.

Sacred Chow
– – – I
227 Sullivan St. (bet. Bleecker & W. 3rd Sts.), 212-337-0863;
www.sacredchow.com
Recently relocated to NYU territory, this venerable vegetarian coffee
shop/prepared foods specialist is also a full-service restaurant; expect
a cheap, all-kosher vegan menu served in a low-lit space.

S'Agapo
22 15 19 $33
34-21 34th Ave. (35th St.), Queens, 718-626-0303
You "may need a dictionary" to converse with the Greek waiters at
this "no-frills" Astoria Hellenic, but the modestly priced "food needs
no translation", especially its signature, "grilled-to-perfection" fish;
regulars eschew the "dowdy" interior and request "outdoor seating."

Sahara ◐
21 14 15 $26
2337 Coney Island Ave. (bet. Aves. T & U), Brooklyn, 718-376-8594;
www.saharapalace.com
It's "no wonder they keep expanding" at this "gigantic" Gravesend
Turk that pulls in "loud, bustling" crowds with its "festive" air and "huge
platters" of "tasty" vittles; sure, the "decor's tacky" and service
"erratic", but in return prices are "fantastic."

SAIGON GRILL ◐
23 9 16 $21
620 Amsterdam Ave. (90th St.), 212-875-9072
1700 Second Ave. (88th St.), 212-996-4600
www.saigongrill.com
There's "always a mob" at these crosstown Vietnamese siblings
thanks to their "flavorful, exotic" fare priced "insanely cheap"; if
"zero decor" and "mediocre service" are off-putting, there's always
"lightning-fast" delivery.

Sakura Café
– – – M
388 Fifth Ave. (bet. 6th & 7th Sts.), Brooklyn, 718-832-2970
The name translates as cherry blossom, and everything at this new
Park Slope Japanese reflects a light, subtle touch, from the plates to
the signature rice flavored with the flower; expect delicate home
cooking and reasonably priced sushi.

Sala
22 21 18 $35
344 Bowery (Great Jones St.), 212-979-6606
35 W. 19th St. (bet. 5th & 6th Aves.), 212-229-2300
www.salanyc.com
"Top-of-the-line tapas" and a "dark", "cavernous basement" make for
a nightly "party after 10 PM" at this "snazzy" NoHo Spaniard where
the "sangria keeps flowing"; the newer Flatiron outpost may be "not
as romantic", but it's every bit as "chill."

Salaam Bombay
21 17 18 $34

317 Greenwich St. (bet. Duane & Reade Sts.), 212-226-9400;
www.salaambombay.com
"Less crowded than you'd expect", this "old-style" TriBeCa Indian is
best known for its "high-quality lunch buffet", bargain-priced at $13.95;
but some say "tired" decor and "service that could be friendlier" have
made it a "shadow" of its former self.

Sal Anthony's
17 16 17 $37

55 Irving Pl. (bet. 17th & 18th Sts.), 212-982-9030
Sal Anthony's Lanza
168 First Ave. (bet. 10th & 11th Sts.), 212-674-7014
Sal Anthony's S.P.Q.R.
133 Mulberry St. (bet. Grand & Hester Sts.), 212-925-3120
www.salanthonys.com
"You don't last this long without delivering the goods", and this
"longtime" Italian trio still turns out solid, classic repasts that are a
"good value" – provided that you overlook the "touristy" Little Italy
crowd and somewhat "stale" settings.

Sala Thai ●
20 13 18 $27

1718 Second Ave. (bet. 89th & 90th Sts.), 212-410-5557
A "tried-and-true" neighborhood "staple", this Upper East Side Thai
dispenses "better-than-average" food that's "such a bargain"; the
weak link is its "seedy charm" (how about some "new furniture"?).

Salsa y Salsa
18 14 14 $25

206 Seventh Ave. (bet. 21st & 22nd Sts.), 212-929-2678
This "straight-up" Chelsea Mexican seduces "fun-loving locals" with
"flavorful", "reasonably priced" specialties and carefully crafted
cocktails; most sidestep the "tiny", "tacky" setting in favor of the
"outdoor tables" with "people-watching" possibilities.

Salt ⊠
22 19 20 $41

58 MacDougal St. (bet. Houston & Prince Sts.), 212-674-4968;
www.saltnyc.com
Salt Bar ●
29A Clinton St. (bet. Houston & Stanton Sts.), 212-979-8471
"Attention to detail" is the hallmark of this SoHo New American
"sleeper", a shaker-size affair with "communal tables" that are "more
intimate than you expect"; its Lower East Side sibling focuses more
on drinking and snacking, though the edibles are equally "amazing."

Salute!
19 19 17 $40

270 Madison Ave. (39th St.), 212-213-3440
For "great energy", it's tough to top this Murray Hill Northern Italian
that lures "masses of businessmen" at lunchtime with "consistent"
cooking; dinner is quieter, except for that "after-work bar scene."

Sambuca
18 15 18 $34

20 W. 72nd St. (bet. Columbus Ave. & CPW), 212-787-5656;
www.sambucanyc.com
"Everyone's in a good mood" at this West Side "homestyle" Italian
featuring "heaping" platters of affordable pasta; it's a lot "like
Carmine's but less crazed", though contras call it a "consistently
inconsistent" exercise in "quantity over quality."

Sammy's Roumanian
20 10 18 $48

157 Chrystie St. (Delancey St.), 212-673-0330
"Heartburn heaven", this "one-of-a-kind" Eastern European serves
"heavy" Jewish fare in a "tacky" Lower East Side basement that feels

like a wild bar mitzvah; just "pace yourself" and "bring your cardiologist (you'll need him)", and you'll have one "hoot" of a good time.

Sandia
▽ 25 | 21 | 21 | $42

111 W. 17th St. (bet. 6th & 7th Aves.), 212-627-3700; www.sandiarestaurant.com
Spanish for 'watermelon', this subterranean Chelsea newcomer serves "inventive" Pan-Latin fare in "sexy" digs done up in think-pink, juicy-fruit hues; fusion cocktail–sipping and small plate–snacking are bringing in "cool" types who appreciate the palatable prices.

Sandobe ◗
19 | 12 | 14 | $24

167 First Ave. (bet. 10th & 11th Sts.), 212-505-3348
"Super-cheap, super-size sushi" is the name of the game at this East Village Japanese that's moved to a "larger space" with mixed results: fans say it's "much improved", foes say it's "lost quality", but the divey digs and "inattentive" service remain constant.

San Domenico
22 | 22 | 22 | $70

240 Central Park S. (bet. B'way & 7th Ave.), 212-265-5959; www.sandomenicony.com
"Upscale and serene", this "civilized" CPS Italian features "elegant", "subtle" fare via chef Odette Fada backed up by smoothly "professional service" supervised by owner Tony May; the "jackets-required" policy and "quite pricey" tabs don't faze the "soigné" set who report it's "great for entertaining clients", especially at the bargain lunch.

San Pietro ⊠
24 | 21 | 23 | $68

18 E. 54th St. (bet. 5th & Madison Aves.), 212-753-9015; www.sanpietro.net
The "flawless" Southern Italian food is "awesome – but so's the bill" – at this "top-drawer" Midtowner where the "CEO-filled" dining room testifies to its reputation as a "power-lunch destination"; it's "quieter at night", although a "warm welcome is assured" at any time.

Santa Fe
18 | 14 | 17 | $37

73 W. 71st St. (bet. Columbus Ave. & CPW), 212-724-0822
Relocated "two blocks north", this Lincoln Center–area Southwesterner still dispenses the "same comforting menu" and "strong margaritas" at the same comfortable prices; but the "antiseptic" new digs strike some as more "cafeteria than dining room."

Sant Ambroeus
▽ 21 | 18 | 20 | $49

1000 Madison Ave. (bet. 77th & 78th Sts.), 212-570-2211
259 W. Fourth St. (Perry St.), 212-604-9254
www.santambroeus.com
A "glittery European crowd" makes for prime people-watching at this fashionable Village Italian famed for its espresso and gelati (plus Milanese items at dinner); champions cheer the recent reopening of its original Madison Avenue flagship.

Sapa
21 | 26 | 19 | $55

43 W. 24th St. (bet. B'way & 6th Ave.), 212-929-1800; www.sapanyc.com
"Stellar" chef Patricia Yeo mans the burners at this "trendy" new Flatiron French-Vietnamese where the cooking lies somewhere between "highly imaginative" and "respectable"; more successful is the "drop-dead gorgeous" room (and loo), though some suggest it's still in the "teething" stage.

Sapori D'Ischia
▽ 26 | 16 | 21 | $45

55-15 37th Ave. (56th St.), Queens, 718-446-1500
"Specialty food shop by day" turned "fine-dining" restaurant after dark, this "hidden gem" in a Woodside "warehouse neighborhood" surprises

with "creative" Southern Italian cooking enhanced by occasional "live opera"; some have even "fallen in love by the dairy case."

Sapphire Indian
| 21 | 18 | 19 | $40 |

1845 Broadway (bet. 60th & 61st Sts.), 212-245-4444; www.sapphireny.com
"Top of the caste", Columbus Circle–area Indian where a "first-class dinner" with "accommodating service" will cost you, but "bargain"-hunters hail the $12.95 "eat-all-you-want" lunch buffet.

Sapporo East ◗
| 22 | 10 | 17 | $24 |

245 E. 10th St. (1st Ave.), 212-260-1330
Reliable quality, "cheap" prices and an "'80s punk rock" soundtrack result in "long", NYU-laden lines at this East Village Japanese; so what if it's "sort of a hole-in-the-wall", it's "too packed to see" anyway.

Sarabeth's
| 21 | 17 | 17 | $31 |

423 Amsterdam Ave. (bet. 80th & 81st Sts.), 212-496-6280
40 Central Park S. (bet. 5th & 6th Aves.), 212-826-5959
Chelsea Mkt., 75 Ninth Ave. (bet. 15th & 16th Sts.), 212-989-2424
1295 Madison Ave. (bet. 92nd & 93rd Sts.), 212-410-7335
Whitney Museum, 945 Madison Ave. (75th St.), 212-570-3670
www.sarabeth.com
"Swamped at brunch, dead at dinner", these "homespun" Americans offer "bed and breakfast food" in "girlie", "tea shoppe" settings; for those who find the morning lines "too much trouble", insiders tout the "snazzy new CPS location" where it's "easier to get a table."

Saravanaas
| – | – | – | M |

81 Lexington Ave. (26th St.), 212-679-0204; www.saravanaas.com
The first East Coast branch of a successful Southern India chain, this bright, modern Gramercy newcomer serves vegetarian cuisine; its moderate pricing makes everything even tastier.

Sardi's ◗
| 16 | 21 | 19 | $50 |

234 W. 44th St. (bet. B'way & 8th Ave.), 212-221-8440; www.sardis.com
This "touristy" Theater District "landmark" has been around "for a million years" and is more celebrated for its famous caricatures of show folk than for its "tired", "expensive" Continental fare; but even if it's a "shadow of its former self", it's still a popular party venue.

Sarge's Deli ◗
| 19 | 8 | 14 | $22 |

548 Third Ave. (bet. 36th & 37th Sts.), 212-679-0442;
www.sargesdeli.com
"Nosh" around the clock at this always-open Murray Hill "pastrami palace" where "huge portions" of "kosher-ish" "Jewish soul food" is vended; what with the "cracked upholstery" and "grumpy", "battle-tested" staff, regulars report "delivery's the way to go."

SAUL
| 26 | 19 | 24 | $51 |

140 Smith St. (bet. Bergen & Dean Sts.), Brooklyn, 718-935-9844
"Haute" meets "homey" at Saul Bolton's "exceptional" Boerum Hill New American where the "fantastic" food and "thoughtful wine list" are "Manhattan worthy", the room "understated" and the staff "aims to please"; if a bit "high end for Smith Street", it's still a "bargain given the quality."

Savann
| 19 | 15 | 18 | $38 |

414 Amsterdam Ave. (bet. 79th & 80th Sts.), 212-580-0202;
www.savannrestaurant.com
"Intimate" and "relaxed", this Upper West Side French-Med offers "better-than-expected" vittles and "good-value" pricing (especially that $21.95 early-bird); the only question is "why isn't it more crowded?"

Savoia
21 | 17 | 17 | $28

277 Smith St. (bet. Degraw & Sackett Sts.), Brooklyn, 718-797-2727
The brick-oven "pizza is the best thing to order" at this Carroll Gardens Southern Italian that's like "Naples without traveling" thanks to its "deliciously authentic" cooking; on the downside is that "spacey" staff.

Savore
▽ 21 | 18 | 24 | $44

200 Spring St. (Sullivan St.), 212-431-1212
"Old-world hospitality" is the strong suit of this "sophisticated" SoHo Tuscan that's "always excellent" yet often "empty"; a new wine room in back showcases an "outstanding selection" that complements the smartly served, "savory" cooking.

Savoy
23 | 20 | 23 | $53

70 Prince St. (Crosby St.), 212-219-8570
Upstairs is "cozy-elegant" and downstairs "more casual" at this SoHo Med–New American where chef Peter Hoffman's "innovative" use of Greenmarket items makes for "delightful" (albeit "expensive") dining; the "soothing" vibe and "gracious" staff are always "in season."

Scaletta
21 | 18 | 22 | $49

50 W. 77th St. (bet. Columbus Ave. & CPW), 212-769-9191;
www.scalettaristorante.com
As "civilized" and "sedate" as its "mature", *Golden Girls* following, this West Side Northern Italian features "consistently good" food plus service with "old-world charm"; though "not exciting" enough for some, regulars rejoice "you can actually hear your guests" here.

Scalinatella ◑
24 | 16 | 21 | $70

201 E. 61st St. (3rd Ave.), 212-207-8280
Despite the "grottolike" basement location, this "authentic" East Side Capri-style Italian shines with "heavenly food and service"; but it sure "ain't cheap", particularly its "endless list of specials."

SCALINI FEDELI ⊠
26 | 25 | 25 | $78

165 Duane St. (bet. Greenwich & Hudson Sts.), 212-528-0400;
www.scalinifedeli.com
Chef-owner Michael Cetrulo "keeps them coming back" to his "luxury" TriBeCa Northern Italian with tableside visits, "swoon-inducing cuisine", "white-glove service" and "romantic" environs (a "great use of the old Bouley space"); just be sure to "save up", since such "flawlessness" can be "extremely expensive."

Schiller's ◐
19 | 20 | 17 | $35

131 Rivington St. (Norfolk St.), 212-260-4555; www.schillersny.com
This "wildly popular" Keith McNally Lower East Side Eclectic is always jammed with "Bergdorf blondes" who "come for the scene" but stay for the "guilty pleasures" menu; that "double take"–worthy bathroom makes up for the "airport runway" din.

Scopa
18 | 16 | 16 | $38

79 Madison Ave. (28th St.), 212-686-8787; www.scoparestaurant.com
"Excellent thin-crust pizza" and "delicious" small plates highlight the menu of this "airy" Gramercy Italian, whose "Romanesque dining room" is dominated by an "enormous bar"; what with the "iffy", "mood-swing" service, some "prefer its take-out offshoot" next door.

Scottadito Osteria Toscana ⊅
▽ 21 | 21 | 19 | $36

788A Union St. (bet. 6th & 7th Aves.), Brooklyn, 718-636-4800;
www.scottadito.com
Park Slope's latest "secret weapon" is this "charming" new Tuscan, a "cozy", "brick"-lined affair with a "rustic" feel that's echoed on the

"delicious" menu; everything's "attractive" here (except for the "cash-only" policy), but for best results "eat in the wine cellar."

SEA

| 22 | 22 | 17 | $23 |

75 Second Ave. (bet. 4th & 5th Sts.), 212-228-5505
114 N. Sixth St. (Berry St.), Brooklyn, 718-384-8850 ◗

www.spicenyc.net
The Williamsburg half of this Thai duo "looks like a million bucks" with "swings", "crazy bathrooms" and a "dance club vibe"; though not as "flamboyant", its tiny East Village sibling shares its reputation as a "cheapskate's paradise" and "tastes just as good."

Sea Grill ⊠

| 24 | 24 | 23 | $60 |

Rockefeller Ctr., 19 W. 49th St. (bet. 5th & 6th Aves.), 212-332-7610;
www.theseagrillnyc.com
Credit the "knockout views" of Rock Center's skating rink and the "exceptional" cooking for this "sophisticated" seafooder's "special-occasion" reputation; while prices may be "hefty" and the crowd "touristy", it works for locals who want to pretend they're "on vacation."

Second Avenue Deli ◗

| 23 | 10 | 15 | $24 |

156 Second Ave. (10th St.), 212-677-0606; www.2ndavedeli.com
Pastrami "perfumes the air" and arrives "piled sky-high on rye" at this "quintessential" East Village kosher deli "landmark" that's been making folks feel like chopped liver for over 50 years; "kvetch"-as-kvetch-can service comes with the territory.

Secretes

| – | – | – | E |

513 E. Sixth St. (bet. Aves. A & B), 212-228-2775
Don't confuse this romantic boîte with an ordinary tapas bar; its avant-garde chef presents a compact but ambitious roster of Eclectic bites meant to titillate, not satiate – despite prices that suggest otherwise.

Sensa

| – | – | – | M |

676 Sixth Ave. (21st St.), 212-807-0615
A former Rao's chef is in the kitchen at this new Flatiron eatery, but rather than red sauce it's Med- and Asian-inflected New American fare that's on offer here; the sense-pleasing setting includes a sexy black-lit dining room, shimmering white-tiled bar and big corner windows.

Seppi's ◗

| 18 | 16 | 17 | $44 |

Le Parker Meridien, 123 W. 56th St. (bet. 6th & 7th Aves.), 212-708-7444;
www.seppisnewyork.com
"Despite the Italian-sounding name", this French bistro serves "reliable" fare in a "convenient" Midtown space; "late-night" hours (till 2 AM) balances out the "iffy service" and "nondescript" decor.

Serafina ◗

| 19 | 16 | 15 | $37 |

Dream Hotel, 210 W. 55th St. (B'way), 212-315-1700
38 E. 58th St. (bet. Madison & Park Aves.), 212-832-8888 ⊠
29 E. 61st St. (bet. Madison & Park Aves.), 212-702-9898
393 Lafayette St. (4th St.), 212-995-9595
1022 Madison Ave., 2nd fl. (79th St.), 212-734-2676
www.serafinarestaurant.com
"Designer pizza" and "fabulous people-watching" are on the modestly priced menu of this Italian quintet; still, the "swarms" sometimes buzz "too loud", and "surly" service threatens to "spoil la dolce vita."

Serendipity 3 ◗

| 19 | 20 | 15 | $27 |

225 E. 60th St. (bet. 2nd & 3rd Aves.), 212-838-3531; www.serendipity3.com
"Indulge your inner child" at this East Side cafe/toy shop "institution" that's not celebrated for its "decent", affordable Americana but

rather for its "sinful desserts" – especially its "signature frozen hot chocolate" that's worth the weight and the "hours" on line.

Sette ◐

| | 19 | 17 | 17 | $38 |

191 Seventh Ave. (bet. 21st & 22nd Sts.), 212-675-5935; www.nycrg.com
"Good standards", a "sleek, chic setting" and fair prices make this Chelsea Italian a "great date spot"; yet some feel it "lacks soul", with "nothing special" going on either food- or service-wise.

Sette Enoteca e Cucina

| | – | – | – | M |

207 Seventh Ave. (3rd St.), Brooklyn, 718-499-7767
New Park Slope Southern Italian eatery/wine bar offering fish, meat and poultry from a wood-burning oven; a vaguely rustic setting, enclosed sidewalk seating and affordable vinos heighten its local allure.

Sette Mezzo ◐⇗

| | 23 | 15 | 20 | $59 |

969 Lexington Ave. (bet. 70th & 71st Sts.), 212-472-0400
"Reservations are passed down in patrons' wills" at this "clubby" Italian where the "improbably good" Italian fare draws the "nobility of the East Side"; since it accepts plastic from no one, "bring plenty of cash."

Seven ◐⊠

| | 18 | 16 | 17 | $39 |

350 Seventh Ave. (bet. 29th & 30th Sts.), 212-967-1919; www.sevenbarandgrill.com
Just the ticket "pre- or post-Garden event", this "busy, busy, busy" New American gets more civilized "after the local cocktail crowd goes home"; while the food is "decent" enough, the "nonattentive" service needs work.

718

| | 23 | 22 | 20 | $38 |

35-01 Ditmars Blvd. (35th St.), Queens, 718-204-5553
"Left Bank chic" comes to Astoria at this "destination" bistro where "intriguing", Spanish-accented French food is served at "outer-borough prices"; conversely, its success might "account for much of the rise in local real estate values."

71 Clinton Fresh Food

| | 24 | 17 | 21 | $56 |

71 Clinton St. (bet. Rivington & Stanton Sts.), 212-614-6960; www.71clintonfreshfood.com
Renowned for its "inventive", "daring" kitchen, this Lower East Side storefront provides "esoteric" New American fare with "flavor combos that really work"; while the "minimalist", minuscule digs are no surprise in this neighborhood, "big tastes" and a "warm" staff compensate.

71 Irving Place

| | 19 | 18 | 17 | $14 |

71 Irving Pl. (bet. 18th & 19th Sts.), 212-995-5252; www.irvingfarm.com
One of Gramercy Park's perks is this reasonably priced, "picture-perfect neighborhood cafe" usually crowded with "bohemian" types "reading for hours on the same cup of coffee"; the major grounds for complaint is a "staff that's flakier than the desserts."

Sevilla ◐

| | 23 | 15 | 20 | $38 |

62 Charles St. (W. 4th St.), 212-929-3189; www.sevillarestaurantandbar.com
"Ageless" at 65, this Village Spaniard is a "garlic lover's paradise" with "*muy bueno*" dishes, "killer" sangria and "old-school" "tag-team" service; it "hasn't changed in years" (i.e. "still packed, still a bargain"), and the "leftovers reheat wonderfully" at home.

Sezz Medi'

| | 21 | 18 | 18 | $30 |

1260 Amsterdam Ave. (122nd St.), 212-932-2901; www.sezzmedi.com
Tucked away on an "up-and-coming" Morningside Heights block is this student-friendly Mediterranean "oasis" where the "colorful

"presentation" and "European atmosphere" are as "warm" as the "delectable" brick-oven pizzas.

Shaan

22 | 21 | 19 | $39

Rockefeller Ctr., 57 W. 48th St. (bet. 5th & 6th Aves.), 212-977-8400; www.shaanofindia.com
From its "jeweled chandelier" to the "formal", "old-world" service, this "luxe" Indian near Rockefeller Center is a "tasteful" destination; sure, it's a bit "pricey" for the genre, but the $14.95 lunch buffet and the early-bird dinner are "incredible values."

Shaburi

▽ 23 | 21 | 19 | $53

125 E. 39th St. (bet. Lexington & Park Aves.), 212-867-6999; www.shaburi.com
The first U.S. outpost of the Taiwanese chain, this new Murray Hill shabu-shabu/sukiyaki specialist dazzles with a chic bi-level setting and "attentive" service; "unusual", high-quality meats add up to "expensive" tabs, especially since you "cook your own food" here.

Shabu-Shabu 70

19 | 13 | 20 | $35

314 E. 70th St. (bet. 1st & 2nd Aves.), 212-861-5635
"Self-cooking without the cleanup" is the draw at this "been-around-forever" East Side hot-pot (and sushi) purveyor whose eponymous specialty dish reminds some of "Japanese fondue"; "considerate" service and fair pricing keep this "off-the-beaten-path" spot hopping.

Shabu-Tatsu ●

▽ 21 | 13 | 16 | $31

216 E. 10th St. (bet. 1st & 2nd Aves.), 212-477-2972
"Participatory dining" is the thing at this "traditional" East Village Japanese specializing in shabu-shabu and sukiyaki; it's "wholesome" fun for kids and "cook-your-own" types, and prices are affordable, but both the decor and service could use some work.

Shaffer City Oyster Bar & Grill ☒

23 | 15 | 21 | $47

5 W. 21st St. (bet. 5th & 6th Aves.), 212-255-9827; www.shaffercity.com
A "good reminder that NY is a shore town", this "casual" Flatiron spot features "first-rate fish" and an "outstanding raw bar"; "gregarious" chef-owner Jay Shaffer will help treat any cases of "sticker shock."

Shake Shack ⇄

22 | 14 | 12 | $13

Madison Square Park (23rd St.), 212-889-6600; www.shakeshacknyc.com
"Quality fast food" comes to Madison Square Park via this "irresistible" alfresco all-American from Danny Meyer vending "highly addictive" burgers, franks and shakes; despite the "crazy lines", fans are pleased to hear it has extended its season, now open March–December.

Shanghai Cuisine ⇄

▽ 20 | 12 | 12 | $22

89 Bayard St. (Mulberry St.), 212-732-8988
The appeal of this low-budget C-towner comes down to "two words: soup dumplings"; though the rest of its Shanghai-style menu is "authentic" enough, "lackadaisical service", "close quarters" and a cash-only rule can leave a sour taste.

Shanghai Pavilion

22 | 18 | 19 | $34

1378 Third Ave. (bet. 78th & 79th Sts.), 212-585-3388
An "upscale" East Side Shanghainese that's "above average" thanks to a "delicious, creative menu"; the "civilized" verging on "fancy" digs might help explain the slightly high-for-Chinese pricing.

Shark Bar ⇄

▽ 21 | 15 | 18 | $36

307 Amsterdam Ave. (bet. 74th & 75th Sts.), 212-874-8500; www.sharkbar.com
There's "a lot of chow for your buck" at this West Side soul fooder that's "withstood the test of time" thanks to "down-home cooking like

mama used to make"; expect a "gold chain and velour tracksuit"–clad crowd enjoying the "casual" setting.

Sharz Cafe & Wine Bar
`19` `14` `19` `$38`

435 E. 86th St. (bet. 1st & York Aves.), 212-876-7282
A "terrific", "well-priced selection of wine by the glass" lures "mature" types to this "undiscovered" East Side Med that also boasts good food and "cheerful service"; seating can be a little "cramped", however, especially for that "great early-bird special."

Shelly's New York ●
`21` `19` `21` `$54`

104 W. 57th St. (bet. 6th & 7th Aves.), 212-245-2422; www.shellysnewyork.com
"Old-school seafood and steaks" fill out the "retro menu" of Shelly Fireman's "roomy" Midtown duplex equipped with a "mountainous raw bar" downstairs and a "jazz-and-martinis" boîte above; ok, it's "costly", but "risqué art" via Peter Max and Red Grooms is a "funny" distraction.

Sherwood Cafe ●⇄
∇ `19` `22` `16` `$27`

195 Smith St. (bet. Baltic & Warren Sts.), Brooklyn, 718-596-1609; www.sherwoodcafe.com
"Funky" and "festive", this "appealing" Smith Street French serves "comfort bistro food" in a "retro" roadshow setting (with much of its "kitschy" "junk-store" decor for sale); partisans put up with the "relax-and-wait-it-out service" and tout its "fab garden."

Shopsin's
∇ `19` `13` `14` `$23`

54 Carmine St. (bet. Bedford & Bleecker Sts.), 212-924-5160; www.shopsins.com
Like something out of a "sitcom", this Village Eclectic "marches to its own drummer" with a "miles-long menu" and some "arbitrary house rules" (e.g. "no sharing", "no parties over four"); just be "fearless" enough to "brave the moods" of the "irascible chef-owner."

shore
`17` `14` `18` `$38`

41 Murray St. (bet. Church St. & W. B'way), 212-962-3750; www.freshshorecoast.com
Think "clambake" to get the gist of this New England seafooder in TriBeCa serving "simple, down-home" dishes; chowderheads "not impressed" by the "hit-or-miss" food prefer its "classier" sibling, Fresh.

Shorty's on the Half Shell ⊠
`–` `–` `–` `M`

470 Sixth Ave. (bet. 11th & 12th Sts.), 212-243-8226
New England and Maryland mingle with Italy on the menu of this Greenwich Village seafooder decked out with old-time marine memorabilia; neighborly service, a casual bar area and reasonable prices have locals dropping anchor here.

Shula's Steak House
`19` `18` `20` `$57`

Westin NY Times Sq., 270 W. 43rd St. (bet. B'way & 8th Ave.), 212-201-2776; www.donshula.com
A "chain steakhouse" set in a "chain hotel" lobby near Times Square, this "sports-themed" shrine ("hope you like football") naturally caters "primarily to tourists", serving "big" slabs o' meat; foes find "nothing special" going on, save those go-for-broke tabs.

Shun Lee Cafe ●
`21` `17` `18` `$39`

43 W. 65th St. (bet. Columbus Ave. & CPW), 212-769-3888; www.shunleewest.com
"Dim sum at all hours" is the draw at this "busy" West Side Chinese that also offers a variety of dishes that are just as "delicious" but "less expensive than" its more upscale "sister next door"; it's also renowned as a "quick" resource for Lincoln Center–goers.

SHUN LEE PALACE ❶

| 24 | 20 | 22 | $52 |

155 E. 55th St. (bet. Lexington & 3rd Aves.), 212-371-8844
Proving "there is such a thing as upscale Chinese food", Michael Tong's Midtown "institution" combines "striking" surroundings and "silky service" to provide plenty of "panache"; ok, it may come at "Hong Kong real estate prices", but in exchange you get "emperor's-quality" "gourmet" dining that has kept NYers happy for a generation.

Shun Lee West ❶

| 23 | 21 | 21 | $50 |

43 W. 65th St. (bet. Columbus Ave. & CPW), 212-595-8895;
www.shunleewest.com
"Impeccable" cooking and "theatrical" decor have made this "black-lacquered" Lincoln Center–area Chinese a West Side "mainstay" for 25 years; it sure "ain't cheap", but most say it's "worth it", particularly if you enjoy being "handled by the staff as carefully as a Ming vase."

Siam Inn

| 22 | 14 | 20 | $29 |

854 Eighth Ave. (bet. 51st & 52nd Sts.), 212-757-4006; www.siaminn.com
"NY efficiency and Thai charm" come together in the service at this Theater District Asian where "upscale" grub is served for "lowscale" bucks; "very plain decor" leads some to opt for the "excellent delivery."

Siam Square ⊋

| ▽ 23 | 16 | 19 | $26 |

564 Kappock St. (Henry Hudson Pkwy.), Bronx, 718-432-8200;
www.siamsq.com
Regulars "pay extra attention to the specials" at this "delicious" Bronx Thai where the chow comes "just as spicy as you desire"; some find the space "slightly claustrophobic", but "bargain" prices and "authenticity" are sufficient compensations.

Silverleaf Tavern

| 21 | 21 | 21 | $55 |

70 Park Avenue Hotel, 43 E. 38th St. (Park Ave.), 212-973-2550;
www.silverleaftavern.com
A "sleeper in a lacking neighborhood", this "civilized" Murray Hill newcomer purveys an "attractive" American mix of "classic NY dishes with modern twists"; "wacky" decor notwithstanding, locals say it's "much needed" – particularly its "upbeat" bar.

Sipan ❶

| 21 | 18 | 17 | $39 |

702 Amsterdam Ave. (94th St.), 212-665-9929
"Excellent seafood" washed down with "potent pisco sours" help make this "upscale" yet moderately priced Peruvian a "popular" West Side locus; it's a welcome "change of pace" for those seeking "something different", even if service can be a bit on the "slow" side.

Sip Sak ❶⊋

| 20 | 11 | 16 | $21 |

928 Second Ave. (bet. 49th & 50th Sts.), 212-583-1900; www.sip-sak.com
"Wonderfully exotic" Turkish fare comes at "moderate prices" at this UN-area storefront blessed with "BYO" status; so long as you don't mind the "cash-only" rule and rather "peculiar" owner, this one's a "find."

Sistina ❶

| 25 | 18 | 23 | $63 |

1555 Second Ave. (bet. 80th & 81st Sts.), 212-861-7660
"Tuscan titillation" abounds at this "longtime" East Side Northern Italian where *molto bene* food is served by a "top-notch" staff in "airy" digs; sure, it's "expensive" and caters to the "well-heeled", but the "attention to detail" alone is worth it.

66

| 21 | 24 | 20 | $56 |

241 Church St. (Leonard St.), 212-925-0202; www.jean-georges.com
"Almost too chic for words", Jean-Georges Vongerichten's TriBeCa "Chinese moderne" features "cleanly executed" cuisine in a "Zen",

Richard Meier—designed space that's "soothing" enough to cushion the "Diamond Jim Brady" prices; since the menu can be "uneven", wags say the "waiters are the tastiest thing there."

Smith & Wollensky

| 23 | 18 | 20 | $63 |

797 Third Ave. (49th St.), 212-753-1530; www.smithandwollensky.com
Beef eaters agree this "clubby", "man's man" East Side steakhouse is well "worth the high price of admission" given the "gargantuan" portions and "old-fashioned NY" service – or you can always "save a few dollars" at Wollensky's Grill next door (that's also "open later").

Smoked ●

| – | – | – | M |

103 Second Ave. (6th St.), 212-388-0388; www.smokednyc.com
The BBQ frenzy sweeping NYC has arrived in the East Village via this "upscale" spot with a menu that mingles traditional mesquite-grilled ribs and fried chicken with hickory-plank fish and duck confit; the "casual decor" contrasts with the "not so casual prices", however.

Smorgas Chef

| ▽ | 19 | 14 | 17 | $26 |

924 Second Ave. (49th St.), 212-486-1411 ●
53 Stone St. (William St.), 212-422-3500
www.smorgaschef.com
For a "refreshing change of pace", try this Midtown/Downtown Scandinavian duo vending "delicious Swedish meatballs" and "exotic" beverages; the Stone Street branch boasts a particularly "charming setting" on a "historic" lane, evidence of that area's exciting "revival."

Snack

| 23 | 12 | 17 | $23 |

105 Thompson St. (bet. Prince & Spring Sts.), 212-925-1040
Aka the "little engine that could", this "tiny" SoHo Greek may be the size of a "walk-in closet" (with only 16 seats) but puts out food "so delicious you won't care"; naturally, "long waits" come with the territory, so insiders "go during off-hours."

Snack Taverna

| 22 | 17 | 18 | $39 |

63 Bedford St. (Morton St.), 212-929-3499
Snack's "younger, bigger sister", this "charming" Village Greek offers more "upscale" cuisine with "brio" washed down with an "intriguing" list of all-Hellenic wines; while the mood's "friendly" and "sociable", some find it "more precious than necessary."

Soba Nippon

| ▽ | 21 | 15 | 18 | $34 |

19 W. 52nd St. (bet. 5th & 6th Aves.), 212-489-2525; www.sobanippon.com
Buckwheat noodles are the stars at this "modestly priced" Midtown Japanese soba shop, not the "decor that's ready for the museum of '60s restaurant design"; while lunch can be a "hectic" affair, dinner is decidedly more "quiet and serene."

Soba-ya

| 23 | 17 | 19 | $26 |

229 E. Ninth St. (bet. 2nd & 3rd Aves.), 212-533-6966
It "tastes like Japan" at this East Village noodle specialist where the "slurpalicious" soba is smothered in a "tantalizing array of broths" served "hot and cordially"; a "quiet, relaxing atmosphere" takes the sting out of the "serious waits" for entry.

Soho Cantina ●

| ▽ | 19 | 16 | 17 | $35 |

199 Prince St. (bet. MacDougal & Sullivan Sts.), 212-598-0303;
www.sohocantina.com
"Trendy" SoHo taco belle where "tasty" Mexican eats "make up for lacking space", and "fabulous" drinks "make up for the decor"; now if only there was something to compensate for that "where-is-the-waitress?" service.

Soju ⊠⇗
– – – M

145 Atlantic Ave. (bet. Clinton & Henry Sts.), Brooklyn, 718-624-7658;
www.sojurestaurant.com
Locals get convivial on soju and sake cocktails at this Brooklyn Heights
Pan-Asian with a red interior and a courtyard festively strewn with
lights; soaking up any happy-hour excesses are the well-priced rice
bowls that can be customized with chile sauces and peanut pastes.

Solera ⊠
21 | 19 | 20 | $51

216 E. 53rd St. (bet. 2nd & 3rd Aves.), 212-644-1166;
www.soleranyc.com
"Authentic classic Spanish cuisine" is the draw at this Midtown
"standby" with an "array of tapas" plus a "solid list" of wines and
sherries; "gracious service" and an "inviting" duplex setting bode
well for a "romantic" if "expensive" night out.

Solo
▽ 23 | 22 | 21 | $66

Sony Plaza Atrium, 550 Madison Ave. (bet. 55th & 56th Sts.), 212-833-7800;
www.solonyc.com
"You don't have to be Jewish" to enjoy this kosher Midtown Med that's
become a magnet for "Madonna" and the "Kabbalah Center" crowd
thanks to "terrific" food and "chic" digs; ok, "glatt ain't cheap", but
for most, it's "worth the shekels."

Sol y Sombra ◑
– – – I

462 Amsterdam Ave. (bet. 82nd & 83rd Sts.), 212-400-4036
This Upper West Side Spaniard, whose name means 'sun and shade',
serves up myriad tapas for any occasion – whether or not the sun is
shining – plus plenty of Iberian wines to go with them; brick walls, stone-
tile floors and dark-wood tables make a classy backdrop.

Son Cubano ⊠
21 | 21 | 18 | $42

405 W. 14th St. (bet. 9th Ave. & Washington St.), 212-366-1640;
www.soncubanonyc.com
"Conversation is futile" at this "extremely loud" Meatpacking District
Cuban where the "tasty" grub and "old Havana" decor play second
fiddle to the "dancing and partying"; the "could-be-better service" is
more tolerable after a "potent drink" at the "happening bar."

Song ⇗
▽ 20 | 18 | 18 | $22

295 Fifth Ave. (bet. 1st & 2nd Sts.), Brooklyn, 718-965-1108
This "Joya spin-off" features the same "outstanding" selection of
"cheap" Thai chow in a similarly "industrial" setting, this time on Park
Slope's Fifth Avenue Restaurant Row; it's also "just as loud" as its sire,
leading some to suggest "takeout's better."

Sosa Borella
20 | 16 | 18 | $35

832 Eighth Ave. (50th St.), 212-262-7774 ◑
460 Greenwich St. (bet. Desbrosses & Watts Sts.), 212-431-5093
www.sosaborella.com
For "something out of the ordinary", try these Italian-Argentine fusion
specialists in TriBeCa and the Theater District vending very good vittles
at a "decent cost"; sure, they could "use some decor" and "service
can be too casual", but overall, life's "harmonious" here.

SPARKS STEAK HOUSE ⊠
25 | 19 | 21 | $66

210 E. 46th St. (bet. 2nd & 3rd Aves.), 212-687-4855;
www.sparkssteakhouse.com
You get to "watch wheeler-dealers wheel and deal" at this "manly
man" Midtown meat market where "everything's big" – from the steaks'
flavors and the wine list to the dining room and the noise level; it's a

prime example of "how cholesterol should taste", but "bring your checkbook" and a "carefree attitude" to deal with the frequent waits since people are dying to eat here.

Spice
20 | 16 | 16 | $24

199 Eighth Ave. (bet. 20th & 21st Sts.), 212-989-1116
1411 Second Ave. (bet. 73rd & 74th Sts.), 212-988-5348
60 University Pl. (10th St.), 212-982-3758
"Stylish" to a fault, this "very cool" trio lures "slim young things" with "tasty Thai", "mod decor", "loud music" and low prices; "dicey service" and "cramped quarters" are the price of all that "popularity."

SPICE MARKET ◐
22 | 27 | 20 | $56

403 W. 13th St. (9th Ave.), 212-675-2322; www.jean-georges.com
"Another winner in the Vongerichten empire", this "sybaritic" Meatpacking District destination purveys "haute" Thai-Malay street food in a spectacular "theatrical" duplex setting frequented by "tourists early and glamorous folk later on"; despite barbs for "birdlike portions at beastlike prices", it's still "hard as hell to get reservations", and deservedly so.

Spicy & Tasty ⊄
▽ 20 | 12 | 14 | $20

39-07 Prince St. (39th Ave.), Queens, 718-359-1601
"Living up to its name" with a "hodgepodge" of "distinctive dishes", this "super" Flushing Szechuan also manages to do it on the cheap; "doesn't-speak-English" service and not much decor are the trade-offs.

Spigolo
▽ 26 | 17 | 22 | $47

1561 Second Ave. (81st St.), 212-744-1100
Upper Eastsiders report a "nice buzz" emanating from this new Italian offering an "inventive, impeccably prepared" menu in "cramped" quarters; it's "trying hard" and shows "great promise", despite a few worries that "publicity may spoil it."

Spoto's
▽ 20 | 18 | 19 | $32

4005 E. Tremont Ave. (Sampson Ave.), Bronx, 718-828-5613
This Bronx Southern Italian wins cheers for being "family-friendly" and a "good value"; a seasonal menu and outdoor seating add appeal, though some say it "needs to be more consistent."

Spotted Pig ◐
21 | 16 | 16 | $40

314 W. 11th St. (Greenwich St.), 212-620-0393; www.thespottedpig.com
"Getting a table is a contact sport" at this "way too popular" Villager that's always "insanely packed" due to its no-reservations policy; while chef April Bloomfield's Italian-accented British gastro-pub grub is "jolly good", the "disinterested" service is another story; N.B. an expansion and renovation are underway at press time.

Spring Street Natural ◐
18 | 14 | 15 | $28

62 Spring St. (Lafayette St.), 212-966-0290; www.springstreetnatural.com
Featuring an "earnest", "something-for-everyone menu" that's "wholesome but not too much so", this "quasi-landmark" NoLita organic also offers fish and poultry; though it earns points for longevity, and parsimonious pricing, it gets docked for "lethargic" service and plain-Jane looks.

SQC
19 | 14 | 15 | $39

270 Columbus Ave. (bet. 72nd & 73rd Sts.), 212-579-0100; www.sqcnyc.com
"Brunch is a mob scene" at Scott Campbell's West Side New American, but no matter when you go you'll find "well-crafted" dishes and that "unbeatable hot chocolate"; still, friends who think it "should be better" cite "fumbling" service and bland decor.

SRIPRAPHAI ⊅

26 | 11 | 16 | $20

64-13 39th Ave. (bet. 64th & 65th Sts.), Queens, 718-899-9599
"Authenticity seekers" ascend to inexpensive "Thai heaven" at this "hot, hot, hot" Woodside spot where "mild is spicy enough" for neophytes; no longer BYO, they "now serve wine and beer", and since they've "renovated and expanded", it's "a little easier" to get a table.

Stage Deli ◑

20 | 10 | 14 | $26

834 Seventh Ave. (bet. 53rd & 54th Sts.), 212-245-7850;
www.stagedeli.com
If you like it "overstuffed", you'll love this "obligatory", circa-1938 Theater District deli that pioneered the "supersize-me" concept with its "ridiculous", "need-a-nap-afterwards" portions; in short, "come hungry but not often."

Stamatis ◑

22 | 12 | 18 | $28

31-14 Broadway (bet. 31st & 32nd Sts.), Queens, 718-204-8964
29-12 23rd Ave. (bet. 29th & 31st Sts.), Queens, 718-932-8596
These separately owned, "basic" Astoria Greeks share some notable characteristics: "hearty" Hellenic fare, "moderate prices", "charming", "no-frills" atmospheres and a "tendency to run out of their specials."

Stanton Social ☒

▽ 26 | 29 | 21 | $45

99 Stanton St. (bet. Ludlow & Orchard Sts.), 212-995-0099;
www.thestantonsocial.com
The Lower East Side continues to gentrify with this "trendy" new Eclectic where a smartly "earthy" dining room is topped by an amber-lit lounge; the "original" globe-trotting menu arrives small plate–style to encourage sharing, and though pricing is reasonable, it does add up.

Starbucks

12 | 10 | 13 | $9

13-25 Astor Pl. (Lafayette St.), 212-982-3563 ◑
241 Canal St. (Centre St.), 212-219-2725
152-154 Columbus Ave. (67th St.), 212-721-0470 ◑
4 Columbus Circle (enter on 58th St., bet. 8th & 9th Aves.), 212-265-0658
255 Eighth Ave. (enter on 8th Ave., bet. 22nd & 23rd Sts.), 646-638-1571
682 Ninth Ave. (47th St.), 212-397-2288
141-143 Second Ave. (9th St.), 212-780-0024
1642 Third Ave. (92nd St.), 212-360-0425
150 Varick St. (Spring St.), 646-230-9816
77 W. 125th St. (Lenox Ave.), 917-492-2454
www.starbucks.com
Additional locations throughout the NY area
NYers' "love/hate relationship" with these "dime-a-dozen" java joints continues: despite the ongoing brew-haha over its "overpriced, over-roasted" "rocket fuel", some simply "can't live without them", period.

Steak Frites ◑

18 | 16 | 16 | $40

9 E. 16th St. (bet. 5th Ave. & Union Sq. W.), 212-463-7101
"Simple fare well done" says it all about this Union Square French bistro where the eponymous dish is "enjoyable but not spectacular"; similarly, the decor's "a little frayed around the edges" and service is of the "too-many-chiefs, not-enough-Indians" variety.

Stella del Mare ☒

▽ 22 | 17 | 20 | $50

346 Lexington Ave. (bet. 39th & 40th Sts.), 212-687-4425;
www.stelladelmareny.com
"Not on many radar screens", this Murray Hill Italian seafooder is "worth discovering" for its "safe-bet" menu, "pleasant" setting and "efficient" service; just "bring your checkbook": its "gray-haired regulars" report "high prices for the neighborhood."

Stone Park Café
24 | 21 | 21 | $41

324 Fifth Ave. (3rd St.), Brooklyn, 718-369-0082; www.stoneparkcafe.com
"Park Slope's Fifth Avenue restaurant collection" has a new "gem" via this Contemporary American with an "elegantly simple menu" (particularly those "terrific marrow bones"); "well-priced wines" and a staff that "tries hard" add to the "overall positive impression."

Strip House ◐
25 | 22 | 21 | $63

13 E. 12th St. (bet. 5th Ave. & University Pl.), 212-328-0000; www.theglaziergroup.com
There's "plenty of sizzle" at Peter and Penny Glazier's "saucy" Village chop shop, a "dark, hip" joint done up in "ironic" "1950s burlesque" style; it's a "refreshing change" from "standard-issue steakhouses", combining "big juicy" hunks of meat, "attentive" servers and a "happening" vibe into one "terrific", albeit "pricey", package.

SUBA
20 | 26 | 19 | $48

109 Ludlow St. (bet. Delancey & Rivington Sts.), 212-982-5714; www.subanyc.com
"Trendy" types "go for the ambiance" at this "over-the-top" Lower East Side Spaniard renowned for a subterranean dining room "surrounded by a moat"; despite "interesting" cooking from chef Alex Ureña, some report "more scene than cuisine" here.

Sueños
23 | 20 | 19 | $44

311 W. 17th St. (bet. 8th & 9th Aves.), 212-243-1333; www.suenosnyc.com
"Refreshing updates" on traditional Mexican recipes fill out the menu of chef Sue Torres' Chelsea cantina where the "new wave" cooking "goes way beyond tacos"; the "unnecessarily high prices" and waiters "taking a siesta between courses" need work, however.

Sugiyama ◐⊘⌧
27 | 19 | 25 | $89

251 W. 55th St. (bet. B'way & 8th Ave.), 212-956-0670; www.sugiyama-nyc.com
The "attention to detail is amazing" at "genius" chef Nao Sugiyama's "magical" Midtown Japanese featuring perhaps the "best kaiseki on the East Coast" abetted by "warm", caring service; the experience may involve a big chunk of "time and money", but the payoff is "pleasing."

Sultan ◐
19 | 13 | 18 | $35

1435 Second Ave. (bet. 74th & 75th Sts.), 212-861-0200; www.sultan-nyc.com
Spicing up the "boring East Side" is this "Turkish delight" with "solid" cooking at "reasonable prices"; while service is "vague" and the decor "tacky", "summer sidewalk dining" is a "good bet."

Sumile ⌧
23 | 20 | 21 | $63

154 W. 13th St. (bet. 6th & 7th Aves.), 212-989-7699; www.sumile.com
Chef Josh DeChellis' "rarefied aesthetic" is at work at this "minimalist" Village Japanese fusion purveyor that offers "no sushi" but rather a variety of "brilliant" small plates; still, the "little portions" can add up to a "big check."

Superfine
18 | 21 | 17 | $27

126 Front St. (bet. Jay & Pearl Sts.), Brooklyn, 718-243-9005
"Loud and fun", this big Dumbo Med may be "more bar than restaurant" what with the "pool table in the dining room" and "laid-back" service; at least the "simple" food's "flavorful" and the people-watching superfine.

Supper ◐≠
23 | 19 | 17 | $33

156 E. Second St. (bet. Aves. A & B), 212-477-7600; www.supperrestaurant.com
Behind the "deceptively humble name" lies some "delectable" chow at this "inexpensive" East Village Northern Italian; to ease the "long

waits" (they take "no rezzies"), park yourself at the "great wine bar" next door.

Surya
22 | 16 | 19 | $34

302 Bleecker St. (bet. Grove St. & 7th Ave.), 212-807-7770; www.suryany.com
Though insiders say the "vegetarian dishes are best", it's "hard to go wrong" at this "exotic" Village Indian; a "fantastic brunch" and a "cute patio" out back bring in the "upscale masses."

Sushi Ann Ⓢ
▽ 25 | 17 | 22 | $60

38 E. 51st St. (bet. Madison & Park Aves.), 212-755-1780
"Top-of-the-line", "super-fresh sushi" and "delicately prepared rolls" are the highlights of this "relaxing" Midtown Japanese; "impeccable service" and a "comfortable setting" come with the territory – as do the high prices.

Sushiden
24 | 17 | 21 | $53

19 E. 49th St. (bet. 5th & Madison Aves.), 212-758-2700
123 W. 49th St. (bet. 6th & 7th Aves.), 212-398-2800 Ⓢ
www.sushiden.com
"Serious sushi" turns up at these "serene" crosstown twins where the quality – and the prices – "compare with Tokyo"; the "professional", "kimono'd" service makes them "corporate lunch" magnets, not the "uninspired decor."

Sushi Hana ●
22 | 16 | 18 | $35

466 Amsterdam Ave. (bet. 82nd & 83rd Sts.), 212-874-0369
1501 Second Ave. (78th St.), 212-327-0582
www.sushihana.com
For "reliable" sushi that "won't break the bank", locals are happy to have this crosstown Japanese duo; since the Eastsider's decor is "somewhat sterile", regulars head for the "opium den"–esque sake bar around the corner.

SUSHI OF GARI
27 | 11 | 19 | $63

402 E. 78th St. (bet. 1st & York Aves.), 212-517-5340
The food's "so creative" and the prices so high at chef Gari's "avant-garde" East Side Japanese that admirers "don't know if it belongs in a restaurant or a museum guide"; just ignore the "unpretentious surroundings" and prepare for "a wait even on a school night"; P.S. "omakase is the only way to go."

Sushi Rose Ⓢ
19 | 13 | 17 | $35

248 E. 52nd St., 2nd fl. (bet. 2nd & 3rd Aves.), 212-813-1800
Saturday's half-price "steal of a deal" still "packs 'em in" at this East Side Japanese "hidden" atop a flight of stairs; some say it's "not the greatest ambiance" while others feel it's "slipped a notch under a new owner"; stay tuned.

SushiSamba ●
22 | 21 | 17 | $46

245 Park Ave. S. (bet. 19th & 20th Sts.), 212-475-9377
87 Seventh Ave. S. (Barrow St.), 212-691-7885
www.sushisamba.com
Sushi gets a "South American twist" at these "nightclubbish" fusion specialists famed for their "glam" patrons and "Miami-chic" airs; there's a "to-die-for roof deck" at the Village branch, while the Flatiron outlet has added a hot new next-door lounge dubbed Sugarcane.

SUSHI SEKI ●Ⓢ
27 | 14 | 20 | $53

1143 First Ave. (bet. 62nd & 63rd Sts.), 212-371-0238
A "sushi star is born" at this "exceptional" East Side Japanese that's "like Gari" (i.e. "bland decor", "always crowded") but with a bit

"more panache"; sure, it's "expensive" (but "not pretentious"), though it gets bonus points for being "open till 3 AM."

Sushi Sen-nin
24 | 12 | 19 | $49

1420 Third Ave. (bet. 80th & 81st Sts.), 212-249-4992; www.sushisennin.com
The "unique combinations" and "extremely fresh" sushi at this "inventive" Upper Eastsider come in "big portions", but despite "cheap-looking" decor, "you'll definitely pay for it"; N.B. the original Murray Hill outpost has closed but a replacement is in the works.

SUSHI YASUDA ☒
28 | 22 | 24 | $76

204 E. 43rd St. (bet. 2nd & 3rd Aves.), 212-972-1001; www.sushiyasuda.com
"Nirvana" on 43rd Street, this Grand Central–area sushi purveyor showcases the "ethereal" handiwork of "true master" chef Naomichi Yasuda, whose "peerless" performance has again made it the No. 1 Japanese in this *Survey*; the "best does not come cheap", but "first-rate service" and "modern" decor are part of the "superb" package.

Sushi Zen ☒
24 | 20 | 22 | $56

108 W. 44th St. (bet. B'way & 6th Ave.), 212-302-0707; www.sushizen-ny.com
"Fresh is the word" at this Theater District Japanese that feels like the "ocean" is nearby; despite the "Times Square action" outside, it's "surprisingly tranquil" inside so you can count on a truly "Zen experience – until you get the bill."

Swagat Indian Cuisine
▽ 22 | 13 | 20 | $25

411A Amsterdam Ave. (bet. 79th & 80th Sts.), 212-362-1400
"Distinct flavors" and "sweet service" make this West Side Indian "secret" one of those "classic hole-in-the-wall discoveries"; it "may not catch your eye", but it's a "quality" find in a "lacking neighborhood", and has "takeout that travels well."

Sweet Melissa
24 | 18 | 19 | $15

276 Court St. (bet. Butler & Douglass Sts.), Brooklyn, 718-855-3410
75 W. Houston St. (W. Broadway), 212-260-1086
"Tasty pastries" and "heavenly desserts" abound at this "twee" Cobble Hill bakery/tearoom combination; if prices are "a bit steep" and the setup "tiny", the "back garden is bliss in summer" and "makes it all worthwhile"; N.B. the SoHo satellite is new and unrated.

Sweet-n-Tart Cafe ●⊅
20 | 11 | 14 | $17

136-11 38th Ave. (Main St.), Queens, 718-661-3380
Sweet-n-Tart Restaurant
20 Mott St. (Chatham Sq.), 212-964-0380
www.sweetntart.com
"Perfect for beginners", these "dim-sum-meets-the-Internet-Cafe" hybrids serve everything from "tasty Cantonese" to "Hong Kong-style" finger food; despite "tart" service and "no decor", tabs are "dirt cheap"; P.S. at Mott Street, there's "more room" and "more selection."

Swifty's ●
17 | 18 | 17 | $58

1007 Lexington Ave. (bet. 72nd & 73rd Sts.), 212-535-6000; www.swiftysny.com
It's "Mortimer's revisited" at this "clubby, chummy" East Side American where "social X-rays", the "*WWD*" set" and "media eccentrics" convene; if "watching the swells is better than eating the food", the straightforward cuisine easily meets Hamptons standards.

Sylvia's
16 | 11 | 15 | $29

328 Lenox Ave. (bet. 126th & 127th Sts.), 212-996-0660;
www.sylviassoulfood.com
Bring an "empty stomach" to this "famous" Harlem soul fooder known for its "down-home" fare and dive decor; live jazz and gospel brunches

keep it "packed with tourists", however, declining ratings indicate it "ain't what it used to be."

Symposium
18 | 13 | 19 | $23

544 W. 113th St. (bet. Amsterdam Ave. & B'way), 212-865-1011
"Hidden away amid university row houses", this longtime "Columbia staple" serves "homestyle Greek" grub at "student prices"; "flirty old man service" is "part of its charm", but the decor's an "afterthought."

TABLA
26 | 25 | 24 | $60

11 Madison Ave. (25th St.), 212-889-0667; www.tablany.com
There's "luxury all around" at this "polished" duplex off Madison Square Park, where chef Floyd Cardoz offers an "adventurous", Indian-accented New American menu that's served by an "anticipate-your-every-whim" staff; sure, it comes with "NYC price tags", but the downstairs "Bread Bar is less expensive" (and "more low-key"), and there's always that "bargain" $25 prix fixe lunch.

Table d'Hôte
19 | 17 | 19 | $43

44 E. 92nd St. (bet. Madison & Park Aves.), 212-348-8125
"Discriminating diners" find "zero pretension" at this "sweet", "thimble"-size Carnegie Hill French bistro; "imaginative" dishes, "attentive service" and a $22.50 pre-theater "deal" transform what might otherwise be a "tight squeeze" into a "romantic hideaway."

Table XII ⊠
– | – | – | M

Lombardy Hotel, 109 E. 56th St. (Park Ave.), 212-750-5656; www.tablexii.com
The former Etoile space in Midtown is now purveying moderately priced Italian classics in a newly renovated, chandelier-bedecked dining room; there's also a number of private party spaces available.

Taboon
23 | 19 | 19 | $44

773 10th Ave. (52nd St.), 212-713-0271
"Articulate flavors" mark the Med–Middle Eastern menu at this Hell's Kitchen "oasis" known for its "fresh bread from the taboon oven"; "attentive" service and a "festive" air trump its "dodgy" locale.

Taci's Beyti
▽ 23 | 10 | 18 | $23

1955 Coney Island Ave. (bet. Ave. P & Kings Hwy.), Brooklyn, 718-627-5750
Folks "stagger out stuffed" and happy from this Midwood Turkish BYO thanks to its "large servings" for "little cost"; it's always "packed" despite the "plastic plants" and "frantic" but "friendly" service.

Taco Chulo ⊘
– | – | – | I

318 Grand St. (bet. Havemeyer St. & Marcy Ave.), Brooklyn, 718-302-2485; www.tacochulo.com
The latest arrival on Williamsburg's Grand Street, this new *taqueria* purveys inexpensive tacos and other Mexicana made from natural and organic ingredients; airy digs compensate for the cash-only policy.

Taka
▽ 25 | 13 | 20 | $45

61 Grove St. (bet. Bleecker St. & 7th Ave. S.), 212-242-3699
"Hard-core sushi lovers" say this Village Japanese is "not the same" since its namesake owner retired; if the "closetlike" setting is a "bit too intimate" for some, at least the fish remains as "fresh" as ever.

Takahachi
24 | 15 | 21 | $34

85 Ave. A (bet. 5th & 6th Sts.), 212-505-6524 ◗
145 Duane St. (bet. Church St. & W. B'way), 212-571-1830
Well-priced "everyday sushi" and hot dishes are served at this Downtown Japanese duo that makes up in quality what it lacks in variety; "above-the-call-of-duty" service ices the cake.

Taksim

▽ 22 | 13 | 18 | $22

1030 Second Ave. (bet. 54th & 55th Sts.), 212-421-3004; www.taksim.us
"Tasty Turkish tapas" turn up at this "casual" East Midtown BYO where the main courses are "authentic" enough, but regulars say a meal of appetizers is "the way to go"; "fair prices" make the "tight quarters" more bearable.

Taku

– | – | – | M

116 Smith St. (bet. Dean & Pacific Sts.), Brooklyn, 718-488-6269
Ramen reigns at this minimalist Boerum Hill Japanese where the signature version sports Berkshire pork *and* bacon; its midpriced menu also lists numerous small plates plus shochu-infused cocktails.

Tamarind ◗

25 | 23 | 23 | $49

41-43 E. 22nd St. (bet. B'way & Park Ave. S.), 212-674-7400;
www.tamarinde22.com
Indian cuisine "with flair and style" curries favor at this "fashionable", "nonkitschy" Flatiron flight to "Bombay"; it's "higher up the food chain" than most of its rivals, with equally "high-end" prices, so for a cheaper, lighter option, head for the "secret" Tea Room next door.

Tang Pavilion

22 | 16 | 21 | $34

65 W. 55th St. (bet. 5th & 6th Aves.), 212-956-6888
"Classic Shanghai" dishes are the specialty of this "first-rate" Midtown Chinese where the "food and price can't be beat, given the business neighborhood"; the "attentive", "super-fast service" is matched by "incredibly fast takeout."

Tanoreen

▽ 25 | 12 | 20 | $27

7704 Third Ave. (bet. 77th & 78th Sts.), Brooklyn, 718-748-5600;
www.tanoreen.com
Veggie-lovers "keep coming back" to Bay Ridge for the "superlative" Middle Eastern fare and "incredible" selection at this "comfy" cafe; low prices and magnificent "meze make up for the lack of decor."

TAO ◗

22 | 27 | 19 | $54

42 E. 58th St. (bet. Madison & Park Aves.), 212-888-2288;
www.taorestaurant.com
"Suckers for ambiance" report "quite a show" at this "big, booming" Midtown Pan-Asian where an "enormous Buddha" presides over the "hopping scene"; despite "deafening noise", "rushed service" and "DMV"-like waits, the food's "artful" and the crowd "beautiful" enough to justify all the hype; P.S. "lunch is much easier" – and cheaper – but also duller.

Taormina

▽ 21 | 16 | 19 | $39

147 Mulberry St. (bet. Grand & Hester Sts.), 212-219-1007
You can absorb lots of "local color" as well as "good" traditional food at this Little Italy Italian fixture; a few say it's not been the same since former regular John Gotti went away.

Tartine ⊅

22 | 14 | 16 | $27

253 W. 11th St. (W. 4th St.), 212-229-2611
This "*magnifique*" Village French bistro is always "packed" due to its "extremely reasonable" pricing and "no-bookings" rule; if the "weekend waits get irksome", the "BYO policy" compensates.

Taste

▽ 21 | 15 | 20 | $44

1413 Third Ave. (80th St.), 212-717-9798; www.elizabar.com
A "cafeteria on weekdays" turned restaurant/wine bar at night, Eli Zabar's East Side New American "does a lot with a small menu"; as with everything he produces, it offers superior ingredients and service.

TASTING ROOM Ⓩ

| 26 | 17 | 25 | $59 |

72 E. First St. (bet. 1st & 2nd Aves.), 212-358-7831;
www.thetastingroomnyc.com
"Flawlessly executed" New Americana prepared from "super-fresh" "daily changing" ingredients comes in "tasting or sharing portions" at this "high-caliber" East Villager where there's also a "superb" "all-American wine list" and "service beyond compare"; don't mind the "microscopic", 25-seat setting and macro pricing: this place is nothing short of "amazing."

Taverna Kyclades

| 24 | 13 | 18 | $28 |

33-07 Ditmars Blvd. (bet. 33rd & 35th Sts.), Queens, 718-545-8666;
www.tavernakyclades.com
The "buttery" seafood "melts in your mouth" at this "fresh-as-can-be" Astoria Greek that transports you to "Mykonos" for "Queens prices"; the "small" space is eased by "summertime outdoor tables."

TAVERN ON THE GREEN

| 15 | 25 | 17 | $59 |

Central Park W. (bet. 66th & 67th Sts.), 212-873-3200;
www.tavernonthegreen.com
"Central Park meets Disneyland" at this "storybook" West Side American institution where the "picturesque surroundings" make up for any gastronomic deficiencies"; indeed, the Crystal Room's "Fabergé egg" decor alone makes it "a must" for lunch or special occasions; dining in the garden can be delightful, but it's also great for private parties.

Tea & Sympathy

| 20 | 16 | 16 | $24 |

108 Greenwich Ave. (bet. 12th & 13th Sts.), 212-807-8329;
www.teaandsympathynewyork.com
"There will always be a Britain" at this "pint-size" Village tea shop offering everything from "tasty scones" to shepherd's pie; so what if the decor is "more shabby than chic" and the staff serves "more tea than sympathy."

Tea Box Ⓩ

| 21 | 18 | 17 | $30 |

Takashimaya, 693 Fifth Ave. (bet. 54th & 55th Sts.), 212-350-0180
For spent shoppers, this Midtown "sanctuary" in a Fifth Avenue department store basement is "serenity itself"; there's both "afternoon tea" with an Asian twist and a "Zen-like" lunch of "expensive" but "exquisite little bites."

teany ◗

| 19 | 14 | 15 | $16 |

90 Rivington St. (bet. Ludlow & Orchard Sts.), 212-475-9190; www.teany.com
"Socially conscious" types turn up at pop star Moby's Lower East Side vegan cafe for its "healthy" eats and "extensive tea selection", not the "slow", "spacey" service or second-rate space; "there's now a take-out outlet next door."

Telly's Taverna ◗

| 23 | 14 | 17 | $35 |

2813 23rd Ave. (bet. 28th & 29th Sts.), Queens, 718-728-9056
"Amazingly fresh fish grilled to perfection" says it all about this "homestyle" Astoria Greek seafooder; maybe prices are "going up", but the "beautiful" back patio and good food are still a bargain.

Tempo

| 25 | 23 | 23 | $49 |

256 Fifth Ave. (bet. Carroll St. & Garfield Pl.), Brooklyn, 718-636-2020;
www.tempobrooklyn.com
"Manhattan-style dining comes to Park Slope" via this "terrific" new Mediterranean offering "robust flavors" in "big, airy" "SoHo-like" digs; though "service is Brooklyn friendly", locals better "be prepared to spend" like they were in the city.

Tennessee Mountain
16 | 11 | 15 | $30

143 Spring St. (Wooster St.), 212-431-3993; www.tnmountain.com
"Serious eaters" willing to "roll up their sleeves and get their hands dirty" say this SoHo BBQ standby doles out "well-priced", "fall-off-the-bone" ribs and other "solid" "man fare"; but snobs sneer there's "nothing exciting" at this "quantity-not-quality" spot.

Tenzan ●
▽ 25 | 19 | 21 | $30

285 Columbus Ave. (73rd St.), 212-580-7300
7116 18th Ave. (71st St.), Brooklyn, 718-621-3238
www.tenzanny.com
This "modest", but excellent, Upper West Side/Brooklyn sushi duo has "quickly become popular" thanks to an unbeatable formula: "more fish and less rice" at "decent prices"; they're "not discovered yet", making them all the more "delightful."

Teodora
21 | 15 | 19 | $46

141 E. 57th St. (bet. Lexington & 3rd Aves.), 212-826-7101
"They know their pasta" at this "plenty authentic" Midtown Northern Italian with waiters out of "central casting"; upstairs is more "relaxing" than the "cramped" main floor, but either way it's "a bit pricey."

Teresa's
18 | 11 | 14 | $19

103 First Ave. (bet. 6th & 7th Sts.), 212-228-0604
80 Montague St. (Hicks St.), Brooklyn, 718-797-3996
"Diner food with an Eastern European accent" is yours at this pair of dirt-"cheap" Polish coffee shops; regulars advise "stick to the ethnic specialties" (pierogi, blintzes, etc.) and ignore the "dismal" service.

Terrace in the Sky
23 | 25 | 21 | $62

400 W. 119th St. (bet. Amsterdam Ave. & Morningside Dr.), 212-666-9490;
www.terraceinthesky.com
This Morningside Heights rooftop is the "only show in town Uptown" thanks to its "panoramic views", "unobtrusive service" and "classic" (if "pricey") French-Med cuisine; a "live harpist" makes it "perfect for romantic dinners" or celebrations.

Tevere
▽ 25 | 19 | 22 | $54

155 E. 84th St. (bet. Lexington & 3rd Aves.), 212-744-0210;
www.teverenyc.com
"You'd never guess it was kosher" at this "outstanding" Upper East Side Italian where the "food, ambiance and service are all tops"; sure, it can be "crowded" and "pricey", but its "great trattoria" feeling more than compensates.

Texas Smokehouse BBQ
16 | 9 | 14 | $25

438 Second Ave. (25th St.), 212-725-9800
The "smell's enticing" at this Gramercy BBQ vending "solid", "edible" ribs and such for "bargain" tabs; still, connoisseurs citing "drab" digs and "sloppy service" dub it "disappointing."

Thai Pavilion
▽ 23 | 15 | 21 | $21

37-10 30th Ave. (37th St.), Queens, 718-777-5546
The "food's better than the generic atmosphere would suggest" at this "excellent" Astoria Thai; even better, prices are "decent" and the staff "friendly."

Thalassa
23 | 25 | 23 | $58

179 Franklin St. (bet. Greenwich & Hudson Sts.), 212-941-7661;
www.thalassanyc.com
Just as "sophisticated" and maybe "more fun than Milos", this TriBeCa "haute Greek" serves the "freshest fish Downtown" in "airy", "subtly

nautical" environs; since "one dish is better than the next" and service is so "solid", you might even "forget the price."

Thalia ◐ | 20 | 21 | 18 | $46

828 Eighth Ave. (50th St.), 212-399-4444; www.restaurantthalia.com
"Much better" than most pre-theater choices in the area, this "high-ceilinged", stage-lit Hell's Kitchen spot exudes "modern zip" both in its decor and "well-executed" New American menu; despite slightly upscale tabs, many say "you can't go wrong" here.

Thomas Beisl ◑ | 20 | 17 | 18 | $38

25 Lafayette Ave. (Ashland Pl.), Brooklyn, 718-222-5800
It "looks, feels and tastes like Europe" at this "authentic Austrian" bistro in Fort Greene where the "menu's simple", the ambiance "comforting" and the prices "reasonable"; a location "convenient to BAM" is a plus, ditto the "friendly" if sometimes "slow" service.

Thor | – | – | – | E

The Hotel on Rivington, 107 Rivington St. (bet. Essex & Ludlow Sts.), 212-796-8040; www.hotelonrivington.com
Kurt Gutenbrunner (Wallsé) tries something different at this new Lower East Side hotel room featuring seasonal New Americana presented via variously sized plates; the glassed-in atrium setting (complete with skylights offering views of the adjoining tenements) adds a stylish note.

343 | ▽ 17 | 18 | 17 | $45

343 E. 85th St. (bet. 1st & 2nd Aves.), 212-717-6200;
www.restaurant343.com
"Much needed" in underserved Yorkville, this "stylish" New American features a "darn good burger" on its otherwise "limited" menu; though it's "pricey" and still "rough around the edges", locals are "willing to cut it some slack."

Three of Cups ◐ | 20 | 17 | 16 | $25

83 First Ave. (5th St.), 212-388-0059; www.threeofcupsnyc.com
Some "never get past" the brick-oven pizzas at this "budget" East Villager that also offers a "basic" Italian menu; though the "mock-medieval" decor may be deemed "dim" and "dungeonlike", the "eclectic" young crowd is "fun and friendly", especially when in their cups.

360 ⌷ | 23 | 14 | 17 | $37

360 Van Brunt St. (bet. Sullivan & Wolcott Sts.), Brooklyn, 718-246-0360
Don't let the "end-of-the-earth" Red Hook address (and dearth of public transportation) deter you: this underdecorated New French features an "excellent", daily changing menu and an "impeccable", all-organic wine list; the $25 prix fixe dinner "deal" makes the "haughty" service bearable.

Tía Pol | 24 | 17 | 20 | $35

205 10th Ave. (bet. 22nd & 23rd Sts.), 212-675-8805;
www.tiapol.com
"Small plates", a "small space" and "much hype" collide at this red hot new Chelsea Spaniard with "nuanced", *que bueno* tapas à la Barcelona; "mobbed" conditions and "long waits" make everyone "wish it were bigger."

Tides ⌧ | – | – | – | M

102 Norfolk St. (bet. Delancey & Rivington Sts.), 212-254-8855
New Lower East Side seafooder serving a succinct menu at shallow tabs in a tiny space; it's most memorable for its lobster roll and a

ceiling skewered with thousands of bamboo shoots designed to look like sea grass.

Tierras Colombianas ⊄

| 20 | 13 | 19 | $21 |

33-01 Broadway (33rd St.), Queens, 718-956-3012
82-18 Roosevelt Ave. (82nd St.), Queens, 718-426-8868

"Bring your appetite" for the "heaping platters" of "authentic" grub at these "cheap" Queens Colombians where the "entrees are big enough to feed a small country"; for best results, "bring a translator", ignore the "greasy spoon" decor and "don't wear a belt."

Tiramisu ◗

| 18 | 15 | 17 | $34 |

1410 Third Ave. (80th St.), 212-988-9780

"Hearty Italian dishes" plus some notable "brick-oven pizzas" are the draws at this affordable Upper East Side neighborhood "standby"; any deficiencies in decor or service are trumped by sidewalk seating that's "perfect for a nice day."

TOCQUEVILLE

| 25 | 21 | 24 | $65 |

1 E. 15th St. (5th Ave.), 212-647-1515; www.tocquevillerestaurant.com

"Dignified dining" carries on at this "understated", "absolutely adult" Union Square French-American where chef Marco Moreira's "brilliant" menu meets the "highest standards"; sure, you'll "pay for it", but the "calming" ambiance and "your-wish-is-their-command" service more than "justifies the high tabs"; N.B. a recent move to larger digs puts its Decor score in question.

Tommaso's

| ▽ 22 | 17 | 20 | $40 |

1464 86th St. (bet. 14th & 15th Aves.), Brooklyn, 718-236-9883

They treat you like a "relative they actually like" at this Bensonhurst Italian featuring "wonderful", "old-line" dishes and a "great wine selection"; equally memorable is the "opera singing" by owner Thomas Verdillo, who always has a "few arias" ready.

TOMOE SUSHI ⊠

| 27 | 8 | 17 | $38 |

172 Thompson St. (bet. Bleecker & Houston Sts.), 212-777-9346

"Neither rain nor sleet nor snow" deter diehards from this Village Japanese and its "affordable", "monster-size" sushi that "melts in your mouth like buttah"; defying the "nonexistent decor" and "postage stamp"–dimensions, "ouch"-inducing lines wrap "around the block" every single day.

Tomo Sushi & Sake Bar ◗

| 19 | 16 | 17 | $25 |

2850 Broadway (bet. 110th & 111th Sts.), 212-665-2916

"Columbia students" show up for the "good deals" at this "serviceable" Morningside Japanese where "friendly service" distracts from "minimal decor"; some dub it "middle of the road" with "mercurial quality", but it does the job for a "quick", satisfying sushi fix.

Tom's ⊠⊄

| ▽ 19 | 18 | 25 | $14 |

782 Washington Ave. (Sterling Pl.), Brooklyn, 718-636-9738

A "Brooklyn institution for 70 years", this Prospect Heights coffee shop still dishes out "down-home Americana" (i.e. egg creams, lime rickeys) in a wonderful '30s setting; indeed, many wish this daytimer stayed open for dinner.

Tony Luke's

| ▽ 22 | 5 | 13 | $12 |

576 Ninth Ave. (bet. 41st & 42nd Sts.), 212-967-3055; www.tonylukesnyc.com

A cheap "taste of Philly" lands in Hell's Kitchen at this "phantastic" import specializing in cheese steaks and roast pork sandwiches; alright, the decor is "unfortunate" and the service "glacial", but it still satisfies average Joes "jonesing for the real thing."

Tony's Di Napoli

19 | 14 | 17 | $32

1606 Second Ave. (83rd St.), 212-861-8686
147 W. 43rd St. (bet. B'way & 6th Ave.), 212-221-0100 ☾
www.tonysnyc.com

Plate sharers are in "heaven" at these "boisterous" Italians serving family-style feasts for "modest" payouts; many call them the "poor man's Carmine's", with the same "giant" portions and "noise levels."

Topaz Thai

21 | 11 | 16 | $27

127 W. 56th St. (bet. 6th & 7th Aves.), 212-957-8020

"Tasty" vittles at "too-good-to-believe prices" and convenience to Carnegie Hall make up for "not the greatest decor" at this Midtown Thai where the "efficient service has you in-and-out in a flash – whether you want to be or not."

Tosca Café ☾

▽ 20 | 21 | 19 | $32

4038 E. Tremont Ave. (bet. Gerber Pl. & Sampson Ave.), Bronx, 718-239-3300; www.toscanyc.com

As "happening" as it gets in Throgs Neck, this "classic" Italian is one of the area's "most popular" and known for its "reasonable" tabs; not only does the "decor rock", but there's "enchanting" outdoor dining too.

Tossed

18 | 6 | 10 | $13

295 Park Ave. S. (bet. 22nd & 23rd Sts.), 212-674-6700
30 Rockefeller Plaza Concourse (bet. 49th & 50th Sts.), 212-218-2525 🖾
www.tossed.com

"When you want to eat healthy", these simple salad specialists offer "made-to-order" greens with "options galore", so long as you ignore the "absentminded" staff and plain decor; Rock Center is takeout only, while Downtown tosses in dinnertime table service.

Totonno's Pizzeria Napolitano

22 | 10 | 15 | $21

462 Second Ave. (26th St.), 212-213-8800
1544 Second Ave. (bet. 80th & 81st Sts.), 212-327-2800
1524 Neptune Ave. (bet. W. 15th & 16th Sts.), Brooklyn, 718-372-8606 ⊟
www.totonnos.com

"Dream pies" are yours at this pizzeria trio that originated in Coney Island in 1924; as hard as the Manhattan offshoots try, "Brooklyn they're not", though they've got full Italian menus and "better decor."

Tournesol ☾

24 | 15 | 21 | $38

50-12 Vernon Blvd. (bet. 50th & 51st Aves.), Queens, 718-472-4355;
www.tournesolnyc.com

"So friendly and so French – if that's not a contradiction" – this Long Island City bistro serves "authentic", "inexpensive" chow in "tiny", "crowded" digs; indeed, it's so "lovingly run" that some "want to not only eat here but work here" too.

Town

24 | 25 | 23 | $74

Chambers Hotel, 15 W. 56th St. (bet. 5th & 6th Aves.), 212-582-4445;
www.townnyc.com

The crowd's "model-thin" and the dining room "sunken" at this "delovely" Midtown New American where chef Geoffrey Zakarian's "adventurous" cuisine "strikes a balance between classical and creative"; the portions – not the prices – can be a bit "paltry", but "smooth service" sustains the "luxurious" mood.

Trata Estiatorio

22 | 17 | 19 | $51

1331 Second Ave. (bet. 70th & 71st Sts.), 212-535-3800; www.trata.com

"Simply prepared delicious fish" is the calling card of this "rustic" East Side Greek seafooder, a "neighborhood version of Milos" with the same "by-the-pound", "deep-pockets" pricing; a "good value" prix fixe lures in early birds.

Trattoria Alba
20 | 17 | 20 | $39

233 E. 34th St. (bet. 2nd & 3rd Aves.), 212-689-3200
"Pleasant" sums up this "reliable", "old-world" Murray Hill Italian that's "not cutting-edge", but rather more "quiet and dark" with plenty of "senior appeal"; "ample portions", "medium prices" and "warm" service explain its longevity.

Trattoria Dell'Arte ●
22 | 20 | 20 | $53

900 Seventh Ave. (bet. 56th & 57th Sts.), 212-245-9800;
www.redeyegrillgroup.com
Besides the fantastic antipasti bar, this "convivial" Midtown Italian puts "fabulous food" on the plates, "amusing body part art" on the walls and lots of "energy" in the air; proximity to Carnegie Hall makes it a natural before or after a concert, but it's worth a trip anytime.

TRATTORIA L'INCONTRO
26 | 19 | 24 | $45

21-76 31st St. (Ditmars Blvd.), Queens, 718-721-3532;
www.trattorialincontro.com
An Astoria "class act" where chef Rocco Sacramone turns out "superb" Italian dishes – including "endless specials", whose recitation tests the waiter's memory; add in attractive decor and "Queens pricing", and it's easy to see why it's "worth going out of the way for."

Trattoria Pesce & Pasta
18 | 14 | 17 | $30

262 Bleecker St. (bet. 6th Ave. & 7th Ave. S.), 212-645-2993 ●
625 Columbus Ave. (bet. 90th & 91st Sts.), 212-579-7970
1079 First Ave. (59th St.), 212-888-7884 ●
1562 Third Ave. (bet. 87th & 88th Sts.), 212-987-4696 ●
www.pescepasta.com
The "well-prepared" seafood and "basic" pastas are "reliable" (albeit "predictable") at these "steady-as-she-goes" Italians; "affordable" pricing and "accommodating service" are bonuses.

Trattoria Romana
25 | 16 | 21 | $38

1476 Hylan Blvd. (Benton Ave.), Staten Island, 718-980-3113;
www.trattoriaromana.com
For food "like mama used to make", try this "authentic", "zesty" Staten Island Italian; granted, the tables may be "too close together", but "classy service" and decent pricing keep it "busy, busy, busy."

tre dici Ⓩ
– | – | – | M

128 W. 26th St. (bet. 6th & 7th Aves.), 212-243-8183
"Pleasing to both the eye and the palate", this new Italian set on an "out-of-the-way" Chelsea block features "great" cookery abetted by a "small but good wine list"; add in a "knowledgeable" staff and it's got "neighborhood haunt" written all over it.

Tre Pomodori
19 | 12 | 18 | $25

210 E. 34th St. (bet. 2nd & 3rd Aves.), 212-545-7266
There are "no frills" at this Murray Hill Italian, but realists ask "who expects them at these prices?"; it's "well visited by locals" who ignore the "cramped" quarters to focus on the "friendly service" and portions "that could feed a village."

Triangolo ●
22 | 16 | 21 | $37

345 E. 83rd St. (bet. 1st & 2nd Aves.), 212-472-4488;
www.triangolorestaurant.com
This longtime East Side Italian proffers "delicious" pastas in "tiny but charming" digs; prices are relatively low and the "outside tables

great in summer", but for many the big news is that they now take plastic (Amex only).

Tribeca Grill
22	20	21	$55

375 Greenwich St. (Franklin St.), 212-941-3900; www.tribecagrill.com
"Open, spacious" and handsome, this New American grill from Drew Nieporent and Robert De Niro "launched TriBeCa" when it opened 16 years ago; if "not as exciting" as in the past, its "fail-safe" food, "superb wine list" and "efficient" staff keep it as crowded as ever.

Trio ⊠
23	19	22	$43

167 E. 33rd St. (bet. Lexington & 3rd Aves.), 212-685-1001
"Unsung", perhaps due to its "side-street" address, this "seriously delicious" Murray Hill Med exudes "great flair" with "hearty", "unique" offerings including some "authentic Croatian" dishes; nightly "live piano" ices the cake.

Triomphe
25	22	22	$65

Iroquois Hotel, 49 W. 44th St. (bet. 5th & 6th Aves.), 212-453-4233; www.triomphe-newyork.com
"Often overlooked", this "refined", "elegant" Theater District New French has "serious foodies" avidly extolling its "marvelous" menu; though the room and portions are "small", prices are anything but.

Tropica ⊠
21	18	19	$50

MetLife Bldg., 200 Park Ave. (enter on 45th St., bet. Lexington & Vanderbilt Aves.), 212-867-6767; www.tropicany.com
For a bit of Key West in Grand Central, check out this "fanciful" seafooder where an "expense-account" commuter crowd gathers for "Caribbean kicks"; even with the obscure location in the MetLife Building, fans "wish it were open on weekends."

Trump Grille ⊠
–	–	–	M

Trump Tower, 725 Fifth Ave., downstairs garden level (bet. 56th & 57th Sts.), 212-715-7290
Nestled beneath a waterfall on the lower level of Trump Tower, this American comfort fooder turns out breakfast, lunch and dinner in a meandering, multichambered space that attracts everyone from tourists to business types; its easy pricing reflects the laid-back mood.

Tsampa ●
▽ 21	19	18	$25

212 E. Ninth St. (bet. 2nd & 3rd Aves.), 212-614-3226
The "dark" "Zen" setting complements the "wonderful flavors" at this East Village Tibetan known for its "terrific vegetarian choices" (though carnivores also "do fine"); some call the food and mood a bit "spartan", but most agree dining here is more "calming" than Valium.

Tse Yang
23	23	23	$58

34 E. 51st St. (bet. Madison & Park Aves.), 212-688-5447
"Consistently superb" cooking and "doting" service make for a "dreamlike experience" at this "elegant" Midtown Chinese with "fascinating" fish-tank decor; it's famed for both its "spectacular" Peking duck and pricing.

Tsuki
▽ 23	11	17	$38

1410 First Ave. (bet. 74th & 75th Sts.), 212-517-6860
"Terrific" value is the thing at this East Side Japanese where the sushi is so fresh you'd think it was "caught in the back room"; despite "slow" service and dumpy digs, fans still place it on their "weekly rotation."

Tuk Tuk
20	15	17	$21

204 Smith St. (bet. Baltic & Butler Sts.), Brooklyn, 718-222-5598 ⊟

(continued)

Tuk Tuk
49-06 Vernon Blvd. (bet. 49th & 50th Aves.), Queens, 718-472-5597
"Spicy means *really* spicy" at this "cheap" Cobble Hill Thai featuring "hearty home cooking" in a "relaxed" room; while the weekend jazz performances are "questionable", at least the "curries are right on"; N.B. the new Long Island City satellite is unrated and also offers some Vietnamese items.

Tupelo Grill ⊠
▽ **20** | **18** | **18** | **$45**
1 Penn Plaza (33rd St., bet. 7th & 8th Aves.), 212-760-2700; www.tupelogrill.com
"Location, location, location" says it all about this "Madison Square Gardenland" American, a "solid", "civil" spot for "pre-Knicks nibbles" or business lunches; given the "limited" local options, it's a "decent" (albeit "pricey") possibility.

Turkish Cuisine ●
19 | **14** | **18** | **$30**
631 Ninth Ave. (bet. 44th & 45th Sts.), 212-397-9650
Hidden away in Hell's Kitchen, this "quiet", "unpretentious" Turk has "flown under the radar for years" despite its "tasty", "reasonably priced" eats; it sure "ain't fancy", but "they don't rush you" and the appetizers alone "can make a meal."

Turkish Kitchen
23 | **19** | **19** | **$38**
386 Third Ave. (bet. 27th & 28th Sts.), 212-679-6633; www.turkishkitchen.com
Though the ingredients are the usual, "something special happens in the kitchen" of this "fit-for-a-pasha" Gramercy Turk; it looks more "like a hotel bar than an ethnic eatery", and its Sunday brunch has diners "whirling like dervishes."

Turkuaz ●
18 | **20** | **18** | **$33**
2637 Broadway (100th St.), 212-665-9541; www.turkuazrestaurant.com
For "sheer theater", this "over-the-top" Upper West Side Turk "can't be beat" with its "gauzy tented ceiling", "colorful lanterns" and "costumed staff"; that the "consistently good" grub plays second fiddle to all the above is no surprise.

Turquoise
– | – | – | **M**
240 E. 81st St. (bet. 2nd & 3rd Aves.), 212-988-8222
With a name conjuring up the Caribbean, this airy East Side seafood specialist shows off a menu enlivened by Middle Eastern accents that only costs a few clams; sea-green stone walls and a bar made of pebbles add to its beachy feel.

Tuscan Square ⊠
20 | **20** | **17** | **$42**
16 W. 51st St. (bet. 5th & 6th Aves.), 212-977-7777
"Business types" and "Rock Center tourists" like to lunch at this "convenient" Midtown Tuscan featuring "above-average" chow and "open, airy" digs; though it "loses something at dinner" and service "could be better", most agree it provides a good square meal.

Tuscany Grill
23 | **18** | **20** | **$43**
8620 Third Ave. (bet. 86th & 87th Sts.), Brooklyn, 718-921-5633
They do "zippy business" at this Bay Ridge Northern Italian thanks to "tasty" rustic cooking, "welcoming" service and an ambiance that's "like home, only better"; the "intimate" space is particularly "date"-worthy, and ergo "darkly lit."

12th St. Bar & Grill
22 | **19** | **19** | **$35**
1123 Eighth Ave. (bet. 11th & 12th Sts.), Brooklyn, 718-965-9526
Offering "consistent" New Americana at "reasonable prices", this "low-key" Park Slope "staple" is most revered for its "popular" brunch;

most say it "hits all the bases", but a few find it "a bit tired" compared to its newer neighbors.

21 CLUB ☒
22 | 23 | 24 | $66

21 W. 52nd St. (bet. 5th & 6th Aves.), 212-582-7200; www.21club.com
This quintessential NYC institution, a "venerable" former speakeasy, still draws Midtown "power brokers" with its "classic" American menu, "impeccable" service, "old-world panache" and "money-is-no-object" pricing; though it "won't be the same without [retired maitre d'] Bruce Snyder", its traditional "jacket-and-tie" dress code, "priceless bartenders" and "great private rooms" remain; don't miss a tour of the "not-to-be-believed wine cellar."

26 Seats
23 | 17 | 21 | $35

168 Ave. B (bet. 10th & 11th Sts.), 212-677-4787; www.26seats.com
Terrific "traditional French cuisine" comes with an "East Village price tag" at this Avenue B spot that "could use some extra space" ("if only it had 52 seats!"); for best results, be "fashionably thin" or "impossibly romantic", but you'll do well regardless.

Two Boots
18 | 10 | 13 | $14

37 Ave. A (bet. 2nd & 3rd Sts.), 212-505-2276
42 Ave. A (3rd St.), 212-254-1919 ●
74 Bleecker St. (B'way), 212-777-1033 ●
Grand Central, lower level (42nd St. & Lexington Ave.), 212-557-7992
30 Rockefeller Plaza, downstairs (bet. 49th & 50th Sts.), 212-332-8800
201 W. 11th St. (7th Ave. S.), 212-633-9096 ●
514 Second St. (bet. 7th & 8th Aves.), Brooklyn, 718-499-3253
www.twoboots.com
"Crispy crusts", "imaginative toppings" and "wacky-named" pies separate this "taste-of-Louisiana" pizza chain from the competition; the separately managed Park Slope outpost (a magnet for "overactive kids") also offers a full Cajun menu.

212 ●
17 | 17 | 16 | $43

133 E. 65th St. (bet. Lexington & Park Aves.), 212-249-6565; www.212restaurant.com
It's all about "the scene" at this "nightclub-esque" Eastsider frequented by "yummy mummys" by day and "loud Euros" at night; given the quality of the French-Italian food and "snooty service", some say it's the "wrong number", especially if you're a grown-up.

202 Cafe
– | – | – | M

Chelsea Mkt., 75 Ninth Ave. (bet. 15th & 16th Sts.), 646-638-1173
Chelsea Market is the site of this new arrival that combines simple Modern European dining with the high-end wares of designer Nicole Farhi; while the non-food items are pretty pricey, the equally stylish menu is quite affordable.

2 West
▽ 22 | 24 | 23 | $57

Ritz-Carlton Battery Park, 2 West St. (Battery Pl.), 917-790-2525; www.ritzcarlton.com
"Not the easiest place to get to", this "undiscovered" American steakhouse in the "wilds of Battery Park City" features "pricey but delicious" food in "spacious" surroundings; typical Ritz-Carlton "solicitous service" compensates for the lack of a harbor view.

Ubol's Kitchen
▽ 21 | 11 | 21 | $23

24-42 Steinway St. (bet. Astoria Blvd. & 25th Ave.), Queens, 718-545-2874
Folks who like it hot "like the midday sun" like this "spicy" Astoria Thai's "masterfully prepared food", the "next best thing to being in

subscribe to zagat.com

Bangkok"; the "tacky" "neon-beer-sign" decor is offset by fair prices and a "staff that treats you like family."

Ulrika's 22 | 17 | 20 | $44
115 E. 60th St. (bet. Lexington & Park Aves.), 212-355-7069; www.ulrikas.com
A "fine taste of Sweden" near Bloomie's, this "undiscovered" Scandinavian looks like an "upscale Ikea" showroom; maybe the "classic", midpriced menu is "nothing fancy", but it's just the ticket at "Christmastime" or for a "respite after shopping."

Umberto's Clam House ● 19 | 14 | 18 | $34
178 Mulberry St. (Broome St.), 212-343-2053
2356 Arthur Ave. (186th St.), Bronx, 718-220-2526
www.umbertosclamhouse.com
"Old-time Little Italy" thrives at this modestly priced red-sauce "cornerstone" known for "drop-dead" pastas and seafood; while cynics take shots at the "inconsistent" menu and "touristy" digs, fans suggest a visit to the "*molto bene*" Arthur Avenue spin-off.

Una Pizza Napoletana ⊄ ▽ 24 | 9 | 14 | $25
349 E. 12th St. (bet. 1st & 2nd Aves.), 212-477-9950
"It's all about the dough" at this "unusual" East Village pizzeria offering a "limited" selection of whole Neapolitan pies ("four choices, to be exact") and no slices; while the $16.95 price tag is "shockingly expensive" to some, purists praise it as the "most authentic in town."

Uncle Jack's Steakhouse 24 | 19 | 21 | $64
440 Ninth Ave. (bet. 34th & 35th Sts.), 212-244-0005
39-40 Bell Blvd. (40th Ave.), Queens, 718-229-1100
www.unclejacks.com
Two "contenders in the burgeoning steakhouse scene", these Bayside/ Garment District chop shops serve "fabulous" beef in "old-school", "Sinatra-on-the-sound-system" settings; "surly Noo Yawk" staffers and "big-splurge" tabs simply add to the authenticity.

Uncle Nick's 20 | 12 | 16 | $31
747 Ninth Ave. (bet. 50th & 51st Sts.), 212-245-7992
The "good times are contagious" at this "loud" Hell's Kitchen taverna where "super-size portions" of "authentic" Greek grub come at "Astoria prices"; if it's "too busy and bustling" for some, the adjoining Ouzaria is a bit more "leisurely."

UNION SQUARE CAFE 27 | 23 | 26 | $62
21 E. 16th St. (bet. 5th Ave. & Union Sq. W.), 212-243-4020;
www.unionsquarecafe.com
Now in its 20th year and thus one of the "elder statesmen of NYC food", Danny Meyer's "evergreen" New American off Union Square just "gets better with age", starting with chef Michael Romano's "inspired" cooking delivered by a staff that "acts as if your showing up has made their day"; folks in need of a "morale boost" "eat at the bar" when they can't get a table, and leave "happier than when they came in."

UNO Chicago Grill ● 14 | 12 | 14 | $21
432 Columbus Ave. (81st St.), 212-595-4700
220 E. 86th St. (bet. 2nd & 3rd Aves.), 212-472-5656
391 Sixth Ave. (bet. 8th St. & Waverly Pl.), 212-242-5230
South Street Seaport, 89 South St. (Pier 17), 212-791-7999
55 Third Ave. (bet. 10th & 11th Sts.), 212-995-9668
9201 Fourth Ave. (92nd St.), Brooklyn, 718-748-8667
39-02 Bell Blvd. (39th Ave.), Queens, 718-279-4900
107-16 70th Rd. (bet. Austin St. & Queens Blvd.), Queens, 718-793-6700
(continued)

(continued)
Uno Chicago Grill
37-11 35th Ave. (38th St.), Queens, 718-706-8800
www.unos.com
You "won't be hungry" after taking the "deep-dish plunge" at this "family-friendly" pizza franchise where "you know what you're getting", even if real Midwesterners say the "greasy" chow is "hardly authentic"; "tired" decor and "spotty" service come with the territory.

Uovo
— | — | — | M

175 Ave. B (11th St.), 212-475-8686; www.uovo.biz
The East Village's smart eggs roll into this Med-American newcomer to sample its fairly priced, seasonal fare with a focus on fresh Greenmarket ingredients; there's usually a pecking order to obtain the pleasant sidewalk seats.

Upstairs
— | — | — | M

Bouley Bakery & Mkt., 130 W. Broadway, 2nd fl. (Duane St.), 212-608-5829
David Bouley's tri-level TriBeCa culinary complex, just north of his eponymous restaurant, includes this casual, 35-seat eatery serving midpriced sushi and small plates crafted to complement haute cocktails; by day, it serves as a demonstration kitchen for cooking classes.

Uskudar
21 | 11 | 19 | $31

1405 Second Ave. (bet. 73rd & 74th Sts.), 212-988-2641
"Unassuming and unpretentious", this Upper East Side Turkish "delight" may be the "size of a NY closet" (with an "engineering marvel of a restroom"), but remains "packed" thanks to "tasty" cooking and "sweet" service; "what-a-bargain" prices seal the deal.

Utsav
21 | 19 | 19 | $35

1185 Sixth Ave., 2nd fl. (enter on 46th, bet. 6th & 7th Aves.), 212-575-2525
"Hard to find but easy to enjoy", this "white-tablecloth" Theater District Indian is "more inventive" than others in the pack, with "delightfully spacious" digs to boot; it may cost some "additional rupees", so the $14.95 lunch buffet could be the way to go.

Uva ◗
▽ 20 | 23 | 21 | $34

1486 Second Ave. (bet. 77th & 78th Sts.), 212-472-4552
Off to a "great start", this affordable new East Side Italian exudes a "stylish", "European feel" right down to its attractive back garden; "delicious" food, a "lengthy wine list" and late-night hours have made it a hit with "young" folk.

V&T ◗
19 | 8 | 13 | $19

1024 Amsterdam Ave. (bet. 110th & 111th Sts.), 212-666-8051
"Cheap" pizzas and "simple but tasty" pastas have made this crusty Morningside Heights Italian a Columbia student "fixture" for 60 years; indeed, the "pallid" setting and "curmudgeonly waiters" are even beginning to feel "endearing."

Vatan
22 | 24 | 23 | $33

409 Third Ave. (29th St.), 212-689-5666; www.vatanny.com
There are "no decisions" at this Gramercy Indian where "memorable" Gujarati vegetarian dishes just "keep coming" for an all-you-can-eat price of $22.95; "tip-top" service and a wonderfully "campy" village setting ("think India Epcot") augment the "unique experience."

VaTutto
▽ 20 | 19 | 20 | $36

23 Cleveland Pl. (bet. Kenmare & Spring Sts.), 212-941-0286; www.vatutto.com
A "gorgeous garden that transports you to Tuscany" is the star of the show at this NoLita Italian that's also known for its "solid", "no-

nonsense" seasonal menu; inside, it's "homey and cozy", but no matter where you sit, its prices are "moderate."

Vegetarian Paradise

▽ | 20 | 13 | 17 | $19

144 W. Fourth St. (bet. MacDougal St. & 6th Ave.), 212-260-7130
"Endless permutations of faux meat" fill out the menu of this cheap Village Chinese vegetarian that might even "make you like tofu"; despite "abrupt service" and uncertainty about "exactly what you're eating", healthy types tout it as "tried-and-true."

Vela 🖾

▽ | 21 | 21 | 16 | $49

55 W. 21st St. (bet. 5th & 6th Aves.), 212-675-8007; www.velarestaurant.com
Sushi "comes alive" with Brazilian flavors at this "tropical" Flatiron Japanese that attracts a "hip young" following; but critics cite a "trendier-than-thou" staff and a "SushiSamba wannabe" scene, particularly in the wee hours when it morphs into a "nightclub."

Veniero's ◐

| 23 | 13 | 14 | $14

342 E. 11th St. (bet. 1st & 2nd Aves.), 212-674-7070; www.venierospastry.com
Since 1894, this "venerable" East Village Italian "cannoli heaven" has been preparing "sinful" pastries "worth their weight in gold"; so ignore the "indifferent" service and "glacial waits" for a chance to tune in to this "direct channel to the old country."

Vento ◐

| 18 | 19 | 17 | $47

675 Hudson St. (14th St.), 212-699-2400; www.brguestrestaurants.com
Despite the "multilevel" space and wraparound outdoor seating, Steve Hanson's "red-hot" Meatpacking District Italian can be a "zoo" – blame the "sexy vibe" and "hearty" cooking; "aloof" service and "no culinary revelations" suggest it may be still "getting its sea legs."

VERITAS

| 27 | 23 | 26 | $81

43 E. 20th St. (bet. B'way & Park Ave. S.), 212-353-3700; www.veritas-nyc.com
"Getting better with each passing year", Scott Bryan's "impeccable" New American cuisine has become an "equal partner" to the "best wine list out there" at this Flatiron "mecca"; given the "refined" service and "subdued" setting, it's made for "romance", so long as you "bring your wallet" – the prix fixe–only dinner is $72.

Vermicelli

| 20 | 16 | 18 | $30

1492 Second Ave. (bet. 77th & 78th Sts.), 212-288-8868;
www.vermicellirestaurant.com
"Italian-sounding" yet Vietnamese, this "cozy" but "not fancy" Yorkville spot serves "well-prepared" fare to happy locals; doubters declare it's definitely "Second Avenue, not Saigon", though the bargain "box-lunch special" is hard to beat.

Veselka ◐

| 19 | 12 | 14 | $18

144 Second Ave. (9th St.), 212-228-9682; www.veselka.com
"Tasty" Ukranian diner "basics" keep this 24/7 East Villager packed in the wee hours with "cool kids sobering up" on "bargain" pierogi and borscht; a recent "Starbucks-like renovation" draws brickbats, ditto the ever "sullen" service.

Vespa

| 19 | 19 | 20 | $35

1625 Second Ave. (bet. 84th & 85th Sts.), 212-472-2050;
www.barvespa.com
The "charming back garden" is the "real star" of this "casual" East Side Italian where "everyone seems to be on a first date"; while the modestly priced cooking can be "a bit uneven" and the setup "sardine"-like, at least the "novel", "Italian movie–themed" decor is easy to watch.

Via Brasil
18 | 13 | 18 | $38

34 W. 46th St. (bet. 5th & 6th Aves.), 212-997-1158;
www.viabrasilrestaurant.com

"Hearty portions" of "solid" meats and stews beef up the menu of this "casual" Theater District Brazilian that's like a "fast trip to Rio" and always "full of natives"; "wonderful" live music Wednesday–Saturday keeps things shaking here.

Via Emilia ☒⊅
21 | 12 | 17 | $30

240 Park Ave. S. (bet. 19th & 20th Sts.), 212-505-3072; www.viaemilianyc.net

Most "reasonably priced" for its "otherwise expensive" Flatiron neighborhood, this Northern Italian purveys "honest home cooking" abetted by a "wide Lambrusco selection"; "bland" decor and the "no-reservations policy" put some on the via out.

Viand
16 | 7 | 15 | $18

2130 Broadway (75th St.), 212-877-2888 ◗
300 E. 86th St. (2nd Ave.), 212-879-9425 ◗
673 Madison Ave. (bet. 61st & 62nd Sts.), 212-751-6622 ⊅
1011 Madison Ave. (78th St.), 212-249-8250

Popular Uptown coffee shops featuring all the expected menu items and typical diner decor, but salvaged by "faster-than-a-speeding-bullet service" and a mighty "fantastic" turkey sandwich; N.B. the separately owned Yorkville branch is available 24/7.

Via Oreto
21 | 15 | 19 | $43

1121-23 First Ave. (bet. 61st & 62nd Sts.), 212-308-0828; www.viaoreto.com

"They make you feel at home" at this "mama-and-son" East Side trattoria where the "authentic", homemade standards reach their height with Sunday's "worth-the-trip meatballs"; "superb management" gives this "casual" spot a "special touch", even if you can feel it in your billfold.

Via Quadronno
21 | 15 | 16 | $37

25 E. 73rd St. (bet. 5th & Madison Aves.), 212-650-9880;
www.viaquadronno.com

A bona fide "Euro hangout", this "little piece of Milan off Madison" serves three squares a day but insiders hone in on the "unbelievable" panini and "fantastic" Italian coffees; "cramped" and "expensive" is trumped by "chic" here.

ViceVersa ☒
22 | 22 | 22 | $52

325 W. 51st St. (bet. 8th & 9th Aves.), 212-399-9291;
www.viceversarestaurant.com

"Satisfying to both the eye and palate", this "urbane" Northern Italian is the "only reason to eat in the Theater District" for those taken by its "delicious" dishes and "clean, contemporary" look; a "charming garden patio" and delightful host seal the deal.

Vico ◗⊅
21 | 15 | 20 | $52

1302 Madison Ave. (bet. 92nd & 93rd Sts.), 212-876-2222

Very much a "neighborhood club", this Carnegie Hill Italian is "perfect" if you're a regular, though the "consistently good" cooking wins over irregulars too; most "annoying", however, is that "cash-only policy", particularly given the "pretty pricey" tabs.

Victor's Cafe ◗
21 | 19 | 19 | $47

236 W. 52nd St. (bet. B'way & 8th Ave.), 212-586-7714;
www.victorscafe.com

"Just steps from the theaters", this longtime Hell's Kitchen Cuban still draws applause for its "hefty portions" of *maravilloso* chow served in "lively" environs; though a precursor to a host of recent Cuban eateries, it still may be the best.

VietCafé
▽ 21 | 21 | 19 | $34

345 Greenwich St. (bet. Harrison & Jay Sts.), 212-431-5888; www.viet-cafe.com
"Little publicized", this new "upscale" TriBeCa Vietnamese offers "authentic but refined" takes on traditional dishes in a "beautiful", "Saigon-chic" setting (despite the "uncomfortable stools"); a "next-door gallery" displays Viet art and pours cocktails too.

View, The
18 | 25 | 19 | $55

Marriott Marquis Hotel, 1535 Broadway, 47th fl. (bet. 45th & 46th Sts.), 212-704-8900; www.nymarriottmarquis.com
NY's "only revolving restaurant" has been "recently spruced up" and fans say it's "back on top again", crediting the similarly revamped surf 'n' turf menu; of course, the 47th-floor Midtown panorama "dazzles tourists" who may find the sky-high tabs equally stunning.

Villa Berulia
23 | 19 | 25 | $47

107 E. 34th St. (bet. Lexington & Park Aves.), 212-689-1970
"Lovely on all counts" – from the "gracious" staff to the Northern Italian dishes presented in "portions only a mama would serve" – this Murray Hill vet is a "place to linger", even if it's a "little aged around the edges."

Village
20 | 20 | 19 | $40

62 W. Ninth St. (bet. 5th & 6th Aves.), 212-505-3355; www.villagerestaurant.com
"Top-flight" French–New American dishes arrive in "relaxed", "skylit" surroundings at this "spacious" Villager that does a "good impersonation of a bistro"; "midscale" pricing and "friendly" service help make dining here "always a pleasure."

Villa Mosconi ⊠
21 | 16 | 23 | $41

69 MacDougal St. (bet. Bleecker & Houston Sts.), 212-673-0390; www.villamosconi.com
"Frozen in time" in a good way, this "been-there-forever" Village Italian dishes out fairly priced "honest meals" of "red-sauce" basics; the decor may be "left over from the Sinatra days", but the all-weather garden gives it a "small-town" ambiance.

Vince and Eddie's
18 | 17 | 19 | $46

70 W. 68th St. (bet. Columbus Ave. & CPW), 212-721-0068
Particularly "cozy" in winter thanks to several "romantic fireplaces", this West Side American also offers a "pretty garden" in warmer months; year-round, the food is "well prepared" and service "prompt", a good thing given its "convenience to Lincoln Center."

Vincent's ●
21 | 14 | 18 | $31

119 Mott St. (Hester St.), 212-226-8133; www.originalvincents.com
"Some like it hot" at this circa-1904 Little Italy "oldie but goodie" where the famed homemade red sauce can be ordered in temperatures ranging from "medium to oh-my-God"; expect "nostalgia" galore with "gargantuan portions" and "lots of tourists" looking around for *The Sopranos* cast.

Virgil's Real Barbecue ●
20 | 13 | 16 | $32

152 W. 44th St. (bet. B'way & 6th Ave.), 212-921-9494; www.virgilsbbq.com
"Get ready to get messy" at this cheap, "noisy, greasy" Times Square "zoo", a "little bit of Red State in Midtown" where fans "pig out" on "huge portions" of "just-like-Dixie" BBQ; don't mind the "tour bus crowds", and count on being "full for days."

Vittorio Cucina

▽ | 22 | 19 | 21 | $43 |

*308-310 Bleecker St. (bet. Grove St. & 7th Ave. S.), 212-463-0730;
www.vittoriocri.com*

Suprisingly "seldom crowded", this Village Italian standby is known for
its ever-changing menu that "highlights different regional specialties",
not to mention its signature "cheese-wheel pasta", a "marvelous
garden" and "artwork from its chef-owner."

Viva Mar Cafe ●

– | – | – | M |

35-03 Broadway (bet. 35th & 36th Sts.), Queens, 718-278-8700

Boasting a menu that's more creative (yet not much pricier) than its
Hellenic neighbors, this Astoria Med specializes in seafood and serves
it in a bright room; live Greek music on weekends lends a festive feel.

Vivolo

20 | 18 | 20 | $45 |

140 E. 74th St. (bet. Lexington & Park Aves.), 212-737-3533; www.vivolonyc.com

"Solid", "no-surprises" Italian cooking draws an "older, well-heeled"
crowd to this East Side duplex townhouse that's "homey" downstairs
and more "elegant" above; a "gracious" staff, three fireplaces and an
"excellent" $24 early-bird keep patrons pleased.

Vong

23 | 24 | 21 | $60 |

200 E. 54th St. (3rd Ave.), 212-486-9592; www.jean-georges.com

"Mouthwatering" fusion fare, "top-notch" service and an "exotic",
"golden-toned" setting keep Jean-Georges Vongerichten's "showy"
Midtown French-Thai a "perennial favorite"; to make the "child-size
portions" and "expensive" tabs more palatable, fans suggest the
"bargain" lunch and pre-theater prix fixes.

Voyage

▽ | 19 | 20 | 18 | $43 |

117 Perry St. (Greenwich St.), 212-255-9191

It feels like a "friendly cruise ship" aboard this "romantic", nautically
themed Village "hideaway" where the "perfectly prepared" New
American menu arrives in "quiet", "transporting" digs; despite some
"kinks in the service", overall, things are shipshape here.

V Steakhouse

20 | 22 | 21 | $75 |

*Time Warner Ctr., 10 Columbus Circle, 4th fl. (60th St. at B'way),
212-823-9500; www.jean-georges.com*

Jean-Georges Vongerichten's Time Warner Center steakhouse features
Niman Ranch beef and "inventive sauces" served amid "amazing
park views" for only slightly less than the price to "buy the whole
cow"; still, many find this conceptual take on steak "contrived" and
the decor too much like a Vegas "bordello."

Waldy's Wood Fired Pizza

– | – | – | I |

800 Sixth Ave. (bet. 27th & 28th Sts.), 212-213-5042

From Waldy Malouf (Beacon) comes this new Chelsea wood-burning
oven pizzeria vending a variety of gourmet pies topped with organic
ingredients; bare-bones decor and not much seating presumably keep
the prices down and the volume up.

Walker's ●

19 | 14 | 18 | $27 |

16 N. Moore St. (Varick St.), 212-941-0142

TriBeCa types tout the "traditional pub grub" at this historic saloon as
a "step up" from the competition; an atmospheric, circa-1890 setting
and "unbeatable value" keep it especially busy on weekends.

Wallsé ●

26 | 21 | 23 | $62 |

344 W. 11th St. (Washington St.), 212-352-2300; www.wallse.com

It's "Vienna in the Village" at Kurt Gutenbrunner's "*wunderbar*" Austrian
that puts a "haute spin on classic dishes" burnished by an "amazing

wine" list, "genuine" pro service and a "stylish" setting adorned with Julian Schnabel art; sure, it's "pricey", but libertines "loosen their lederhosen and go with the tasting menu."

Water Club
21 | 24 | 21 | $59

East River at 30th St. (enter on E. 23rd St.), 212-683-3333; www.thewaterclub.com
"One-of-a-kind views" are a "precious asset" of this "romantic", nautically decorated American set on an East River barge where the food almost seems incidental to the sights; fans hail it as a "wonderful party" venue, despite the "sinking feeling when the bill comes."

Water's Edge ⊠
22 | 25 | 23 | $60

44th Dr. & East River (Vernon Blvd.), Queens, 718-482-0033; www.watersedgenyc.com
The "only thing they overlook is Manhattan" at this big-bucks Long Island City New American where fans "fall in love" with the "surprisingly good" food and "extraordinary view"; the complimentary water taxi from Midtown is a "great extra."

wd-50 ❷
24 | 21 | 23 | $70

50 Clinton St. (bet. Rivington & Stanton Sts.), 212-477-2900; www.wd-50.com
Bring an "open mind", an "adventurous appetite" and a good credit rating to Wylie Dufresne's "intellectual" Lower East Side American-Eclectic that splits surveyors: acolytes find "substance behind the flash" and award it an "A+ for creativity", while skeptics see it as "more cerebral than succulent"; overall, everyone agrees that the place has a "good vibe."

West Bank Cafe ❷
19 | 16 | 19 | $39

Manhattan Plaza, 407 W. 42nd St. (bet. 9th & 10th Aves.), 212-695-6909
Given its "convenience" to the 42nd Street Off-Broadway theaters, this "informal", "affordable" Hell's Kitchen New American is a magnet for "not-so-famous actors"; the staff's "aware of curtain times", and a new chef and revamped menu show future promise.

Westville ❷
21 | 12 | 17 | $22

210 W. 10th St. (bet. Bleecker & W. 4th Sts.), 212-741-7971
For "home-cooked meals away from home", try this "farm fresh" Village American that "feels like a picnic even in the dead of winter"; "good food for not a lot of money" and a "minuscule" setting explain the inevitable "long lines."

Whole Foods Café
20 | 10 | 11 | $16

Time Warner Ctr., 10 Columbus Circle, downstairs (bet. 58th & 60th Sts.), 212-823-9000
4 Union Square S. (bet. B'way & University Pl.), 212-673-5388
www.wholefoods.com
Think "postmodern Horn & Hardart" to get the gist of these "self-service" Eclectic cafeterias set in NYC's latest "destination groceries"; a "dizzying array" of multinational prepared foods makes up for the "daunting" prime-time lines and "whole paycheck" pricing.

'wichcraft
22 | 11 | 15 | $16

397 Greenwich St. (Beach St.), 866-942-4272
Terminal Warehouse, 224 12th Ave. (bet. 27th & 28th Sts.), 212-780-0577
www.wichcraftnyc.com
"Perfection in sandwich form" is yours at these limited-menu breakfast-and-lunch "godsends" via Craft's Tom Colicchio that "put some magic" into casual daytime dining; ok, the preparations come at "premium prices", but they're certainly "worth the splurge."

Wild Ginger ❶

| 20 | 19 | 18 | $26 |

51 Grove St. (bet. Bleecker St. & 7th Ave. S.), 212-367-7200;
www.wildginger-ny.com

"Decent basics" (including some "spiced-up old favorites") fill out the menu of this "can't-go-wrong" Village Thai boasting "distinctive", "heavy-on-the-bamboo" decor; "gracious service" and "rock-bottom" prices contribute to its "relaxing" mood.

Willie's Steak House ❶

| ▽ 19 | 14 | 20 | $26 |

1832 Westchester Ave. (bet. Taylor & Thieriot Aves.), Bronx, 718-822-9697;
www.williessteakhouse.com

"Popular with families and couples", this longtime, low-budget Spanish steakhouse in the Bronx is an "excellent hangout" provided you don't mind the crowds that come for the "live Latin jazz" on Wednesdays and Saturdays.

Wimp's Sky Café ❶

| ▽ 24 | 21 | 24 | $28 |

29 W. 125th St., 2nd fl. (bet. Lenox & 5th Aves.), 212-410-2296

Cramming a lot into a small space, this Harlem duplex features a downstairs bakery topped by a Southern soul food eatery complete with a martini bar; some find it "surprisingly chic" for the neighborhood, though prices are comfortingly low.

Wogies Bar & Grill ❶

| ▽ 22 | 13 | 18 | $18 |

39 Greenwich Ave. (Charles St.), 212-229-2171; www.wogies.com

"Dynamite" Philly cheese steaks, "piping hot" and slathered "with plenty of goop", are the forte of this very "lively" Village bar and grill; it's best "with an Eagles game on TV" or "people-watching" from its sidewalk tables.

Wo Hop ❶⊟

| 21 | 5 | 13 | $17 |

17 Mott St. (Canal St.), 212-267-2536

"Chinatown's answer to White Castle", this 24-hour "insomniac favorite" "satisfies every craving" after a "rough night of barhopping"; "lightning service", "total steal" pricing and "large portions" of "old-style" Chinese grub "done right" trump the "been-there-forever" "truck-stop" decor.

Wolfgang's Steakhouse

| 25 | 21 | 20 | $68 |

4 Park Ave. (33rd St.), 212-889-3369;
www.wolfgangssteakhouse.com

This "extremely popular" Murray Hill chophouse "clone" from a Luger alumnus boasts an "incredible" porterhouse, "pro service" and an "atmospheric tiled ceiling"; while downsides include "brain-numbing" acoustics, "long waits even with reservations" and "lotsa bucks" price tags, unlike "you know who", "they take plastic."

Wollensky's Grill ❶

| 22 | 17 | 19 | $47 |

201 E. 49th St. (3rd Ave.), 212-753-0444;
www.smithandwollensky.com

"Mostly suits" frequent this more modest Midtown adjunct to Smith & Wollensky offering the "same high-quality" steaks and burgers at lower prices; regulars like its late hours and "Cheers-like" feel but advise "eat outside or leave your elbows at home."

Wondee Siam

| 24 | 8 | 18 | $21 |

792 Ninth Ave. (bet. 52nd & 53rd Sts.), 212-459-9057 ⊟
813 Ninth Ave. (bet. 53rd & 54th Sts.), 917-286-1726

The Thai "food's memorable" even if the settings aren't at this Hell's Kitchen duo, so aesthetes usually "stick to delivery"; in or out, it's worth sampling for "authentic" fare served two ways: "American spicy" or "sweating-bullets spicy."

Won Jo ◐ 21 12 15 $31
23 W. 32nd St. (bet. B'way & 5th Ave.), 212-695-5815;
www.wonjokoreanrestaurant.com
"Perfectly marinated BBQ" highlights the menu of this 24/7 Garment District Korean where the "real wood fires make all the difference"; sure, the grill smell may "follow you home" and it's "very plain" looking, but "reasonable prices" keep the trade brisk.

Woo Lae Oak 23 22 19 $47
148 Mercer St. (bet. Houston & Prince Sts.), 212-925-8200;
www.woolaeoaksoho.com
"Sleek" and "sexy", this "new age" SoHo Korean "hits all the right Saturday night buttons" with a "do-it-yourself" twist: "cooking your food on your own personal grill"; most agree the grub's "a cut above K-town, but it's priced above it" too.

Wu Liang Ye 22 12 16 $28
215 E. 86th St. (bet. 2nd & 3rd Aves.), 212-534-8899
338 Lexington Ave. (bet. 39th & 40th Sts.), 212-370-9648
36 W. 48th St. (bet. 5th & 6th Aves.), 212-398-2308
As "authentic as they come", these Szechuan triplets are a "refreshing contrast" to the usual since they "don't skimp on the spice"; besides "clearing sinuses", they also supply "good value."

Xing ∇ 19 24 20 $32
785 Ninth Ave. (52nd St.), 646-289-3010; www.xingrestaurant.com
"Old-school Chinese" cooking arrives in "sleek", ultra-"modern" digs at this "promising" Hell's Kitchen newcomer; a few wish the "food lived up to the decor", but most feel the price is right and service is more "sweet than sour."

X.O. ⌦ 18 10 12 $15
148 Hester St. (bet. Bowery & Elizabeth St.), 212-965-8645
96 Walker St. (bet. Centre & Lafayette Sts.), 212-343-8339
Ok, there's "little atmosphere" and the "service is from hunger", but this Hong Kong–style Chinese duo compensates with "lots of food to try" at "definitely cheap" tabs; the Walker Street outlet's "main selling point" is its "all-day dim sum."

Xunta ◐ 19 12 14 $27
174 First Ave. (bet. 10th & 11th Sts.), 212-614-0620; www.xuntatapas.com
"Very young" types cram into this low-budget East Village Spanish "crowd-pleaser" famed for "killer sangria" and a "huge selection of tapas"; despite "uncomfortable seating" and interminable waits, it stays "lively" and "noisy."

Yama 25 12 16 $37
38-40 Carmine St. (bet. Bedford & Bleecker Sts.), 212-989-9330
122 E. 17th St. (Irving Pl.), 212-475-0969 ⊠
92 W. Houston St. (bet. La Guardia Pl. & Thompson St.), 212-674-0935 ◐
www.yamarestaurant.com
"Yama mia!"; the "Godzilla-size" pieces of "succulent" sushi match the "monster waits" (but not the "small prices") at this insanely "popular" Japanese trio; if the "long waits" are a turnoff, "yamaniacs" suggest Carmine Street, the only outlet that takes reservations.

Yellow Fin ∇ 23 19 18 $51
20 Ellis St. (Arthur Kill Rd.), Staten Island, 718-317-5700
"Manhattan comes to Staten Island" via this "trendy" New American purveying "creative" dishes; while the prices leave some "gasping for air", it's a good alternative to standard local fare.

York Grill

22 | 20 | 22 | $45

1690 York Ave. (bet. 88th & 89th Sts.), 212-772-0261
The "low-key setting feels high class" at this "earnest" New American "hidden" on the "far East Side" near Gracie Mansion; its "mature" following says it's "much needed" in this "restaurant desert" for its "signature skirt steak" alone.

You-Chun

– | – | – | I

5 W. 36th St. (5th Ave.), 212-563-3737 ●
156-03 Northern Blvd. (156th St.), Queens, 718-461-6511
The house specialty at these inexpensive outposts of a popular Seoul chain is cold noodles served with partially frozen broth, though things warm up when the charcoal grills get going in the evening for yakitori; N.B. the Garment District branch stays open till 4 AM.

Yuca Bar ●

▽ 22 | 16 | 21 | $26

111 Ave. A (7th St.), 212-982-9533; www.yucabarnyc.com
"Funky little" East Villager with an "inventive" Pan-Latin menu that's lubricated by "fantastic sangria" or "refreshing mojitos"; the candlelit, "no-pretensions" setting and "bay windows" overlooking Avenue A draw a "kinda hip" young crowd.

Yujin

▽ 19 | 21 | 18 | $49

24 E. 12th St. (bet. 5th Ave. & University Pl.), 212-924-4283; www.yujinnyc.com
Although "aesthetically pleasing" and offering an "ambitious menu", this Village Japanese "hasn't caught on yet"; some dismiss it as "just another pretty, overpriced place" and dis the "lackadaisical" service.

Yuka

22 | 12 | 20 | $26

1557 Second Ave. (bet. 80th & 81st Sts.), 212-772-9675
The "$18 all-you-can-eat sushi deal" is this Yorkville Japanese's claim to fame; regulars report the rolls are "gigantic", the staff "energetic" and the value "incredible", and only wish they could do something about the "dingy" digs and "long waits."

Yuki Sushi ●

21 | 15 | 20 | $29

656 Amsterdam Ave. (92nd St.), 212-787-8200
"Anything but yuki", this Upper West Side "neighborhood" Japanese lures locals with "inventive rolls" (the peanut avocado in particular) at "good value"; throw in "remember-your-face service" and the "small space" doesn't seem so tight.

Yumcha ●

– | – | – | E

29 Bedford St. (Downing St.), 212-524-6800; www.yumchanyc.com
Set on a quaint Village corner, this "appealing" newcomer serves self-described 'modern haute Chinese' in "stylish" surroundings; its name means 'drink tea', ergo the bar's centerpiece is a chest of exotic flowers waiting to be steeped in its signature brews.

Yura & Co.

20 | 10 | 15 | $23

1292 Madison Ave. (92nd St.), 212-860-8060
1645 Third Ave. (92nd St.), 212-860-8060
1659 Third Ave. (93rd St.), 212-860-8060
These "busy" East Side American bakery/cafes are "better for takeout", given their limited seating; despite "distracted" service and "not much atmosphere", their "addictive, pound-packing" offerings are favorites of "school kids, runners and museumgoers."

Zabar's Cafe ⊟

20 | 6 | 10 | $14

2245 Broadway (80th St.), 212-787-2000; www.zabars.com
Thanks to patrons out of a "Nora Ephron movie" and a "quasi-rude" staff, this "no-frills" West Side adjunct to the gourmet market is a

"very NY" experience; though they serve good stuff, the "lack of charm" (and seats) makes it "better to take it home."

Zarela
21 | 16 | 17 | $40

953 Second Ave. (bet. 50th & 51st Sts.), 212-644-6740; www.zarela.com
"Downstairs if you want to party, upstairs if you want to dine" is the word on Zarela Martinez's beyond-"energetic" East Side cantina; while the Mexican fare is about as good as it gets in NYC, its "kick-ass margaritas" are equally memorable.

Zaytoons
23 | 13 | 17 | $16

472 Myrtle Ave. (bet. Hall St. & Washington Ave.), Brooklyn, 718-623-5522
283 Smith St. (Sackett St.), Brooklyn, 718-875-1880
"Well-made, interesting riffs on a Mideastern theme" turn up at these "flavorful" Brooklyn eateries celebrated for their "fantastically cheap" tabs abetted by a BYO policy; "cramped" settings and "inattentive" staffers are unfortunately part of the package.

Za Za ◗
20 | 16 | 20 | $35

1207 First Ave. (bet. 65th & 66th Sts.), 212-772-9997
"Good Italian food without a lot of fanfare" sums up the scene at this "reliable" midpriced Eastsider where there are "no surprises on the menu", but no one minds much; rather, it's the "pretty garden out back" that seems to stand out most.

Zebú Grill
∇ 21 | 17 | 19 | $35

305 E. 92nd St. (bet. 1st & 2nd Aves.), 212-426-7500; www.zebugrill.com
It helps to be "in the mood for meat" at this "charming little" Upper East Side Brazilian where "top-notch churrasco" is the signature dish; "modest" pricing, "powerhouse cocktails" and a "warm welcome" enhance its "relaxed", "neighborhood" feel.

Zen Palate
19 | 16 | 16 | $26

2170 Broadway (bet. 76th & 77th Sts.), 212-501-7768
663 Ninth Ave. (46th St.), 212-582-1669
34 Union Sq. E. (16th St.), 212-614-9291
www.zenpalate.com
"They do amazing things to approximate meat" at this vegetarian chainlet where "health nuts" can't get over "what they do with tofu"; even if a few feel the "food needs more pizzazz", the "bargain" tabs lure them in "now and Zen."

Zeytin
19 | 18 | 17 | $38

519 Columbus Ave. (85th St.), 212-579-1145
"Am I in Constantinople?" ask transported Westsiders at this Turkish spot where the "caliber of the food is high" enough to make it a "potential up-and-comer"; trouble is, "service can be a crapshoot", though "reasonable pricing" is a constant.

Zeytuna
18 | 14 | 13 | $16

59 Maiden Ln. (William St.), 212-742-2436
161 Maiden Ln. (Front St.), 212-514-5858
"Selection, selection, selection" is the draw at these "Financial District versions of Zabar's" offering "serve-yourself" Eclectic offerings in "upscale food court" settings; although the "quality varies wildly", at least you'll "never get bored."

Zipi Zape
∇ 20 | 18 | 20 | $28

152 Metropolitan Ave. (Berry St.), Brooklyn, 718-599-3027
The "pickings are good" (albeit on the "small" side, portionwise) at this Spanish tapas outlet in Williamsburg, where the "staff is sweet"

and the sangria "spicy"; prices can "add up quickly", but at least it's a zippy "change of pace."

Zócalo
| | 20 | 15 | 17 | $36 |

174 E. 82nd St. (bet. Lexington & 3rd Aves.), 212-717-7772
Grand Central, lower level (42nd St. & Vanderbilt Ave.), 212-687-5666
www.zocalo.us
There's "real life to the food" at this "higher-end" East Side Mexican (and its "handy-for-commuters" Grand Central spin-off); though it's "a bit pricey", the "strong margaritas" help ease the pain.

Zoë
| | 21 | 19 | 19 | $45 |

90 Prince St. (bet. B'way & Mercer St.), 212-966-6722
The food's "consistently good" at this "consistently crowded" SoHo New American "standard" where "weary shoppers get nourishment"; fans like "watching the cooks at work" in the open kitchen, and report that brunch is especially "top-notch."

Zona Rosa ⊠
| | 19 | 17 | 19 | $42 |

40 W. 56th St. (bet. 5th & 6th Aves.), 212-247-2800;
www.zonarosarestaurant.com
"Refreshingly light takes on Mexican cuisine" turn up at this "upscale" Midtown duplex where the "intimate" downstairs dining room is crowned by a bar stocked with "high-end" tequila; sure, it's a tad "pricey" but that's because it's "out of the ordinary."

Zucco Le French Diner ◑⊟
| | – | – | – | I |

188 Orchard St. (bet. Houston & Stanton Sts.), 212-677-5200
The brainchild of a colorful French ex-journalist, this shoebox-size facsimile of a Parisian cafe on the Lower East Side lures expats and locals for relaxed coffee talk with an appealing pop soundtrack as background; the kitchen turns out light fare and hearty *plats du jour.*

Zum Schneider ⊟
| | 18 | 16 | 16 | $25 |

107 Ave. C (7th St.), 212-598-1098; www.zumschneider.com
"Bavaria" lands in Alphabet City at this "raucous", "no-pretensions" German where the grub is "hearty" enough to offset the beer; "outdoor grazing" and "cheap" tabs compensate for the "slow service."

Zum Stammtisch
| | 23 | 20 | 20 | $34 |

69-46 Myrtle Ave. (bet. 69th Pl. & 70th St.), Queens, 718-386-3014;
www.zumstammtisch.com
Sure, the "year-round Oktoberfest atmosphere can be daunting", but this "authentic" Glendale German pleases most with its *wunderbar* chow and "kitschy", "old beer hall feel"; it's "one of the last of its kind" and thus "worth the trip to the edge of Queens."

Zuni ◑
| | 17 | 13 | 17 | $31 |

598 Ninth Ave. (43rd St.), 212-765-7626; www.zuniny.com
An "easygoing" mood prevails at this "tried-and-true" Hell's Kitchen New American where the food's "reliable", the service "pleasant" and the cost "reasonable"; since it "never seems to be busy", "pre-theater dining is less stressful" than at many of its neighbors.

Zutto
| | 23 | 18 | 20 | $37 |

62 Greenwich Ave. (bet. 7th Ave. S. & W. 11th St.), 212-367-7204 ⊠
77 Hudson St. (Harrison St.), 212-233-3287
www.sushizutto.com
"Quality sushi and creative rolls" jazz up the menu of this "modest" Japanese duo; surveyors split on the cost – "pretty reasonable" versus the "usual NYC pricing" – but otherwise laud the "try-to-please" staffs and "consistently good" kitchens.

Indexes

CUISINES
LOCATIONS
SPECIAL FEATURES

CUISINES

(Restaurant Names, Food ratings and neighborhoods)

Afghan
Afghan Kebab Hse./18/multi. loc.

African
Les Enfants Terribles/21/Low E Side

American (New)
Abigael's/20/Garment
Above/19/W 40s
Aesop's Tables/22/Staten Is.
Alias/21/Low E Side
Amuse/–/Chelsea
Angus McIndoe/17/W 40s
Annisa/27/G Vil.
Applewood/23/Park Slope
Arabelle/25/E 60s
Aureole/27/E 60s
Bar Americain/24/W 50s
barmarché/18/NoLita
Battery Gardens/19/Fin. District
Beacon/22/W 50s
BED New York/17/Chelsea
Biltmore Room/24/Chelsea
Bistro Ten 18/19/W 100s
Black Duck/19/Gramercy
BLT Prime/27/Gramercy
Blue Hill/26/G Vil.
Blue Ribbon/25/multi. loc.
Blue Ribbon Bakery/24/G Vil.
Boat House/17/E 70s
Bridge Cafe/21/Fin. District
Bruckner B&G/–/Bronx
Bull Run/19/Fin. District
Butter/18/G Vil.
Café Botanica/20/W 50s
Cafe S.F.A./18/E 40s
Café St. Bart's/15/E 50s
CamaJe/22/G Vil.
Candela/18/Union Sq.
Caviar Russe/25/E 50s
Chemist Club/–/E 40s
Chestnut/21/Carroll Gdns.
Chop't Creative/21/multi. loc.
Cibo/20/E 40s
Cité Grill/20/W 50s
Cocotte/22/Park Slope
Columbus Bakery/19/W 80s
Compass/21/W 70s
Cornelia St. Cafe/19/G Vil.
Craft/26/Flatiron
Craftbar/23/Flatiron
Croton Reservoir/19/W 40s

Cub Room/17/SoHo
davidburke/donatella/25/E 60s
Deborah/21/G Vil.
Diner/23/Williamsburg
District/20/W 40s
dominic/19/TriBeCa
Downtown Atlantic/20/Boerum Hill
Duane Park Cafe/22/TriBeCa
DuMont/23/Williamsburg
Duvet/17/Flatiron
East of Eighth/17/Chelsea
Eatery/19/W 50s
Eleven Madison/26/Gramercy
elmo/15/Chelsea
Essex/18/Low E Side
Etats-Unis/25/E 80s
Fifty Seven 57/23/E 50s
Five Front/21/Dumbo
Five Points/22/NoHo
Fives/21/W 50s
44/19/W 40s
44 & X Hell's Kit./21/W 40s
Fred's at Barneys/20/E 60s
Freemans/21/Low E Side
Garden Cafe/28/Prospect Heights
Giorgio's/Gramercy/23/Flatiron
good/21/G Vil.
Gotham B&G/27/G Vil.
Grace/20/TriBeCa
Gramercy Tav./28/Flatiron
Grocery/27/Carroll Gdns.
Harlem Grill/–/Harlem
Harrison/24/TriBeCa
Hearth/24/E Vil.
Heights Cafe/17/Bklyn Hts.
Henry's End/26/Bklyn Hts.
HK/19/Garment
Hope & Anchor/19/Red Hook
Ian/23/E 80s
Ici/21/Ft. Greene
Ida Mae/21/Garment
Inside/24/G Vil.
Isabella's/20/W 70s
Jane/22/G Vil.
Jerry's/19/SoHo
Josephina/19/W 60s
Josephs Citarella/23/W 40s
Kitchen/Cocktails/–/Low E Side
Kitchen 82/22/21/multi. loc.
Knickerbocker B&G/20/G Vil.
Landmark Tavern/–/W 40s
Lenox Room/19/E 70s

Levana/18/W 60s
Lever House/23/E 50s
Little Giant/26/Low E Side
Maggie Brown/21/Clinton Hill
Magnolia/20/Park Slope
March/26/E 50s
Mark's/23/E 70s
Mas/25/G Vil.
Melt/–/Park Slope
Mercer Kitchen/22/SoHo
Metrazur/20/E 40s
Modern, The/25/W 50s
Monkey Bar/18/E 50s
Morrell Wine Bar/20/W 40s
My Most Favorite/18/W 40s
New Leaf/22/Wash. Hts. & Up
Night and Day/–/Park Slope
NoHo Star/18/NoHo
Norma's/26/W 50s
North Sq./23/G Vil.
Oceana/26/E 50s
Océo/18/W 40s
One/18/Meatpacking
One if by Land/23/G Vil.
101/19/multi. loc.
Ouest/25/W 80s
Paloma/–/Greenpoint
Parish & Co./21/Chelsea
Park Avalon/20/Flatiron
Park Ave. Cafe/24/E 60s
Patroon/20/E 40s
Pearl Room/23/Bay Ridge
per se/28/W 60s
Philip Marie/21/G Vil.
Picket Fence/20/Ditmas Pk.
Place/22/G Vil.
Poetessa/21/E Vil.
Pop Burger/19/Meatpacking
Prune/25/E Vil.
Rachel's American/18/W 40s
Red Café/21/Park Slope
Red Cat/24/Chelsea
Redeye Grill/21/W 50s
Regency/19/E 60s
Relish/21/Williamsburg
Riingo/19/E 40s
River Café/26/Dumbo
Riverdale Garden/22/Bronx
Riverview/20/LIC
Rose Water/25/Park Slope
Salt/22/multi. loc.
Saul/26/Boerum Hill
Savoy/23/SoHo
Seven/18/Chelsea
71 Clinton Fresh/24/Low E Side
Shaffer City/23/Flatiron
Silverleaf Tavern/21/Murray Hill

SQC/19/W 70s
Stone Park Café/24/Park Slope
Tabla/26/Gramercy
Taste/21/E 80s
Tasting Room/26/E Vil.
Tea Box/21/E 50s
Thalia/20/W 50s
Thor/–/Low E Side
343/17/E 80s
Tocqueville/25/Union Sq.
Town/24/W 50s
Tribeca Grill/22/TriBeCa
12th St. B&G/22/Park Slope
Union Sq. Cafe/27/Union Sq.
Uovo/–/E Vil.
Veritas/27/Flatiron
View/18/W 40s
Village/20/G Vil.
Voyage/19/G Vil.
Water's Edge/22/LIC
wd-50/24/Low E Side
West Bank Cafe/19/W 40s
'wichcraft/22/multi. loc.
Yellow Fin/23/Staten Is.
York Grill/22/E 80s
Zoë/21/SoHo
Zuni/17/W 40s

American (Traditional)

Alexandra/20/G Vil.
Algonquin/16/W 40s
Alias/21/Low E Side
American Grill/19/Staten Is.
Annie's/17/E 70s
Barking Dog/16/multi. loc.
Bayard's/24/Fin. District
Bliss/22/Sunnyside
Boat Basin Cafe/12/W 70s
Brennan & Carr/19/Sheepshead Bay
Brooklyn Diner/16/W 50s
Bryant Park/17/W 40s
Bubba Gump/14/W 40s
Bubby's/18/multi. loc.
Cafeteria/18/Chelsea
Chadwick's/21/Bay Ridge
Chat 'n Chew/17/Union Sq.
Chelsea Grill/19/multi. loc.
Coffee Shop/16/Union Sq.
Comfort Diner/16/multi. loc.
Corner Bistro/23/G Vil.
Cupping Room/17/SoHo
Diner 24/17/Chelsea
E.A.T./19/E 80s
EJ's Luncheonette/16/multi. loc.
Elaine's/12/E 80s
Elephant & Castle/18/G Vil.
Embers/22/Bay Ridge

ESPN Zone/12/W 40s
Fairway Cafe/20/W 70s
Friend of a Farmer/17/Gramercy
Good Enough to Eat/20/W 80s
Gravy/–/Boerum Hill
Grilled Cheese/20/Low E Side
Hard Rock Cafe/11/W 40s
Heartland Brew./14/multi. loc.
Home/20/G Vil.
Houston's/20/multi. loc.
Hudson Cafeteria/18/W 50s
Jackson Hole/17/multi. loc.
Jekyll & Hyde/10/W 50s
J.G. Melon/20/E 70s
Joe Allen/17/W 40s
Lodge/–/Williamsburg
Lorenzo's/22/Staten Is.
LoSide/–/Low E Side
Luke's B&G/17/E 70s
Mama's Food /21/E Vil.
Maremma/–/G Vil.
Marion's Cont./17/NoHo
Mars 2112/9/W 50s
Mayrose/15/Flatiron
McHales/20/W 40s
Melba's/–/Harlem
MetroCafe/18/Flatiron
Michael Jordan's/21/E 40s
MJ Grill/18/Fin. District
Neary's/16/E 50s
Odeon/18/TriBeCa
Once Upon a Tart/20/SoHo
O'Neals'/17/W 60s
Parsonage/21/Staten Is.
Penelope/22/Murray Hill
Pershing Sq./15/E 40s
Pete's Tavern/13/Gramercy
P.J. Clarke's/18/E 50s
Popover Cafe/18/W 80s
Raymond's Cafe/19/Chelsea
Rock Center Cafe/19/W 50s
Roll-n-Roaster/19/multi. loc.
Sarabeth's/21/multi. loc.
Sensa/–/Flatiron
Serendipity 3/19/E 60s
Shake Shack/22/Flatiron
Swifty's/17/E 70s
Tavern on Green/15/W 60s
Tom's/19/Prospect Heights
Trump Grille/–/E 50s
Tuk Tuk/20/LIC
Tupelo Grill/20/Garment
21 Club/22/W 50s
2 West/22/Fin. District
Uno Chicago/14/multi. loc.

Vince & Eddie's/18/W 60s
Walker's/19/TriBeCa
Water Club/21/Murray Hill
Westville/21/G Vil.
Wollensky's Grill/22/E 40s
Yura & Co./20/E 90s

Argentinean

Azul Bistro/23/Low E Side
Cambalache/–/E 60s
Chimichurri Grill/22/W 40s
Hacienda Argentina/20/E 70s
Mundo/–/Astoria
Novecento/22/SoHo
Pampa/21/W 90s
Sosa Borella/20/multi. loc.

Asian

Aja/21/E 50s
Arabelle/25/E 60s
Asia de Cuba/24/Murray Hill
Bright Food Shop/20/Chelsea
Cafe Asean/22/G Vil.
Chance/21/Boerum Hill
China Grill/23/W 50s
Chino's/20/Gramercy
Chow Bar/20/G Vil.
Citrus Bar & Grill/20/W 70s
Friendhouse/19/E Vil.
Gobo/23/G Vil.
Hispaniola/21/Wash. Hts. & Up
Koi/24/W 40s
Lotus/17/Meatpacking
Nana/21/Park Slope
O.G./24/E Vil.
Plate NYC/19/NoLita
Roy's NY/24/Fin. District
Ruby Foo's/19/multi. loc.
Sandia/25/Chelsea
Tao/22/E 50s

Australian

Eight Mile Creek/19/Little Italy

Austrian

Café Sabarsky/22/E 80s
Danube/27/TriBeCa
Thomas Beisl/20/Ft. Greene
Wallsé/26/G Vil.

Bakeries

Amy's Bread/24/multi. loc.
City Bakery/22/Flatiron
Columbus Bakery/19/multi. loc.
La Bergamote/26/Chelsea
Le Pain Quotidien/20/multi. loc.
Once Upon a Tart/20/SoHo
Yura & Co./20/E 90s

Barbecue

Blue Smoke/21/Gramercy
Bone Lick Pk. BBQ/14/G Vil.
Brother Jimmy BBQ/16/multi. loc.
Daisy May's BBQ/23/W 40s
Dallas BBQ/15/multi. loc.
Dinosaur BBQ/22/Harlem
Pearson's BBQ/16/E 80s
Rib/–/G Vil.
RUB BBQ/19/Chelsea
Smoked/–/E Vil.
Tennessee Mtn./16/SoHo
Texas Smoke BBQ/16/Gramercy
Virgil's Real BBQ/20/W 40s

Belgian

Café de Bruxelles/20/G Vil.
Le Pain Quotidien/20/multi. loc.
Markt/19/Meatpacking
Petite Abeille/19/multi. loc.

Brazilian

BarBossa/–/NoLita
Casa/23/G Vil.
Caviar & Banana/18/Flatiron
Churra. Plata./22/multi. loc.
Circus/20/E 60s
Coffee Shop/19/Union Sq.
Green Field Churra./19/Corona
Malagueta/26/Astoria
Rice 'n' Beans/20/W 50s
Vela/21/Flatiron
Via Brasil/18/W 40s
Zebú Grill/21/E 90s

Burmese

Mingala Burmese/20/multi. loc.

Cajun

Bayou/18/Harlem
Delta Grill/19/W 40s
French Quarter/–/Gramercy
Great Jones Cafe/22/NoHo
Jacques-Imo's/18/multi. loc.
Mara's Homemade/18/E Vil.
107 West/17/multi. loc.
Two Boots/18/Park Slope

Californian

Michael's/22/W 50s

Caribbean

A/23/W 100s
Brawta Caribbean/20/Boerum Hill
Don Pedro's/21/E 90s
Ideya/21/SoHo
Ivo & Lulu/24/SoHo
Negril/20/multi. loc.

Cheese Steaks

BB Sandwich/19/G Vil.
Carl's Steaks/22/multi. loc.
Philly Slim's/22/W 50s
Tony Luke's/22/W 40s
Wogies B&G/22/G Vil.

Chinese

(* dim sum specialist)
A&B Lobster King/19/Ctown
Au Mandarin/19/Fin. District
Bill Hong's/23/E 50s
Café Evergreen*/20/E 60s
Canton/24/Ctown
Chef Ho's/22/E 80s
Chiam*/21/E 40s
China 1/17/E Vil.
Chin Chin/23/E 40s
Diamond on Eighth*/23/Sunset Park
Dim Sum Go Go*/21/Ctown
Dumpling Man/19/E Vil.
Eastern King/–/E 70s
East Lake*/21/Flushing
East Manor*/20/Flushing
Empire Szechuan*/15/multi. loc.
Evergreen Shan.*/18/multi. loc.
Excellent Dumpling/19/Ctown
Flor de Mayo/20/multi. loc.
Fuleen Sea./24/Ctown
Golden Unicorn*/20/Ctown
Goodies/20/Ctown
Grand Sichuan/22/multi. loc.
Happy Buddha/–/Flushing
Hip Hop Chow/–/E Vil.
HSF*/19/Ctown
Hunan Park/20/W 70s
Ivy's Cafe/20/W 70s
Jing Fong*/18/Ctown
Joe's/22/multi. loc.
Lili's Noodle/17/multi. loc.
Mainland/–/E 60s
Mandarin Court*/20/Ctown
Mee Noodle Shop/17/multi. loc.
Mr. Chow/23/E 50s
Mr. K's/24/E 50s
New Green Bo/23/Ctown
Nice*/21/Ctown
NoHo Star/18/NoHo
Ollie's/16/multi. loc.
Oriental Garden*/24/Ctown
Our Place*/21/multi. loc.
Peking Duck/22/multi. loc.
Phoenix Garden/22/Murray Hill
Pig Heaven/19/E 80s
Ping's Seafood*/21/multi. loc.
Rickshaw Dumpling/17/Flatiron
Shanghai Cuisine/20/Ctown

Shanghai Pavilion/22/E 70s
Shun Lee Cafe*/21/W 60s
Shun Lee Palace/24/E 50s
Shun Lee West/23/W 60s
66*/21/TriBeCa
Spicy & Tasty/20/Flushing
Sweet-n-Tart*/20/multi. loc.
Tang Pavilion/22/W 50s
Tse Yang/23/E 50s
Veg. Paradise*/20/G Vil.
Wo Hop/21/Ctown
Wu Liang Ye/22/multi. loc.
Xing/19/W 50s
X.O.*/18/Ctown
Yumcha/–/G Vil.

Coffeehouses

Cafe Lalo/20/W 80s
Edgar's Cafe/19/W 80s
Ferrara/22/Little Italy
French Roast/15/multi. loc.
Grey Dog's Coffee/22/G Vil.
Le Pain Quotidien/20/multi. loc.
Omonia Cafe/18/multi. loc.
Once Upon a Tart/20/SoHo
71 Irving Place/19/Gramercy
Starbucks/12/multi. loc.

Coffee Shops/Diners

Burger Heaven/16/multi. loc.
Chat 'n Chew/17/Union Sq.
Comfort Diner/16/multi. loc.
Diner/23/Williamsburg
Diner 24/17/Chelsea
Edison Cafe/15/W 40s
EJ's Luncheonette/16/multi. loc.
Empire Diner/15/Chelsea
Florent/19/Meatpacking
Googie's/14/E 70s
Gravy/–/Boerum Hill
Junior's/17/multi. loc.
LoSide/–/Low E Side
Mayrose/15/Flatiron
Tom's/19/Prospect Heights
Veselka/19/E Vil.
Viand/16/multi. loc.

Colombian

Tierras Colomb./20/multi. loc.

Continental

Café Pierre/22/E 60s
Caffé/Green/21/Bayside
Cebu/22/Bay Ridge
Chadwick's/21/Bay Ridge
El Rey del Marisco/–/Bronx
Four Seasons/26/E 50s
Jack's Lux. Oyster/25/E Vil.

Kings' Carriage Hse./20/E 80s
Marion's Cont./17/NoHo
Paris Commune/18/G Vil.
Park Place/20/Bronx
Parsonage/21/Staten Is.
Petrossian/25/W 50s
Russian Samovar/19/W 50s
Sardi's/16/W 40s

Creole

Bayou/18/Harlem
Creole/20/Harlem
Delta Grill/19/W 40s
French Quarter/–/Gramercy
Jacques-Imo's/18/multi. loc.
Mara's Homemade/18/E Vil.

Cuban

Agozar!/18/NoHo
Asia de Cuba/24/Murray Hill
Azucar/–/W 50s
Cabana/21/multi. loc.
Cafe Con Leche/17/multi. loc.
Café Habana/23/NoLita
Calle Ocho/21/W 80s
Cuba/21/G Vil.
Cuba Cafe/19/Chelsea
Cubana Café/20/multi. loc.
Havana Alma/22/G Vil.
Havana Central/17/multi. loc.
Havana Chelsea/21/Chelsea
Son Cubano/21/Meatpacking
Victor's Cafe/21/W 50s

Delis

Artie's Deli/18/W 80s
Barney Greengrass/24/W 80s
Ben's Kosher Deli/18/multi. loc.
Carnegie Deli/21/W 50s
Ess-a-Bagel/24/multi. loc.
Katz's Deli/23/Low E Side
Mill Basin Deli/22/Mill Basin
Sarge's Deli/19/Murray Hill
Second Ave Deli/23/E Vil.
Stage Deli/20/W 50s
Zabar's Cafe/20/W 80s

Dessert

Amy's Bread/24/multi. loc.
Cafe Lalo/20/W 80s
Café Sabarsky/22/E 80s
Caffe Rafaella/18/G Vil.
ChikaLicious/25/E Vil.
Edgar's Cafe/19/W 80s
Ferrara/22/Little Italy
Junior's/17/multi. loc.
La Bergamote/26/Chelsea
Lady Mendl's/21/Gramercy

Cuisines

My Most Favorite/*18/W 40s*
Omonia Cafe/*18/multi. loc.*
Once Upon a Tart/*20/SoHo*
Park Ave. Cafe/*24/E 60s*
Payard Bistro/*24/E 70s*
Serendipity 3/*19/E 60s*
Sweet Melissa/*24/multi. loc.*
Veniero's/*23/E Vil.*

Dominican

Cafe Con Leche/*17/multi. loc.*
El Malecon/*21/multi. loc.*
Hispaniola/*21/Wash. Hts. & Up*
It's Dominican/*19/Chelsea*

Eastern European

Sammy's Roum./*20/Low E Side*

Eclectic

Alice's Tea Cup/*19/multi. loc.*
Biltmore Room/*24/Chelsea*
B. Smith's/*18/W 40s*
Cal. Pizza Kitchen/*16/E 60s*
Carol's Cafe/*25/Staten Is.*
China Grill/*23/W 50s*
Chubo/*22/Low E Side*
Delegates Dining Rm./*18/E 40s*
Dishes/*21/E 40s*
East Buffet/*19/Flushing*
East of Eighth/*17/Chelsea*
5 Ninth/*20/Meatpacking*
Gobo/*23/E 80s*
Hudson Cafeteria/*18/W 50s*
Josephina/*19/W 60s*
Josie's/*20/multi. loc.*
Kitchen/Cocktails/*–/Low E Side*
Lady Mendl's/*21/Gramercy*
La Flor Bakery/*24/Woodside*
Ludo/*–/E Vil.*
Maggie Brown/*21/Clinton Hill*
Native/*19/Harlem*
NoHo Star/*18/NoHo*
Nook/*24/W 50s*
Océo/*18/W 40s*
Orbit East Harlem/*20/Harlem*
Public/*21/NoLita*
Pump Energy Food/*19/multi. loc.*
Punch/*19/Flatiron*
Radha/*–/Low E Side*
Rice/*21/multi. loc.*
Schiller's/*19/Low E Side*
Secretes/*–/E Vil.*
Shopsin's/*19/G Vil.*
Stanton Social/*26/Low E Side*
Upstairs/*–/TriBeCa*
wd-50/*24/Low E Side*
Whole Foods Café/*20/multi. loc.*
Zeytuna/*18/Fin. District*

Egyptian

Casa La Femme/*20/E 50s*

English

(See also Fish and Chips)
Spotted Pig/*21/G Vil.*
Tea & Sympathy/*20/G Vil.*

Ethiopian

Ethiopian Rest./*–/E 80s*
Ghenet/*21/NoLita*
Meskerem/*20/multi. loc.*

European

August/*23/G Vil.*
Bette/*–/Chelsea*
Employees Only/*18/G Vil.*
202 Cafe/*–/Chelsea*

Filipino

Cendrillon/*20/SoHo*
Kuma Inn/*21/Low E Side*

Fish and Chips

A Salt & Battery/*18/multi. loc.*
ChipShop/CurryShop/*19/multi. loc.*

French

A.O.C. Bedford/*24/G Vil.*
Arabelle/*25/E 60s*
Asiate/*23/W 60s*
Au Bon Pain/*14/multi. loc.*
Au Coin du Feu/*–/NoLita*
Barbès/*22/Murray Hill*
Bayard's/*24/Fin. District*
BED New York/*17/Chelsea*
Bouillabaisse 126/*23/Carroll Gdns.*
Breeze/*–/W 40s*
Brick Cafe/*20/Astoria*
Café Boulud/*27/E 70s*
Café des Artistes/*22/W 60s*
Cafe Gitane/*21/NoLita*
Café Pierre/*22/E 60s*
Chanterelle/*27/TriBeCa*
Cité Grill/*20/W 50s*
Cocotte/*22/Park Slope*
Danal/*21/E Vil.*
Darna/*20/W 80s*
Django/*20/E 40s*
FireBird/*21/W 40s*
Fives/*21/W 50s*
Fleur de Sel/*25/Flatiron*
44/*19/W 40s*
Gavroche/*19/G Vil.*
Geisha/*23/E 60s*
Hue/*18/G Vil.*
Ici/*21/Ft. Greene*
Indochine/*21/E Vil.*

Ivo & Lulu/24/SoHo
Jack's Lux. Oyster/25/E Vil.
Jolie/21/Boerum Hill
Kitchen Club/23/NoLita
Komegashi/21/Flatiron
La Baraka/21/Little Neck
La Bergamote/26/Chelsea
La Boîte en Bois/20/W 60s
La Grenouille/27/E 50s
La Mirabelle/21/W 80s
Landmarc/23/TriBeCa
Le Bernardin/28/W 50s
L'Ecole/24/SoHo
Le Colonial/21/E 50s
Le Perigord/25/E 50s
Le Refuge Inn/25/Bronx
Les Enfants Terribles/21/Low E Side
Loulou/24/Ft. Greene
Mark's/23/E 70s
Mercer Kitchen/22/SoHo
Modern, The/25/W 50s
Montrachet/26/TriBeCa
Once Upon a Tart/20/SoHo
Park Terrace/21/Wash. Hts. & Up
per se/28/W 60s
Picholine/27/W 60s
Picnic Market/23/W 100s
René Pujol/22/W 50s
Sapa/21/Flatiron
718/23/Astoria
Sherwood Cafe/19/Boerum Hill
Terrace in Sky/23/W 100s
26 Seats/23/E Vil.
Vong/23/E 50s
Zucco/–/Low E Side

French (Bistro)

A/23/W 100s
Alouette/20/W 90s
A.O.C./18/G Vil.
Bacchus/20/Downtown
Banania Cafe/21/Cobble Hill
BarTabac/18/Boerum Hill
Belleville/20/Park Slope
Bistro 61/20/E 60s
Bistro Cassis/21/Chelsea
Bistro du Nord/19/E 90s
Bistro du Vent/21/W 40s
Bistro Les Amis/20/SoHo
Bistro Le Steak/17/E 70s
Bistro St. Mark's/21/Park Slope
Brasserie Julien/17/E 80s
Café du Soleil/23/W 100s
Cafe Joul/18/E 50s
Cafe Loup/18/G Vil.
Cafe Luluc/19/Cobble Hill
Cafe Luxembourg/21/W 70s

Cafe Un Deux/16/W 40s
CamaJe/22/G Vil.
Capsouto Frères/24/TriBeCa
Casimir/20/E Vil.
Chelsea Bistro/21/Chelsea
Chez Jacqueline/20/G Vil.
Chez Josephine/21/W 40s
Chez Michallet/23/G Vil.
Chez Napoléon/20/W 50s
Cornelia St. Cafe/19/G Vil.
Cosette/20/Murray Hill
Country Café/20/SoHo
db Bistro Moderne/25/W 40s
Deux Amis/20/E 50s
Epicerie/20/Low E Side
Félix/18/SoHo
Flea Market Cafe/20/E Vil.
Florent/19/Meatpacking
French Roast/15/multi. loc.
Frère Jacques/19/Murray Hill
Gascogne/23/Chelsea
Jarnac/22/G Vil.
Jean Claude/23/SoHo
Jean-Luc/20/W 80s
JoJo/25/E 60s
Jubilee/21/E 50s
Jules/20/E Vil.
La Belle Vie/17/Chelsea
La Bonne Soupe/18/W 50s
La Goulue/20/E 60s
La Lunchonette/22/Chelsea
La Mangeoire/19/E 50s
La Mediterranée/18/E 50s
La Petite Auberge/20/Gramercy
La Ripaille/19/G Vil.
Le Bilboquet/20/E 60s
Le Boeuf/Mode/20/E 80s
Le Charlot/19/E 60s
Le Gamin/20/multi. loc.
Le Gigot/25/G Vil.
Le Jardin Bistro/21/NoLita
Le Madeleine/20/W 40s
L'Entrecote/20/E 50s
Le Pescadou/18/SoHo
Le Refuge/21/E 80s
Le Rivage/20/W 40s
Le Sans Souci/21/Astoria
Le Singe Vert/19/Chelsea
Le Tableau/23/E Vil.
L'Express/17/Flatiron
Le Zinc/19/TriBeCa
Lucien/22/E Vil.
Madison Bistro/19/Murray Hill
Metropol/18/G Vil.
Mon Petit Cafe/19/E 60s
Montparnasse/20/E 50s
Moutarde/18/Park Slope

Odeon/18/TriBeCa
Paradou/19/Meatpacking
Paris Commune/18/G Vil.
Paris Match/–/E 60s
Park Bistro/21/Gramercy
Pascalou/20/E 90s
Pastis/21/Meatpacking
Patois/20/Carroll Gdns.
Payard Bistro/24/E 70s
Pigalle/17/W 40s
Provence/21/SoHo
Quatorze Bis/21/E 70s
Quercy/23/Cobble Hill
Raga/22/E Vil.
Raoul's/23/SoHo
Rouge/20/Forest Hills
Seppi's/18/W 50s
Steak Frites/18/Union Sq.
Table d'Hôte/19/E 90s
Tartine/22/G Vil.
Tournesol/24/LIC
Village/20/G Vil.

French (Brasserie)

Artisanal/23/Murray Hill
Balthazar/23/SoHo
Brasserie/20/E 50s
Brasserie 8½/21/W 50s
Brasserie Julien/17/E 80s
Brasserie LCB/24/W 50s
Café Gray/25/W 60s
Jacques Brasserie/18/E 80s
L'Absinthe/22/E 60s
Le Marais/20/W 40s
Le Monde/17/W 100s
Les Halles/21/multi. loc.
Marseille/20/W 40s
Nice Matin/20/W 70s
Orsay/18/E 70s
Pershing Sq./15/E 40s
Pigalle/17/W 40s
Rue 57/19/W 50s

French (New)

Aix/23/W 80s
Alain Ducasse/27/W 50s
Atelier/27/W 50s
Bouley/28/TriBeCa
Daniel/28/E 60s
Elephant/21/E Vil.
14 Wall Street/19/Fin. District
Jean Georges/27/W 60s
JoJo/25/E 60s
Métisse/20/W 100s
Orsay/18/E 70s
Pascalou/20/E 90s
Perry Street/–/G Vil.

Petrossian/25/W 50s
Savann/19/W 70s
360/23/Red Hook
Tocqueville/25/Union Sq.
Triomphe/25/W 40s
212/17/E 60s
Village/20/G Vil.

German

Hallo Berlin/19/W 40s
Heidelberg/18/E 80s
Killmeyer Bavarian/18/Staten Is.
Rolf's/17/Gramercy
Zum Schneider/18/E Vil.
Zum Stammtisch/23/Glendale

Greek

Agnanti/27/Astoria
Ammos/–/Astoria
Avra Estiatorio/24/E 40s
Cávo/19/Astoria
Demetris Seafood/23/Astoria
Eliá/26/Bay Ridge
Elias Corner/22/Astoria
En Plo/22/W 70s
Ethos/21/Murray Hill
Greek Kitchen/18/W 50s
Ithaka/21/E 80s
Kyma/18/W 40s
Meltemi/18/E 50s
Metsovo/17/W 70s
Milos/26/W 50s
Molyvos/23/W 50s
Niko's Med. Grill/19/W 70s
Omonia Cafe/18/multi. loc.
Onera/25/W 70s
Periyali/25/Flatiron
Ploes/23/Astoria
Pylos/23/E Vil.
S'Agapo/22/Astoria
Snack/23/SoHo
Snack Taverna/22/G Vil.
Stamatis/22/Astoria
Symposium/18/W 100s
Taverna Kyclades/24/Astoria
Telly's Taverna/23/Astoria
Thalassa/23/TriBeCa
Trata Estiatorio/22/E 70s
Uncle Nick's/20/W 50s

Hamburgers

Better Burger/15/multi. loc.
Big Nick's Burger/17/W 70s
Blue 9 Burger/19/E Vil.
Boat Basin Cafe/12/W 70s
Burger Heaven/16/multi. loc.

burger joint/Parker M./24/W 50s
Burger Joint/21/Gramercy
Chelsea Grill/19/multi. loc.
Corner Bistro/23/G Vil.
Cozy Soup/Burger/18/G Vil.
db Bistro Moderne/25/W 40s
Five Front/21/Dumbo
Hard Rock Cafe/11/W 40s
Island Burgers/22/W 50s
Jackson Hole/17/multi. loc.
J.G. Melon/20/E 70s
Luke's B&G/17/E 70s
McHales/20/W 40s
Peter Luger/28/Williamsburg
Piper's Kilt/20/multi. loc.
P.J. Clarke's/18/E 50s
Pop Burger/19/Meatpacking
Rare B&G/21/Murray Hill
Shake Shack/22/Flatiron
12th St. B&G/22/Park Slope
Wollensky's Grill/22/E 40s

Hawaiian
Roy's NY/24/Fin. District

Hot Dogs
F & B/19/multi. loc.
Gray's Papaya/20/multi. loc.
Papaya King/20/multi. loc.

Ice Cream Parlor
Emack & Bolio's/25/multi. loc.
L & B Spumoni/23/Bensonhurst
Serendipity 3/19/E 60s

Indian
Adä/24/E 50s
Amma/23/E 50s
Angon on the Sixth/23/E Vil.
Babu/23/G Vil.
Baluchi's/18/multi. loc.
Banjara/23/E Vil.
Bay Leaf/20/W 50s
Bombay Palace/19/W 50s
Bombay Talkie/20/Chelsea
Brick Lane Curry/21/E Vil.
Bukhara Grill/21/E 40s
Cafe Spice/18/multi. loc.
Chennai Garden/22/Gramercy
ChipShop/CurryShop/19/Park Slope
Chola/24/E 50s
Copper Chimney/--/Gramercy
Curry Leaf/21/multi. loc.
Dakshin Indian/21/E 80s
Darbar/21/E 40s
Dawat/24/E 50s
Delhi Palace/24/Jackson Hts.
dévi/25/Flatiron

Diwan/22/E 40s
Hampton Chutney/23/SoHo
Haveli/21/E Vil.
Indus Valley/23/W 100s
Jackson Diner/22/Jackson Hts.
Jewel of India/21/W 40s
Khyber Grill/21/E 50s
Mughlai/19/W 70s
Pongal/21/multi. loc.
Radha/--/Low E Side
Raga/22/E Vil.
Salaam Bombay/21/TriBeCa
Sapphire Indian/21/W 60s
Saravanaas/--/Gramercy
Shaan/22/W 40s
Surya/22/G Vil.
Swagat Indian/22/W 70s
Tabla/26/Gramercy
Tamarind/25/Flatiron
Utsav/21/W 40s
Vatan/22/Gramercy

Irish
Landmark Tavern/--/W 40s
Neary's/16/E 50s
Piper's Kilt/20/multi. loc.

Israeli
Azuri Cafe/23/W 50s
Rectangles/--/E 70s

Italian
(N=Northern; S=Southern)
Abboccato/23/W 50s
Acappella (N)/24/TriBeCa
Acqua Pazza/21/W 50s
Al Di La (N)/26/Park Slope
Aleo (N)/22/Flatiron
Al Forno Pizza/20/E 70s
Alfredo of Rome (S)/19/W 40s
Aliseo Osteria/23/Prospect Heights
Alto (N)/24/E 50s
Ama (S)/23/SoHo
Amarone/19/W 40s
Amici Amore I/21/Astoria
Angelina's/23/Staten Is.
Angelo's/Mulberry (S)/22/Little Italy
ápizz/24/Low E Side
Areo/24/Bay Ridge
Arezzo (N)/22/Flatiron
Arqua (N)/23/TriBeCa
Arté (N)/17/G Vil.
Arté Café/18/W 70s
Arturo's Pizzeria/22/G Vil.
Assaggio (N)/19/W 80s
Babbo/27/G Vil.
Baldoria/21/W 40s

Cuisines

Bamonte's/*22/Williamsburg*
Baraonda (N)/*18/E 70s*
Barbetta (N)/*20/W 40s*
Barbuto/*19/G Vil.*
Barolo (N)/*18/SoHo*
Bar Pitti (N)/*22/G Vil.*
Basso Est/*21/Low E Side*
Basta Pasta/*21/Flatiron*
Becco (N)/*21/W 40s*
Bella Blu (N)/*19/E 70s*
Bella Via/*20/LIC*
Bellavitae/*24/G Vil.*
Bellini/*22/E 50s*
Bello (N)/*20/W 50s*
Belluno (N)/*21/Murray Hill*
Beppe/*23/Flatiron*
Bettola/*21/W 70s*
Bianca (N)/*23/NoHo*
Bice (N)/*20/E 50s*
Biricchino (N)/*20/Chelsea*
Bivio (N)/*18/G Vil.*
Bolzano's/*–/W 40s*
Bond 45/*19/W 40s*
Boom (S)/*19/SoHo*
Borgo Antico/*19/G Vil.*
Bottega del Vino/*21/E 50s*
Bottino (N)/*19/Chelsea*
Bravo Gianni/*23/E 60s*
Bread Tribeca (N)/*18/TriBeCa*
Bricco (S)/*19/W 50s*
Brick Cafe (N)/*20/Astoria*
Brio/*18/E 60s*
Bruculino (S)/*18/W 70s*
Bruno/*23/E 50s*
Cacio e Pepe (S)/*22/E Vil.*
Café Fiorello/*20/W 60s*
Cafe Trevi (N)/*18/E 80s*
Caffe Bondi (S)/*22/Staten Is.*
Caffe Buon Gusto/*18/multi. loc.*
Caffe Cielo (N)/*20/W 50s*
Caffe Grazie/*18/E 80s*
Caffe Linda/*19/E 40s*
Caffé/Green (N)/*21/Bayside*
Caffe Rafaella/*18/multi. loc.*
Campagnola (S)/*24/E 70s*
Canaletto (N)/*21/E 60s*
Cara Mia/*20/W 40s*
Carino (S)/*21/E 80s*
Carmine's (S)/*20/multi. loc.*
Casa Mia/*20/Gramercy*
Cascina/*18/W 40s*
Caserta Vecc. (S)/*21/Carroll Gdns.*
Celeste (S)/*24/W 80s*
Cellini (N)/*22/E 50s*
Centolire (N)/*20/E 80s*
'Cesca (S)/*24/W 70s*
Chelsea Ristorante (N)/*20/Chelsea*

Chianti/*22/Bay Ridge*
Cibo (N)/*20/E 40s*
Cinque Terre (N)/*19/Murray Hill*
Cipriani Dolci/*18/E 40s*
Cipriani Dwntn (N)/*21/SoHo*
Coco Pazzo (N)/*23/E 70s*
Col Legno (N)/*19/E Vil.*
Coppola's/*19/multi. loc.*
Cortina (N)/*19/E 70s*
Crispo (N)/*23/G Vil.*
Cucina di Pesce (N)/*18/E Vil.*
Da Andrea (N)/*24/G Vil.*
Da Antonio/*22/E 50s*
Da Ciro/*21/Murray Hill*
Da Filippo (N)/*21/E 60s*
da Giacomo/*23/E 60s*
Da Nico/*20/Little Italy*
Da Silvano (N)/*22/G Vil.*
Da Tommaso (N)/*21/W 50s*
Da Umberto (N)/*24/Chelsea*
Dazies/*21/Sunnyside*
DeGrezia/*23/E 50s*
Della Rovere/*21/TriBeCa*
De Marco's/*18/G Vil.*
Divino (N)/*19/E 80s*
dominic/*19/TriBeCa*
Dominick's (S)/*23/Bronx*
Don Giovanni/*18/multi. loc.*
Don Peppe (N)/*25/Ozone Park*
Due (N)/*21/E 70s*
Ecco/*22/TriBeCa*
Elaine's/*12/E 80s*
Elio's/*22/E 80s*
El Rancho/*–/Bronx*
English is Italian/*20/E 40s*
Ennio & Michael/*22/G Vil.*
Enzo's (S)/*23/Bronx*
Erminia (S)/*25/E 80s*
Esca (S)/*24/W 40s*
etcetera etcetera/*22/W 40s*
Falai/*24/Low E Side*
F & J Pine (S)/*22/Bronx*
Felidia (N)/*25/E 50s*
Ferdinando's (S)/*22/Carroll Gdns.*
Ferrara/*22/Little Italy*
Fiamma Osteria/*24/SoHo*
50 Carmine (N)/*22/G Vil.*
F.illi Ponte/*20/TriBeCa*
Finestra/*19/E 70s*
Fino (N)/*21/multi. loc.*
Fiorentino's (S)/*20/Gravesend*
Firenze (N)/*19/E 80s*
Fontana di Trevi (N)/*20/W 50s*
Fragole/*22/Carroll Gdns.*
Frank (S)/*23/E Vil.*
Frankies 457/*22/Carroll Gdns.*
Franny's/*23/Prospect Heights*

Fred's at Barneys (N)/20/E 60s
Fresco by Scotto (N)/23/E 50s
Fresco on the Go (N)/20/E 50s
Gabriel's (N)/22/W 60s
Gargiulo's (S)/22/Coney Island
Gennaro/24/W 90s
Giambelli (N)/21/E 50s
Gigino Trattoria/21/TriBeCa
Gigino/Wagner/19/Fin. District
Gino (S)/19/E 60s
Giorgione/21/SoHo
Giovanni (N)/21/W 50s
Giovanni 25 (N)/22/E 80s
Girasole/22/E 80s
Gnocco Caffe (N)/23/E Vil.
Gonzo/21/G Vil.
Googie's/14/E 70s
Grace's Trattoria/19/E 70s
Grifone (N)/23/E 40s
Grotta Azzurra (S)/17/Little Italy
Gusto/–/G Vil.
Hearth/24/E Vil.
I Coppi (N)/22/E Vil.
Il Bagatto/24/E Vil.
Il Bastardo/–/Chelsea
Il Buco/23/NoHo
Il Cantinori (N)/22/G Vil.
Il Corallo/23/SoHo
Il Cortile/23/Little Italy
Il Fornaio/21/Little Italy
Il Gattopardo (S)/24/W 50s
Il Giglio (N)/26/TriBeCa
Il Menestrello/22/E 50s
Il Monello (N)/23/E 70s
Il Mulino (S)/27/G Vil.
Il Nido (N)/23/E 50s
Il Palazzo/23/Little Italy
Il Postino/22/E 40s
Il Riccio (S)/22/E 70s
Il Tinello (N)/23/W 50s
Il Vagabondo (N)/18/E 60s
Il Valentino (N)/18/E 50s
'ino/24/G Vil.
'inoteca/23/Low E Side
Intermezzo/19/Chelsea
I Tre Merli (N)/18/multi. loc.
I Trulli (S)/23/Gramercy
John's 12th St./19/E Vil.
Joseph's (N)/21/Fin. District
Julian's (S)/18/W 50s
La Bottega/18/Chelsea
La Cantina (S)/22/G Vil.
La Cantina Toscana (N)/23/E 60s
La Focaccia (N)/22/G Vil.
La Giara/20/Murray Hill
La Gioconda/22/E 50s
La Grolla (N)/21/W 70s

Lake Club/16/Staten Is.
La Lanterna/21/G Vil.
L'Allegria (N)/18/W 40s
La Locanda Vini/22/W 40s
Lamarca (S)/20/Gramercy
La Masseria (S)/22/W 40s
La Mela/19/Little Italy
La Pizza Fresca (N)/23/Flatiron
La Rivista/19/W 40s
Lattanzi/22/W 40s
Lavagna/24/E Vil.
La Vela (N)/18/W 70s
La Villa Pizzeria/22/multi. loc.
La Vineria (S)/21/W 50s
Lentini/20/E 80s
Lento's/19/multi. loc.
Le Zie 2000 (N)/22/Chelsea
Lil' Frankie Pizza/23/E Vil.
L'Impero/26/E 40s
Lisca (N)/20/W 90s
Locanda Vini/Olii (N)/22/Clinton Hill
Lorenzo's/22/Staten Is.
Lo Scalco/26/TriBeCa
Luca (N)/20/E 80s
Luna Piena/18/E 50s
Lupa (S)/26/G Vil.
Lusardi's (N)/24/E 70s
Luxia/19/W 40s
Macelleria (N)/20/Meatpacking
Madison's/21/Bronx
Magnifico (N)/20/Chelsea
Malatesta Tratt. (N)/21/G Vil.
Manducatis/23/LIC
Manetta's/23/LIC
Mangia/20/multi. loc.
Mangiarini/19/E 80s
Marco Polo/20/Carroll Gdns.
Maremma/–/G Vil.
Maria Pia/20/W 50s
Marinella/23/G Vil.
Mario's (S)/21/Bronx
Maruzzella/21/E 70s
Maurizio Trattoria (N)/22/G Vil.
Max (S)/24/multi. loc.
Mediterraneo (N)/18/E 60s
Mezzaluna/20/E 70s
Mezzogiorno/20/SoHo
Minetta Tavern (N)/19/G Vil.
Miss Williamsburg/20/multi. loc.
Moda (S)/19/W 50s
Naima (S)/–/Chelsea
Nanni (N)/24/E 40s
Naples 45 (S)/17/E 40s
Nello (N)/20/E 60s
Nero/17/Meatpacking
Nick's/23/multi. loc.
Nicola's/22/E 80s

Nino's (N)/*23/multi. loc.*
Nino's Positano/*21/E 40s*
Nocello (N)/*21/W 50s*
Nonna/*20/W 80s*
Noodle Pudding/*25/Bklyn Hts.*
Notaro (N)/*20/Murray Hill*
Novitá (N)/*23/Gramercy*
One 83 (N)/*20/E 80s*
101/*19/Bay Ridge*
Onju/*20/E Vil.*
Orso/*22/W 40s*
Osso Buco (N)/*16/multi. loc.*
Osteria al Doge (N)/*21/W 40s*
Osteria del Circo (N)/*22/W 50s*
Osteria del Sole (S)/*22/G Vil.*
Osteria Gelsi (S)/*23/Garment*
Osteria Laguna (N)/*20/E 40s*
Osteria Stella (N)/*21/W 50s*
Otto/*22/G Vil.*
Pace/*21/TriBeCa*
Palm (N)/*24/multi. loc.*
Panino'teca 275/*24/Carroll Gdns.*
Paola's/*22/E 80s*
Paper Moon (N)/*18/E 50s*
Park Side/*25/Corona*
Parma (N)/*22/E 70s*
Pasquale's Rigoletto/*24/Bronx*
Pasticcio/*20/Murray Hill*
Patsy's (S)/*21/W 50s*
Paul & Jimmy's/*19/Gramercy*
Peasant/*22/NoLita*
Pellegrino's/*23/Little Italy*
Pepe . . . To Go/*21/multi. loc.*
Pepolino (N)/*25/TriBeCa*
Perbacco/*25/E Vil.*
Pescatore/*19/E 50s*
Petaluma/*18/E 70s*
Pete's Downtown/*19/Dumbo*
Petrosino (S)/*20/Low E Side*
Piadina (N)/*20/G Vil.*
Piano Due/*–/W 50s*
Piccola Venezia/*25/Astoria*
Piccolo Angolo/*25/G Vil.*
Pietrasanta (N)/*19/W 40s*
Pietro's (N)/*23/E 40s*
Pinocchio/*23/E 90s*
Pisticci (S)/*24/W 100s*
Pó/*25/G Vil.*
Poetessa/*21/E Vil.*
Pomodoro Rosso/*21/W 70s*
Ponticello (N)/*23/Astoria*
Portofino Grille/*20/E 60s*
Portofino's/*20/Bronx*
Positano (S)/*20/Little Italy*
Primavera (N)/*24/E 80s*
Primola/*23/E 60s*
Puttanesca/*18/W 50s*

Quartino (N)/*21/multi. loc.*
Quattro Gatti/*19/E 80s*
Queen/*23/Bklyn Hts.*
Rainbow Room (N)/*20/W 40s*
Rao's (S)/*21/Harlem*
Regional/*–/W 90s*
Remi/*22/W 50s*
Re Sette/*21/W 40s*
Risotteria/*21/G Vil.*
Roberto Passon/*23/W 50s*
Roberto's/*27/Bronx*
Roc/*22/TriBeCa*
Rocco (S)/*20/G Vil.*
Rossini's (N)/*22/Murray Hill*
Rughetta (S)/*23/E 80s*
Sal Anthony's/*17/multi. loc.*
Salute! (N)/*19/Murray Hill*
Sambuca (S)/*18/W 70s*
San Domenico/*22/W 50s*
San Pietro (S)/*24/E 50s*
Sant Ambroeus (N)/*21/multi. loc.*
Sapori D'Ischia (S)/*26/Woodside*
Savoia (S)/*21/Carroll Gdns.*
Savore/*21/SoHo*
Scaletta (N)/*21/W 70s*
Scalinatella/*24/E 60s*
Scalini Fedeli (N)/*26/TriBeCa*
Scopa (N)/*18/Gramercy*
Scottadito (N)/*21/Park Slope*
Serafina/*19/multi. loc.*
Sette/*19/Chelsea*
Sette Enoteca (S)/*–/Park Slope*
Sette Mezzo/*23/E 70s*
Sistina (N)/*25/E 80s*
Sosa Borella/*20/multi. loc.*
Spigolo/*26/E 80s*
Spoto's (S)/*20/Bronx*
Spotted Pig/*21/G Vil.*
Stella del Mare (N)/*22/Murray Hill*
Supper (N)/*23/E Vil.*
Table XII/*–/E 50s*
Taormina/*21/Little Italy*
Teodora (N)/*21/E 50s*
Tevere/*25/E 80s*
Three of Cups (S)/*20/E Vil.*
Tiramisu/*18/E 80s*
Tommaso's/*22/Dyker Heights*
Tony's Di Napoli (S)/*19/multi. loc.*
Tosca Café/*20/Bronx*
Totonno Pizza/*22/multi. loc.*
Tratt. Alba (N)/*20/Murray Hill*
Tratt. Dell'Arte (N)/*22/W 50s*
Trattoria L'incontro/*26/Astoria*
Tratt. Pesce/*18/multi. loc.*
Tratt. Romana/*25/Staten Is.*
tre dici/*–/Chelsea*
Tre Pomodori (N)/*19/Murray Hill*

Triangolo/*22/E 80s*
Tuscan Square (N)/*20/W 50s*
Tuscany Grill (N)/*23/Bay Ridge*
Two Boots/*18/E Vil.*
212/*17/E 60s*
Umberto's/*19/multi. loc.*
Uva/*20/E 70s*
V&T/*19/W 100s*
VaTutto/*20/NoLita*
Veniero's/*23/E Vil.*
Vento/*18/Meatpacking*
Vespa/*19/E 80s*
Via Emilia (N)/*21/Flatiron*
Via Oreto (S)/*21/E 60s*
Via Quadronno (N)/*21/E 70s*
ViceVersa (N)/*22/W 50s*
Vico/*21/E 90s*
Villa Berulia (N)/*23/Murray Hill*
Villa Mosconi (N)/*21/G Vil.*
Vincent's (S)/*21/Little Italy*
Vittorio Cucina/*22/G Vil.*
Vivolo/*20/E 70s*
Za Za (N)/*20/E 60s*

Jamaican

Aki/*25/G Vil.*
Maroons/*22/Chelsea*
Mo-Bay/*20/multi. loc.*

Japanese

(* sushi specialist)
Aki/*25/G Vil.*
Aki Sushi*/*19/multi. loc.*
Asiate/*23/W 60s*
Bar Masa*/*23/W 60s*
bluechili*/*20/W 50s*
Blue Ribbon Sushi*/*26/multi. loc.*
Bond Street*/*25/NoHo*
Butai/*–/Gramercy*
Cube 63*/*25/Low E Side*
Donguri/*27/E 80s*
Eastern King*/*–/E 70s*
Empire Szechuan*/*15/multi. loc.*
EN Japanese/*22/G Vil.*
Fushimi*/*24/Staten Is.*
Gari*/*25/W 70s*
Geisha/*23/E 60s*
Gyu-Kaku/*–/E Vil.*
Haikara Grill/*21/E 60s*
Hakata Grill/*20/W 40s*
Haru*/*21/multi. loc.*
Hasaki*/*24/E Vil.*
Hatsuhana*/*24/E 40s*
Hedeh/*24/NoHo*
Honmura An/*26/SoHo*
Ichiro*/*22/E 80s*
Inagiku/*23/E 40s*

Iron Sushi*/*20/multi. loc.*
Ivy's Cafe/*20/W 70s*
Japonica*/*22/G Vil.*
Jewel Bako*/*26/E Vil.*
Kai/*26/E 60s*
Katsu-Hama/*22/E 40s*
Kitchen Club/*23/NoLita*
Kodama*/*18/W 40s*
Koi*/*25/E Vil.*
Komegashi/*21/Flatiron*
Korea Palace/*18/E 50s*
Ko Sushi*/*19/multi. loc.*
Kuruma Zushi*/*27/E 40s*
Lan*/*23/E Vil.*
Masa*/*27/W 60s*
Matsuri/*23/Chelsea*
Maxie/*23/Murray Hill*
Megu/*24/TriBeCa*
Menchanko-tei/*19/multi. loc.*
Minado/*19/Murray Hill*
Mishima*/*23/Murray Hill*
Mizu Sushi*/*23/Flatiron*
Momofuku Noodle/*20/E Vil.*
Momoya*/*–/Chelsea*
Monster Sushi*/*19/multi. loc.*
Nëo Sushi*/*23/W 80s*
Ninja/*–/TriBeCa*
Nippon*/*22/E 50s*
Nobu*/*28/multi. loc.*
Nobu 57*/*–/W 50s*
Omen/*24/SoHo*
Ono*/*20/Meatpacking*
Ony*/*18/G Vil.*
Osaka/*24/Cobble Hill*
Ota-Ya/*23/E 80s*
Planet Thailand*/*21/Williamsburg*
Poke*/*26/E 80s*
Riingo*/*19/E 40s*
Roppongi*/*21/W 80s*
Rue 57*/*19/W 50s*
Sachiko's/*23/Low E Side*
Sakura Café*/*–/Park Slope*
Sandobe*/*19/E Vil.*
Sapporo East*/*22/E Vil.*
Shaburi*/*23/Murray Hill*
Shabu-Shabu 70*/*19/E 70s*
Shabu-Tatsu/*21/E Vil.*
Soba Nippon*/*21/W 50s*
Soba-ya/*23/E Vil.*
Sugiyama/*27/W 50s*
Sumile/*23/G Vil.*
Sushi Ann*/*25/E 50s*
Sushiden*/*24/multi. loc.*
Sushi Hana*/*22/multi. loc.*
Sushi of Gari*/*27/E 70s*
Sushi Rose*/*19/E 50s*
SushiSamba*/*22/multi. loc.*

Sushi Seki*/27/E 60s
Sushi Sen-nin*/24/E 80s
Sushi Yasuda*/28/E 40s
Sushi Zen*/24/W 40s
Taka*/25/G Vil.
Takahachi/24/multi. loc.
Taku/–/Boerum Hill
Tea Box/21/E 50s
Tenzan/25/multi. loc.
Tomoe Sushi*/27/G Vil.
Tomo Sushi*/19/W 100s
Tsuki*/23/E 70s
Vela/21/Flatiron
Yama*/25/multi. loc.
Yujin*/19/G Vil.
Yuka*/22/E 80s
Yuki Sushi*/21/W 90s
Zutto/23/multi. loc.

Jewish
Artie's Deli/18/W 80s
Ben's Kosher Deli/18/Bayside
Edison Cafe/15/W 40s
Mo Pitkin's/–/E Vil.
Sammy's Roum./–/Low E Side
Second Ave Deli/23/E Vil.

Korean
(* barbecue specialist)
Bann*/–/W 50s
Cho Dang Gol*/23/Garment
DoHwa*/21/G Vil.
Dok Suni's/21/E Vil.
Eemo/–/E Vil.
Franchia/23/Murray Hill
Gahm Mi Oak/22/Garment
Hangawi/25/Murray Hill
Kang Suh*/20/Garment
Korea Palace/18/E 50s
Kori/21/TriBeCa
Kum Gang San*/21/multi. loc.
Mandoo Bar/19/multi. loc.
Mill Korean/20/W 100s
Won Jo*/21/Garment
Woo Lae Oak*/23/SoHo
You-Chun/–/multi. loc.

Kosher
Abigael's/20/Garment
Azuri Cafe/23/W 50s
Ben's Kosher Deli/18/multi. loc.
Chennai Garden/22/Gramercy
Darna/20/W 80s
Haikara Grill/21/E 60s
Happy Buddha/–/Flushing
Le Marais/20/W 40s
Levana/18/W 60s
Mill Basin Deli/22/Mill Basin

My Most Favorite/18/W 40s
Park East Grill/23/E 80s
Pongal/21/multi. loc.
Prime Grill/21/E 40s
Quintessence/20/multi. loc.
Rectangles/–/E 70s
Sacred Chow/–/G Vil.
Second Ave Deli/23/E Vil.
Solo/23/E 50s
Tevere/25/E 80s

Lebanese
Al Bustan/20/E 50s

Malaysian
Nyonya/23/multi. loc.
Penang/19/multi. loc.
Spice Market/22/Meatpacking

Mediterranean
Aesop's Tables/22/Staten Is.
Akdeniz/22/W 40s
Aleo/22/Flatiron
Alta/22/G Vil.
A.O.C. Bedford/24/G Vil.
Beast/18/Prospect Heights
Bello Sguardo/21/W 70s
Beyoglu/21/E 80s
Black Betty/19/Williamsburg
Bouterin/20/E 50s
Café Botanica/20/W 50s
Cafe Centro/19/E 40s
Café du Soleil/23/W 100s
Cafe Ronda/19/W 70s
Convivium Osteria/25/Park Slope
Cru/25/G Vil.
Danal/21/E Vil.
Dee's Pizza/23/Forest Hills
Django/20/E 40s
En Plo/22/W 70s
Epices du Traiteur/20/W 70s
Extra Virgin/23/G Vil.
Fig & Olive Kitchen/–/E 60s
Five Points/22/NoHo
Frederick's Madison/–/E 60s
Harrison/24/TriBeCa
Hemsin/22/Sunnyside
Il Buco/23/NoHo
Isabella's/20/W 70s
Jarnac/22/G Vil.
Les Moules/–/Astoria
Ludo/–/E Vil.
Mangia/20/multi. loc.
Marseille/20/W 40s
Meet/17/Meatpacking
Moda/19/W 50s
Neptune Room/23/W 80s
Nice Matin/20/W 70s

Cuisines

Nick and Toni's/*18/W 60s*
Niko's Med. Grill/*19/W 70s*
Nisos/*18/Chelsea*
Olives/*22/Union Sq.*
Park/*16/Chelsea*
Petrosino/*20/Low E Side*
Picholine/*27/W 60s*
Place/*22/G Vil.*
Provence/*21/SoHo*
Red Cat/*24/Chelsea*
Ribot/*–/E 40s*
Savann/*19/W 70s*
Savoy/*23/SoHo*
Sezz Medi'/*21/W 100s*
Sharz Cafe/*19/E 80s*
Solera/*21/E 50s*
Solo/*23/E 50s*
Superfine/*18/Dumbo*
Taboon/*23/W 50s*
Taci's Beyti/*23/Midwood*
Tempo/*25/Park Slope*
Terrace in Sky/*23/W 100s*
Trio/*23/Murray Hill*
Uncle Nick's/*20/W 50s*
Uovo/*–/E Vil.*
Viva Mar Cafe/*–/Astoria*

Mexican
Alma/*22/Carroll Gdns.*
Blockhead Burrito/*18/multi. loc.*
Bonita/*22/Williamsburg*
Bright Food Shop/*20/Chelsea*
Café Frida/*20/W 70s*
Café Habana/*23/NoLita*
Centrico/*–/TriBeCa*
Chipotle/*19/multi. loc.*
Cosmic Cantina/*19/E Vil.*
Diablo Royale/*–/G Vil.*
Dos Caminos/*21/multi. loc.*
El Parador Cafe/*21/Murray Hill*
El Paso Taqueria/*21/E 90s*
Hell's Kitchen/*23/W 40s*
Itzocan/*25/multi. loc.*
Ixta/*19/Gramercy*
La Esquina/*–/NoLita*
La Flor Bakery/*24/Woodside*
La Palapa/*20/multi. loc.*
Lucy's Latin Kit./*18/Flatiron*
Lupe's East L.A. Kitchen/*–/TriBeCa*
Mamá Mexico/*20/multi. loc.*
Mary Ann's/*15/multi. loc.*
Maya/*23/E 60s*
Maz Mezcal/*21/E 80s*
Mercadito/*24/multi. loc.*
Mex. Mama/*24/G Vil.*
Mexican Radio/*20/NoLita*
Mi Cocina/*23/G Vil.*

Pampano/*24/E 40s*
Rocking Horse/*21/Chelsea*
Rosa Mexicano/*23/multi. loc.*
Salsa y Salsa/*18/Chelsea*
Soho Cantina/*19/SoHo*
Sueños/*23/Chelsea*
Taco Chulo/*–/Williamsburg*
Zarela/*21/E 50s*
Zócalo/*20/multi. loc.*
Zona Rosa/*19/W 50s*

Middle Eastern
Black Betty/*19/Williamsburg*
Mamlouk/*22/E Vil.*
Miriam/*–/Park Slope*
Moustache/*22/multi. loc.*
Olive Vine Cafe/*18/Park Slope*
Taboon/*23/W 50s*
Tanoreen/*25/Bay Ridge*
Zaytoons/*23/multi. loc.*

Moroccan
Barbès/*22/Murray Hill*
Cafe Gitane/*21/NoLita*
Cafe Mogador/*22/E Vil.*
Casbah Rouge/*–/W 100s*
Country Café/*20/SoHo*
Darna/*20/W 80s*
Le Souk/*17/E Vil.*
Park Terrace/*21/Wash. Hts. & Up*

Noodle Shops
Bao Noodles/*20/Gramercy*
Big Wong/*22/Ctown*
Great NY Noodle/*21/Ctown*
Honmura An/*26/SoHo*
Kelley & Ping/*17/SoHo*
Lili's Noodle/*17/multi. loc.*
Mee Noodle Shop/*17/multi. loc.*
Menchanko-tei/*19/multi. loc.*
Momofuku Noodle/*20/E Vil.*
New Bo-Ky/*22/Ctown*
Nooch/*15/Chelsea*
Ollie's/*16/multi. loc.*
Ony/*18/G Vil.*
Pho Bang/*21/multi. loc.*
Pho Viet Huong/*21/Ctown*
Republic/*18/Union Sq.*
Soba Nippon/*21/W 50s*
Soba-ya/*23/E Vil.*
Sweet-n-Tart/*20/multi. loc.*

Nuevo Latino
Beso/*20/Park Slope*
Cabana/*21/multi. loc.*
Calle Ocho/*21/W 80s*
Citrus Bar & Grill/*20/W 70s*
Esperanto/*21/E Vil.*

Cuisines

Hispaniola/21/Wash. Hts. & Up
Luz/–/Ft. Greene
Paladar/18/Low E Side
Raices/–/Astoria
Sabor/18/E 80s

Pan-Asian

bluechili/20/W 50s
Cendrillon/20/SoHo
Kelley & Ping/17/Gramercy
Kuma Inn/21/Low E Side
Nooch/15/Chelsea
O.G./24/E Vil.
Rain/21/W 80s
Republic/18/Union Sq.
Ruby Foo's/19/multi. loc.
Soju/–/Bklyn Hts.

Pan-Latin

Bogota Latin/–/Park Slope
Mo Pitkin's/–/E Vil.
Plate NYC/19/NoLita
Sandia/25/Chelsea
Yuca Bar/22/E Vil.

Persian/Iranian

Persepolis/21/E 70s

Peruvian

Coco Roco/20/Park Slope
Flor de Mayo/20/multi. loc.
Lima's Taste/21/multi. loc.
Mancora/19/multi. loc.
Nobu/28/TriBeCa
Nobu 57/–/W 50s
Sipan/21/W 90s

Pizza

Al Forno Pizza/20/E 70s
Angelo's Pizza/21/multi. loc.
ápizz/24/Low E Side
Arturo's Pizzeria/22/G Vil.
Bella Blu/19/E 70s
Cal. Pizza Kitchen/16/E 60s
Cascina/18/W 40s
Caserta Vecc./21/Carroll Gdns.
Dee's Pizza/23/Forest Hills
De Marco's/18/G Vil.
Denino's/25/Staten Is.
Di Fara/27/Midwood
Don Giovanni/18/multi. loc.
Fornino/21/Williamsburg
Franny's/23/Prospect Heights
Gonzo/21/G Vil.
Grimaldi's/26/Dumbo
Joe's Pizza/24/multi. loc.
John's Pizzeria/22/multi. loc.
La Bottega/18/Chelsea

L & B Spumoni/23/Bensonhurst
La Pizza Fresca/23/Flatiron
La Villa Pizzeria/22/multi. loc.
Lento's/19/multi. loc.
Lil' Frankie Pizza/23/E Vil.
Little Italy Pizza/22/multi. loc.
Lombardi's/25/NoLita
Mediterraneo/18/E 60s
Mezzaluna/20/E 70s
Naples 45/17/E 40s
Nick's/23/multi. loc.
Otto/22/G Vil.
Patsy's Pizzeria/21/multi. loc.
Peperoncino/19/Park Slope
Pinch, Pizza/19/Gramercy
Pintaile's Pizza/19/multi. loc.
Pizza Gruppo/26/E Vil.
Pizza 33/23/multi. loc.
Posto/23/Gramercy
Savoia/21/Carroll Gdns.
Sezz Medi'/21/W 100s
Three of Cups/20/E Vil.
Totonno Pizza/22/multi. loc.
Two Boots/18/multi. loc.
Una Pizza Nap./24/E Vil.
Uno Chicago/14/multi. loc.
V&T/19/W 100s
Waldy's Pizza/–/Chelsea

Polish

Teresa's/18/multi. loc.

Portuguese

Alfama/23/G Vil.
Luzia's/17/W 80s

Puerto Rican

La Taza de Oro/18/Chelsea

Russian

FireBird/21/W 40s

Sandwiches

Amy's Bread/24/multi. loc.
Artie's Deli/18/W 80s
Au Bon Pain/14/multi. loc.
Barney Greengrass/24/W 80s
BB Sandwich/19/G Vil.
Bread/18/NoLita
Brennan & Carr/19/Sheepshead Bay
Carl's Steaks/22/Murray Hill
Carnegie Deli/21/W 50s
Columbus Bakery/19/E 50s
Cosí/17/multi. loc.
Dishes/21/E 40s
E.A.T./19/E 80s
El Rancho/–/Bronx
Ess-a-Bagel/24/multi. loc.

Grey Dog's Coffee/22/G Vil.
Grilled Cheese/20/Low E Side
Hale & Hearty Soup/19/multi. loc.
Katz's Deli/23/Low E Side
Nicky's Viet./22/E Vil.
Panino'teca 275/24/Carroll Gdns.
Peanut Butter/Co./20/G Vil.
Press 195/20/Park Slope
Roll-n-Roaster/19/multi. loc.
Sarge's Deli/19/Murray Hill
Second Ave Deli/23/E Vil.
71 Irving Place/19/Gramercy
Stage Deli/20/W 50s
Sweet Melissa/24/multi. loc.
Tossed/18/multi. loc.
'wichcraft/22/multi. loc.
Zabar's Cafe/20/W 80s

Scandinavian
AQ Cafe/21/Murray Hill
Aquavit/25/E 50s
Smorgas Chef/19/multi. loc.
Ulrika's/22/E 60s

Seafood
Acqua Pazza/21/W 50s
Aquagrill/26/SoHo
Atlantic Grill/22/E 70s
Avra Estiatorio/24/E 40s
Black Duck/19/Gramercy
Black Pearl/–/E Vil.
BLT Fish/22/Flatiron
Blue Fin/22/W 40s
Blue Star/20/Cobble Hill
Blue Water/24/Union Sq.
Bond 45/19/W 40s
Bouillabaisse 126/23/Carroll Gdns.
Brooklyn Fish Camp/–/Park Slope
Bubba Gump/14/W 40s
City Crab/17/Flatiron
City Hall/21/TriBeCa
City Lobster/18/W 40s
coast/20/Fin. District
da Giacomo/23/E 60s
Demetris Seafood/23/Astoria
Docks Oyster Bar/19/multi. loc.
Elias Corner/22/Astoria
El Rey del Marisco/–/Bronx
En Plo/22/W 70s
Erawan/23/Bayside
Esca/24/W 40s
Fish/21/G Vil.
Foley's Fish Hse./20/W 40s
Francisco's Centro/20/Chelsea
fresh/24/TriBeCa
Fuleen Sea./24/Ctown

Gramercy 24/21/Gramercy
Grill Room/20/Fin. District
Harlem Grill/–/Harlem
Jack's Lux. Oyster/25/E Vil.
Jake's Steakhouse/24/Bronx
Josephs Citarella/23/W 40s
Kam Chueh/25/Ctown
Lake Club/16/Staten Is.
Le Bernardin/28/W 50s
Le Pescadou/18/SoHo
Lobster Box/19/Bronx
London Lennie's/20/Rego Park
Lure Fishbar/22/SoHo
Manhattan Ocean/24/W 50s
Marina Cafe/19/Staten Is.
Mary's Fish Camp/24/G Vil.
McCormick & Schmick/19/W 50s
Meltemi/18/E 50s
Mermaid Inn/22/E Vil.
Milos/26/W 50s
Minado/19/Murray Hill
Minnow/22/Park Slope
Moran's Chelsea/19/Chelsea
Morton's Steak/24/E 40s
Neptune Room/23/W 80s
Novecento/22/SoHo
Oceana/26/E 50s
Ocean Grill/23/W 70s
Oriental Garden/24/Ctown
Oyster Bar/21/E 40s
Pampano/24/E 40s
Pearl Oyster/27/G Vil.
Pearl Room/23/Bay Ridge
Pescatore/19/E 50s
Ping's Seafood/21/multi. loc.
Portofino's/20/Bronx
Redeye Grill/21/W 50s
Red Garlic/20/W 50s
Roy's NY/24/Fin. District
Sea Grill/24/W 40s
Shaffer City/23/Flatiron
Shelly's NY/21/W 50s
shore/17/TriBeCa
Shorty's Half Shell/–/G Vil.
Stella del Mare/22/Murray Hill
Taverna Kyclades/24/Astoria
Telly's Taverna/23/Astoria
Thalassa/23/TriBeCa
Tides/–/Low E Side
Trata Estiatorio/22/E 70s
Tropica/21/E 40s
Turquoise/–/E 80s
Umberto's/19/Little Italy
View/18/W 40s
Water's Edge/22/LIC

Small Plates

(See also Spanish tapas specialist)

Alta/22/G Vil.
Beast/18/Prospect Heights
Bellavitae/24/G Vil.
Bello Sguardo/21/W 70s
Butai/–/Gramercy
Casa Mono/25/Gramercy
Chino's/20/Gramercy
Cru/25/G Vil.
EN Japanese/22/G Vil.
Grace/20/TriBeCa
'ino/24/G Vil.
'inoteca/23/Low E Side
One/18/Meatpacking
Perbacco/25/E Vil.
Plate NYC/19/NoLita
Rocking Horse/21/Chelsea
Scopa/18/Gramercy
Secretes/–/E Vil.
Stanton Social/26/Low E Side
Sumile/23/G Vil.
Taste/21/E 80s
Tasting Room/26/E Vil.

Soul Food

Amy Ruth's/23/Harlem
Charles' Southern/24/Harlem
Hip Hop Chow/–/E Vil.
Kitchenette/20/multi. loc.
Miss Mamie's/Maude's/21/Harlem
Mo-Bay/20/multi. loc.
Old Devil Moon/19/E Vil.
Pink Tea Cup/20/G Vil.
Shark Bar/21/W 70s
Sylvia's/16/Harlem
Wimp's Sky Café/24/Harlem

Soup

Cozy Soup/Burger/18/G Vil.
Hale & Hearty Soup/19/multi. loc.

South African

Madiba/18/Ft. Greene

South American

Boca Chica/20/E Vil.
Cafe Ronda/19/W 70s
Don Pedro's/21/E 90s
Paladar/18/Low E Side
Sabor/18/E 80s
SushiSamba/22/multi. loc.

Southern

Amy Ruth's/23/Harlem
Brother Jimmy BBQ/16/multi. loc.
B. Smith's/18/W 40s
Charles' Southern/24/Harlem
Duke's/16/Gramercy
Earl's/15/Murray Hill
Gravy/–/Boerum Hill
Great Jones Cafe/22/NoHo
Harlem Grill/–/Harlem
Hip Hop Chow/–/E Vil.
Ida Mae/21/Garment
Jezebel/19/W 40s
Kitchenette/20/multi. loc.
Londel's/19/Harlem
Maroons/22/Chelsea
Melba's/–/Harlem
Miss Mamie's/Maude's/21/Harlem
Old Devil Moon/19/E Vil.
Pearson's BBQ/16/E 80s
Pink Tea Cup/20/G Vil.
Rib/–/G Vil.
Smoked/–/E Vil.
Sylvia's/16/Harlem
Wimp's Sky Café/24/Harlem

Southwestern

Agave/20/G Vil.
Canyon Road/20/E 70s
Cilantro/17/multi. loc.
Cowgirl/16/G Vil.
Los Dos Molinos/18/Gramercy
Mesa Grill/24/Flatiron
Miracle Grill/19/multi. loc.
Santa Fe/18/W 70s

Spanish

(* tapas specialist)

Alcala*/22/E 40s
Azafran*/21/TriBeCa
BarBossa/–/NoLita
Barna/–/Gramercy
Bolo*/23/Flatiron
Cafe Español/19/G Vil.
Casa Mono/25/Gramercy
El Charro Español/23/G Vil.
El Cid*/22/Chelsea
El Faro/22/G Vil.
El Pote/21/Murray Hill
El Quijote/19/Chelsea
Euzkadi/20/E Vil.
Flor de Sol/20/TriBeCa
Francisco's Centro/20/Chelsea
Joe's Place/–/Bronx
La Paella*/20/E Vil.
Luzia's/17/W 80s
Ñ*/21/SoHo
Pipa*/21/Flatiron
Sala*/22/multi. loc.
718/23/Astoria
Sevilla/23/G Vil.
Solera*/21/E 50s

Sol y Sombra*/–/W 80s
Suba*/20/Low E Side
Tía Pol*/24/Chelsea
Willie's Steak/19/Bronx
Xunta*/19/E Vil.
Zipi Zape*/20/Williamsburg

Steakhouses

Angelo & Maxie's/21/Flatiron
Austin's Steak/21/Bay Ridge
Ben & Jack's/–/E 40s
Ben Benson's/22/W 50s
Bistro Le Steak/17/E 70s
BLT Prime/27/Gramercy
BLT Steak/24/E 50s
Bobby Van's Steak/23/multi. loc.
Bond 45/19/W 40s
Bull & Bear/20/E 40s
Capital Grille/23/E 40s
Carne/19/W 100s
Chemist Club/–/E 40s
Christos/22/Astoria
Churra. Plata./22/multi. loc.
Cité/22/W 50s
City Hall/21/TriBeCa
Del Frisco's/24/W 40s
Delmonico's/22/Fin. District
Dylan Prime/24/TriBeCa
Embers/22/Bay Ridge
Erawan/23/Bayside
Fairway Cafe/20/W 70s
Frankie & Johnnie/21/multi. loc.
Frank's/21/Chelsea
Gallagher's Steak/21/W 50s
Green Field Churra./19/Corona
Grill Room/20/Fin. District
Hacienda Argentina/20/E 70s
Haikara Grill/21/E 60s
Jake's Steakhouse/24/Bronx
Keens Steak/23/Garment
Knickerbocker B&G/20/G Vil.
Le Marais/20/W 40s
Les Halles/21/multi. loc.
Macelleria/20/Meatpacking
Maloney & Porcelli/23/E 50s
Manhattan Grille/20/E 60s
MarkJoseph Steak/24/Fin. District
Michael Jordan's/21/E 40s
Monkey Bar/18/E 50s
Moran's Chelsea/19/Chelsea
Morton's Steak/24/E 40s
Napa/Sonoma/21/Whitestone
Nebraska Steak/21/Fin. District
Nick & Stef Steak/20/Garment
Old Homestead/23/Meatpacking
Outback Steak/15/multi. loc.
Palm/24/multi. loc.

Pampa/21/W 90s
Park East Grill/23/E 80s
Patroon/20/E 40s
Peter Luger/28/Williamsburg
Pietro's/23/E 40s
Post House/24/E 60s
Prime Grill/21/E 40s
Rothmann's/21/E 50s
Roth's Westside Steak/19/W 90s
Ruth Chris Steak/24/W 50s
Shelly's NY/21/W 50s
Shula's Steak/19/W 40s
Smith & Wollensky/23/E 40s
Sparks Steak/25/E 40s
Steak Frites/18/Union Sq.
Strip House/25/G Vil.
Tupelo Grill/20/Garment
2 West/22/Fin. District
Uncle Jack's Steak/24/multi. loc.
View/18/W 40s
V Steakhouse/20/W 60s
Willie's Steak/19/Bronx
Wolfgang's Steak/25/Murray Hill
Wollensky's Grill/22/E 40s

Tearooms

Alice's Tea Cup/19/multi. loc.
Lady Mendl's/21/Gramercy

Tex-Mex

Burritoville/17/multi. loc.
Cowgirl/16/G Vil.
Mary Ann's/15/multi. loc.
107 West/17/multi. loc.

Thai

Bann Thai/20/Forest Hills
bluechili/20/W 50s
Breeze/–/W 40s
Chanpen Thai/19/W 50s
Cyclo/18/E Vil.
Elephant/21/E Vil.
Erawan/23/Bayside
Highline/20/Meatpacking
Holy Basil/23/E Vil.
Jaiya Thai/21/Gramercy
Jasmine/20/E 80s
Joya/23/Cobble Hill
Kin Khao/21/SoHo
Kittichai/23/SoHo
Klong/21/E Vil.
Land/22/W 80s
Lemongrass Grill/17/multi. loc.
Lime Leaf/18/W 100s
Long Tan/19/Park Slope
Pam Real Thai/23/W 40s
Peep/21/SoHo
Planet Thailand/21/Williamsburg

Pongsri Thai/20/multi. loc.
Prem-on Thai/22/G Vil.
Pukk/22/E Vil.
Q, a Thai Bistro/21/Forest Hills
Red Garlic/20/W 50s
Regional Thai/18/multi. loc.
River/18/W 70s
Royal Siam/18/Chelsea
Sala Thai/20/E 80s
SEA/22/multi. loc.
Siam Inn/22/W 50s
Siam Square/23/Bronx
Song/20/Park Slope
Spice/20/multi. loc.
Spice Market/22/Meatpacking
Sripraphai/26/Woodside
Thai Pavilion/23/Astoria
Topaz Thai/21/W 50s
Tuk Tuk/20/multi. loc.
Ubol's Kitchen/21/Astoria
Vong/23/E 50s
Wild Ginger/20/G Vil.
Wondee Siam/24/W 50s

Tibetan
Tsampa/21/E Vil.

Tunisian
Epices du Traiteur/20/W 70s

Turkish
Akdeniz/22/W 40s
Ali Baba/23/Murray Hill
Bereket/20/Low E Side
Beyoglu/21/E 80s
Dervish Turkish/19/W 40s
Hemsin/22/Sunnyside
Kapadokya/20/Bklyn Hts.
Mundo/–/Astoria
Pasha/21/W 70s
Sahara/21/Gravesend
Sip Sak/20/E 40s
Sultan/19/E 70s
Taci's Beyti/23/Midwood
Taksim/22/E 50s
Turkish Cuisine/19/W 40s
Turkish Kitchen/23/Gramercy
Turkuaz/18/W 100s
Uskudar/21/E 70s
Zeytin/19/W 80s

Ukrainian
Veselka/19/E Vil.

Vegetarian
(* vegan)
Angelica Kitchen*/20/E Vil.
Candle 79*/23/E 70s
Candle Cafe*/21/E 70s
Chennai Garden/22/Gramercy
Chop't Creative/21/multi. loc.
Counter/21/E Vil.
Franchia/23/Murray Hill
Gobo*/23/multi. loc.
Hangawi*/25/Murray Hill
Happy Buddha/–/Flushing
Pongal/21/multi. loc.
Pukk/22/E Vil.
Pure Food + Wine*/20/Gramercy
Quartino/21/NoHo
Quintessence*/20/multi. loc.
Radha*/–/Low E Side
Sacred Chow/–/G Vil.
Saravanaas/–/Gramercy
Spring St. Natural/18/NoLita
teany*/19/Low E Side
Tsampa/21/E Vil.
Vatan/22/Gramercy
Veg. Paradise/20/G Vil.
Zen Palate/19/multi. loc.

Venezuelan
Caracas Arepa/22/E Vil.
Flor's Kitchen/19/multi. loc.

Vietnamese
Anh/20/Gramercy
Bao Noodles/20/Gramercy
Bao 111/23/E Vil.
Boi/21/E 40s
Cyclo/18/E Vil.
Doyers Viet./22/Ctown
Hue/18/G Vil.
Indochine/21/E Vil.
L'Annam/18/multi. loc.
Le Colonial/21/E 50s
MeKong/18/multi. loc.
Miss Saigon/18/E 80s
Monsoon/19/W 80s
Nam/22/TriBeCa
New Pasteur/21/Ctown
Nha Trang/23/Ctown
Nicky's Viet./22/E Vil.
O Mai/23/Chelsea
Pho Bang/21/multi. loc.
Pho Viet Huong/21/Ctown
River/18/W 70s
Saigon Grill/23/multi. loc.
Sapa/21/Flatiron
Tuk Tuk/20/LIC
Vermicelli/20/E 70s
VietCafé/21/TriBeCa

Yemenite
Rectangles/–/E 70s

Manhattan

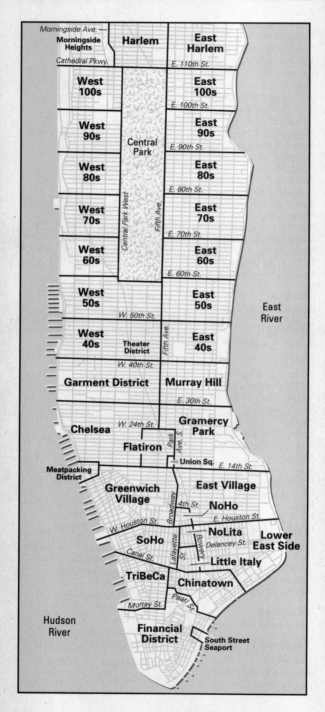

subscribe to zagat.com

LOCATIONS

(Restaurant name followed by its street location.
A=Avenue, s=Street, e.g. 1A/116s=First Ave. at 116th St.;
3A/82-3s=Third Ave. between 82nd & 83rd Sts.)

MANHATTAN

Chelsea
(24th to 30th Sts., west of 5th;
14th to 24th Sts., west of 6th)
Amuse *18s/6-7A*
Amy's Bread *9A/15-6s*
BED New York *27s/10-1A*
Bette *23s/9-10A*
Better Burger *8A/19s*
Biltmore Room *8A/24-5s*
Biricchino *29s/8A*
Bistro Cassis *14s/7-8A*
Bombay Talkie *9A/21-22s*
Bottino *10A/24-5s*
Bright Food Shop *8A/21s*
Burritoville *23s/7-8A*
Cafeteria *7A/17s*
Chelsea Bistro *23s/8-9A*
Chelsea Grill *8A/16-7s*
Chelsea Ristorante *8A/15-6s*
Cuba Cafe *8A/20-1s*
Dallas BBQ *8A/23s*
Da Umberto *17s/6-7A*
Diner 24 *8A/15s*
Don Giovanni *10A/22-3s*
East of Eighth *23s/7-8A*
El Cid *15s/8-9A*
elmo *7A/19-20s*
El Quijote *23s/7-8A*
Empire Diner *10A/22s*
F & B *23s/7-8A*
Francisco's Centro *23s/6-7A*
Frank's *16s/9-10A*
Gascogne *8A/17-8s*
Grand Sichuan *9A/24s*
Hale & Hearty Soup *9A/15-6s*
Havana Chelsea *8A/19-20s*
Il Bastardo *7A/21-2s*
Intermezzo *8A/20-1s*
It's Dominican *19s/6-7A*
La Belle Vie *8A/19-20s*
La Bergamote *9A/20s*
La Bottega *9A/17s*
La Lunchonette *10A/18s*
La Taza de Oro *8A/14-5s*
Le Gamin *15s/7-8A*
Le Singe Vert *7A/19-20s*

Le Zie 2000 *7A/20-1s*
Magnifico *9A/22s*
Maroons *16s/7-8A*
Mary Ann's *8A/16s*
Matsuri *16s/9A*
Momoya *7A/21s*
Monster Sushi *23s/6-7A*
Moran's Chelsea *10A/19s*
Naima *27s/10-1A*
Negril *23s/8-9A*
Nisos *8A/19s*
Nooch *8A/17s*
O Mai *9A/19-20s*
Parish & Co. *9A/22-3s*
Park *10A/17-8s*
Patsy's Pizzeria *23s/8-9A*
Pepe Giallo To Go *10A/24-5s*
Petite Abeille *18s/6-7A*
Pizza 33 *multi. loc.*
Pongsri Thai *23s/6-7A*
Rafaella on 9th *9A/21s*
Raymond's Cafe *7A/15-6s*
Red Cat *10A/23-4s*
Regional Thai *7A/22s*
Rocking Horse *8A/19-20s*
Royal Siam *8A/22-3s*
RUB BBQ *23s/7-8A*
Salsa y Salsa *7A/21-2s*
Sandia *17s/6-7A*
Sarabeth's *9A/15-6s*
Sette *7A/21-2s*
Seven *7A/29-30s*
Spice *8A/20-1s*
Starbucks *8A/22-3s*
Sueños *17s/8-9A*
Tía Pol *10A/22-3s*
tre dici *26s/6-7A*
202 Cafe *9A/15-6s*
Waldy's Pizza *6A/27-8s*
'wichcraft *12A/27-8s*

Chinatown
(Bet. Hester & Pearl Sts.,
bet. Bowery & Bway)
A&B Lobster King *Mott/Bowery*
Big Wong *Mott/Bayard-Canal*
Canton *Division/Bowery-Market*

Dim Sum Go Go *Bway/Chatham*
Doyers Viet. *Doyers/Chatham*
Evergreen Shan. *Mott/Bayard-Canal*
Excellent Dumpling *Lafayette/Canal*
Fuleen Sea. *Division/Bowery*
Golden Unicorn *E. Bway/Catherine*
Goodies *E. Bway/Catherine-Oliver*
Grand Sichuan *Canal/Bowery*
Great NY Noodle *Bowery/Bayard*
HSF *Bowery/Bayard-Canal*
Jing Fong *Elizabeth/Bayard-Canal*
Joe's *multi. loc.*
Kam Chueh *Bowery/Bayard-Canal*
Mandarin Court *Mott/Bayard-Canal*
New Bo-Ky *Bayard/Mott-Mulberry*
New Green Bo *Bayard/Elizabeth*
New Pasteur *Baxter/Bayard-Canal*
Nha Trang *multi. loc.*
Nice *Bway/Catherine-Market*
Oriental Garden *Elizabeth/Bayard*
Peking Duck *Mott/Chatham Sq.-Pell*
Pho Bang *multi. loc.*
Pho Viet Huong *Mulberry/Bayard*
Ping's Seafood *Mott/Bayard-Pell*
Pongsri Thai *Bayard/Baxter*
Shanghai Cuisine *Bayard/Mulberry*
Starbucks *Canal/Centre*
Sweet-n-Tart *Mott/Chatham*
Wo Hop *Mott/Canal*
X.O. *multi. loc.*

East Village

(14th to Houston Sts.,
east of Bway)
Angelica Kitchen *12s/1-2A*
Angon on the Sixth *6s/1-2A*
A Salt & Battery *2A/4-5s*
Baluchi's *2A/6s*
Banjara *1A/6s*
Bao 111 *Ave. C/7-8s*
Black Pearl *Ave. A/Houston-2s*
Blue 9 Burger *3A/12s*
Boca Chica *1A/1s*
Brick Lane Curry *6s/2A*
Burritoville *2A/8-9s*
Cacio e Pepe *2A/11-2s*
Cafe Mogador *St. Marks/Ave A.-1A*
Caracas Arepa *7s/1A*
Casimir *Ave. B/6-7s*
ChikaLicious *10s/1-2A*
China 1 *Ave. B/4s*
Chipotle *St. Marks/2-3A*
Col Legno *9s/2-3A*
Cosmic Cantina *3A/13s*
Counter *1A/6-7s*
Cucina di Pesce *4s/Bowery-2A*
Cyclo *1A/12-3s*

Dallas BBQ *2A/St. Marks*
Danal *10s/3-4A*
Dok Suni's *1A/St. Marks-7s*
Dumpling Man *St. Marks/Ave. A-1A*
Eemo *1A/6-7s*
Elephant *1s/1-2A*
Emack & Bolio's *Cooper/6-7s*
Esperanto *Ave. C/9s*
Euzkadi *4s/1A*
Flea Market Cafe *Ave. A/9s*
Flor's Kitchen *1A/9-10s*
Frank *2A/5-6s*
Friendhouse *3A/12-3s*
Gnocco Caffe *10s/Aves.A-B*
Grand Sichuan *St. Marks/2-3A*
Gyu-Kaku *Cooper/Astor-4s*
Hasaki *9s/2-3A*
Haveli *2A/5-6s*
Hearth *12s/1A*
Hip Hop Chow *2A/7s-St. Marks Pl.*
Holy Basil *2A/9-10s*
I Coppi *9s/Ave.A-1A*
Il Bagatto *2s/Aves. A-B*
Indochine *Lafayette/Astor-4s*
Itzocan *9s/Ave.A-1A*
Jack's Lux. Oyster *5s/2-3A*
Jewel Bako *multi. loc.*
John's 12th St. *12s/2A*
Jules *St. Marks/1-2A*
Klong *St. Marks/2-3A*
Koi *2A/11s*
Lan *3A/10-1s*
La Paella *9s/2-3A*
La Palapa *St. Marks/1-2A*
Lavagna *5s/Aves. A-B*
Le Gamin *5s/Aves. A-B*
Le Souk *Ave. B/3-4s*
Le Tableau *5s/Aves. A-B*
Lil' Frankie Pizza *1A/1-2s*
Lima's Taste *13s/Ave. A-1A*
Lucien *1A/1-2s*
Ludo *1s/1-2A*
Mama's Food *3s/Aves. A-B*
Mamlouk *4s/Aves. A-B*
Mancora *1A/6s*
Mara's Homemade *6s/1-2A*
Mary Ann's *2A/5s*
Max *Ave. B/3-4s*
Mee Noodle Shop *1A/13s*
Mercadito *Ave. B/11-2s*
Mermaid Inn *2A/5-6s*
Mingala Burmese *7s/2-3A*
Miracle Grill *1A/6-7s*
Miss Williamsburg *10s/1-2A*
Momofuku Noodle *1A/10-1s*
Mo Pitkin's *Ave. A/2-3s*
Moustache *10s/Ave. A-1A*

Nicky's Viet. *2s/Ave. A*
O.G. *6s/Aves. A-B*
Old Devil Moon *12s/Ave. A-B*
Onju *4s/1-2A*
Perbacco *4s/Ave. A-B*
Pizza Gruppo *Ave. B/11-2s*
Poetessa *2A/5-6s*
Prune *1s/1-2A*
Pukk *1A/4-5s*
Pylos *7s/Ave. A-1A*
Quintessence *10s/Ave. A-1A*
Raga *6s/Ave. A-1A*
Roll-n-Roaster *3A/11s*
Sal Anthony's *1A/10-1s*
Sandobe *1A/10-1s*
Sapporo East *10s/1A*
SEA *2A/4-5s*
Second Ave Deli *2A/10s*
Secretes *6s/Aves. A-B*
Shabu-Tatsu *10s/1-2A*
Smoked *2A/6s*
Soba-ya *9s/2-3A*
Starbucks *2A/9s*
Supper *2s/Aves. A-B*
Takahachi *Ave. A/5-6s*
Tasting Room *1s/1-2A*
Teresa's *1A/6-7s*
Three of Cups *1A/5s*
Tsampa *9s/2-3A*
26 Seats *Ave. B/10-1s*
Two Boots *multi. loc.*
Una Pizza Nap. *12s/1-2A*
Uno Chicago *3A/10-1s*
Uovo *Ave. B/11s*
Veniero's *11s/1-2A*
Veselka *2A/9s*
Xunta *1A/10-1s*
Yuca Bar *Ave. A/7s*
Zum Schneider *Ave. C/7s*

East 40s

Alcala *46s/1-2A*
Au Bon Pain *42s/Lex-Park*
Avra Estiatorio *48s/Lex-3A*
Ben & Jack's *44s/2-3A*
Bobby Van's Steak *Park/46s*
Boi *44s/2-3s*
Brother Jimmy BBQ *42s/Vanderbilt*
Bukhara Grill *49s/2-3A*
Bull & Bear *Lex/49s*
Burger Heaven *multi. loc.*
Cafe Centro *Park/45s-Vanderbilt*
Cafe S.F.A. *5A/49-50s*
Cafe Spice *42s/Vanderbilt*
Caffe Linda *49s/Lex-3A*
Capital Grille *46s/Lex-3A*

Chemist Club *41s/Mad-Park*
Chiam *48s/Lex-3A*
Chin Chin *49s/2-3A*
Chipotle *44s/Lex-3A*
Cibo *2A/41-2s*
Cipriani Dolci *42s/Vanderbilt*
Comfort Diner *45s/2-3A*
Darbar *46s/Lex-3A*
Delegates Dining Rm. *1A/45s*
Dishes *multi. loc.*
Diwan *48s/Lex-3A*
Django *Lex/46s*
Docks Oyster Bar *3A/40s*
English is Italian *3A/40s*
Grifone *46s/2-3A*
Hale & Hearty Soup *multi. loc.*
Haru *Park/48s*
Hatsuhana *multi. loc.*
Il Postino *49s/1-2A*
Inagiku *49s/Lex-Park*
Jacques-Imo's *42s/Vanderbilt*
Junior's *42s/Vanderbilt*
Katsu-Hama *47s/5A-Mad*
Kuruma Zushi *47s/5A-Mad*
L'Impero *Tudor City/42-3s*
Little Italy Pizza *43s/5A-Mad*
Mamá Mexico *49s/2-3A*
Mangia *48s/5A-Mad*
Mee Noodle Shop *2A/49s*
Menchanko-tei *45s/Lex-3A*
Metrazur *42s/Park*
Michael Jordan's *Vanderbilt/43-4s*
Morton's Steak *5A/45s*
Nanni *46s/Lex-3A*
Naples 45 *Park/45s*
Nino's Positano *2A/47-8s*
Osteria Laguna *42s/2-3A*
Oyster Bar *42s/Vanderbilt*
Palm *2A/44-5s*
Pampano *49s/2-3A*
Patroon *46s/Lex-3A*
Pepe Rosso Caffe *Lex/42s*
Pershing Sq. *42s/Park*
Pietro's *43s/2-3A*
Prime Grill *49s/Mad-Park*
Ribot *3A/48s*
Riingo *45s/2-3s*
Sip Sak *2A/49-50s*
Smith & Wollensky *3A/49s*
Smorgas Chef *2A/49s*
Sparks Steak *46s/2-3A*
Sushiden *49s/5A-Mad*
Sushi Yasuda *43s/2-3A*
Tropica *45s/Lex-Park*
Two Boots *42s/Lex*
Wollensky's Grill *49s/3A*
Zócalo *42s/Vanderbilt*

East 50s

Adä 58s/2-3A
Aja 1A/58s
Al Bustan 3A/50-1s
Alto 53s/5A-Mad
Amma 51s/2-3A
Angelo's Pizza 2A/55s
Aquavit 55s/Mad-Park
Au Bon Pain Lex/52-3s
Baluchi's 53s/2-3A
Bellini 52s/2-3A
Bice 54s/5A-Mad
Bill Hong's 56s/2-3A
Blockhead Burrito 2A/50-1s
BLT Steak 57s/Lex-Park
Bobby Van's Steak 54s/Lex-Park
Bottega del Vino 59s/5A-Mad
Bouterin 59s/1A-Sutton
Brasserie 53s/Lex-Park
Bruno 58s/2-3A
Burger Heaven multi. loc.
Burritoville 3A/52s
Cafe Joul 1A/58-9s
Café St. Bart's 50s/Park
Caffe Buon Gusto 2A/53-4s
Casa La Femme 1A/58-9s
Caviar Russe Mad/54-5s
Cellini 54s/Mad-Park
Chipotle 52s/Lex-3A
Chola 58s/2-3A
Chop't Creative 56s/Mad-Park
Columbus Bakery 1A/52-3s
Cosí 56s/Mad-Park
Da Antonio 55s/Lex-3A
Dawat 58s/2-3A
DeGrezia 50s/2-3A
Deux Amis 51s/1-2A
Ess-a-Bagel 3A/50-1s
F & B 52s/Lex-3A
Felidia 58s/2-3A
Fifty Seven 57 57s/Mad-Park
Four Seasons 52s/Lex-Park
Fresco by Scotto 52s/Mad-Park
Fresco on the Go 52s/Mad-Park
Giambelli 50s/Mad-Park
Grand Sichuan 2A/55-6s
Houston's 53s/54s & 3A
Il Menestrello 52s/5A
Il Nido 53s/2-3A
Il Valentino 56s/1-2A
Jubilee 54s/1-2A
Khyber Grill 58s/2-3A
Korea Palace 54s/Lex-Park
La Gioconda 53s/2-3A
La Grenouille 52s/5A-Mad
La Mangeoire 2A/53-4s
La Mediterranée 2A/50-1s

Le Colonial 57s/Lex-3A
L'Entrecote 1A/57-8s
Le Perigord 52s/FDR-1A
Lever House 53s/Mad-Park
Luna Piena 53s/2-3A
Maloney & Porcelli 50s/Mad-Park
March 58s/1A-Sutton
Meltemi 1A/51s
Monkey Bar 54s/Mad-Park
Montparnasse 51s/2-3A
Mr. Chow 57s/1-2A
Mr. K's Lex/51s
Neary's 57s/1A
Nippon 52s/Lex-3A
Oceana 54s/Mad-Park
Our Place 55s/Lex-3A
Outback Steak 56s/2-3A
Paper Moon 58s/Mad-Park
Peking Duck 53s/2-3A
Pescatore 2A/50-1s
P.J. Clarke's 3A/55s
Pump Energy Food 3A/50s
Rosa Mexicano 1A/58s
Rothmann's 54s/5A-Mad
San Pietro 54s/5A-Mad
Serafina 58s/Mad-Park
Shun Lee Palace 55s/Lex-3A
Solera 53s/2-3A
Solo Mad/55-6s
Sushi Ann 51s/Mad-Park
Sushi Rose 52s/2-3A
Table XII 56s/Park
Taksim 2A/54-5s
Tao 58s/Mad-Park
Tea Box 5A/54-5s
Teodora 57s/Lex-3A
Tratt. Pesce 1A/59s
Trump Grille 5A/56-7s
Tse Yang 51s/Mad-Park
Vong 54s/3A
Zarela 2A/50-1s

East 60s

Arabelle 64s/Mad
Aureole 61s/Mad-Park
Baluchi's 1A/63s
Bistro 61
Bravo Gianni 63s/2-3A
Brio Lex/61s
Burger Heaven Lex/62s
Cabana 3A/60-1s
Café Evergreen 1A/69-70s
Café Pierre 61s/5A
Cal. Pizza Kitchen 60s/2-3A
Cambalache 64s/1A-York
Canaletto 60s/2-3A
Circus 61s/Lex-Park

Locations

Da Filippo *2A/69-70s*
da Giacomo *64s/Lex*
Daniel *65s/Mad-Park*
davidburke/donatella *61s/Lex-Park*
Fig & Olive Kitchen *Lex/62s*
Frederick's Madison *Mad/65-6s*
Fred's at Barneys *Mad/60s*
Geisha *61s/Mad-Park*
Gino *Lex/60-1s*
Haikara Grill *63s/2-3A*
Hale & Hearty Soup *Lex/64-5s*
Il Vagabondo *62s/1-2A*
Jackson Hole *64s/2-3A*
John's Pizzeria *64s/1A-York*
JoJo *64s/Lex-3A*
Kai *Mad/68-9s*
L'Absinthe *67s/2-3A*
La Cantina Toscana *1A/60-1s*
La Goulue *Mad/64-5s*
Le Bilboquet *63s/Mad-Park*
Le Charlot *69s/Mad-Park*
Le Pain Quotidien *Lex/63-4s*
Mainland *3A/64s*
Manhattan Grille *1A/63-4s*
Maya *1A/64-5s*
Mediterraneo *2A/66s*
Mon Petit Cafe *Lex/62s*
Nello *Mad/62-3s*
Paris Match *65s/Mad-Park*
Park Ave. Cafe *63s/Lex-Park*
Patsy's Pizzeria *multi. loc.*
Pongal *1A/63-4s*
Portofino Grille *1A/63-4s*
Post House *63s/Mad-Park*
Primola *2A/64-5s*
Regency *Park/61s*
Scalinatella *61s/3A*
Serafina *61s/Mad-Park*
Serendipity 3 *60s/2-3A*
Sushi Seki *1A/62-3s*
212 *65s/Lex*
Ulrika's *60s/Lex-Park*
Viand *Mad/61-2s*
Via Oreto *1A/61-2s*
Za Za *1A/65-6s*

East 70s

Afghan Kebab Hse. *2A/70-1s*
Aki Sushi *York/75-6s*
Al Forno Pizza *2A/77-8s*
Annie's *3A/78-9s*
Atlantic Grill *3A/76-7s*
Baraonda *2A/75s*
Barking Dog *York/77s*
Bella Blu *Lex/70-1s*
Bistro Le Steak *3A/75s*
Boat House *72s/CPD N.*

Brother Jimmy BBQ *2A/77-8s*
Burritoville *2A/77-8s*
Café Boulud *76s/5A-Mad*
Caffe Buon Gusto *77s/2-3A*
Campagnola *1A/73-4s*
Candle 79 *79s/Lex-3A*
Candle Cafe *3A/74-5s*
Canyon Road *1A/76-7s*
Cilantro *1A/71s*
Coco Pazzo *74s/5A-Mad*
Cortina *2A/75-6s*
Dallas BBQ *3A/72-3s*
Due *3A/79-80s*
Eastern King *2A/72-3s*
EJ's Luncheonette *3A/73s*
Finestra *York/73s*
Googie's *2A/78s*
Grace's Trattoria *71s/2-3A*
Hacienda Argentina *75s/1-2A*
Haru *3A/76s*
Il Monello *2A/76-7s*
Il Riccio *79s/Lex-3A*
Iron Sushi *78s/1-2A*
J.G. Melon *3A/74s*
Ko Sushi *2A/70s*
Lenox Room *3A/73-4s*
Le Pain Quotidien *multi. loc.*
Luke's B&G *3A/79-80s*
Lusardi's *2A/77-8s*
Mark's *77s/5A-Mad*
Maruzzella *1A/77-8s*
Mary Ann's *2A/78-9s*
Mezzaluna *3A/74-5s*
Mingala Burmese *2A/72-3s*
Nino's *1A/72-3s*
Orsay *Lex/75s*
Parma *3A/79-80s*
Payard Bistro *Lex/73-4s*
Persepolis *2A/74-5s*
Petaluma *1A/73s*
Pintaile's Pizza *York/76-7s*
Quatorze Bis *79s/1-2A*
Rectangles *1A/74s*
Regional Thai *1A/77s*
Sant Ambroeus *Mad/77-8s*
Sarabeth's *Mad/75s*
Serafina *Mad/79s*
Sette Mezzo *Lex/70-1s*
Shabu-Shabu 70 *70s/1-2A*
Shanghai Pavilion *3A/78-9s*
Spice *2A/73-4s*
Sultan *2A/74-5s*
Sushi Hana *2A/78s*
Sushi of Gari *78s/1A-York*
Swifty's *Lex/72-3s*
Trata Estiatorio *2A/70-1s*

Tsuki *1A/74-5s*
Uskudar *2A/73-4s*
Uva *2A/77-8s*
Vermicelli *2A/77-8s*
Viand *Mad/78s*
Via Quadronno *73s/5A-Mad*
Vivolo *74s/Lex-Park*

East 80s
Baluchi's *multi. loc.*
Better Burger *2A/84s*
Beyoglu *3A/81s*
Blockhead Burrito *2A/81-2s*
Brasserie Julien *3A/80-1s*
Burger Heaven *3A/86s*
Café Sabarsky *5A/86s*
Cafe Trevi *1A/81-2s*
Caffe Grazie *84s/5A-Mad*
Carino *2A/88-9s*
Centolire *Mad/85-6s*
Chef Ho's *2A/89-90s*
Cilantro *2A/88-9s*
Dakshin Indian *1A/88-9s*
Divino *2A/80-1s*
Donguri *83s/1-2A*
E.A.T. *Mad/80-1s*
Elaine's *2A/88-9s*
Elio's *2A/84-5s*
Emack & Bolio's *1A/81-2s*
Erminia *83s/2-3A*
Etats-Unis *81s/2-3A*
Ethiopian Rest. *York/83-4s*
Firenze *2A/82-3s*
Giovanni 25 *83s/5A-Mad*
Girasole *82s/Lex-3A*
Gobo *3A/81s*
Heidelberg *2A/85-6s*
Ian *86s/1-2s*
Ichiro *2A/87-8s*
Ithaka *86s/1-2A*
Jackson Hole *2A/83-4s*
Jacques Brasserie *85s/2-3A*
Jasmine *2A/84s*
Kings' Carriage Hse. *82s/2-3A*
Ko Sushi *York/85s*
Le Boeuf/Mode *81s/E. End-York*
Lentini *2A/81s*
Le Pain Quotidien *Mad/84-5s*
Le Refuge *82s/Lex-3A*
Lili's Noodle *3A/84-5s*
Luca *1A/88-9s*
Mangiarini *2A/82-3s*
Maz Mezcal *86s/1-2A*
Miss Saigon *3A/80-1s*
Nicola's *84s/Lex*
One 83 *1A/83-4s*
Ota-Ya *2A/81-2s*

Our Place *3A/82s*
Paola's *84s/2-3A*
Papaya King *86s/3A*
Park East Grill *2A/81-2s*
Pearson's BBQ *81s/Lex-3A*
Penang *2A/83s*
Pig Heaven *2A/80-1s*
Pintaile's Pizza *York/83-4s*
Poke *85s/1-2A*
Primavera *1A/82s*
Quattro Gatti *81s/2-3A*
Rughetta *85s/1-2A*
Sabor *2A/89s*
Saigon Grill *2A/88s*
Sala Thai *2A/89-90s*
Sharz Cafe *86s/1A-York*
Sistina *2A/80-1s*
Spigolo *2A/81s*
Sushi Sen-nin *3A/80-1s*
Taste *3A/80s*
Tevere *84s/Lex-3A*
343 *85s/1-2A*
Tiramisu *3A/80s*
Tony's Di Napoli *2A/83s*
Totonno Pizza *2A/80-1s*
Tratt. Pesce *3A/87-8s*
Triangolo *83s/1-2A*
Turquoise *81s/2-3A*
Uno Chicago *86s/2-3A*
Vespa *2A/84-5s*
Viand *86s/2A*
Wu Liang Ye *86s/2-3A*
York Grill *York/88-9s*
Yuka *2A/80-1s*
Zócalo *82s/Lex-3A*

East 90s & 100s
(Bet. 90th & 110th Sts.)
Barking Dog *3A/94s*
Bistro du Nord *Mad/93s*
Brother Jimmy BBQ *3A/93s*
Don Pedro's *2A/96s*
El Paso Taqueria *multi. loc.*
Itzocan *Lex/101s*
Jackson Hole *Mad/91s*
Mary Ann's *2A/93s*
Nick's *2A/93-4s*
Osso Buco *3A/93s*
Pascalou *Mad/92-3s*
Pinocchio *1A/90-1s*
Pintaile's Pizza *91s/5A-Mad*
Sarabeth's *Mad/92-3s*
Starbucks *3A/92s*
Table d'Hôte *92s/Mad-Park*
Vico *Mad/92-3s*
Yura & Co. *multi. loc.*
Zebú Grill *92s/1-2A*

Locations

Financial District
(South of Murray St.)
Au Bon Pain *multi. loc.*
Au Mandarin *Vesey/Bway*
Battery Gardens *Battery Park*
Bayard's *Hanover/Pearl*
Bridge Cafe *Water/Dover*
Bull Run *William/Pine*
Burritoville *Water/Broad*
Chipotle *Bway/Whitehall*
coast *Liberty/Church*
Cosí *Vesey/W. Side Hwy.*
Delmonico's *Beaver/Williams*
Fino *Wall/Pearl*
14 Wall Street *Wall/Broad-Bway*
Gigino/Wagner *Battery/West*
Grill Room *Liberty/West Side Hwy.*
Hale & Hearty Soup *Broad/Beaver*
Joseph's *Hanover/Pearl*
Lemongrass Grill *William/Maiden*
Les Halles *John/Bway-Nassau*
Lili's Noodle *North End/Vesey*
Little Italy Pizza *Park Pl./Bway*
Mangia *Wall/Broad-William*
MarkJoseph Steak *Water/Peck Slip*
MJ Grill *John/Cliff-Pearl*
Nebraska Steak *Stone/Broad-Bway*
Roy's NY *Washington/Albany-Carlisle*
Smorgas Chef *Stone/William*
2 West *West/Battery Pl.*
Zeytuna *multi. loc.*

Flatiron District
(Bet. 14th & 24th Sts.,
6th Ave. & Park Ave. S.,
excluding Union Sq.)
Aleo *20s/5A*
Angelo & Maxie's *Park S./19s*
Arezzo *22s/5-6A*
Basta Pasta *17s/5-6A*
Beppe *22s/Bway-Park S.*
BLT Fish *17s/5-6A*
Bolo *22s/Bway-Park S.*
Caviar & Banana *22s/Bway-Park S.*
Chipotle *6A/21-2s*
City Bakery *18s/5-6A*
City Crab *Park S./19s*
Comfort Diner *23s/5-6A*
Cosí *multi. loc.*
Craft *19s/Bway-Park S.*
Craftbar *Bway/19-20s*
dévi *18s/Bway-5A*
Duvet *21s/5-6A*
Fleur de Sel *20s/Bway-5A*
Giorgio's/Gramercy *21s/Bway*
Gramercy Tav. *20s/Bway-Park S.*

Haru *Park S./18s*
Kitchen 82/22 *22s/Bway-Park S.*
Komegashi *Bway/21-2s*
La Pizza Fresca *20s/Bway-Park S.*
Le Pain Quotidien *19s/Bway-Park S.*
L'Express *Park S./20s*
Lucy's Latin Kit. *18s/Bway-Park S.*
Mangia *23s/5-6A*
Mayrose *Bway/21s*
Mesa Grill *5A/15-6s*
MetroCafe *21s/Bway-Park S.*
Mizu Sushi *20s/Bway-Park S.*
Outback Steak *23s/5-6A*
Park Avalon *Park S./18-9s*
Periyali *20s/5-6A*
Pipa *19s/Bway-Park S.*
Pump Energy Food *21s/Bway-Park*
Punch *Bway/20-1s*
Rickshaw Dumpling *23s/5-6A*
Sala *19s/5-6A*
Sapa *24s/Bway-6A*
Sensa *6A/21s*
Shaffer City *21s/5-6A*
Shake Shack *Mad Sq. Pk./23s*
SushiSamba *Park S./19-20s*
Tamarind *22s/Bway-Park S.*
Tossed *Park S./22-3s*
Vela *21s/5-6A*
Veritas *20s/Bway-Park S.*
Via Emilia *Park S./19-20s*

Garment District
(30th to 40th Sts., west of 5th)
Abigael's *Bway/38-9s*
Au Bon Pain *34s/7A*
Ben's Kosher Deli *38s/7-8A*
Burritoville *39s/9A*
Chipotle *34s/8A*
Cho Dang Gol *35s/5-6A*
Cosí *7A/36-7s*
Frankie & Johnnie *37s/5-6A*
Gahm Mi Oak *32s/Bway-5A*
Gray's Papaya *8A/37s*
Hale & Hearty Soup *7A/35s*
Heartland Brew. *5a/34s*
HK *9A/39s*
Ida Mae *38s/Bway-6A*
Kang Suh *Bway/32s*
Keens Steak *36s/5-6A*
Kum Gang San *32s/Bway-5A*
Mandoo Bar *32s/Bway-5A*
Nick & Stef Steak *33s/7-8A*
Osteria Gelsi *9A/38s*
Pump Energy Food *38s/Bway-6A*
Tupelo Grill *33s/7-8A*
Uncle Jack's Steak *9A/34-5s*

Won Jo *32s/Bway-5A*
You-Chun *36s/5A*

Gramercy Park
(24th to 30th Sts., east of 5th;
14th to 24th Sts., east of Park)
Aki Sushi *27s/Lex-Park S.*
Anh *3A/26-7s*
Baluchi's *29s/Lex-Park S.*
Bao Noodles *2A/22-3s*
Barna *Park S./26s*
Black Duck *28s/Lex-Park S.*
BLT Prime *22s/Lex-Park S.*
Blue Smoke *27s/Lex-Park S.*
Burger Joint *3A/19-20s*
Butai *18s/Irving-Park S.*
Casa Mia *24s/2-3A*
Casa Mono *Irving/17s*
Chennai Garden *27s/Lex-Park S.*
Chino's *3A/16-7s*
Copper Chimney *28s/Lex-Park S.*
Coppola's *3A/27-8s*
Curry Leaf *Lex/27s*
Dos Caminos *Park S./26-7s*
Duke's *19s/Park S.*
Eleven Madison *Mad/24s*
Empire Szechuan *3A/27-8s*
Ess-a-Bagel *1A/21s*
French Quarter *25s/Lex-Park S.*
Friend of a Farmer *Irving/18-9s*
Gramercy 24 *3A/24s*
Houston's *Park S./27s*
I Trulli *27s/Lex-Park S.*
Ixta *29s/Mad-Park S.*
Jaiya Thai *3A/28s*
Kelley & Ping *3A/25s*
Lady Mendl's *Irving Pl./17-8s*
Lamarca *22s/3A*
L'Annam *3A/28s*
La Petite Auberge *Lex/27-8s*
Les Halles *Park S./28-9s*
Los Dos Molinos *18s/Irving-Park S.*
Novitá *22s/Lex-Park S.*
Park Bistro *Park S./28-9s*
Paul & Jimmy's *18s/Irving-Park S.*
Pete's Tavern *18s/Irving*
Petite Abeille *20s/1A*
Pinch, Pizza *Park S./28-9s*
Pongal *Lex/27-8s*
Pongsri Thai *2A/18s*
Posto *2A/18s*
Pure Food + Wine *Irving/17-8s*
Rice *Lex/28s*
Rolf's *3A/22s*
Sal Anthony's *Irving/17-8s*
Saravanaas *Lex/26s*
Scopa *Mad/28s*

71 Irving Place *Irving/18-9s*
Tabla *Mad/25s*
Texas Smoke BBQ *2A/25s*
Totonno Pizza *2A/26s*
Turkish Kitchen *3A/27-8s*
Vatan *3A/29s*
Yama *17s/Irving*

Greenwich Village
(Houston to 14th Sts., west of
Bway, excluding NoHo and
Meatpacking District)
Agave *7A S./Charles-W. 10s*
Aki *4s/Barrow-Jones*
Alexandra *Hudson/Barrow-Morton*
Alfama *Hudson/Perry*
Alta *W. 10s/5-6A*
Amy's Bread *Bleecker/Leroy*
Annisa *Barrow/7A S.-W. 4s*
A.O.C. *Bleecker/Grove*
A.O.C. Bedford *Bedford/Downing*
Arté *9s/5A-University*
Arturo's Pizzeria *Houston/Thompson*
A Salt & Battery *Greenwich A/12-3s*
Au Bon Pain *8s/Mercer*
August *Bleecker-Charles-W. 10s*
Babbo *Waverly/MacDougal-6A*
Babu *MacDougal/Bleecker-W. 3s*
Barbuto *Washington/Jane-W. 12s*
Bar Pitti *6A/Bleecker-Houston*
BB Sandwich *3s/MacDougal-6A*
Bellavitae *Minetta/MacDougal-6A*
Bivio *Hudson/Horatio*
Blue Hill *Washingtion Pl./Wash. Sq.*
Blue Ribbon Bakery *Downing/
  Bedford*
Bone Lick Pk. BBQ *Greenwich A/
  Bank*
Borgo Antico *13s/5A-University*
Burritoville *Bleecker/7A S.*
Butter *Lafayette/Astor Pl.-4s*
Cafe Asean *10s/Greenwich-6A*
Café de Bruxelles *Greenwich A/13s*
Cafe Español *multi. loc.*
Cafe Loup *13s/6-7A*
Cafe Spice *University/10-1s*
Caffe Rafaella *7A S./Charles-W. 10s*
CamaJe *MacDougal/Bl.-Houston*
Casa *Bedford/Commerce*
Chez Jacqueline *MacDougal/Blckr*
Chez Michallet *Bedford/Grove*
Chipotle *8s/Bway-University*
Chow Bar *4s/W. 10s*
Cornelia St. Cafe *Cornelia/Blckr*
Corner Bistro *4s/Jane*
Cosí *multi. loc.*
Cowgirl *Hudson/W. 10s*

Locations

Cozy Soup/Burger *Bway/Astor*
Crispo *14s/7-8A*
Cru *5A/9s*
Cuba *Thompson/Bleecker*
Cubana Café *Thompson/Prince*
Da Andrea *Hudson/Perry-W. 11s*
Da Silvano *6A/Bleecker-Houston*
Deborah *Carmine/Bedford-Bleecker*
De Marco's *Houston/MacDougal*
Diablo Royale *10s/Bleecker-W. 4s*
DoHwa *Carmine/Bedford-7A S.*
EJ's Luncheonette *6A/9-10s*
El Charro Español *Charles/7A S.*
Elephant & Castle *Greenwich A/6-7s*
El Faro *Greenwich s/Horatio*
Emack & Bolio's *7A/13-4s*
Empire Szechuan *multi. loc.*
Employees Only *Hudson/Christopher*
EN Japanese *Hudson/Leroy*
Ennio & Michael *La Guardia/W. 3s*
Extra Virgin *W/ 4s/Charles-Perry*
50 Carmine *Carm./Bedford-Blckr*
Fish *Bleecker/Jones*
Flor's Kitchen *Waverly/6-7A*
French Roast *6A/11s*
Gavroche *14s/7-8A*
Gobo *6A/8s-Waverly Pl.*
Gonzo *13s/6-7A*
good *Greenwich A/Bank-W. 12s*
Gotham B&G *12s/5A-University*
Gray's Papaya *6A/8s*
Grey Dog's Coffee *Carmine/Bedford*
Gusto *Greenwich A/Perry*
Havana Alma *Christopher/Bedford*
Home *Cornelia/Bleecker-W. 4s*
Hue *Charles/Bleecker*
Il Cantinori *10s/Bway-University*
Il Mulino *3s/Sullivan-Thompson*
'ino *Bedford/Downing-6A*
Inside *Jones/Bleecker-W. 4s*
I Tre Merli *W. 10s/7A*
Jane *Houston/La Guardia-Thompson*
Japonica *University/12s*
Jarnac *12s/Greenwich s*
Joe's Pizza *Carmine/Bleecker-6A*
John's Pizzeria *Bleecker/6A-7A S.*
Knickerbocker B&G *University/8-9s*
La Cantina *8A/Jane*
La Focaccia *Bank/W. 4s*
La Lanterna *MacDougal/W. 3-4s*
L'Annam *University/13s*
La Palapa *6A/Washington Pl.-W. 4s*
La Ripaille *Hudson/Bethune-W. 12s*
Le Gigot *Cornelia/Bleecker-W. 4s*
Lemongrass Grill *multi. loc.*
Le Pain Quotidien *5A/8s*

Lima's Taste *Christopher/Bedford*
Lupa *Thompson/Bleecker-Houston*
Malatesta Tratt. *Washington/Christopher*
Mandoo Bar *Univ./10-1s*
Maremma *10s/Bleecker-Hudson*
Marinella *Carmine/Bedford*
Mary's Fish Camp *Charles/W. 4s*
Mas *Downing/Bedford-Varick*
Maurizio Trattoria *13s/5-6A*
Mercadito *7A-S./Grove*
Meskerem *MacDougal/Bleecker-3s*
Metropol *W. 4s/10s*
Mex. Mama *Hudson/Charles*
Mi Cocina *Jane/Hudson*
Minetta Tavern *MacDougal/3s*
Miracle Grill *Bleecker/Bank-11s*
Monster Sushi *Hudson/Charles*
Moustache *Bedford/Barrow-Grove*
Negril *3s/La Guardia-Thompson*
North Sq. *Waverly/MacDougal*
One if by Land *Barrow/7A S.-4s*
Ony *6A/Washington Pl.-W. 4s*
Osso Buco *University/11-2s*
Osteria del Sole *4s/Perry*
Otto *5A/8s*
Papaya King *14s/7A*
Paris Commune *Bank/Greenwich*
Patsy's Pizzeria *University/10-1s*
Peanut Butter/Co. *Sullivan/Bleecker*
Pearl Oyster *Cornelia/Bleecker*
Pepe Verde To Go *Hudson/Perry-11s*
Perry Street *Perry/West St.*
Petite Abeille *Hudson/Barrow*
Philip Marie *Hudson/11s*
Piadina *10s/5-6A*
Piccolo Angolo *Hudson/Jane*
Pink Tea Cup *Grove/Bleecker*
Place *4s/Bank-W. 12s*
Pó *Cornelia/Bleecker-W. 4s*
Prem-on Thai *Houston/MacDougal*
Rib *West/Clarkson-Leroy*
Risotteria *Bleecker/Morton*
Rocco *Thompson/Bleecker-Houston*
Sacred Chow *Sullivan/W. 3s*
Sant Ambroeus *W. 4s/Perry*
Sevilla *Charles/W. 4s*
Shopsin's *Carmine/Bleecker-6A*
Shorty's Half Shell *6A/11-2s*
Snack Taverna *Bedford/Morton*
Spotted Pig *W11s/Greenwich s*
Starbucks *Astor/Lafayette*
Strip House *12s/5A-University*
Sumile *13s/6-7A*
Surya *Bleecker/Grove-7A S.*
SushiSamba *7A S./Barrow*

Taka *Grove/Bleecker-7A S*
Tartine *11s/W. 4s*
Tea & Sympathy *Greenwich A/12-3s*
Tomoe Sushi *Thompson/Bl.- Houston*
Tratt. Pesce *Bleecker/6A-7A S.*
Two Boots *11s/7A S.*
Uno Chicago *6A/8s-Waverly Pl.*
Veg. Paradise *4s/MacDougal*
Village *9s/5-6A*
Villa Mosconi *MacDougal/Houston*
Vittorio Cucina *Bleecker/Grove-7A*
Voyage *Perry/Greenwich s*
Wallsé *11s/Washington*
Westville *10s/Bleecker-W. 4s*
Wild Ginger *Grove/Bleecker-7A S.*
Wogies B&G *Greenwich A/Charles*
Yama *multi. loc.*
Yujin *12s/5A-University*
Yumcha *Bedford/Downing*
Zutto *Greenwich A/7A S.-W. 11s*

Harlem/East Harlem
(Bet. 110th & 157th Sts.,
excluding Columbia U. area)
Amy Ruth's *116s/Lenox-7A*
Bayou *Lenox/125-26s*
Charles' Southern *8A/151s*
Creole *3A/118s*
Dinosaur BBQ *131s/12A*
Harlem Grill *ACP/132-3s*
Londel's *FDB/139-40s*
Melba's *114s/8A*
Miss Mamie's/Maude's *multi. loc.*
Mo-Bay *125s/5A-Lenox A*
Native *118s/Lenox*
Orbit East Harlem *1A/116s*
Papaya King *125s/Lenox-7A*
Patsy's Pizzeria *1A/117-8s*
Rao's *114s/Pleasant*
Starbucks *125s/Lenox*
Sylvia's *Lenox/126-7s*
Wimp's Sky Café *125s/Lenox-5A*

Little Italy
(Bet. Canal & Delancey Sts.
& Bowery & Lafayette St.)
Angelo's/Mulberry *Mulberry/Grand*
Da Nico *Mulberry/Broome-Grand*
Eight Mile Creek *Mulberry/Prince*
Ferrara *Grand/Mott-Mulberry*
Grotta Azzurra *Broome/Mulberry*
Il Cortile *Mulberry/Canal-Hester*
Il Fornaio *Mulberry/Grand-Hester*
Il Palazzo *Mulberry/Grand-Hester*
La Mela *Mulberry/Broome-Grand*
Nyonya *Grand/Mott-Mulberry*

Pellegrino's *Mulberry/Grand-Hester*
Pho Bang *Mott/Broome-Grand*
Positano *Mulberry/Canal-Hester*
Sal Anthony's *Mulberry/Grand*
Taormina *Mulberry/Grand-Hester*
Umberto's *Mulberry/Broome*
Vincent's *Mott/Hester*

Lower East Side
(Houston to Canal Sts.,
east of Bowery)
Alias *Clinton/Rivington*
ápizz *Eldridge/Rivington-Stanton*
Azul Bistro *Stanton/Suffolk*
Basso Est *Orchard/Stanton*
Bereket *Houston/Orchard*
Chubo *Clinton/Houston-Stanton*
Cube 63 *Clinton/Rivington-Stanton*
Epicerie *Orchard/Rivington-Stanton*
Essex *Essex/Rivington*
Falai *Clinton/Rivington-Stanton*
Freemans *Rivington/Bowery-Chrystie*
Grilled Cheese *Ludlow/Houston*
'inoteca *Rivington/Ludlow*
Katz's Deli *Houston/Ludlow*
Kitchen/Cocktails *Orchard/Houston*
Kuma Inn *Ludlow/Delancey-Riv.*
Les Enfants Terribles *Canal/Ludlow*
Little Giant *Orchard/Broome*
LoSide *Houston/Allen-Eldridge*
Paladar *Ludlow/Houston-Stanton*
Petrosino *Norfolk/Houston*
Radha *Ludlow/Houston-Stanton*
Sachiko's *Clinton/Houston-Stanton*
Salt *Clinton/Houston-Stanton*
Sammy's Roum. *Chrystie/Delancey*
Schiller's *Rivington/Norfolk*
71 Clinton Fresh *Clinton/Rivington*
Stanton Social *Stanton/Ludlow*
Suba *Ludlow/Delancey-Rivington*
teany *Rivington/Ludlow-Orchard*
Thor *Rivington/Essex-Ludlow*
Tides *Norfolk/Delancey-Riv.*
wd-50 *Clinton/Rivington-Stanton*
Zucco *Orchard/Houston-Stanton*

Meatpacking District
(Gansevoort to 15th Sts.,
west of 9th Ave.)
5 Ninth *9A/Gansevoort*
Florent *Gansevoort/Wash.*
Highline *Washington/Little W. 12s*
Lotus *14s/9A-Washington*
Macellaria *Gansevoort/Greenwich*
Markt *14s/9A*
Meet *Gansevoort/Washington*

Locations

Nero *Gansevoort/Greenwich*
Old Homestead *9A/14-5s*
One *Little W. 12s/9A*
Ono *9A/13s*
Paradou *Little W. 12s/Greenwich s*
Pastis *9A/Little W. 12s*
Pop Burger *9A/14-5s*
Son Cubano *14s/9A-Washington*
Spice Market *13s/9A*
Vento *Hudson/14s*

Murray Hill
(30th to 40th Sts., east of 5th)
Ali Baba *34s/2-3A*
AQ Cafe *Park/37-8s*
Artisanal *32s/Mad-Park*
Asia de Cuba *Mad/37-8s*
Barbès *36s/5A-Mad*
Barking Dog *34s/Lex-3A*
Belluno *Lex/39-40s*
Better Burger *3A/37s*
Blockhead Burrito *3A/33-4s*
Carl's Steaks *3A/34s*
Cinque Terre *38s/Mad-Park*
Cosette *33s/Lex-3A*
Da Ciro *Lex/33-4s*
Earl's *3A/37s*
El Parador Cafe *34s/1-2A*
El Pote *2A/38-9s*
Ethos *3A/33-4s*
Evergreen Shan. *38s/5A-Mad*
Fino *36s/5A-Mad*
Franchia *Park/34-5s*
Frère Jacques *37s/5A-Mad*
Grand Sichuan *Lex/33-4s*
Hangawi *32s/5A-Mad*
Iron Sushi *3A/30-1s*
Jackson Hole *3A/35s*
Josie's *3A/37s*
La Giara *3A/33-4s*
Lemongrass Grill *34s/Lex-3A*
Madison Bistro *Mad/37-8s*
Maxie *3A/34-5s*
Mee Noodle Shop *2A/30-31s*
Minado *32s/5A-Mad*
Mishima *Lex/30-1s*
Notaro *2A/34-5s*
Pasticcio *3A/30-1s*
Patsy's Pizzeria *3A/34-5s*
Penelope *Lex/30s*
Phoenix Garden *40s/2-3A*
Pizza 33 *3A/33s*
Pump Energy Food *31s/Lex-Park S.*
Rare B&G *Lex/37s*
Rossini's *38s/Lex-Park*
Salute! *Mad/39s*
Sarge's Deli *3A/36-7s*

Shaburi *39s/Lex-Park*
Silverleaf Tavern *38s/Park*
Stella del Mare *Lex/39-40s*
Tratt. Alba *34s/2-3A*
Tre Pomodori *34s/2-3A*
Trio *33s/Lex-3A*
Villa Berulia *34s/Lex-Park*
Water Club *30s/E. 23s*
Wolfgang's Steak *Park/33s*
Wu Liang Ye *Lex/39-40s*

NoHo
(Bet. Houston & 4th Sts.,
Bowery & Bway)
Agozar! *Bowery/Bleecker*
Au Bon Pain *Bway/3s*
Bianca *Bleecker/Bowery*
Bond Street *Bond/Bway-Lafayette*
Five Points *Gr. Jones/Lafayette*
Great Jones Cafe *Gr. Jones/Bowery*
Hedeh *Great Jones/Bowery*
Il Buco *Bond/Bowery-Lafayette*
Marion's Cont. *Bowery/4s-Gr. Jones*
NoHo Star *Lafayette/Bleecker*
Quartino *Bleecker/Elizabeth*
Sala *Bowery/Great Jones*
Serafina *Lafayette/4s*
Two Boots *Bleecker/Bway*

NoLita
(Bet. Delancey & Houston
Sts., Bowery & Lafayette St.)
Au Coin du Feu *Lafayette/Spring*
BarBossa *Elizabeth/Houston-Prince*
barmarché *Spring/Elizabeth*
Bread *Spring/Elizabeth-Mott*
Cafe Gitane *Mott/Prince*
Café Habana *Prince/Elizabeth*
Ghenet *Mulberry/Houston-Prince*
Kitchen Club *Prince/Mott*
La Esquina *Kenmare/Lafayette*
Le Jardin Bistro *Clev./Kenmare*
Lombardi's *Spring/Mott-Mulberry*
MeKong *Prince/Mott-Mulberry*
Mexican Radio *Cleveland/Kenmare*
Peasant *Elizabeth/Prince-Spring*
Plate NYC *Elizabeth/Houston-Prince*
Public *Elizabeth/Prince*
Rice *Mott/Prince-Spring*
Spring St. Natural *Spring/Lafayette*
VaTutto *Clev./Kenmare-Spring*

SoHo
(Bet. Canal & Houston Sts.,
west of Lafayette St.)
Ama *MacDougal/King-Prince*
Aquagrill *Spring/6A*

Balthazar *Spring/Bway-Crosby*
Baluchi's *Spring/Sullivan-Thompson*
Barolo *W. Bway/Broome-Spring*
Bistro Les Amis *Spring/Thompson*
Blue Ribbon *Sullivan/Prince-Spring*
Blue Ribbon Sushi *Sullivan/Prince*
Boom *Spring/Bway-Wooster*
Cendrillon *Mercer/Broome-Grand*
Chipotle *Varick/Houston-King*
Cipriani Dwntn *W. Bway/Broome*
Country Café *Thompson/Broome*
Cub Room *Sullivan/Prince*
Cupping Room *W. Bway/Broome*
Dos Caminos *W. Bway/Houston*
Emack & Bolio's *Houston/W. Bway*
Félix *W. Bway/Grand*
Fiamma Osteria *Spring/6A-Sullivan*
Giorgione *Spring/Greenwich-Hudson*
Hampton Chutney *Prince/Bway*
Honmura An *Mercer/Houston-Prince*
Ideya *W. Bway/Broome-Grand*
Il Corallo *Prince/Sullivan*
I Tre Merli *W. Bway/Houston-Prince*
Ivo & Lulu *Broome/6A-Varick*
Jean Claude *Sullivan/Houston*
Jerry's *Prince/Greene-Mercer*
Kelley & Ping *Greene/Prince*
Kin Khao *Spring/Thompson-W. Bway*
Kittichai *Thompson/Broome-Spr.*
L'Ecole *Bway/Grand*
Le Pain Quotidien *Grand/Greene*
Le Pescadou *King/6A*
Little Italy Pizza *Varick/Charlton*
Lure Fishbar *Mercer/Prince*
Mercer Kitchen *Prince/Mercer*
Mezzogiorno *Spring/Sullivan*
Ñ *Crosby/Broome-Grand*
Novecento *W. Bway/Broome-Grand*
Omen *Thompson/Prince-Spring*
Once Upon a Tart *Sullivan/Houston*
Peep *Prince/Sullivan-Thompson*
Penang *Spring/Greene-Mercer*
Pepe Rosso To Go *Sullivan/Houston-Prince*
Provence *MacDougal/Prince*
Raoul's *Prince/Sullivan-Thompson*
Salt *MacDougal/Houston-Prince*
Savore *Spring/Sullivan*
Savoy *Prince/Crosby*
Snack *Thompson/Prince-Spring*
Soho Cantina *Prince/MacDougal*
Starbucks *Varick/Spring*
Sweet Melissa *Houston/W. Bway*
Tennessee Mtn. *Spring/Wooster*
Woo Lae Oak *Mercer/Houston*
Zoë *Prince/Bway-Mercer*

South Street Seaport

Cabana *South/Fulton-John*
Heartland Brew. *South/Fulton*
Quartino *Peck/Water*
Uno Chicago *South/Pier 17*

TriBeCa
(Bet. Canal & Murray Sts., west of Bway)

Acappella *Hudson/Chambers*
Arqua *Church/White*
Azafran *Warren/Greenwich-W. Bway*
Bouley *W. Bway/Duane*
Bread Tribeca *Church/Walker*
Bubby's *Hudson/N. Moore*
Burritoville *Chambers/Chambers*
Capsouto Frères *Washington/Watts*
Carl's Steaks *Chambers/Bway*
Centrico *W. Bway/Franklin*
Chanterelle *Harrison/Hudson*
Churra. Plata. *Bway/Franklin-White*
City Hall *Duane/Church-W. Bway*
Danube *Hudson/Duane-Reade*
Della Rovere *W. B'way/Beach*
dominic *Greenwich/Harrison-Jay*
Duane Park Cafe *Duane/Hudson*
Dylan Prime *Laight/Greenwich*
Ecco *Chambers/Church-W. Bway*
F.illi Ponte *Desbrosses/W. Side Hwy.*
Flor de Sol *Greenwich/Franklin*
fresh *Reade/Church-W. Bway*
Gigino Trattoria *Greenwich/Duane*
Grace *Franklin/Church-W. Bway*
Harrison *Greenwich s/Harrison*
Il Giglio *Warren/Greenwich-W. Bway*
Kitchenette *W. Bway/Warren*
Kori *Church/Franklin-Leonard*
Landmarc *W. Bway/Leonard-Worth*
Le Zinc *Duane/Church-W. Bway*
Lo Scalco *Church/Lispenard-Walker*
Lupe's East L.A. Kitchen *6A/Watts*
Mary Ann's *W. Bway/Chambers*
Megu *Thomas/Church-W. Bway*
Montrachet *W. Bway/Walker-White*
Nam *Reade/W. Bway*
Ninja *Hudson/Duane-Reade*
Nobu *Hudson/Franklin*
Odeon *W. Bway/Duane-Thomas*
Pace *Hudson/N. Moore*
Pepolino *W. Bway/Canal-Lispenard*
Petite Abeille *W. Bway/Duane*
Roc *Duane/Greenwich s*
Salaam Bombay *Green. s/Duane*
Scalini Fedeli *Duane/Greenwich s*
shore *Murray/Church-W. Bway*
66 *Church/Leonard*

Sosa Borella *Greenwich s/Watts*
Takahachi *Duane-Church/W. Bway*
Thalassa *Franklin/Greenwich*
Tribeca Grill *Greenwich/Franklin*
Upstairs *W. Bway/Duane*
VietCafé *Greenwich s/Harrison-Jay*
Walker's *N. Moore/Varick*
'wichcraft *Greenwich s/Beach*
Zutto *Hudson/Harrison*

Union Square
(Bet. 14th & 17th Sts., Union
Sq. E. & W.)
Au Bon Pain *Union Sq. E/14s*
Blue Water *Union Sq. W./16s*
Candela *16s/Irving-Park S.*
Chat 'n Chew *16s/5A-Union Sq. W*
Chop't Creative *17s/Bway-5A*
Coffee Shop *Union Sq. W./16s*
Havana Central *17s/Bway-5A*
Heartland Brew. *Union Sq. W./16s*
Olives *Park S./17s*
Republic *Union Sq. W./16-7s*
Spice *University/10s*
Steak Frites *16s/5A-Union Sq. W.*
Tocqueville *15s/5A*
Union Sq. Cafe *16s/5A-Union Sq. W.*
Whole Foods Café *Union Sq. S.*
Zen Palate *Union Sq. E./16s*

Washington Hts. & Up
(North of W. 157th St.)
Dallas BBQ *Bway/166s*
El Malecon *Bway/175s*
Empire Szechuan *Bway/170-71s*
Hispaniola *181s/Cabrini Blvd.*
New Leaf *M. Corbin/190s*
107 West *187/Ft. Wash.-Pinehurst*
Park Terrace *Bway/Isham-207s*
Piper's Kilt *Bway/207s*

West 40s
Above *42s/7-8A*
Akdeniz *46s/5-6A*
Alfredo of Rome *49s/5-6A*
Algonquin *44s/5-6A*
Amarone *9A/47-8s*
Amy's Bread *9A/46-7s*
Angus McIndoe *44s/Bway-8A*
Au Bon Pain *8A/40-1s*
Baldoria *49s/Bway-8A*
Barbetta *46s/8-9A*
Becco *46s/8-9A*
Better Burger *9A/42-3s*
Bistro du Vent *42s/9-10A*
Blue Fin *Bway/47s*

Bolzano's *B'way/45s*
Bond 45 *45s/6-7A*
Breeze *9A/45-46s*
Bryant Park *40s/5-6A*
B. Smith's *46s/8-9A*
Bubba Gump *Bway/43-4s*
Burritoville *9A/44s*
Cafe Un Deux *44s/Bway-6A*
Cara Mia *9A/45-6s*
Carmine's *44s/Bway-8A*
Cascina *9A/45-6s*
Chelsea Grill *9A/46-7s*
Chez Josephine *42s/9-10A*
Chimichurri Grill *9A/43-4s*
Chipotle *42s/5-6A*
Churra. Plata. *49s/8-9A*
City Lobster *49s/6-7A*
Così *42s/5-6A*
Croton Reservoir *40s/Bway-6A*
Daisy May's BBQ *11A/46s*
db Bistro Moderne *44s/5-6A*
Del Frisco's *6A/49s*
Delta Grill *9A/48s*
Dervish Turkish *47s/6-7A*
District *46s/6-7A*
Don Giovanni *44s/8-9A*
Edison Cafe *47s/Bway-8A*
Esca *43s/9A*
ESPN Zone *Bway/42s*
etcetera etcetera *44s/8-9A*
FireBird *46s/8-9A*
Foley's Fish Hse. *7A/47-8s*
44 *44s/5-6A*
44 & X Hell's Kit. *10A/44s*
Frankie & Johnnie *45s/Bway-8A*
Hakata Grill *48s/Bway-8A*
Hale & Hearty Soup *42s/5-6A*
Hallo Berlin *10A/44-5s*
Hard Rock Cafe *Bway/43s*
Haru *43s/Bway-8A*
Havana Central *46s/6-7A*
Heartland Brew. *43s/Bway-6A*
Hell's Kitchen *9A/46-7s*
Jewel of India *44s/5-6A*
Jezebel *9A/45s*
Joe Allen *46s/8-9A*
John's Pizzeria *44s/Bway-8A*
Josephs Citarella *6A/49s*
Kodama *45s/8-9A*
Koi *40s/5-6A*
Kyma *46s/8A*
L'Allegria *9A/44s*
La Locanda Vini *9A/49-50s*
La Masseria *48s/Bway-8A*
Landmark Tavern *11A/46s*
La Rivista *46s/8-9A*
Lattanzi *46s/8-9A*

Le Madeleine *43s/9-10A*
Le Marais *46s/6-7A*
Le Rivage *46s/8-9A*
Little Italy Pizza *45s/5-6A*
Luxia *48s/8-9A*
Marseille *9A/44s*
McHales *8A/46s*
Meskerem *47s/9-10A*
Monster Sushi *46s/5-6A*
Morrell Wine Bar *49s/5-6A*
My Most Favorite *45s/Bway-6A*
Océo *49s/Bway-8A*
Ollie's *44s/Bway-8A*
Orso *46s/8-9A*
Osteria al Doge *44s/Bway-6A*
Pam Real Thai *49s/9-10A*
Pietrasanta *9A/47s*
Pigalle *8A/48s*
Pongsri Thai *48s/Bway-8A*
Rachel's American *9A/43-4s*
Rainbow Room *49s/5-6A*
Re Sette *45s/5-6A*
Ruby Foo's *Bway/49s*
Sardi's *44s/Bway-8A*
Sea Grill *49s/5-6A*
Shaan *48s/5-6A*
Shula's Steak *43s/7-8A*
Starbucks *9A/47s*
Sushiden *49s/6-7A*
Sushi Zen *44s/Bway-6A*
Tony Luke's *9A/41-2s*
Tony's Di Napoli *43s/Bway-6A*
Tossed *Rock Plz./49-50s*
Triomphe *44s/5-6A*
Turkish Cuisine *9A/44-5s*
Two Boots *Rock Plz./49-50s*
Utsav *46s/6-7A*
Via Brasil *46s/5-6A*
View *Bway/45-6s*
Virgil's Real BBQ *44s/Bway-6A*
West Bank Cafe *42s/9-10A*
Wu Liang Ye *48s/5-6A*
Zen Palate *9A/46s*
Zuni *9A/43s*

West 50s

Abboccato *55s/6-7A*
Acqua Pazza *52s/5-6A*
Afghan Kebab Hse. *9A/51-2s*
Aki Sushi *52s/8-9A*
Alain Ducasse *58s/6-7A*
Angelo's Pizza *multi. loc.*
Atelier *CPS/6A*
Au Bon Pain *55s/6-7A*
Azucar *8A/56s*
Azuri Cafe *51s/9-10A*
Baluchi's *56s/Bway-8A*

Bann *50s/8-9A*
Bar Americain *52s/6-7A*
Bay Leaf *56s/5-6A*
Beacon *56s/5-6A*
Bello *9A/56s*
Ben Benson's *52s/6-7A*
Blockhead Burrito *50s/8-9A*
bluechili *51s/8A-Bway*
Bombay Palace *52s/5-6A*
Brasserie 8½ *57s/5-6A*
Brasserie LCB *55s/5-6A*
Bricco *56s/8-9A*
Brooklyn Diner *57s/Bway-7A*
burger joint/Parker M. *56s/6-7A*
Café Botanica *CPS/6-7A*
Cafe Spice *55s/5-6A*
Caffe Cielo *8A/52-3s*
Carnegie Deli *7A/55s*
Chanpen Thai *9A/51s*
Chez Napoléon *50s/8-9A*
China Grill *53s/5-6A*
Cité *51s/6-7A*
Cité Grill *51s/6-7A*
Cosí *Bway/51s*
Da Tommaso *8A/53-4s*
Eatery *9A/53s*
Fives *5A/55s*
Fontana di Trevi *57s/6-7A*
Gallagher's Steak *52/Bway-8A*
Giovanni *55s/5-6A*
Grand Sichuan *9A/50-1s*
Greek Kitchen *10A/58s*
Hale & Hearty Soup *56s/5-6A*
Heartland Brew. *6A/51s*
Hudson Cafeteria *58s/8-9A*
Il Gattopardo *54s/5-6A*
Il Tinello *56s/5-6A*
Island Burgers *9A/51-2s*
Jekyll & Hyde *6A/57-8s*
Joe's *56s/5-6A*
Julian's *9A/53-4s*
La Bonne Soupe *55s/5-6A*
La Vineria *55s/5-6A*
Le Bernardin *51s/6-7A*
Le Pain Quotidien *7A/58s*
Lili's Noodle *7A/56-7s*
Mangia *57s/5-6A*
Manhattan Ocean *58s/5-6A*
Maria Pia *51s/8-9A*
Mars 2112 *Bway/51s*
McCormick & Schmick *52s/6-7A*
Mee Noodle Shop *9A/53s*
Menchanko-tei *55s/5-6A*
Michael's *55s/5-6A*
Milos *55s/6-7A*
Moda *52s/6-7A*

Locations

Modern, The *53s/5-6A*
Molyvos *7A/55-6s*
Nino's *58s/6-7A*
Nobu 57 *57s/5-6A*
Nocello *55s/Bway-8A*
Nook *9A/50s*
Norma's *57s/6-7A*
Osteria del Circo *55s/6-7A*
Osteria Stella *50s/6-7A*
Palm *50s/Bway-8A*
Patsy's *56s/Bway-8A*
Petrossian *58s/7A*
Philly Slim's *9A/52-3s*
Piano Due *51s/6-7A*
Pump Energy Food *55s/5-6A*
Puttanesca *9A/56s*
Redeye Grill *7A/56s*
Red Garlic *8A/54-5s*
Remi *53s/6-7A*
René Pujol *51s/8-9A*
Rice 'n' Beans *9A/50-1s*
Roberto Passon *9A/50s*
Rock Center Cafe *50s/5-6A*
Rue 57 *57s/6A*
Russian Samovar *52s/Bway-8A*
Ruth Chris Steak *51s/6-7A*
San Domenico *CPS/Bway-7A*
Sarabeth's *CPS/5-6A*
Seppi's *56s/6-7A*
Serafina *55s/Bway*
Shelly's NY *57s/6-7A*
Siam Inn *8A/51-2s*
Soba Nippon *52s/5-6A*
Sosa Borella *8A/50s*
Stage Deli *7A/53-4s*
Starbucks *58s/8-9A*
Sugiyama *55s/Bway-8A*
Taboon *10A/52s*
Tang Pavilion *55s/5-6A*
Thalia *8A/50s*
Topaz Thai *56s/6-7A*
Town *56s/5-6A*
Tratt. Dell'Arte *7A/56-7s*
Tuscan Square *51s/5-6A*
21 Club *52s/5-6A*
Uncle Nick's *9A/50-1s*
ViceVersa *51s/8-9A*
Victor's Cafe *52s/Bway-8A*
Whole Foods Café *Col Cir./60s*
Wondee Siam *multi. loc.*
Xing *9A/52s*
Zona Rosa *56s/5-6A*

West 60s

Asiate *Col Cir./60s*
Bar Masa *Col Cir./60s*
Café des Artistes *67s/Col.-CPW*

Café Fiorello *Bway/63-4s*
Café Gray *Col Cir./60s*
Empire Szechuan *Col./68-9s*
Gabriel's *60s/Bway-Col.*
Hale & Hearty Soup *Rock Plz./49s*
Jean Georges *CPW/60-1s*
Josephina *Bway/63-4s*
La Boîte en Bois *68s/Col.-CPW*
Levana *69s/Bway-Col.*
Masa *Col Cir./60s*
Meskerem *Amsterdam/67s*
Nick and Toni's *67s/Bway-Col.*
Ollie's *Bway/67-8s*
O'Neals' *64s/Bway-CPW*
per se *Col Cir./60s*
Picholine *64s/Bway-CPW*
Rosa Mexicano *Col./62s*
Sapphire Indian *Bway/60-1s*
Shun Lee Cafe *65s/Col.-CPW*
Shun Lee West *65s/Col.-CPW*
Starbucks *Col./67s*
Tavern on Green *CPW/66-7s*
Vince & Eddie's *68s/Col.-CPW*
V Steakhouse *Col Cir./60s*

West 70s

Alice's Tea Cup *73s/Amst.-Col.*
Arté Café *73s/Amst.-Col.*
Baluchi's *Col./73-4s*
Bello Sguardo *Amst./79-80s*
Bettola *Amst./79-80s*
Big Nick's Burger *Bway/77s*
Boat Basin Cafe *79s/Hudson River*
Bruculino *Col./70s*
Burritoville *72s/Amst.-Col.*
Café Frida *Col./77-8s*
Cafe Luxembourg *70s/Amst.-W. End*
Cafe Ronda *Col./71-2s*
'Cesca *75s/Amst.*
Citrus Bar & Grill *Amst./75s*
Compass *70s/Amst.-West End*
Coppola's *W. 79s/Amst.-Bway*
Cosí *Bway/76s*
Dallas BBQ *72s/Col.-CPW*
Emack & Bolio's *Amst./78-9s*
Empire Szechuan *72s/Bway-W. End*
En Plo *77s/Columbus*
Epices du Traiteur *70s/Col.*
Fairway Cafe *Bway/74s*
Gari *Columbust/77-8s*
Gray's Papaya *Bway/72s*
Hunan Park *Col./70-1s*
Isabella's *Col./77s*
Ivy's Cafe *72s/Bway-Col.*
Jacques-Imo's *Columbus/77s*
Josie's *Amst./74s*
La Grolla *Amst./79-80s*

La Vela *Amst./77-8s*
Le Pain Quotidien *72s/Col.-CPW*
Metsovo *70s/Col.-CPW*
Mughlai *Col./75s*
Nice Matin *79s/Amst.*
Niko's Med. Grill *Bway/76s*
Ocean Grill *Col./78-9s*
Onera *79s/Amsterdam-Bway*
Pasha *71s/Col.-CPW*
Patsy's Pizzeria *74s/Col.-CPW*
Penang *Columbus/71s*
Pomodoro Rosso *Col./70-1s*
River *Amst./76-7s*
Ruby Foo's *Bway/77s*
Sambuca *72s/Col.-CPW*
Santa Fe *71s/Col.-CPW*
Savann *Amst./79-80s*
Scaletta *77s/Col.-CPW*
Shark Bar *Amst./74-75s*
SQC *Col./72-3s*
Swagat Indian *Amst./79-80s*
Tenzan *Columbus/73s*
Viand *Bway/75s*
Zen Palate *Bway/76-7s*

West 80s

Aix *Bway/88s*
Artie's Deli *Bway/82-3s*
Assaggio *Col./82-3s*
Barney Greengrass *Amst./86-7s*
Brother Jimmy BBQ *Amst./80-1s*
Cafe Con Leche *Amst./80-1s*
Cafe Lalo *83s/Amst.-Bway*
Calle Ocho *Col./81-2s*
Celeste *Amst./84-5s*
Columbus Bakery *Col./82-3s*
Darna *Col./89s*
Docks Oyster Bar *Bway/89-90s*
Edgar's Cafe *84s/Bway-West End*
EJ's Luncheonette *Amst./81-2s*
Flor de Mayo *Amst./83-4s*
French Roast *Bway/85s*
Good Enough to Eat *Amst./83-4s*
Haru *Amst./80-1s*
Jackson Hole *Col./85s*
Jean-Luc *Col./84-5s*
Kitchen 82/22 *Col./82s*
La Mirabelle *86s/Amst.-Col.*
Land *Amsterdam/81-2s*
Luzia's *Amst./80-1s*
Monsoon *Amst./81s*
Nëo Sushi *Bway/83s*
Neptune Room *Amst./84-5s*
Nonna *Columbus/85s*
Ollie's *Bway/84s*
Ouest *Bway/83-4s*

Popover Cafe *Amst./86-7s*
Quintessence *Amst./87-8s*
Rain *82s/Amst.-Col.*
Roppongi *Amst./81s*
Sarabeth's *Amst./80-1s*
Sol y Sombra *Amst./82-3s*
Sushi Hana *Amst./82-3s*
Uno Chicago *Col./81s*
Zabar's Cafe *Bway/80s*
Zeytin *Columbus/85s*

West 90s

Alouette *Bway/97-8s*
Cafe Con Leche *Amst./95-6s*
Carmine's *Bway/90-1s*
El Malecon *Amst./97-8s*
Empire Szechuan *Bway/97s*
Gennaro *Amst./92-3s*
Lemongrass Grill *Bway/94-5s*
Lisca *Amsterdam/92-3s*
Mary Ann's *Bway/90-1s*
Pampa *Amst./97-8s*
Regional *Bway/98-9s*
Roth's Westside Steak *Col./93s*
Saigon Grill *Amst./90s*
Sipan *Amst./94s*
Tratt. Pesce *Col./90-1s*
Yuki Sushi *Amst./92s*

West 100s

(See also Harlem/East Harlem)
A *Col./106-7s*
Bistro Ten 18 *Amst./110s*
Café du Soleil *Bway/104s*
Carne *Bway/105s*
Casbah Rouge *Bway/110-1s*
Empire Szechuan *Bway/100s*
Flor de Mayo *Bway/101s*
Indus Valley *Bway/100s*
Kitchenette *Amst./122-23s*
Le Monde *Bway/112-13s*
Lime Leaf *Bway/108s*
Mamá Mexico *Bway/101-2s*
Max *Amst./123s*
Métisse *105s/Amst.-Bway*
Mill Korean *Bway/112-3s*
Ollie's *Bway/116s*
107 West *Bway/107-8s*
Picnic Market *Bway/101s*
Pisticci *La Salle/Bway*
Sezz Medi' *Amst./122s*
Symposium *113s/Amst.-Bway*
Terrace in Sky *119s/Morningside*
Tomo Sushi *Bway/110-11s*
Turkuaz *Bway/100s*
V&T *Amst./110-11s*

BRONX

Alice's Tea Cup *City Island A/
    Hawkins*
Bruckner B&G *Bruckner/3A*
Dominick's *Arthur/Crescent-E. 187s*
El Malecon *Bway/231s*
El Rancho *Tremont/Park*
El Rey del Marisco *Webster/175s*
Enzo's *Williamsbridge/Neill*
F & J Pine *Bronxdale/White Plains*
Jake's Steakhouse *Bway/242s*
Joe's Place *Westchester/Thieriot*
Le Refuge Inn *City Is./Beach-Cross*
Lobster Box *City Island/Belden*
Madison's *Riverdale/258s*
Mario's *Arthur/184-86s*

Park Place *Mosholu/Bway*
Pasquale's Rigoletto *Arthur/
    Crescent*
Piper's Kilt *231s/Albany Crescent*
Portofino's *City Island A/Cross*
Riverdale Garden *Manh. Coll./242s*
Roberto's *Crescent/Hughes*
Siam Square *Kappock/Henry Hudson*
Spoto's *Tremont/Sampson*
Tosca Café *Tremont/Sampson-
    Gerber*
Umberto's *Arthur/186s*
Willie's Steak *Westchester/Taylor-
    Thieriot*

BROOKLYN

Bay Ridge

Areo *3A/84-5s*
Austin's Steak *5A/90s*
Cebu *3A/88s*
Chadwick's *3A/89s*
Chianti *3A/86s*
Eliá *3A/86-7s*
Embers *3A/95-6s*
Lento's *3A/Ovington*
Omonia Cafe *3A/76-7s*
101 *4A/100-1s*
Pearl Room *3A/82s*
Tanoreen *3A/77-8s*
Tuscany Grill *3A/86-7s*
Uno Chicago *4A/92s*

Bensonhurst

L & B Spumoni *86s/W.10-11s*

Boerum Hill

BarTabac *Smith/Dean*
Brawta Caribbean *Atlantic/Hoyt*
Chance *Smith/Butler*
Downtown Atlantic *Atlantic/Bond*
Gravy *Smith/Atlantic-Pacific*
Jolie *Atlantic/Hoyt-Smith*
Saul *Smith/Bergen-Dean*
Sherwood Cafe *Smith/Baltic*
Taku *Smith/Dean-Pacific*

Borough Park

Tenzan *18A/71s*

Brooklyn Heights

Caffe Buon Gusto *Montague/Henry*
Chipotle *Montague/Court*
ChipShop/CurryShop *Atlantic/
    Clinton-Henry*

Curry Leaf *Remsen/Clinton-Court*
Hale & Hearty Soup *Court/Remsen*
Heights Cafe *Montague/Hicks*
Henry's End *Henry/Cranberry*
Kapadokya *Montague/Clinton-Henry*
Noodle Pudding *Henry/Cranberry*
Queen *Court/Livingston*
Soju *Atlantic/Clinton-Henry*
Teresa's *Montague/Hicks*

Carroll Gardens

Alma *Columbia/Degraw*
Baluchi's *Smith/Degraw*
Bouillabaisse 126 *Union/Hicks*
Caserta Vecc. *Smith/Baltic-Butler*
Chestnut *Smith/Degraw-Sackett*
Ferdinando's *Union/Columbia-Hicks*
Fragole *Court/Carroll-1 Pl.*
Frankies 457 *Court/4 Pl.-Luquer*
Grocery *Smith/Sackett-Union*
Marco Polo *Court/Union*
Panino'teca 275 *Smith/Degraw*
Patois *Smith/Degraw-Douglass*
Savoia *Smith/Degraw-Sackett*
Zaytoons *Smith/Sackett*

Clinton Hill

Locanda Vini/Olii *Gates/Cambridge*
Maggie Brown *Myrtle/Washington*

Cobble Hill

Banania Cafe *Smith/Douglass*
Blue Star *Court/Degraw-Kane*
Cafe Luluc *Smith/Baltic*
Cubana Café *Smith/Degraw*
Joya *Court/Warren*
Lemongrass Grill *Court/Dean-Pac.*

Mancora *Smith/Warren-Wyckoff*
Osaka *Court/Degraw-Kane*
Quercy *Court/Baltic*
Sweet Melissa *Court/Butler*
Tuk Tuk *Smith/Baltic-Butler*

Coney Island
Gargiulo's *15s/Mermaid-Surf*
Totonno Pizza *Neptune/W. 15-6s*

Ditmas Park
Picket Fence *Cortel./Argyle-Rugby*

Downtown
Bacchus *Atlantic/Bond*
Dallas BBQ *Livingston/Hoyt-Smith*
Junior's *Flatbush/DeKalb*

Dumbo
Bubby's *Main/Plymouth-Franklin*
Five Front *Front/Old Fulton*
Grimaldi's *Old Fulton/Front-Water*
Pete's Downtown *Water/Old Fulton*
Rice *Washington/Front-York*
River Café *Water/Furman-Old Fulton*
Superfine *Front/Jay-Pearl*

Dyker Heights
Outback Steak *86s/15A*
Tommaso's *86s/14-5A*

Fort Greene
Ici *DeKalb/Clermont-Vand.*
Loulou *DeKalb/Adelphi-Clermont*
Luz *Vanderbilt/Myrtle-Willoughby*
Madiba *DeKalb/Adelphi-Carlton*
Mo-Bay *DeKalb/Ashland*
Thomas Beisl *Lafayette/Ashland*
Zaytoons *Myrtle/Hall-Washington*

Gravesend
Fiorentino's *Ave. U/McDonald-West*
Sahara *Coney Island A/Aves. T-U*

Greenpoint
Paloma *Greenpoint/Franklin-West*

Midwood
Di Fara *Ave. J/E. 14-15s*
Taci's Beyti *Coney Island/Ave. P*

Mill Basin
La Villa Pizzeria *Ave. U/66-7s*
Mill Basin Deli *Ave. T/58-9s*

Park Slope
Al Di La *5A/Carroll*
Applewood *11s/7-8A*
Belleville *5A/5s*
Beso *5A/Union*
Bistro St. Mark's *St. Marks/Flatbush*

Blue Ribbon *5A/1s-Garfield*
Blue Ribbon Sushi *5A/1s-Garfield*
Bogota Latin *5A/Lincoln-St. John's*
Brooklyn Fish Camp *5A/Degraw*
ChipShop/CurryShop *5A/6-7s*
Coco Roco *5A/6-7s*
Cocotte *5A/4s*
Convivium Osteria *5A/Bergen*
Joe's Pizza *7A/Carroll-Garfield*
La Villa Pizzeria *5A/1s-Garfield*
Lemongrass Grill *7A/Berkeley*
Long Tan *5A/Berkeley-Union*
Magnolia *6A/12s*
MeKong *5A/Garfield*
Melt *Bergen/5s-Flatbush*
Minnow *9s/6-7A*
Miracle Grill *7A/4s*
Miriam *5A/Prospect*
Moutarde *5A/Carroll*
Nana *5A/Lincoln-St. John's*
Night and Day *5A/President*
Olive Vine Cafe *multi. loc.*
Peperoncino *5A/St. Marks*
Press 195 *5A/Sackett-Union*
Red Café *5A/Prospect*
Rose Water *Union St./6A*
Sakura Café *5A/6-7s*
Scottadito *Union/6-7A*
Sette Enoteca *7A/3s*
Song *5A/1-2s*
Stone Park Café *5A/3s*
Tempo *5A/Carroll-Garfield*
12th St. B&G *8A/11-2s*
Two Boots *2s/7-8A*

Prospect Heights
Aliseo Osteria *Vanderbilt/Prospect*
Beast *Bergen/Vanderbilt*
Franny's *Flatbush/Prospect*
Garden Cafe *Vanderbilt/Prospect*
Le Gamin *Vanderbilt/Dean*
Tom's *Washington/Sterling*

Red Hook
Hope & Anchor *Van Brunt/Wolcott*
360 *Van Brunt/Dikeman-Wolcott*

Sheepshead Bay
Brennan & Carr *Nostrand/Ave. U*
Roll-n-Roaster *Emmons/29s*

Sunset Park
Diamond on Eighth *8A/60s*
Nyonya *8A/54s*

Williamsburg
Bamonte's *Withers/Lorimer-Union*
Black Betty *Metropolitan/Havemeyer*

Bonita *Bedford/S. 2-3s*
Diner *Bway/Berry*
DuMont *Union/Devoe-Metropolitan*
Fornino *Bedford/N. 7s*
Lodge *Grand/Havemeyer*
Miss Williamsburg *Kent/N. 3s*

Peter Luger *B'way/Driggs*
Planet Thailand *N. 7s/Bedford-Berry*
Relish *Wythe/Metropolitan-N. 3s*
SEA *N. 6s/Berry*
Taco Chulo *Grand/Havemeyer-Marcy*
Zipi Zape *Metropolitan/Berry*

QUEENS

Astoria
Agnanti *Ditmars/19s*
Amici Amore I *Newtown/30s*
Ammos *Steinway/20A-20R*
Brick Cafe *33s/31A*
Cávo *31A/42s*
Christos *23A/41s*
Demetris Seafood *Bway/32-3s*
Elias Corner *31s/24A*
Emack & Bolio's *31s/Ditmars-21A*
Le Sans Souci *Bway/44-5s*
Les Moules *Ditmars/35s*
Malagueta *36A/28s*
Mundo *Bway/32s*
Omonia Cafe *Bway/33s*
Piccola Venezia *28A/42s*
Ploes *Bway/33s*
Ponticello *Bway/46-7s*
Raices *Steinway/25-28A*
S'Agapo *34A/35s*
718 *Ditmars/35s*
Stamatis *multi. loc.*
Taverna Kyclades *Ditmars/33-4s*
Telly's Taverna *23A/28-9s*
Thai Pavilion *30A/37s*
Tierras Colomb. *Bway/33s*
Trattoria L'incontro *31s/Ditmars*
Ubol's Kitchen *Steinway/Astoria-25A*
Uno Chicago *35A/38s*
Viva Mar Cafe *Bway/35-6s*

Bayside
Ben's Kosher Deli *26A/211s*
Caffé/Green *Cross Is./Clearview*
Erawan *multi. loc.*
Jackson Hole *Bell Blvd./35A*
Outback Steak *Bell/26A*
Uncle Jack's Steak *Bell/40A*
Uno Chicago *Bell Blvd./39A*

Corona
Green Field Churra. *Northern/108s*
Park Side *Corona/51A*

Elmhurst
Outback Steak *Queens Blvd./56A*
Pho Bang *Bway/Elmhurst*
Ping's Seafood *Queens/Goldsmith*

Flushing
East Buffet *Main/Maple*
East Lake *Main/Franklin*
East Manor *Kissena/Laburnum*
Happy Buddha *37A/Main-Prince*
Joe's *37A/Main-Union*
Kum Gang San *Northern Blvd./Union*
Pho Bang *Kissena/Main*
Spicy & Tasty *Prince/39A*
Sweet-n-Tart *38s/Main*
You-Chun *Northern/156s*

Forest Hills
Bann Thai *Austin/Yellowstone*
Cabana *70/Austin-Queens Blvd.*
Dee's Pizza *Metropolitan/74A*
Nick's *Ascan/Austin-Burns*
Q, a Thai Bistro *Ascan/Austin-Burns*
Rouge *70R/Austin*
Uno Chicago *70 Rd./Austin-Queens*

Glendale
Zum Stammtisch *Myrtle/69 Pl.-70s*

Howard Beach
La Villa Pizzeria *153A/82-3s*

Jackson Heights
Afghan Kebab Hse. *37A/74-5s*
Delhi Palace *74s/Roosevelt-37A*
Jackson Diner *74s/Roosevelt-37A*
Jackson Hole *Astoria/ 70s*
Tierras Colomb. *Roosevelt/82s*

Little Neck
La Baraka *Northern Blvd/Little Neck*

Long Island City
Bella Via *Vernon/48A*
Manducatis *Jackson/47A*
Manetta's *Jackson/49A*
Riverview *49A/Center*
Tournesol *Vernon/50-1A*
Tuk Tuk *Vernon/49-50A*
Water's Edge *44 Dr. & East River*

Ozone Park
Don Peppe *Lefferts Blvd./135A*

Rego Park
London Lennie's *Woodhav./Fleet*

Sunnyside
Bliss *Skillman/46s*
Dazies *Queens Blvd./40s*
Hemsin *Queens Blvd./39 Pl.*

Whitestone
Napa/Sonoma *149s/15A*

Woodside
La Flor Bakery *Roosevelt/53s*
Sapori D'Ischia *37A/56s*
Sripraphai *39A/64-5s*

STATEN ISLAND

Aesop's Tables *Bay/Maryland*
American Grill *Forest/Bard-Hart*
Angelina's *Jefferson/Annadale*
Caffe Bondi *Hylan/Dongan Hills*
Carol's Cafe *Richmond/Four Corners*
Denino's *Pt. Richmond/Hooker*
Fushimi *Richmond/Lincoln*
Killmeyer Bavarian *Arthur Kill/ Sharrotts*

Lake Club *Clove/Victory*
Lento's *multi. loc.*
Lorenzo's *South/Staten Island Expwy*
Marina Cafe *Mansion/Hillside*
101 *Richmond/Amboy*
Parsonage *Arthur Kill/Clarke*
Tratt. Romana *Hylan/Benton*
Yellow Fin *Ellis/Arthur Kill*

SPECIAL FEATURES

(Indexes list the best in each category. Multi-location restaurants' features may vary by branch.)

Breakfast
(See also Hotel Dining)
A Salt & Battery
Balthazar
Barney Greengrass
Brasserie
Bubby's
Cafe Con Leche
Cafe Luxembourg
Cafe Mogador
Café Sabarsky
Carnegie Deli
City Bakery
City Hall
Cupping Room
Diner 24
E.A.T.
Florent
14 Wall Street
Good Enough to Eat
Googie's
HK
Katz's Deli
Kitchenette
Mayrose
Michael's
Naples 45
Nice Matin
NoHo Star
Pastis
Payard Bistro
Penelope
Pershing Sq.
Rue 57
Sant Ambroeus
Second Ave Deli
Tartine
Taste
Teresa's
Veselka

Brunch
Aix
Applewood
Aquagrill
Aquavit
Artisanal
Balthazar
Beacon
Bistro St. Mark's
Blue Water
Bubby's
Café Botanica
Café de Bruxelles
Café des Artistes
Cafe Luxembourg
Capsouto Frères
Celeste
Cornelia St. Cafe
Danal
davidburke/donatella
Eleven Madison
Five Points
Gascogne
Home
Isabella's
JoJo
Le Gigot
Les Halles
Manhattan Grille
Mark's
Mesa Grill
Miracle Grill
Odeon
One
Ouest
Pastis
Patois
Petrossian
Pipa
Provence
Prune
Public
Rainbow Room
River Café
Rocking Horse
Sapa
Schiller's
Sette Enoteca
718
Spotted Pig
Spring St. Natural
SQC
Sylvia's
Tartine
Taste
Tribeca Grill
Wallsé
Water Club
Zoë

Buffet Served
(Check availability)

Aquavit
Bay Leaf
Bombay Palace
Brick Lane Curry
Bukhara Grill
Charles' Southern
Chennai Garden
Chola
Churra. Plata.
Curry Leaf
Dakshin Indian
Darbar
Delegates Dining Rm.
Delhi Palace
Diwan
East Buffet
Fives
Green Field Churra.
Jackson Diner
Jewel of India
Khyber Grill
La Baraka
Mangia
Minado
Rainbow Room
Roy's NY
Salaam Bombay
Sapphire Indian
Shaan
Shark Bar
Surya
Turkish Kitchen
Turkuaz
Utsav
View
Water Club

BYO
A
Afghan Kebab Hse.
Amy Ruth's
Angelica Kitchen
Brawta Caribbean
Comfort Diner
Di Fara
Hemsin
La Taza de Oro
Mandarin Court
Nook
Olive Vine Cafe
Philly Slim's
Pho Bang
Phoenix Garden
Pink Tea Cup
Poke

Quintessence
Sweet Melissa
Taci's Beyti
Tanoreen
Tartine
Tea & Sympathy
Wo Hop
Wondee Siam
Zaytoons

Celebrations
Beacon
BLT Fish
BLT Prime
Bond 45
Bouley
Café Botanica
Café des Artistes
Café Gray
'Cesca
Daniel
FireBird
Four Seasons
Fresco by Scotto
Gotham B&G
Komegashi
La Grenouille
Le Bernardin
Lobster Box
Mark's
Mas
Matsuri
Megu
Mercer Kitchen
Modern, The
Molyvos
Nobu 57
Odeon
Olives
One if by Land
Ouest
Palm
Park Ave. Cafe
Peter Luger
Petrossian
Provence
Rainbow Room
Raoul's
Redeye Grill
River Café
Rosa Mexicano
Ruby Foo's
San Domenico
Sea Grill
Tavern on Green
Terrace in Sky
Tratt. Dell'Arte

View
Water Club
Water's Edge

Celebrity Chefs

Aix, *Didier Virot*
Alain Ducasse, *Alain Ducasse, T. Esnault*
Alto, *Scott Conant*
Annisa, *Anita Lo*
Aquavit, *Marcus Samuelsson*
Artisanal, *Terrance Brennan*
Aureole, *Charlie Palmer*
Babbo, *Mario Batali*
Bar Americain, *Bobby Flay*
Barbuto, *Jonathan Waxman*
Bayard's, *Eberhard Müller*
Beacon, *Waldy Malouf*
Beppe, *Cesare Casella*
Biltmore Room, *Gary Robins*
BLT, *Laurent Tourondel*
Blue Hill, *Daniel Barber*
Bouley, *David Bouley*
Brasserie LCB, *J.J. Rachou*
Café Boulud, *Daniel Boulud*
Café Gray, *Gray Kunz*
Chanterelle, *David Waltuck*
Coco Pazzo, *Mark Strausman*
Craft, *Tom Colicchio*
Cru, *Shea Gallante*
Daniel, *Daniel Boulud*
Danube, *David Bouley*
davidburke/donatella, *D. Burke*
dévi, *S. Saran, H. Mathur*
English is Italian, *Todd English*
Esca, *David Pasternack*
Felidia, *Lidia Bastianich*
Fleur de Sel, *Cyril Renaud*
Gotham B&G, *Alfred Portale*
Gramercy Tav., *Tom Colicchio*
Harrison, *Jimmy Bradley*
Hearth, *Marco Canora*
Jean Georges, *J.G. Vongerichten*
Landmarc, *Marc Murphy*
Le Bernardin, *Eric Ripert*
Les Halles, *Anthony Bourdain*
L'Impero, *Scott Conant*
March, *Wayne Nish*
Maremma, *Cesare Casella*
Mas, *Galen Zamarra*
Masa, *Masayoshi Takayama*
Matsuri, *Tadashi Ono*
Mesa Grill, *Bobby Flay*
Modern, The, *Gabriel Kreuther*
Nobu, *Nobu Matsuhisa*
Oceana, *Cornelius Gallagher*
Olives, *Todd English*

Ouest, *Tom Valenti*
per se, *Thomas Keller*
Picholine, *Terrance Brennan*
Pure Food + Wine, *M. Kenney*
Red Cat, *Jimmy Bradley*
Sapa, *Patricia Yeo*
Spotted Pig, *April Bloomfield*
Suba, *Alex Ureña*
Sueños, *Sue Torres*
Sushi of Gari, *Gari Sugio*
Tabla, *Floyd Cardoz*
Thor, *Kurt Gutenbrunner*
Tocqueville, *Marco Moreira*
Town, *Geoffrey Zakarian*
Union Sq. Cafe, *Michael Romano*
Veritas, *Scott Bryan*
Wallsé, *Kurt Gutenbrunner*
wd-50, *Wylie Dufresne*
Zarela, *Zarela Martinez*

Cheese Trays

Alain Ducasse
Alto
A.O.C. Bedford
Artisanal
Babbo
Café Gray
Chanterelle
Craft
Cru
Daniel
Etats-Unis
Gramercy Tav.
Mas
Mercer Kitchen
Olives
Onera
Otto
per se
Picholine
Tasting Room

Chef's Table

Alain Ducasse
Bao 111
Barbuto
Brasserie Julien
Café Gray
Col Legno
Daniel
Hemsin
Il Buco
Komegashi
Maloney & Porcelli
Megu
Olives
Park Ave. Cafe

Patroon
Remi
Smith & Wollensky

Child-Friendly
(See also Theme places)
Alice's Tea Cup
Amy Ruth's
Artie's Deli
Barking Dog
Boat House
Brennan & Carr
Bubby's
Cafe Un Deux
Carmine's
Comfort Diner
Cowgirl
Dallas BBQ
EJ's Luncheonette
Friend of a Farmer
Gargiulo's
Good Enough to Eat
Googie's
Grilled Cheese
Junior's
L & B Spumoni
London Lennie's
Miss Mamie's/Maude's
Peanut Butter/Co.
Rock Center Cafe
Rossini's
Sammy's Roum.
Sarabeth's
Serendipity 3
SQC
Sylvia's
Tavern on Green
Tony's Di Napoli
Virgil's Real BBQ
Zum Stammtisch

Cool Loos
Brasserie
Butter
Compass
Duvet
ESPN Zone
44
Matsuri
Megu
Nooch
Ono
Paradou
Pastis
Peep
P.J. Clarke's
Prem-on Thai

Pukk
Sapa
Schiller's
SEA
Tao
wd-50

Dancing
Cávo
Lotus
Rainbow Room
Tavern on Green

Entertainment
(Call for days and times of performances)
Alfama (fado/jazz)
Blue Fin (jazz)
Blue Smoke (jazz)
Blue Water (jazz)
Café Pierre (piano player/singer)
Chez Josephine (jazz/piano)
Delta Grill (blues/jazz/zydeco)
FireBird (harp/piano)
Flor de Sol (Spanish bands)
Ideya (salsa)
Jules (jazz)
Knickerbocker B&G (jazz)
La Lanterna (jazz)
La Lunchonette (accordion/ singer)
Londel's (jazz)
Madiba (South African bands)
Marion's Cont. (burlesque)
Ñ (flamenco)
Rainbow Room (orchestra)
River Café (piano)
Russian Samovar (Russian)
Sandia (jazz)
Shelly's NY (jazz)
Son Cubano (Cuban bands)
Sylvia's (blues/gospel/jazz)
Tavern on Green (DJ/piano)
Tommaso's (piano/singers/opera)
Walker's (jazz)
West Bank Cafe (singer)

Fireplaces
Adä
Bayard's
Caffé/Green
Chelsea Bistro
Chemist Club
Cornelia St. Cafe
I Trulli
Jack's Lux. Oyster
Keens Steak
La Lanterna

Special Features

Landmark Tavern
Loulou
March
Metsovo
Moran's Chelsea
One if by Land
Patois
per se
Piccola Venezia
Place
Portofino Grille
René Pujol
Savoy
Vince & Eddie's
Vivolo

Lenox Room, *Tony Fortuna*
Neary's, *Jimmy Neary*
Nino's, *Nino Selimaj*
Paola's, *Paola Marracino*
Primavera, *Nicola Civetta*
Rao's, *Frank Pellegrino*
San Domenico, *Tony May*
Tasting Room, *Renée Alevras*
Tocqueville, *Jo-Ann Makovitzky*
Tommaso's, *Thomas Verdillo*

Game in Season

Aesop's Tables
Aquavit
Babbo
Bayard's
Beacon
Beppe
Café des Artistes
Café Gray
'Cesca
Craft
Daniel
Eight Mile Creek
Felidia
Four Seasons
Gascogne
Henry's End
Il Mulino
I Trulli
Jean Georges
La Grenouille
Levana
Madiba
Ouest
Peasant
Piccola Venezia
Picholine
River Café
Saul
Tocqueville

Gracious Hosts

Canton, *Eileen Leong*
Chanterelle, *Karen Waltuck*
Chez Josephine, *J.C. Baker*
Chin Chin, *James Chin*
davidburke, *Donatella Arpaia*
Fresco by Scotto, *Marion Scotto*
Jewel Bako, *Grace & Jack Lamb*
Kitchen Club, *Marja Samsom*
La Grenouille, *Charles Masson*
La Mirabelle, *Annick Le Douaron*

Historic Places
(Year opened; * building)

1794 Bridge Cafe*
1837 Delmonico's*
1851 Bayard's*
1864 Pete's Tavern
1868 Landmark Tavern
1868 Old Homestead
1880 Veniero's
1884 P.J. Clarke's
1885 Keens Steak
1887 Peter Luger
1888 Katz's Deli
1890 Walker's*
1892 Ferrara
1896 Rao's
1900 Bamonte's
1902 Algonquin
1902 Angelo's/Mulberry
1904 Ferdinando's
1904 Vincent's
1906 Barbetta
1907 Gargiulo's
1908 Barney Greengrass
1908 Grotta Azzurra
1908 John's 12th St.
1912 Frank's
1913 Oyster Bar
1917 Café des Artistes
1919 Mario's
1921 Sardi's
1922 Rocco
1924 Totonno Pizza
1925 El Charro Español
1926 Frankie & Johnnie
1926 Lento's
1926 Palm
1927 El Faro
1927 Gallagher's Steak
1929 Empire Diner
1929 John's Pizzeria
1929 21 Club
1930 El Quijote
1931 Café Pierre
1932 Patsy's Pizzeria
1932 Pietro's

1934 Papaya King
1934 Rainbow Room
1936 Tom's
1937 Carnegie Deli
1937 Denino's
1937 Minetta Tavern
1938 Brennan & Carr
1938 Heidelberg
1938 Stage Deli
1938 Wo Hop
1939 L & B Spumoni
1941 Sevilla
1943 Burger Heaven
1944 Patsy's
1945 Gino
1945 V&T
1946 Lobster Box
1947 Delegates Dining Rm.
1950 Junior's
1950 Marion's Cont.
1950 Paul & Jimmy's
1953 McHales
1954 Pink Tea Cup
1954 Second Ave Deli
1954 Serendipity 3
1954 Veselka
1955 Bill Hong's

Hotel Dining

(Best of many)
Alex Hotel
  Riingo
Algonquin Hotel
  Algonquin
Blakely Hotel
  Abboccato
Bryant Park Hotel
  Koi
Chambers Hotel
  Town
City Club Hotel
  db Bistro Moderne
Dylan Hotel
  Chemist Club
Elysée Hotel
  Monkey Bar
Essex House
  Alain Ducasse
  Café Botanica
Gansevoort Hotel
  Ono
Hotel on Rivington, The
  Thor
Hudson Hotel
  Hudson Cafeteria
Iroquois Hotel
  Triomphe

Le Parker Meridien
  burger joint/Parker M.
  Norma's
  Seppi's
Lowell Hotel
  Post House
Mandarin Oriental Hotel
  Asiate
Maritime Hotel
  La Bottega
  Matsuri
Mark Hotel
  Mark's
Marriott Financial Ctr.
  Roy's NY
Marriott Marquis Hotel
  View
Mercer Hotel
  Mercer Kitchen
Morgans Hotel
  Asia de Cuba
Muse Hotel
  District
Peninsula Hotel
  Fives
Pierre Hotel
  Café Pierre
Plaza Athénée Hotel
  Arabelle
Regency Hotel
  Regency
Renaissance NY Hotel
  Foley's Fish Hse.
Ritz-Carlton Battery Park
  2 West
Ritz-Carlton Central Park
  Atelier
Royalton Hotel
  44
60 Thompson
  Kittichai
Surrey Hotel
  Café Boulud
Time Hotel
  Océo
Trump Int'l Hotel
  Jean Georges
Waldorf-Astoria
  Bull & Bear
  Inagiku
Westin NY Times Sq.
  Shula's Steak
W Times Square Hotel
  Blue Fin
W Union Sq.
  Olives

Jacket Required

(* Tie also required)
Alain Ducasse
Alto
Atelier
Aureole
Café Pierre
Daniel
Delegates Dining Rm.
Four Seasons
Jean Georges
La Grenouille
Le Bernardin
per se
Picholine
Rainbow Room*
River Café
San Domenico
21 Club*

Jury Duty

(Near Foley Sq.)
Arqua
Big Wong
Bouley
Bread Tribeca
Bridge Cafe
City Hall
Da Nico
Dim Sum Go Go
Duane Park Cafe
Ecco
Excellent Dumpling
Goodies
Great NY Noodle
HSF
Il Cortile
Il Fornaio
Il Palazzo
Le Zinc
New Bo-Ky
New Green Bo
New Pasteur
Nha Trang
Odeon
Oriental Garden
Peking Duck
Pho Viet Huong
Shanghai Cuisine
Taormina
Wo Hop

Late Dining

(Besides most diners and
delis; weekday closing hour)
Arturo's Pizzeria (1 AM)
Balthazar (1 AM)

Bao 111 (2 AM)
Baraonda (1 AM)
barmarché (2 AM)
BarTabac (1 AM)
Bereket (24 hrs.)
Big Nick's Burger (24 hrs.)
Blue Ribbon (2 AM)
Blue Ribbon Sushi (2 AM)
Brennan & Carr (1 AM)
Bubba Gump (1 AM)
Café Fiorello (2 AM)
Cafe Lalo (2 AM)
Cafeteria (24 hrs.)
Carnegie Deli (4 AM)
Cávo (2 AM)
Cebu (3 AM)
Chelsea Grill (4 AM)
Chez Josephine (1 AM)
China 1 (2 AM)
Coffee Shop (5:30 AM)
Corner Bistro (3:30 AM)
Cosí (1 AM)
Cosmic Cantina (5 AM)
Cozy Soup/Burger (24 hrs.)
Diablo Royale (1 AM)
Diner 24 (24 hrs.)
East Lake (2 AM)
Edgar's Cafe (1 AM)
Eight Mile Creek (1 AM)
Elaine's (2 AM)
El Malecon (24 hrs.)
El Rancho (2 AM)
El Rey del Marisco (2 AM)
Empire Diner (24 hrs.)
Employees Only (3:30 AM)
Florent (5 AM)
Frank (1 AM)
French Roast (24 hrs.)
Fuleen Sea. (4 AM)
Gahm Mi Oak (24 hrs.)
Grace (4 AM)
Gravy (2 AM)
Gray's Papaya (24 hrs.)
Great NY Noodle (3:30 AM)
Grotta Azzurra (2 AM)
Havana Central (1 AM)
HK (1 AM)
'ino (2 AM)
'inoteca (3 AM)
I Tre Merli (1 AM)
Jackson Hole (varies)
J.G. Melon (2:30 AM)
Joe's Place (1 AM)
Kam Chueh (3:30 AM)
Kang Suh (24 hrs.)
Knickerbocker B&G (1 AM)
Kum Gang San (24 hrs.)

La Bottega (1 AM)
La Lanterna (3 AM)
L'Allegria (1 AM)
La Mela (2 AM)
Landmarc (2 AM)
Le Souk (2 AM)
L'Express (24 hrs.)
Lil' Frankie Pizza (2 AM)
Lima's Taste (1 AM)
Lodge (2 AM)
Ludo (4 AM)
Luke's B&G (2 AM)
Macelleria (1 AM)
Metropol (2 AM)
Ñ (2 AM)
Neary's (1 AM)
Omen (1 AM)
Omonia Cafe (2 AM)
One (1 AM)
Orbit East Harlem (1 AM)
Papaya King (2 AM)
P.J. Clarke's (3 AM)
Planet Thailand (1 AM)
Pop Burger (4 AM)
Raoul's (2 AM)
Roll-n-Roaster (1 AM)
Sabor (2 AM)
Sahara (5 AM)
Sandobe (1:30 AM)
Sarge's Deli (24 hrs.)
Schiller's (2 AM)
Seppi's (2 AM)
Sol y Sombra (2 AM)
Spotted Pig (2 AM)
Stage Deli (2 AM)
Stamatis (1 AM)
SushiSamba (1 AM)
Sushi Seki (3 AM)
Three of Cups (1 AM)
212 (1 AM)
Umberto's (4 AM)
Uno Chicago (varies)
Uva (1 AM)
Veselka (24 hrs.)
Vincent's (2 AM)
Walker's (1 AM)
West Bank Cafe (1 AM)
Wogies B&G (2 AM)
Wo Hop (24 hrs.)
Wollensky's Grill (2 AM)
Won Jo (24 hrs.)
Zucco (2 AM)

Artisanal
Balthazar
Bar Masa
Beast
Biltmore Room
Blue Fin
Boat Basin Cafe
Boat House
Bond Street
Brick Cafe
Bryant Park
Cafe Luxembourg
City Hall
Dos Caminos
Eight Mile Creek
Four Seasons
Geisha
Gotham B&G
Grace
Gramercy Tav.
HK
Il Bastardo
'inoteca
Jean Georges
Keens Steak
Le Colonial
Lenox Room
L'Impero
Ludo
Luz
Maloney & Porcelli
Mark's
Odeon
One
Paper Moon
Park
Park Avalon
Pastis
Piano Due
Sala
Scopa
Sensa
Shelly's NY
Stanton Social
Stone Park Café
Tao
Town
212
Wollensky's Grill

Meet for a Drink
(Most top hotels, bars and the following standouts)
Algonquin
Amuse

Natural/Organic
(Places specializing in organic, local ingredients)
A
Angelica Kitchen
Applewood
Better Burger

Special Features

Blue Hill
Candle 79
Candle Cafe
Chennai Garden
Chestnut
Cho Dang Gol
Chop't Creative
Cosmic Cantina
Counter
Craft
Gobo
Grocery
Happy Buddha
Ivo & Lulu
Josephina
Josie's
Luxia
Mas
New Leaf
Parish & Co.
Perry Street
Popover Cafe
Pure Food + Wine
Quartino
Quintessence
Sacred Chow
Saul
Savoy
Spring St. Natural
SQC
Tasting Room
360
Tocqueville
Tsampa
Zebú Grill

Noteworthy Newcomers (247)

(Name, cuisine; * not open at press time, but looks promising)

Abboccato, *Italian*
Agata/Valentina Food*, *Italian*
Alcala, *Basque*
Alexandra, *American*
Alto, *Italian*
Ama, *Italian*
American Masala*, *Indian/Amer.*
Ammos, *Greek*
Angon on the Sixth, *Indian*
Applewood, *American*
Artemis*, *Greek*
Aspen*, *American*
Au Coin du Feu, *French*
Azucar, *Cuban*
Babu, *Indian*
Bann, *Korean*

Bar Americain, *brasserie*
BarBossa, *Med./Brazilian*
Barbounia*, *Greek/Turkish*
barmarché, *American*
Barna, *Spanish*
Beast, *Mediterranean*
BED New York, *American*
Bellavitae, *Italian*
Ben & Jack's, *Steakhouse*
Bette, *European*
BG, Bergdorf Goodman*, *Amer.*
Bistro 61, *French*
Bistro du Vent, *French bistro*
Black Pearl, *Seafood*
Bliss, *American*
BLT Fish, *Seafood*
BLT Prime, *Steakhouse*
Bogota Latin, *Latin*
Bolzano's, *Italian*
Bombay Talkie, *Indian*
Bond 45, *Italian*
Bone Lick Pk. BBQ, *Barbecue*
Bottega del Vino, *Italian*
Bouchon Bakery*, *American*
Bouillabaisse 126, *French*
Breeze, *Thai/French*
Brooklyn Fish Camp, *Seafood*
Buddakan*, *Asian*
Burger Joint, *burgers*
Butai, *Japanese*
Café d'Alsace*, *French*
Café du Soleil, *French bistro*
Cambalache, *Argentine*
Camino Sur*, *South American*
Casbah Rouge, *Moroccan*
Caviar & Banana, *Brazilian*
Centrico, *Mexican*
Cercle Rouge*, *French/American*
Chemist Club, *American*
Chinatown*, *Chinese*
Chino's, *Asian*
coast, *Seafood*
Colors*, *American*
Cookshop*, *American*
Copper Chimney, *Indian*
Country*, *American*
Craftsteak*, *Steakhouse*
Creole, *Creole*
da Giacomo, *Italian*
Dani*, *Italian*
Della Rovere, *Italian*
Del Posto*, *Italian*
De Marco's, *pizza*
De Medici*, *Italian*
dévi, *Indian*
Diablo Royale, *Mexican*
Dinosaur BBQ, *Barbecue*

D'Or Ahn*, *European*
Dumpling Man, *Chinese*
Duvet, *Eclectic*
Earl Monroe's*, *Southern*
Eastern King, *Chinese/Japanese*
Eemo, *Korean*
El Rancho, *American*
Employees Only, *Med.*
English is Italian, *Italian*
EN Japanese, *Japanese*
etcetera etcetera, *Med.*
European Union*, *Gastropub*
Falai, *Italian*
Fatty Crab*, *Malaysian/SE Asian*
Fig & Olive Kitchen, *Med.*
Fornino, *Italian*
Frankies 457, *Italian*
Frederick's Madison, *Med.*
Freemans, *American*
French Quarter, *Cajun*
Fuel Grill*, *American*
Gari, *Japanese*
Ginger*, *Chinese*
Gordon Ramsay*, *French*
Gramercy 24, *Seafood*
Gravy, *American Diner*
Gusto, *Italian*
Gyu-Kaku, *Japanese bbq*
Happy Buddha, *Veg. Chinese*
Harlem Grill, *American*
Hedeh, *Japanese*
Hip Hop Chow, *Chinese/Southern*
Il Bastardo, *Italian*
In Tent*, *Mediterranean*
It's Dominican, *Dominican*
Jefferson Grill*, *American*
Jimmy's*, *European*
Jolie, *French*
Jovia*, *American*
Kellari*, *Greek*
Khyber Grill, *Indian*
Kitchen/Cocktails, *American*
Klong, *Thai*
Koi, *Asian*
Komegashi, *Japanese*
La Esquina, *Mexican*
La Masseria, *Italian*
Land, *Thai*
L'Atelier de Joël Robuchon*, *French*
Le Sans Souci, *French bistro*
Les Moules, *Mediterranean*
Le Vallon Rouge*, *French*
Lisca, *Italian*
Little Giant, *American*
Lodge, *American*
Loft*, *Mediterranean*

Lo Scalco, *Italian*
LoSide, *American Diner*
Ludo, *Med./Int'l*
Lure Fishbar, *Seafood*
Luz, *Nuevo Latino*
Maggie Brown, *American*
Mainland, *Chinese*
Maremma, *Italian/American*
Maroons Smoke Shack*, *BBQ*
Maxie, *Japanese*
Megu -Trump World*, *Japanese*
Melba's, *Southern*
Melt, *American*
Mercadito, *Mexican*
Metropol, *French bistro*
Mint*, *Indian*
Miriam, *Med./Middle Eastern*
Modern, The, *French/Amer.*
Momofuku Noodle, *Japanese*
Momoya, *Japanese*
Mo Pitkin's, *Judeo-Latino*
Morimoto*, *Japanese*
Mundo, *Turkish/Argentine*
Naima, *S. Italian*
Nero, *Italian*
Nicky's Viet., *Vietnamese*
Night and Day, *American*
Ninja, *Japanese Fusion*
Nobu 57, *Japanese/Peruvian*
Nonna, *Italian*
Nooch, *Noodle shop*
Noodle Bar*, *Asian*
Olea*, *Mediterranean*
Onera, *Greek*
Onju, *Italian*
Ono, *Japanese*
Orchard, The*, *American*
Orto*, *Italian*
Osteria Gelsi, *Italian*
Pair of 8's*, *American*
Palá*, *Pizza*
Paloma, *American/Eclectic*
Parea*, *Greek*
Paris Match, *French bistro*
Park Terrace, *French bistro*
Peacock Alley*, *French*
Perry Street, *French*
Philly Slim's, *cheesesteaks*
Piano Due, *Italian*
P.J. Clarke's-Hudson*, *Pub*
Picnic Market, *French*
Plate NYC, *Chinese/Latin*
Ploes, *Greek*
Poetessa, *Italian*
Porcao*, *Brazilian Steakhouse*
Prem-on Thai, *Thai*
Press 195*, *Italian*
Pukk, *Thai*

Special Features

Radha, *Vegetarian*
Raices, *Nuevo Latino*
Regional, *Italian*
Rib, *Southern*
Ribot, *Mediterranean*
Rickshaw Dumpling, *Chinese*
Roberto Passon, *Italian*
Roe*, *Asian*
RUB BBQ, *Barbecue*
Sachiko's, *Japanese*
Sakura Café, *Japanese*
Sandia, *Nuevo Latino*
Sapa, *French/Vietnamese*
Saravanaas, *Indian*
Sascha*, *French*
Scarlatto*, *Italian*
Scottadito, *Italian*
Secretes, *Eclectic*
Sensa, *American*
Sette Enoteca, *Italian*
Shaburi, *Japanese*
Shorty's Half Shell, *Seafood*
Silverleaf Tavern, *American*
Smoked, *Barbecue*
Social NY*, *Asian*
Sol y Sombra, *Spanish Tapas*
Song, *Thai*
Spigolo, *Italian*
Stanton Social, *International*
STK*, *Steakhouse*
Stone Park Café, *American*
Table XII, *Italian*
Taco Chulo, *Mexican*
Taku, *Japanese*
Tazza*, *Italian*
Telepan*, *American*
Tempo, *Med.*
Thompson HQ.*, *American*
Thor, *American*
343, *American*
Tides, *Seafood*
Tony Luke's, *cheesesteaks*
tre dici, *Italian*
Trestle on 10th*, *American*
Turquoise, *Seafood*
24 Prince*, *American*
202 Cafe, *European*
Una Pizza Nap., *Pizza*
Uovo, *Med./American*
Upstairs, *Eclectic*
Uva, *Italian*
Via*, *Italian*
VietCafé, *Vietnamese*
Viva Mar Cafe, *Med.*
Waldy's Pizza, *Pizza*
Wimp's Sky Café, *Southern*
Xing, *Chinese*

You-Chun, *Korean*
Yumcha, *Chinese*
Zucco, *French Diner*

Outdoor Dining
(G=garden; P=patio;
S=sidewalk; T=terrace)
Aesop's Tables (G)
Aleo (G)
Alma (T)
A.O.C. (G)
Aquagrill (T)
Barbetta (G)
Barolo (G)
Bar Pitti (S)
Battery Gardens (G, P, T)
Blue Hill (G, P)
Blue Water (T)
Boat Basin Cafe (P)
Boat House (T)
Bolzano's (P)
Bone Lick Pk. BBQ (S)
Bottino (G)
Bryant Park (G, P, S)
Cacio e Pepe (G, S)
Cafe Centro (S)
Café Fiorello (S)
Café St. Bart's (T)
Caffe Rafaella (S)
Caviar & Banana (T)
Cávo (G, P)
Chestnut (G)
Coffee Shop (S)
Convivium Osteria (G)
Da Nico (G, S)
Da Silvano (S)
East of Eighth (G)
Employees Only (G)
Esca (P)
Five Front (G)
Gascogne (G)
Gavroche (G)
Gigino Trattoria (S)
Gigino/Wagner (P)
Gnocco Caffe (G)
Grocery (G)
I Coppi (G)
Il Gattopardo (P)
Il Palazzo (S)
Isabella's (S)
I Trulli (G)
La Bottega (T)
La Lanterna (G)
Lattanzi (G, T)
Le Jardin Bistro (G)
Le Refuge (G)
L'Impero (P)

Long Tan (G)
Loulou (G)
Luxia (G)
March (T)
Markt (S, T)
Miracle Grill (G)
Modern, The (T)
New Leaf (P)
Ocean Grill (S)
One (S)
Ono (G, S)
Pace (T)
Pampano (T)
Panino'teca 275 (G)
Paradou (G)
Park (G)
Pastis (T)
Patois (G)
Pete's Tavern (S)
Pure Food + Wine (G)
Ribot (T)
River Café (G)
Riverview (P)
Rock Center Cafe (T)
Sahara (G)
Sea Grill (G)
Sherwood Cafe (G, P)
Surya (G)
Sweet Melissa (G, S)
Tartine (S)
Tavern on Green (G)
Terrace in Sky (T)
VaTutto (G)
Vento (S)
ViceVersa (G)
Vittorio Cucina (G)
Water Club (P)
Water's Edge (P)
Wollensky's Grill (S)
Zum Schneider (G, S)

People-Watching

Alto
Angus McIndoe
Asia de Cuba
Babbo
Balthazar
Barbuto
Bar Pitti
Bette
Bice
Blue Water
Da Silvano
Elio's
Freemans
Fresco by Scotto
Il Cantinori

Indochine
Joe Allen
Koi
La Grenouille
Matsuri
Mercer Kitchen
Mr. Chow
Nam
Nobu
Nobu 57
Pastis
Perry Street
Sardi's
Schiller's
Sensa
Spice Market
212

Power Scenes

Bar Americain
Bayard's
Ben Benson's
BLT Prime
Bobby Van's Steak
City Hall
Coco Pazzo
Daniel
Delmonico's
Elio's
44
Four Seasons
Fresco by Scotto
Gabriel's
Gallagher's Steak
Gotham B&G
Jean Georges
Keens Steak
La Grenouille
Le Bernardin
Michael's
Nobu
Nobu 57
Peter Luger
Rao's
Regency
Smith & Wollensky
Sparks Steak
21 Club

Private Rooms/Parties

(Call for capacity)
Alain Ducasse
Arabelle
Barbetta
Battery Gardens
Bayard's
Beacon

BLT Fish
BLT Prime
BLT Steak
Blue Hill
Blue Water
Café Gray
Capital Grille
Cellini
Centolire
City Hall
Compass
Daniel
Danube
Del Frisco's
Delmonico's
Duvet
Eleven Madison
English is Italian
EN Japanese
ESPN Zone
Fiamma Osteria
F.illi Ponte
FireBird
Four Seasons
Fresco by Scotto
Gabriel's
Geisha
Gramercy Tav.
Il Buco
Il Cortile
'inoteca
Jean Georges
Jezebel
Josephs Citarella
Keens Steak
La Grenouille
Landmark Tavern
Le Bernardin
Le Perigord
Lever House
Le Zie 2000
L'Impero
Lo Scalco
Maloney & Porcelli
March
Matsuri
Megu
Michael's
Mi Cocina
Milos
Modern, The
Moran's Chelsea
Mr. Chow
Mr. K's
Nobu 57
Oceana
Park

Park Ave. Cafe
Periyali
per se
Picholine
Redeye Grill
Remi
Re Sette
Riingo
River Café
Rock Center Cafe
Sambuca
Scopa
Shelly's NY
Solo
Sparks Steak
Tao
Tavern on Green
Terrace in Sky
Thalassa
Tocqueville
Tribeca Grill
21 Club
212
Vento
Water Club
Water's Edge

Pubs/Microbreweries
(See Zagat NYC Nightlife)
Angus McIndoe
Bridge Cafe
Corner Bistro
Heartland Brew.
Jackson Hole
J.G. Melon
Joe Allen
Keens Steak
Landmark Tavern
Luke's B&G
Markt
McHales
Moran's Chelsea
Neary's
Pete's Tavern
Piper's Kilt
P.J. Clarke's
Spotted Pig
Walker's
Wollensky's Grill

Quick Bites
Amy's Bread
A Salt & Battery
Azuri Cafe
BB Sandwich
Bereket
Brennan & Carr

Burritoville
Carl's Steaks
ChipShop/CurryShop
City Bakery
Columbus Bakery
Cosí
Cosmic Cantina
Cozy Soup/Burger
Daisy May's BBQ
Dishes
F & B
Fresco on the Go
Good Enough to Eat
Gray's Papaya
Grilled Cheese
Hale & Hearty Soup
Hampton Chutney
'ino
Joe's Pizza
La Esquina
Papaya King
Press 195
Pump Energy Food
Quintessence
Rice 'n' Beans
Risotteria
Shake Shack
Westville
Whole Foods Café
'wichcraft
Zabar's Cafe

Quiet Conversation

Alto
Arabelle
Asiate
Atelier
Café Botanica
Café Pierre
Chanterelle
Fleur de Sel
Il Gattopardo
Jean Georges
Kai
Kings' Carriage Hse.
La Grenouille
Le Bernardin
March
Mark's
Masa
Mr. K's
per se
Petrossian
Picholine
Terrace in Sky
Tocqueville
Tsampa

Raw Bars

Aquagrill
Atlantic Grill
Balthazar
Bar Americain
BLT Fish
Blue Fin
Blue Ribbon
Blue Star
Blue Water
Brooklyn Fish Camp
City Crab
City Hall
coast
Docks Oyster Bar
Fish
Josephs Citarella
Le Pescadou
London Lennie's
Lure Fishbar
Markt
McCormick & Schmick
Mercer Kitchen
Mermaid Inn
Milos
Neptune Room
Ocean Grill
Oyster Bar
Plate NYC
Sapa
Shaffer City
Shelly's NY
shore

Romantic Places

Aix
Alain Ducasse
Alma
Asiate
Aureole
Barbetta
BED New York
Biltmore Room
Blue Hill
Boat House
Café des Artistes
Café Pierre
Candela
Capsouto Frères
Casa La Femme
Chanterelle
Chez Josephine
Chez Michallet
Convivium Osteria
Danal
Danube
davidburke/donatella

Special Features

Duvet
Erminia
FireBird
Gascogne
Il Buco
Jezebel
JoJo
Kitchen Club
La Grenouille
La Lanterna
Le Gigot
Le Refuge
Le Refuge Inn
L'Impero
Ludo
March
Mark's
One if by Land
Periyali
Petrossian
Piano Due
Piccola Venezia
Place
Primavera
Provence
Rainbow Room
River Café
Scalini Fedeli
Spice Market
Suba
Terrace in Sky
View
Water Club
Water's Edge

Senior Appeal

Arabelle
Barbetta
Café des Artistes
Embers
Fontana di Trevi
Il Nido
La Goulue
La Mangeoire
Le Perigord
Mark's
Pietro's
René Pujol
Rossini's
Sardi's
Tavern on Green

Singles Scenes

Angelo & Maxie's
Artisanal
Asia de Cuba
Atlantic Grill
Balthazar

Baraonda
BED New York
Blue Fin
Blue Ribbon
Boca Chica
Bonita
Brasserie 8½
Bryant Park
Butter
Cabana
Canyon Road
Cité Grill
Citrus Bar & Grill
Coffee Shop
Diner 24
Dos Caminos
Duvet
East of Eighth
Elephant
elmo
Employees Only
Essex
Grace
Heartland Brew.
Houston's
Hudson Cafeteria
Ideya
Isabella's
Jane
Joya
Koi
La Esquina
La Goulue
Le Zinc
Madiba
Maloney & Porcelli
Marion's Cont.
Markt
Mesa Grill
Monkey Bar
One
Otto
Park Avalon
Pastis
Pete's Tavern
Pipa
Punch
Ruby Foo's
Schiller's
Scopa
Shark Bar
Spice Market
Suba
Tao
Town
Tribeca Grill
Zarela

Sleepers
(Good to excellent food, but little known)
Adä
Akdeniz
Aliseo Osteria
Austin's Steak
Bacchus
Belluno
Brawta Caribbean
Caserta Vecc.
Cebu
Chance
Country Café
Dakshin Indian
Darbar
Diamond on Eighth
El Paso Taqueria
Franchia
Ghenet
Giovanni 25
Haikara Grill
Havana Alma
Ivo & Lulu
Joseph's
Kam Chueh
Kitchen Club
Kuruma Zushi
La Cantina
La Cantina Toscana
Lentini
Lima's Taste
Loulou
Maurizio Trattoria
Nippon
Nook
One 83
Orbit East Harlem
Park East Grill
Picket Fence
Pinocchio
Pizza Gruppo
Raga
Red Café
Savore
Solo
Sushi Ann
Taci's Beyti
Tanoreen
Tenzan
Tevere
Tsampa
Tsuki
2 West
Veg. Paradise
Vittorio Cucina

Wogies B&G
Yuca Bar
Zipi Zape

Sunday Best Bets
(See also Hotel Dining)
Aquagrill
Aquavit
Artisanal
Balthazar
Bar Americain
Blue Hill
Blue Ribbon
Blue Water
Bouley
Café de Bruxelles
Café des Artistes
Chez Michallet
Coco Pazzo
davidburke/donatella
Five Points
Gotham B&G
Gramercy Tav.
Komegashi
La Mediterranée
Lupa
Luxia
Mesa Grill
Mi Cocina
Moran's Chelsea
Odeon
Onera
Ouest
Our Place
Peter Luger
Piccolo Angolo
Picholine
Prune
River Café
Solo
Tavern on Green
Tratt. Dell'Arte
Tribeca Grill
Union Sq. Cafe
Water Club
Zoë

Tasting Menus
($ minimum)
Alain Ducasse (225)
Alto (115)
Amma (50)
Annisa (68)
Aquavit (100)
Asiate (95)
Aureole (89)
Babbo (59)

Special Features

Barbuto (55)
Blue Hill (68)
Bond Street (60)
Bouley (85)
Chanterelle (115)
Chubo (56)
Cru (85)
Daniel (125)
Danube (85)
davidburke/donatella (85)
dévi (60)
Diwan (55)
Eleven Madison (65)
Esca (65)
FireBird (100)
Fleur de Sel (82)
Four Seasons (125)
Frederick's Madison (68)
Gramercy Tav. (98)
Grocery (70)
Hearth (74)
Hedeh (70)
Ian (75)
Il Buco (85)
Inagiku (90)
Jack's Lux. Oyster (75)
Jean Georges (125)
JoJo (65)
Josephs Citarella (65)
Kai (200)
Komegashi (75)
La Grenouille (115)
Le Bernardin (150)
Le Perigord (75)
Le Tableau (45)
L'Impero (100)
Lo Scalco (48)
Lupa (60)
March (75)
Mas (95)
Masa (350)
Moda (80)
Modern, The (105)
Montrachet (79)
Ninja (80)
Nobu (80)
Oceana (110)
Olives (72)
One if by Land (79)
Onera (75)
Payard Bistro (68)
per se (175)
Petrossian (55)
Philip Marie (85)
Picholine (125)
Pó (48)

River Café (95)
San Domenico (75)
Scalini Fedeli (90)
Scottadito (50)
71 Clinton Fresh (60)
Solera (65)
Solo (85)
Spigolo (60)
Suba (55)
Sueños (50)
Sugiyama (68)
Sumile (120)
SushiSamba (69)
Sushi Zen (75)
Tabla (79)
Taka (60)
Terrace in Sky (97)
Tocqueville (75)
Triomphe (75)
21 Club (70)
Ulrika's (75)
View (75)
Vong (68)
Wallsé (70)
wd-50 (95)

Tea Service

Alice's Tea Cup
Bombay Talkie
Café Pierre
Cafe S.F.A.
Danal
Franchia
Kai
Kings' Carriage Hse.
Lady Mendl's
Mark's
North Sq.
Payard Bistro
Sant Ambroeus
Sarabeth's
Sweet Melissa
Tea & Sympathy
Tea Box
teany
202 Cafe

Theme Restaurants

Brooklyn Diner
Bubba Gump
Cowgirl
ESPN Zone
Hard Rock Cafe
Jekyll & Hyde
Mars 2112
Ninja
Shula's Steak

Transporting Experiences

Asiate
Balthazar
Bayard's
Boat House
Café des Artistes
Chez Josephine
FireBird
Il Buco
Jezebel
Keens Steak
La Grenouille
Le Colonial
Masa
Matsuri
Megu
Ninja
One if by Land
per se
Rainbow Room
Rao's
Suba
Tao
Tavern on Green
Vatan
Water's Edge

Trendy

Balthazar
Bar Americain
BED New York
Bette
Bistro du Vent
Casa Mono
'Cesca
davidburke/donatella
Duvet
Employees Only
EN Japanese
5 Ninth
Freemans
Highline
'inoteca
Jack's Lux. Oyster
Koi
La Esquina
L'Impero
Lure Fishbar
Matsuri
Modern, The
Nobu 57
Ono
Pastis
Perry Street
RUB BBQ
Schiller's
Shake Shack

Spice Market
Spotted Pig
Stanton Social
Suba

Views

Alma
Asiate
Battery Gardens
BED New York
Boat Basin Cafe
Boat House
Bryant Park
Café Gray
Cafe S.F.A.
Caffé/Green
Cipriani Dolci
Delegates Dining Rm.
Foley's Fish Hse.
Gigino/Wagner
Grill Room
Hispaniola
Lake Club
Lobster Box
Marina Cafe
Metrazur
Michael Jordan's
per se
Pete's Downtown
Rainbow Room
River Café
Riverview
Rock Center Cafe
Sea Grill
Tavern on Green
Terrace in Sky
View
V Steakhouse
Water Club
Water's Edge

Visitors on Expense Account

Alain Ducasse
Bouley
Chanterelle
Craft
Daniel
Del Frisco's
Four Seasons
Il Mulino
Jean Georges
Kuruma Zushi
Masa
Megu
Milos
Nobu 57

Special Features

One if by Land
per se
Petrossian

Waterside

Alma
Battery Gardens
Boat House
Cabana
Caffé/Green
Grimaldi's
Lake Club
Lobster Box
Marina Cafe
Pete's Downtown
River Café
Riverview
Water Club
Water's Edge

Winning Wine Lists

Alain Ducasse
Aureole
Babbo
Barbetta
Barolo
Bayard's
Bottega del Vino
Bouley
Capital Grille
Chanterelle
Chiam
Cité
Craft
Cru
Daniel
Danube
Del Frisco's
Eleven Madison

Felidia
Fleur de Sel
Four Seasons
Gotham B&G
Gramercy Tav.
Il Buco
'inoteca
I Trulli
Jean Georges
Landmarc
Le Bernardin
Le Perigord
L'Impero
Maloney & Porcelli
Manhattan Ocean
March
Michael's
Montrachet
Oceana
Olives
Otto
Oyster Bar
per se
Piccola Venezia
Picholine
Post House
River Café
Scalini Fedeli
Smith & Wollensky
Sparks Steak
Tasting Room
Tavern on Green
Tocqueville
Tribeca Grill
21 Club
Union Sq. Cafe
Veritas
Water Club

Wine Vintage Chart

This chart is designed to help you select wine to go with your meal. It is based on the same 0 to 30 scale used throughout this *Survey*. The ratings (prepared by our friend **Howard Stravitz,** a law professor at the University of South Carolina) reflect both the quality of the vintage and the wine's readiness for present consumption. Thus, if a wine is not fully mature or is over the hill, its rating has been reduced. We do not include 1987, 1991–1993 vintages because they are not especially recommended for most areas. A dash indicates that a wine is either past its peak or too young to rate.

	'85	'86	'88	'89	'90	'94	'95	'96	'97	'98	'99	'00	'01	'02	'03	'04
WHITES																
French:																
Alsace	24	–	22	27	27	26	25	25	24	26	23	26	27	25	22	–
Burgundy	26	25	–	24	22	–	28	29	24	23	26	25	24	27	23	24
Loire Valley	–	–	–	–	–	20	23	22	–	24	25	26	27	25	23	–
Champagne	28	25	24	26	29	–	26	27	24	23	24	24	22	26	–	–
Sauternes	21	28	29	25	27	–	21	23	25	23	24	24	28	25	26	–
German	–	–	25	26	27	25	24	27	26	25	25	23	29	27	25	25
California (Napa, Sonoma, Mendocino):																
Chardonnay	–	–	–	–	–	–	–	–	–	–	24	25	28	27	26	–
Sauvignon Blanc/Sémillon	–	–	–	–	–	–	–	–	–	–	–	–	27	28	26	–
REDS																
French:																
Bordeaux	24	25	24	26	29	22	26	25	23	25	24	28	26	23	25	23
Burgundy	23	–	21	24	26	–	26	28	25	22	27	22	25	27	24	–
Rhône	–	–	26	29	29	24	25	22	24	28	27	27	26	–	25	–
Beaujolais	–	–	–	–	–	–	–	–	–	–	–	24	–	25	28	25
California (Napa, Sonoma, Mendocino):																
Cab./Merlot	27	26	–	–	28	29	27	25	28	23	26	22	27	25	24	–
Pinot Noir	–	–	–	–	–	–	–	–	24	24	25	24	27	28	26	–
Zinfandel	–	–	–	–	–	–	–	–	–	–	–	–	26	26	28	–
Italian:																
Tuscany	–	–	–	–	25	22	25	20	29	24	28	24	26	24	–	–
Piedmont	–	–	24	26	28	–	23	26	27	25	25	28	26	18	–	–
Spanish:																
Rioja	–	–	–	–	26	26	24	25	22	25	25	27	20	–	–	–
Ribera del Duero/Priorat	–	–	–	–	26	26	27	25	24	26	26	27	20	–	–	–